**Foreign Relations of the
United States, 1964–1968**

Volume XVI

Cyprus; Greece;
Turkey

Editor   James E. Miller

General Editor   David S. Patterson

United States Government Printing Office
Washington
2000

DEPARTMENT OF STATE PUBLICATION 10644

OFFICE OF THE HISTORIAN

BUREAU OF PUBLIC AFFAIRS

For sale by the U.S. Government Printing Office
Superintendent of Documents, Mail Stop: SSOP, Washington, DC 20402-9328
ISBN 0-16-045085-3

Preface

The *Foreign Relations of the United States* series presents the official documentary historical record of major foreign policy decisions and significant diplomatic activity of the United States Government. The series documents the facts and events that contributed to the formulation of policies and includes evidence of supporting and alternative views to the policy positions ultimately adopted.

The Historian of the Department of State is charged with the responsibility for the preparation of the *Foreign Relations* series. The staff of the Office of the Historian, Bureau of Public Affairs, plans, researches, compiles, and edits the volumes in the series. This documentary editing proceeds in full accord with the generally accepted standards of historical scholarship. Official regulations codifying specific standards for the selection and editing of documents for the series were first promulgated by Secretary of State Frank B. Kellogg on March 26, 1925. These regulations, with minor modifications, guided the series through 1991.

A new statutory charter for the preparation of the series was established by Public Law 102–138, the Foreign Relations Authorization Act, Fiscal Years 1992 and 1993, which was signed by President George Bush on October 28, 1991. Section 198 of P.L. 102–138 added a new Title IV to the Department of State's Basic Authorities Act of 1956 (22 USC 4351, *et seq.*).

The statute requires that the *Foreign Relations* series be a thorough, accurate, and reliable record of major United States foreign policy decisions and significant United States diplomatic activity. The volumes of the series should include all records needed to provide comprehensive documentation of major foreign policy decisions and actions of the United States Government. The statute also confirms the editing principles established by Secretary Kellogg: the *Foreign Relations* series is guided by the principles of historical objectivity and accuracy; records should not be altered or deletions made without indicating in the published text that a deletion has been made; the published record should omit no facts that were of major importance in reaching a decision; and nothing should be omitted for the purposes of concealing a defect in policy. The statute also requires that the *Foreign Relations* series be published not more than 30 years after the events recorded. The editor is convinced that this volume, which was compiled in 1992–1993, meets all regulatory, statutory, and scholarly standards of selection and editing.

Structure and Scope of the Foreign Relations Series

This volume is part of a subseries of volumes of the *Foreign Relations* series that documents the most important issues in the foreign policy of the 5 years (1964–1968) of the administration of Lyndon B. Johnson. The subseries presents in 34 volumes a documentary record of major foreign policy decisions and actions of President Johnson's administration. This volume documents U.S. policy toward Cyprus, Greece, and Turkey.

Principles of Document Selection for the Foreign Relations Series

In preparing each volume of the *Foreign Relations* series, the editors are guided by some general principles for the selection of documents. Each editor, in consultation with the General Editor and other senior editors, determines the particular issues and topics to be documented either in detail, in brief, or in summary.

The following general selection criteria are used in preparing volumes in the *Foreign Relations* series. Individual compiler-editors vary these criteria in accordance with the particular issues and the available documentation. The editors also apply these selection criteria in accordance with their own interpretation of the generally accepted standards of scholarship. In selecting documentation for publication, the editors gave priority to unpublished classified records, rather than previously published records (which are accounted for in appropriate bibliographical notes).

Selection Criteria (in general order of priority):

1. Major foreign affairs commitments made on behalf of the United States to other governments, including those that define or identify the principal foreign affairs interests of the United States;

2. Major foreign affairs issues, commitments, negotiations, and activities, whether or not major decisions were made, and including dissenting or alternative opinions to the process ultimately adopted;

3. The decisions, discussions, actions, and considerations of the President, as the official constitutionally responsible for the direction of foreign policy;

4. The discussions and actions of the National Security Council, the Cabinet, and special Presidential policy groups, including the policy options brought before these bodies or their individual members;

5. The policy options adopted by or considered by the Secretary of State and the most important actions taken to implement Presidential decisions or policies;

6. Diplomatic negotiations and conferences, official correspondence, and other exchanges between U.S. representatives and those of other governments that demonstrate the main lines of policy implementation on major issues;

7. Important elements of information that attended Presidential decisions and policy recommendations of the Secretary of State;

8. Major foreign affairs decisions, negotiations, and commitments undertaken on behalf of the United States by government officials and representatives in other agencies in the foreign affairs community or other branches of government made without the involvement (or even knowledge) of the White House or the Department of State;

9. The main policy lines of intelligence activities if they constituted major aspects of U.S. foreign policy toward a nation or region or if they provided key information in the formulation of major U.S. policies, including relevant National Intelligence Estimates and Special National Intelligence Estimates as may be declassified;

10. The role of the Congress in the preparation and execution of particular foreign policies or foreign affairs actions;

11. Economic aspects of foreign policy;

12. The main policy lines of U.S. military and economic assistance as well as other types of assistance;

13. The political-military recommendations, decisions, and activities of the military establishment and major regional military commands as they bear upon the formulation or execution of major U.S. foreign policies;

14. Diplomatic appointments that reflect major policies or affect policy changes.

Sources for the Foreign Relations Series

The *Foreign Relations* statute requires that the published record in the *Foreign Relations* series include all records needed to provide comprehensive documentation on major U.S. foreign policy decisions and significant U.S. diplomatic activity. It further requires that government agencies, departments, and other entities of the U.S. Government engaged in foreign policy formulation, execution, or support cooperate with the Department of State Historian by providing full and complete access to records pertinent to foreign policy decisions and actions and by providing copies of selected records. Many of the sources consulted in the preparation of this volume have been declassified and are available for review at the National Archives and Records Administration. The declassification review and opening for public review of all Department of State records no later than 30 years after the events is mandated by the *Foreign Relations* statute. The Department of State and other record sources used in the volume are described in detail in the section on Sources below.

*Focus of Research and Principles of Selection for Foreign Relations, 1964–1968,
Volume XVI*

The editor of the volume sought to present documentation illuminating responsibility for major foreign policy decisions in the U.S. Government, with emphasis on the President and his advisers. The documents include memoranda and records of discussions that set forth policy issues and options and show decisions or actions taken. The emphasis is on the development of U.S. policy and on major aspects and repercussions of its execution rather than on the details of policy execution.

Lyndon Johnson's personal involvement in the making of foreign policy decisions relating to Cyprus, Greece, and Turkey was intermittent and tended to focus on Cyprus during the 1964 and 1967 crises on the island republic. The editor sought to document his role as far as possible. Although the foreign policy record of the Johnson administration is voluminous, many internal discussions between Johnson and his advisers apparently were not recorded. President Johnson's involvement as well as that of Secretary of State Rusk in the policy process often had to be pieced together from a variety of sources.

Major topics covered in this volume include: 1) U.S. efforts to maintain the cohesion of the NATO alliance by avoiding outbreaks of violence on Cyprus that would provoke clashes between Greece and Turkey; 2) attempts of U.S. policymakers to devise a compromise solution for Cyprus that would meet the requirements of its major regional partners; 3) a growing U.S. involvement in Greece's internal politics as a result of a major constitutional crisis between political forces led by George and Andreas Papandreou on one side and a conservative coalition under the leadership of King Constantine II on the other; and 4) the U.S reaction to the Greek military coup of April 1967 and imposition of a dictatorship in Greece. Coverage of bilateral U.S.-Turkish relations focuses on the Cyprus issue.

The editor included a selection of intelligence estimates and analyses seen by high-level policymakers, especially those that were made available to President Johnson.

Editorial Methodology

The documents are presented chronologically according to Washington time or, in the case of conferences, in the order of individual meetings. Memoranda of conversation are placed according to the time and date of the conversation, rather than the date the memorandum was drafted.

Editorial treatment of the documents published in the *Foreign Relations* series follows Office style guidelines, supplemented by guidance from the General Editor and the chief technical editor. The source text is reproduced as exactly as possible, including marginalia or other notations, which are described in the footnotes. Texts are transcribed and printed according to accepted conventions for the publication of historical documents in the limitations of modern typography. A heading has been supplied by the editors for each document included in the volume. Spelling, capitalization, and punctuation are retained as found in the source text, except that obvious typographical errors are silently corrected. Other mistakes and omissions in the source text are corrected by bracketed insertions: a correction is set in italic type; an addition in roman type. Words or phrases underlined in the source text are printed in italics. Abbreviations and contractions are preserved as found in the source text, and a list of abbreviations is included in the front matter of each volume.

Bracketed insertions are also used to indicate omitted text that deals with an unrelated subject (in roman type) or that remains classified after declassification review (in italic type). The amount of material not declassified has been noted by indicating the number of lines or pages of source text that were omitted. Entire documents withheld for declassification purposes have been accounted for and are listed by headings, source notes, and number of pages not declassified in their chronological place. The amount of material omitted from this volume because it was unrelated to the subject of the volume, however, has not been delineated. All brackets that appear in the source text are so identified by footnotes.

The first footnote to each document indicates the document's source, original classification, distribution, and drafting information. This note also provides the background of important documents and policies and indicates whether the President or his major policy advisers read the document. Every effort has been made to determine if a document has been previously published, and, if so, this information has been included in the source footnote.

Editorial notes and additional annotation summarize pertinent material not printed in the volume, indicate the location of additional documentary sources, provide references to important related documents printed in other volumes, describe key events, and provide summaries of and citations to public statements that supplement and elucidate the printed documents. Information derived from memoirs and other first-hand accounts has been used when appropriate to supplement or explicate the official record.

Advisory Committee on Historical Diplomatic Documentation

The Advisory Committee on Historical Diplomatic Documentation, established under the *Foreign Relations* statute, reviews records, advises, and makes recommendations concerning the *Foreign Relations* series. The Advisory Committee monitors the overall compilation and editorial process of the series and advises on all aspects of the preparation and declassification of the series. Although the Advisory Committee does not attempt to review the contents of individual volumes in the series, it does monitor the overall process and makes recommendations on particular problems that come to its attention.

The Advisory Committee reviewed the declassification review decisions for this volume.

Declassification Review

The Information Response Branch of the Office of IRM Programs and Services, Bureau of Administration, Department of State, conducted the declassification review of the documents published in this volume. The review was conducted in accordance with the standards set forth in Executive Order 12958 on Classified National Security Information and applicable laws.

Under Executive Order 12958, specific information may be exempt from automatic declassification after 25 years if its release could be expected to:

1) reveal the identity of a confidential human source, or reveal information about the application of an intelligence source or method, or reveal the identity of a human intelligence source when the unauthorized disclosure of that source would clearly and demonstrably damage the national security interests of the United States;

2) reveal information that would assist in the development or use of weapons of mass destruction;

3) reveal information that would impair U.S. cryptologic systems or activities;

4) reveal information that would impair the application of state of the art technology within the U.S. weapon system;

5) reveal actual U.S. military war plans that remain in effect;

6) reveal information that would seriously and demonstrably impair relations between the United States and a foreign government, or seriously and demonstrably undermine ongoing diplomatic activities of the United States;

7) reveal information that would clearly and demonstrably impair the current ability of U.S. Government officials to protect the President, Vice President, and other officials for whom protection services, in the interest of national security, are authorized;

8) reveal information that would seriously and demonstrably impair current national security emergency preparedness plans; or

9) violate a statute, treaty, or international agreement.

The principle guiding declassification review is to release all information, subject only to the current requirements of national security as embodied in law and regulation. Declassification decisions entailed concurrence of the appropriate geographic and functional bureaus in the Department of State, other concerned agencies of the U.S. Government, and the appropriate foreign governments regarding specific documents of those governments.

The final declassification review of this volume, which began in 1993 and was completed in 1999, resulted in the decision to withhold about .4 percent of the documentation proposed for publication; 1 document was withheld in full. A determination to acknowledge discussions in Washington about a proposed covert operation was made by a High-Level Panel consisting of senior officials from the Department of State, the National Security Council, and the Central Intelligence Agency. The Panel's determination was followed by the release of associated documentation proposed for publication.

The Office of the Historian is confident, on the basis of the research conducted in preparing this volume and as a result of the declassification review process described above, that the documentation and editorial notes presented here provide an accurate account of U.S. policy toward Cyprus, Greece, and Turkey during the 1964–1968 period.

Acknowledgments

The editor wishes to acknowledge the assistance of officials at the Lyndon B. Johnson Library of the National Archives and Records Administration, especially David C. Humphrey, Regina Greenwell, and Charlaine Burgess, who provided key research assistance. The editor also wishes to acknowledge the assistance of historians at the Central Intelligence Agency, particularly Michael Warner.

James E. Miller collected documentation for this volume and selected and edited it, under the general supervision of former General Editor Glenn W. LaFantasie. He also prepared the lists of names, sources, and abbreviations. Vicki E. Futscher and Rita M. Baker did the copy and technical editing, and Susan C. Weetman coordinated the final declassification review. Do Mi Stauber prepared the index.

William Slany
The Historian
Bureau of Public Affairs

December 1999

Johnson Administration Volumes

Following is a list of the volumes in the *Foreign Relations* series for the administration of President Lyndon B. Johnson. The titles of individual volumes may change. The year of publication is in parentheses after the title.

Print Volumes

I	Vietnam, 1964 (1992)
II	Vietnam, January–June 1965 (1996)
III	Vietnam, July–December 1965 (1996)
IV	Vietnam, 1966 (1998)
V	Vietnam, 1967
VI	Vietnam, January–August 1968
VII	Vietnam, August–December 1968
VIII	International Monetary and Trade Policy (1998)
IX	International Development and Economic Defense Policy; Commodities (1997)
X	National Security Policy
XI	Arms Control and Disarmament (1997)
XII	Western Europe
XIII	Western Europe Region (1995)
XIV	Soviet Union
XV	Germany and Berlin (1999)
XVI	Cyprus; Greece; Turkey (1999)
XVII	Eastern Europe; Austria; Finland (1996)
XVIII	Arab-Israeli Dispute, 1964–1967
XIX	Six-Day War
XX	Arab-Israeli Dispute, 1967–1968
XXI	Near East Region; Arab Peninsula
XXII	Iran (1999)
XXIII	Congo
XXIV	Africa (1999)
XXV	South Asia
XXVI	Indonesia; Malaysia-Singapore; Philippines
XXVII	Mainland Southeast Asia; Regional Affairs
XXVIII	Laos (1998)
XXIX	Korea; Japan
XXX	China (1998)
XXXI	Central and South America; Mexico
XXXII	Dominican Crisis; Cuba; Caribbean
XXXIII	Organization of Foreign Policy; United Nations
XXXIV	Energy Diplomacy and Global Issues (1999)

Contents

Sources

The editors of the *Foreign Relations* series have complete access to all the retired records and papers of the Department of State: the central files of the Department; the special decentralized files ("lot files") of the Department at the bureau, office, and division levels; the files of the Department's Executive Secretariat, which contain the records of international conferences and high-level official visits, correspondence with foreign leaders by the President and Secretary of State, and memoranda of conversations between the President and Secretary of State and foreign officials; and the files of overseas diplomatic posts. When this volume was being compiled, the Department of State records consulted were still under the custody of the Department, and the footnotes citing Department of State files suggest that the Department is the repository. By the time of publication, however, all the Department's indexed central files for these years have been permanently transferred to the National Archives and Records Administration (Archives II) at College Park, Maryland. Many of the Department's decentralized office (or lot) files covering this period, which the National Archives deems worthy of permanent retention, are in the process of being transferred from the Department's custody to Archives II.

The editors of the *Foreign Relations* series also have full access to the papers of President Johnson and other White House foreign policy records. Presidential papers maintained and preserved at the Presidential libraries include some of the most significant foreign affairs-related documentation from the Department of State and other Federal agencies including the National Security Council, the Central Intelligence Agency, the Department of Defense, and the Joint Chiefs of Staff.

In preparing this volume, the editor made extensive use of Presidential papers and other White House records at the Lyndon B. Johnson Library. The bulk of the foreign policy records at the Johnson Library are in the country files and other component parts of the National Security File. The editor also made extensive use of the Papers of George Ball and Robert Komer, two officials who were deeply involved in policy-making for the region in the first half of the Johnson administration.

Thanks to the leadership of the Johnson Library, the Department of State historians had full access to the audiotapes of President Johnson's telephone conversations. These audiotapes include substantial numbers of telephone conversations between President Johnson and Secretary of State Rusk, Secretary of Defense McNamara, the President's Special Assistant for National Security Affairs McGeorge Bundy, and key members of Congress. The editor of this volume selected for publication five audiotapes of President Johnson's telephone conversations dealing with

Cyprus. The editor prepared transcripts of all or parts of these conversations. Although the transcripts give the substance of the conversations, readers are urged to consult the recordings for a full appreciation of those dimensions that cannot be captured fully in a transcription, such as the speakers' inflections and emphases that may convey nuances of meaning.

Second in importance only to the White House records at the Johnson Library were the records of the Department of State. Because White House interest in the region tended to be limited to periods of crisis, the Ambassadors in the three countries played a major role in the formulation of policy. The volume includes a large selection of telegraphic correspondence between the Embassies and the Department of State. Telegrams also provide the most complete and accurate record of the two Ball missions to the region in the spring of 1964, Dean Acheson's mediation effort on Cyprus that took place in Geneva in the summer of 1964, and the Cyrus Vance mediation of November–December 1967. Finally, U.S. reactions during recurrent crises in Cyprus and at the time of the Greek coup and the December 1967 counter coup of King Constantine are most thoroughly documented in telegraphic exchanges.

The Department's central files contain the cable traffic recording U.S. diplomatic relations with Cyprus, Greece, and Turkey; memoranda of diplomatic conversations; and memoranda proposing action or providing information. Some important documents are found only in the Department's lot files. The Conference Files maintained by the Executive Secretariat contain briefing materials as well as records of conversations. Documentation on initiatives that were not approved is often found only in desk or bureau files. The Ball Papers include summaries of telephone conversations and other useful documentation. Greek and Cyprus Desk Files include a large selection of correspondence, especially the so-called "Official Informal" letters that passed between diplomats in the field and the Department of State's Office of Greek, Turkish, and Iranian Affairs (GTI), which provide critical insights into policy-making.

The Central Intelligence Agency provides the Department of State historians access to intelligence documents from records in its custody and at the Presidential libraries. This access is arranged and facilitated by the CIA's History Staff, part of the Center for the Study of Intelligence, pursuant to a May 1992 memorandum of understanding.

This volume includes a number of intelligence records. Among the intelligence records reviewed for the volume were those in country and intelligence files at the Johnson Library, the files of the Directors of Central Intelligence especially John McCone, CIA intelligence reports and summaries, retired files of the Department of State's Bureau of Intelligence and Research containing National Intelligence Estimates, and the INR Historical Files.

Almost all of this documentation has been made available for use in the *Foreign Relations* series thanks to the consent of the agencies mentioned, the assistance of their staffs, and especially the cooperation and support of the National Archives and Records Administration.

The following list identifies the particular files and collections used in the preparation of this volume. The declassification and transfer to the National Archives of the Department of State records is in process, and many of those records are already available for public review at the National Archives. The declassification review of other records is going forward in accordance with the provisions of Executive Order 12958, under which all records over 25 years old, except file series exemptions requested by agencies and approved by the President, should be reviewed for declassification by 2000.

Unpublished Sources

Department of State

Central Files. See National Archives and Records Administration below.

Lot Files. These files have been transferred or will be transferred to the National Archives and Records Administration at College Park, Maryland, Record Group 59.

Cyprus Desk Files: Lot 66 D 277

> Records maintained by the Officer in Charge of Cyprus Affairs of the Bureau of Near Eastern and South Asian Affairs for 1964.

Cyprus Desk Files: Lot 67 D 412

> Records maintained by the Officer in Charge of Cyprus Affairs of the Bureau of Near Eastern and South Asian Affairs for 1965.

Cyprus Desk Files: Lot 70 D 416

> Records maintained by the Officer in Charge of Cyprus Affairs of the Bureau of Near Eastern and South Asian Affairs for 1967.

Cyprus Desk Files: Lot 72 D 59

> Records maintained by the Officer in Charge of Cyprus Affairs of the Bureau of Near Eastern and South Asian Affairs for 1968.

Greek Desk Files: Lot 66 D 277

> Records maintained by the Officer in Charge of Greek Affairs of the Bureau of Near Eastern and South Asian Affairs for 1964.

Greek Desk Files: Lot 67 D 192

> Records maintained by the Officer in Charge of Greek Affairs of the Bureau of Near Eastern and South Asian Affairs for 1965.

Greek Desk Files: Lot 69 D 15

> Records maintained by the Officer in Charge of Greek Affairs of the Bureau of Near Eastern and South Asian Affairs for 1966.

Greek Desk Files: Lot 69 D 553

Records maintained by the Officer in Charge of Greek Affairs of the Bureau of Near Eastern and South Asian Affairs for 1967.

Greek Desk Files: Lot 71 D 6

Records maintained by the Officer in Charge of Greek Affairs of the Bureau of Near Eastern and South Asian Affairs for 1968.

INR Files

Files maintained by the Bureau of Intelligence and Research.

National Archives and Records Administration, College Park, MD

Record Group 59, Records of the Department of State

Central Files

AID 4 GREECE, economic assistance issues
POL GREECE-US, political relations with Greece
POL TUR-US, political relations with Turkey
POL 1 GREECE, general policy relating to Greece.
POL 2 GREECE, general information on Greece
POL 2-1 GREECE, weekly activities reports on Greece
POL 7 GREECE, visits by Greek officials
POL 7 US-VANCE, Cyprus peacekeeping mediation
POL 12-6 GREECE, internal political affairs
POL 14 GREECE, internal political affairs
POL 15-1 GREECE, internal political affairs
POL 23-9 GREECE, coups and civil disturbances
POL 23-8 CYPRUS, civil disturbances
POL 27 CYPRUS, unrest and civil disturbances
POL 27-14 , CYPRUS-UN, UN peacekeeping activities
DEF TUR, defense arrangements
DEF 15 CYP, defense arrangements

Lot Files

Ball Papers: Lot 74 D 272

Records of Under Secretary of State George Ball, 1961–1966.

Conference Files: Lot 66 D 110

Collection of documentation on international conferences abroad attended by the President, Secretary of State, or other U.S. officials, May 1961–December 1964.

Conference Files: Lot 66 D 347

Collection of documentation on international conferences abroad attended by the President, Secretary of State, or other U.S. officials for 1965.

Conference Files: Lot 67 D 586

Collection of documentation on international conferences abroad attended by the President, Secretary of State, or other U.S. officials, September 1966–April 1967.

Conference Files: Lot 68 D 453

Collection of documentation on international conferences abroad attended by the President, Secretary of State, or other U.S. officials, May 1967–January 1968.

Conference Files: Lot 69 D 182

> Collection of documentation on international conferences abroad attended by the President, Secretary of State, or other U.S. officials for 1968.

Secretary's Memoranda of Conversation: Lot 65 D 330

> Memoranda of conversation of the Secretary and Under Secretary of State, 1961–1964.

SIG Files: Lot 74 D 164

> Records of the Senior Interdepartmental Group.

S/S-NSC Files: Lot 70 D 265

> Master set of papers pertaining to National Security Council meetings, including policy papers, position papers, and administrative documents, 1961–1966.

S/S-NSC Files: Lot 72 D 316

> Master file of National Security Action Memorandums (NSAMs), 1961–1968.

S/S-NSC Files: Lot 72 D 318

> Cabinet and National Security Council records, 1966–1968.

Record Group 84, Records of Diplomatic and Consular Posts

Athens Post Files: Lot 71 A 2420

> Records of the Embassy in Athens, 1964–1966.

Athens Post Files: Lot 72 A 5030

> Records of the Embassy in Athens, 1967–1968.

Central Intelligence Agency

DCI Files: Job 80–B01676R

DCI Files: Job 80–B01285A

CIA Executive Registry, Intelligence Information Cables

Lyndon Baines Johnson Library, Austin, Texas

Papers of Lyndon B. Johnson

National Security File
> Country File
> Files of Robert W. Komer
> NSC Meetings File
> Memos to the President
> Files of McGeorge Bundy

Special Files
> Meeting Notes Files
> President's Office File
> Recordings and Transcripts of Telephone Conversations and Meetings
> Tom Johnson's Notes of Meetings

Other Personal Papers

Ball Papers

Published Sources

Ball, George W. *The Past Has Another Pattern.* New York: Norton, 1982.

Papandreou, Andreas. *Democracy at Gunpoint: The Greek Front.* New York: Doubleday, 1970.

C. L. Sulzberger, *Age of Mediocrity: Memoirs and Diaries, 1963–1972.* New York, Macmillan, 1973.

U.S. National Archives and Records Administration. *Public Papers of the Presidents of the United States: Lyndon Baines Johnson, 1964–1968.* 4 volumes. Washington, D.C.: U.S. Government Printing Office.

U.S. Department of State, Department of State *Bulletin.* Washington, D.C.: U.S. Government Printing Office.

————. *American Foreign Policy: Current Documents, 1959–1964.* Annual volumes. Washington, D.C.: U.S. Government Printing Office.

Abbreviations

AID, Agency for International Development
AKEL, Anorthotikon Komma Ergazo Laou (Reform Party of the Working People) (Cyprus)
AMF, Allied Multilateral Force

BNA, Office of British Commonwealth and Northern European Affairs, Bureau of European Affairs, Department of State

CA, circular airgram
CAS, controlled American source
CENTO, Central Treaty Organization
CGUSAREUR, Commanding General, U.S. Army, Europe
CIA, Central Intelligence Agency
CINCEUR, Commander in Chief, Allied Forces, Europe
CINCMEAFSA, Commander in Chief, Middle East/South Asia and Africa South of the Sahara
CINCSTRIKE, Commander in Chief, Strike Command
CINCUSNAVEUR, Commander in Chief, U.S. Navy, Europe
cirtel, circular telegram
COMSIXTHFLEET, Commander, U.S. Navy Sixth Fleet

DCM, Deputy Chief of Mission
Deptel, Department of State telegram
Depcirtel, Department of State circular telegram
DIA, Defense Intelligence Agency

EAM, Ethnikon Apeleftherikon Meteron (National Liberation Front)
EDA, Elliniki Dimokratiki Aristera (Greek Democratic Left)
Embtel, Embassy telegram
ERE, Ethniki Pizopastiti Enosis (National Radical Union)
EUR, Bureau of European Affairs, Department of State
Exdis, executive distribution only
EXIM, Export-Import Bank

FonMin, Foreign Minister
FonSec, Foreign Secretary

G, Office of the Deputy Under Secretary of State for Political Affairs
GAGS, Greek Army General Staff
GOG, Government of Greece
GOT, Government of Turkey
GTI, Office of Greek, Turkish, and Iranian Affairs, Bureau of Near Eastern and South Asian Affairs, Department of State

HICOM, High Commissioner

ICJ, International Court of Justice at The Hague
ICRC, International Committee of the Red Cross
IDEA, Ieros Desmos Ellinon Axiomatikon (Sacred Bond of Greek Officers)
IERAX (Hawk) 2, code name for NATO Internal Security Plan
IMF, International Monetary Fund

INR, Bureau of Intelligence and Research, Department of State
IO, Bureau of International Organization Affairs, Department of State
IRG, Interdepartmental Review Group

JCS, Joint Chiefs of Staff
JP, Justice Party
JUSMAG, Joint U.S. Military Advisory Group

Limdis, limited distribution only
LANDSOUTHEAST, NATO Land Forces Command, Southeastern Europe
L/UNA, Division of United Nations Affairs, Office of the Legal Adviser, Department of
State

MAP, Military Assistance Program
memcon, memorandum of conversation
MLF, Multilateral Force

NAC, North Atlantic Council
NATO, North Atlantic Treaty Organization
NEA, Bureau of Near Eastern and South Asian Affairs, Department of State
NDGS, National Defense General Staff
NIE, National Intelligence Estimate
Noforn, No foreign dissemination
NSC, National Security Council

OAS, Organization of American States
OASD, Office of the Assistant Secretary of Defense for International Security Affairs
OECD, Organization for Economic Cooperation and Development
OSD, Office of the Secretary of Defense

PKF, peacekeeping force
PM, Prime Minister; Bureau of Politico-Military Affairs, Department of State
POLAD, Political Adviser
PolOff, political officer
Polto, series indicator for telegrams from the U.S. Mission to the North Atlantic Treaty Or-
ganization
PriMin, Prime Minister

RPP, Republican People's Party (Turkey)

S, Office of the Secretary of State
SACEUR, Supreme Allied Commander, Europe
SC, United Nations Security Council
Secto, series indicator for telegrams from the Secretary of State when he is away from
Washington
Secun, series indicator for telegrams from the Under Secretary of State when he is away
from Washington
SHAPE, Supreme Headquarters, Allied Forces, Europe
SIG, Senior Interdepartmental Group
SNIE, Special National Intelligence Estimate
S/S, Executive Secretariat, Office of the Secretary of State
SYG, United Nations Secretary-General

TAF, Turkish Air Force
TAG, series indicator for telegrams

TCPA, Turkish Cypriot Provisional Administration

telcon, telephone conversation

TGS, Turkish General Staff

TOG, series indicator for telegrams to the Under Secretary of State

Topol, series indicator for telegrams to the U.S. Mission to the North Atlantic Treaty Organization

Tosec, series indicator for telegrams to the Secretary of State when he is away from Washington

Tovan, series indicator for telegrams to Cyrus Vance

TUG, series indicator for telegrams to Geneva for Cyprus mediator Dean Acheson

U, Office of the Under Secretary of State for Political Affairs

UK, United Kingdom

UN, United Nations

UNFICYP, United Nations Force in Cyprus

UNGA, United Nations General Assembly

UNP, Office of United Nations Programs, Bureau of International Organization Affairs, Department of State

UNPKF, UN Peacekeeping Force

USAREUR, U.S. Army, Europe

USARMA, U.S. Army Attaché

USDOCOSouth, Documents officer, Allied Forces, Southeastern Europe

USG, United States Government

USIB, U.S. Intelligence Board

USRO, U.S. Mission to the North Atlantic Treaty Organization and European Regional Organizations

USUN, U.S. Mission to the United Nations in New York

Vanto, series indicator for telegrams from Cyrus Vance

VOA, Voice of America

WE, Office of Western European Affairs, Bureau of European Affairs, Department of State

Z, Zulu time (Greenwich mean time)

Persons

Acheson, Dean, former Secretary of State and Presidential mediator for Cyprus, June–September 1964

Anderson, Robert, Office of the Under Secretary of State

Andreadis, Stratis (George), Greek businessman

Anghelis, General Odysseus, Chief of Staff, Greek Armed Forces, 1967–1968

Anschuetz, Norbert, Deputy Chief of Mission, Embassy in Greece to July 1967

Antonakos, Vice Marshal Georgios, Greek Air Force, 1964–1967

Apostolakis, Christos, Greek Minister of Labor, April–December 1967

Arnaoutis, Major Michele, Aide de Camp to King Constantine of Greece

Baker, John, U.S. Mission to the United Nations, New York

Ball, George W., Under Secretary of State to September 1966; Permanent Representative to the United Nations, June–September 1968

Barham, Richard W., Officer in Charge of Greek Affairs, Department of State, 1965–1967

Battle, Lucius D., Assistant Secretary of State for Near Eastern and South Asian Affairs from April 1967

Bayulken, Haluk, Director General of Turkish Ministry of Foreign Affairs

Belcher, Taylor, Ambassador to Cyprus from May 1964

Bernardes, Carlos, Permanent Representative of Brazil to the United Nations; UN Secretary-General's Representative in Cyprus, 1964

Bitsios, Dimitrios, Chief of Cabinet to King Constantine of Greece

Bracken, Katherine W., Director of the Office of Greek, Turkish, and Iranian Affairs, Department of State, to May 1966; Chief of Political Section, Embassy in Greece, from June 1966

Brewster, H. Daniel, Chief of the Political Section, Embassy in Greece, to October 1965; Director of the Office of Greek Affairs, Department of State, from July 1966

Brosio, Manlio, Secretary General of NATO from August 1964

Bruce, David K.E., Ambassador to Great Britain

Buffum, William B., Deputy Assistant Secretary of State for International Organization Affairs from September 1965; Deputy Representative to the United Nations from January 1967

Bunche, Ralph, Under Secretary-General of the United Nations for Political Affairs

Bundy, McGeorge, Special Assistant to the President for National Security Affairs to February 1966

Bundy, William P., Assistant Secretary of Defense for International Security Affairs until March 1964; thereafter Assistant Secretary of State for Far Eastern Affairs

Burchinal, Lieutenant General David, Director of Joint Staff, Joint Chiefs of Staff, to 1966

Burdett, William C., Deputy Assistant Secretary of State for European Affairs to June 1964

Burns, John H., Political Adviser to the Supreme Commander, Allied Powers Europe, to September 1965

Burris, Phillip, Embassy in Italy to September 1965

Butler, Richard A., British Secretary of State for Foreign Affairs to October 1964

Caccia, Sir Harold, Permanent Under Secretary, British Foreign Office Caglayangil, Ihsan Sabri, Turkish Foreign Minister from October 1965

Canellopoulos (also Kanellopoulos), Panayiotis, leader of the National Radical Union (ERE); Greek Prime Minister, April 1967

Caramanlis (also Karamanlis), Constantine, former Greek Prime Minister

Carter, Lieutenant General Marshall S., Deputy Director, Central Intelligence Agency

Cash, Frank E. Jr., Counselor for Military Affairs, Embassy in Turkey, from July 1964

Chapman, General Leonard, Commandant of the U.S. Marine Corps
Chayes, Abram, Legal Adviser of the Department of State
Choidas, Constantine, Chief of Greek Royal Political Bureau to 1965
Christian, George, President Johnson's Press Secretary from 1966
Churchill, George T., Officer in Charge of Turkish Affairs, Department of State, October 1964–July 1966
Cleveland, Harlan, Assistant Secretary of State for International Organization Affairs to August 1965; Permanent Representative to the North Atlantic Treaty Organization from September 1965
Clerides, Glaufkos, Speaker of the Cypriot Parliament
Constantine II (also Konstantine), King of Greece from February 1964
Costopoulos (also Kostopoulos), Stavros, Greek Foreign Minister, February 1964–July 1965; Minister of Defense, July 1965–December 1966
Crawford, William A., Special Assistant for International Affairs to the Supreme Allied Commander, Europe, October 1965–April 1967

Davis, Nathaniel, member, National Security Council Staff
Day, Arthur D., Office of United Nations Programs, Bureau of International Organization Affairs, Department of State
Day, John G., Political Officer, Embassy in Greece, to August 1968
De Gaulle, Charles, President of France
Denktash, Rauf, chief negotiator for the Turkish Cypriot community in 1968 intercommunal talks
Demirel, Suliman, Turkish Prime Minister from October 1965
Dillon, Robert S., Second Secretary of the Embassy in Turkey
Douglas Home, Sir Alec, British Prime Minister to October 1964
Dovas, Lieutenant General Konstantinos, Greek Army (retired), former Chief of King's Household

Economides, Marcos, Executive Secretary, Greek Foreign Ministry
Economou-Gouras, Paul, Greek Foreign Minister, April–December 1967
Edwards, Don, U.S. Congressman (D–Calif.)
Elekdag, Sukru, Turkish Ministry of Foreign Affairs
Erim, Nihan, chief Turkish negotiator at 1964 Geneva talks on Cyprus
Erkin, Feridun.C., Turkish Foreign Minister to February 1965.
Erselman, Brigadier General Andreas, Third Corps, Greek Army
Esenbel, Melih, Turkish Ambassador to the United States

Farmakis, Nikos, journalist; former member of the Greek Parliament
Federenko, Nikolai, Soviet Permanent Representative to the United Nations
Finletter, Thomas K., Permanent Representative to the North Atlantic Council to September 1965. Folsom, Robert S., Country Director for Cyprus, Department of State
Fowler, Henry H., Secretary of the Treasury from April 1965
Fraser, Donald, Congressman (D–Minn.)
Frederika of Hanover, Queen of Greece to February 1964, thereafter Queen Mother of Greece
Freeman, William, First Secretary of the Embassy in Turkey, June 1964–September 1966
Freshman, C. Arnold, Embassy in Italy, July 1965–July 1967
Fulbright, J. William, Jr., Senator (D–Arkansas)

Garoufalias, Petros, Greek Minister of Defense, February 1964–July 1965
Gennimatas, General Ioannis, Chief of Staff, Greek Army, 1964
Georkadjis, Polykarpos, Cypriot Minister of Defense and Interior
Glazos, Manlios, leader of the Greek Democratic Left Party (EDA)

Goldberg, Arthur, Permanent Representative to the United Nations, July1965–June 1968
Gore, Sir David Ormsby (Lord Harlech), British Ambassador to the United States to 1965
Greenhill, Denis, Minister of the British Embassy in Washington
Grivas, Lieutenant General George, Commander, Cyprus National Guard
Gromyko, Andrei A., Soviet Foreign Minister
Gyani, General Prem Singh, Commander, UN Peacekeeping Force in Cyprus, March–June 1964

Handley, William J., Deputy Assistant Secretary of State for Near Eastern and South Asian Affairs, September 1964–October 1967
Hare, Raymond A., Ambassador to Turkey to August 1965; Assistant Secretary of State for Near Eastern and South Asian Affairs, September 1965–October 1966.
Harriman, W. Averell, Under Secretary of State for Political Affairs to March 1965; Ambassador at Large from March 1965
Hart, Parker T., Ambassador to Turkey, July 1965–October 1968
Helms, Richard, Director of Central Intelligence from June 1966
Howison, John M., Director of the Office of Turkish Affairs, Department of State, July 1966–October 1968

Iakovos, Orthodox Archbishop of North and South America
Inonu, Ismet, Turkish Prime Minister to February 1965
Ioannides, Lieutenant Colonel Dimitrios, Chief of Greek Military Police (ESA) from April 1967
Isik, Hasan, Turkish Foreign Minister, February–October 1965

Jacovides, Andreas, Political Director, Cypriot Ministry of Foreign Affairs
James, Alan G., Political Section, Mission to the North Atlantic Treaty Organization and European Regional Organizations
Jernegan, John D., Deputy Assistant Secretary of State for International Organization Affairs to June 1965
Jessup, John, Consul General at Thessaloniki to October 1966
Johnson, Lyndon Baines, President of the United States
Johnson, Tom, White House Press Officer

Karamanlis, *see* Caramanlis
Katzenbach, Nicholas deB., Under Secretary of State from September 1966
Khrushchev, Nikita S., First Secretary of the Soviet Communist Party and Chairman of the Council of Ministers of the USSR until October 1964
King, Gordon D., Officer in Charge of Cypriot Affairs, Department of State, to May 1965
Knight, Ridgway B., Ambassador to Belgium from July 1965
Kohler, Foy D., Ambassador to the Soviet Union to November 1966; thereafter Deputy Under Secretary of State for Political Affairs
Kokkas, Panos, Greek publisher
Kollias, Constantine, Greek Prime Minister, April–December 1967
Komer, Robert W., Member of the National Security Council Staff; Ambassador to Turkey from October 1968
Konstantine, *see* Constantine
Koren, Henry T., Deputy Director, Office of Southeast Asian Affairs, Department of State, to April 1964
Kostantopoulos, Savvas, Greek publisher
Kosygin, Alexei, Vice Chairman of the Soviet Council of Ministers until October 1964; thereafter Chairman (Premier)
Kutchuk, Fazil, Vice President of Cyprus
Kyprianou, Spyros, Cypriot Foreign Minister

Labouisse, Henry R., Ambassador to Greece to May 1965
Ladas, Lieutenant Colonel Ioannis, Greek military conspirator
Lakas, Lieutenant Colonel Antonios, Greek military conspirator
Lambrakis, Christos, Greek publisher
Lazaris, Lieutenant Colonel Ioannis, Greek military conspirator
Lemnitzer, General Lyman L., Supreme Commander, Allied Powers, Europe; also Commander, U.S. European Command
Liarrkos, Major General Sotirios, Greek Army officer
Lyssarides, Vassos, Socialist Party leader in Cyprus and personal physician to Archbishop Makarios

Makarezos, Lieutenant Colonel Nicholas, organizer of the 1967 military coup in Greece; Minister of Economic Coordination from April 1967
Makarios III, Orthodox Archbishop of Cyprus; President of Cyprus
Marie, Anne, of Denmark, Queen of Greece from February 1964
Markezinis, Spiros, Greek politician
Marks, Leonard, Director of the U.S. Information Agency
Martin, Paul, Canadian Foreign Minister to April 1968
Matsas, Alexander A., Greek Ambassador to the United States
McCaskill, Charles W., Cyprus Desk Officer, Department of State, June 1965–August 1967
McCone, John A., Director of Central Intelligence to April 1965
McFarland, George A., Consular-Political Officer, Embassy in Cyprus, to August 1965; Political Officer, Embassy in Turkey, September 1965–August 1967
McKiernan, Thomas, Deputy Chief of Mission, Embassy in Cyprus, to August 1964
McNamara, Robert S., Secretary of Defense to February 1968
McNaughton, John T., Assistant Secretary of Defense for International Security Affairs from March 1964
Menemencioglu, Turgut, Turkish Ambassador to the United States
Menon, Krishna, former Indian Foreign Minister
Mercouri, Melina, actress, proponent of democracy in Greece
Mexis, Lieutenant Colonel Antonios, Greek military conspirator; Secretary General of the Ministry of Social Welfare after April 1967
Mitsotakis, Konstantine, Greek Finance Minister, February 1964–July 1965

Natzinas, Lieutenant General Alexandros, Greek Army (retired)
Nikolareisis (also Nikolareizis), Demitiros, Greek Ambassador to Yugoslavia and Chief negotiator for Greece at 1964 Geneva talks on Cyprus
Nitze, Paul H., Under Secretary of Defense
Novas, George, Speaker of the Greek Parliament, February 1964–July 1965; Greek Prime Minister from July 1965

Palamas, Christos (Christian), Greek Permanent Representative to the North Atlantic Treaty Organization to August 1967; thereafter Greek Ambassador to the United States
Panaghoulis, Alexander, attempted assassin of Greek Prime Minister Papadopoulos, August 1968
Papadatos, Lieutenant General Christos, Greek Army officer
Papademas, Costas, Counselor, Cypriot Embassy in Washington
Papadopoulos, Lieutenant Colonel Constantine, Greek military conspirator
Papadopoulos, Lieutenant Colonel George, organizer of the 1967 Greek military coup; Minister to the Greek Prime Minister, April–December 1967; Prime Minister from December 1967
Papadopoulos, Tassos, Cypriot Minister of Labor
Papaligouras, Panayiotis, Greek Minister of Defense from April 1967

Papandreou, Andreas, Minister to the Greek Prime Minister, February–November 1964, Alternate Minister of Economic Coordination, February–July 1965

Papandreou, George, Greek Prime Minister, February 1964–July 1965

Papathanassiades, General Theodosius, Chief of Military Staff to King Constantine II of Greece

Pappas, Tom, Greek-American industrialist

Paraskevopoulos, John, Greek Prime Minister, December 1966–March 1967

Patsouros, Lieutenant Colonel Theodoros, Greek military conspirator

Pattakos (also Patakos), Brigadier Stylianos, organizer of the April 1967 Greek military coup; Greek Minister of the Interior from April 1967

Pearson, Lester, Canadian Prime Minister to April 1968 Perides, General George, Greek Army officer

Peurifoy, John H., Ambassador to Greece, September 1950–August 1953

Pezmazoglu, John, Deputy Governor of the Bank of Greece

Pipilus, General Ioannis, Chief of Greek Army Staff to 1964

Pipinelis, Panayiotis, Greek Foreign Minister from December 1967

Plaza Lasso, Galo, UN mediator in Cyprus, 1964–1965

Rallis, George, Greek Minister of Public Order, April 1967

Read, Benjamin H., Special Assistant to the Secretary of State, Executive Secretary, Department of State

Reedy, George E., Press Secretary to President Johnson, 1964–1965

Ritchie, Charles, Canadian Ambassador to the United States, 1962–1966

Rockwell, Stuart W., Deputy Assistant Secretary of State for Near Eastern and South Asian Affairs from September 1966

Rolz-Bennett, José, Special Representative of the UN Secretary-General for Cyprus, 1964; Under Secretary-General for Special Political Affairs from 1965

Rossides, Zenon, Cypriot Permanent Representative to the United Nations and Ambassador to the United States

Rostow, Walt W., Counselor and Chairman of the Policy Planning Council, Department of State, until April 1966; thereafter Special Assistant to the President

Roufogalis, Lieutenant Colonel Michael, Deputy Chief, Greek Central Intelligence Agency

Rowan, Carl, Ambassador to Finland to February 1964; Director of the U.S. Information Agency, February 1964–October 1965

Rusk, Dean, Secretary of State

Sampson, Nicos, Greek Cypriot publisher and political activist

Sandys, Duncan, British Minister of Defense to October 1964

Sisco, Joseph J., Assistant Secretary of State for International Organization Affairs from September 1965

Smith, Bromley, Executive Secretary of the National Security Council

Sossides, John, Diplomatic Adviser to Greek Prime Minister George Papandreou, 1964

Spandikakis, Lieutenant General Gregory, Chief, Greek Army General Staff, to April 1967; thereafter Deputy Prime Minister and Minister of Defense

Springsteen, George S., Special Assistant to the Under Secretary of State to September 1966; Deputy Assistant Secretary of State for European Affairs from October 1966 Stamatelopoulos, Lieutenant Colonel Dimitrios, Greek military conspirator

Stephanopoulos, Stephen, Greek Prime Minister, September 1965–December 1966

Sunay, Cedvet, President of Turkey from March 1966

Stein, Robert A., Adviser to the Bureau of Near Eastern and South Asian Affairs, Department of State

Stevenson, Adlai E., Permanent Representative to the United Nations to July 1965

Stikker, Dirk, Secretary General of the North Atlantic Treaty Organization, 1961–1964

Talbot, Phillips H., Assistant Secretary of State for Near Eastern and South Asian Affairs to September 1965; Ambassador to Greece from October 1965
Taylor, General Maxwell D., Chairman of the Joint Chiefs of Staff to 1964
Thant, U, UN Nations Secretary-General
Thimayya, General, Commander, UN Forces in Cyprus (UNFICYP) from July 1964
Thompson, Llewellyn H., Ambassador to the Soviet Union from December 1966
Toumbas, Admiral John, Greek Foreign Minister, May–December 1966
Tsasakos, Lieutenant Colonel Ilias, Chief of Greek Air Force Security
Tsatsos, Constantine, Greek Parliamentary Deputy
Tsirimokos, Elias, Greek Prime Minister from August 1965; Foreign Minister and Deputy Prime Minister, August 1965–April 1966
Tuomioja, Sakari Severi, UN mediator on Cyprus, March–July 1964
Turkmen, Ilter, Chairman of Policy Planning, Turkish Foreign Ministry
Tyler, William R., Assistant Secretary of State for European Affairs to May 1965

Urguplu, Ali Suat, Turkish Prime Minister, February–ober 1965

Vagenas, Lieutenant Colonel George, Director of the Greek Army General Staff
Valenti, Jack, Special Assistant to the President
Vance, Cyrus, Deputy Secretary of Defense to June 1967; Presidential mediator for Cyprus, November–ember 1967
Venizelos, Sophocles, Greek Parliamentary Deputy; deputy leader of the Center Union Party until February 1964.
Vigderman, Alfred G., Counselor for Political Affairs, Embassy in Greece to August 1966

Wehmeyer, Donald A., Division of Near Eastern and Asian Affairs, Office of the Legal Adviser, Department of State
Wheeler, General Earle, U.S. Army Chief of Staff until July 1, 1964; thereafter Chairman of the Joint Chiefs of Staff
Wilkins, Fraser, Ambassador to Cyprus to May 1964
Wood, Chalmers, Director of the Office of Cyprus Affairs, Department of State, August 1966–May 1967

Yost, Charles W., Deputy Permanent Representative to the United Nations from September 1965

Zoitakis, General George, Regent of Greece from December 1967
Zolotas, Zenophone, Governor of the Bank of Greece 30

U.S. Covert Actions and Counter-Insurgency Programs

In compliance with the *Foreign Relations of the United States* statute to include in the *Foreign Relations* series comprehensive documentation on major foreign policy decisions and actions, the editors have sought to present essential documents regarding major covert actions and intelligence activities. In order to provide readers with some organizational context on how covert actions and special intelligence operations in support of U.S. foreign policy were planned and approved within the U.S. Government, the following note is offered. It describes, on the basis of previously-declassified documents, the changing and developing procedures during the Truman, Eisenhower, Kennedy, and Johnson Presidencies.

Management of Covert Actions in the Truman Presidency

The Truman administration's concern over Soviet "psychological warfare" prompted the new National Security Council to authorize, in NSC 4-A of December 1947, the launching of peacetime covert action operations. NSC 4-A made the Director of Central Intelligence responsible for psychological warfare, establishing at the same time the principle that covert action was an exclusively Executive Branch function. The Central Intelligence Agency (CIA) certainly was a natural choice but it was assigned this function at least in part because the Agency controlled unvouchered funds, by which operations could be funded with minimal risk of exposure in Washington.[1]

CIA's early use of its new covert action mandate dissatisfied officials at the Departments of State and Defense. The Department of State, believing this role too important to be left to the CIA alone and concerned that the military might create a new rival covert action office in the Pentagon, pressed to reopen the issue of where responsibility for covert action activities should reside. Consequently, on June 18, 1948, a new NSC directive, NSC 10/2, superseded NSC 4-A.

NSC 10/2 directed CIA to conduct "covert" rather than merely "psychological" operations, defining them as all activities "which are conducted or sponsored by this Government against hostile foreign

---

[1] NSC 4-A, December 17, 1947, printed in *Foreign Relations*, 1945–1950, Emergence of the Intelligence Establishment, Document 257.

states or groups or in support of friendly foreign states or groups but which are so planned and executed that any US Government responsibility for them is not evident to unauthorized persons and that if uncovered the US Government can plausibly disclaim any responsibility for them."

The type of clandestine activities enumerated under the new directive included: "propaganda; economic warfare; preventive direct action, including sabotage, demolition and evacuation measures; subversion against hostile states, including assistance to underground resistance movements, guerrillas and refugee liberations [sic] groups, and support of indigenous anti-Communist elements in threatened countries of the free world. Such operations should not include armed conflict by recognized military forces, espionage, counter-espionage, and cover and deception for military operations."[2]

The Office of Policy Coordination (OPC), newly established in the CIA on September 1, 1948, in accordance with NSC 10/2, assumed responsibility for organizing and managing covert actions. OPC, which was to take its guidance from the Department of State in peacetime and from the military in wartime, initially had direct access to the State Department and to the military without having to proceed through CIA's administrative hierarchy, provided the Director of Central Intelligence (DCI) was informed of all important projects and decisions.[3] In 1950 this arrangement was modified to ensure that policy guidance came to OPC through the DCI.

During the Korean conflict the OPC grew quickly. Wartime commitments and other missions soon made covert action the most expensive and bureaucratically prominent of CIA's activities. Concerned about this situation, DCI Walter Bedell Smith in early 1951 asked the NSC for enhanced policy guidance and a ruling on the proper "scope and magnitude" of CIA operations. The White House responded with two initiatives. In April 1951 President Truman created the Psychological Strategy Board (PSB) under the NSC to coordinate government-wide psychological warfare strategy. NSC 10/5, issued in October 1951, reaffirmed the covert action mandate given in NSC 10/2 and expanded CIA's authority over guerrilla warfare.[4] The PSB was soon abolished by the incoming Eisenhower administration, but the expansion of CIA's co-

---

[2] NSC 10/2, June 18, 1948, printed ibid., Document 292.

[3] Memorandum of conversation by Frank G. Wisner, "Implementation of NSC-10/2," August 12, 1948, printed ibid., Document 298.

[4] NSC 10/5, "Scope and Pace of Covert Operations," October 23, 1951, in Michael Warner, editor, *The CIA Under Harry Truman* (Washington, D.C.: Central Intelligence Agency, 1994), pp. 437–439.

vert action writ in NSC 10/5 helped ensure that covert action would remain a major function of the Agency.

As the Truman administration ended, CIA was near the peak of its independence and authority in the field of covert action. Although CIA continued to seek and receive advice on specific projects from the NSC, the PSB, and the departmental representatives originally delegated to advise OPC, no group or officer outside of the DCI and the President himself had authority to order, approve, manage, or curtail operations.

NSC 5412 Special Group; 5412/2 Special Group; 303 Committee

The Eisenhower administration began narrowing CIA's latitude in 1954. In accordance with a series of National Security Council directives, the responsibility of the Director of Central Intelligence for the conduct of covert operations was further clarified. President Eisenhower approved NSC 5412 on March 15, 1954, reaffirming the Central Intelligence Agency's responsibility for conducting covert actions abroad. A definition of covert actions was set forth; the DCI was made responsible for coordinating with designated representatives of the Secretary of State and the Secretary of Defense to ensure that covert operations were planned and conducted in a manner consistent with U.S. foreign and military policies; and the Operations Coordinating Board was designated the normal channel for coordinating support for covert operations among State, Defense, and CIA. Representatives of the Secretary of State, the Secretary of Defense, and the President were to be advised in advance of major covert action programs initiated by the CIA under this policy and were to give policy approval for such programs and secure coordination of support among the Departments of State and Defense and the CIA.[5]

A year later, on March 12, 1955, NSC 5412/1 was issued, identical to NSC 5412 except for designating the Planning Coordination Group as the body responsible for coordinating covert operations. NSC 5412/2 of December 28, 1955, assigned to representatives (of the rank of assistant secretary) of the Secretary of State, the Secretary of Defense, and the President responsibility for coordinating covert actions. By the end of the Eisenhower administration, this group, which became known as the "NSC 5412/2 Special Group" or simply "Special Group," emerged as the executive body to review and approve covert action programs initiated

---

[5] William M. Leary, editor, *The Central Intelligence Agency: History and Documents* (The University of Alabama Press, 1984), p. 63; the text of NSC 5412 will be printed in *Foreign Relations, 1950–1960*, Development of the Intelligence Community, scheduled for publication in 2000.

by the CIA.[6] The membership of the Special Group varied depending upon the situation faced. Meetings were infrequent until 1959 when weekly meetings began to be held. Neither the CIA nor the Special Group adopted fixed criteria for bringing projects before the group; initiative remained with the CIA, as members representing other agencies frequently were unable to judge the feasibility of particular projects.[7]

After the Bay of Pigs failure in April 1961, General Maxwell Taylor reviewed U.S. paramilitary capabilities at President Kennedy's request and submitted a report in June which recommended strengthening high-level direction of covert operations. As a result of the Taylor Report, the Special Group, chaired by the President's Special Assistant for National Security Affairs McGeorge Bundy, and including Deputy Under Secretary of State U. Alexis Johnson, Deputy Secretary of Defense Roswell Gilpatric, Director of Central Intelligence Allen Dulles, and Chairman of the Joint Chiefs of Staff General Lyman Lemnitzer, assumed greater responsibility for planning and reviewing covert operations. Until 1963 the DCI determined whether a CIA-originated project was submitted to the Special Group. In 1963 the Special Group developed general but informal criteria, including risk, possibility of success, potential for exposure, political sensitivity, and cost (a threshold of $25,000 was adopted by the CIA), for determining whether covert action projects were submitted to the Special Group.[8]

From November 1961 to October 1962 a Special Group (Augmented), whose membership was the same as the Special Group plus Attorney General Robert Kennedy and General Taylor (as Chairman), exercised responsibility for Operation Mongoose, a major covert action program aimed at overthrowing the Castro regime in Cuba. When President Kennedy authorized the program in November, he designated Brigadier General Edward G. Lansdale, Assistant for Special Operations to the Secretary of Defense, to act as chief of operations, and Lansdale coordinated the Mongoose activities among the CIA and the Departments of State and Defense. CIA units in Washington and Miami had primary responsibility for implementing Mongoose operations, which included military, sabotage, and political propaganda programs.[9]

NSAM No. 303, June 2, 1964, from Bundy to the Secretaries of State and Defense and the DCI, changed the name of "Special Group 5412" to

---

[6] Leary, *The Central Intelligence Agency: History and Documents*, pp. 63, 147–148; *Final Report of the Select Committee To Study Governmental Operations With Respect to Intelligence Activities, United States Senate*, Book I, *Foreign and Military Intelligence* (1976), pp. 50–51. The texts of NSC 5412/1 and NSC 5412/2 will be printed in *Foreign Relations*, 1950–1960, Development of the Intelligence Community, scheduled for publication in 2000.

[7] Leary, *The Central Intelligence Agency: History and Documents*, p. 63.

[8] Ibid., p. 82.

[9] See *Foreign Relations*, 1961–1963, vol. X, Documents 270 and 278.

"303 Committee" but did not alter its composition, functions, or responsibility. Bundy was the chairman of the 303 Committee.[10]

The Special Group and the 303 Committee approved 163 covert actions during the Kennedy administration and 142 during the Johnson administration through February 1967. The 1976 Final Report of the Church Committee, however, estimated that of the several thousand projects undertaken by the CIA since 1961, only 14 percent were considered on a case-by-case basis by the 303 Committee and its predecessors (and successors). Those not reviewed by the 303 Committee were low-risk and low-cost operations. The Final Report also cited a February 1967 CIA memorandum that included a description of the mode of policy arbitration of decisions on covert actions within the 303 Committee system. CIA presentations were questioned, amended, and even on occasion denied, despite protests from the DCI. Department of State objections modified or nullified proposed operations, and the 303 Committee sometimes decided that some agency other than CIA should undertake an operation or that CIA actions requested by Ambassadors on the scene should be rejected.[11]

Special Group (Counter-Insurgency)

In March 1961 early in the administration of President Kennedy, a Counter-Guerrilla Task Force under CIA Deputy Director for Plans Richard Bissell was set up. In December the Bissell Task Force completed its report "Elements of US Strategy To Deal With Wars of National Liberation." NSC Staff member Robert Komer proposed to Bundy that "high-level responsibility" for coordinating counter-insurgency activities should be assigned to "Taylor and the Special Group," separate from the mechanism for implementing NSC 5412/2.[12]

On January 18, 1962, President Kennedy signed NSAM No. 124, which established the Special Group (Counter-Insurgency) to be composed of the Military Representative of the President (Taylor) as Chairman, the Attorney General, Deputy Under Secretary of State for Political Affairs, Deputy Secretary of Defense, Chairman of the Joint Chiefs of Staff, the Director of Central Intelligence, the President's Special Assistant for National Security Affairs, and the Administrator of AID. The task of Special Group (CI) would be "to assure unity of effort and the use of all available resources with maximum effectiveness in preventing and

---

[10]Text of NSAM No. 303 will be printed in *Foreign Relations, 1964–1968*, vol. X, scheduled for publication in 2000.

[11] *Final Report of the Select Committee To Study Governmental Operations With Respect to Intelligence Activities, United States Senate* Book I, *Foreign and Military Intelligence*, pp. 56–57.

[12]*Foreign Relations, 1961–1963*, vols. VII, VIII, IX, Microfiche Supplement, Document 249, and Richard M. Bissell, *Reflections of a Cold Warrior* (New Haven, CT: Yale University Press, 1996), p. 149.

resisting subversive insurgency and related forms of indirect aggression in friendly countries." The Special Group (CI) was to confine itself to establishing broad policies and give oversight to country or regional interagency task forces. An annex to NSAM No. 124 assigned Thailand, Vietnam, and Laos to the initial cognizance of the Special Group (CI).[13]

The Special Group (CI) held its first meeting on January 18, 1962, and subsequently held weekly 2-hour meetings with no substitute members allowed. Although members may have preferred that the Special Group (CI) act as a separate executive body to carry out its decisions, the decisions were coordinated with the various executive departments and agencies within the existing chain of command. General Taylor served as Chairman until he became Chairman of the Joint Chiefs of Staff in October 1962 when Deputy Under Secretary of State U. Alexis Johnson succeeded him.[14]

Throughout much of 1962, Special Group (CI) received extensive briefings on the situations in Vietnam, Laos, Thailand, Iran, Indonesia, and other countries faced with what the Group regarded as "internal defense problems." After much debate and interagency drafting, an agreed Special Group (CI) policy statement on counter-insurgency was set forth in a State Department report of September 1962, entitled "United States Overseas Internal Defense Policy." The policy expressed in the report, which was approved by President Kennedy in NSAM No. 182, included the presumption that counter-insurgency programs (referred to as "internal defense programs" in the report) should not be limited to military measures but should also involve as necessary such additional dimensions as economic development, police control, and effective local government.[15]

In the course of its existence until 1966, Special Group (CI) spurred the establishment of extensive training courses on counter-insurgency throughout the government; promoted the responsibility of interagency "country teams" in the countries concerned to develop "Internal Defense Plans;" examined and reshaped programs for advising, supplying, and training paramilitary and military forces in developing countries; encouraged the redirection and expansion of government programs to equip police forces in developing countries; agreed on programs to encourage the local military in these countries to undertake their own "civic action" programs; asked for additional government

---

[13] For text of NSAM No. 124, see *Foreign Relations*, 1961–1963, vol. VIII, Document 68.

[14] Memorandum by McCone, August 17, 1962, published ibid., 1961–1963, vols. VII, VIII, IX, Microfiche Supplement, Document 277, and U. Alexis Johnson, *The Right Hand of Power* (Englewood Cliffs, NJ: Prentice-Hall, Inc., 1984), p. 330.

[15] "United States Overseas Internal Defense Policy," September 1962, and NSAM No. 182 are printed, respectively, in *Foreign Relations*, 1961–1963, vols. VII, VIII, IX, Microfiche Supplement, Document 279, and ibid., vol. VIII, Document 105.

weapons research for counter-insurgency operations; urged the Agency for International Development to coordinate economic assistance programs with military civic action programs; and urged the CIA to increase its intelligence and counter intelligence activity in target countries.[16]

On October 15, 1963, General Taylor, signing as Chairman of the JCS, addressed a memorandum to members of the Special Group (CI) entitled "U.S. Support of Foreign Paramilitary Forces," which concluded that U.S. policy to support the Honduran Civil Guard had resulted in the overthrow of the constitutional government. Taylor observed that the Honduras experience suggested that U.S. programs in other countries should be reviewed to determine whether similar potentially dangerous situations were being fostered, and he recommended that "interagency working groups which monitor internal defense plans" review these programs and report to the Special Group (CI).[17]

On January 17, 1966, General Taylor wrote to President Johnson recommending that the Special Group (CI) "be converted into an agency for supporting the Secretary of State in discharging his broadened responsibilities for the direction, coordination, and supervision of overseas affairs." In NSAM No. 341, March 2, 1966, President Johnson assigned to the Secretary of State the "authority and responsibility to the full extent permitted by law for the overall direction, coordination, and supervision of interdepartmental [counter subversion] activities of the United States government overseas." A Senior Interdepartmental Group (SIG), chaired by the Under Secretary of State, was established to assist the Secretary of State in discharging his responsibilities. Assistant Secretaries of State would chair interdepartmental regional groups (IRGs) within the SIG structure to coordinate regional planning and actions.[18]

W. Averell Harriman, chairman of the former Special Group (CI), wrote on March 7, 1966, to Under Secretary George Ball that "real progress has been made in that field. We have learned from mistakes and know considerably more about the matters on which to concentrate."[19] Counter-insurgency doctrine in the areas supervised by the Secretary of State was re-defined in a SIG-approved paper of May 23, 1968.[20]

---

[16] See Johnson, *The Right Hand of Power,* pp. 330–339.

[17] Memorandum from Taylor to Special Group (CI), October 15, 1963, published in *Foreign Relations,* 1961–1963, vols. VII, VIII, IX, Microfiche Supplement, Document 300.

[18] Memorandum from Taylor to President Johnson, January 17, 1966, NSAM No. 341, and other documentation on the origins of the SIG will be printed in *Foreign Relations,* 1964-1968, vol. XXXIII, scheduled for publication in 2000.

[19] Scheduled for publication ibid.

[20] Editorial note to be printed ibid., vol. X, scheduled for publication in 2000.

THE BALL MISSIONS AND MEETINGS AT WASHINGTON, JANUARY–JUNE 1964

1. Memorandum of Conversation[1]

Washington, January 24, 1964.

SUBJECT

Cyprus

PARTICIPANTS

Sir David Ormsby Gore, British Ambassador
Nigel Trench, Counselor, British Embassy

The Secretary
The Under Secretary
Phillips Talbot, Assistant Secretary, NEA
William C. Burdett, Deputy Assistant Secretary, EUR
Henry T. Koren, SEA

The Ambassador said that the outlook both for the London conference[2] and the situation on the island was very black. The Greeks and Turks in London were poles apart, and the Cypriot Turks were very nervous about their position. If there were a breakdown in London and a flare-up in Cyprus, very strong measures would have to be taken. He asked the Secretary's opinion on the relative merits of a UN "peace-keeping" mission and a force drawn from NATO countries. He mentioned that the Greek Foreign Minister had suggested a NATO force.

The Secretary replied he wasn't fully advised on the question and could not give a final answer now, but he could see advantages in discussing it in NATO, which might produce some pressure on the Greeks and Turks. If the three guarantor powers plus Cyprus so requested, he could see some advantage in using troops from NATO powers. He thought it would probably be best not to have any such force under the NATO label, but it might be better to draw on the NATO nations rather than put the matter to the UN. The Secretary said he could give no answer on the question of a U.S. contingent. He pointed out we have some 17,000 troops in Turkey and if our troops were in Cyprus shooting at Turks, we might run into some serious trouble in Turkey,

---

[1] Source: Department of State, Secretary's Memoranda of Conversation: Lot 65 D 330. Secret. Drafted by Koren and approved in S on February 8.

[2] Reference is to the January 15–February 5 meeting of representatives of the Government of Cyprus, Turkish Cypriots, and representatives of the three guarantor powers: Greece, Turkey, and the United Kingdom.

where they might begin shooting at us. He also mentioned our interest in the security of our important installations on Cyprus.

The Secretary continued he hoped they could keep talking in London. The Ambassador reiterated that the situation in the island was bad and the talks deadlocked. If fighting broke out Turkey might take some precipitate action. Mr. Burdett said that EUR's feeling was that the gravity of the situation and the many complications of using troops from NATO countries made it desirable that Cyprus be a first priority for UK troops. The Secretary observed that there should be a note of caution on priorities in view of the serious and spreading situation in East Africa. If the situation quickly went bad UK troops were the only and best way; but otherwise troops from some NATO countries acceptable to both the Greeks and Turks might be used. He mentioned Norway as an example.

2.   Telephone Conversation Between President Johnson and the Under Secretary of State (Ball)[1]

Washington, January 25, 1964, 2:05 p.m.

GWB:[2] any bad news from any other part of the world, but the situation in Cyprus has been getting worse in the last few days.

LBJ: Yeah, I'm reading it.

GWB: The British Ambassador was in to see me this morning[3] and he said that they're not prepared to continue alone to try to carry this because of the political problem they find themselves in—the history of the hatred of the British on both the Greeks' and Turks' side as far as the local population is concerned. And that he wanted us to agree with them on a

---

[1] Source: Johnson Library, Recordings and Transcripts, Recording of Telephone Conversation between President Johnson and Ball, January 25, 1964, 2:05 p.m., Tape F64.07, Side B, PNO 4. No classification marking. This transcript was prepared by the Office of the Historian specifically for this volume.
[2] The recording of the conversation begins in mid-sentence.
[3] At a noon meeting, Ambassador Ormsby Gore reported on the lack of progress at the London four-power talks and on the "disturbing" situation on Cyprus. He informed U.S. representatives that the British Government wanted to internationalize the problem either through NATO or U.N. intervention in the crisis. A memorandum of conversation of this meeting is ibid. Ball passed the substance of the meeting to President Johnson in a 2:10 p.m. telephone conversation. The President directed Ball to "try to get NATO—not the U.N." (Johnson Library, Ball Papers, Telephone Conversations, Cyprus Pre-Trip)

proposal to try and internationalize the arrangement. Now, this would mean one of two things—

LBJ: NATO going in or the UN?

GWB: No. Getting a NATO force to go in or going to the UN. The UN would be very bad because it would—

LBJ: I'd try to get NATO to go in if I could.

GWB: Well.

LBJ: I think that the British are getting to where they might as well not be British anymore if they can't handle Cyprus.

GWB: Well, I've, they're—we put it to them very strong as to whether this was on the basis that they were spread too thin in which case we might relieve some of their forces from, even from Germany. But the—what Ormsby Gore says—and this checks with our own advice—is that putting additional British forces in is probably just going to make the situation worse rather than better.

Now, I'm meeting with Bob McNamara at five o'clock.[4] In the meantime, we're having this thing looked at by the Joint Chiefs—

LBJ: I'll be available and I'll talk to you—

GWB: We'll have a recommendation—

LBJ: —and I would say off-hand that I would have NATO—try to get NATO in there. And I think the UN's out, but I'd tell the British that there might as well not be a Britain anymore if they can't handle Cyprus.

GWB: Right. Well, this is—what we're taking a hard look at—

LBJ: And I'd let them relieve whatever they needed in Germany to put there rather than NATO. But they won't do it, then we go to NATO. I don't agree that it's going to make it worse, because they can—I'm ashamed of them, but go ahead and let's take NATO.

GWB: Well, we'll have a recommendation for you. Bob and I are getting together at five and [unintelligible].

[Here follows discussion of the situation in Panama.]

---

[4] See footnote 2, Document 3.

3.   Memorandum of Conference With President Johnson[1]

Washington, January 25, 1964, 6:30 p.m.

SUBJECT

Cyprus

OTHERS PRESENT

Acting Secretary Ball, Secretary McNamara, General Taylor, Mr. Valenti, Mr. Komer, Mr. Bromley Smith

Prior to the meeting with the President, the following met in the Cabinet Room from 5:00 to 6:30 PM:[2]

State: Acting Secretary Ball, Under Secretary Harriman, Mr. Cleveland, Mr. Talbot, Mr. Burdett, Mr. Chayes, Mr. Jernegan
Defense: Secretary McNamara, General Taylor, Mr. William Bundy, Admiral Chew, Captain Conkey, Mr. Sloan
CIA: General Carter
White House: Mr. Bromley Smith, Mr. Komer

Acting Secretary Ball reviewed the current situation in Cyprus and the British request that we send U.S. troops as part of an allied force to Cyprus.[3] The discussion centered around the attached draft telegram[4] as being the preferred course of action because of disadvantages associated with taking the question to the UN or taking it to the North Atlantic Council.

Mr. Ball reviewed for the President the planning which had been done in the State and Defense Departments since the British démarche. He recalled that the British had been told of our great reluctance to consider the use of U.S. combat troops, but that the British Prime Minister had again requested us to participate in an allied force as the only way to alter a rapidly deteriorating situation in Cyprus which the British were not prepared to continue to deal with alone.

Secretary Ball said an appeal to the UN had been ruled out as the worst possible alternative. The UN might set up a peacekeeping force which would be beyond our control and in which the Russians and the Yugoslavs would undoubtedly want to participate. A NATO solution was not possible because Cyprus is not a member of NATO even though,

---

[1] Source: Johnson Library, National Security File, Files of McGeorge Bundy, Miscellaneous Meetings. Top Secret. Drafted by Bromley Smith.

[2] A memorandum of this discussion is in Department of State, Secretary's Memoranda of Conversation: Lot 65 D 330.

[3] See footnote 3, Document 2.

[4] Not found.

if the worst happened, two NATO allies would be fighting each other. The tripartite negotiations of the three guarantor powers, U.K., Greece and Turkey, have broken down in London. Prime Minister Inonu is in charge of a weak government in Ankara and may have trouble keeping civilian control of the Turkish military. In Athens, where there is a caretaker government, there may be a military coup. The prospect of such a coup would be greatly increased by serious fighting in Cyprus.

Mr. Ball recommended that we ask the British government to send a ranking military officer to Washington tomorrow in order to obtain more information about their proposed allied intervention force. He said the group would postpone until tomorrow at least making a recommendation on whether or not we should join the U.K. in seeking to establish a military force composed of troops from NATO countries. He suggested that the President might want to talk to the leaders of Congress tomorrow. He summarized the guidelines which would govern our participation in an allied force as follows:

1. The U.S. would make a token contribution—a battalion of 1200 men.
2. The bulk of the force would be British.
3. Two other NATO allies would make token contributions equal to the U.S. contribution.
4. The force would not go into Cyprus until it was large enough to be "adequate" to the need. We do not now know whether the British figure of 10,000 men would be adequate.
5. The military mission of the force would be specifically defined. The British would command the force.

Mr. Ball discussed whether General Lemnitzer should go to Ankara and later to Athens. He said the Turkish military may move in the next two or three days. The Turks have promised us that they will consult before they intervene in Cyprus. But if there were a massacre involving a large number of Turkish Cypriots, the Turkish military might jump off immediately. The civil government in Turkey is very weak and the military may force its hand.

President Makarios may on his own take the case to the UN Security Council. We doubt that any serious resolution could come out of the Security Council unless major fighting broke out or unless the Turkish government intervened militarily.

Ambassador Bruce has reported that the British consider the Cyprus situation more serious and much more important than the Malaysia crisis. They recall the agony of the last time they attempted to keep peace in Cyprus. They have two major bases in Cyprus which they intend to defend. If civil strife outside the bases becomes too great for them to handle, their present plan is to withdraw their troops within the bases and wait out the situation. If major reenforcements of British troops were sent to Cyprus, the Conservatives know that they would be severely attacked by the Labor Party in an election period. The British are also sensitive to the fact that they were the colonial power prior to their withdrawal from Cyprus and that, therefore, they are a hostage to the past.

The President said if the British had election problems, he had problems with the U.S. citizens of Greek background.

Mr. Ball replied that the Greek Government had favored the intervention of allied forces.

The President referred to the fact that our elections are coming and that the prospect of sending U.S. troops into Cyprus is one to face only as a last resort.

Secretary McNamara said that the unfortunate part of the situation was that the only solution to the problem in Cyprus was to force the Greek Cypriots to do something they did not want to do, namely, not increase their control over the Turkish Cypriots by revising the existing Constitution and agreements.

The President asked everyone to go slow on any plan to use U.S. troops in Cyprus. He said there is nothing we can do which will not end up in our losing. Mr. Ball acknowledged that there was no good solution to the problem. He said that if it were necessary to reenforce the original U.S. complement, all participants would contribute to the reenforcement in the same percentage. Secretary McNamara said that if we do go in, the percentage of our participation is the extent of our share of the operation. He thought that 6500 men would have to be put in by others and he did not know where these troops were coming from. Our share would be no more than 1200 men.

General Taylor said that if we do put in our troops, we would provide our own supplies and our own logistic backup. We would ask that each participant do the same.

The President said that perhaps we would have to go through a blood bath in Cyprus before we could take any U.S. military action. He asked whether it were not possible for someone else to go in, such as a neutral or Nasser.

Mr. Ball responded by saying that Makarios wants a neutral such as Nasser or a UN group with neutrals because he is convinced that the neutrals will favor him over the Turks in Cyprus.

The President said General Lemnitzer could tell the Turks not to go into Cyprus and the same thing to the Greeks. We have been holding up numerous situations around the world and we are not going to walk out, but we don't expect others to walk out either. General Lemnitzer should tell Inonu how we feel. Mr. Ball suggested that General Lemnitzer also talk to the military directly because Inonu may not be in full control of the Turkish military.

The President said we should give no encouragement to the U.K. to think that we would join in an allied force. He then asked what would happen if we did not go in.

Mr. Ball replied that the situation might blow up with the result that two NATO allies would be fighting each other. It was also possible that Makarios would ask the UN to come in and a UN peacekeeping force would have Communist elements in it.

Secretary McNamara pointed out that the Greeks in Cyprus out-number the Turks four to one. He repeated his earlier statement that a political settlement would mean forcing the Greeks to do something they did not now wish to do.

The President asked what else we could do—was a conference pos-sible? Could we get people discussing their problems around a table? Mr. Ball replied that the London tripartite conference had blown up. The U.S. had no status in that conference because it was composed of the three guarantor powers. It is difficult to talk to the Greeks and the Turks because of the weakness of these governments. The views of the Greeks and the Turks are more crystallized and farther apart as the result of the conference in London than before.

The President said it would be necessary to shove him very hard to get him to agree to send U.S. troops to Cyprus. We must do more in a dip-lomatic way than we have so far.

Mr. Ball said that both the Turkish and Greek Foreign Ministers were in London and it would be possible for Ambassador Bruce to talk to them there.[5] The President agreed.

The President said we should ask the British to send more troops to Cyprus. We have helped them in the past and they must now continue to carry this burden in Cyprus.[6] We should hold off replying to the British until after we hear from General Lemnitzer.

Bromley Smith[7]

---

[5] Bruce reported on his talks with British officials in telegrams 3499 from London, January 25, and 3510 from London, January 26. (Department of State, Central Files, POL 23–8 CYP) Details on the talks and Bruce's views are in the Bruce Diary, January 26 and 27, 1964. (Ibid., Bruce Diaries: Lot 64 D 327)

[6] Ball told Ormsby Gore during a meeting at 7:15 p.m. that the United States was not prepared to commit troops to a Cyprus operation, but would provide the United Nations with logistical support. The memorandum of their conversation is ibid., Secretary's Memo-randa of Conversation: Lot 65 D 330.

[7] Printed from a copy that bears this typed signature.

4.   Editorial Note

At approximately 6:35 p.m., January 28, 1964, Acting Secretary of State George Ball called President Johnson with the outline of a "plan" for Cyprus that would involve sending to Cyprus a contingent of 1,200 U.S. soldiers as part of a 10,000-man NATO peacekeeping force designed to facilitate mediation of the crisis by separating the warring parties. Ball indicated that the plan had the approval of Secretary of Defense McNamara. The President expressed continued skepticism about the utility of sending U.S. troops to the island:

LBJ: Why do we want to put something in?
GWB: I think that, the word we've had all through the day is that there's danger of a blow up. That the situation.
LBJ: That's the danger. They're just trying to make us move and get into something we can't get out of, I think.
GWB: Well, the point of this plan is that if we move in a very limited liability manner.
LBJ: I'd like to move you or Harriman or somebody—Bobby Kennedy, or Bob McNamara or somebody—I'd like to move them over there and let them make an all out diplomatic effort. Maybe put an airplane carrier or two there, but not. That island's already overcrowded.

In response Ball stressed that the United States should avoid becoming the mediator in Cyprus: "Anyone who settles this is going to come down hard on the Greeks." The United States should stay in the background. Ball then outlined a proposal for a Western European mediator, a 3-month cease-fire to permit mediation to proceed, and the inclusion of a 1,200 man U.S. contingent in the peacekeeping force. After answering a number of questions regarding the activities of U.S. officials, the President authorized further exploration of the Ball plan. (Johnson Library, Recordings and Transcripts, Recording of Telephone Conversation between President Johnson and Acting Secretary Ball, January 28, 1964, 6:35 p.m.?, Tape 64.08, Side B, PNO 1)

At 6:45 p.m. the President telephoned Secretary McNamara to get his views on the Ball plan. The Secretary of Defense suggested that no decision be made until "we've heard from Lem" [General Lyman Lemnitzer]. (Ibid., Recording of Telephone Conversation Between President Johnson and Secretary McNamara, January 28, 1964, 6:45 p.m., Tape 64.08, Side B, PNO 2)

The President telephoned Ball to relay McNamara's views at approximately 6:48 p.m. Ball responded: "Fine." (Ibid., Recording of Telephone Conversation Between President Johnson and Acting Secretary Ball, January 28, 1964, 6:48 p.m.?, Tape 64.08, Side B, PNO 3)

5.   **Telegram From the Supreme Allied Commander, Europe (Lemnitzer) to Secretary of Defense McNamara[1]**

Paris, January 30, 1964, 2134Z.

ALO 17. 1. I arrived in Athens at 1145 local, 29 January, where I was met by General Pipilis, Chief of the Defense General Staff, and the various service chiefs. After a short press conference at the airport with a large number of press, I departed for a conference with Prime Minister Paraskevopoulos with the understanding that General Pipilis was to accompany me. When we arrived in the Prime Minister's office, Pipilis was summarily dismissed, and the conference, which lasted about an hour, consisted only of the Prime Minister with an interpreter and myself and my executive officer. As a result of his dismissal from my conference with the Prime Minister, General Pipilis later expressed the fear that the Prime Minister might be pursuing a different line than the Defense Ministry and my executive officer was specifically queried by him regarding content of the Prime Minister's remarks.

2. After lunch with Defense Minister Papanikolopoulos and the Chiefs of Staff, I had a two-hour discussion with them at the Defense Ministry, followed by a one-hour conference with the Crown Prince substituting for his father, who was ill. All parties concerned voiced views which were substantially the same.

3. In opening all my conferences, I explained the purpose of my visit along the same lines as I had the day before with the Turks,[2] highlighting, of course, the disastrous consequences of a military clash over Cyprus between two NATO allies.

4. The common thread which the Greeks pursued in all of our conversations was that the Turks were determined to abrogate the 1955 treaty[3] and that they would settle for nothing less than full self-determination for Turkish Cypriots and partition of the island of Cyprus. Furthermore, the Greeks maintained that the Turks were pushing things to an explosive state by their large concentration of forces at Iskenderun and by their continuing inflammatory remarks in the state-controlled press and radio. As a consequence, Greek public opinion has been

---

[1] Source: Johnson Library, National Security File, Country File, Cyprus, Vol. 2. Secret; Noforn. Repeated to USDOCOSouth for Admiral Russell, Athens, and Ankara and passed to the Department of State. The source text is the Department of State copy. The Chairman of the JCS had requested that Lemnitzer visit Athens and Ankara to "calm the situation" in telegram 4559, January 27. (Ibid.)

[2] Lemnitzer reported on his talks with Turkish officials in an unnumbered telegram to Secretary of Defense McNamara, January 29. (Ibid.)

[3] Apparently a reference to the 1959 agreements establishing an independent Cyprus; for texts, see *American Foreign Policy: Current Documents, 1959*, pp. 765–775.

greatly aroused and has now reached the fever pitch of 1940 when neither the King, nor the government, nor anyone else, could hold the Greek people in check.

5. To reduce these tensions and to resolve the current crisis, the Defense Minister listed the following requirements:

a. Dispersion of the heavy concentration of forces in southern Turkey, or, failing that,
b. Introduction of an allied force to Cyprus of sufficient size to maintain peace and security.
c. Stationing of the Sixth Fleet around Cyprus to police the waters and prevent a Turkish invasion.

6. Of these requirements, the dispersal of Turkish forces at Iskenderun is regarded by the Greeks as the most imperative and the most immediate since they look upon this concentration as a Sword of Damocles which could prevent any productive steps. If however, none of the requirements is met, then the Greeks would be compelled to take prompt counter-action. The precise nature of this counter-action was not disclosed.

7. With regard to the allied force, Greece is quite willing to withdraw its forces from Cyprus if the Turks will do likewise. In response to my specific question as to whether they would object to leaving both Turkish and Greek forces there if an allied force went in, the Defense Minister responded that he would have no objection to this if it were necessary. As to command of the allied force, the Defense Minister stated that the question had not been thoroughly studied but that they would prefer to see an American commander.

8. I informed the Greeks that I had been notified through appropriate NATO Commanders of Turkish movement of forces and that I was convinced that I would continue to be kept informed. I stated that even though naval units of both Greece and Turkey were not under NATO command, I had received notification of the movement of Turkish naval units from the Black Sea to Iskenderun. With regard to the build-up of ground forces, I stated that there was not any repositioning of additional combat units in the Iskenderun area, but that any increase in combat strength there related only to the build-up to 100 percent strenth of the 39th Division which was normally based at Iskenderun. I stressed the importance of Greece following the NATO procedures for reporting and consultation and was assured that such procedures would be followed and that, in no case, would Greece take any unilateral action without prior consultation.

9. In general, I did not find Greek officials as calm as the Turks. Emotion is running high, aggravated by a sense of frustration stemming from the all-too-obvious military advantages of the Turks in the Cyprus area and the feeling among the military that they cannot look to their

caretaker government for decisive leadership. On the other hand, they gave every indication that they sincerely hope to find a peaceful solution to the Cyprus problem. The disadvantages under which they labor are likely to militate against any precipitate, unilateral moves by Greece.

10. I departed Athens at 1830 local and arrived in Paris at 0100 30 Jan. En route I stopped at Naples for a conference with Admiral Russell to give him more detailed information regarding my visits.[4]

---

[4] The Embassy in Athens reported in telegram 1122, January 30, that Lemnitzer had succeeded in "lowering temperature" in Athens. (Johnson Library, National Security File, Country File, Cyprus, Vol. 2)

---

6.   Telegram From the Department of State to the Embassy in Turkey[1]

Washington, February 8, 1964, 8:41 p.m.

781. Personal for Hare from Ball. Embtel 1002.[2] I am deeply concerned by the delay in Turkish reply and indications they want to do some legalistic nitpicking. In working out revised proposals, we were particularly concerned that any rewording, or any revising of plan should not compromise Turkish interests.[3]

When reply is delivered, if it appears Turks are presenting their "objections" because of resentment at Sandys–Kyprianou conversation and misinterpretation of "Sandys proposals", emphasize that nitpicking at this time is disastrous course.

Their worry over getting relief supplies through can be alleviated more rapidly by getting the international force on the island immediately rather than haggling over terms of reference. We cannot understand their objection to "international force". Main point of forces from

---

[1] Source: Department of State, Central Files, POL 23–8 CYP. Secret; Immediate. Drafted by Bracken, cleared by Ball, and approved by Talbot.

[2] Telegram 1002, February 8, reported Turkish objections to any further concessions to the Government of Cyprus on the creation of a U.N. peacekeeping force. (Ibid.)

[3] On January 31, the United States and United Kingdom made a joint proposal to the parties concerned for the establishment of a peacekeeping force in Cyprus drawn from NATO countries. For text, see *American Foreign Policy: Current Documents, 1964*, p. 556.

NATO countries with possibly a non-NATO country (which would have to be acceptable to GOT) is preserved. Committee of Ambassadors from first meant representatives of governments having forces stationed on the Island. It was always planned that liaison with Government of Cyprus and with two communities would take place in Cyprus. There is nothing in the proposal in our view that prejudices either Turkey's treaty rights or the position of the Vice President under the constitution.

Seek to have Turks concur in presentation to Makarios and Kutchuk and phrase their "objections" as observations or points as GOG did in first go-round. If they insist on tampering with details as conditions they must understand they are endangering whole operation.

Rusk

---

7.   Telegram From the Embassy in Turkey to the Department of State[1]

Ankara, February 9, 1964, 1 p.m.

1004. For Ball from Hare. Deptel 781.[2] Immediately on receipt reftel I went see Erkin and we had very down to earth talk. In essence his line was similar that of Tuluy, maintaining GOT had agreed original proposals despite sacrificing very important points. Fact that Makarios had done opposite and that adjusted proposals drafted so as take his conditions into consideration necessitates GOT present its views in order regain balance. Furthermore GOT has Parliament looking over its shoulder and already under pressure for having been too supine. Paper giving GOT response would be given me and British Ambassador at two o'clock.[3] He said most important points would be application of all treaty provisions (para numbered two of Embtel 1002)[4] and reference to "Gov-

---

[1] Source: Department of State, Central Files, POL 23–8 CYP. Secret; Immediate. Repeated to London. Passed to the White House, JCS, OSD, CIA, USUN, CINCEUR, and CINCSTRIKE.

[2] Document 6.

[3] The text of the note was transmitted in telegram 1005 from Ankara, February 9. (Department of State, Central Files, POL 23–8 CYP)

[4] See footnote 2, Document 6.

ernment of Cyprus", existence of which GOT does not recognize, should just refer to Archbishop Makarios and Dr Kucuk by name (para numbered four of Embtel). I commented along following lines:

1) Revision of proposals made with Turkish interests in mind and represents no derogation of them.

2) GOT may have problems re proposals but so do we. Matter is urgent and if time lost discussing detailed points whole effort could collapse, including our own steps to be helpful.

3) Purpose of presenting revised proposals was to obtain GOT acquiescence in order present them to Cypriots. In so doing we of course expected GOT would make comments and observations as Greeks had done but I trusted these would not involve changes in document itself but would rather be for information and clarification.

4) Point re general validity of treaty provisions represents no substantive problem since it has been our view from beginning that proposals do not affect such provisions. We have so stated repeatedly and I could now say so again under authority of message from Ball.

5) Point re "Government of Cyprus" was quite another matter since, regardless of GOT reservations, we just could not put ourselves in position of challenging legal status of GOC. We recognize that GOC not functioning normally but that is practical, not legal, consideration. Fact that proposals had been submitted to Kucuk as well as Makarios was illustrative this point.

At end, Erkin said GOT reply would cover number of points, including proposed revisions of text but that point regarding general application of treaty provisions was most important.

Referring to my previous warning re danger of delay involved in redrafting, I asked whether these suggestions would be in the form of requirements for GOT acquiescence or as expression of what they would want if possible arrange. Erkin replied that we would be given paper and would be up to us what to do with it. I asked what this meant in terms of submission of proposals to GOC. To be specific, could paper go forward even if decided changes inadvisable? Erkin replied "What else can you do?"

This not too satisfactory but better than expected. At any rate your message afforded timely opportunity to get crack at Erkin and give him time do a little thinking before seeing him this afternoon.

Hare

8.   Telegram From the Embassy in the United Kingdom to the Department of State[1]

London, February 9, 1964, midnight.

3824. Following is uncleared memcon of Under Sec Ball's talk with Cypriot FonMin Kyprianou:

1. Under Sec and Amb Bruce met 1730 today with Kyprianou at AmEmbassy. Kyprianou was accompanied by Cyprus HICOM in London Soteriades. Under Sec explained US concern with Cyprus problem prompted primarily by our concern with peace. We believe establishment peace-keeping force, coupled with mediator concept, offers best way to proceed. US participation in force depends on working out acceptable arrangements to avoid entangling problem in cold war and on willingness of GOC to accept and request such force. Under Sec asked for GOC's frank views re US participation.

2. Kyprianou affirmed GOC reply given earlier remains basic GOC view.[2] GOC has no objection in principle to participation by any country. It is not the force that will provide permanent peace. If it is necessary have such a force because UK not prepared assume full responsibility, GOC believes it should be under Security Council. GOC has no wish create further complications. In its view, however, such force needed primarily for external purposes. Once danger of intervention is removed, atmosphere will automatically improve. Greeks will know no need exists to prepare for invasion; Turks will know they cannot hope for intervention. Influence and interference of outsiders primarily responsible for present troubled situation. Turkey more to blame than Greece. While primary purpose of such force should be to deter outside aggression, internal peace-keeping obviously also desirable. Force should assist GOC restore normal conditions.

3. If these are to be missions of force, it preferable force be under Security Council. Cyprus is small country with bitter past experience. If force under Security Council aegis, Cypriot public opinion will find it much more palatable. Kyprianou stressed GOC not trying blackmail. It remains ready discuss question before going to SC. Once agreement reached on composition of force, GOC wonders why US and UK should consider it dangerous go to Security Council.

---

[1] Source: Department of State, Central Files, POL 23–8 CYP. Confidential; Flash. Repeated to Athens for Ball. Relayed to the White House, JCS, OSD, CIA, USUN, CINCEUR, and CINCSTRIKE.

[2] In a February 2 statement to the London conference, Kyprianou announced that the Government of Cyprus accepted the idea of a NATO peacekeeping force in principle, but insisted that it operate under the authority of the United Nations. Subsequently, President Makarios outlined further objections to a NATO force under U.N. aegis. For text of Makarios' February 4 statement, see *American Foreign Policy: Current Documents, 1964,* p. 557.

4. Under Sec explained part of problem revolves about meaning of "under Security Council." We do not object to some connection with Security Council. We are seeking work out with other objective and competent countries establishment of force able to provide both power and a psychological framework designed to restore calm while political solution is being sought. Rather than inject question of composition of force into cold war politics at UN, we believe composition should be pre-arranged before going to Security Council. Formula by which link with Security Council is established is important. We do not wish make force subject of Soviet veto. Also, it is impractical to organize force if Security Council is going to be asked finance it because of already existing controversy revolving about Article 19. To get into this range of questions will merely delay its organization. We think it possible agree with GOC on a force where each participating govt pays its own way. We would also agree with GOC on what nations should participate. Thereafter, we see no reason why matter could not be brought to Security Council in manner where Soviet veto and cold war confrontation are avoided.

5. Kyprianou disclaimed GOC responsibility for present situation. He then alluded to various other factors which allegedly increased tension. Manner in which proposal prepared and projected in Cyprus, with other nations and press apparently apprised before GOC, increased suspicions. Under Sec noted original idea was Greek. HMG had called Greek proposal to our attention. In order to test its feasibility, we have explored it with other govts. Kyprianou insisted GOC equally interested party and should have been consulted earlier. Greeks had told GOC it was not their proposal, although GOC knows it was. With respect to force itself, Kyprianou said once agreement is reached on composition, GOC wants to go to Security Council. It would explain its desire is to place pre-arranged force under Security Council control. He wondered if Soviets would in fact veto such force since they appear to be trying assist GOC.

6. Under Sec pointed out "under Security Council" can embrace Security Council "taking note," "reporting," etc. What did GOC have in mind? Kyprianou replied Security Council should authorize SYG to have the right to control the force within the scope of agreed terms of reference. Security Council should be competent to take decisions with respect to the force if called upon to do so by SYG, GOC or the participating countries. The Security Council might also have the mission of working out terms of reference for the force. He envisaged a two-stage procedure. The Security Council should first pass a resolution asking all states to refrain from threatening independence, territorial integrity and sovereignty of Cyprus. GOC would inform Security Council that talks are also taking place on the composition of a force about which it would report back to Security Council once agreement is reached. Such proce-

dure would have a calming effect in Cyprus. Security Council endorsement, in GOC's view, is a deterrent. Kyprianou added he was thinking of going to New York on Wednesday or Thursday to initiate Security Council action, although his trip might be postponed until Saturday. Under Sec said we will have to examine Kyprianou's idea. Meanwhile, he hoped we might move forward on composition and terms of reference of force.

7. Kyprianou also suggested SYG might, even in absence any specific proposal, go to Cyprus himself for a day. He need have no specific mission, but would simply seek inform himself of situation. This too would have calming effect. Kyprianou said he had instructed Rossides to sound out SYG on this. Did we have any objection?

Under Sec said he would want to consider this further with his UN experts. His initial impression was that there should be no objection.

8. With respect to US participation, Kyprianou thought this would be inadvisable. GOC would not object, but US participation would adversely affect the "popularity" of the US in Cyprus and could give rise to public feelings against the US. Under Sec pointed out that we must consider if any force can in fact be organized on viable basis if US does not participate. If force could be organized without us, we would prefer it. We have been inclined to doubt that it can. Many nations who speak boldly of peace-keeping force become less so when it comes to paying for it. Some states have said they will join only if US does so. In any case, there is no intention of taking any action without full agreement of GOC.

9. Kyprianou contended that, psychologically, if force had come in context of political settlement, it might not have been viewed differently in Cyprus. Fact is, however, that it developed while London talks were taking place, thereby heightening Cypriot suspicions. He asked Under Sec if US has formed any views re political settlement.

Under Sec replied that on basis our knowledge of Cyprus situation, we have not felt able to contribute any useful suggestions at this time. Kyprianou then asked what purpose of mediator would be? Under Sec pointed out it was not proposed he try to put American ideas into effect. His task would be to sound out all interested parties and seek to persuade them come to some mutually agreeable settlement. Kyprianou was skeptical about mediator's prospects. He opined that if there were some way to get Greece and Turkey out of picture, chances of success would be greater. He recalled that ten years ago enosis might have been better arrangement. Through no fault of Greek Cypriots, it could not be worked out. Such "radical solution" probably not possible now.

10. Under Sec told Kyprianou he planned meet with Sandys again and, together with Sandys, might perhaps be able to hold second meeting with Kyprianou later. During subsequent talk with Sandys, it became clear that further discussions with Greeks desirable before saying any-

thing more to Kyprianou. Under Sec then telephoned Kyprianou to explain his inability meet with him again today and his wish to reflect further on Kyprianou's observations. Under Sec said he hoped be in Nicosia sometime Tuesday and suggested Kyprianou might wish to consider meeting him there. Kyprianou will probably do so.

Bruce

9.   Telegram From the Embassy in Greece to the Department of State[1]

Athens, February 10, 1964, 10 p.m.

1197. For Secretaries of State and Defense and Ambassador Stevenson from Under Secretary.

I have had useful detailed discussions today with Hare, Labouissse and Wilkins. In sum, they reinforce and support the tentative views of the overall situation I expressed yesterday. (Athens 1184)[2]

1. I am now even firmer in my view that the US should not put troops in Cyprus. Wilkins (who supports wholeheartedly views contained in Athens 1184)[3] together with his Army Attaché [*less than 1 line of source text not declassified*] are all convinced Makarios does not want Americans. They fear US forces would be special target of hit and run tactics of Greek Cypriots. According to Wilkins, Pickard also agrees that US troops would be singled out more than other Western powers because of our position of leadership in NATO.

We explored possible ways that US military support might be provided while minimizing exposure of US forces on assumption some form of US involvement may be useful or even necessary to keep Turks from standing down. This included possibility of putting US troops in

---

[1] Source: Department of State, Central Files, POL 23–8 CYP. Confidential; Immediate; Exdis. Repeated to USUN. Passed to the White House, CIA, JCS, OSD, CINCEUR, and CINCSTRIKE.

[2] Telegram 1184, February 10, reported Ball's view that the United States should not put troops in Cyprus and should avoid taking a firm public position on the issue so that the United Kingdom, Greece, or Turkey would not back off from their commitments. (Ibid.) A summary of this telegram was provided to President Johnson in a February 10 memorandum from Bundy. (Johnson Library, National Security File, Files of McGeorge Bundy, Lunch with President)

[3] In telegram 685 from Nicosia, February 8, Wilkins warned that the British plan would fail to win Cypriot acceptance and urged U.S. support of a peacekeeping force under U.N. aegis with the participation of forces from both Greece and Turkey. (Department of State, Central Files, POL 23–8 CYP)

British bases on standby basis. However, we concluded this not desirable since US unit would be thrown into breach at such time as serious fighting broke out, which would be worse than being in from beginning.

2.   Today's discussion highlighted importance and delicacy of handling Turks so as to minimize adverse repercussions on our relations and to dampen any desire they may have to intervene in Cyprus unilaterally. As a result, it is more than ever important that responsibility for our non-participation be placed squarely on Makarios' back. As Hare puts it, US failure to participate in an international force would remove keystone to arch, so far as Turks are concerned.

It seems increasingly likely that Makarios will cooperate with us on this since opinion of our Nicosia [*less than 1 line of source text not declassified*] is that Makarios could not survive acceptance of US troops. He believes Cypriot "fighters" would throw him out if he tried it.

3.   What are the alternatives to plan as presently agreed by all but GOC? We concluded best alternative we can probably hope to achieve is modest international force under UK com and made up of Benelux, Scandinavian countries, Canada and possibly Ireland.

Force would be approved by SC but not put under its control. While such force not as effective militarily as original concept, it would provide political deterrent and help spread responsibility as UK desires. If Makarios wants such a force—and there is still real doubt that he wants any international force at all—a prearranged deal along these lines might be feasible. Hare is clear, however, that this fallback—while probably the best we can hope for—would cause Turks great anguish.

4.   If we are to keep the Turks from feeling we have sold them down the river, we must make strongest effort to avoid any suggestion we are weakening in our decision to contribute US contingent to international force. Any leak or suggestion from any US source indicating such weakening would be catastrophic.[4]

5.   Kyprianou told me in London that GOC was planning—before dealing with question of international force—to seek Security Council confirmation of "territorial integrity and independence of Cyprus". This was confirmed by Greek FonMin this afternoon[5] who added information that Makarios planned to go personally to New York for that purpose but had agreed to defer this junket until after Greek election next Sunday (February 16). I described to FonMin how I am tentatively planning to deal with this proposal when I meet Makarios. However, I would

---

[4] In telegram 789 to Ankara, February 10, Secretary Rusk responded: "First purely personal reaction your telegram is that Turks might be saved if there is U.S. naval or air participation not involving U.S. ground troops." (Ibid.)

[5] Ball reported on his meeting with Foreign Minister Palamas in telegram 1199 from Athens, February 10. (Ibid.)

appreciate suggestion of Ambassador Stevenson and Department as to best tactic. I have in mind saying following to Makarios:

a. We have been the major support of the United Nations from the beginning while certain other nations that make great pretense of interest in Cypriot situation have consistently sabotaged UN and failed to provide financial support for its peacekeeping efforts.

b. We are practical nation and trust that Makarios will take a hard look at the practical consequences of his proposed action.

c. A move toward the Security Council on this issue will almost certainly result in the interjection of cold war politics. It will provide the forum for charges of genocide against Cypriots while speeches in Security Council will only serve to inflame passions that are already too high.

d. We must concentrate on first things first and that means getting agreement on international force before involving Security Council.

Obviously this ploy may not work. Makarios apparently has naive idea that Security Council is like General Assembly and filled with Afro-Asian pals. If he insists on going ahead, however, we could probably not frontally oppose kind of resolution Cypriots have in mind. We should seek to finesse it by developing formulation we could support. In that event, each member of Council would put its own interpretation on language. Net result might be resolution putting Security Council on record that all parties concerned must keep their shirts on and avoid action that would exacerbate situation.

6. We also grappled briefly and inconclusively with nature of long-term settlement. All were in full agreement we should not get into middle of mediating process. If there is a solution it is certainly not in sight in near furture. Movement of population within federation seems offer some possibility but has the great draw-back of being rational and therefore not feasible. Best we can hope for in foreseeable future is to help keep lid on boiling cauldron and thus prevent southern wing of NATO from blowing up.

Tomorrow I go to Ankara to begin process of preparing Turks for turn down by Makarios and possible modest UN force alternative described above.

I plan to see Makarios Wednesday.[6] I have asked Wilkins to get categoric assurances from Makarios there will be no demonstration as condition precedent to my visit.[7]

Labouisse

---

[6] In telegram 793 to Ankara, February 11, the Department of State commented that Makarios had an "exaggerated idea" of what he could get from a Security Council meeting without U.S. and British support and provided Ball with a series of talking points designed to impress on Makarios the limits and dangers of over-reliance on this approach. (Ibid.)

[7] In telegram 355 from Nicosia, February 11, Wilkins reported that he had Makarios' assurances that no demonstrations would take place during Ball's visit. (Ibid.)

10.   Telegram From the Embassy in Turkey to the Department of State[1]

Ankara, February 11, 1964, 6 p.m.

1017. From Under Secretary. We met this morning first with Foreign Minister Erkin and then went with him for session with PM Inonu. In both cases, I explained our interest in problem of Cyprus, our concern over its dangers and our support for peacekeeping-mediator proposals. At same time I made clear we and other non-guarantor powers could only participate if Makarios agreed, and I indicated considerable concern at what I understood to be his rather negative attitude. Said I was going to Nicosia tomorrow and intended to press hard for his agreement. They asked what could be done if he refused, to which I replied that this would depend upon nature of his refusal. We had no specific present plans in this regard.

I also discussed report that Makarios plans to appeal to UN after Greek elections are over and seek resolution warning against aggression or interference with independence and territorial integrity of Cyprus. Assured them I intended try to dissuade him from this and make point that there should be reference to Security Council only after full agreement reached among parties concerned. Turks agreed premature Security Council debate would be harmful and wished me well in my efforts.

I emphasized that continuing tense situation on island and Makarios' idea of rushing to UN made it imperative for us to get quick decision and that I would work hard to this end. Was prepared stay over day or two in Nicosia if satisfactory answer not forthcoming tomorrow.

Erkin asked about Greek position. I said they supported peacekeeping plan but had told me they had little influence on Makarios. Erkin questioned latter statement, but we said our own information from various sources confirmed it. He commented some Greek moves had been displeasing to Turkey, but government exercised restraint despite heavy pressures on it to act, including severe criticism by Parliamentary opposition. I said we appreciated this and told him Greek Foreign Minister Palamas had himself expressed admiration for restraint displayed by Inonu.

Erkin indicated he fully realized dangers Turkish intervention, saying British would withdraw and Greeks would intervene "not with us but against us".

---

[1] Source: Department of State, Central Files, POL 23–8 CYP. Secret; Priority. Repeated to Nicosia, London, USUN, and Athens. Passed to the White House, CIA, JCS, OSD, CINC-EUR, and CINCSTRIKE.

He asked whether we intended answer Soviet note. I said we were studying question, thought British answer was good one.[2] Erkin commented Turkey would have something to say about note[3] and referred to TASS articles criticizing Turkish position, which he said were particularly annoying because Soviet Ambassador had promised his government would support Turkey.

Both Inonu and Erkin remarked position Turkish community in Cyprus was getting worse rather than better, "massacres" still continuing. Longer international force delayed, worse situation would get, because Makarios and associates have "no scruples left". Inonu added, Turks have no confidence in guarantee enforced solely by British, although British have enough troops on island for purpose. Problem was British instructions to their troops. They were instructed not to shoot but confine themselves to giving advice which was not enough. Asked if British could not be induced to act more effectively, I said I would talk to them about it.

They asked for our suggestions for proposed mediator, and I mentioned names of van Roijen, Plimsoll, van Kleffans. Said Spaak and Lange probably out of consideration because both occupied in important full time positions. Inonu said he was not familiar with first three names but made no suggestions of his own. Expressed hope man chosen would have full opportunity to learn facts and would realize Turkish community cannot be left to mercies of Makarios.

Erkin asked our reactions to proposed Turkish changes in joint proposals. I said we had given them consideration and thought we had been able to meet most important points. Jernegan would meet later with Foreign Office officials to explain what we had done.

Hare

---

[2] For text of the Soviet note and the U.S. reply, see Department of State *Bulletin,* March 23, 1964, pp. 446–448. For text of the British reply, see *The New York Times*, February 9, 1964.

[3] The Turkish reply was released on February 25. A copy is in the Johnson Library, National Security File, Files of Robert W. Komer, Cyprus.

11.   Telegram From the Embassy in Cyprus to the Department of State[1]

Nicosia, February 13, 1964, 1:45 a.m.

732. Dept pass White House and Defense. For President, Secretaries of State and Defense and Ambassador Stevenson from Under Secretary.

1. In the last few days, we have succeeded in clearing our Cyprus proposals with the British, Greek and Turkish Governments. This has required a substantial output of persuasion.

2. I spent the day today largely with Archbishop Makarios and his colleagues. I had two long meetings—one this morning and one this afternoon.[2]

3. While we were meeting, fighting was going on at various points in the island yielding a number of dead and wounded, both Greek and Turk. This is a daily occurrence. Cyprus is a battlefield. We travel about Nicosia with police escorts, followed by RAF units with sub-machine guns. There is a pervasive atmosphere of imminent crisis.

4. Our morning meeting consisted largely of my own long and hard-boiled presentation. Makarios seemed willing to consider our proposal. This afternoon the psychotic element in the Cyprus drama fully emerged and the atmosphere chilled.

5. At the conclusion of lengthy technical discussions, Makarios indicated that in spite of my most vigorous arguments he was going ahead with his foolish plan of sending an expedition to ask the Security Council to try to undermine the Treaties of Guarantee by seeking a resolution reaffirming the territorial integrity and political independence of Cyprus. He indicated quite casually that he would deal with the creation of an international force at some later date.

6. In view of the fact that the murder rate is rising steadily and that the tempo of fighting is increasing, such conduct by Makarios is criminally foolhardy.

---

[1] Source: Department of State, Central Files POL 23–8 CYP. Secret; Immediate; Exdis. Repeated to USUN. Passed to the White House, JCS, OSD, CIA, CINCEUR, and CINCSTRIKE.

[2] Detailed reports of the morning discussions were transmitted in telegrams 726 and 727 from Nicosia, February 12. (Ibid.) Ball presented Makarios with an "adjusted proposal." The text of this proposal was transmitted in circular telegram 1482, February 12. (Ibid.) The Embassy provided a detailed report on the afternoon discussions in telegrams 728 and 731 from Nicosia, February 12. (Ibid.) Makarios presented Ball with the text of the Cypriot proposal "preconditioning" acceptance of an international peacekeeping force. This document was transmitted in telegram 742 from Nicosia, February 13. (Ibid.) Ball also met with Vice President Kuchuk in the interval between his two sessions with Makarios. The Embassy reported on this meeting in telegram 729 from Nicosia, February 12. (Ibid.)

7. In view of this, the British High Commissioner and I told off Makarios and his extremist ministers in a manner unfamiliar to diplomatic discourse. In an exchange which lasted 45 minutes or more, we painted a lurid picture of the consequences that would entail from the folly he has proposed.

8. When the discussion got past the boiling point, I proposed that we adjourn until Thursday morning, to which the Archbishop agreed.

9. I think we shook the Archbishop. Even his beard seemed pale. But the big question is whether he is really in command of the situation. The two ministers who led the discussion on the Cypriot side—Clerides and Papadopoulos—are fanatical and over the edge. They reflect the death wish that seems endemic in this wretched island. Both also have some Communist coloration in their backgrounds.

10. The question we face tonight is who is in charge? If the Archbishop is as scared as I think he is, we may be able to salvage something tomorrow morning. I plan to see him alone before the meeting. But if he is a prisoner of his own folly—which seems likely—he will commit Cyprus in the morning to a disaster course.

11. The issue that must be faced is the only simple question in this complex situation. Is the Cypriot Government prepared to work with us and other countries in organizing an international force immediately? Or does it want to throw the issues into the United Nations in the hope of attracting enough Soviet bloc and Afro-Asian support to embarrass the Turks while the island continues to fall apart?

12. As of tonight, Cyprus is very near civil disintegration. I talked with the Commander of the British Forces, General Young, this noon and he felt despondent and frustrated: A battle occurred today in a town that has heretofore been quiet; something on the order of 5,000 Turks are encircled. There have been casualties on both sides. The pace is accelerating and a general bloodbath just over the horizon.

13. Against this background, I told Makarios that if he did not proceed immediately to organize an international peace force, he would condemn his country to total anarchy. But I have little confidence that he is enough of a free man to act rationally—even if he had the will to do so.

14. I have sent him word through covert channels that if he would agree to the organization of an international force immediately, we and the British would help him achieve one. We would call on the Commonwealth countries and on some of the Western European neutrals. If he would postpone throwing his problems into the Security Council until after such a force had been agreed, order might be restored and the situation salvaged. In that event, we would talk to the Turks and try to hold up their hand while efforts were made to develop a formula for a general settlement. Such a force cld not involve US troops.

15. I hope we can agree on something but I am not too sanguine.

16. The position of Turkey in this affair is a critical one. From my talks in Ankara, I am persuaded that if Makarios is enough of a fool to go to the Security Council and try for a resolution designed to hamstring the Turks in exercising their rights of intervention, without first dealing with the internal situation through the organization of an international force, he is likely to trigger an incisive Turkish reaction. The Turks may move, and the Greeks will respond.

17. Our only hope, it seems to me, is to scare Makarios sufficiently to compel him to concentrate on the creation of an international force that will stop carnage. If he does not do so—and I will know tomorrow—we have some hard decisions to make. I have promised the Turks and Greeks to report on our meetings here.

18. One possibility of preventing a Greco-Turkish war is to persuade both governments to exercise the rights of unilateral intervention granted them under the 1960 Treaties of Guarantee and move into Cyprus peacefully and together in order to stop the destruction of the Greek and Turkish communities. This obviously would not be feasible until after the Greek elections which take place on Sunday.

19. For the moment, we have considerable influence with Inonu, who has made clear to me his gratitude for the US manifestations of interest in the Cyprus situation. Hopefully we may be able to establish a relation of confidence with whatever new government emerges from the Greek elections.

20. I have the impression that Britain, as the third guarantor power, would be willing to associate itself with a peaceful joint intervention by Greece and Turkey and would simultaneously increase present British troop strength in Cyprus.

21. To arrange a common action by Greece and Turkey would require considerable diplomatic skill and the maximum use of our leverage. Yet I am inclined tonight to think this may be about the only remaining hope of preventing a major collision of two of our NATO allies—if, as I fear he will, Makarios turns out to be a prisoner or a fool or both.

22. I am sending you this cable tonight not with the thought of immediate instructions, since it is hard to make a definite plan until we know the full results of tomorrow's meeting with Makarios. I must emphasize, however, that the atmosphere at this end of the Mediterranean is supercharged and that an explosion may be imminent. I shall try tomorrow to send you more considered recommendations as to the options open to us and the immediate actions we should take.

Wilkins

12.   Memorandum of Conversation[1]

Washington, February 13, 1964, 10:55 a.m.

SUBJECT

Situation in Cyprus

PARTICIPANTS

British
Sir Alec Douglas-Home, Prime Minister of Great Britain
R.A. Butler, Secretary of State for Foreign Affairs
Sir David Ormsby Gore, British Ambassador
Sir Harold Caccia, Permanent Under Secretary, Foreign Office
N. Henderson, Private Secretary to Mr. Butler
Tom Bridges, Second Private Secretary to Mr. Butler
Denis Greenhill, Minister, UK Embassy
M. Hadow, Press Secretary, Foreign Office

US
The President
The Secretary of State
Governor Harriman, Under Secretary of State for Political Affairs
David K.E. Bruce, Ambassador to Great Britain
McGeorge Bundy, Special Assistant to the President for National Security Affairs
William R. Tyler, Assistant Secretary, EUR
Richard I. Philips, Director, P/ON
M. Gordon Knox, Deputy Director, BNA

Secretary Rusk reviewed the situation in Cyprus. He pointed out that Archbishop Makarios had seemed willing to see a peace-keeping force composed not of troops from NATO states (except for the UK), but from the Commonwealth and from nations like Sweden. Mr. Butler remarked that the idea of such an alternative force was hopeful. Secretary Rusk said that Mr. Ball would see Makarios again the morning of the 14th. Meanwhile, reports of heavy fighting in the southern part of the island were disturbing, however, and Secretary Rusk stated that Mr. Ball would proceed on the 14th to Ankara to counsel prudence to the Turkish government.

Mr. Butler remarked that the Cypriot government would surely bring the issue before the Security Council and the Cypriot delegate, Rossides, would introduce a resolution. If it were unreasonable, the British and the US could be negative and would have the votes. If the resolution were reasonable and two-sided, we could be reasonable about it.

---

[1] Source: Department of State, Presidential Memoranda of Conversation: Lot 66 D 149. Secret. Drafted by Knox and approved in S on February 20 and in the White House on February 24. The meeting was held in the White House. The source text is marked "Part I of II." Prime Minister Home visited the United States February 12–14.

Secretary Rusk remarked that the best and most likely kind of resolution which would get a majority at the Security Council was one of the "don't fight, talk" resolutions which are customary in the Security Council under circumstances such as now prevail in Cyprus. The US and UK could back such a resolution in order to head off other ones of the sort the Cypriot government would want. Namely, one to cast a shadow on the Treaty of Guarantee.

Sir Alec doubted that Makarios can control matters in Cyprus any longer. He hoped that Canada would continue to be one of the states making up the peace-keeping force.

Secretary Rusk referred to the fact that the Turks, Greeks and British have forces on the island by right; this could be a concept which could be used to keep Makarios from calling in forces from Egypt or the Soviet Bloc, for example, which have no right on the island.

Sir Alec supposed that if the Turkish army invaded Cyprus, the British government would call on it to stop at a certain line. The British forces certainly would not fight a NATO ally.

The President suggested that it would be important to have the Turkish and Greek armies agree not to fight each other, should their governments decide to send forces to occupy portions of Cyprus. It would also be desirable that each side should protect the other's minority population. He recalled that Queen Frederika of Greece had told him during her recent visit to Washington that the Greek Army would move to Cyprus if the Turkish Army did.[2]

He then asked Sir Alec what motivates Makarios.

Sir Alec called Makarios a stinker of the first water. He wants a central government in Cyprus which would rob the Turkish minority of its rights. Makarios seemed to rely on a Soviet promise that it will keep the Turks from invading the island.

Sir Harold Caccia stated that any action of this sort by Russia against Turkey would bring NATO into action.

Mr. Rusk observed that this was a matter of extreme danger. Before there would be a response to a Soviet action affecting the Soviet-Turkish border the question would be in the Security Council.

---

[2] Queen Frederika visited Washington on January 27. Her comments on Cyprus were reported in a memorandum from Komer to the President, January 27. (Johnson Library National Security File, Country File, Greece, Vol. 1)

13.   Telegram From the Embassy in Turkey to the Department of State[1]

Ankara, February 14, 1964, 6 p.m.

1031. For Read from Hainy. Following uncleared memo of conversation with Makarios. From Under Secretary. Mr. Pickard and I called on the Archbishop this morning.[2] I reiterated the concern of the USG for the situation in Cyprus not merely because of the loss of life on the island but the threat to peace which was posed. I expressed my disappointment that we had not been able to arrive at an agreement on concrete measures but stated that my government was not prepared to abandon efforts to contribute to an alleviation of the dangers that threatened.

I said that I had been instructed to return to Washington today by way of the capitals of Turkey and Greece. I would try to use what influence we had to persuade the governments in Ankara and in Athens to exercise restraint. Of course, the effectiveness of that would depend on the absence of any incidents on the island. Before leaving I had been asked to obtain the assurances of the Archbishop that he would make a public declaration of the determination of his government to restore peace and order and to take effective measures toward that end.

I said that I did not intend to discuss further the question of the application by the GOC to the Security Council but could only reiterate my regret that they were pursuing this course before taking effective steps to bring about an international force that could contribute toward peace. I said also that the Archbishop and I had established, I thought, a basis of personal friendship during the past three days and that I felt it necessary to say to him that the debate in the Security Council in the manner in which the issue was being presented by the GOC would have a lamentable effect on the world's conception not merely of the Government of Cyprus but of the leadership of the Archbishop.

Pickard then went on to say that he had also proposed to his government that he should return to London via Ankara and Athens to discuss the future of the British peace-keeping force on the island. He said that it was impossible for the British forces to carry out their tasks in present circumstances unless it was clear beyond all doubt that it was the intention of the Government of Cyprus to restrain their forces and avoid such attacks as have happened in Limassol.

---

[1] Source: Department of State, Central Files, POL 23–8 CYP. Confidential; Immediate. Repeated to Athens, London, and USUN. Passed to the White House, JCS, OSD, CIA, CINCEUR, and CINCSTRIKE.

[2] Sir Cyril Pickard, Assistant Under Secretary of State for the Commonwealth Relations Office, was Acting U.K. High Commissioner for Cyprus. Pickard's report to his government on this meeting was transmitted in telegram 748 from Nicosia, February 14. (Ibid.)

The Archbishop had previously given assurance that the govern-ment forces would not retaliate even if attacked. In fact, however, an attack had been carried out in Limassol with very little provocation from the Turks. Peace could only be kept by the Cypriots themselves and no force however it was composed could do the job keeping the peace unless it was the intention of the Cypriots to find a peaceful basis of liv-ing together.

The Archbishop again reiterated his assurances about the peaceful intentions of the Cypriot Government. He agreed, however, that the present basis for peace-keeping was totally inadequate and that there must be discussion of practical measures to restore the life of the commu-nity on a normal basis. He undertook to proceed with such discussions immediately on Pickard's return from London and to do his utmost to establish a basis of confidence with the Turks which would enable a return to normal conditions on the island.

Pickard stressed that this required compromise on the Greek side as well as on the side of the Turks. There was no question of forcing the Turks to comply with Greek requirements. What was required was an overall negotiated agreement on practical measures for restoring life on the island to normal. It was only on the basis of such a settlement that a peace-keeping force would have any reality.

The Archbishop accepted all this and undertook as a practical first step himself to visit Limassol in order to give public expression to his concern that the peace should be kept on both sides.

We left the meeting on the basis of a firm undertaking from the Arch-bishop that he will get to work at once on practical ways of reassuring and finding a basis for returning conditions to normality on the island.

The Archbishop also promised to make some form of public decla-ration asserting his government's intention to keep the peace.

The Archbishop was undoubtedly sincere and on the face of it the proposal of working out the details of practical measures for peacekeep-ing is a sensible next step. It would, however, be a mistake to underesti-mate the great difficulties of bringing any such discussions to a conclusion acceptable to both sides.

I did not discuss the compromise plan at all with Makarios, and in view of Turkish and British anxieties, I believe the less said regarding it the better for the moment.

Hare

14. Telegram From the Department of State to the Embassy in Turkey[1]

Washington, February 14, 1964, 8:48 p.m.

817. Following highlights telecon between Secretary and Under Secretary (in Ankara) February 14, 1830Z, are in addition verbatim portion sent action Paris repeated info other posts.[2]

Under Secretary reported meetings with Inonu and Erkin showed PriMin under enormous pressure which greatly intensified after bloody Limassol affair. However he determined act in consultation with US and wishes withhold any decisive action until after disposition Cypriot case in UN provided there no new incidents. It clear situation extremely precarious but Under Secretary trusts PriMin's assurances he will not move before telling US unless something occurs making intervention imperative.

Under Secretary stated PriMin presented several questions and wants answers before Monday:

1. What will US reaction be if Russians want intervene?
2. How should GOT act during UN consideration this matter?
3. If US advises patience, what will be advice to all other parties concerned in order maintain even temporary peace and security?
4. Will US release Turkey's troops from NATO command to be available and ready?
5. In case nobody intervenes except Turks, may GOT expect attitude benevolence and neutrality US Government?
6. Wish clear-cut indication as soon as possible US's UN tactics and close cooperation with Turk Ambassador Washington who will handle in UN.

In addition, two questions put to British Ambassador: if troubles go on in Cyprus what will UK do? Is UK ready exercise its right intervention with Turkey?

Commenting on UN tactics (transmitted separately)[3] Under Secretary said this exactly right course which can make major contribution hold back Turks. Stated he had made clear to PriMin it would disastrously prejudice chances defeating Cypriot UN move if Turks took action giving credence GOC claim Cyprus was in imminent danger Turk aggression, and that request to NATO for release Turk NATO contingents on standby basis would be exploited by GOC in UN and make

---

[1] Source: Department of State, Central Files, POL 23–8 CYP. Secret; Exdis. Drafted by Bracken, cleared by Burdett, and approved by Talbot. Also sent to Athens and repeated to London, Nicosia, Paris for USRO, and USUN.

[2] A transcript of the telephone conversation is ibid.

[3] Ball's comments were transmitted in telegram 816 to Ankara, February 14. (Ibid.)

efforts defeat GOC tactics immensely more difficult. He had told PriMin emphatically US would never support resolution questioning Treaty Guarantee and expressed confidence that by working together we can defeat GOC ploy, and assured PriMin closest consultation.

Under Secretary asked if Turks could be told of plans for preemptive move to SC on Saturday.

Secretary noted Caccia and Dean were with him and that Limassol casualties not as great as first reported. Gave first reaction some of GOT questions as follows:

See no prospect Russians would attempt intervene Cyprus but assume Western powers including US would find way prevent. Noted other possibility of Soviet pressure on Turkey in event Turkey moved unilaterally under Treaty would raise gravest questions for NATO generally and underscores necessity finding answer Cyprus problem which would prevent that contingency.

Believe US and Turkey should act in closest harmony during period UN consideration and all parties, especially UK, should make maximum effort keep situation calm.

Added that presumably British will shortly answer questions put to British Ambassador since PriMin has returned London.

Re UN tactics, Secretary stated we contemplate British letter will go SC President Saturday afternoon but no SC meeting before Monday because of Greek elections. Said Turks must not give publicity to British letter since could have adverse effect on Greek elections.

Emphasized importance that Greeks not be informed of British letter before its approximate time of delivery which roughly 1430 Saturday NY time.

Noted that possibility Soviet pressures on Turkey underscored necessity closest Turkish consultation in NATO re Cyprus. Mentioned planned Saturday meeting NAC on Cyprus and suggested Turks should keep closest touch with Secretary General Stikker.

Secretary suggested Under Secretary proceed on itinerary to Athens. British Ambassadors Athens Ankara would inform GOG and GOT at appropriate time Saturday re British letter to SC.[4] Ambassador Hare could at same time give suggested assurances to Turks, and that Under Secretary need not discuss British SC letter either capital.

Rusk

---

[4] In telegram 1227 from Ankara, February 15, Ball reported that he had explained the "preemptive initiative" to Turkish officials during an evening meeting. (Ibid.)

15.   Telegram From the Department of State to the Embassy in the United Kingdom[1]

Washington, February 18, 1964, 5:55 p.m.

5185. Please deliver the following letter from the President to Prime Minister Douglas-Home: *Begin verbatim text.*

Dear Prime Minister:

I have had a good talk with George Ball about the impressions he gained on his trip and we have given further thought to the explosive situation stemming from the troubles in Cyprus.

George Ball reports he had a particularly useful meeting with Rab Butler and Duncan Sandys and I am glad to find that there is no difference in our appraisals of the Cyprus crisis.[2]

I think you were wise to beat the Cypriots to the Security Council.[3] It seems very likely that we should be able to prevent the use of the Council to scrap the guarantee treaty. I hope we can also obtain a satisfactory resolution for the creation of an international force. However, the Council may well be heading into a mean and protracted debate, and I fear that an international force will not be landed in Cyprus quickly.

Meanwhile, there is the increasing nervousness of the Turks. In more than three hours of conversation with Inonu, George Ball came away convinced, as you know, that the Turks are poised to intervene and that they will certainly move if a further nasty incident like Limassol should occur. In that event, we would be in for deep trouble since the Greeks have made it clear that they will not stand down.

I conclude from all this that we cannot safely depend merely on the results of the Security Council action. Even an international force may not secure order in Cyprus. As your own people on the Island have pointed out quite perceptively no peacekeeping force will be able to maintain order unless something can be done to change the attitude of the two communities—and the encouragement each is getting from the mainland. Yet Turkish passions will not subside, even with a force in being, if the killing continues.

For that reason, I would strongly urge you to give serious thought to convening the guarantor powers under Article IV of the Treaty for a sum-

---

[1] Source: Department of State, Central Files, POL 23–8 CYP. Confidential; Immediate; Exdis. Drafted and approved by Ball and cleared by Komer for the White House. Repeated to Ankara and Athens.

[2] Ball reported on this meeting in telegram 3969 from London, February 16. (Ibid.)

[3] On February 15, following Makarios' formal rejection of the U.S.–U.K. proposals for an international military force, the British Government requested a Security Council meeting to discuss Cyprus. See *American Foreign Policy: Current Documents, 1964*, pp. 561–562.

mit conference within the next few days. There are clear advantages in acting promptly. First, we need immediate insurance against a unilateral Turkish move. Second, we have, at long last, a Greek Government with a solid majority. Papandreou is rumored in the press this morning as possibly intending to get together with the Turks as his first order of business. This may well be the psychological moment for an effort to break the impasse.

I should think that the subject matter of such a summit meeting could well be the security problem in Cyprus and support for the international force in the United Nations. At the same time, I think you might use such a meeting to develop standby contingency arrangements against the possibility that the Turks may be stimulated by events into a unilateral move.

Such arrangements could take the form of a pledge from each of the guarantor powers that, if one party felt compelled to move, it would confer with the other two powers to make arrangements by which the move would be made on a tripartite basis. Military representatives of the three countries could work out plans for some kind of a combined operation— perhaps along the lines suggested in a paper which George Ball gave to Rab Butler and Duncan Sandys in London.[4]

If such a meeting were to be held, it might be useful to ask the United States to send observers in order that we could add our influence to yours in injecting some rationality into the present situation. If you thought this a good idea, I would be glad to send George Ball and perhaps General Maxwell Taylor.

Of course, it is important that whatever the guarantor powers do as a group should reinforce rather than cut across the current effort in New York to establish the basis for an international peacekeeping force. Both the draft resolution you expect to put into the Security Council and the ideas floated by U Thant include the provision that the guarantor powers should reach agreement, along with the Government of Cyprus, on details of a peacekeeping plan. I have no doubt that a meeting of guarantor powers could be fitted into the track now being pursued in the United Nations.

With my strong feeling that time is of the essence, I am at your disposal to help in any possible way to avoid the fearful consequences of a Greek-Turkish war. Sincerely, *End verbatim text.*

Rusk

---

[4] Ball flew to London on February 14. His "Action Plan for Cyprus" was transmitted in telegram 3961 from London, February 16. (Department of State, Central Files, POL 23–8 CYP)

16.   Message From President Johnson to Prime Minister
        Papandreou[1]

Washington, February 20, 1964.

I have sent you separately my congratulations on your landslide victory in the elections.[2] We are particularly happy that a government can now be formed soonest with a clear majority, because of the grave crisis which confronts the Western Alliance over Cyprus.

Truly, this is a time which requires the closest collaboration of all the allies concerned if we are to surmount the crisis. The US, because of its deep commitment to the NATO alliance, will do whatever it can to help. Nor are we pressing for any specific long-range solution. On the contrary, as we have repeatedly sought to make clear, the United States has no position on terms of any final settlement. What we all need immediately is the reestablishment of law and order so that the parties can proceed to the search for solutions acceptable to all.

And let me assure you that we are neither favoring Turkey at the expense of Greece nor vice versa. Our interest is—as it has been since 1947—that of supporting the security and well-being of two close NATO allies. As we see it, the common need of Greece, Turkey, the US, and the UK to stick together is paramount.

It will take the highest statesmanship on all sides, but especially in Athens and Ankara, to prevent a wholly unnecessary debacle—and one which threatens the very security of both Greece and Turkey—from being precipitated by the Cypriot extremists of both sides.

For this reason I am grateful that you won by a majority that gives you the necessary freedom of action, because we count heavily on the wise heads of you and Inonu to help find some way of stopping the drift toward communal tragedy. I have seen with interest reports that you may have been considering a new effort in partnership with Inonu, and while I do not know the details of what you may have in mind, I do want to say that in principle nothing could be more helpful than joint action by

---

[1] Source: Johnson Library, National Security File, Files of Robert W. Komer, Cyprus. Secret. A copy of the message was transmitted in telegram 943 to Athens, February 20. (Department of State, Central Files, POL 23–8 CYP) The President also addressed similar letters on the Cyprus issue to Prime Minister Inonu and President Makarios. The text of the February 21 letter to Makarios is in the Johnson Library, National Security File, Special Head of State Correspondence, Cyprus. The text of the letter to Inonu was transmitted in telegram 848 to Ankara, February 20. (Department of State, Central Files, POL 23–8 CYP)

[2] A copy of Johnson's message is in the Johnson Library, National Security File, Country File, Greece, Papandreou. In telegram 1261 from Athens, February 19, the Embassy commented that the main characteristic of the new Papandreou government was its "moderate nature," noting that Papandreou had placed conservatives in key positions. (Department of State, Central Files, POL 15–1 GREECE)

the leaders of Greece and Turkey in the spirit which I am sure you have in mind.

In this critical period it is important that our representatives keep in close touch with each other, in Nicosia and New York as well as Athens and Washington. We recognize the special responsibilities which Greece, Turkey, and the United Kingdom must continue to bear, but you may count on us as well.[3]

Sincerely,

Lyndon B. Johnson[4]

---

[3] In a February 27 response, Prime Minister Papandreou stated his opposition to direct negotiations between himself and Inonu, reaffirmed his opposition to the use of force to settle the Cyprus issue, and called for close consultations. (Ibid., POL 23–8 CYP)

[4] Printed from a copy that bears this typed signature.

---

17. Telegram From the Embassy in Greece to the Department of State[1]

Athens, February 21, 1964, 3 p.m.

1272. Cyprus.

1. I called on PriMin last night. I found him looking tired but mentally alert. After I extended our congratulations on his great political victory, we immediately got down to discussion Cyprus problem.

2. I recalled to him that our only interest was reestablishment law and order so that parties concerned could work out political solution in atmosphere of calm. For our part, we had no pre-conceived ideas of what ultimate solution should be—this was matter for parties concerned. Papandreou indicated he understood and appreciated our position, but said that many considered we were supporting Turks. He smilingly added that if the US fully supported the "right", we would have to take sides—Greece's—for London–Zurich Accords had created impossible

---

[1] Source: Department of State, Central Files, POL 23–8 CYP. Secret; Immediate. Repeated to USUN, Ankara, London, and Nicosia. Passed to the White House, COA, JCS, OSD, CINCEUR, and CINCSTRIKE.

situation. I suggested one of reasons for public misunderstanding was irresponsible and wholly misleading articles in Greek press which led the public to believe that US either had ulterior motives or was supporting Turkey versus Greece. I pointed out that Paraskevopoulos caretaker govt had either been unwilling or unable tell facts to public.

3. While on the subject of our support of GOT position, I said that it was obvious we could not accept the view—apparently advanced by Makarios—that the SC could amend or nullify treaties. This could only be accomplished through negotiation of the interested parties. Papandreou nodded assent. I stressed that, even though we took above position on treaty, we had been using very strong pressure on GOT not to exercise "right of intervention."

4. I then went on to say that, during these past days, the situation on the island had deteriorated and was extremely dangerous. Not only was Makarios apparently acting on very bad advice, but individual guerrilla bands were growing in strength and independence. Consequently it was of transcending importance that peacekeeping force be organized and despatched quickly and, meanwhile, that every effort be made to prevent further violence on the island. In view great danger confronting us all, I added that it was indeed fortunate that Papandreou had achieved his overwhelming electoral victory, for this put him in key position to play constructive and decisive role on Cyprus question; his election could well prove turning point in history as he was probably only man who could move problem toward solution.

5. After we agreed on need for peace force and also on fact this only temporary expedient, I said it seemed to me only hope for any solution, long or short term, was agreement between Greece and Turkey—certainly no permanent solution could be found without their agreement. Meanwhile, what could Papandreou do to get Makarios in hand and also control Greek-Cypriot irregular leaders? This was essential and extremely urgent.

6. Papandreou said first that he already moved to gain control over Greek Cypriots as he had told me he would do if elected. He repeated his statement to me of last week (Embtel 1205)[2] that it was inadmissible for Greece's future to be decided by Makarios and stated firmly that he intended to enforce discipline on Greek Cypriots. To achieve this, he had been in touch with Makarios and had also just that afternoon met with General Grivas and a "representative" of Cypriot Interior Minister Georgatzis; he expected Georgatzis to arrive during the night. He also said he was contacting Sampson, Lyssarides and the Commander of the Greek forces in Cyprus, Col. Petridies. He said he would demand that Greek

---

[2] Dated February 11. (Ibid.)

Cypriots undertake no violence against Turk Cypriots unless attacked first. He stressed importance GOT holding Turk Cypriots in check. Otherwise, he seemed confident that he could exert the necessary control over the Greek Cypriots to create an atmosphere leading to negotiations.

7.   The PriMin agreed completely that first step was to bring about peace and calm atmosphere in which negotiations could take place. However, he said long-term solution requires removal of Greek and Turkish forces from Cyprus; their presence there, facing one another was unnatural and created constant tension. Their place should be taken by an international force, he continued, that would stay as long as needed. Long term solution would require "international" guarantee rather than present impossible system. He did not spell out "international" but seemed to have in mind a UN guarantee of some sort (I don't think he would rule out NATO) which would give "complete" guarantees to Turk Cypriots for protection of their minority rights (he repeated word "complete" several times).

8.   Papandreou said he thought time had come when Grivas could play constructive role in Cyprus; he observed that as Makarios' prestige was going down, Grivas' was going up. However, he emphasized that he did not want to play one off against the other, and that it was essential that they cooperate or the Communists would gain. He apparently had not thought through how Grivas' appearance on scene would affect British or Turks. He seemed to be toying with idea that Grivas would pull all irregular elements together and ensure discipline, leaving Makarios as President—for the moment at least. This is all in "feeling out" stage and I doubt that Papandreou sees clear path ahead as yet.

9.   I stressed again that it was vital that there be understanding between Greece and Turkey. He agreed and said that if he were to meet Inonu, he would tell him that it is insane to consider war between Greece and Turkey; however, he added that if Turks "open door to insane asylum, then he would have to accompany Inonu inside." I did not press him on meeting with Inonu, since I thought it would be counter-productive to do so at that particular moment. However, I have very definite impression he would go along with meeting if we can set proper stage. President's letter to Brit PriMin may show the way, but this should be researched by Brits.

10. Papandreou expressed optimism about outcome of talks at UN; he said info he had received during afternoon sounded promising. He strongly favors giving U Thant proposals a good try.

11. *Comment:* I was impressed by speed with which Papandreou has started action aimed at gaining control of Greek Cypriots as he had told me he would in our meeting last week. He seemed fully cognizant of dangers involved in Cyprus crisis and said several times he wanted to move Cyprus from the "danger" status to the "problem" status. Whether

he can really gain control of Greeks on island remains to be seen, but he apparently is confident that he can and is going to make real college try. Meanwhile, I urge that we restate to Turks importance controlling their brethren on island in order prevent incidents such as those mentioned in Nicosia's 405.[3]

Labouisse

---

[3] Telegram 405 from Nicosia, December 29, 1963, reported the Ambassador's talk with Clerides. (Ibid., POL 25 CYP)

---

18.   Telegram From the Department of State to the Embassy in Greece[1]

Washington, February 24, 1964, 8:46 p.m.

933. We are pleased to see from urtels 1279 and 1280[2] that Papandreou (a) aware of Communist dangers in Cyprus; (b) working on Makarios to accept U Thant proposal; and (c) agrees that main thing now is for Greeks and Turks to sit down together and work out solution.

Dept gratified at constructive dialogue which you have conducted with Papandreou since election. We are anxious have you continue full and frank exchange with him on all aspects of Cyprus problem both to establish mutual confidence and to create positive atmosphere for eventual Greco-Turkish (or tripartite) meeting. This connection, we wish give him our appraisal of current situation in New York, as follows:

As we read situation at UN, there has been substantial agreement among all concerned on same basic elements accepted in earlier US–UK proposal, to wit, need for international peacekeeping force and need for mediator. However, in our judgment, prospects are extremely remote that SC session will result in any kind of action giving reality to either of these two concepts. Reason for this perfectly clear: Makarios remains

---

[1] Source: Department of State, Central Files, POL 23–8 CYP. Confidential; Priority. Drafted by Buffum and Sisco; cleared by Bracken, Talbot, and Cleveland; and approved by Ball. Repeated to Ankara, Nicosia, London, and USUN.

[2] Telegrams 1279 and 1280, February 20, reported on discussions with Papandreou regarding Cyprus. (Ibid.)

obdurate in opposing any UN resolution which does not have effect of negating Treaty of Guarantee. He presumably has Soviet veto in his pocket and we assume will not hesitate to use it. We and the UK, on the other hand, are equally determined that SC shall not be exploited to nullify Treaty of Guarantee, and most members of Council agree this should not be the case. We are not seeking get SC reaffirm Treaty of Guarantee; however, we cannot agree to type of resolution sought by Makarios which by completely ignoring Treaty and by giving an international force mandate that appears to be directed against Turkish intervention has effect of negating Treaty.

We hope GOG is under no illusion about futility of Makarios' efforts get kind of action from Council he wants. (We assume Bitsios has so reported to Athens.) Only way we can see to prevent total impasse at UN is if Makarios relents in his position. We hope GOG doing what it can get him adopt more flexible attitude toward SC resolution. SC President Bernardes (Brazil) is now consulting with non-permanent SC members in hope of working out a formula which both sides can accept. We wish them well in this endeavor, but looking at problem realistically, we are convinced Bernardes will fare no better than U Thant has unless Makarios prepared abandon his objective of getting SC to vitiate Treaty.

Our present assessment is that efforts to get an acceptable resolution in Council may run for another two or three days. But we deeply concerned that if SC produces nothing, as we anticipate, vacuum may be created in which there will be further violence in Cyprus and renewed temptation for Turks to move in. We would be interested in any thoughts Papandreou has on possible lines of approach to Inonu. We glad he planned to see Turkish Ambassador and would be interested to learn whether he did so and what came of meeting. If US, as friend of both sides, can in any way facilitate Greek-Turkish dialogue, we shall be most happy to do so.

With future course of events in Cyprus murky in face of almost certain Council inaction, we would warmly welcome any thoughts Papandreou has on steps that might be taken now to avoid a dangerous vacuum when deadlock reached in SC.

FYI: We think an early Papandreou–Inonu meeting would be best next step. This could be without prejudice to later participation of UK (and US) if this proves desirable. We believe such meeting could provide vehicle for keeping lid on situation in Cyprus and convincing Makarios to accept international peacekeeping force along lines of Thant Plan.[3] Possible outcome of such meeting could be to: (a) address an appeal to Makarios to take all possible measures to maintain law and order; (b)

---

[3] This plan, which was rejected, proposed establishment of an international peacekeeping force and provided for a mediator under special circumstances. For text, see U.N. Doc. S/5554, February 15, 1964.

urge him to accept international force along lines of Thant Plan; and (c) reassure Makarios, as in Allied Plan, that rights of intervention under Treaty of Guarantee would be suspended for period during which international force operating and while mutually-agreed mediator was seeking political solution. We also believe that Makarios' willingness accept international peacekeeping force along lines of Thant Plan would be decisively influenced if the Greeks and Turks could make clear to him that alternative to such an international peacekeeping force would be tripartite military intervention under Treaty of Guarantee. Confronted with choice between international force along lines of Thant Plan and tripartite military intervention, Makarios might well see former as lesser of two evils.

We have outlined the above rather fully to give you the flavor of our present tentative thinking. We leave it to your discretion as to how much of this would be appropriate for you to reveal to Papandreou at this time. We would like you to see Papandreou soonest, largely in context of an exchange of views on where we are in New York, and to have you probe further possibility of an early high-level meeting.[4] End FYI.

Rusk

---

[4] In telegram 1298 from Athens, February 26, Labouisse reported he had passed on the Department's views to Papandreou who outlined his efforts to restrain Makarios and stressed the need for the United States to restrain Turkey. (Ibid)

---

19.   Telegram From the Department of State to the Embassy in the United Kingdom[1]

Washington, February 26, 1964, 6:05 p.m.

5393. For Ambassador from Under Secretary. Would you please deliver the following message from me to Messrs. Butler and Sandys:

Begin verbatim text

Denis Greenhill has told me[2] of your plan to approach the Greek and Turkish Governments tomorrow to urge a meeting between Papandreou and Inonu. I told him that we would ask our Ambassadors in the two capitals to coordinate with yours in order to give whatever reinforcement seemed useful.

---

[1] Source: Department of State, Central Files, POL 23–8 CYP. Secret; Immediate; Exclusive Distribution. Drafted and approved by Ball and cleared by Burdett and Jernegan. Repeated to Ankara, Athens, USUN, DOD, and the White House.

[2] At a noon meeting at the Department of State; a memorandum of their conversation is ibid.

While I see great virtue in a bilateral meeting, I am not at all sanguine it can be achieved at this point. Our own tentative soundings have indicated that it will be difficult for either Papandreou or Inonu to move without at least some third party invitation and a juridical excuse for conferring.

I would strongly urge, therefore, that if the answer is negative—as I fear it will be—you consider going back promptly with a request for tripartite consultation under Article 4 of the Treaty of Guaranty. As I read this Article, consultation is not merely a privilege, but an obligation of the parties—if there is reason to believe that the state of affairs under the constitution has been altered. In order to bring the Greeks along it might well be necessary to suggest that Makarios and Kutchuck be invited to participate in the consultation.

Alternatively, we might propose to Inonu that the Turks themselves extend the invitation for tripartite consultation. This would have, however, two disadvantages. First, based on my conversations with Erkin, I doubt that the Turks would be prepared to call for a tripartite consultation unless it were clearly understood that this was a prelude to tripartite intervention. Second, the Greeks might be less responsive to a Turkish request for consultation than to an invitation from your Government.

I feel more than ever that some move of this kind is imperative. It seems evident that the Greek Cypriot game is to try to keep the United Nations proceedings going. This is a forum where they can draw support from their Communist friends. It provides them with insulation against a Turkish move while eroding Turkish intervention rights.

Bernardes, the President of the Security Council, is trying to work out a compromise resolution before Thursday afternoon. If the Cypriots continue to dig in, however, I think it may become apparent by then that no resolution can be forthcoming. The Cypriots are exploiting to the maximum Soviet and Czech support. Kyprianou has played the Council skillfully, and there is developing evidence of softness on the part of the Ivory Coast and Morocco. The increasing pro-Makarios line being pursued by Bitsios is having its effect on the Council members.

Meanwhile, in Cyprus Makarios is moving with his characteristic Byzantine deviousness. The regularizing of 5,000 irregulars looks to us as an effort to lay a basis for a request that your troops be withdrawn. There is plenty of evidence that Makarios does not want a peace-keeping force of any kind. By asking the withdrawal of British forces, he would probably discourage countries from contributing components even if the Security Council should produce a satisfactory resolution.

If Makarios can keep the matter going in New York, he probably feels that he can deal with the Turkish Cypriots without much fear of Turkish intervention—particularly with his exaggerated belief in the nature of Soviet assistance.

Against this background, we see his call for the disarmament of the population as laying the basis for a move to disarm the Turkish Cypriots. In this connection we have good report that Papadoupulos made speech on the 24th to the Patriotic Front Deputies saying GOC has decided definitely to rely fully on Soviet support having lost hope in UN.

All these events in Nicosia have certainly not been lost on Ankara, which is presumably feeling an increasing claustrophobia. I do not think we can count on Inonu holding the line, once it becomes clear that an international force is not on. And, if the Turks sense the erosion of their treaty rights to intervene, they may feel compelled to move before it is too late.

All of these considerations seem to me to urge a tripartite meeting if Bernardes is not successful and if we cannot secure the promise of an immediate bilateral Greek-Turkish dialogue. Such a meeting would seem to offer several opportunities:

(a) To convince Makarios that the Turks mean business and that he is playing too risky a game;
(b) To press Makarios to accept and support an international peace-keeping force along the lines of the Thant plan; and
(c) To undertake contingency planning for a possible tripartite intervention as an alternative to unilateral Turkish move.

I do not think I am being alarmist in feeling a deep sense of urgency. I cannot believe that the arms build-up in Cyprus can continue much longer without grave danger of an explosion.

I think it very likely that if the Security Council fades out and the Cypriots prove unable to secure an emergency General Assembly meeting the present superficial calm will give way to a bloodbath. *End verbatim text.*[3]

For Ankara: Would appreciate your comments on foregoing together with results your soundings with GOT on its views and possible actions as result of developments in Security Council and on Cyprus.[4]

For Athens: You are requested to comment similarly.[5]

Rusk

---

[3] In telegram 4189 from London, February 27, Bruce reported that he delivered Ball's message to Caccia who outlined British doubts about the utility of a guarantor powers' meeting and suggested that a Makarios–Inonu summit might jolt the Greek Cypriots to their senses. (Ibid.)

[4] In telegram 1090 from Ankara, February 28, the Embassy reported that Turkish patience with Makarios was wearing thin, but the Turks remained receptive to the idea of a "high level meeting" with Greek officials. (Ibid.)

[5] In telegram 1306 from Athens, February 27, the Embassy reported that Papandreou was unwilling to enter into direct high-level talks with the Inonu government and would probably oppose any proposal involving action by the guarantor powers. (Ibid.)

20.   Telegram From the Embassy in Greece to the Department of State[1]

Athens, February 27, 1964, 5 p.m.

1302. 1. I think we have reached a stage which warrants reevaluation of some aspects of our policy and tactics dealing with the Cyprus question. Our main concern has been to prevent a situation from developing which would embroil two of our allies, thus precipitating NATO disaster. To this end, our basic drive thus far has been to gain time and keep the Turks from making a military move on Cyprus which the Greeks would inevitably feel bound to counter. We have consequently worked for measures which would effectively suppress violence on the island and thus deprive the Turks of the provocation which might trigger off a legally justified intervention on their part. In order to avoid antagonizing either of these two allies of the US, we have studiously avoided taking a position as to the form or the shape of a final settlement of the Cyprus problem. We have said many times that the solution is a matter for the parties concerned. This was probably the proper stand for us to take at first, but is it right and is it good enough to meet the situation which faces us today?

2. It must no doubt be difficult for the more sophisticated to believe that the US has been willing to accept an important role in the efforts to bring peace to the island without also attempting to form a considered judgment as to how the matter ought to be settled on a long-term basis. In our conversations, PriMin Papandreou has been probing for a US position and obviously does not believe that we do not have one. In fact (as has become increasingly clear during UN debate) our studious avoidance to take a position is in itself a position—one that is inevitably interpreted as favoring the existing set of arrangements rather than acknowledging the pace of events and the impetus to change the agreements which have been established and theoretically govern Cyprus. Moreover, while continuing to adhere to this noncommittal attitude of neutrality on the question of a long-term solution, we have been supporting—in effect if not in words—the Turkish insistence that the Treaty of Guarantee affords the Turks a legal cover for intervention. We are thus inevitably taken to be supporting not only the Treaty of Guarantee but the other aspects of the London and Zurich Agreements as well—in short, the status quo.

3. It has already been vividly and painfully demonstrated that the present arrangements for Cyprus do not work and will in due course

---

[1] Source: Department of State, Central Files, POL 23–8 CYP. Secret; Priority. Repeated to Ankara, Nicosia, London, and USUN. Relayed to the White House, CIA, JCS, OSD, CINCEUR, and CINCSTRIKE.

have to be changed. In Cyprus, in Greece, and at the UN, the pressure for "self-determination" is increasingly strong. I do not see how the US can ultimately escape agreeing to the application of more self-determination for Cyprus than is presently permitted in the existing arrangements without laying itself open to the charge of moral inconsistency. Only last Saturday the communiqué issued after President Johnson's meeting with Pres. Lopez Mateos reaffirmed "support of the principle of self-determination of all peoples and of its corollary, non-intervention. They agreed . . . to promote the acceptance of such principles, not only with words but with deeds, in the Americas and throughout the world."[2]

4. Much more will be heard in UN halls and out, from the Soviet and Afro-Asian blocs, and indeed from the Greeks, on the necessity for applying the principle of self-determination to Cyprus. Will it not then become increasingly embarrassing for us to avoid taking stand? In the end our strategy of neutrality (generally interpreted as support of the existing arrangements) will not only hurt us in the UN but spread the wrong impression about US policy around the world. Here in Greece, adherence to this strategy over a long period of time, with the resulting vocal reactions in the press, among the public and in government circles, may do serious and lasting damage to US-Greek relations that will have repercussions more far-reaching than Cyprus.

5. Since it seems to me that we will inevitably be driven to conceding in the end that the present arrangements cannot be made to work, would it not be well to make a virtue of necessity by saying at once that, in our opinion, the agreements will, in due course, have to be altered by negotiations between the interested parties? I believe that this would clear the air considerably, put us in a less uncomfortable position to deal with Makarios, the Greeks and the neutral and Soviet blocs—thus improving the chances for the creation of a peace force—and give some negotiating substance to future discussions between Greeks and Turks. While, in the recent past, the cruelty of the Greek Cypriot irregulars toward the Turkish minority and the deviousness of Makarios have damaged the majority's case for control by it of the island's affairs, the fact remains that the Greek Cypriot 82 percent majority has the right to a preponderant voice in determining what the island's government and policies ought to be.

6. Obviously, the Turks will hardly welcome this evolution in our position. We can, I believe, relieve some if not all of their concern by emphasizing that our position in favor of modifying the agreements is rigidly conditioned on complete protection of the rights of the Turkish Cypriot minority—rights which, however, cannot include a veto over

---

[2] For full text of the statement, see *Public Papers of the Presidents of the United States: Lyndon B. Johnson, 1964*, Book I, pp. 303–305.

the 82 percent majority's right to control its foreign affairs, defense and taxes. This guarantee of the rights of the minority would, in the first stage, have to be insured by the presence and appropriate authority of an international force. Such a force would have to stay on the island long enough to make sure, for the future, that the Government of Cyprus would not and could not use the principle of self-determination as a means of destroying or oppressing the Turkish minority.

7. While the course of action proposed may not curb overnight the neutralist and leftward drift of the island's present government, I believe that it would somewhat restore the position of the West in Cyprus and make the island a less open target for Communist intrigue and penetration. It would make it easier for the US to maneuver amidst changing events. Our first step ought to be an acknowledgement that the present arrangements have less chance than ever to become workable in practice. (The setting up of the London conference and the subsequent Anglo-American suggestions for appointing a mediator implied, in a sense, that changes were needed.) Our main goal should continue to be the elimination of communal strife through the dispatch of an international force or in any other way that might appear practicable. Looking further ahead, it may be that, in the end a NATO guarantee or some other form of association of the island with the West will become desirable and feasible—for a Cyprus remaining a permanent apple of discord between Greeks and Turks would continue to be a grave threat to Western and US interests.

8. The foregoing observations and recommendations have been set down in full awareness that

(a) A shift in our public position in the direction of self-determination will be taken as a victory for Makarios (who bears such heavy responsibility for the present impasse), and
(b) That if the Turkish minority were to continue to be permitted to retain a degree of control over the island's affairs out of proportion to its voting strength, it might help frustrate neutralist and leftist tendencies on the island. (The Greeks, of course, argue forcefully that continuation of present situation is driving Cyprus into Communist arms.)

Although these considerations are important and must be weighed, I firmly believe that the United States stands to lose less by modifying our position along lines suggested.[3]

Labouisse

---

[3] Telegram 880 from Nicosia, February 29, endorsed Labouisse's arguments, adding that the United States "should not abandon hope of finding basis of cooperation with Greek Cypriots" that would permit a settlement protecting the legitimate interests of both Cypriot communities. In telegram 906 to Athens, March 4, Ball responded that while Cypriot constitutional arrangements appeared unworkable, the United States continued to insist that changes could not come through Security Council actions. (Both in Department of State, Central Files, POL 23–8 CYP)

21.   Telegram From the Embassy in Cyprus to the Department of State[1]

Nicosia, March 3, 1964, 4 p.m.

898. Makarios told me this morning GOC had decided accept draft SC resolution on Cyprus submitted by five non-permanent members (USUN's 3246 to Department).[2]

He said Clerides had telephoned him from New York last night to recommend some minor changes. Clerides had told him USSR very disturbed about provision that commander of peace-keeping force would be appointed by and report to SYG because USSR felt bound by Congo precedent in that commander should be appointed by and report to SC. Makarios commented he would ask Soviet Ambassador Ermoshin request USSR not to veto resolution on this basis.

Since Makarios obviously expected some reply, I commented that it was quite understandable USSR would take such a position because it could thus hope, through threat or use of SC veto, to exercise continuing, if negative, influence on development of Cyprus problem for its own purposes. After mentioning Soviet abuse of veto in past, I reminded Makarios of analogous situation existing under Constitution of Republic of Cyprus. Under this constitution Turkish minority in House of Representatives could never by themselves procure adoption of legislation but were in position, through exercise of veto, to prevent adoption of legislation which majority of House considered necessary for good of country. Makarios nodded agreement.

Makarios, who usually appears reposed, seemed unusually relaxed today but did not, it will be noticed, miss opportunity to discredit a pretender (Clerides) in American eyes.

McKiernan

---

[1] Source: Department of State, Central Files, POL 23–8 CYP. Confidential; Immediate. Repeated to USUN, Ankara, Athens, London, and Paris for USRO. Passed to the White House, CIA, JCS, OSD, CINCEUR, and CINCSTRIKE.

[2] Not printed. (Ibid.) For text of Security Council Resolution 186 (1964), adopted unanimously on March 4 (U.N. Doc. S/5575), see *American Foreign Policy: Current Documents, 1964*, pp. 566–567. The resolution recommended that the Secretary-General create a peacekeeping force in Cyprus and designate a mediator to promote a peaceful solution.

22.   Telegram From the Department of State to the Embassy in Cyprus[1]

Washington, March 7, 1964, 6:26 p.m.

621. After interview with Secretary reported separate telegram,[2] Kyprianou, Clerides, and Rossides had brief talk with President March 6. President expressed hope machinery set up by SC would be sufficient to work out Cyprus problem. Thought it was best we could hope for and stressed extreme importance of peaceful settlement, remarking that most people would rather talk things out than fight. He expressed regret there had been misunderstanding of U.S. attitude. Sent his regards and best wishes to Makarios.

As in prior talk with Secretary, Kyprianou emphasized need for unitary state in Cyprus "with everyone equal" and understanding that Greece and Turkey should have nothing to do with Cyprus.

President commented that unfortunately neither Greek Cypriots nor Turkish Cypriots seemed to think this way. Greek Cypriots thought of themselves as Greek just as much as Turkish Cypriots thought of themselves as Turkish. Feelings ran high on both sides not only on island but in Greece and Turkey as well. Kyprianou stuck to his position.

Conversation was amicable throughout.

Rusk

---

[1] Source: Department of State, Central Files, POL 23–8 CYP. Confidential. Drafted and approved by Jernegan and cleared by Komer for the White House. Also sent to Ankara, Athens, London, and USUN.

[2] Telegram 619 to Nicosia, March 7. (Ibid.)

---

23.   Telegram From the Department of State to the Mission to the United Nations[1]

Washington, March 9, 1964, 9:05 p.m.

2377. There are number important points which we believe need to be pursued re establishment and operation of UN Force in Cyprus:

---

[1] Source: Department of State, Central Files, POL 23–8 CYP. Confidential. Drafted by Buffum and Moffitt, cleared by Jernegan and Cleveland, and approved by Ball. Also sent to Nicosia and repeated to Ankara, Athens, London, Stockholm, Copenhagen, Helsinki, Dublin, and Ottawa.

1) Three month period for which force established is absolute minimum within which we can reasonably expect mediator to make any headway toward permanent settlement. It therefore desirable that date at which writ for force starts to run not begin prematurely. We note that Cypriots themselves consider logical date for three-month period to begin is date of placement of UN troops in Cyprus rather than date res adopted. We hope Thant will bear this in mind by formally designating establishment of force only when he has sizable contingents (2,000 to 3,000 non-UK troops) on the ground. If UK has not yet turned over British units to SYG control, as London's 4357[2] would indicate, this should give U Thant additional time to maneuver on effective date on which UN force becomes operative.

2) Septel deals with question size UK contribution to UN.[3] In discussions with SYG and Bunche, you authorized draw on this message to indicate our views on this subject.

3) We understand Sweden insists it not be only neutral country and hope SYG continuing press Irish and Finns to contribute at least some troops. (We understand Brazil will probably not contribute troops because of domestic considerations, and in view of their extraordinarily high per diem requirements would not be disposed to push them to participate.)

4) We concerned that as things are now going SYG will not be able muster minimum force of 10,000 men unless UK keeps all its present forces in Cyprus and we assume they will be most reluctant if not totally unwilling to do so. We find it difficult believe that Cypriots would not accept Danish contingent if they can accept UK and Canada. Since Danes apparently willing and eager serve, we think SYG should at least urge Cypriots reconsider question Danish participation.

5) Major problem which will confront force once it established is precise terms of engagement under which it will operate. We note that Canadians, Swedes, and UK concerned on this score. It is unrealistic to expect that countries will put their troops into field under SYG's command until they know more clearly than they are told in SC res what ground rules are under which troops will be used.

One of most difficult questions likely to be what UN force should do re armed irregulars and Greek Cypriot police. Makarios will undoubtedly try use UN Force to help disarm Turkish Cypriots. Any such move, of course, would be totally unacceptable in Ankara. Since dispute in case is between two communities in Cyprus, UN would need to operate in even-handed fashion and can hardly lend itself to disarming one party to

---

[2] Dated March 6. (Ibid.)

[3] In telegram 5722 to London, March 9, the Department expressed concern about the size of the proposed British troop contribution to the peacekeeping force. (Ibid.)

dispute while leaving other in control of security force. Alternatively, Makarios might try use his augmented police force to disarm Turkish Cypriots while UN Force is on the ground, assuming latter will restrain Turks from invading Cyprus. This would pose much more difficult problem since Makarios would argue this is exercise of sovereign powers of GOC. In fact, of course, Constitution gives Turkish Cypriots veto power in field of security, and use of police force clearly falls within this provision. UN could refuse permit disarming of Turk Cypriots by police since this would inevitably lead to violence between communities and SC res calls on UN Force to prevent recurrence fighting.

6) With a mandate of only 3 months and resolution directing force "to use its best efforts to prevent a recurrence of fighting and as necessary contribute to maintenance and restoration of law and order and a return to normal conditions", UN's role would be that of UN policeman. That is, UN Force should interpose itself between two communities preventing hostilities, arranging cease-fires and taking any other steps it finds necessary to maintain law and order. This will involve certain amount initiative on part of UN Force and necessitate practical cooperation from both communities.

7) We assume that—unlike Congo where use of force authorized in certain specified circumstances—UN Force in Cyprus would use force only in self-defense.

8) There may also be danger that Makarios will seek to exploit the phrase "return to normal conditions" as meaning that Turkish Cypriots will have to be moved back to domiciles where they were located before current fighting began; he may argue that de facto partition has been created and must be abolished if "normal conditions" are to prevail. We assume UN would not lend itself to any effort at forced population movement. Turk Cypriots deserted mixed villages in fear for their lives and would resist any attempt send them back. For UN to do anything to abet such effort would be widely regarded as pro-Makarios move.

Request USUN discuss foregoing questions as appropriate with U Thant, Bunche and Rikhye, urging that they clarify UN policy as soon as possible so that potential contributors will know what to expect re utilization their forces.

For Nicosia

Appreciate any comments you have on foregoing.[4] In addition without going into details of above, request you seek Pickard's views on problems to be anticipated in connection with UN Force and suggestions for coping with them.

Rusk

---

[4] In telegram 936 from Nicosia, Belcher expressed his view that Makarios would seek to limit the powers of the peacekeeping force. (Ibid.)

24.   Telegram From the Embassy in Turkey to the Department of State[1]

Ankara, March 10, 1964, 2:13 p.m.

1143. Embtel 1136.[2] I had rather expected that completeness with which reftel and Embtel 1134[3] covered GOT misgivings re Cyprus would give breathing space for their consideration but on contrary I was again called in by Erkin this morning for presentation which, from standpoint of intensity and gravity, unequalled since that of Christmas day.

As I came in Erkin had report in his hand of new attacks this morning by Greeks in western part of Cyprus using mortars, bazookas, heavy machine guns, etc. At first I assumed this was immediate cause of his agitation but it later came out that he had asked see me before receiving this report on basis of general deterioration of situation on island, including presumed death of large number of Turk hostages, and increased dissatisfaction with implementation of resolution. Specific points mentioned were:

1. GOT had always assumed that Turkish contingent would be included in peace force but it now learns that GOG has told SYG it prepared withdraw its contingent and that, at their instigation together with GOC, SYG has confirmed he considering their recommendation that withdrawal of Greek contingent be accompanied by that of Turks. GOT is lodging strong protest with SYG on this point.

2. Report received yesterday which causes GOT have increased reservations re Gyani[4] since appears that he has made statements to effect that Turks must as minority give in to Greeks; that he has seen much of Makarios and Greek Ministers but Kucuk practically ignored; that he has been available to Greek journalists but only received Turks reluctantly, etc. In circumstances, GOT will advise SYG it remains unconvinced that Gyani man for job but will give him benefit of doubt for time being. However, if events should give reason for dissatisfaction, GOT will say so publicly and give reasons.

3. Specification of qualification for mediator mentioned reftel will now be followed by clear-cut refusal to accept [garble—Gyani?].

---

[1] Source: Department of State, Central Files, POL 23–8 CYP. Confidential; Priority. Repeated to USUN, Athens, Nicosia, London, and Paris. Passed to the White House, CIA, JCS, OSD, CINCEUR, and CINCSTRIKE.

[2] Telegram 1136, March 8, reported Turkish concerns about the Secretary-General's proposals for a Cyprus settlement. (Ibid.)

[3] Telegram 1134, March 7, reported on Barnes' farewell talks with senior Turkish officials. (Ibid.)

[4] Lieutenant General Prem Singh Gyani, the Secretary-General's Personal Representative in Cyprus since January 17 and his nominee to command the peacekeeping force.

4. Deterioration of situation in Cyprus is direct result of SC resolution. We can now see what "additional measures" mentioned in Article 2 really mean.

5. GOT addressing notes to SYG, UK and US stressing need for British forces in Cyprus being more effective in peacekeeping until new force arrives.

6. Cabinet met this morning and was very dissatisfied with way things going.

7. GOT listened to our advice re exerting restraint and then accepting resolution, only to find itself in steadily deteriorating situation.

8. Throughout crisis Inonu has been very patient but this morning he said for first time that situation approaching point where Turkey would be forced intervene unless effective measures taken to bring it under control, and asked Erkin so advise me.

I spent some time trying reassure Erkin and at same time ferret out what had happened since we talked on Saturday to generate so much heat. Among other things I stressed danger of becoming overly exercised re reports from Cyprus which had been notoriously inaccurate in past; observed that BBC and VOA this morning credited Gyani with having been helpful in effecting a cease-fire in Paphos area; said I still felt GOT had been wise accept resolution and would be stretching things pretty far for GOC to attempt justify recent incidents under Article 2, etc.[5]

In end Erkin was perhaps a little less tense but there was certain note of finality on which conversation closed that was disturbing. I hope I am not imagining things but impression Erkin seemed to be trying convey was that GOT had gone long way with us but was now finding situation very hard to bear and might have to strike out on own unless present trend reversed both in New York and in Cyprus.

British Amb Allen immediately followed me and we compared notes afterward. Apparently conversation covered same points including message from Inonu, and, although Erkin had begun on lower key, he had ended on bitter note that GOT now in backwash of resolution it should not have approved and at loss defend itself before Turkish people and Parliament. (Fact that High Military Council opened semi-annual meeting here this morning and had Cyprus as first item on agenda may have been another contributing factor.)

Allen and I carefully checked our memories on Inonu message concerning possible intervention and agreed it did not reflect indication of intention to intervene but rather that intervention could become necessary unless something done to avert present deterioration in New York and Cyprus and that it was especially up to UK and US to see that action taken.

---

[5] Reference is to Article 2 of the Treaty of Guarantee signed at London on February 19, 1959. For text, see *American Foreign Policy: Current Documents, 1959*, p. 770.

Comment: It is possible that conversation which Barnes happened have simultaneously with SecGen Bayramoglu[6] may cast some light on what troubling Turks, at least as far as we concerned. After expressing similar unhappiness re resolution and other developments, Bayramoglu wondered whether we still as interested in Cyprus as before or whether now that resolution was passed, we would not be inclined pull out. If, as possible, this may be doubt which Erkin hesitated mention, it could partially explain vigor of his approach, i.e., to try to keep us interested while at same time seeking goad British to bear down harder until peace force arrives.

In sum, this may not be crisis but no doubt that we have some very restive Turks on our hands and that it would be helpful if we could do something to make them feel our interest is continuing and active.[7]

Hare

---

[6] Barnes' talk with Bayramoglu was reported in telegram 1134.

[7] In telegram 934 to Ankara, March 10, the Department replied that while it agreed with the Turkish position on the right to intervention, it believed that more attention needed to be paid to putting a peacekeeping force into place. The telegram also urged the Embassy to stress the need for cooperation with the U.N. efforts to establish a peacekeeping force and outlined steps the United States had taken to promote peaceful resolution of the problem. (Department of State, Central Files, POL 23–8 CYP)

---

25.   Circular Telegram From the Department of State to All Posts[1]

Washington, March 12, 1964, 11:06 p.m.

1675. 1. Critic Message from Ankara,[2] repeated to you by Department, told of warning Turks have given to Makarios,[3] that they would move if attacks on Turkish Cypriots did not stop. Ambassador Hare asked for 24 hours consultation, and Erkin said he would so recommend.

---

[1] Source: Department of State, Central Files, POL 23–8 CYP. Confidential; Immediate. Drafted by Cleveland, cleared by Burdett, and approved by Jernegan. Also sent to the White House, JCS, and CIA.

[2] Dated March 12. Hare reported that the Turkish Government had sent an ultimatum to the Cypriot Government to impose an immediate cease-fire or face unilateral intervention by Turkey. (Ibid.)

[3] The text of the Turkish message was transmitted to the Department of State in telegram 1161 from Ankara, March 13. (Ibid.)

2. Secretary spoke with Ralph Bunche at UN Headquarters directly. Bunche reported substance of above to SYG and Canadian Fon-Min Paul Martin who there with SYG at the time.

3. In subsequent telecon directly with Paul Martin, Secretary gave him substance of Ambassador Hare's reports, and asked him to start Canadian troops moving toward Cyprus, even if they had to stage through some Near Eastern base or British sovereign bases in Cyprus. (When President called Prime Minister Pearson earlier in day, Pearson had said only obstacle immediate movement ready Canadian battalion was need for SYG's assurance some other countries (other than British) would also be participating in international force.) Martin said he would "see what we can do immediately."

4. In absence British Ambassador, Under Secretary called in British Minister Greenhill Thursday evening, gave him substance of report from Ankara and indications of Turkish troop movements. Under Secretary said we should move along several lines simultaneously. Rapid formulation of UN force was one route being vigorously pursued. But seemed to us moment had now come for calling of summit conference under Treaty of Guarantee, Greece, Turkey, UK (and possibly Makarios and Kutchuk) previously agreed with UK to be useful fall-back at some stage of game.

5. Greenhill said as we knew London had been thinking along same lines. He asked where we thought conference should be held. Under Secretary said he remembered British suggestion was to hold it in Geneva. Under Secretary and Greenhill agreed Makarios and Kutchuk would need to be invited, and Greenhill mentioned also representative of SYG. (If held in Geneva, Spinelli would be obvious choice.)

6. Under Secretary noted Makarios in Athens for funeral. British said their understanding was Archbishop intended stay in Athens until Friday but British had offered fly him back to Nicosia via RAF whenever he wished. Greenhill, as own idea, suggested SYG might go to Nicosia to help calm things down. US reaction to this idea was inconclusive. Under Secretary said regardless of what was done, summit meeting nevertheless was not in conflict with any UN moves at this juncture.

For London: Ambassador Bruce should press British on immediate summit as political deterrent to Turkish action.[4]

For Nicosia and Athens: You should convey to Makarios and Papandreou and Clerides our judgment that Turks are serious, and that immediate turning off of violence is essential.[5] Note that Greek Cypriots

---

[4] In telegram 4474 from London, March 13, Bruce reported that the British Government did not think a Greek-Turkish summit meeting would prove useful. (Ibid.)

[5] In telegram 1392 from Athens, March 13, Labouisse reported that Costopoulos was irritated with the Turkish action but had cautioned moderation on the Cypriot Government. (Ibid.) In telegram 956 from Nicosia, March 13, Belcher reported that Acting President Clerides stated that every effort was being made to secure a cease-fire. (Ibid.)

demonstrated during entire period of Security Council session that they had sufficient control to insure relative absence of bloodshed on Island.

For Paris USRO: Ambassador Finletter may inform Stikker of developments stressing that it is for his personal information only and not for NATO action.

For Ottawa: Press Canadians for immediate action moving troops toward Cyprus. Martin said he would let us know through Embassy Ottawa what action being taken.[6]

Rusk

---

[6] Telegram 1196 from Ottawa, March 13, recommended inviting the Canadian Government to any peace conference on Cyprus. (Ibid.)

---

26.   National Security Action Memorandum No. 286[1]

Washington, March 12, 1964.

TO

The Secretary of State
The Secretary of Defense
The Director, Bureau of the Budget

SUBJECT

United Nations Cyprus Force

The President has decided that the U.S. will provide troop airlift free of cost to the United Nations where countries contributing forces to the United Nations Cyprus Force are unable to furnish their own transportation. The President expects that this particular airlift will be absorbed within the airlift capability of the Department of Defense and that no additional funds will be required by the Department.

McGeorge Bundy[2]

---

[1] Source: Johnson Library, National Security File, Files of Robert W. Komer, Cyprus. Confidential. A copy was sent to Komer.

[2] Printed from a copy that bears this typed signature.

27.   Telegram From the Embassy in Cyprus to the Department of State[1]

Nicosia, March 23, 1964, 9 p.m.

1015. During discussion this morning, Makarios reviewed recent political and military developments. Makarios thought that peak of crisis had passed, that worst difficulties were behind him and that, although further troubles could be expected, situation would improve from now on. Discussion of political and military situation revolved around three aspects:

1. Creation and establishment of PKF in Cyprus: PKF was now settled. It would become clear during next two weeks whether it would be successful or not. PKF cooperation with GOC and nature of its terms of reference were essential to success.

2. Mediator: Makarios said name of Sakari Severi Tuomioja had been suggested. Tuomioja was agreeable to GOC, Greece and Britain.[2] He had not yet heard whether he was acceptable to Turkey. Makarios said he was "pessimistic mediation would soon result in political settlement." It depended on whether Turkish Cypriots would be willing to return to their villages and not insist on some form of partition or federation. Success or failure of Mediator would begin to emerge within one month.

3. Return of Greek and Turkish Cypriots to their homes and jobs: Some estimates were that there were now 6,000 displaced Greek Cypriots and 45,000 or 50,000 Turkish Cypriots and it was estimated former would increase to 20,000 and latter to 80,000 within next month or so. Makarios thought these estimates high, but nevertheless figures were substantial for Cyprus. It was important all Cypriots, especially Turkish Cypriots, have confidence in government and return to their homes and jobs. Makarios hoped those Turkish Cypriots who did not wish to do so might go to Turkey.

He said GOC would assist all Cypriots, including Turkish Cypriots, in various necessary ways to return to their homes and jobs. Cost of rebuilding homes would be formidable. Makarios hoped international financial assistance would be available. GOC had been losing one million pounds monthly in income during recent troubles and he hoped it would soon be possible resume development program.

---

[1] Source: Department of State, Central Files, POL 23–8 CYP. Confidential. Repeated to Ankara, Athens, London, Paris for USRO, and USUN. Passed to the White House, JCS, OSD, CIA, CINCEUR, and CINCSTRIKE.

[2] Secretary-General Thant announced Tuomioja's appointment on March 25. For text of the statement, see U.N. Doc. S/5625 and Corr. 1.

I said attitude of GOC toward needy Cypriots, including Turkish Cypriots, was most statesmanlike and would indicate to world GOC was ready to take care of all of its people rather than only one segment.

I added I had been disappointed, following my return from US, to read articles in Greek Cypriot press indicating US activities were being curtailed and Greek Cypriots being let go for purpose of bringing economic pressure on GOC. This type of analysis was wholly inaccurate. I wished to assure him there had been no change in attitude of USG toward Cyprus and that we continued ready to help Cyprus with its economic development as we could within scope of our resources.

It had been necessary to suspend some programs such as Peace Corps and to curtail others such as technical assistance for time being because American staff could not function in many parts of Cyprus because of present difficulties and because Greek Cypriot press continued to foment anti-Americanism by charging that US was pro-Turkish. Fact of matter was US was not only friendly to Turkey, but also to Greece and to Britain and especially to Cyprus. I hoped Makarios would use his influence with press to explain true American attitude and thus bring stop to this unfriendly criticism which might have unsettling effect on friendly relations which had been built up between US and Cyprus over years.

Makarios said he understood true situation and realized US had always been friendly to Cyprus. Makarios ducked issue of Greek Cypriot press by saying American press (especially *Christian Science Monitor*) seemed to be unfriendly to Cyprus. I commented it was not exactly fair comparison. Greek Cypriot press might be expected to respond to suggestions from him more readily than American press would respond to suggestions from us.

Wilkins

28.   Telegram From the Department of State to the Embassy in Cyprus[1]

Washington, March 28, 1964, 2:54 p.m.

699. Ankara's 1254 to Dept; Nicosia's 1035 to Dept; Nicosia's 1039 to Dept.[2] Agree with Embassy Nicosia's conclusion reftel that Makarios' action in appointing acting ministers to replace Turks designed underscore Turk non-participation and strengthen formal GOC control Turkish-allocated ministries. This connection, Cyprus UN PermRep Rossides has informed SC President that civil servants who "deliberately refuse report to office" could not expect "continue indefinitely be paid out of public funds".

Timing these Greek-Cypriot tactics is interesting. Makarios apparently fully understands that (1) Turk-Cypriots could strengthen their case and weaken his by participation, (2) that such participation was not likely while security forces were primarily GOC and British, and (3) that formal establishment UNFICYP is strategic moment for Kutchuk to insist on participation. He appears to have made moves re Denktash and acting minister appointments to goad Turks into frittering away energies in protests and legal arguments until opportunity has passed. Makarios' tactics will probably succeed if Turk-Cypriots continue to sit on hands and feel sorry for themselves.

If Kutchuk would return to his office because of UN presence, he could be serious embarrassment to Makarios. Even if Makarios could insist successfully that all measures of GOC taken during Kutchuk's absence are legal and not subject to Vice-President's veto, he would have difficulty not forwarding future bills or measures to Kutchuk as required by constitution. His only effective alternatives would appear to be: (1) to maintain that Kutchuk was rebel who tried to set up separate Turk-Cypriot administration and therefore had lost authority in government (difficult argument to sustain if GOC has, as it claims, been sending invitations to Kutchuk and other Turk-Cypriot officials to attend scheduled meetings) or (2) to maneuver Turk-Cypriots into holding back from participation until too late.

He appears to be operating under second alternative. With each passing day that his tactics perpetuate Turk-Cypriots boycott of govern-

---

[1] Source: Department of State, Central Files, POL 23–8 CYP. Confidential. Drafted by Gordon D. King; cleared by NEA, UNP, and BNA; and approved by Jernegan. Also sent to Ankara and repeated to Athens, London, and USUN.

[2] Telegram 1254 from Ankara, March 27, reported Turkish press reaction to Makarios' refusal to permit Denktash to return to Cyprus. (Ibid.) Telegram 1035 from Nicosia, March 27, reported that Makarios' appointment of "temporary" ministers appeared to avoid violation of the Cypriot Constitution. (Ibid., POL 15 CYP) Telegram 1039 from Nicosia, March 28, reported negative Turkish Cypriot reaction to Makarios' actions. (Ibid.)

ment, he increases general acceptance GOC as presently constituted, strengthens his contention that Turk-Cypriots are insurgents and weakens ability UN to remain neutral between two communities.

In this connection, British Embassy informs us GOT has asked HMG to intercede with Makarios and protest to UNSYG on behalf Denktash. HMG has informed GOT British forces Cyprus part of UNFICYP and they cannot make independent intercessions with GOC. (FYI. UKUN, however, has been instructed to call Denktash problem to attention SYG on humanitarian grounds. End FYI.) Turk Embassy informed Dept of GOT concern re Denktash but made no request for USUN action and Dept plans none.

For Nicosia: Explore problem with UK HICOM and in your discretion reiterate points made in Deptel 668[3] to Kutchuk and Turk-Cypriot leaders as to advantage renewed participation government. Re Rossides claim regarding payments, would appreciate clarification on situation since other reports indicate Turks paying relief because no salaries paid by GOC to absentee Turk-Cypriots.[4]

For Ankara: In your discretion, discuss Turk-Cypriot non-participation further with GOT. We would be interested any indications GOT is planning or willing actively push Turk-Cypriot leadership into participation.[5]

Rusk

---

[3] Telegram 668 to Nicosia, March 18, stressed the need to get Turkish Cypriot support for UNFICYP. (Ibid., POL 23–8 CYP)

[4] In telegram 1051 from Nicosia, April 1, the Embassy reported the British believed that Turkish Cypriot leaders preferred partition as a solution and would avoid returning to the Cabinet. It also reported that Turkish Cypriot civil servants who failed to report to work were not being paid. (Ibid.)

[5] In telegram 1278 from Ankara, the Embassy reported Turkish assurances that they were urging Turkish Cypriot Ministers to rejoin meetings of the Makarios government. (Ibid.)

29.   Telegram From the Embassy in Cyprus to the Department of State[1]

Nicosia, April 7, 1964, 3 p.m.

1078. Cyprus mediation. Deptel 707.[2] Department may recall that during 1959 Constitution-drafting period I was reporting from Nicosia that Rube Goldberg contraption could work, but only given magnanimity on part of Greeks and good will from all.

So much has happened since then to show that neither quality has many exponents on this unhappy island that another attempt at a patchwork solution can only breed further trouble. Situation obviously calls for drastic action involving major effort by NATO allies to support solution based on security needs of area, but also recognizing generally accepted democratic principle of majority rule.

Our own ideas as to once-for-all (para 5 Deptel 707) solution somewhat like Alexander's approach to Gordian Knot, although without resultant "partition" as in myth. Our recommendations will require considerable selling to GOT since we are proposing recognize Greek Cypriot ascendancy and intransigence and their insistence on a solution in accord with generally accepted standards of self-determination based on majority rule. On this basis following proposals submitted as outline of plan designed achieve over-all peace and security in area.

1. Constitutional framework providing for one person-one vote majority rule, with elections on basis of proportional representation.
2. Adequate safeguards for minorities (perhaps as with Swedes in Finland).
3. Cyprus to be tied to Greece either by enosis or in some "associated" status such as Puerto Rico. Greece would at minimum control foreign policy and defense, perhaps leaving other facets of government to Cypriots.

Would seem that only through some such device could GOT be convinced that security interests being preserved and safeguarded. Do not see how independent Cyprus with strong Communist Party organization could be accepted by Turks. Cyprus could continue to be "used" in one way or another as shuttlecock in Soviet-Western cold war in the area. Only as part of Greece and thereby included in NATO security system could GOT fears be mitigated. Part of such concept could be transferring

---

[1] Source: Department of State, Central Files, POL 23–8 CYP. Secret. Repeated to Ankara, Athens, London, Paris for USRO, and USUN.

[2] Telegram 707 to Nicosia, April 1, stressed the Department of State's desire for a quick solution to the Cyprus problem and requested comments on the shape of a permanent political solution to the Cyprus question. (Ibid.)

of Izmir joint Greek-Turkish headquarters to one of British bases (probably Dhekelia) and UK giving up sovereignty over all or most of area in favor of NATO base on sovereign "Greek" territory.

Whatever Mediator may propose that would be acceptable to Greek Cypriots in their present ascendant position will require major selling effort with Turks, and in this respect Greek Ambassador Delivanis correct in his statement to Ambassador Wilkins (Embtel 1070)[3] that US must play major persuasive role—but this does not mean that efforts other NATO partners will not be needed.

Further factor which Embassy considers essential to any lasting solution is some form of assisted emigration for Turks who are convinced they can no longer live with Greeks in Cyprus. This should involve setting up of commission to handle transfer of properties on equitable basis as well as other details of moves, including some provision for compensation for damages. Agree with Department's observations para 3 Deptel re best course of action for Mediator except with regards manner handling proposals once formulated. Experience with Cyprus "solutions" which presented publicly or leaked in some fashion not encouraging in past and no reason believe one or other side would not act same way now, particularly given existing inflamed and emotional situation.

At very least, believe proposals should be worked out and accepted by GOG and GOT (USUN's 3598 to Department)[4] before being "surfaced" in effort bring international pressure on Cypriots. (This would require support of Erkin's desire for Greek-Turkish "summit" meeting—Ottawa's 1270 to Department.)[5]

We must bear in mind how sensitive is Cypriot pride and how convinced Greeks here are of right and justice their cause—and that they can win out eventually even if this means going to UNGA.

In summary, advantages we see in enosis or "associated" status would be:

1. Tie Cyprus firmly to West, thus eliminating security concerns of UK, Turkey and ourselves.
2. Reduce danger of further growth of Communism on island.
3. End nuisance of Cypriot "neutralist" foreign policy maneuvering.

---

[3] Telegram 1070 from Nicosia, April 5, reported that Delivanis appeared to be taking a harder political line after his return from consultations in Athens. (Ibid., POL 17 GR–CYP)

[4] Telegram 3598 from USUN, April 2, reported USUN's belief that the mediation should be carried forward with a minimum of public comment. (Ibid., POL 23–8 CYP)

[5] Telegram 1270 from Ottawa, April 1, reported that the Canadian Government was interested in an active U.S. mediation role in Cyprus. (Ibid.)

4. Remove constant irritant in Greek politics and same time weaken Soviet ability exploit issue in Greece.

5. Effect set-back for Soviet (and UAR) policy in area, which is adamantly opposed to enosis.

6. Give us friendly government with which to negoiate satisfactory status for our communications facilities.[6]

Belcher

---

[6] In telegrams 1510 from Athens, April 8, and 1315 from Ankara, April 8, the Embassies reported similar conclusions: that either independence or enosis was the only likely solution to the Cyprus issue and that union with Greece would require political concessions to Turkey. (Ibid.)

---

30.   Telegram From the Embassy in Cyprus to the Department of State[1]

Nicosia, April 8, 1964, 3 p.m.

1085. In conversation yesterday with Acting FonMin Soulioti, she brought up role of Mediator. She said GOC had not as yet made any contribution in way of written draft, although she admitted that two statements by Makarios to govt mouthpiece Cyprus news agency (reported separately)[2] could be interpreted as laying groundwork for Mediator's understanding of GOC position.

For instance, they had not prepared any new draft Constitution, although some thought had been devoted to this. She indicated her preoccupation with certain difficulties involved in persuading Turkish Cypriots and GOT accept Greek Cypriot line regarding "adequate safeguards for minority." She said it all very well to spell out minority rights including free access to government jobs on basis of merit, etc., etc., but when it came to describing method of guaranteeing application these rights, she ran up against seemingly insuperable difficulties. What recourse would Turks have in event they claimed discrimination? Constitutional Court had not proved effective under old regime and no

---

[1] Source: Department of State, Central Files, POL 23–8 CYP. Confidential. Repeated to Ankara, Athens, London, Paris for USRO, and USUN.

[2] In telegram 1084 from Nicosia, April 8. (Ibid., POL 15–1 CYP)

reason believe it would necessarily be so under any new setup. International supervisory group for appeals would be distasteful infringement of sovereignty and difficult sell to Greek Cypriots. She admitted to sense of frustration, particularly since she recognized how vital this aspect of problem was.

I agreed that under present circumstances of distrust and consequent lack of confidence, it would be difficult persuade Turks that law would be administered impartially, but suggested that there must be numerous examples in other countries where experience of minority problems could be drawn upon. In fact, experience of Swedish minority in Finland might be instructive. I also took opportunity to play on old theme of restoration of confidence in Turkish community by cessation of harassment of Turks attempting to move in Nicosia area. I said I recognized there was harassment on both sides, but with UN here, surely government could assume posture of magnanimity and put onus for continuation of efforts keep two communities apart on Turks. Mrs. Soulioti agreed that this might be useful gambit, but that there had been a continued hardening of Greek attitude towards Turkish community in view of unwillingness see UN open Kyrenia Road and restore freedom of access Iozablesia itself. I commented that I too had noted an increasingly hard line in talking to Ministers and other leading members of Greek Cypriot community.

This took form of maintaining that until such time as there was political settlement satisfactory to Greeks or at least until Turkish community here recognized fact that GOC was undisputed government, there was no possibility of Turkish Ministers or even Turkish civil servants returning to work. Mrs. Soulioti said that she did not go this far, but that unless there was freedom of access for Greeks who have legitimate business in present Turkish-controlled areas. (i.e., area north of Nicosia and Kyrenia Road), she saw no reason why Turks should be allowed come back to work in government in Greek area. (This strong attitude reflects position taken by Makarios in farewell conversation with Ambassador Wilkins and me reported in Embtel 1060.)[3]

I find it very disturbing that Greek Cypriots seem determined push on with hard line. We note series of event such as refusal allow Denktash free access to Cyprus, appt of acting Ministers, treaty denunciation, pressure on Turk Army contingent all seemingly designed with some idea of "unconditional surrender" and thereby complicating already almost impossible problem faced by Mediator.

---

[3] Dated April 2. (Ibid., POL 1 CYP–US)

Both Ambassador Wilkins and I have preached rather forlornly a policy of moderation and restoration of confidence with Makarios as well as his Ministers.

Would it not be desirable do what we can to reinforce presumed GOG desires to do same when Archbishop visits Athens this weekend?

Following telegram gives our assessment reasons for visit at this time.[4]

Belcher

---

[4] In telegram 1086 from Nicosia, April 8, Belcher reported that Makarios' proposed visit was apparently part of a Greek campaign to pressure him into a more moderate line that would also meet the demands of more pro-enosis Ministers in his Cabinet. (Ibid., POL 7 CYP) Makarios visited Greece April 11–15.

---

31.   Telegram From the Embassy in Greece to the Department of State[1]

Athens, April 10, 1964, 8 p.m.

1527. 1. I called on PriMin today at his home to introduce Anschuetz, new DCM.

Conversation devoted largely to Cyprus. I expressed our satisfaction along lines of Dept's 1172[2] for Papandreou's restrained reaction to recent Turkish moves (i.e. abrogation 1930 Treaty etc.)[3] and stressed need continued moderation on Greek side, particularly since events moving in Greek favor. I said in order create conditions conducive to ultimate settlement it essential that damage to Turkish prestige be held to minimum and that his cooperation in restraining Makarios this regard would be essential. I pointed out that US had made conscious effort following Cuban crisis to spare Khrushchev as much humiliation as possible.

---

[1] Source: Department of State, Central Files, POL 23–8 CYP. Confidential. Repeated to Ankara, London, Nicosia and Thessaloniki.

[2] Telegram 1172, April 9, instructed the Embassy to suggest that Papandreou extend an "olive branch" to Turkey in order to facilitate a favorable settlement of the Cyprus issue. (Ibid.)

[3] The 1930 Treaty of Friendship, Commerce, and Navigation. (125 LTS 371)

2. PriMin agreed emphatically. He said that in his recent message to Inonu—which he said was verbal one—he had stated that he recognized Cyprus presented Turkish Govt with foreign and domestic political problems (as it did for Greece), that it was difficult for either country to retreat publicly from respective positions, but that two countries must think of overall general interests in reaching final settlement. Message emphasized importance to both countries of continued Greek-Turkish friendship and that it was essential to resolve Cyprus question in order that these relations could continue. Papandreou said that Inonu had agreed but had commented that Cyprus treaties must be honored.

3. I reiterated importance of preventing Makarios from following line which would only provoke Turks. In reply, PriMin said he agreed completely, and said that he now has established "complete discipline" over Makarios. He asserted he regretted Makarios' trip to Athens at present time,[4] so soon after Makarios' denunciation of alliance treaties, since it might be considered "conspiracy" between two leaders. PriMin said his own prestige was now at high point in Cyprus itself. In response to question he expressed opinion that if vote for enosis were held in Cyprus now, it would be unanimously supported by Cypriot public, whereas two months ago—before his accession to power—Greece's position was such that majority would have opposed enosis.

4. I said I hoped he would caution Makarios about taking any action against Turkish unit on island. He agreed, and said he had already forbidden Makarios to do such thing and would reaffirm this warning when they met. Papandreou said he was holding Makarios responsible for the irregular Greek-Cypriot forces as well as the police. The PriMin said his plan was for Greek unit to remain in its camp (to which it had already retired) and then for the UN to pressure the Turks to do same—in this way, he pointed out, Turks would be isolated if they refused to follow suit.

5. PriMin in his frequent references to Makarios spoke disparagingly of Archbishop. He said laughingly that while Makarios was concerned with personal, temporal triumph, he preferred that Makarios be a sacrifice to "the cause of Hellenism," following which he would be prepared to accord Makarios a hero's role in Hellenic history. Papandreou continued that vis-à-vis himself Makarios had lost greatly in recent weeks. When Anschuetz noted that Makarios had met recently with Bishop of Kyrenia,[5] PriMin said this was proof of Makarios' present weak position, since Bishop was Makarios' old rival, and never in the past would he have consented to meet with him.

---

[4] See footnote 4, Document 30.
[5] Bishop Kyprianos, a strong proponent of enosis.

Concerning role for Grivas, Papandreou said he preferred not to have General go to island since he would rally support against Makarios and thus divide Cypriot struggle. He said it was essential that unity be preserved.

6.   PriMin then went on to discuss his policy for Cyprus. He said that in order not provoke Turks he would not push for enosis at this point, or even self-determination. Rather, he would press idea of "independence" which he felt was principle that no one could oppose. The new character of this independence would necessitate the abolishment of all recent treaties which had been proved unworkable. However, the final settlement should provide full and complete rights for minority, protected by international guarantees. Self-determination and enosis would follow naturally since independent state could take any action it wished. He noted that Krishna Menon, in UN, had spoken against enosis, and that world opinion would be solidly behind principle of independence but might balk at enosis with Greece as part of settlement. By demanding complete independence rather than enosis or self-determination defeat for Turks would be softened and victory for Makarios would be more modest. PriMin seemed to feel enosis would be even less palatable to Turks at present time than solution based on "independence."

7.   Papandreou said he would cooperate with us in policy of "moderation" re Cyprus question. However, he stressed again need for quick settlement, since "time hurts." He said he had told Makarios, and he would repeat it, that Greek Cypriots must avoid all provocation and that, even if a Greek is killed, not to make reprisal but call upon UN. He emphasized that policy of Greek Govt was "peace" and he would make every effort to achieve that goal. PriMin said we must give full support to UN Mediator in his effort to find "democratic" solution.

8.   PriMin then went on to stress importance for West of a quick end to Cyprus question. He said it was unfortunate that Cypriot crisis had occurred at all since it had given Khrushchev opportunity to pose as champion of people struggling for liberty, while US and Britain were cast in light of opposing it. He continued that Communists had exploited this fact to hilt, not only in Greece and Cyprus, but throughout world and had scored point in world ideological battle. He noted that Khrushchev in particular had increased his prestige by supporting the "peaceful way" against Chinese on one hand while posing as champion of liberation movement on other. The longer the Cyprus crisis remains unsettled the greater the gain to international Communism.

9.   At this point Papandreou noted newspaper report of a possible Khrushchev visit to Cyprus. He said he was going to tell Makarios such a visit was completely out of question.

10. PriMin said he was deeply pleased by fact Greek public opinion undergoing change for better in recent weeks regarding Americans due to report about change in UN policy towards Cyprus. He said he understood perfectly difficulty of US position, which was to steer impartial course between two trusted allies and he could understand our reluctance to take sides. However, as between two friends this policy could only be determined on basis essential merits of case and justice of cause. In case of Cyprus it was impossible for 18 percent of population in Cyprus to run country at expense of majority 82 percent.

11. PriMin said he was concerned about position Greek communities in Turkey, but he did not think it fruitful to talk of exodus of Istanbul Greeks. Concerning Patriarch, he said he personally would not mind transfer of the Patriarchy to Mt. Athos, but that the Communists were pushing for the expulsion of the Patriarch, so that Moscow could lay claim to world leadership of Orthodoxy. This, he said, made him uneasy, since religion was one of main stakes in world ideological battle between Communists and democracy.

12. PriMin then launched attack against British policy in Cyprus. While he understood US position, he could not understand British, which had been "frantically" pro-Turkish. When I noted Turks were criticizing British also, he said that was because Turks wanted even more support. He referred in passing to newspaper reports that British had undermined MacArthur position against Chinese in Korea and added that British policy could not be trusted.

Comment: PriMin was in great form and did most of the talking in 75 minute session. His optimistic mood reflects the feeling here that the Greek cause is winning out. We believe we must take with a grain of salt his assertions about his control over Makarios until we have more proof of it than we have at the moment. He seemed acutely aware of the domestic Turkish problem regarding Cyprus which I think explains moderation of Greek responses up to present point. On other hand, it seemed clear that he had done little thinking about ways to sweeten pill for Turks if final settlement goes against Turk interests.

We have reservations about Papandreou's estimate of preference for solution based on independent Cyprus rather than on union with Greece. His policy seems designed more to satisfy Afro-Asian bloc and exigencies of UN tactics rather than to appease Turks. We interpret his solution as meaning that under circumstances, "independence" solution would be enforced by weight of UN opinion and thereby hopefully avoid direct confrontation between Greece and Turkey which would be provoked by solution based on self-determination or enosis.

Labouisse

32.   Telegram From the Department of State to the Embassy in Turkey[1]

Washington, April 11, 1964, 4:27 p.m.

1076. Acting Secretary Ball gave following response to Turk Ambassador's request for US views on Turk Government's intention request SC consideration recent developments on Cyprus:

1.   Question of calling SC meeting essentially GOT decision. USG would not oppose meeting if GOT decides call SC. However, we do not see constructive results; in fact, we see risk discussion might be turned against Turks and in particular focus on position Turk contingent. In that event, we are not sure SC action would be a good one, since SC might insist on Turk contingent's returning to barracks.

2.   We have considered whether there are ways in which we could limit SC consideration to debate and airing of issue. We doubt SC consideration can be limited to this. Our Embassy in Ankara indicates your Government has in mind a simple res making it clear Makarios is offending party. We doubt such res could be obtained. At best, res would be even-handed exhortation to both sides and, more likely, res would seek to pressure GOT move its contingent to barracks.

3.   As result careful study and appraisal, we suggest following steps as alternatives:

a.   that GOT send letter for circulation to Members SC stating its views and reserving right to call meeting at later date;
b.   that GOT continue its informal démarches with SYG in New York and with Gyani, with view to bringing end to incidents and pressing UN take action to find ways give relief to some localities where Turk-Cypriots find themselves in difficult position;
c.   in view indications that SYG appreciates Turk concern over pullback to barracks, perhaps GOT should make counter-proposal to UN which might be suggestion that Turk contingent move into encampment near road rather than into barracks;
d.   USG will increase our consultation efforts both in New York and in Nicosia to be as helpful as possible. In particular, USG prepared press UN see what further it can do with respect Turk localities and villages under siege and to urge UN have its force interpret its mandate as vigorously as possible. In addition, we would consider any other steps that GOT might develop.

---

[1] Source: Department of State, Central Files, POL 23–8 CYP. Confidential; Priority. Drafted by Helseth, cleared by Sisco, and approved by Talbot. Also sent to Nicosia and USUN and repeated to London, Paris for USRO, Oslo, and Athens.

4. We see certain encouraging signs, perhaps because we in position get more accurate information than Turk Ambassador in Nicosia and perhaps because of our close relations with Gyani. These include:

a. while it true UN plans use joint patrols employing Greek-Cypriot policemen in Greek quarters, UN also plans use Turk-Cypriot policemen in Turk quarters;

b. UN seeking increase number its forces and to get them in place as well as develop a non-Cypriot police contingent which should contribute further to stabilizing situation. (specific mention was made of Austrian police increment);

c. UN has stated its readiness to provide adequate security for Turk members of Government so that Vice President and Ministers can attend meetings, although we recognize impediments Makarios has placed in this regard;

d. we understand your Government has now received confirmation that UN force, and not Cypriot police, has taken over one road.

Menemencioglu responded he pleased hear about international police contingent. Police force currently monopoly Greek-Cypriots. Constitution provides for 2,000 police force, of which 600 should be Turk-Cypriots. Turk-Cypriots no longer in force, and Makarios had illegally increased size of police force by 5,000 without consultation with Vice President. Ambassador understood Gyani had said he could accept as legitimate police with appropriate authority only those persons who had card identifying themselves as such issued by Makarios. Ambassador said it obvious no Turk-Cypriots could obtain such a card from Makarios and that, therefore, no Turk-Cypriot could be recognized by Gyani as policeman, even former 600 Turk policemen.

Talbot said he assumed UN would not have told us they would use Turk police unless they had plans to do so. (Would appreciate USUN and Nicosia comment on question UN acceptance of cards issued by Makarios as evidence member of police force. If this is system envisaged, how can Turk-Cypriot police obtain card?)

Menemencioglu said his Government very unhappy and worried about Makarios' visit Athens. GOC seeking Greek assistance in getting Turk contingent off island. In response Acting Secretary's question, Ambassador said his Government views possibility Grivas return Cyprus as serious. Ambassador continued he personally very unhappy with Greek Government's actions. He said GOG had at no time condemned Makarios' actions; in fact, Papandreou had encouraged Makarios by saying Greeks would stand with Cypriots to the end. No Greek has said anything against the bloody actions of Makarios. It is Papandreou, he continued, who brought Makarios and Grivas together. Situation would be grave if Grivas went Cyprus since it would mean encouragement of military action. GOG should emulate GOT action following anti-Greek riots Istanbul 1955 when GOT condemned these riots, paid damages, passed parliamentary res against action, and had Greek flag, which torn down during riots, raised with military honors by Cabinet Minister. GOG has not acted this way, and has instead closely associated itself with Makarios with result that situation in Cyprus now out of hand. In conclusion, Ambassador said emphatically that Makarios should not do anything rash about Turkish contingent.

Ambassador said he would convey USG views to his Government, which he was sure would be most appreciative. In particular, GOT would appreciate our increased activity at the UN and in Nicosia. He would also hope this would include Athens. Acting Secretary said we have in mind further consultations with Greek Government.

Acting Secretary stated that Belcher arriving Ankara Monday for two-day visit. He believed Belcher should have opportunity discuss current situation with GOT. (Ankara please arrange appropriate meetings with Turk officials for Belcher.)

Comment: While we agree final para Ankara's 1335,[2] unlikely, as indicated above, SC meeting could be limited and directed in order obtain results GOT wants. You may wish convey above position to Erkin. All addressees may use appropriately with respective Foreign Offices or in event Turkish démarche.

Menemencioglu seemed gratified receive alternative proposals.

Ball

---

[2] Telegram 1335, April 10, reported Erkin's views on the possibility of successful Cyprus negotiations. The final paragraph reads: "In this context, projected SC meeting, despite our reservations, might be used to advantage if properly directed and also afford appropriate opportunity for us to reassert our interest." (Ibid.)

---

33.   Telegram From the Department of State to the Mission to the United Nations[1]

Washington, April 14, 1964, 7:08 p.m.

2670. Re Cyprus. *For USUN:* Following aspects of Cyprus situation give cause for concern. In view seriousness of problem, including current reports Turkish contingent under fire, request you raise matter directly with SYG. (Nicosia's 1114[2] just received reinforces this concern.)

---

[1] Source: Department of State, Central Files, POL 23–8 CYP. Confidential. Drafted by Buffum and Moffitt, cleared by Jernegan and Sisco, and approved by Sisco. Also sent to Ankara and Nicosia and repeated to London, Athens, Stockholm, Dublin, Ottawa, Helsinki, Copenhagen, and to USDOCOSouth (Naples) for POLAD.
[2] Telegram 1114 from Nicosia, April 14, transmitted the "terms of reference" for UNFICYP. (Ibid.)

1. While Dept considers Aide-Mémoire (S/5653)[3] issued by SYG generally good directive to UN Force, we both surprised and concerned by that section which deals with reaction of UNFICYP when unit arrives at scene of actual conflict. As we understand para, it would in effect give both parties veto over effective UNFICYP action in circumstances described. Either side could refuse interposition of UN Force, and whoever enjoyed advantage at time likely do so, thereby nullifying UN's peacekeeping potential. We disagree with Narasimhan's view that UNFICYP mandate less broad than that of UNOC. March 4 Resolution calls upon UN Force prevent recurrence fighting and contribute to restoration and maintenance law and order and return normal conditions. Certainly this mandate sufficiently broad permit UNFICYP unit commanders insist on cease-fire and, if this refused, interpose force between combatants or take any other action necessary end fighting. We recall that Bunche explicitly envisaged this possibility in conversation with Yost March 16. (Urtel 3400)[4]

We understand, of course, that document having been made public, it not feasible get it modified on public record in near future. We would hope, however, that in actual practice UNFICYP will exert every reasonable effort in stopping violence. Perhaps this could be accomplished by insuring that Gyani encouraged interpret liberally phrase interposition should not "normally" be done if not acceptable to those involved in conflict. It is for him to determine what is norm for situation. At minimum he should be given to understand he has broad flexibility in interpreting force directive. Should be emphasized to Thant that, if UN Force action limited as in para cited above, this would practically give Greek Cypriots carte blanche to bring Turk Cypriot community to its knees since they enjoy such numerical superiority. Clearly this is not intent of SC res.

(Dept notes Rolz-Bennett statement UNFICYP directives stronger than those of UK Force. This does not appear to square with our understanding of role UK troops during Limassol and Ktima episodes and explicit UK authority to fire on individuals crossing truce line in Nicosia. You may wish check this with UKUN.)

2. Dept disturbed also by almost daily eruptions fighting in Cyprus and fact that Greek Cypriot forces apparently continue move about at will in their campaign against Turk Cypriots. These forces today estimated to number 15,000, or more than twice planned strength of UNFICYP. (Rolz-Bennett assertion UN Force now at 7,000 does not agree

---

[3] Dated April 10; for text, see *American Foreign Policy: Current Documents, 1964*, pp. 573–575.

[4] Telegram 3400 from USUN, March 16, reported the intention of U.N. officials to interpose UNFICYP troops between the factions in Cyprus. (Department of State, Central Files, POL 23–8 CYP)

with our figures which place operational strength at less than 5,500.) We recognize impracticability seeking disarm Greek Cypriot forces. We believe, however, that unless they are soon disbanded or otherwise stopped from continuing their campaign against Turk Cypriots, UNFICYP will not be able successfully carry out its mission. We believe Makarios cannot be permitted flout SC res and intent by continuing maintain or utilize what amounts to small army of armed guerrillas. GOC accepted terms of SC res and should be held to them. We think that Thant should make an appeal to Makarios, either publicly or privately. There is urgent need as deterrent, lest situation get out of hand, for some concrete step by UN demonstrating its intent take vigorous action.

As you note (USUN 3719),[5] Ankara becoming disillusioned with UN role in Cyprus, and we can expect further protests from GOT unless UN acts effectively re guerrilla force. Dept would make same points re Turk irregulars but would be unrealistic call for their disbandment while numerically superior Greek Cypriots move about with impunity. We recognize number of recent incidents actually provoked by Turk Cypriots, but feel burden of evidence makes clear Greek Cypriot intention bend Turk Cypriots to their will.

3. We note (USUN's 3719) that SYG is continuing his efforts bring Greek and Turkish contingents under Gyani's command and Eralp statement GOT would accept this provided Turk contingent not ordered to return to barracks. We see immediate problem as need to move Turk contingent from Kyrenia road area making it possible open this road to regular traffic. We understand UN prepared assure GOT that road, which runs through Turk business and residential areas, would be patrolled by UN Force and not Greek Cypriot police. We can appreciate SYG's unwillingness publicly accept any conditions to placing contingent under UN command. We feel might accomplish this through suggestion you have already made, i.e., that contingent not be asked return to barracks but be permitted encamp in location which would clear Kyrenia road without forcing GOT lose face by appearing bow to UN request which essentially same as that made by Makarios on March 29 prior to repudiating Treaty of Alliance.

Dept feels it important that problem of Turk contingent be resolved quickly. Ankara has put Makarios on notice that any move against contingent would bring vigorous response. Although GOG appears understand serious consequences any incident involving contingent and has probably made this clear to Makarios, there is always possibility fractious Greek Cypriot irregulars who not completely controllable may provoke situation to which Ankara would feel called on react.

---

[5] Telegram 3719 from USUN, April 13, reported the U.N. estimate of the military situation on Cyprus and on subsequent discussions of Yost with Turkish officials. (Ibid.)

Please also suggest that SYG defer publication next report to SC if possible until GOT responds to our suggestions re putting its contingent under Gyani.

Request you inform Eralp of efforts we making with UN and urge he strongly recommend to Ankara that GOT adopt liberal attitude toward placing Turkish contingents under UN command.

For Ankara: You authorized inform GOT we making repeated démarches with UN in effort assure that SC res of March 4 equitably implemented and that Turks on Cyprus given fair play. With GOT suggest you stress generally satisfactory nature of force directive, which Eralp has also recognized (see USUN's tel 3719).

In addition to standard urging that Turks do nothing rash now that UNFICYP nearing full effectiveness, you should strongly urge GOT agree give serious consideration to making counter proposals re location of Turk force which mentioned to Turk Ambassador Saturday by Acting Secretary Ball.[6] There may be other ways that Turks can develop to put force under Gyani without requiring it return barracks.

For Nicosia: Request you maintain particularly close contact with Turkish Ambassador in effort improve his reporting to Ankara.

Would also appreciate your evaluation of performance of UN Force during most recent incidents.

Ball

---

[6] See Document 32.

---

34.   Telegram From the Military Attaché in Turkey to the Department of the Army[1]

Ankara, April 16, 1964, 1645Z.

C–92. No foreign dissem except Canada and UK. DA for ACSI. Pass to State. On occasion Turkish party for US National War College students, ARMA had following conversation with General Sunalp, TGS Operations Chief. Resuming where he left off in conversation reported

---

[1] Source: Department of State, Central Files, POL 23–8 CYP. Confidential. Repeated to DIA, USCINCEUR, USAREUR, USDOCOSouth (Naples), USDOCOLandSouth (Izmir), Nicosia, Athens, and the Department of State. The source text is the Department of State copy.

my C–84 airgram,[2] Sunalp stated Turks not concerned about Cypriot real estate and although they abhorred continued killing Turk Cypriots, their major preoccupation danger from highly effective Cypriot Communist organization. GOT policy now to be that this essentially a Turk-Greek matter and that GOT approach will be put all possible pressure on GOG. When I protested that this likely drive the two nations farther apart rather than facilitate mutually acceptable solution Cyprus, he replied that to contrary due centuries of experience with Greeks, Turks regard this as only method force Greeks collaborate. He likened Greece to house cat which would defy man until forced in corner from which no escape where man could pin it down and if necessary kill it. Current series of GOT anti-Greek actions designed force Greece into this corner. He protested that from the outset Turks had tried to get the Greeks to solve the problem jointly with Turkey without avail and present measures seem only solution. I remarked that Turkey's much publicized preparations for amphibious operations had seemed to me to have exactly the opposite effect and that in fact, the Greeks had shown no indication of willingness cooperate but rather favor a withdrawal even when they expressed greatest concern over reported exchange of Turkish troops for border guards in Thrace. He replied that Turkey would not move into northern Greece in any case as such an operation would have no value for them. He said he felt that should the Turks undertake a military operation, it might very possibly be against one of the Greek islands. In further development of the theme that Turks must have some sort of a face saving solution before too long and that if the US does not take steps to assist in the realization of such a solution, Turkey will do so herself, he said somewhat ominously "I tell you that there will be action—maybe tomorrow, maybe next week, maybe next month, but there will be action".

Comment:

1. General response Turkish senior officers (notably Admiral Eyiceoglu, J–2) (General Atalay, J–3) to queries War College students on Cyprus situation was one of continuation Turk military feeling close affinity US military, nor was there any indication this feeling would diminish despite political developments. One gets the impression that all briefed and reiterating same party line and that in fact, Turks desperately seeking any measures reach solution to the problem without too much loss of face and still hoping against hope US will be able assist. Sunalp's remarks probably part of larger design scare us into doing something to keep Turks from taking action inimical to NATO interests. We assessed earlier threats to conduct amphibious operation on Cyprus as same technique and they may be trying it once again.

---

[2] Not found.

2.   Both Atalay and Sunalp depart Ankara 19 April for CENTO conference Washington. Both speak excellent English and this might provide good opportunity further exploitation these sources.

---

35.   Telegram From the Embassy in Cyprus to the Department of State[1]

Nicosia, April 22, 1964, 9 a.m.

1133. Tuomioja told me yesterday evening UN mediation effort is at "impasse" following his discussions at Ankara April 18–19 and his first working meeting with Makarios April 20.

Both Turkish Cypriots and GOT have told Tuomioja federation is only acceptable solution. Federation they have now defined as division of island into Turkish area in north and Greek area in south with compulsory population exchange. Tuomioja lent me in confidence copy of memorandum from Kutchuk setting forth "Principles of Federal Constitution of Republic of Cyprus." Text in next following telegram.[2] Tuomioja said he received very similar communication from GOT. GOT adamant that Turkish Cypriots are "separate community" and not "minority."

Tuomioja sounded out GOT views on enosis as lesser evil than independent Cyprus ruled by Greek majority. GOT refused contemplate enosis under any circumstances. GOT argued continued presence of Turkish troops on Cyprus essential for security of Turkey although there no objection to presence of Greek troops also.

Visit to Ankara gave Tuomioja more vivid realization of Turkey's interest in Cyprus. He seems to have been very much impressed by Turkish military strength and readiness to intervene and twice commented that Greek Cypriots did not know what great risks they were taking and that Turkish forces could sweep island in two days. He also commented favorably on Inonu's political wisdom and restraint.

Re possible "summit" meeting of Inonu and Papandreou, Tuomioja said Inonu was not opposed in principle but thought way would have to be prepared by meetings at lower level. Tuomioja himself thought such

---

[1] Source: Department of State, Central Files, POL 23–8 CYP. Secret; Priority. Repeated to Ankara, Athens, London, Paris for USRO, and USUN.

[2] Telegram 1134 from Nicosia, April 22. (Ibid.)

meeting might eventually be useful or even necessary, but felt he should first have more time to explore possibilities of mediation.

Tuomioja discussed Turkish federation proposal with Makarios showing latter copy of Kutchuk's memorandum. Makarios rejected Turkish proposal out of hand, evidently arguing federation identical with partition and insisting Turkish Cypriots had to be satisfied with normal minority rights.

Present situation Tuomioja described as "total impasse," with "no light at end of tunnel." While he admitted all concerned might be starting at beginning positions from which they might retreat as mediation progressed, he appeared seriously concerned about rigidity of Turks and Greek Cypriots and by their apparent willingness to run risk of war not only on island but also between Turkey and Greece. Tuomioja professed to be at loss to understand how there could be such bitter animosity between nationalities who had every interest in maintaining friendship and who have no basic ideological differences. He added that pessimism would not, however, be consistent with his role as Mediator. Citing as his motto for present situation Finnish saying that "the pigs will come home with the frost," he expressed hope that decline of island's economy and increased difficulties of living would gradually make Cypriots on either side more tractable. He thought there might be moderate elements in both communities whose voices are yet to be heard. He furthermore took note of value of UNFICYP political staff's efforts to restore some normality to intercommunal relations.

Tuomioja confirmed that he will go to Athens for talks with GOG next weekend. He thought he might find more divergence between Greek and Greek Cypriot views than between Turk and Turkish Cypriot. He will also go on to London and to Paris, where he will report to U Thant April 29.

He was expecting his political advisor Robin Miller (New Zealand) to arrive last night.

At end of our conversation I asked Mediator whether there was anything we could do to help. He replied "no, not yet" and then added wryly "except to have your government keep persuading Greece and Turkey not to go to war."

McKiernan

36.   Telegram From the Department of State to the Mission to the United Nations[1]

Washington, April 28, 1964, 5:38 p.m.

2779. Our sense of the situation in Cyprus based on reliable intelligence is:

(a) That the Greek Cypriots are undertaking the attack on St. Hilarion Castle as a systematic operation designed to test the strength and will of the UN Force. If this attack succeeds it will almost certainly lead to a series of systematic attacks in order to achieve a fait accompli to present to the Mediator.

(b) At same time there is a developing Gotterdammerung spirit among the Turkish Cypriots that may at almost any moment result in a widespread and suicidal violence which could quickly lead to civil war throughout Island.

(c) We believe that events can rapidly get out of hand unless: First, the UN Force moves quickly and vigorously to take all necessary steps to stop St. Hilarion action. Second, SYG issues strong and unambiguous statement calling on Makarios to call off Greek Cypriots. Third, SYG sends strong private appeal to Papandreou urging him exercise necessary restraint on Makarios.

(d) The consequences of failure to act definitively would not only be tragic and dangerous situation in Cyprus; it could discredit UN peacekeeping for future and could well lead to Turkish intervention with all frightful consequences which that would entail.

We suggest you also make following additional concrete suggestions:

1. Urge SYG to send instructions to Gyani to have UN Force exercise greater initiative;

2. If UN Force needs more equipment to increase mobility and cope with situation, it should seek such assistance;

3. Reiterate strongly our interpretation of the mandate based on Security Council Resolution of 4 March 1964; and

4. Make two suggestions contained in paragraph 6 and penultimate paragraph of Nicosia's 1161, repeated USUN 386.[2] You should fill in Bunche confidentially, particularly on Nicosia's comments re immediate

---

[1] Source: Department of State, Central Files, POL 23–8 CYP. Confidential; Immediate. Drafted and approved by Sisco and cleared by Jernegan. Also sent to Athens and Nicosia and repeated to Ankara, London, Ottawa, and Paris.

[2] Telegram 1161 from Nicosia, April 27, reported on the difficulties UNFICYP faced in trying to enforce a peace settlement in Cyprus. (Ibid.)

need of high-level political adviser who can be helpful to Gyani. We are glad to learn that SYG's report indicates UN desires to go ahead in this regard.

Confirming Ball–Sisco–Plimpton telecon,[3] you should support Canadian initiative and urge strongly that SYG go to Nicosia. While we doubt SYG will feel he can go at this time, it should help convince him at least take kind of actions cited above.[4]

Rusk

---

[3] No record of this telephone conversation has been found.

[4] Telegram 3928 from USUN, April 29, reported that Yost had raised with Bunche the issues outlined in this telegram. (Department of State, Central Files, POL 23–8 CYP)

---

37.   Memorandum for the Record[1]

Washington, April 29, 1964.

SUBJECT

    President's Meeting with Turkish Foreign Minister Erkin

PARTICIPANTS

    Foreign Minister F. C. Erkin   The President
    Ambassador T. Menemencioglu   Asst. Secretary P. Talbot
                                        R. W. Komer

The President, after greeting Erkin cordially, said with emphasis that he wished to commend the Turks on how they had acted with such great restraint and statesmanship in recent weeks. He knew what a trial the Cyprus crisis was to Turkey and how lucky we all were to have so great a man as Inonu at the helm during such a period. "So don't lose your heads now," he said to Erkin. "It's always darkest just before the dawn. Give the UN a little more time to work out a solution." Erkin agreed that Turkey had acted with "great restraint" but "we must avoid that the bill should now be paid by Turkey." Erkin said he had told his Prime Minister the previous night how very pleased he was with his talks here and with the US attitude.

The President came back to the theme of how it was important to avoid a shooting war over Cyprus. War, as he put it, solves nothing. Our

---

[1] Source: Johnson Library, National Security File, Country File, Turkey, Vol. 1. Secret. Drafted by Komer. The source text is marked "Draft."

experience has been that the UN can finally work something out which will be acceptable to all parties in situations like these. But if people start shooting, the whole situation is changed. Other powers are drawn in and a new and far graver problem is created.

Erkin pointed out that so far Turkey had refrained from exercising their undoubted right of action in this case. Now that the UN was there, it was "not possible for us to intervene any more."

"Inonu is a hero", the President said. We applaud him and his policies. We will do anything we can to support the UN in working out a peaceful solution. Let's try everything to avoid a clash. Some solution can and must be found. The President analogized to the problem of our railway settlement. It had taken five years but we finally settled it last week. We salute Inonu and were tremendously grateful that he had acted with such statesmanship at a time when others did not display the same qualities. Erkin interjected that "our antagonist took advantage of our moderation and is seeking to inflict humiliation on us." The President granted that they were bullies but world opinion would know what they had done. He wished Erkin to tell Inonu that the President was his friend; he, the President, remembered extremely well his visit to Ankara and how he and Inonu had been waylaid by the crowds.

Returning again to the importance of avoiding a shooting war, the President commented that we are worried about some signs of Turkish preparations, for example, the cancellation of leaves. Erkin explained that "we have to be prepared." The President replied that he should tell Inonu right away of our admiration for him and how we count on his continued retraint. "Tell Inonu", he said, "I haven't got a better friend. And I'm proud of your people. We are always going to be stout allies." Erkin again assured him that the Turks would not intervene.

The President then told Messrs. Talbot and Komer to see what we could do with the Greeks and Cypriots. When Senator Fulbright was in Athens we could send him to Papandreou and tell him how concerned we were.[2] Talbot mentioned that we had just urged restraint on the Greek

---

[2] On May 2, President Johnson asked Senator J. William Fulbright, Chairman of the Senate Foreign Relations Committee, to visit Athens and Ankara for the purpose of "reinforcing" U.S. efforts to preserve peace in the Aegean region. The President outlined his objectives in sending Fulbright in a May 6 press conference statement; for text, see *American Foreign Policy: Current Documents, 1964*, p. 577.

Fulbright visited London May 4–6, Athens May 6–7, Ankara May 7–8, The Hague and Copenhagen May 8–13. He reported to the President on his trip on May 15. In telegram 1304 to Athens, May 2, the Department of State informed the Embassy that in addition to "fact finding," Fulbright would seek in talks with Papandreou and Inonu, "To move GOG to restrain Greek Cypriots more effectively and to assure GOT that its policy of restraint is appreciated and will prove fruitful. He will avoid any impression that USG has preconceived plans for ultimate solution." (Department of State, Central Files, POL 7 US/FULBRIGHT) Documentation on the Fulbright mission is ibid., Greek Desk Files: Lot 67 D 192, POL 7–Visits, Fulbright.

Government the previous night. The President's view was that we should be as tough as necessary. The Greeks must not humiliate the Turks. We should go in and press Makarios as well. When Talbot commented that we had used up most of our leverage with Makarios, the President's reaction was that we should use up whatever was left if necessary.

Foreign Minister Erkin expressed his great appreciation for the President's words and assured him that his message to Inonu would be sent immediately. Ambassador Menemencioglu mentioned that the Turks had a second bit of good news while here—they had been assured by the Department of State that the US would not support any solution which would humiliate Turkey. The President fully agreed.

As Foreign Minister Erkin left, the President gave him two medallions, one for the Prime Minister and one for himself, as a token of his admiration for Prime Minister Inonu and for the Turkish nation.

R.W. Komer[3]

---

[3] Printed from a copy that bears this typed signature.

---

38.   Telegram From the Embassy in Cyprus to the Department of State[1]

Nicosia, May 4, 1964, 6 p.m.

1189. Saw Makarios and after exchange of pleasantries regarding my confirmation by Senate,[2] I raised points set forth in Deptel 807.[3]

I explained that during my stay in Washington I had been particularly impressed by fact that very difficult situation in island was a matter of great concern at highest levels USA. I said President himself was kept

---

[1] Source: Department of State, Central Files, POL 23–8 CYP. Secret. Repeated to Ankara, Athens, London, Paris for USRO, and USUN.

[2] Belcher's appointment as Ambassador to Cyprus was confirmed by the Senate on May 1.

[3] Telegram 807, April 30, instructed Belcher to inform Makarios of both the U.S. concern about the situation on Cyprus and its support for U.N. peacekeeping and mediation efforts. (Department of State, Central Files, POL 23–8 CYP)

fully informed of developments on day-to-day basis and that he had taken personal interest in events in Cyprus. Said we were pledged to support UN efforts find solution and added that one of most difficult events to place in proper perspective had been fighting around St. Hilarion which appeared to have been deliberate use of force to gain purely military objective during time when all govts concerned had been pledged to carry out terms of SC res.

The President said he could appreciate fact that fighting at St. Hilarion might not be fully explicable to people abroad but that in his view this was defensible objective on part of his govt (Gen Pantelides, Comander of Home Guard, had made similar presentation to me just before going in see President). He claimed that Turks had been extending their positions both to east and west of Castle and that UN had appeared unwilling or powerless to stop them. He added that UN appeared to be acting as "conciliatory commission" rather than peace-keeping force. He asked what might be expected on the part of Greek Cypriots in face of this sort of "provocation" which was not so easily identifiable as gun fire. Quiet infiltration by Turks in effort to consolidate their hold on northern range was more difficult pinpoint than outright hositility involving gun fire. Having accomplished objective of rolling back Turkish forward positions, he had issued the statement claiming Greeks had reached their objective and they had no need to take the Castle itself.

He added that something had to be done about continued harassing indiscriminate fire from Castle into Karmi village. Roll-back helped but probably would not completely stop. (*Comment:* Turks were extending positions and have been firing into Karmi but Greeks have accomplished more than mere roll-back. They now command Turk airfield at Krini as well as Aghirda and other villages on south slope.)

I said that everyone in Washington had been much relieved and encouraged at recent statements by both himself and Dr. Kutchuk of renewed determination to cooperate with UN in creating a situation which might be more conducive to finding of a political solution.

In discussing need to avoid further violence and take steps restore confidence among Turk Cypriots I raised question of SecGen's report.[4] President said that he felt that this was a very useful report and that his govt was ready to cooperate in every possible way toward achievement of UNSYG's objectives. He did say that there would be great difficulty with some of items mentioned, in particular reintegration of police force and the opening of area north of Nicosia. With regard to Kyrenia Road, I said I hoped that some compromise might be worked out whereby his govt would not necessarily insist on Greek Cypriot patrols but might as first step agree to merely UN patrols. His Beatitude said he was prepared

---

[4] For text of this report, dated April 29, see U.N. Doc. S/5671. Annex I to the report is printed in *American Foreign Policy: Current Documents, 1964*, pp. 576–577.

cooperate on this point but that he felt UN presence would not be suffi-cient to permit Greek community to use road. He pointed to fact that the road through Kokkina area was presently being patrolled by UN but there were many new Turkish fortifications and Greeks were most reluc-tant to use it.

We discussed arrival of Gen Karayannis[5] and Archbishop indicated that there were two purposes in bringing him here. First was establish-ment of discipline among various fighter elements in hope of avoiding undirected and dangerous action by irresponsible elements within armed groups. Second was to create disciplined, well-trained and well equipped force which could meet at least for time the external threat posed by possibility of Turkish invasion. He said Karayannis was not needed for purpose of bringing Greek Cypriot force efficiency up to enable it control Turkish Cypriots. They were already in position to do so.

We discussed briefly question of General Grivas with me expressing opinion that it was perhaps better that objective be accomplished through Gen Karayannis because of predictably adverse Turkish reac-tion to Grivas' return. The Archbishop agreed but added that in his own opinion General would not have directed his energies against Turks but on contrary would purposely have asserted restraining influence on those elements in fighter group who were particularly anti-Turkish.

Archbishop said he had had very interesting talk with Mediator after his return from Ankara confirming that he had received from Mr. Tuomioja written copy of Turkish position as given in Ankara. He said that Turkish position was so far from anything which could be consid-ered by Greeks that he feared Mediator's job would require much longer time than anyone had at first expected. He was seeing him Monday or Tuesday when he returned from his trip to Athens, Paris and London and he hoped there might be something more encouraging to tell me when he next saw me. President reiterated his oft-repeated pledge that he hoped work with Mediator Gyani in spirit of cooperation and in atmosphere of peace and tranquillity.

Conversation concluded with reference to my looking forward to an early opportunity present credentials once signed copy arrived from Washington.

As usual, Archbishop was pleasant, witty and the soul of reason. However, I have no reason be encouraged believe he will keep his word to the letter, although I doubt we shall see more such direct actions as that at St. Hilarion unless there is direct provocation.

Belcher

---

[5] Newly-appointed Commander of the Cypriot National Guard.

39.   Telegram From the Embassy in Greece to the Department of State[1]

Athens, May 6, 1964, 7 p.m.

1663. DCM, who prior to my return last night acting as Chargé, called on FonMin Costopoulos yesterday evening at latter's request. Pilavakis, Director Fourth Political Division (including Cyprus affairs), was also present.

Conversation, which lasted almost three-quarters of an hour, was dominated by highly emotional recapitulation by Costopoulos of well-established GOG theses on Cyprus question.

Costopoulos began by saying that he was speaking as friend and that he would like to know what is real mission Senator Fulbright. It must be clearly understood that Greece cannot be expected to make further sacrifice with regard to Cyprus problem. Greece had received the visits of Ball, Tuomioja, Stikker and now Fulbright; Mr. Rusk and the Canadian Minister for External Affairs had only that morning requested to see Costopoulos at The Hague—obviously in connection with Cyprus. There is no reason in justice why Greece should be called upon to abandon the basic principles of democracy in Cyprus because Turks are obstructing self-determination and exerting unjustifiable pressures in other areas of Greek-Turkish relations.

DCM replied he was certain FonMin appreciated personal stature as well as key position of Senator Fulbright in conduct American foreign relations, that Fulbright was coming principally reflect deep concern felt at highest levels of USG with regard possibility increasing deterioration in Greek-Turkish relations and to inform himself at first hand with regard to views of GOG. He emphasized Senator Fulbright not coming to propose a solution and that USG strongly supports role of UN Mediator in evolving political solution.

Costopoulos spoke with considerable heat and bitterness regarding recent emergency session of NAC and Birgi's attack[2] during session. He said he wanted USG clearly to understand Greek-Turkish confrontation during forthcoming Ministerial Meeting would be catastrophic and that precise consequences might be difficult to anticipate. History of Greek-Turkish relations did not begin only in December 1963, and in the event that this question became a matter of debate in the NATO Ministerial

---

[1] Source: Department of State, Central Files, POL 23–8 CYP. Secret; Priority. Repeated to London, Ankara, Nicosia, and Paris for USRO.

[2] At a May 2 special meeting of the North Atlantic Council, Turkish Permanent Representative Nuri Birgi read a long statement attacking Greece's support for Makarios. Polto 1593 from Paris, May 2, reported on Birgi's statement and the Greek response. (Ibid.)

Meeting, Greeks would be forced open long dossier of grievances against Turks. Costopoulos was particularly bitter in his references to Stikker. GOG had been shocked hear NATO SYG say that in event of a Greek-Turkish conflict it would be difficult for NATO allies to intervene and that foreign aid would likely be terminated.[3] Costopoulos said GOG had impression Stikker's activities were encouraging Turks pursue an intransigent policy, and that even though as a legal proposition there might not be an obligation for NATO allies intervene, it was impossible to consider that the allies (by inference the US) could stand aside indifferent to the moral obligation support Greece in event of Turkish attack.

DCM said that he was confident NATO SYG not encouraging Turks adopt more aggressive attitude but that Stikker expressing personal point of view based on his own responsibilities to the Alliance. Moreover, Stikker was personally convinced that GOT on verge of military intervention at moment of attacks on Saint Hilarion. US is well aware that open debate during NATO Ministerial Meeting might well not be constructive but that we do hope that it might be possible during forthcoming meeting to create situation where Greek-Turkish discussions on bilateral issues might be contemplated. Visit is precisely in order to avoid intolerable circumstances in which US would be placed in event of Greek-Turkish hostilities that US bending every effort to encourage restraint on respective parties and wholeheartedly supporting efforts of UN Mediator. US believed enhanced effectiveness of UNFICYP, the recent statements of Makarios, and Papandreou's recent intervention with Makarios would produce circumstances in which more rational atmosphere would prevail in Cyprus and make more rapid rehabilitation of situation possible. USG had been gravely concerned at moment of Greek-Cypriot attacks in Kyrenia Road area that Turkish military intervention might occur. Because of impossible situation which would have been created in event of Greek-Turkish hostilities USG had intervened with Papandreou and Inonu and President Johnson had asked Senator Fulbright to visit Athens and Ankara. Moreover, although GOG quite naturally separates Cyprus problem from other Greek-Turkish bilateral problems, it is perfectly apparent that GOT possesses capability of exercising tremendous pressures on Greek interests in Istanbul and elsewhere. Consequently, we must proceed in full recognition of tactical situation as it exists and in such a manner as to limit damage to Greek interests, to Greek-Turkish relations and to Alliance.

Costopoulos alluded to recent Khrushchev statement regarding Cyprus,[4] pointing out Soviets are very skillfully taking position which

---

[3] Stikker made this point to both Greek and Turkish officials. (Telegram 1651 from Athens, May 2; ibid.)

[4] In a May 4 interview in *Izvestia*, Chairman Khrushchev supported Makarios' position.

would commend itself to Greek opinion. DCM acknowledged GOG faced with delicate political problem in attempting to prevent Communists and extreme leftist elements in Cyprus and in Greece from monopolizing strong nationalist role and exploiting deep-seated popular emotions on this issue. Costopoulos suggested that if Greece were abandoned by all of her allies in her search for democratic solution to the Cyprus problem, it would be only natural for the Greek people to look with increasing favor on those who were prepared to support them, i.e. USSR. He also observed that if the situation deteriorated further it would not be British, concerning whose policies all Greeks are cynical, but the Americans who would be held responsible in public mind.

Comment: Although courteous, Costopoulos was so deeply emotional that comprehensive, rational discussion would not have been possible. GOG obviously suffering from deep-seated apprehension that Greece will be called upon to make unacceptable sacrifices (exchange of populations, territory, etc.) as price for Cyprus settlement. There is little question Fulbright visit following that of Stikker and recent more cheerful utterances of Erkin following Washington talks present themselves in Greek eyes as preliminaries to such a maneuver. In light volatile quality Costopoulos' presentation, we concur Department's effort (set forth Paris Topol 1695)[5] encourage discussion Greek-Turkish problems through bilateral conversations rather than in plenary NAC session.

Labouisse

---

[5] Topol 1695, May 4, cautioned that continued discussion within NATO forums could further exacerbate tensions between Greece and Turkey and suggested instead that Stikker encourage a direct meeting between the Greek and Turkish Foreign Ministers during the NATO Ministerial Meeting at The Hague May 12–14. (Department of State, Central Files, POL 23–8 CYP)

40.   Telegram From the Embassy in Cyprus to the Department of State[1]

Nicosia, May 7, 1964, noon.

1201. Embtel 1136.[2] Tuomioja called on me yesterday evening and gave quite discouraging account of mediation efforts to date.

In Ankara Tuomioja had found GOT adamant on "federation" which would separate Greek and Turkish communities. In Athens GOG had said it would accept any solution acceptable to other parties and had talked "nonsense" about "majority rule" and "self-determination" while professing to reject enosis. In London HMG had "no policy", and this seemed to be position of USA as well. Turkish Cypriots repeatedly refused discuss, even on hypothetical basis, anything but their "federation" proposal. Makarios had not yet furnished promised written proposals re guarantees of Turkish Cypriot rights, but would probably do so within week.

Since mediation getting nowhere, Tuomioja said he plans proceed wrap up activities here, at least for present. He intends, without waiting for Makarios' proposals, to put to both Makarios and Kutchuk certain written questions re measures to guarantee Turkish Cypriot rights. He believes Turkish Cypriots may well not reply. He will give them two weeks and then will submit his report to UNSYG. He is determined return to his post in Stockholm, where he can "meditate in comfort", in mid-June. There he will remain available if developments warrant further intervention by Mediator.

Tuomioja had little to say about contents of his report, probably because he has not yet finished putting his thoughts in order. He did say that as international lawyer he condemned repudiation of international agreements "whether by Russians, Hitler, or Makarios" and would so state in report. He also seemed be pondering idea of recommending proposal for solution which would proceed from Constitution of 1960 but would give Greek Cypriots more in way of majority rule while assuring greater protection of Turkish Cypriot rights and security by providing for (1) quasi-federal system under which "five or six" areas with predominantly Turkish population would have certain measure of autonomy in communal matters, (2) long-term UN observer role, and international participation in or supervision of court system.

---

[1] Source: Department of State, Central Files, POL 23–8 CYP. Confidential. Repeated to Ankara, Athens, London, Paris for USRO, and USUN.

[2] Telegram 1136, February 2, reported on Cypriot student demonstrations against "NATO intervention" in Cyprus. (Ibid.)

Since he had not yet decided whether he should do so, I urged Tuomioja make concrete recommendation for solution in his report, as this would at least provide impetus for further discussion of negotiated solution. Tuomioja said he saw advantages of specific recommendation.

Asked for his views on possibility of progress on "UN Program for Cyprus" annexed to UNSYG's April 29 report to UNSC,[3] Tuomioja again expressed pessimism and said he would like to be able give UNFICYP Commander Gyani at least some moral support but could not.

Comment: I believe Tuomioja would give considerable weight to any proposal for solution to which USG was prepared lend its support, but I recognize complexity of our interests in this area make it very difficult commit ourselves to such proposal in time to influence mediation. Failing this, we can best assist Tuomioja by redoubling our efforts to make clear to GOT that one cannot in Cyprus, any more than in other former colonial areas, successfully impose any solution—especially an undemocratic one—on population which is prepared to fight, is assured of assistance from outside, and believes it can mobilize world opinion on own behalf in UN. Turkish position on island is being steadily weakened, in comparison to growing Greek Cypriot resources, as present situation continues, and Turkish community's best hope is to cut its losses by reasonable compromise. Continued smuggling of arms to Turkish Cypriot forces would seem at best futile effort and one which can only lead to bloodier clashes as time wears on with no solution.

I urgently recommend Secretary make these points in meeting with Erkin May 11 and attempt persuade Erkin be more responsive to Mediator's honest efforts find some middle way. If Tuomioja fails, next round of discussion of Cyprus question will undoubtedly take place in atmosphere even less conducive to reaching political settlement and will probably find Turkish position further eroded while that of Greeks strengthened through inevitable appeal to UNGA where Afro-Asian and Communist support probably assured.[4]

Belcher

---

[3] See footnote 4, Document 38.

[4] In telegram 837 to Nicosia, May 8, the Department of State expressed concern regarding Tuomioja's plans for the mediation and instructed Belcher to discourage any public statement by the Mediator of his findings. (Department of State, Central Files, POL 23–8 CYP)

41.   Telegram From the Department of State to Secretary of State Rusk, at The Hague[1]

Washington, May 10, 1964, 3:25 p.m.

Tosec 27. For Secretary from Acting Secretary. Disturbing developments in the Cyprus situation lead me to think that you should probably have some talks in The Hague with key NATO Foreign Ministers, looking toward possible common action at the appropriate point. In this telegram I shall try to sum up the situation as I see it.

1. Tuomioja, the Finnish Mediator, while a reticent man, has given some vague foreshadowing of his thinking. Proceeding from the Constitution of 1960, he is considering proposals that would give the Greek Cypriots more in the way of majority rule. In order to assure the Turk Cypriots of their rights and security, he is toying with the idea of (a) a quasi-federal system under which five or six areas with predominant Turkish populations would have a certain autonomy in communal affairs and (b) a long-term UN observer and international participation in or supervision of the court system.

2. While this represents progress over what appeared as his first thoughts, I am confident that the Turks would not presently be prepared to accept a solution along these lines.

3. While it is not entirely clear what his plans are (and there are conflicting stories) Tuomioja has indicated to us that he intends to put both to Makarios and Kutchuk written questions regarding measures to guarantee Turkish Cypriot rights. He will give the parties about two weeks to respond. He believes Turkish Cypriots may not reply. He intends then to submit his report to UNSYG. Thereafter he will return to his post in Stockholm where he can "mediate in comfort" until mid-June and remain unless developments warrant further intervention by the Mediator.

4. Tuomioja's proposed course of action could result in a gravely dangerous situation. Makarios might well make the heroic gesture of agreeing to accept the Mediator's proposals. Kutchuk would almost certainly reject them. Makarios would then go into the Security Council and demand that they be given effect. The GOG would almost certainly have to support Makarios and the USG and other NATO governments would face the discomfort of having to vote against the proposals of the UN Mediator.

---

[1] Source: Department of State, Central Files, POL 27 CYP. Secret; Immediate; Limdis. Drafted by Ball and cleared by Talbot and Bracken. Repeated to London, Nicosia, Ankara, Athens, and Paris for USRO. Secretary Rusk was attending the NATO Ministerial Meeting May 12–14.

5. The Soviet Government would presumably seek to play a double game of supporting Makarios while at the same time exploiting the growing disenchantment of the Turks. What the Soviet Union is most afraid of is "enosis" which could lead to the presence of NATO in Cyprus.

6. Under the circumstances we have instructed Belcher to emphasize to Tuomioja that he should not put in a non-agreed report. If he feels it necessary to make a report in the near future, he should simply state his inability to reach an agreed solution and indicate his determination to continue the effort. USUN is also making the same representations to the SYG.

7. Even if Tuomioja goes along with this formula, we shall face serious problems in the SC. There are only six weeks to go until the present resolution runs out. Makarios will use the occasion of the further extension of UNFICYP in June to try to put further hamstringing conditions on the use of the UN force. We shall have great difficulty getting the members contributing forces to agree to supply further financial support and we shall be hard put to scratch around and find the necessary money. Troops will be difficult to hold and replacements even more difficult to find. A number of countries will wish to withdraw their units and there is a danger that the SYG will have to reach farther out to less desirable suppliers. We shall have difficulty holding Tuomioja to a longer term than the initial three months.

8. All of this confusion is made to order for Makarios, who has already shown a notable ability to do mischief in the SC. He may make an effort to get a special meeting of the UNGA called in order to achieve an even better forum.

9. Meanwhile time is not running on our side. The GOT is getting in a mood of greater moroseness and despondency and the Turk-Cypriots are capable of a kind of Gotterdammerung psychology that could lead to a blow-up all over the Island.

10. There seems to me only one sensible procedure and that is for the Greek and Turkish Governments to move into the situation and take charge of it. From Papandreou's talk with Fulbright and from other sources there are indications of an increasing Greek Government disenchantment with Makarios. I find Papandreou's repeated references to "enosis" a healthy sign. From the point of view of all of NATO, we should regard "enosis" as a useful component in any final solution since it would mean that a NATO government would have charge of the Island rather than the wolf in priest's clothing. Obviously, "enosis" would be possible only if some provision were made for those Turk-Cypriots to leave who wanted to leave. In order to make this palatable to the GOT there would have to be some kind of territorial concessions by Greece.

11. I doubt that there is much efficacy in trying to get Erkin and Costopoulos together in The Hague. But I do think that you might wish to have talks with some of the other Foreign Ministers in order to prepare their minds for possible joint pressure on both Papandreou and Inonu directed at persuading them to take matters in their own hands and work out an agreed solution somewhere down the line. Papandreou seems confident that he can bring off "enosis" by providing some kind of a plebiscite on the Island. While a Greek Cyprus would be hard for the Turks it would certainly be better for their interests than Cuba off their shores.

12. I have talked with both Harlech and Charles Ritchie about these matters and have told them that I would suggest to you that you have some conversations in this spirit with some of the other Ministers. I think you will find both Butler and Paul Martin prepared for this.

13. Meanwhile you might suggest to some of the other Foreign Ministers that Tuomioja's role is to be that of quiet mediator and that they should make this clear to him. Nothing could be worse for our purposes than a report by the Mediator that would give the initiative to Makarios and drive the Turks into a greater sense of isolation and despondency.

Ball

---

42.   Telegram From Secretary of State Rusk to the Department of State[1]

The Hague, May 11, 1964, 4 p.m.

Secto 12. For the Acting Secretary. In my talk with Costopoulos this morning[2] he said that he planned to make a statement this afternoon on Cyprus which would call for a stronger UN role in keeping the peace in Cyprus. I have not seen an advance copy of his statement but will relay it as soon as one is available. I asked him what President Makarios would think about such a stronger UN role and he replied "it doesn't matter what President Makarios thinks about it." There may be many hookers in

---

[1] Source: Department of State, Central Files, POL 23–8 CYP. Secret; Priority; Exdis.
[2] A memorandum of this conversation was transmitted in Secto 13, May 11. (Ibid.)

his statement when actually made but it might provide some leverage for further strengthening of UN Force operations of a sort which would reassure the Turks. I leave it to you to follow up with UN if the Greek statement offers a further handle to take hold of.[3]

Costopoulos confirmed that Greece considers the Treaty of Guarantee to be still in effect but insisted that Article IV does not authorize unilateral Turkish intervention. He offered to have this point adjudicated. From Turkish point of view I would suppose adjudication would be interpreted as an attempt to throw doubt on Turkish rights during protracted period. On the other hand, it is just possible that some form of general adjudication as to the continuing validity and interpretation of the treaties might provide a means to put certain prestige factors on ice for a period if adjudication were to be applied to issues of interest to both sides. This is a very long shot but I mention it for Department's consideration.

Reporting officer's account of my talk with Erkin will be sent separately.[4] After that conversation Erkin drew me aside and affirmed Inonu's interest in talks with Greek Government although there seemed to be a strong implication that such talks would have to be on the basis of recognizing the validity of existing treaties. Erkin then expressed dismay over the prospect of a greatly deteriorating situation in Cyprus at the end of the period of UN responsibility and said that Turkey may be forced to intervene. He asked me whether, in that event, the US will support Turkey. I reminded him that the President had referred to intervention as a "last resort" but that, in any event, a direct answer to his question could only be given by the President. I said that situation would constitute no solution and would be the very catastrophe which all of us should now work to prevent. I added that it might be necessary for the UN forces to remain beyond the period of their initial engagement in order to forestall the deterioration he feared. I did not get the impression that he was warning me of imminent military action by Turkey.

Rusk

---

[3] In the statement, Costopoulos stressed the desire of the Greek Government to contribute to a solution of the Cyprus problem that would provide "Cypriots of Turkish origin" with every protection of law. He also stated that Greece would support any U.N. body that would provide long-term guarantees of the rights of Turkish Cypriots. The text of Costopoulos' statement was transmitted in Secto 21, May 12. (Ibid.)

[4] Transmitted in Secto 19, May 12. (Ibid.) A memorandum of the conversation regarding Cyprus is ibid., Conference Files: Lot 66 D 110, CF 2397.

43.   Telegram From the Embassy in Turkey to the Department of State[1]

Ankara, May 12, 1964, 9 p.m.

1517. At informal family lunch today with only the Inonus, Metin Tokers and ourselves present, for which invitation only extended yesterday and which obviously intended to afford occasion discuss Cyprus, Inonu was model of courtesy and hospitality but burden of his remarks constituted heavy fare indeed.

Inonu began by saying everything had been tried to no avail and future dark. He was at wits end to know where turn. As far as he knew conversation of Erkin with Secretary[2] had not brought out anything new and Greeks opposing discussion Cyprus in NATO Council. It was dismal business. He had done his best explain situation as seen here but still wondered if Washington really understood. At times we had seemed lose interest. I said that, referring first to his last comment, I could say Washington did understand matter but action must of necessity be suited to circumstance. If we had been less active for a time it had been in order give UN opportunity function effectively but when its performance seemed lagging we had not hesitated renew efforts.

Regarding what to do next, I said had always been my conviction that mistake to think of Cyprus as just thing in itself and that closer consultation in past between Ankara and Athens might have spared us much of present grief. I realized that consultation now more difficult but, difficult or not, it seemed necessary step in seeking solution. Could Inonu tell me if Erkin might be seeing Greek FonMin in Hague?

Inonu said he too had always favored direct talks with Athens and there had been some hope under previous Greek govts but Papandreou had now elected identify himself completely with Makarios. Talking with one would be same as talking with other. Regarding Erkin, no reason why he shouldn't talk with Greek counterpart but Greek officials very high and mighty these days and didn't know whether would be possible.

I said all this seemed be getting nowhere and asked if Inonu as man of great experience could not identify certain areas where effort might be made break through present barriers.

It was at this point that Inonu delivered what he apparently intended be punch-line of conversation by saying that time for persua-

---

[1] Source: Department of State, Central Files, POL 23–8 CYP. Secret; Immediate. Repeated to Nicosia, Athens, London, and USUN. Passed to the White House.

[2] See the last paragraph of Document 42.

sion now passed; no longer any role for "the old statesman," as matter now stand there are only two alternatives, either submit to Makarios or beat some sense into his head by force.

At this point we were called to lunch but afterward I asked what Inonu meant by using force to bring Makarios to see reason. He said he meant military force; it wouldn't be necessary to invade all of island, merely occupy part of it. This was something Makarios could understand.

I said needless point out this would probably result in Greek intervention, clash between Greek and Turkish forces and possible escalation of conflict to full-scale war between Greece and Turkey.

Inonu replied decision would be up to GOG. GOT prepared in either contingency.

I observed that, if only possible think of matter in terms of surrender or war, obvious that Turkey's friends could support neither but I had gained different impression in conversation with Fulbright in which I had understood Inonu to have endorsed idea of strengthening peacekeeping function in order establish security which would in turn permit quiet negotiation.

Inonu said this correct and he still felt that way but doubted it would work. Must look facts in face. Service which USG might render would be to make Turkish determination clear to Athens.

I said this still opened no path toward solution and in this connection questioned accuracy of Inonu's assumption in equating Makarios and Papandreou so completely. Information available to me did not indicate that situation so monolithic but rather that there were various aspects which might be exploited to advantage with Athens if communication could just be established. Furthermore there seemed to be certain change in pattern of Makarios' behavior recently which might be more hopefully interpreted. Addressing himself to Makarios first, Inonu said he too had noted certain recent changes but now clear from bitter experience that Makarios is crafty schemer and that such changes merely for tactical deception.

Regarding Athens he was also dubious but, if it wished make contribution, it could announce clearly its recognition of validity of existing treaties. If this done and given several years time eventual solution could be worked out. Such an announcement would completely clear atmosphere.

Adverting again to our attitude, Inonu said he had been greatly troubled by apparent falling off of our interest following Ball Mission and also by persistent reports that USG favoring enosis as solution. This now cleared up but he still felt Washington not fully aware of depth of Turkish despair in finding road out of Cyprus imbroglio and its determination to use force if necessary. If I could convey this depth of feeling to Washington and it, in turn, could convince Athens our conversation would have served useful purpose.

Comments: As is usually case, much of foregoing repetitive and even punch-line re time for persuasion being passed and preparedness intervene by force was reformulation of standard theme. However, when this latter evaluated in terms of emphasis on strategic importance of Cyprus during Fulbright talks and of insistence that GOT could not allow Cyprus slip away as had other coastal islands, regardless of whether Cyprus became unitary state or devolved to Greece, there would seem to be strong indication that policy decision has been reached or is in making in accord with which GOT will insist on some form of Turkish presence on Cyprus or right of custodianship as essential ingredient in any solution involving abrogation of present treaties. As of now this is still somewhat dim shape emerging from mist but its outline has seemed to have become increasingly clear of late. If this correct and if—if such policy rigidly held, it is obvious that certain mixes which have been tentatively considered to meet Turkish requirements would no longer fill bill. Admittedly, this still somewhat "iffy" but trend seems increasingly strong.

In so saying I am also mindful that Inonu may have correctly assumed that his remarks would be promptly reported to Hague as background for discussions there. Even so, I should still hesitate to discount them on that score, given Inonu's reputation for multiple purpose action.[3]

Hare

---

[3] In telegram 1563 from Ankara, May 26, Hare commented that while Inonu's statements were intended to maintain Turkey's international bargaining position, they were not intended for domestic consumption. (Department of State, Central Files, POL 23–8 CYP)

---

44.   Telegram From the Embassy in Greece to the Department of State[1]

Athens, May 18, 1964, 8 p.m.

1722. 1.   In rereading recent telegrams on Cyprus I have observed that whereas serious thought is being given by us to an eventual solution

---

[1] Source: Department of State, Central Files, POL 23–8 CYP. Secret; Limdis. Repeated to Ankara.

involving enosis as preferable to "unfettered independence", this possibility has been linked at time with the suggestion of some kind of territorial concession to Turkey by Greece. As has been reported from here, I consider that question of territorial concession is out of the picture not only for Papandreou govt but for any other Greek Govt. All Greek politicians, govt and opposition, stand as one on this issue. It is difficult to envisage Greek politicians being brought to agree to what could be termed a partition of Greece when all are so dead set against a partition of Cyprus.

2. On the other hand, Papandreou and some other influential Greeks have expressed their awareness of the importance of trying to find something which might avoid or at least minimize feeling of "humiliation" on part of GOT, but none of them have been very helpful in pointing way. Unfortunately, so long as the Greeks are convinced that "justice" is on their side and that the UN will support their view of justice, there is precious little initiative to be expected from them to date. The only proposals to this end which Papandreou has advanced have been (a) his suggestion that enosis would meet Turkey's security worries by having Cyprus become part of NATO; (b) that a formula be devised for continued UN presence on island to ensure minority rights; (c) that adequate compensation be paid to all Cypriots who wish to leave island; and (d) that GOT be helped financially.

3. This would doubtless be considered cold fare by the Turks, even if an enosis solution should include establishment of a NATO base in Cyprus, manned in part by Turkish soldiers. The only other thing which I believe to be in the realm of realism so far as the Greeks are concerned relates to Greek interests in Istanbul. The sacrificing of those interests, which is in fact already going on, might help salve Turkish feelings as well as providing ways of life for such of the non-rural Turk-Cypriot population as may leave Cyprus. The Greeks would, in first instance, certainly oppose a population move, but this would not be the determinant, particularly as GOT can throw the Greek population out at any time. Moreover, I believe that many Greeks are already reconciled to elimination of the Greek community.

4. The removal of the Patriarchate would present much more serious problem, but should not be ruled out if, in fact, it would help assuage the Turks for loss of position in Cyprus and lead to settlement without more bloodshed. One imporant politician not in the government has suggested to me the possibility of establishing the island of Patmos as sovereign seat of the Patriarchate, with cession of island by Greece and adequate international financing to create proper facilities. A few Greeks are privately talking of these terms, but this is highly unpopular concept for most. Any settlement involving removal of Patriarchate would have

to be most carefully and quietly developed and suggestions should definitely not come from us.

5. I recognize that foregoing does not meet GOT desiderata and may not greatly advance prospects of a Cyprus solution. However, I feel it imporant that the Department appreciate that in our view concession of territory to Turkey would not be acceptable as element in any solution. Furthermore, in view of increasing tensions within Center Union and strong nationalist line on Cyprus taken by extreme left, it is doubtful whether Papandreou could make any meaningful concession to Turks at this juncture.

Labouisse

45.   Telegram From the Department of State to the Mission to the United Nations[1]

Washington, May 21, 1964, 7:44 p.m.

3018. Cyprus—Hostage Problem. Ref: Nicosia's 1244, 1254.[2] Dept agrees with Emb Nicosia that increased hostage taking by Greek Cypriots, and particularly likelihood that sizeable number those taken recent days are dead, has serious implications for efforts restore law and order on Cyprus and establish conditions under which rational efforts resolve basic political problem could be undertaken. We fear that when news breaks, as it doubtless will soon, that sizeable number of Turk Cypriots abducted have been killed, Turk Cypriot forces in Cyprus may respond by abducting and shooting Greek Cypriots or otherwise lashing out with acts of violence. Hostage taking and executions also fodder for militant elements Turkey and could stimulate further GOT moves against Greek community Istanbul and lead to renewed threat of intervention.

---

[1] Source: Department of State, Central Files, POL 23–8 CYP. Confidential. Drafted by Moffit; cleared by Jernegan, Buffum, and L/UNA; and approved by Sisco. Repeated to Nicosia, London, Athens, and Ankara.

[2] Telegram 1244, March 15, reported the shared concern of U.S. and British officials in Cyprus about a renewal of the fighting. (Ibid.) Telegram 1254, May 20, reported that the issue of hostages "has been brought to head" by the announcement that 74 of the 91 Turkish Cypriots taken hostage by Greek Cypriots were unaccounted for. The telegram outlined efforts of U.N. officials to secure the release of the hostages. (Ibid.)

To try head off or blunt these ominous possibilities, we believe would be desirable for SYG call in Rossides and Bitsios and impress on them serious view which he takes of abductions. SYG could launch his démarche by stressing that SC resolutions March 4 and 11 call on all UN member states, including GOC, take no action likely to worsen situation in Cyprus and requests GOC in line its responsibilities for maintaining law and order in Cyprus to take "all additional measures necessary" stop violence and bloodshed. SYG could state forthrightly that large scale abductions which have thus far gone unpunished reflect clear failure GOC live up to its responsibilities under resolutions.

Since we could not be sure Rossides would faithfully reflect seriousness of SYG démarche, we believe it would be extremely important that Thant impress on Bitsios grave implications of hostage taking and probable killing of hostages. SYG could emphasize to Bitsios that, given support for Greek Cypriots by GOG, abductions and probable killings can only lead to further deterioration in Greco-Turkish relations and play into hands militant elements on all sides. We would hope Bitsios would get message and that GOG would in turn drive home to Makarios that abductions must cease and that hostages still living must be released.

As Galo Plaza will presumably be returning Cyprus next few days,[3] we feel would also be useful that he carry strong message from SYG to Makarios along lines suggested démarche in New York and adding, in accordance last paragraph Nicosia 1254, that GOC has obligation to take whatever steps necessary prevent further abductions. Message might refer to reports that some or all those abducted have been executed, and ask that Makarios effect release of hostages still in hands Greek Cypriots. In light Makarios sensitivity foreign criticism and his vanity re personal image, such message might infer that, unless Makarios acts, SYG may feel compelled make public statement condemning abductions.

You requested suggest foregoing course either directly to SYG or through Bunche and urge that SYG act upon it while Galo Plaza in New York. Suggest you indicate we find abductions and potential trouble stemming therefrom particularly disquieting since through efforts of UNFICYP number and scale of incidents has been significantly reduced and gratifying progress being made on civil side particularly harvesting scheme. We believe would be desirable for Galo Plaza, with his on-the-spot knowledge, sit in on SYG meetings with Rossides and Bitsios; in case of former to ensure that Cyprus Rep does not attempt gloss over this serious matter, and with Bitsios to put in perspective seriousness abduction problem for UN peacekeeping effort and work of mediator. We have been impressed by Galo Plaza's quick grasp of Cyprus situation. State-

---

[3] On May 11, Secretary-General Thant informed the Security Council that Galo Plaza was going to Cyprus as his Special Representative.

ments made by him both public and in meetings with Cypriot leaders have, we feel, struck just the right note.

Rusk

---

46.   Letter From the Ambassador to Cyprus (Belcher) to the Deputy Assistant Secretary of State for Near Eastern and South Asian Affairs (Jernegan)[1]

Nicosia, May 21, 1964.

Dear Jack:

The Greek Cypriot leaders have made clear they intend to use the UN as a forum to press their case both in the Security Council in June and in the General Assembly in the autumn, by which time they expect Tuomioja's mediation efforts will have failed. They expect to have adequate support not only to get the item on the agenda but also to secure endorsement of the general principles they espouse: an independent, unitary state; majority control; minority safeguards; right of self-determination. If this is secured, they will proceed, with or without Turkish Cypriot cooperation, to draw up a new constitution, have it endorsed by plebiscite, and implement it.

The Cyprus problem would remain, but in an altered state. The Greek Cypriots would have international moral endorsement of their efforts along the above lines, and conversely, justification for continued Turkish Cypriot legalistic opposition to these efforts would be thrown into doubt, particularly if convincing security guarantees were provided.

It appears inevitable that the GOC will seek General Assembly endorsement of the above principles, which underlie our own system and which command the obvious dedication of the overwhelming majority of the Cyprus population. The vote on some such resolution will obviously pose a difficult problem for the USG. The Soviet Union and East Europeans will have no such scruples as we and can pose as the "true supporters of democracy" unless we can find some way to appear

---

[1] Source: Department of State, Cyprus Desk Files: Lot 67 D 412, Letters from Post—1964. Secret; Official–Informal.

on the positive side of the debate and the vote. While recognizing the very difficult problem this may pose vis-à-vis Ankara, we believe it would be harmful to our overall interests here and elsewhere for the US to oppose such a resolution or abstain. To prepare for this likely eventuality, we believe the United States should commence now to plan a policy evolution which would permit positive endorsement rather than awkward abstention. It might be well for us to coordinate such an effort with the British, who will presumably be in a similar position at the General Assembly because of the need to protect their Sovereign Base Areas.

I realize this will have to be undertaken with considerable finesse in view of the assurances given Erkin that the United States will exert maximum effort in the UN and among the parties concerned to see that justice is done and that Turkey does not suffer humiliation. The obvious problem here is the interpretation of what constitutes "humiliation." The GOT can be expected to interpret this as broadly as possible. For our part, I believe we should from the first make clear that the key word is justice, and in our view a just solution must accord with the political facts of the situation in Cyprus. In this context, we should exert our maximum efforts to see that the wording, specific details and manner of presentation of any specific proposals are such as to avoid offense or humiliation to the GOT. Aside from the proceedings at an early Security Council meeting, I have in mind of course, the probability that Tuomioja will, as a minimum, make a report of his views on settlement to U Thant. As suggested in my tel 1235 to the Department,[2] the use of his report by SYG is something we would want to influence.

Aside from considerations of face, the principal fears of both the GOT and the Turkish Cypriot Community appear to revolve around the question of security. To win even reluctant Turkish acquiescence to a Cyprus solution, some promise of security must be held out to Turkish Cypriots and Turks alike. Specific discussion of ways to cope with Turkish Cypriot and GOT security problems would demonstrate our appreciation of their legitimate concern in this area and should at the same time lead their thinking into more productive and realistic examination of practical problems rather than the present immobilism of extreme and adamant positions which ignore the political, economic and arithmetical realities of this Island.

Sincerely yours,

Toby

---

[2] Telegram 1235 from Nicosia, May 14, reported Tuomoija's views of the likely contents of his report to the Secretary-General. (Ibid.)

47.   Telegram From the Embassy in Cyprus to the Department of State[1]

Nicosia, May 22, 1964, 6 p.m.

1265. Deptel 860.[2] Arms procurement. There is little doubt that GOC is determined to obtain substantial armaments. Most contacts here, including Swedish and Finnish Chargés, agree with our assessment that UAR will be principal source, but financed by Soviets. We have received information (ARMA tel) that UAR-trained Greek Cypriots will be flying UAR-supplied aircraft. In addition, British-trained ground control parties were also trained to fly so they are available at least for light aircraft already purchased. Information received today [*less than 1 line of source text not declassified*] indicates Soviet Ambassador's two calls on Makarios this week concerned arms to be purchased on long-term credits. Shopping list reportedly being prepared by General Karayannis and our informant says "anything goes".

We agree UN cannot allow this problem go unnoticed and believe best course would be to suggest SYG at least issue strong statement condemning not only GOC and Turkish Cypriots for action in attempting build up forces at this time, but also condemning those nations which furnish arms.

In practical terms, however, we doubt he would get far with such an "appeal". (Gyani tells me he has urged SYG go further, having placed arms control question at top priority. He says Plaza agrees and will present forceful case to U Thant.) In first place, smuggling can probably continue largely undetected. Secondly, GOC is apt to argue that as legal government it has authority and responsibility to secure arms needed for national defense. We expect they may put this argument in connection with demand that SC resolution not only instruct UNFICYP to help GOC put down "rebellion", but also state UNFICYP will be used to defend Cyprus in case Turkish "aggression" unless, of course, GOT will give further guarantee of no intervention while UNFICYP here. When SC does not comply, GOC will probably cite lack of guarantee against Turkish intervention as justification for continued arms acquisition.

Of course, arms acquired under this rubric can also be used against Turkish Cypriots. Swedish Chargé Bundy fears this is real purpose of armaments and believes problem cannot be ignored by SYG.

---

[1] Source: Department of State, Central Files, POL 23–8 CYP. Secret. Repeated to Ankara, Athens, London, Paris for USRO, USUN, and Cairo.

[2] Telegram 860 to Nicosia, May 20, stated U.S. opposition to the introduction of armaments on the island and speculated that Makarios was maneuvering to lay the groundwork for an agreement with the Soviet Union on arms supplies. (Ibid.)

In connection with SC consideration of arms problem, GOC is certain to raise question of Turkish clandestine arms and personnel shipments through Mansoura–Kokkina area, west of Morphou Bay area. Minister of Labour Papadopoulos told me yesterday that GOC was about to insist UNPKF do something to stop smuggling or GOC would be forced to take action. Said both arms and men coming in from Turkey in increasing numbers and UN unable or unwilling to stop. I pointed out UN efforts to stop it would mean clash with Turkish Cypriot fighter groups and I doubted Swedish contingent would take such action. (Swedish Chargé later confirmed this.) Papadopoulos was insistent GOC could not permit traffic to continue. He went on to say that Minister of Interior Georkadjis had documentary evidence of complicity Turkish Ambassador in smuggling arrangements and that this might be used in UN proceedings.

Despite these complicating factors, I do not see how we can sit idly by and take no notice of GOC plans to exacerbate situation with extensive arms purchases. Therefore, come what may, we should urge SYG to make representations GOC, as well as to Greece and Turkey, to cooperate in stopping arms race on island. Naturally, appeal should be addressed to other nations as well, and if additional, usable information re UAR and Soviet implication in deals can be developed, statement can be directed at them specifically. (Eventually, of course, as equipment begins arrive, source will be obvious.)

We might also consider utility of requesting NATO embargo on arms to island as in keeping with SC resolution of March 4. This would embarrass Greece and Turkey, but would at least dry up certain other sources. In this connection, Israeli Ambassador says there is blanket prohibition by his government.

Have also spoken to British HICOMer Bishop and Finnish Chargé Kawin, both of whom have sent strong reports their governments along foregoing lines.

All this is something which can be discussed with Plaza in New York on his return from Quito.[3]

Belcher

---

[3] Topol 1822 to Paris, May 26, instructed the Representative to the North Atlantic Treaty Organization to avoid any discussion of a NATO arms embargo since it would cause further deterioration of relationships with Greece, Turkey, and the Greek Cypriots without affecting Makarios' ability to procure arms. (Ibid.)

48.   **Telegram From the Embassy in Cyprus to the Department of State**[1]

Nicosia, May 28, 1964, 6 p.m.

1282. During call on President made at my request, following observations worth reporting:

1. UN SC meeting. GOC will favor three months' extension of UNFI-CYP and, despite rumors to contrary appearing in press will request no changes in terms of reference. (Min Labour told me later this latter point still not finalized.) Possibly due to recent unfortunate incidents involving individual British soldiers as well as considerable anti-British feeling current on island, GOC may request reduction in number UK soldiers in PKF. President has hopes that by concentrating British UN troops in Limassol and Larnaca areas where situation much more [*worse?*] than elsewhere any further incidents can be avoided.

2. Arms procurement and conscription. Makarios said reports of GOC plans to obtain arms grossly exaggerated in press. Obviously GOC has no need for "heavy bombers, etc." He had need, however, for fast patrol vessels, but so far was unable to obtain torpedo boats by purchase in West; therefore might have to turn to Soviets. Pointed out that he had now five planes in Air Force, including two helicopters. Said "all but one are yours, none are from the Soviet." (This confirmed in previous reports from Embassy and ARMA.) We did not discuss possibility of jet fighters or already-reported arrivals of light arms. With regard to conscription bill, President said that bill basically designed to establish control and discipline and would incorporate and break up various private groups such as Lyssarides' and Sampson's under over-all control of General Karayannis. Training program would include initially 16,000, but present plans did not provide for eventual army of anything like that size.

Said they had considered expanding police force, but had rejected this as being more expensive than creating small standing army. Said he had in mind force of 3,000 to 5,000, but this might be somewhat larger, perhaps as high as 8,000, and hoped that there would be no need for more in order control situation here vis-à-vis Turkish Cypriots. When I mentioned hostage problem and my encouragement at recent editorials calling on Greek Cypriots to use restraint and not take vengeance on innocent people, Archbishop said he had instigated press items and added further strong condemnation such acts. Said he hoped conscription and new armed forces would put stop to such irresponsibility. Noted also that no further acts committed since his appeal. Added that

---

[1] Source: Department of State, Central Files, POL 23–8 CYP. Confidential. Repeated to Ankara, Athens, London, Paris for USRO, and USUN.

Red Cross had now found another 30 of those allegedly taken prior to May 11 incidents in Famagust. Said he had asked Kutchuk to issue statement on 30, but reply negative and he now would put matter on public record. (We checking this out with ICRC reps.)

3. Apparent growth of Soviet influence. I said we could understand GOC looking with favor on Soviet offers of assistance when country apparently in danger. However, I recalled that on previous occasion he had said that basic orientation of GOC and majority of people of Cyprus was and would remain with West.

Bearing this in mind, I said number of recent developments appeared to be pointing in other direction: Aside from arms question, there had been Aeroflot agreement, recently completed temporary air agreement with East Germany, establishment here of Cuban Mission, and possibility that Soviet petroleum products would be entering island through contract with electricity authority. President said he considered these were minor developments, and he could assure me that he would continue to act with utmost caution re possible entanglements with USSR. (This obviously means one thing to him and another to us.) With regard to Cuba, he gave me same argument as FonMin (previously reported) and he described air agreements as of little significance except that he was hopeful that East German agreement might possibly involve development in tourism. He said he was hopeful that contract for electricity authority would go to already established private firm here, but he thought it would be difficult to exclude low bidding firm simply on basis that their source of supply was Soviet Union. (It was apparent that he was reluctant to see electricity authority used as means to introduce sizable amounts of Soviet petroleum products, but he was at loss to see just how this might be prevented except perhaps through interpretation of bids based on price, experience and service.)

4. Easing of tensions in Nicosia. President said that in discussions yesterday with UNFICYP POLAD Flores re withdrawal of Greek and Turkish Cypriot positions from demarcations along Green Line, he (Markarios) had made radical proposal as follows: instead of 100-yard withdrawal by each side, if UN would take over several posts which he had designated on map, Greek Cypriots would dismantle all their positions. I said this was most encouraging development and expressed hope it would work out. President said he did not see how Turks could refuse UN offer to take over their posts as long as Greek side withdrew completely. (We shall follow this up with Flores.)

Our meeting was in private, extremely cordial and it was agreed we should meet at least every fortnight for general discussion.

Belcher

49.   Telegram From the Department of State to the Embassy in Cyprus[1]

Washington, June 1, 1964, 6:55 p.m.

885. We seem to detect just the beginnings of thinking in both Athens and Ankara that a territorial quid pro quo might be an ingredient in an eventual settlement of the Cyprus problem. We are anxious that these very fragile seeds be permitted to germinate and nothing be done which would interfere with process. This connection, we would want to be certain of UN Mediator's plans.

For Nicosia: Your 1221[2] cited Tuomioja as saying he felt two months be required for him to prepare report to SYG. Your 1235[3] seemed suggest that Tuomioja's report, when submitted, would include his ideas on solution but that substantive part of report would be confidential and it would be for SYG decide whether make that part public. If you believe there any prospect Tuomioja will submit report before SC meeting, you requested urge that report (1) either contain no recommendations for solution, or (2) any such recommendations be in confidential section of report and report for public record be along lines suggested in penultimate para Deptel 2890.[4]

For USUN: Your tel 4096[5] indicates Bunche appears understand danger of surfacing any recommendations re solution unless there were agreement among parties that such recommendations could serve as basis for negotiations, and that, in absence such agreement, Tuomioja should not attempt submit report for some months. We note also that SYG at meeting with representatives of troop contributing countries May 22 expressed view that mediator should give himself six months and said he would discourage Tuomioja from producing report too soon. SYG also said he felt an early report might prejudice prospects for extension UNFICYP mandate. We assume from this that SYG would not present substantive report on mediation efforts to SC or, in any event, not a report with recommendations or proposals for settlement. You requested to confirm this assumption with Bunche or SYG. If you feel there is any doubt on this, or any change in their thinking, suggest you

---

[1] Source: Department of State, Central Files, POL 23–8 CYP. Secret; Priority; Limdis. Drafted by Moffit, cleared by Jernegan and Buffum, and approved by Cleveland. Also sent to USUN and repeated to London, Ankara, and Athens.

[2] Dated May 11. (Ibid.)

[3] See footnote 2, Document 46.

[4] Telegram 2890 to USUN was also sent to Nicosia as telegram 837; see footnote 4, Document 40.

[5] Dated May 13. (Department of State, Central Files, POL 23–8 CYP)

again emphasize to them dangers of surfacing even vague outline Tuomioja's thinking re solution as expressed Deptel 2890 and your 4029.[6]

Ball

---

[6] Telegram 4029 from USUN discussed and analyzed Tuomioja's proposal. (Ibid.)

**50.   Telegram From the Embassy in Turkey to the Department of
State[1]**

Ankara, June 4, 1964, 6 p.m.

Critic 2. Immediately on receipt info transmitted [*document number
not declassified*][2] I asked see Erkin urgently and was received at once.

Without revealing knowledge CAS report I said that as result
constant association with Cyprus problem one tended develop certain
sensitivity to situation and I somehow had feeling something out of ordinary might be in wind. Could he give me reading since I would not wish
be caught unaware. Also referred our understanding his assurance to
President.

Erkin said in talks with Tuomioja latter had said Makarios intent on
pursuing his objectives regardless consequences. Fault lay with USG and
UK for not having been sufficiently active and Turk cause lost unless two
governments did something.

Erkin then added present situation on island very critical and Cabinet meeting at 8:30 (local time) tonight to decide what to do. I asked if
intervention might be decided. Erkin said that possible.

I then said it was understandable but definite instructions warn
most seriously against intervention and I gave reasons, adding that I had
also been somewhat encouraged recently by reports from Athens indi-

---

[1] Source: Department of State, Central Files, POL 23–8 CYP. Secret; Flash; Limdis.
Received at 12:19 p.m. Repeated to Athens, Nicosia, London, and Paris. Passed to USUN
and to U.S. Intelligence Board agencies.

[2] Dated June 4. It reported a Turkish official statement that following Makarios' rejection of his June 3 request for a Cabinet meeting to find ways to end the bloodshed, Vice President Kutchuk would proclaim the independence of certain Turkish Cypriot enclaves and
request a Turkish intervention that would occur on June 5 or 6. (Ibid.)

cating Papandreou was pondering some formula which might meet Turkish needs.

Erkin said he had heard nothing of more encouraging nature from Athens but, if there was anything firm, it could have important effect on decision of Cabinet tonight and he would endeavor postpone meeting for an hour in order to afford opportunity for us to communicate anything which we might have.

I then asked what Erkin meant by indicating agreement that we and British should have been more diligent. Erkin said support in Athens of Turkish demand for federation or "double enosis." This essential and such ideas as exchange of population or giving Turks "some small island" out of question.

Erkin also said he had thought our attitude toward enosis had been clarified in Washington but he alleged have information that American official sources in Nicosia were in fact stating enosis was our approved policy.

Hope you or Athens can give me something urgently which I can convey to Erkin in effort deter precipitate action.

On leaving FonOff I by chance ran into Inonu and approached him in similar manner but Erkin apparently got wind that we were talking and joined us to say he had explained situation to me and would fill in Inonu. I told him make sure stress gravity our concern of intervention contemplated. He said he would.

I have never seen Inonu more relaxed, even jovial.

He did however confirm that situation critical.

Contents this tel must in no circumstances be revealed to other than Americans.

Hare

---

51.   Memorandum of Telephone Conversation[1]

Washington, June 4, 1964, 12:45 p.m.

SUBJECT

Possible Turkish Government Decision on Intervention in Cyprus

PARTICIPANTS

Turgut Menemencioglu, Turkish Ambassador

The Secretary

---

[1] Source: Department of State, Central Files, POL 23–8 CYP. Secret; Exdis. Drafted by Bracken and approved in S on June 15.

The Secretary apologized for taking up a matter over the telephone with the Ambassador but since time was of the essence he was taking the liberty to do so. He said that the President had asked him to call the Ambassador most urgently and say that the President is gravely concerned by a statement which the Foreign Minister made to our Ambassador to the effect that a cabinet meeting was scheduled for approximately 8:30 p.m. at which the question of intervention in Cyprus could be decided. We have considered we have had a flat assurance through the Foreign Minister such a step would not be taken and that there would be full consultation with allies.We would find this a very, very grave departure from our understandings and would have a serious effect on the problem of our security commitments with our allies. The President asked most urgently that we urge in the gravest terms that we have an opportunity for consultations on these matters.

The Turkish Ambassador responded that it was very difficult for him to get through quickly to Ankara and asked if the Secretary was also sending a message to Ambassador Hare. The Secretary replied in the affirmative, adding that he was requesting the Ambassador to exert every effort as well.[2] Intervention would create most serious difficulties and we consider it cannot be done without consultation with allies. The Ambassador said he would attempt to get in touch with Ankara immediately.

---

[2] Telegram 1285 to Ankara, June 4, 1:15 p.m., instructed Hare to see Inonu immediately, "calling him out of cabinet meeting if necessary" to express U.S. opposition to a military intervention in Cyprus and to "use all arguments in your arsenal to pull them back from any such decision and to insist upon consultation." (Ibid.)

---

52.   Telegram From the Embassy in Greece to the Embassy in Turkey[1]

Athens, June 4, 1964, 9:30 p.m.

336. Ref: Ankara's 500.[2]

1. We have nothing "firm" from Athens to offer Erkin. Embtel 1812 (333 to Ankara)[3] contains confidential report Tuomioja–Papandreou

---

[1] Source: Department of State, Central Files, POL 23–8 CYP. Secret; Flash. Repeated to the Department of State, Nicosia, London, and Paris for USRO. Received in the Department of State at 3:44 p.m. and passed to the White House. The source text is the Department of State copy.

[2] Critic 2 from Ankara (Document 50) was repeated to Athens as telegram 500.

[3] Dated June 4. (Department of State, Central Files, POL 23–8 CYP)

meeting yesterday, which indicates Papandreou still holding to line of enosis. We continue to believe there is no chance of Greek support partition or federation of Cyprus, as apparently demanded by Erkin, although there could likely be guarantees for Turkish minority of Lausanne Treaty type. Other possibilities are those suggested Embtels 1722 and 1759 (318 and 325 to Ankara),[4] but even these cannot be put forward as having Greek approval.

2. Required action for moment seems to me is for Turks to tell Kucuk firmly not to attempt establish de facto partition. I must emphasize that if Turks move to intervene on island, Greeks will react promptly and in force. GOT should be left under no misapprehension on this score.

Labouisse

---

[4] Telegram 1722 is dated May 18. (Ibid.) Telegram 1759 has not been found.

---

53.   Telegram From the Embassy in Turkey to the Department of State[1]

Ankara, June 5, 1964, 1 a.m.

1598.   Have just completed three hour conversation with Inonu while Cabinet waited. From start it was made clear that decision firm as far as Inonu concerned. Only thing wanted from us was understanding attitude on grounds that purpose was to move into only part of island as only way to reduce problem to manageable proportions. We would see and agree once operation carried out. Argument was tough and sometimes got on very sensitive ground with Inonu holding ground firmly and saying not only Cyprus but our relationship could hinge on agreement with Turkish decision. When Inonu made another move to join Cabinet I said was certain what I had been told would be great disappointment to President who has stressed importance of consultation and was only being given opportunity to agree or disagree on single proposition. This could hardly be called consultation.

---

[1] Source: Department of State, Central Files, POL 23–8 CYP. Secret; Flash; Limdis; Noforn. Repeated to Athens, Nicosia, London, and Paris for USRO. Passed to the White House, JCS, OSD, CIA, and USUN. The time of transmission on the source text is 1 p.m., which is incorrect.

Inonu and Erkin said that failure carry through as planned would cause great let down and results could be disastrous. Why hadn't we put questions which could be answered? What would I suggest?

I said what we needed was time make our views known. Inonu asked how much time. I said twenty-four hours in belief that request for longer delay would be refused. Inonu agreed, saying would be difficult call off plans at this stage but that he would do so. He must however stress importance of strict secrecy. This I assured. Longer tel follows[2] but this is guts of discussion and is being sent as preliminary report so you can get wheels turning since we shall need strongest and most forthcoming assurances and arguments possible if we are to head Turks off.

Although we didn't finish till eleven o'clock they asked for our reply by nine o'clock (local time) tomorrow night.

Hare

---

[2] Telegram 1599 from Ankara, June 5. (Ibid.)

---

54.   Telegram From the Department of State to the Embassy in Turkey[1]

Washington, June 5, 1964, 12:15 a.m.

1296. Deliver Inonu soonest following message from President:

"Dear Mr. Prime Minister:

I am gravely concerned by the information which I have had through Ambassador Hare from you and your Foreign Minister that the Turkish Government is contemplating a decision to intervene by military force to occupy a portion of Cyprus. I wish to emphasize, in the fullest friendship and frankness, that I do not consider that such a course of action by Turkey, fraught with such far-reaching consequences, is consistent with the commitment of your Government to consult fully in advance with us. Ambassador Hare has indicated that you have postponed your decision for a few hours in order to obtain my views. I put to you personally whether you really believe that it is appropriate for your

---

[1] Source: Johnson Library, National Security File, Head of State Correspondence, Turkey, Prime Minister Inonu. Secret; Flash; Exdis. Drafted and approved by Rusk and cleared by Bundy for the White House. Repeated to London, Nicosia, Athens, and Paris, also for USRO.

Government, in effect, to present an ultimatum to an ally who has demonstrated such staunch support over the years as has the United States for Turkey. I must, therefore, first urge you to accept the responsibility for complete consultation with the United States before any such action is taken.

It is my impression that you believe that such intervention by Turkey is permissible under the provisions of the Treaty of Guarantee of 1960. I must call your attention, however, to our understanding that the proposed intervention by Turkey would be for the purpose of supporting an attempt by Turkish Cypriot leaders to partition the Island, a solution which is specifically excluded by the Treaty of Guarantee. Further, that Treaty requires consultation among the Guarantor Powers. It is the view of the United States that the possibilities of such consultation have by no means been exhausted in this situation and that, therefore, the reservation of the right to take unilateral action is not yet applicable.

I must call to your attention, also, Mr. Prime Minister, the obligations of NATO. There can be no question in your mind that a Turkish intervention in Cyprus would lead to a military engagement between Turkish and Greek forces. Secretary of State Rusk declared at the recent meeting of the Ministerial Council of NATO in The Hague that war between Turkey and Greece must be considered as 'literally unthinkable.'[2] Adhesion to NATO, in its very essence, means that NATO countries will not wage war on each other. Germany and France have buried centuries of animosity and hostility in becoming NATO allies; nothing less can be expected from Greece and Turkey. Furthermore, a military intervention in Cyprus by Turkey could lead to a direct involvement by the Soviet Union. I hope you will understand that your NATO Allies have not had a chance to consider whether they have an obligation to protect Turkey against the Soviet Union if Turkey takes a step which results in Soviet intervention without the full consent and understanding of its NATO Allies.

Further, Mr. Prime Minister, I am concerned about the obligations of Turkey as a member of the United Nations. The United Nations has provided forces on the Island to keep the peace. Their task has been difficult but, during the past several weeks, they have been progressively successful in reducing the incidents of violence on that Island. The United Nations Mediator has not yet completed his work. I have no doubt that the general membership of the United Nations would react in the strongest terms to unilateral action by Turkey which would defy the efforts of the United Nations and destroy any prospect that the United Nations

---

[2] For text of the May 12 statement, see Department of State *Bulletin*, June 1, 1964, pp. 850–852.

could assist in obtaining a reasonable and peaceful settlement of this difficult problem.

I wish also, Mr. Prime Minister, to call your attention to the bilateral agreement between the United States and Turkey in the field of military assistance. Under Article IV of the Agreement with Turkey of July 1947,[3] your Government is required to obtain United States consent for the use of military assistance for purposes other than those for which such assistance was furnished. Your Government has on several occasions acknowledged to the United States that you fully understand this condition. I must tell you in all candor that the United States cannot agree to the use of any United States supplied military equipment for a Turkish· intervention in Cyprus under present circumstances.

Moving to the practical results of the contemplated Turkish move, I feel obligated to call to your attention in the most friendly fashion the fact that such a Turkish move could lead to the slaughter of tens of thousands of Turkish Cypriots on the Island of Cyprus. Such an action on your part would unleash the furies and there is no way by which military action on your part could be sufficiently effective to prevent wholesale destruction of many of those whom you are trying to protect. The presence of United Nations forces could not prevent such a catastrophe.

You may consider that what I have said is much too severe and that we are disregardful of Turkish interests in the Cyprus situation. I should like to assure you that this is not the case. We have exerted ourselves both publicly and privately to assure the safety of Turkish Cypriots and to insist that a final solution of the Cyprus problem should rest upon the consent of the parties most directly concerned. It is possible that you feel in Ankara that the United States has not been sufficiently active in your behalf. But surely you know that our policy has caused the liveliest resentments in Athens (where demonstrations have been aimed against us) and has led to a basic alienation between the United States and Archbishop Makarios. As I said to your Foreign Minister in our conversation just a few weeks ago,[4] we value very highly our relations with Turkey. We have considered you as a great ally with fundamental common interests. Your security and prosperity have been a deep concern of the American people and we have expressed that concern in the most practical terms. You and we have fought together to resist the ambitions of the communist world revolution. This solidarity has meant a great deal to us and I would hope that it means a great deal to your Government and to your people. We have no intention of lending any support to any solution of Cyprus which endangers the Turkish Cypriot community. We have not been able to find a final solution because this is, admittedly, one of the

---

[3] For text of the agreement on economic and technical cooperation, signed in Ankara on July 12, 1947, and entered into force the same day, see 61 Stat. 2953.

[4] See Document 37.

most complex problems on earth. But I wish to assure you that we have been deeply concerned about the interests of Turkey and of the Turkish Cypriots and will remain so.

Finally, Mr. Prime Minister I must tell you that you have posed the gravest issues of war and peace. These are issues which go far beyond the bilateral relations between Turkey and the United States. They not only will certainly involve war between Turkey and Greece but could involve wider hostilities because of the unpredictable consequences which a unilateral intervention in Cyprus could produce. You have your responsibilities as Chief of the Government of Turkey; I also have mine as .President of the United States. I must, therefore, inform you in the deepest friendship that unless I can have your assurance that you will not take such action without further and fullest consultation I cannot accept your injunction to Ambassador Hare of secrecy and must immediately ask for emergency meetings of the NATO Council and of the United Nations Security Council.

I wish it were possible for us to have a personal discussion of this situation. Unfortunately, because of the special circumstances of our present Constitutional position, I am not able to leave the United States. If you could come here for a full discussion I would welcome it. I do feel that you and I carry a very heavy responsibility for the general peace and for the possibilities of a sane and peaceful resolution of the Cyprus problem. I ask you, therefore, to delay any decisions which you and your colleagues might have in mind until you and I have had the fullest and frankest consultation.

Sincerely, Lyndon B. Johnson"[5]

Rusk

---

[5] The letter was released by the White House in January 1966 and printed in *Middle East Journal* 20 (1966), pp. 386–393.

55.   Telegram From the Embassy in Turkey to the Department of State[1]

Ankara, June 5, 1964, 7 p.m.

1609. Deptel 1296.[2] Have just returned from presenting President's letter to Inonu who read carefully, said disagreed with certain points which he would explain later but that he agreed with final sentence to effect that GOT would delay any action on understanding there would be full and frank discussion with view reaching peaceful solution of Cyprus problem. Added would present this for Cabinet approval tonight but seemed regard their acceptance as taken for granted.

Said considered it important let public know that intervention postponed at our request and that American Government would assume active role in effort settle problem between allies, and asked my approval. I said unable give carte blanche but would be glad submit to Washington such text as GOT might propose.[3]

Further details in separate tel but gist is GOT agrees forego intervention on condition we take active interest in seeking solution.[4]

General Lemnitzer was seeing PriMin immediately after I left.[5]

Hare

---

[1] Source: Department of State, Central Files, POL 23–8 CYP. Secret; Flash. Repeated to London, Paris for USRO, Athens, and Nicosia and to the White House, OSD, CIA, and JCS.

[2] Document 54.

[3] The White House released a statement before the Turkish Government could provide suggested language. The text of the U.S. statement was transmitted in telegram 1460 to Athens, June 5. (Department of State, Central Files, POL 23–8 CYP) In telegram 1617 from Ankara, June 6, Hare reported that Erkin had unsuccessfully sought a joint follow-up statement. (Ibid.)

[4] Telegram 1616 from Ankara, June 6. (Ibid.)

[5] Lemnitzer reported on his meeting with Inonu in an unnumbered telegram to the Department of Defense, June 5. (Ibid.)

56.   Telegram From the Embassy in Cyprus to the Department of State[1]

Nicosia, June 6, 1964, 1 p.m.

1322. Ankara tel sent Dept 1609.[2] Latest Turkish invasion threat may well be climax of Cyprus crisis. Our acceptance of larger measure of responsibility for efforts find solution can be significant new element in problem. Whether our deeper involvement was precalculated objective of Turkish exercise or only way Turks could find out of impasse is not yet clear, but in either case we should seize resulting situation as opportunity to be exploited to fullest in effort achieve lasting settlement.

In planning role we are to play, I would hope Dept shares our belief it essential we keep eye on political, economic and demographic facts of life and avoid being drawn into quid pro quo with Turks which would involve our support of a Turk Cypriot solution in exchange for their agreement not to intervene.

June 5 exercise in Ankara may have been designed in part to take Inonu off hook politically and shift blame for Turkish inaction to us. In itself, this is not bad. We can accept that onus, but we must be wary of dangers of going beyond this possibly becoming involved in support of an unrealistic plan for federation or in giving some general assurance of support which could be interpreted as guaranteeing Turkish satisfaction in Cyprus.

GOT has called for us to become substantively involved. In so doing we must play it straight with GOT, pulling no punches in our analysis that the facts clearly require an essentially Greek solution, that partition or federation is anathema to 80 percent of population and therefore politically and practically infeasible, and that the prime problem will be to devise arrangements to give maximum protection to Turk Cypriot and GOT security interests. This is moment to grasp nettle and tell GOT plainly we believe security interests would best be insured by association of Cyprus with Greece—a NATO ally, a more mature and responsible state, and one whose interests are in no way served by perpetuation of difficulties with Turkey.

We can no longer remain on sidelines, expressing hope for solution satisfactory to both sides. There is no such solution. Unitary, Greek-run

---

[1] Source: Department of State, Central Files, POL 23–8 CYP. Secret. Repeated to London, Athens, Ankara, USUN, and Paris for Under Secretary Ball and USRO. Passed to the White House, JCS, OSD, and CIA. Ball visited Paris and London for meetings with President de Gaulle and senior British officials, and Geneva for a speech to the International Trade Conference June 4–7.

[2] Document 55.

state, closely associated with Greece (perhaps with defense, foreign affairs and guarantees of minority rights left in hands of GOG) would offer following palpable advantages:

1. It should be acceptable to majority of Cyprus population.

2. It would allow us at least in Security Council and elsewhere to displace solution as defender of justice on Cyprus (c.f. my letter to Jernegan), thus stemming dangerous slide to the left here.

3. It would provide best guarantee available for security both of Turk Cypriots and Turkey, bringing island within NATO sphere and removing motive for further equivocating GOC role re East and West which has so encouraged growth of Communist influence on island.

4. It should contribute to improvement of Greek-Turkish relations, as GOG would have every reason to assure Turk Cypriot rights and reestablishment law and order on Cyprus. Partition, federation or hermaphrodite London–Zurich type solution would only guarantee continuing trouble on Cyprus.

Would seem that situation resulting from most recent crisis gives opportunity for new initiative in effort end once and for all this problem so fraught with danger to US and our allies, not to mention people of Cyprus.

If Inonu accepts invitation or if UK–US consultations considered advisable, I believe situation on island such that I could be available for consultation in connection therewith.

Foregoing dictated prior to Tuomioja meeting reported following telegram, but substance that meeting only supports above thesis.[3]

Belcher

---

[3] Belcher reported on his meeting with Tuomioja in telegram 1323 from Nicosia, June 6. (Department of State, Central Files, POL 23–8 CYP)

57.   Telegram From the Embassy in Greece to the Department of State[1]

Athens, June 8, 1964, 10 p.m.

1844. 1. In absence Prime Minister in Crete I had talks with FonMin Costopoulos on Saturday and again Sunday evening and covered points mentioned in Deptels 1446, 1456 and 1464.[2] I started by saying the events were causing USG to play more active role in Cyprus matter, observing that Turks wanted this and I understood Tuomioja and Greeks also did, provided this done within framework UN. We wanted to be helpful but needed help from parties themselves—and particularly Greeks and we must work closely together in finding way out of morass. I then made entirely clear how deeply concerned we were about recent developments, and stressed once more deadly seriousness situation to Greeks as well as to Cyprus and West. I recognized that, for political reasons, Papandreou felt himself in difficult position to oppose Makarios publicly at this time, but pointed out that GOG's open support of Makarios coupled with such things as its failure publicly to protest at time of Saint Hilarion and in connection with hostages following Famagusta had left bad impression and that GOT seemed justified in assuming Makarios calling tune and Greece willingly following. It was therefore most important that something be done which would indicate an atmosphere of reasonableness on part of Greek Govt. I mentioned possibility of GOG influencing Makarios to have talks with Kucuk, delay in introducing conscription, and suspend reported importation heavy armaments.

2. Costopoulos expressed great appreciation for what USG had done. When I said this wasn't the point, he replied that Greece would like to do something to help, but Turks made it very difficult. Latest Turkish threats were justification for Makarios' worries and his actions. However, Costopoulos assured me Greeks had urged Makarios to talk with Kucuk—not under conditions set by Kucuk but just to have general discussion. Makarios had refused, saying it would serve no purpose with Kucuk and Turk Cypriots in present frame of mind.

---

[1] Source: Department of State, Central Files, POL 23–8 CYP. Secret; Priority; Limit Distribution. Repeated to Ankara, London, Nicosia, Paris for USRO, USUN, the White House, CIA, JCS and OSD.

[2] Telegram 1446 to Athens, June 5, instructed the Embassy to urge the Greek Government to relieve pressures in the region through action with the Greek Cypriots and gestures toward Turkey. (Ibid.) Telegram 1456 to Athens, June 5, instructed the Embassy to urge Papandreou to press Makarios for some concessions toward the Turkish Cypriot community in order to reduce tensions. (Ibid.) Telegram 1464, June 6, instructed the Embassy to reiterate that the United States had less leverage with Turkey after restraining it and urge that Greece take concrete actions to lower levels of tension. (Ibid.)

Costopoulos then referred to alleged heavy armaments imports and assured me that as of present time no deals had been made and the main thing Cypriots wanted was torpedo boats ("possibly three"). He believed Cypriots would stop at that and we could pass this on confidentially, but he added he could not guarantee what Makarios might do in future. He shied away from conscription issue. He then referred to an earlier conversation and said Cuba not setting up establishment in Nicosia.

3. Concerning the current Turkish threat, Costopoulos was of two minds. I believe he understands seriousness of situation, but he also harbors theories re GOT motivations which have somewhat offsetting effect. In first place, he believes—as do many Greeks—threat was timed for Senatorial elections—"it would not be first time they have done this."

But in his opinion, even more important motivation was probably related to Turks' "spoiled child" complex in which they seek to obtain concessions from USG to support GOT in return for latter's better behavior. I acknowledge that these might be factors in matter, but that GOG would be making frightful error in judgment if it underestimated Turkish feelings and deadly reality of Greece's danger. It was only President Johnson's very strong message and Inonu's statesmanship that had saved terrible catastrophe so far. I spoke of Inonou's internal problems and repeated need to find some way of preventing Turkish humiliations. I also strongly urged that GOG caution press against playing "bluff" theme it has used in past. He said he agreed with what I had said: his govt has been trying to influence Makarios along reasonable lines but there was not much it could effectively do in circumstances.

4. Costopoulos reverted to my remark about internal political considerations curtailing Papanderou's freedom of action re Cyprus. He said this was entirely true but was only part of story. More important was fact that if GOG did not go along publicly with Makarios, then game might well be lost to the Soviets who were smartly supporting nationalistic aspirations, both here and in Cyprus. Situation was becoming more and more dangerous and only choice was between "a Mediterranean Cuba and NATO" (i.e. enosis). There was no hope of handling the Communist threat through partition or federation. This would only aggravate matters and play into hands of Communists. It was much better for Turkey's security interests, as well as for Greece and Cyprus, to have Cyprus part of Greece with NATO base and with "Greek Govt monarch rather than someone like Lysarrides or worse in control." Latter was only realistic alternative to enosis.[3]

---

[3] In telegram 1845 from Athens, June 8, Labouisse reported that based on his talk with Costopoulos and others he believed that a limited possibility of a Greek-Turkish accord based on enosis and a strictly controlled Turkish base on Cyprus existed. (Ibid.)

5. I said it would be very difficult for Inonu and Turks to swallow such a proposal and pressed again for some other Greek suggestions. He acknowledged problem, but repeated there was only one sensible and effective solution in Western interests. It was useless to expect Greece to cede territory to Turkey to achieve this end. He did volunteer, however, that a population movement might be possible, although he asserted that movement of Greek population and of Patriarchate from Istanbul would cause extreme agonies for Greek people and it was possible that no govt could approve it.

6. I again asked about possibility of talks between Greeks and Turks to which Costopoulos replied that talks between Papandreou and Inonu or between him and Erkin should not be held without proper preparation. On his return from The Hague, he had suggested to Papandreou that Greek and Turk Ambassadors meet in some unspecified spot for discussions but Papandreou had turned this down at the time. I obtained impression that there was possibility of making some headway on this front and I shall continue probing.[4]

7. It came out during talk that Greeks believe that Tuomioja leaning toward Greek concept of satisfactory solution. Costopoulos had received report that USUN opposed to Tuomioja filing report of his own views with Security Council. He asked if this was USG position. I replied in the affirmative, saying that I understood Tuomioja's job that of a mediator and that if he could not find agreed solution, he should keep on trying and should not come out with a personal opinion favoring one extreme or the other; this could only serve to cause trouble at this juncture.

8. At end, Costopoulos said that Greece had been informed during day (Sunday) that Kucuk was about to assert sovereignty over certain areas of Cyprus in expectation that Turkey (and possibly Pakistan and Iran) would support his action by some sort of recognition. His intelligence was that this would take place during Inonu's absence in the States—probably in next couple of days. I said we had heard rumors about possible Kucuk action few days ago and this had given rise to some of our concern. I hoped new rumors were just old ones catching up. Costopoulos said that Greek Cypriots would have to react forcefully against Turkish Cypriots if Kucuk took such action. I strongly urged that in any such event GOG should use every possible influence to have Makarios refer matter to SC without resorting to force. He agreed and was to talk to Kyprianou about it.

Labouisse

---

[4] In telegram 1851, June 10, Labouisse reported that the Greeks were ready to begin secret Ambassadorial-level discussions with Turkey. (Ibid.)

58.   Telegram From the Embassy in the United Kingdom to the
Department of State[1]

London, June 9, 1964, 6 p.m.

6120. Deptel 7854.[2] In as much as Under Secretary Ball did not have
opportunity raise subject of reftel with British during his crowded visit
to London, Jernegan, Sisco and Eilts raised it today with Dodson (Counselor, Central Dept) and Wood of FonOff. We stressed that while appre-
ciating great difficulties under which British soldiers are laboring in
Cyprus, US is convinced that British element in UNPKF is key to success
of peacekeeping effort. Any suggestion therefore of reduction of size
British component creates greatest misgivings in US. We believe 7,000
man UNPKF needed to carry out mission and are concerned that UNPKF
troop strength is slipping below this minimum level.

Dodson said HMG is operating on premise that UNPKF is essential
to peace of Eastern Mediterranean and acknowledged that British element is major factor therein. Same time HMG has been concerned about
treatment meted out to British troops by Cypriots and at suggestion that
Makarios may attempt blackball further British military participation in
UNPKF. In this connection, he cited Georgatizis statement following
arrest of RAF Airman Marley that latter's activities called into question
further utility of British element in UNPKF, and more recent comment of
Kyprianou to UK HICOM that GOC has not yet decided whether British
should remain in UNPKF. Dodson pointed out HMG would not wish
public rebuff by GOC re British participation.

Dodson said British element is now some 1800 strong. He claimed
reduction of British element has in past been geared into availability
other units from elsewhere. He said HMG has now taken policy decision
that it is willing to continue in UNPKF, but for tactical reasons connected
with its unwillingness incur GOC rebuff, has told SYG continuation UK
participation depends entirely on him. By playing reluctant, HMG
believes SYG more likely make clear importance British element to success of UNPKF. Re numbers, Dodson claimed Gyani came up with
suggestion only 1200 British troops needed, e.g. one infantry battalion,
two armored scout car squadrons and supporting troops. This estimate
based on Gyani's apparent belief additional Irish or Danish troops will
become available. HMG now awaiting word from SYG re his wishes on
British participation.

---

[1] Source: Department of State, Central Files, POL 23–8 CYP. Secret. Repeated to Nicosia, Athens, Ankara, USUN, and Geneva for Ball.

[2] Telegram 7854 to London, May 29, instructed the Ambassador to stress U.S. concern
regarding plans for British troop reductions in Cyprus. (Ibid.)

We stressed to Dodson that Dept has no information to suggest GOC might seek to blackball British participation. We reiterated great importance USG attaches to such British participation. We recalled two British troop reductions had taken place without our being consulted. We emphasized our strong hope that before any further reductions are decided upon, HMG consult with us. We also emphasized any further British reductions should be phased into availability other units and noted our impression SYG not likely obtain any substantial increase in other national contingents.

Dodson claimed British troop reductions arranged by UK military officer (Bailey) working with Rikhye in New York and seemed to assume matter should have been discussed with us there. He took note our point, however, and we are hopeful British now appreciate more fully great importance we attach to matter and will in future keep in closer touch with us on this one.

Bruce

---

59.   Telephone Conversation Between President Johnson and Secretary of State Rusk[1]

Washington, June 9, 1964, 6:30 p.m.

Operator: Hello.

O: Secretary Rusk, please.

O: Yes, who's calling?

O: The President.

O: Thank you.

MF: Miss Fehmer.

O: Miss Fehmer, Secretary Rusk for the President.

MF: Thank you.

LBJ: Get me Secretary Rusk.

MF: He's on the phone.

LBJ: Hello? Mr. Secretary?

DR: Hello?

---

[1] Source: Johnson Library, Recordings and Transcripts, Recording of a Telephone Conversation Between President Johnson and Secretary Rusk, June 9, 1964, 6:30 p.m., Tape 64.31, Side A, PNO 2 and 3. No classification marking. This transcript was prepared by the Office of the Historian specifically for this volume.

LBJ: How'd you get along?

DR: Alright with Fulbright, Hickenlooper, and Dirksen.[2] I was not able to get a hold of Halleck, who is out of town, and Bill Bundy was up with the House Foreign Affairs Committee. And I will check with them. I haven't been able to reach them this afternoon.

LBJ: Alright.

DR: But, uh, but the others were alright. They had no problem.

LBJ: Uh-huh, alright, now—

DR: Now, I've got a call in for George Ball. Mr. President, I think the problem here is that we need to get him back to be sure that we are all on the same track here and to see where we are going. That's my concern about that. If he goes to Athens at this point, it could stimulate a good deal of excitement without putting one foot forward. I don't think Ball is in a position yet to begin to move toward a solution to this thing. And, uh, we, our talks in London have not produced, ah enough agreement between us and the British about how we proceed here.[3] I just think that since he now is not planning to stop off in London but he was planning to come right on back, that we've got to let him do it even though by the weekend we might want to send him out to the area.

LBJ: Alright. Now what's the, if you can't produce it while he is over there, how is he going to produce it here?

DR: Well, I think that . . .

LBJ: With the British?

DR: I think, the point is that we—that you and he and I and our people working on this should come to a final conclusion on what we ought to shoot for. And there is not a conclusion on that at the moment, and the conclusion that they have been talking about in London is something that will almost guarantee the Turks would intervene and this is what concerns me.

LBJ: Uh-huh.

DR: We're not giving the Turks enough of a break here in the kind of solution that they have been talking about—in London.

LBJ: Well, is it necessary for him to get back here to do that? Is he an integral part of our—?

DR: Oh, I think that it would be extremely helpful to me because he is our most experienced man on this problem.

LBJ: Uh-huh.

DR: And he could take a real leadership on it.

---

[2] According to Rusk's Appointment Book, he met at 4:45 p.m. with the three Senators at the New Senate Office Building. (Ibid.) There was no indication of the topic of the meeting.

[3] See Document 58.

LBJ: I think it's a lot bigger problem to send him after he gets back over there than let him go while he's there, don't you?

DR: Uh-huh, well—

LBJ: It looks like it's just a routine thing, if he's there now. He's been touring all over the continent.[4] But ah—

DR: There's another piece of information on this. The Greek Cypriot Prime Minister[5] has just arrived in New York to ask for a Security Council meeting on this subject, so that is likely to take the play away from other matters here for a brief time.

LBJ: Uh-huh. Well, is that good?

DR: Ah, I think so, sir. I—

LBJ: Looks like we need some time to get some solutions, don't we?

DR: I think we do need some time here. This is one of the most—

LBJ: I'll defer to your judgment. If I were Secretary of State, I'd send him to Greece and say, "Now, Mr. Prime Minister, here is what happened. We were notified that they were going in and invade that night. We prevailed on them not to do it. We don't think that things are going as they ought to there and we are very concerned about what's going to happen so we—our people are concerned. And we appeal to you to exercise whatever influence you've got with Makarios to try to let the United Nations work this thing out for you instead of shooting at them and arresting them and capturing them and running off with them. And we just think that if you don't take some leadership here and move in, as we had to move in with Turkey, that this is going to be a very bloody bath." And now I don't know what other specific proposals other than urging him to do that, but it seems to me, then that would give us something to say to the Turks that we've made an appeal to them and personally sent our man. Now if you think that he ought to come back before he does that, why—

DR: I think that if you said that to the Greek Ambassador when he brings you that message,[6] that would be, that would have the greatest weight and influence in Athens. But let me talk to George Ball and get his judgment on this point.

LBJ: Alright. Ok. That's good. And I don't think, though, that Inonu is going to think that's much—for me to talk to this little ambassador here.

DR: Uh-huh.

LBJ: I think that if he thinks that this man has crossed the waters and gone to Athens and put the heat on them just like we put the heat on the

---

[4] See footnote 1, Document 56.
[5] Foreign Minister Kyprianou.
[6] See Document 62.

Turks, that he'll think we are sincere and genuine and we're really working at it and not going to sleep on it.

DR: Yes. Now there is a press report out of Ankara that Inonu is replying and conditionally accepting your invitation.

LBJ: Uh-huh.

DR: I don't know what that kind of press leak means, but if he were to come here in the next few days, I think that would be an important step.

LBJ: Well, I look at it the other way. I think that the last thing we want him to do is let me be the peacemaker and later wind up on my lap. I think we ought to carry it right to Ankara and Athens. Now that's my country-boy approach to it.

DR: Alright.

LBJ: And I think that we got in trouble the other night when we suggested to him that if he—I couldn't come over there, but I'd be glad to see him but we were absolutely desperate and I let that go.[7]

DR: Right.

LBJ: But when I got home and thought about it a little bit, I thought, "Now what in the hell is Lyndon Johnson doing inviting this big mess right in his lap?" Bad enough for George Ball to go to them and see him without the President calling him over here. Because I have no solution. I can't propose anything. He'll come over here looking for heaven and he'll find hell.

DR: Well, his message—if it's a conditional message—will probably have that kind of thing in it and would be the basis for deferring until we get some further feeling out of it.

LBJ: Well, my feeling is—and I don't want to be arbitrary and I won't be a bit disappointed if he comes on—but I think you ought to let him know—

DR: Yeah.

LBJ: —that I think that, in the light of this strong message I sent to the Turks—

DR: Right.

LBJ: —that I need to follow through with the Greeks, and the easiest and simplest and least-noticed way to do it is while he's there to spend two hours doing it.

DR: Right.

LBJ: Then I wouldn't hesitate the slightest to say to them, "Now, we're going on and appeal to the Turks to hold this thing in abeyance," and he can go tell the Turks what he'd done—

---

[7] See Document 54.

DR: Uh-huh.

LBJ: —and although you wouldn't have any final solution or division, you would have at least kept faith and made an effort and followed through on what I told them in this wire instead of saying we went off and went to sleep.

DR: Right. Well, let me talk to George and see.[8]

LBJ: Ok.

DR: Thank you.

LBJ: Bye.

---

[8] No record of this conversation was found.

---

60.   Letter From Prime Minister Papandreou to President Johnson[1]

Athens, June 9, 1964.

Dear Mr. President,

The Honorable Henry Labouisse, Ambassador of the United States in Athens has imparted to Mr. S. Costopoulos, the Greek Minister of Foreign Affairs, the concern of the American Government in view of information about an imminent Turkish landing in Cyprus. He also informed Mr. Costopoulos of the action taken by the American Government with the Government of Turkey, in order to avert the landing.

The Greek Government wishes to express its warm thanks for this appropriate and wise initiative of the President of the United States, which agrees with the tradition of the American Nation as well as with the mission of the United States as leader of the Free World.

We do not know if the above step has been decisively effective. Information is reaching us that Turkey persists in the policy of landing and is preparing for it; and that, in order to justify the landing, she is staging the proclamation, by the very small Turkish minority of Cyprus, of a federative or an independent State.[2]

---

[1] Source: Department of State, Central Files, POL 23–8 CYP. No classification marking. The source text is a copy of the letter given to Secretary Rusk by the Greek Embassy on June 9; it is typed on Greek Embassy stationery. Rusk passed it to the President at lunch the same day. Ambassador Matsas formally presented the original of the letter to President Johnson at a June 11 meeting; see Document 62.

[2] In telegram 1848 from Athens, June 9, 5 p.m., the Embassy reported that a "revived atmosphere of crisis gripped Athens" as a result of renewed reports of Turkish preparations for an invasion of Cyprus. (Department of State, Central Files, POL 23–8 CYP)

The Greek Government has repeatedly declared and reasserts today that its policy is peace; but, in case of aggression, it will be defense.

The Greek Government most assuredly regards a Turkish landing in Cyprus as an aggression; because the resolution of the Security Council of the 4th of March would thus be violated and also because such an action aims at the strangulation of the rights of the great Greek majority of the island.

This will be one of the consequences of an eventual Turkish landing: a Greek-Turkish conflict and the dissolution of the Southeastern flank of NATO. But this will not be the only consequence. Communism will become omnipotent within the island of Cyprus; and, we unfortunately fear, within Greece, where, with our policies, we have reduced it to 12%. Besides, it is inevitable and human that the Greeks of Cyprus, threatened by a Turkish invasion tolorated by the Allies, should seek help wherever they can find it. And it is known, under the present circumstance, whence this help will be offered. An objective assessment of the future, unfortunately leads to the certain forecast that, under these conditions, Cyprus will end into another Cuba and that the Greek Government will no longer be in a position to exercise any restraining influence.

We feel that a critical hour has struck and we regard it our duty to define responsibilities before the Greek nation, before the Free World to which we belong, as well as before History. And this is the meaning of the present message.

Yours sincerely,

George A. Papandreou[3]

---

[3] Printed from a copy that bears this typed signature.

61.   Telegram From the Embassy in Cyprus to the Department of State[1]

Nicosia, June 10, 1964, 1 p.m.

1347. Embtel 1346.[2] Greek and Turkish Cypriots look on forthcoming SC meeting on Cyprus as crucial test of US attitudes, influence and abilities. After events of June 5, all parties consider we are now deeply involved and look for us to take positive position in New York. It is common belief our policy on Cyprus has changed, but SC will be regarded as acid test of this belief.

Reading the political temper in Cyprus, we believe either emergency or scheduled SC meeting may prove major watershed in Greek Cypriot attitudes. As we have reported with increasing frequency, Communists have been going all out to enmesh Greek Cypriots by espousing principles of freedom and democracy, offering assistance and promising support. Having a favorably conditioned audience, the Communists have up to this point made extensive progress with most elements of Greek Cypriot society. Their accomplishments have been impressive and give cause for serious concern, but thus far we estimate them to be generally shallow in nature. The fickle, politically immature Greek Cypriots could quickly change their view of their "real friends", if given the occasion.

The show down which now appears to be at hand, would threaten to give Communist accomplishments in Cyprus a deeper, more lasting character where permanent damage might be done to the orientation of the Greek Cypriot leadership as well as many other elements of the society.

Given this ticklish situation, the problem for the US will be how to handle itself on policy without alienating the Greek Cypriots and giving the Soviets the opening for which they hope. In this circumstance perhaps it would be best to let troop contributing countries carry the ball on sensitive terms of reference issue (assuming discussion this issue cannot be avoided) where US involvement in substance would probably range us among opponents of GOC.

There is, however, one point where US might be able to make major productive contribution to work of SC, a contribution which relates to principal concern of Greek Cypriots about threat of Turkish military

---

[1] Source: Department of State, Central Files, POL 23–8 CYP. Secret. Repeated to Ankara, Athens, London, Paris for USRO, the White House, JCS, CIA, and OSD.

[2] Telegram 1346 from Nicosia, June 10, reported the observations of the Syrian Ambassador on the U.S. position following President Johnson's actions to prevent an invasion of Cyprus. (Ibid.)

intervention. If US could produce as its contribution a Turkish commitment not to intervene in Cyprus for the duration of UN involvement, this would be major accomplishment which should go far toward re-establishing our damaged position here.

Belcher

---

62.   Memorandum of Conversation[1]

Washington, June 11, 1964.

SUBJECT

President's Meeting with Greek Ambassador Matsas

PARTICIPANTS

The President
His Excellency Alexander Matsas, Ambassador of Greece
Phillips Talbot, Assistant Secretary for Near Eastern and South Asian Affairs
Robert W. Komer, The White House

After the President greeted Ambassador Matsas cordially, the Ambassador said he understood that the President had already taken action on the letter now being formally delivered. However, Matsas had no report as yet on the Ball conversation in Athens.[2] The President then carefully read Prime Minister Papandreou's letter.[3]

The President made clear our position on the Cyprus crisis. Outside powers could not solve it. The Greeks and Turks must settle it themselves. He believed the Prime Minister of Greece should get together with Prime Minister Inonu, or have some representative talk with the Turks. We had told Turkey that there could not be war but we didn't know how long this would stick. Moreover, we were "disappointed" that the Greek Government had not taken the initiative to meet and talk with the Turks. It was much more dangerous not to get together than to

---

[1] Source: Department of State, Ball Papers: Lot 74 D 272, Memcons Other Than Visits. Secret; Limited Distribution. Drafted by Talbot and Komer and approved in the White House on June 15.
[2] See Document 64.
[3] Document 60.

get together. As we saw it, there were two requirements for a solution: (a) whatever was done must be permanent; (b) the solution could not be humiliating to either side. It was much more dangerous not to have a solution. War could help nobody. Therefore, the President continued, he had told Ball to urge Papandreou to take the initiative in getting together somehow with the Turks. The US people were becoming quite worried over the Cyprus problem; they couldn't understand why "two of our close allies were growling at each other." As for Makarios, he didn't seem to care. He thought he had the Greeks supporting him. Meanwhile, the Soviets were meddling and fully expected to win in the end. So we thought the Greeks must show some statesmanship and get moving toward agreement.

The President returned to the theme of American public attitudes. Some Americans were already wondering if they should go to Europe and to the Eastern Mediterranean now. There was no reason why Turkey and Greece couldn't agree to talk about their problem. It would be dangerous if they did not. To repeat, this solution should be permanent and not humiliating to either side. We had gone to the aid of Greece and Turkey in the Truman Doctrine. We had helped through the years, and wanted to help now. But Greece and Turkey must grasp the problem. We had stopped the Turks from moving, but we couldn't drop the matter there. We wanted to see them at the conference table. Greece should take the initiative.

The Ambassador asked what response his government had given to Ball. The President replied that they seemed to be considering our démarche. But he urged a Greek initiative. Action was what was needed.

Matsas explained that the chief need as his government saw it was to stop the constant threats of invasion. The President interrupted him, saying we had stopped it already but couldn't stop it always. We had acted vigorously when trouble was imminent, but we might not be able to stop the Turks again.

Ambassador Matsas agreed there were still dangers ahead. His government had disturbing reports in the last day or so, including reported overflights of Rhodes. The President replied, "If I can't get you to talk, I can't keep the Turks from moving."

Matsas again sought to explain the Greek position. He reported that the whole trouble lay in the continuing Turkish threat to invade Cyprus. The President interjected: "Or in your support of what Makarios is doing—or in arms imports." The Ambassador replied that otherwise Makarios would have felt isolated. There were two dangers: The Greek-Turkish tensions and the risk of Makarios drifting to "the other side." Both are the consequence of the Turkish threats. If only the US could secure Turkish agreement not to invade, then tensions would be reduced and there would be no need for arms imports to Cyprus, etc. etc. The

President emphasized that we could not get the threat called off until the Greeks had agreed to talk. This called for statesmanship. Papandreou was a statesman. Matsas should tell his Prime Minister to call Inonu today and arrange a meeting. We had done everything we could. Our troubles around the world these days were not our own; our troubles turned out to be mostly disputes between our allies. Certainly Greece and Turkey would not be justified in destroying NATO over this issue.

Matsas asked if the President thought it impossible to get the Turks not to invade. The President said: "Nothing is impossible if people will act." But Papandreou must act in this case if we were to have peace and not war. Matsas tried to point out again that Turkish agreement not to invade was the key to the situation. The President said bluntly that we could not get the Turks to turn off until there was some basis on which to argue with them. He noted that the Greek Government was apparently willing to have secret talks (this surprised Matsas who was obviously unaware of this. So Mr. Komer confirmed that the Foreign Minister had said secret talks were possible). Matsas then asked whether any US proposals had been mentioned by Ball. The President said that we were not going to make proposals ourselves at this point. Any US proposals would be seized upon by one side or the other and used to blame us. We want the Greeks and Turks to start making proposals to each other. This should be a matter between the two of them. Matsas added: "And the Cypriots." Matsas said that "talks are difficult under the threat of invasion." The President immediately came back: "Of course they're difficult. But it's more difficult to talk after an invasion. Get together and work something out. If not, all NATO will become involved."

The Ambassador contended that the Greeks from the beginning had sought to keep the dispute damped down and avoid actions which increased the threat of hostilities. He gave examples of proposals advanced to the British, cooperating with the UN, etc. In contrast, he said, the Turks have done everything to spread the dispute, as by their treatment of the Greeks in Istanbul. The President said he thought Papandreou should appoint someone and talk with Inonu immediately. Talk was far better than the way of the jungle. Matsas attempted to return to the theme of calling the Turks off. The President interrupted him again saying: "I have only a temporary hold-off. What we want is for your Prime Minister to sit down with the Turkish Prime Minister and work out an agreement. Our people are getting terribly worried." Matsas said that temporary cessation of the invasion threat won't solve the problem: it won't keep Makarios from building up arms supplies. The President responded that nothing would. The President said: "The Turks are the only ones I have gotten to do anything till now. All I want is for the Greek Prime Minister to sit down and talk. This is not so difficult." He pointed out that by just this means he had gotten the railroad strike settled in ten days. But Greece always wants Turkey to do something to ease tensions and Turkey always wants Greece to do something. What was the Greek program for settling the crisis?

Matsas described the desire for a fully independent state with self-determination and guarantees of minority rights. He noted this was a "compromise" position (i.e. not enosis). He asked what the President thought of this approach. The President said that we couldn't negotiate for the Turks. All we wanted was for Greece to get together with them. It wasn't up to us to say what agreement should be reached. "We stopped an invasion the other night. Now we want a conference. Let's start discussing this thing." He again mentioned the problem of American tourists going to the threatened area. It was easier to talk than to fight. The President told the Ambassador: "You will only be admired for saying 'let's talk'." It was a matter of the Biblical injunction, "Come let us reason together." Matsas said he would so report to his government.

The President then changed tactics and pointed out the strong American affection for Greece. The President himself would like to travel there again soon with his family. But there could not be a war. We had turned off the Turks. Now we want talks. As Speaker Rayburn had said, "It's always better to talk than fight." Matsas tried once more to press the theme that the US or the UN Security Council should get the Turks to call off their invasion threats. The President said, "Let's see what you can do for us and we will see what we can do for you." Matsas sought to inquire whether this meant the President would get Turkey to agree permanently not to invade. The President carefully avoided any such commitment. He said: "I made a positive request of the Turks and they said that even though they didn't agree they would comply. I now make a positive request to you to talk. If you comply, we will then make some suggestions to the Turks. That's better than fighting." The President did not tell him what these suggestions would be, but promised that if Papandreou would try to bring Greece and Turkey together, we would help all we could to move things along to an agreement. Otherwise we'd have a disaster.

The President asked Matsas to tell his Prime Minister of the President's deep sense of friendship for him and for Greece. The President was counting heavily on Papandreou. We did not want the US people to get the idea that Makarios was "using" the Greeks. "Greece must avoid at all costs humiliating its ally Turkey. Even in the Cuban missile crisis, we always left the enemy a way out. With an ally it was even more important to leave a way out."

The President observed that negotiating with Makarios was impossible. Makarios wasn't interested in the security of the West. But Greece, Turkey, and the US were. Matsas interjected that Greece could not negotiate without Makarios. The President indicated understanding that the

Cypriots would have to be consulted at some point but the important thing was Greek-Turkish agreement. Greece talked about its responsibilities to the Greek Cypriots. Didn't the Greeks see that the fate of 100,000 Turkish Cypriots was a matter of honor for Inonu too?

Ambassador Matsas assured the President that he would promptly inform his Government.

63.   Telegram From the Mission to the United Nations to the Department of State[1]

New York, June 11, 1964, 8 p.m.

4455. SC—Cyprus. Cypriot FonMin Kyprianou called with PermRep Rossides on Stevenson June 11. Fol are highlights:

1. Kyprianou stressed that principal reason he decided for time being not call urgent SC mtg was his awareness Pres Johnson's efforts with GOT which he did not wish upset as he hopeful it would produce something. Stevenson emphasized seriousness present situation stressing GOT concern with Cypriot arms imports, conscription, disappearance hostages, ties with SovBloc. Situation deteriorating and there need work actively for solution agreeable to all parties before situation deteriorates further. Said he hoped GOC had given thought to this as obvious that in any solution no party will get everything it wants.

2. Kyprianou responding to Stevenson mention of GOC moves cited provocative GOT acts (including use UK soldiers for smuggling) leading to GOC arms and conscription decisions and defended these as right and duty of GOC. Stevenson said situation difficult to control. Was worse than in March and GOC had not exercised restraint he had hoped, or avoided provocations as he hoped. Kyprianou stressed GOC had avoided number of moves and Rossides provided chapter and verse on Turk contingent, "rebels" at Hilarion, obstruction on Kyrenia Road.

3. Yost stressed need create feeling of confidence among Turk Cypriots. Kyprianou replied "If GOT wants them have confidence they'll have it. Their unease ordered by Ankara. Everything calm where GOT not stirring them up." Turk Cypriot discontent is manufactured as result long-

---

[1] Source: Department of State, Central Files, POL 23–8 CYP. Confidential. Repeated to Nicosia, London, Athens, Ankara, and Paris for USRO.

standing GOT partition plan of which GOC amassing more and more evidence. Denied arms imports and conscription designed have any effect on Turk Cypriots stating they reaction to: (1) invasion threats; (2) need to discipline Greek Cypriot forces. In response Stevenson question, Kyprianou said regular GOC army would disarm irregular Greek Cypriots.

4. Stevenson again stressed seriousness of situation mentioning GOT fear of new "Cuba." Kyprianou said this new idea but Rossides emphasized Greek Cypriot Communists few and without arms and nationalists in control. Nationalists got main outside support from Sov-Bloc as result Western lack of sympathy.

5. Stevenson asked Kyprianou state of negots with Sovs and Czechs on arms. Kyprianou, hesitating somewhat, denied there were such negots. Rossides noted GOC would abandon arms acquisition if SC guaranteed territorial integrity. Kyprianou defended acquisition of arms "from US or anywhere," not necessarily from Sovs and Czechs.

6. In reply Stevenson query on SC, Kyprianou said 1) not abandon idea urgent mtg; 2) planned in regular mtg raise question Turk threat, exit of Turk contingent along with Greek.

7. Yost stressed GOT feeling that they have been pushed back steadily from Zurich agreements and cannot tolerate this, particularly in view of method by which this done. Kyprianou noted initial method was negots.

8. Stevenson emphasized US effectiveness in restraining GOT diminishing because of GOC moves, urged Kyprianou "bend over backwards avoid provocations", saying would be wise not take any actions which would exacerbate Turk feelings and plan quiet SC mtg instead to extend UNFICYP on basis SYG report and then might be possible move forward toward solution. Kyprianou countered asking how fact recent GOT preparations can be hidden and mentioned expanding SC mandate to include UN guarantee against attack. Stevenson remarked this unlikely.

9. Referring ideas in press for population exchange, Kyprianou stressed Turk Cypriots wanted return to villages but cannot because of Turk Cypriot terrorists' threats. With choice, only 20 per cent would leave Cyprus, he said. Yost suggested offering reassurances in SC to Turk Cypriots to improve atmosphere but Kyprianou responded that this would be admitting GOT threats justified.

10. Referring again GOT threats, Kyprianou said "We not importing planes and tanks to fight Turk Cypriots." Went on describe Mansoura as center smuggling of Turk arms and men which GOC cannot and UN does not stop, implying this would be exposed in SC and would have been publicly described previously except for bearing it has on trial UK airman.

11. Rossides called for "bold move"—dismantling all fortifications by both sides leaving security to UNFICYP.

12. On problem hostages, Kyprianou said there had been regrettable incidents but not as many as charged. Claimed many on Turk list solely in Ankara or hidden in villages. Claimed Kutchuk had not deplored hostage taking as Makarios had and had no accounting for 39 Greek hostages.

13. Stevenson suggested further talk prior SC mtg. Again stressed US efforts with GOT. Urged avoiding clamorous SC mtg in order move on to next step.

Comment: Fol mtg, MisOff encountered Asiroglu (Turkey), informed him that Kyprianou testing idea of calling for withdrawal Turk contingent, SC guarantee for Cyprus but that Stevenson had argued strongly against it. Expressed hope Kyprianou would find similar discouragement elsewhere. Asiroglu stated he confident in Norway, UK, perhaps France. MisOff suggested he talk to others particularly Bernardes, prior his departure for consultation. MisOff stressed Stevenson urging non-polemic mtg. Asiroglu had earlier told MisOff GOT not now planning bring Turk Cypriot leaders to New York but would do so if solution warranted it.

Barring new developments, present expectation SC finish apartheid June 17 and take up Cyprus June 17 or 18 on basis SYG report. SYG had not yet called for mtg on financial contributions presumably because Comptroller still having difficulties figuring up estimates for present and future periods as UK and Swedish bills coming in and being argued.[2]

Stevenson

---

[2] In telegram 4470 from USUN, June 12, the Mission added that Kyprianou also argued that enosis would provide Turkey with the best guarantee about future Cypriot political orientation to the West. (Ibid.)

64.   Memorandum From the Under Secretary of State (Ball) to President Johnson[1]

Washington, June 11, 1964.

SUBJECT

The Cyprus Problem

My conversations in Athens and Ankara[2] have led me to reappraise the play of forces in the Cyprus problem and to modify my thinking as to where we should go from here.

Athens

The significant impressions I gained in Athens are the following:

1.   For the first time the Greek Government is scared—scared at the reality of the danger of a Greek-Turkish war and at the progressive extension of Communist control in Cyprus.

2.   The GOG is fed up with Makarios. Papandreou wants to deal him out of any settlement talks. (This is a marked change from a few months ago when the GOG was insisting that Cyprus could not be discussed without Makarios participating.)

3.   The GOG is now pleading for a strong American intervention in the search for a settlement. (This again contrasts sharply with its earlier attitude when it supported Makarios' efforts to exclude us from a serious role in the Cyprus situation.)

There were strong indications that Papandreou would like to have the USG force a settlement on the GOG that it could accept only with the excuse of outside pressure.

Ankara

On the Turkish side, Inonu is doing everything possible to maneuver us into taking responsibility for bringing about a settlement. The Turks are clearly frightened of the Cyprus situation. They are perplexed and sad. They also want us to force a settlement on them—provided adequate face-saving aspects can be devised.

Washington

Under these circumstances we are now in position for the first time to bring the Cyprus matter to a conclusion if we are prepared to invest time, energy and prestige. The alternatives are dismal.

---

[1] Source: Johnson Library, National Security File, Country File, Cyprus, Vol. 7. Secret.
[2] Ball visited Athens and Ankara June 10–11. Documentation on the visits is in Department of State, Central File POL 23–8 CYP. Ball's account of the trip is in *The Past Has Another Pattern*, pp. 352–355.

The UN is totally unable to make even a beginning on a solution. Tuomioja has flopped around for three months and has achieved nothing whatever except to discredit himself with the Greek and Turkish Governments. This is not altogether his fault since the UN holds no cards in this game. Moreover, it is under the disability of having to genuflect to the Makarios Government. But Tuomioja quite clearly has operated on the wrong assumption—that the Cyprus problem was an affair between the two communities on the Island and not an argument between Greece and Turkey. His efforts to work out a solution from the vantage point of Nicosia were doomed to failure. It would have made quite as much sense for a mediator to try to solve the Kashmir problem by sitting for three months in Kashmir.

U Thant knows that the UN cannot succeed in settling this question. Tuomioja is sick of it and wants out. I think it altogether likely that we could get their tacit acquiescence to a vigorous USG initiative.

Quite obviously Papandreou needs a far greater shock than I was able to give him Wednesday night but I made a start. We need to lay on a crash effort to bring the GOG up short. But the GOG is a hard nut to crack and we are far from being home with this one.

Even so there are indications that Papandreou is ready to start low-level conversations with the GOT. Certainly the GOT is dying for a chance to start talking with the Greeks. But it won't occur without us. Both Papandreou and Inonu indicated quite clearly to me that they envisaged a successful negotiation only under active USG tutelage. I am convinced that a meeting between representatives of the two Governments, without the active presence of the USG, would be likely to lead only to a deepening crystallization of positions. Certainly this was the result when Sandys tried it out in London last January.

Recommendation

I think therefore, that the central thrust of our effort should be directed at bringing representatives of the two Governments together with a strong USG representative as a catalyst—under quiet conditions. The pattern, in other words, would not be unlike that which we followed successfully in disposing of the West New Guinea problem.[3]

I doubt that the United States should try to put forward any plan for settlement. Certainly it should not do so at the outset of negotiations. The Greek and Turkish Governments are now latched on to enosis and double enosis respectively. There should be room for bargaining under these circumstances. In fact, Erkin made it clear that there was—so far as the GOT was concerned.

---

[3] Reference is to Ellsworth Bunker's role in the 1962 Netherlands-Indonesian talks regarding West New Guinea.

I would suggest, as one possibility, that we think of trying to arrange a meeting at some quiet, neutral spot such as the Villa Bellagio on Lake Como where representatives of the two Governments—perhaps at the Ambassadorial level—would be brought together with a respected but hard-boiled American, such as Dean Acheson, who knows the score and is not afraid to use American pressure.

Every effort should be made to keep this meeting secret, although we should quietly tell the British and perhaps U Thant what we were doing. Given the present state of Greek feelings, I think it possible that Papandreou could be persuaded to arrange this without letting the word pass to Makarios.

As a condition to our undertaking this, we should exact from the two Governments a firm commitment to try to hold still the two communities on the Island pending the outcome.

I think we must put this show on the road right away. Time is definitely not running on our side. We can get Turkish approval when Inonu comes to Washington. Meanwhile we should give thought to whether Papandreou might not be invited to pay us a visit.[4]

George W. Ball

---

[4] In telegram 1513 to Athens, June 13, the Department of State instructed Labouisse to sound out Papandreou about a visit to Washington. (Department of State, Central Files, POL 7 GREECE) A letter of invitation was transmitted in telegram 1513 to Athens, June 13. (Ibid.) The letter was delivered on June 14.

---

65.   Memorandum of Conversation[1]

Washington, June 12, 1964, 11:45 a.m.

SUBJECT

US–UK Approach to UN Secretary General Regarding Cyprus

PARTICIPANTS

His Excellency the Right Honorable The Lord Harlech, British Embassy
Mr. Patrick R.H. Wright, First Secretary, British Embassy
Under Secretary George W. Ball
Assistant Secretary Harlan Cleveland (IO)
Mr. George Springsteen (U)
Deputy Assistant Secretary John D. Jernegan (NEA)

---

[1] Source: Department of State, Central Files, POL 23–8 CYP. Secret; Exdis; TUG. Drafted by Jernegan.

Mr. Ball explained to the Ambassador our revised view on double enosis, saying that we now thought it should be put forward to the Greeks and Turks as a serious basis for discussion (rather than dismissing it too quickly from consideration, as had been implied during the discussions in London June 8).[2] He also explained that he did not think it would be well to have the mediator make the proposals of enosis and double enosis to the parties.

We were giving serious thought to doing some "arm twisting" with the Greeks and Turks to induce them to negotiate realistically for a settlement. Prime Minister Inonu was probably coming to Washington and we planned to invite Prime Minister Papandreou as well. The President would bear down on both of them. Our tentative plan of action after that would be to get Greek and Turkish representatives together with an American representative as a third party. This meeting, which should be kept absolutely secret, would have as its object to hammer out an agreement which the mediator could then pick up and work on. We thought this plan had a chance of success because Mr. Ball had found during his most recent visit to Athens and Ankara that both Papandreou and Inonu had a changed attitude and wanted the United States to take an active direct role in bringing about a settlement.

We and the British should, therefore, tell U Thant and the mediator that we were going to make a real effort to get the problem settled, as it must be, between Athens and Ankara. We would not ask U Thant and the mediator to propose any bases for solutions to the Greeks and Turks (as had been contemplated in the papers worked out in London). We would just let Tuomioja keep on doing what he is doing now, for the time being.

Lord Harlech said he would tell London we thought it would not be helpful for the mediator to take any initiative.

It was agreed that the Department would prepare a new draft of proposed instructions to Ambassadors Stevenson and Dean in New York, and send a copy urgently to Lord Harlech for transmission to London.[3]

---

[2] Rusk's conclusion that "hard bargaining" might result in "enosis plus territorial and other compensation to Turkey," was reported in Unsec 32 to Geneva, June 9. (Ibid.)

[3] The instructions embodying Ball's comments were sent to the Embassy in London in telegram 8231, June 12. (Ibid.) Telegram 8250 to London, June 12, reported that Lord Harlech had informed the Department of State that the British Government could not take immediate action on the U.S. proposals because many senior Cabinet officials were away from London. (Ibid.)

66.   Telegram From the Embassy in Cyprus to the Department of State[1]

Nicosia, June 12, 1964, 3 p.m.

1357. Athens 1845 to Dept.[2] We assume comments desired are our views on feasibility of new approach to Cyprus problem in form of secret bilateral negotiations between Greece and Turkey with objective of agreement on union of Cyprus with Greece compensated by some mix of following elements: minor Greek territorial concession to Turkey, emigration of Greek minority from Turkey (with assisted voluntary emigration of Turkish Cypriots to Turkey?), transfer of Patriarchate from Istanbul, and Turkish military base on Cyprus.

We not only concur that it would be useful explore this possibility but also believe satisfactory settlement can only be achieved along these lines.

At same time we wish point out that, while Turkish Cypriots have no alternative to accepting whatever deal Turkey may make, Greek Cypriots have greater independence from Greece. Despite their protestations about Panhellenism, it might take considerable persuasion to win Greek Cypriot acceptance of some elements of deal along lines suggested above.

While there has been marked intensification of enosis agitation in recent months, two very significant elements of Greek Cypriot community are at best lukewarm and at worst hostile toward it. Makarios and GOC officials obviously have vested interest of being large fish in small puddle. A strong and apparently growing Communist movement would obviously resist submersion and probable suppression in Greece. Coalition of these two elements would be quite likely insist in first instance on "full sovereignty", "self determination", "neutrality rather than NATO" as dodges for avoiding enosis. For this reason we believe that, if enosis is agreed on as basis for solution, every effort must be made bring it about as integral part of immediate settlement rather than agreeing on "full independence" or "self-determination" on understanding Cyprus state will wither away and enosis will inevitably occur.

We would not anticipate any serious Greek Cypriot opposition (though there would probably be a lot of noisy protest) about Greek territorial cessions elsewhere or about population movements. Greek Cyp-

---

[1] Source: Department of State, Central Files, POL 23–8 CYP. Secret; Limdis. Repeated to Ankara, Athens, London, Paris, USUN, OSD, CIA, JCS, and the White House.

[2] Telegram 1845, June 8, reported that Greece remained firm on its ultimate objective of enosis but recognized the need for some limited concessions to Turkey and counted on the United States to achieve a mediated settlement. (Ibid.)

riot attitude is wholly self-centered. On other hand, we would expect strong resistance to Turkish base on island, in part as desecration of "holy soil" but even more out of fear it would be used as center for agitation among remaining Turkish community. Limited Turkish military presence might eventually be palatable if it were on NATO base within what is now British sovereign base area.

Another area in which Greek Cypriots might demonstrate independence of Greece, as recent history makes only too clear, is by reneging on agreement once made in order attempt eliminate any special concessions to Turkey or Turkish Cypriots on island. Fact Greek Cypriots cannot be trusted makes it all the more important enosis be part immediate settlement and not as goal to which settlement might eventually open way. Considering Cypriot temperament, strong Communist influences, resentments arising from current strife, and widespread holding of arms, we have every reason to expect Cyprus to be source of difficulties for years to come. It is certainly far preferable this be internal Greek problem rather than international problem of type now facing us.

Belcher

67.   Telegram From the Embassy in Greece to the Department of State[1]

Athens, June 13, 1964, 9 p.m.

1891. Embassy notes with interest Istanbul's 72[2] quoting Turk Press Attaché Athens Karaoglou to effect that Turkish invasion Cyprus would result in "immediate fall" Papandreou government and his substitution by military junta. If this belief also held by important GOT officials, Embassy believes it important clear up what appears to us to be misreading of situation. Our reading is that in event Turkish invasion Cyprus and subsequent Papandreou military response, government would have full backing of Greek nation. In our judgment only if government were to fail to take some action satisfactory to injured Greek pride would there be

---

[1] Source: Department of State, Central Files, POL 23–8 CYP. Confidential. Repeated to London, Ankara, Istanbul, Nicosia, and USDOCOSouth (Naples) for Burris.

[2] Dated June 6. (Ibid.)

threat to Papandreou's continuance in office. It should be noted that there is no important element in Greek political life calling for more "moderate" approach to Cyprus problem; on contrary, Papandreou being attacked by both right and extreme left for not pushing Greek and Greek Cypriot cause more vigorously. Opposition (ERE) press, for example, accuses Papandreou of "retreating" in face of US pressure to seek quick solution Cyprus question.

In any case, it important that senior GOT officials not labor under mistaken belief that Papandreou ahead of press and public in following "hard" line vis-à-vis Cyprus question. On contrary, in view inflamed public opinion here, great test for PriMin will come if and when he agrees to compromise settlement on Cyprus which falls short Greek demands. It conceivable that if he agreed to what public opinion considered "sell-out" on Cyprus, his many enemies within and without party might combine to bring him down. In that event, successor would almost certainly be figure with more intransigent view Cyprus settlement. In sense, Papandreou now paying for fact that during last two electoral campaigns he tried win votes by riding Cypriot tiger and attacking Caramanlis administration for "sell-out" of London and Zurich Agreements. Although he avoided stating exactly what final solution he expected to achieve, public led to believe that Papandreou victory would result in Cypriot independence and enosis, if not immediately at least eventually. Thus, when and if Papandreou sits down to serious negotiations public opinion will expect him to deliver on at least part of his promises, explicit or implied.

To reiterate: in our view Papandreou would have full support of nation in military response to Turkish invasion. (Although once heat of battle passed there might be second thoughts about how Greece was maneuvered into such position.) Only if he failed to take some dramatic action would his position be jeopardized. In such case his successor would undoubtedly be advocate of harder line. However, in view Papandreou's character—as well as his stated commitments to respond to Turk "attack"—it highly unlikely that he would follow passive course under such circumstances.

Labouisse

68.   **Telegram From the Embassy in Greece to the Department of State**[1]

Athens, June 14, 1964, 11 p.m.

1898. I saw Papandreou this morning accompanied by Brewster. After preliminaries, I handed over President's letter.[2] Papandreou read it carefully and said he would be glad to accept, and that June 24 and 25 would be satisfactory provided Inonu had then left. He stressed that it would be most embarrassing if they were both there at same time and made this point a flat condition. He feels it would be most awkward if both were there at same time and they did not see one another, and he does not consider it politically feasible to have a meeting with Inonu at this time.

I believe that Papandreou is sincere in his belief that an over-lapping with Inonu would cause real difficulties, and I strongly recommend that the President set the date for Papandreou's arrival and meeting with him so as to avoid possible over-lapping.

Papandreou then went on to say that, as practical politicians, President Johnson and he would not want to have a meeting which failed. He said that he had tried to make the Greek position clear to me in previous conversations and to Mr. Ball last week. He hoped the President would understand that the Greek position had been formulated "objectively" and on the basis of principles of justice. I responded that it was not my understanding that President Johnson had in mind reaching a definite solution of the Cyprus problem during the proposed discussions. He was not attempting to short-circuit the UN. The purpose of the talks was to exchange views on ways to move toward a solution. He replied that he was not posing this as a condition to a meeting but he thought the President would want to know his views. He said he would put these in a letter which he would deliver to me this evening.

The PriMin then proceeded to outline his position, very much in the same way he has done on previous occasions and with Mr. Ball. There was nothing new in his presentation, except for his emphasis on fact that entry of Soviets in picture had made Cyprus issue a great deal more far-reaching than simply a Greek-Turkish problem. From the "security" point of view, the only hope was "Natofication," including a NATO base which could have Turkish NATO personnel. From "moral" viewpoint there should be self-determination. The present limited independence

---

[1] Source: Department of State, Central Files, POL 23–8 CYP. Secret; Immediate; Exdis. Repeated to London, USUN, Nicosia, and Ankara and passed to the White House, JCS, OSD, and CIA.

[2] See footnote 4, Document 64.

should be lifted and self-determination exercised in the form of a plebiscite (resulting in union with Greece) to take place before the UN forces leave the island; i.e., within three months. He stressed that an independent Cyprus would mean a Cuba and a partitioned Cyprus would lead inevitably to conflict between the 400,000 Greeks and the 100,000 Turks which would only continue the crisis situation.

He asked what I thought about this. Reverting to his security argument, I suggested that Turks might well think double enosis would best serve purpose. He replied that even if he should order partition the population of the island would not accept it and civil war and chaos would ensue. In both cases the Communists would be the winners. Only by a close link with the West could this be averted.

I observed that even though his arguments might sound "objective" to many, there was still an important psychological factor and political realities which Inonu had to face. I suggested that if Menderes had been able to negotiate a deal which disallowed enosis, it would be expecting a lot for Inonu to accept it. I repeated the question I had often posed to him—what could be done to meet Inonu half way? He came to his "security" argument, repeating that the new factor since 1959 was that Sov Union was on scene and would be muddying waters. He felt that the US should stress heavily to Inonu that Natofication would achieve the security of the island within the NATO framework and Turkey would not have a Cuba off its southern shore. This solution could also get Makarios out of the way which should be helpful to the Turkish Govt with its problem of face. Also, compensation could be provided for the Turk Cypriots who wanted to move to the mainland, and further economic aid from the West might be promised. He underlined (more for US benefit, I think, than for the Turks) that this solution would be a lasting one and arrived at within framework of democratic principles.

I pressed him on score as to whether compensation he was offering would be adequate to meet the Turkish political and psychological problem facing Inonu. He had nothing to add to above. When I touched briefly on question of possible territorial exchanges based on news reports he took standard Greek line that giving up islands such as Chios, Mytilini or Samos would be inconceivable. It would lead to revolution in Greece.

Our talk, which was highly informal (no other Greeks present) and friendly throughout, did not touch on displacement of Istanbul population and Patriarchate.[3]

---

[3] In telegram 1899 from Athens, June 14, Labouisse reported that he had also told Papandreou that sending Grivas to Cyprus at this point could have deleterious effects. Papandreou had agreed with this analysis. (Department of State, Central Files, POL 23–8 CYP)

As to publicity concerning the visit, he stated that until he had sent a formal reply of acceptance and had received further word from us, he would not make any statement. He would parry questions with formula "I have received no formal invitation." Publicity from US side should be held up also, pending consideration of content of formal letter, which will be cabled as soon as received. Meanwhile, I shall appreciate comments re date of meeting in light paras 1 and 2 above.[4]

Labouisse

---

[4] In telegram 1516 to Athens, June 15, the Department of State informed the Embassy that June 24–25 was satisfactory for a Papandreou visit and that it would arrange for Inonu's departure prior to Papandreou's arrival. (Ibid., POL 7 GREECE)

---

69.   Telegram From the Embassy in Cyprus to the Department of State[1]

Nicosia, June 18, 1964, 7 p.m.

1377. Deptel 951.[2] Regret Deptel 942[3] not received (although serviced) when I called on Makarios this afternoon. Came in while at palace. With regard SC proceedings,[4] he said Kyprianou will go along with resolution merely extending term of UNFICYP. Said he realizes both sides want changes in terms of reference and would like see resolution continuing some condemnation, either direct of indirect, of other side, but it highly unlikely be possible obtain such res and therefore GOC will not attempt it. I said this would assist in avoiding probable acrimonious debate if other procedure followed. Said my govt would be pleased to hear that this was GOC plan. Makarios went on to say, however, that GOC presentation would have to refer to Turkish invasion threats and to most recent events in Mansoura–Kokkina area where for to him inexpli-

---

[1] Source: Department of State, Central Files, POL 23–8 CYP. Confidential. Repeated to Ankara, Athens, London, USUN, and Paris for USRO.

[2] Telegram 951, June 17, outlined U.S. strategy for the U.N. Security Council meeting on Cyprus. (Ibid.)

[3] Telegram 942, June 14, outlined U.S. strategy for establishing the proper atmosphere for talks in Washington with Inonu and Papandreou. (Ibid., POL 7 TUR)

[4] Reference is to the upcoming Security Council debate on the extension of UNFICYP for a further 3 months.

cable reasons Turks have picked this time to create new and dangerous situation. I urged him to try keep Kyprianou speech in as low key as possible.

While Deptel 942 not available and hence I unable act on specific suggestions, most of them covered indirectly. Items covered were Inonu visit; my frequent consultations his Ministers and himself; support for UN effort; gave credit several recent moves including offer Green Line pull-back; urged him make some unilateral gesture even in face Turkish actions in Mansoura area in effort improve Greek Cypriot image abroad and this particularly in his interest at this moment of SC meeting.

With regard Mansoura and events of last two days,[5] Makarios in most apparent show of anger I have yet seen said he would not permit Turks to take over small Greek villages in area. Said he had reports that UN had urged villagers at Mosphili to evacuate, but when they had inquired whether they should do so, he had refused allow them. Said he will move to protect Greeks if UN cannot do so and if Turks did nothing.

In this regard, he expressed oft-repeated Greek Cypriot position that UN not forceful enough in preventing such incidents and in particular in this northwest area they apparently unable control smuggling of arms and people by Turks. He said if present situation continues much longer or if today's incident becomes more serious, he will move to isolate area from rest of island. In this connection said he had told Plaza (Embtel 1356)[6] that he could not wait "long" for UN to open Kyrenia and Xeropolis Roads. When he said he would close all roads to Turks if these two roads not opened, I said I was sure he had estimated far better than I what probable reaction of Turks might be to such action. Said he had and (contrary to what he told Plaza) he expected they would react violently, but he was prepared to take consequences since present situation intolerable.

When he went on to say he was more pessimistic now than he had been in some months, I said this distressed me since he was usually optimistic. I asked him what he thought probable GOT reaction might be to any such action on his part, particularly in view of present delicate situation in which GOT leadership found itself. At this point he asked me whether USG really thought that Turks had intended invade two weeks ago. I said that this was matter of conjecture for some, but that we were satisfied they had intended do so and it was only with greatest possible pressure that we had dissuaded them. Expressed hope that we would not have to try again.

---

[5] On June 16, the heaviest fighting since April broke out in Nicosia and Tyllonia. At the same time Turkish Cypriot spokesmen began charging that the United Nations and its representatives were not conducting themselves in an impartial manner.

[6] Telegram 1356, June 12, reported on Galo Plaza's discussions with Makarios. (Department of State, Central Files, POL 23–8 CYP)

I said might be useful for me see Kutchuk and urge him use restraint to avoid new crisis. Archbishop told me feel free give "Vice President" full account his statements to me. Am seeing Gyani and Plaza tonight and will concert with them before seeing Kutchuk.[7]

We ended conversation by agreeing that at his usual Thursday evening press conference, he would say that I had called on him to inquire about GOC plans with regard to resolution and to express USG's support for three-month extension of UNFICYP and our willingness to provide another $2 million for expenses.

Belcher

[7] Belcher reported on these talks in telegrams 1381, June 19, and 1395, June 23. (Ibid.)

70. Telegram From the Department of State to the Embassy in the United Kingdom[1]

Washington, June 21, 1964, 5:52 p.m.

8463. For Bruce. We see coming week as crucial in long-smoldering Cyprus crisis. If Inonu and Papandreou talks should fail to yield constructive results, critical new situation might confront us as early as next week. Even while Turkish and Greek Prime Ministers here, impact of Grivas' presence on Cyprus or of communal clashes on island could add complications.[2] Role played by British will have great significance during these days. We sense UKG would prefer avoid facing hard contingencies that may lie ahead, and we look to you to help strengthen their realism and readiness to take any difficult actions that may become necessary.

On June 20, Under Sec Ball called in British Ambassador to explain how we view upcoming talks with Inonu and Papandreou.[3] Ball said our objective is to get Greeks and Turks into serious high-level discussions in

[1] Source: Department of State, Central Files, POL 23–8 CYP. Secret; Priority; Exdis–TUG. Drafted by Bracken, Jernegan, and Talbot; cleared by Ball; and approved by Talbot.

[2] Grivas returned to Cyprus on June 17. The Greek Government announced his return on June 21.

[3] A memorandum of this conversation is in Department of State, Central Files, POL 23–8 CYP.

presence distinguished American. Dean Acheson has agreed to undertake this task. We estimate Turks will agree, but Papandreou will be more difficult. We expect tell Papandreou close vote of confidence in Ankara[4] ominous sign that Turks deeply frustrated. If no movement on Cyprus, Inonu could fall. We should be under no illusions that Turks might then move militarily, whatever we said to them. If Turks moved there would be no question of stopping them with Sixth Fleet or other military means, because we would not fight our allies.

Object in taking this line will be to demonstrate to Papandreou what dangers Greece, Turkey and Western world could face on very short notice unless Greece and Turkey able to compromise their positions. Assuming Inonu will by then have agreed to talks, Papandreou will be told flatly that he will be risking security of his country and of Alliance unless he also agrees to substantive talks.

Harlech agreed Greeks must face up to dangers. US should "make their flesh creep" by spelling out prospects and making them understand US would not stop Turkish intervention if it were started contrary to American advice.

Ball raised question of British plans for such contingency. He returned to discussions of last February when London had agreed to consider possible tripartite intervention should Turks move. Harlech drew back fast from that particular suggestion. He left impression British would want no part of fresh military intervention in Cyprus. He did not think HMG had ever agreed to intervention though there had been talk of trying to get Turks and Greeks to limit their advances should they land on island.

On June 21 Ball met with General Taylor and Sec McNamara to review contingencies on which State–Defense planning should focus in immediate future.[5]

Our contingency problem is what US and UK could do if Inonu and Papandreou talks should result in impasse and if Inonu's moderation was then eclipsed by more activist Turkish forces, leading to Turkish military intervention in Cyprus. This could now occur without our getting much advance warning. In any case we not at all certain we could turn Turks off again even if we had notice.

This would obviously be war nobody could win. We do not see how Greeks could stop Turkish landing or put effective Greek forces on Cyprus. Nonetheless, Greek and Greek Cypriots could harass Turkish action, delay actual landing of total Turkish force and plunge island into bloodbath. If Greeks widened attack to mainland areas, consequences

---

[4] The Inonu government survived a vote of confidence on June 19 by a vote of 199 to 195.

[5] No record of this converstion has been found.

could be disastrous. Meanwhile UNSC activity would be intense. Western security interests could only be seriously jeopardized and none but Soviets could gain, whether or not they threatened to intervene militarily in Turkey or Cyprus.

Turks, if they moved, would hold they acting legally under Article IV of Treaty after failure of Guarantor Powers to take effective joint action to restore constitutional position. Greeks of course would take opposite stand. In this situation posture and actions of UK could have determining effect. We believe plan proposed by Ball in February still has merit, but will be glad to hear any alternatives British may wish to put forward. In any case, we hope British studying this contingency carefully, for if Turks move it is clear US and UK will need to set their courses fast and to lead their public attitudes appropriately. US and UK must obviously stay in close consultation.

We are also looking urgently at possible Soviet actions in event of military operations over Cyprus, and hope British are doing same. Role of UN also needs study.

More immediate question is impact of return of Grivas to island. We assume British will be extremely agitated; British EmbOff suggested today UK might even withdraw contingent from UNFICYP. We appreciate Grivas' presence reopens old wounds and we know how sensitive British public is to his earlier role. However, relationships have changed and it is conceivable Grivas could impose more discipline on Greek Cypriot irregulars, correct slide toward Soviets, extend hand of friendship to Turks and protect them from Greek Cypriot extremists, and actually contribute to solution of British difficulties on island. However this may be, it is going to be hard enough—yet essential—to calm down Turkish fears of Grivas and to forestall any rash Turkish reaction. It is equally essential that British not let appearance of Grivas upset our careful preparations to bring Inonu and Papandreou to effective substantive talks. Do try to persuade them of this.

Rusk

---

71.   Editorial Note

Prime Minister Inonu and Prime Minister Papandreou visited Washington June 22–23 and June 24–25, 1964, respectively, for talks with U.S. officials. Prime Minister Inonu arrived in the United States on June 21 and spent the evening at Williamsburg, Virginia. He met with President Johnson at 10:30 a.m. on June 22 and held subsequent discussions with U.S. officials before departing for New York and meetings at the United Nations on the evening of June 23. For text of statements by President Johnson and Prime Minister Inonu, see *Public Papers of the Presidents of the United States: Lyndon B. Johnson, 1964*, Book II, pages 798–801.

Prime Minister Papandreou arrived in Washington on June 24, following an overnight stay at Williamsburg, for a meeting with the President. He held talks with other U.S. officials June 24–25, prior to departing for New York for discussions at the United Nations. For text of statements by President Johnson and the Greek Prime Minister, see ibid., pages 811–812, 814–816, and 818–819.

Andreas Papandreou, the Prime Minister's son and Alternate Minister for Coordination, discussed the talks in Washington and New York in *Democracy at Gunpoint*, pages 133–136. Ball's recollection of the meeting is in *The Past Has Another Pattern*, page 355. Documentation is in the Johnson Library, National Security File, County Files, Cyprus, Vol. 8; ibid., Ball Papers, Telephone Conversations, Cyprus; Department of State, Central File POL 23–8 CYP; ibid., Conference Files: Lot 66 D 110, CF 2415–2417; and ibid., Ball Files: Lot 74 D 272, Papandreou and Inonu Visits.

---

72.   Memorandum of Conversation[1]

Washington, June 22, 1964, 11 a.m.

SUBJECT

Cyprus Situation and Greek-Turkish Relations

PARTICIPANTS

United States	*Turkey*
The President	Prime Minister Inonu
Under Secretary of State Ball	Foreign Minister Erkin
Ambassador Raymond A. Hare	Ambassador Menemencioglu
Semih Ustun—interpreter	

The President welcomed Prime Minister Inonu and thanked him for coming to Washington to discuss Cyprus and the Greek-Turkish dispute.

---

[1] Source: Department of State, Conference Files: Lot 66 D 110, CF 2415. Secret; Exdis. Drafted by Greene and approved in U on July 24 and in the White House on July 28. The meeting was held at the White House.

The President said these questions have been of great concern to the United States and although the United States does not have ready answers for the many problems of the world, it is the responsibility of statesmen to meet and seek ways to find solutions.

As for Cyprus, the President said we do not have a magic formula to offer, but we are prepared to assist Greece and Turkey in finding a solution. He emphasized it would be unwise to engage in hostilities before making every effort to settle the dispute peacefully. He said that with this in mind, we are ready to make available the services of former Secretary of State Dean Acheson to sit down with Greek and Turkish representatives for quiet and frank talks at Camp David. The President was hopeful that such talks could narrow the gap between the two countries.

Prime Minister Inonu replied that these talks could make possible an exchange of opinions and that in principle he had no objections to the President's kind offer.

Under Secretary Ball said the talks would be most effective if each country sent a highly responsible official short of the most senior ranks, but still a man holding the complete confidence of his Prime Minister. He said that the participation of responsible and trusted officials below the Foreign Minister level and the use of the special facilities afforded by Camp David would make it much easier to keep the talks completely secret. Foreign Minister Erkin and Mr. Ball agreed that the two Foreign Ministers might join the talks at a later date.

The Prime Minister asked when the talks could begin, and the President replied the sooner the better, perhaps within one week. Prime Minister Inonu and Mr. Ball each expressed some optimism that the talks might quickly help clear the air.

Prime Minister Inonu again expressed his thanks for the President's help, but added that every time during recent months when there had seemed to be hope for a peaceful settlement, something had developed to block it. He said the President should know that he may have to overcome resistance on the Greek side to the proposed talks. He agreed with the President that there are no gainers in war, but pointed out that Greece appears to be acting under the impression that it can win an easy victory on Cyprus. The Prime Minister said if there is to be a solution satisfactory to both sides, Prime Minister Papandreou must decide that he wants one.

The President commented he had no illusions that his talks with the Greeks would be easy, but he would do his best.

Foreign Minister Erkin raised the subject of the Turkish-Cypriot refugees, now homeless and unable to return to their old villages. He suggested settling the refugees in new homes where they are now. Under Secretary Ball said the Greeks might interpret such a move as de facto partition, thus making the situation more difficult. He pointed out that the International Red Cross could help in the immediate problems of the refugees, and said the United States would view such assistance with sympathy.

Mr. Ball said we may have a new asset on Cyprus in the person of General Thimayya, the new commander of the United Nations force on the island.[2] The Prime Minister said similar sentiments had been expressed when General Gyani was appointed to the same position.

Foreign Minister Erkin said the Cyprus situation would become serious indeed should the Turkish army contingent on the island be attacked. The President assured the Turkish officials he would do his utmost to persuade the Greek Prime Minister that the issues must be settled peacefully and that Mr. Papandreou should use his influence to maintain tranquility on the island.

The President concluded by saying that Mr. Acheson would be present at Mr. Ball's luncheon the following day and that further details on the proposed talks could be discussed then.

---

[2] On June 20, Secretary-General Thant announced that Thimayya would replace Gyani as commander of UNFICYP. Thimayya assumed command on July 8.

---

73.   Memorandum of Conversation[1]

Washington, June 23, 1964.

SUBJECT

Cyprus

PARTICIPANTS

(See attached list on page 4)[2]

Mr. Ball opened the main conversation by saying that the United States did not want to put forward a formal solution for the Cyprus prob-

---

[1] Source: Department of State, Conference Files: Lot 66 D 110, CF 2415. Secret; Exdis–TUG. Drafted by Jernegan and approved in U on July 13. The meeting was held during a luncheon aboard the Presidential yacht S.S. *Sequoia* on the Potomac River.

[2] Not printed. Prime Minister Inonu, Foreign Minister Erkin, and Ambassador Menemencioglu were accompanied by five Turkish officials. Under Secretary of State Ball and former Secretary of State Acheson were accompanied by Talbot, Jernegan, and Springsteen.

lem but to start by identifying the elements of a possible solution. The Turks, he said think that double enosis would be the best answer whereas the Greeks think that enosis is the solution. For the United States to say now that either of these or certain modifications of either was to be preferred would not be useful. He hoped that Mr. Acheson could push matters forward during the anticipated detailed discussions to come later and that at some time in the future we might then decide to propose something specific to the parties.

Mr. Acheson said he did not consider that these discussions should be regarded as a "lawyer's dispute". There was no sense in simply trying to score points on each other. This was not the way to make progress. Rather, it would be wiser to explore separately the vital elements which each country had at stake in this issue. For example, Turkey seemed to have three major concerns:

1) Turkey's national dignity and prestige;
2) Turkey's physical security, the question of the degree to which Cyprus in unfriendly hands would be a menace to Turkey;
3) The welfare of the Turkish Cypriots, the security of their lives and property. (He remarked that when the crisis arose this last concern had seemed to be Turkey's principal worry, but he thought now it had receded into third place.)

Similarly, Mr. Acheson would propose to ask the Greeks to consider what was *vital* to their national interests, not merely what they would like to have. After doing this with both parties, he would propose that they try to develop a solution from these bases, instead of starting with broad concepts like enosis and double enosis. After these first steps, Mr. Acheson suggested all concerned must decide how to handle Archbishop Makarios and the Cypriots, who were somewhat less than responsible.

Dr. Erim[3] commented that Mr. Acheson's proposed method was a rational approach to a final solution but that the question remained how to preserve security on the Island until a solution could be reached. Mr. Ball replied that a condition to the talks must be that both Ankara and Athens would exert every effort to keep things quiet on the Island. Mr. Acheson added that he hoped the discussions would be very short and the security problem would not be with us for long. Dr. Erim said we could not count on a quick solution, to which Mr. Ball replied that we must not start with the expectation that the talks would be protracted,

---

[3] Dr. Nihat Erim, Chairman of the Foreign Relations Committee of the Turkish National Assembly.

the situation was too urgent. Mr. Ball foresaw three problems during the talks:

1) Maintenance of security on the Island;
2) Possible disruptive activities by Makarios;
3) Possible Communist activity.

Therefore, we must hurry things along. Mr. Acheson concurred heartily, stressing that the present state of affairs would not permit long negotiations of the type which eventually resulted in the Austrian State Treaty; the situation was too explosive. Foreign Minister Erkin interjected that even next week we might have a moral collapse of Turkish Cypriots.

Mr. Ball said that we would like to have the talks begin right after July 4th. There was no dissent. He also suggested that Camp David would be the best site for the talks. Again there was no dissent.

Erkin urged that we try to make sure the Greeks don't leak news of our plan to Makarios. Mr. Ball said we would do our best but could not guarantee anything.

At various times during the conversation, Turkish representatives voiced special concern not only about the general prospect for security on the Island but also about the situation of the displaced Turkish Cypriots who had left their homes. They asserted that relief for these people had been inadequate and that they were living in a state of dire need. Further, the British relief agencies would be withdrawing from the picture at the end of this month. The American side expressed belief that the International Red Cross would carry forward. The Turks expressed doubts on this and pointed out that the IRC can work only through the local government; if the local government were not willing to cooperate, nothing would be done. The American side gave general assurances of support for the relief effort.

The Turks further asserted that the Greek-Cypriot authorities were threatening to prevent the resupplying of the Turkish Army contingents on Cyprus and that this unit would soon exhaust its present stocks. They asked for American help on this problem, which was promised.

Most of the balance of the discussion was concerned with the wording of the joint communiqué. The text of the final draft as issued is attached.[4]

At one point Mr. Ball asked how the Turks interpreted the return of General Grivas to Cyprus. Erkin commented that it was not a good sign from a Turkish point of view, and others made similar remarks, but there

---

[4] Not printed. For text of the joint communiqué issued on June 23, see *American Foreign Policy: Current Documents, 1964*, p. 582.

was no noticeable excitement or special disturbance on the part of the Turks.

Summary: The conversation confirmed agreement on the following points:

1) Provided the Greek Government also agreed, Turkey would participate in secret talks with the Greeks and Mr. Acheson directed toward agreement on a final and permanent solution of the Cyprus dispute.

2) These talks should begin at Camp David promptly after July 4th.

3) The Turkish representative would be Dr. Nihat Erim. (Dr. Erim remarked that he was scheduled to come to the United States later this summer on a leader grant and that this could be given as the reason for his return here when he came for the talks.)

4) In the meantime, the United States would do its best to assist in assuring the welfare of the Turkish-Cypriot refugees.

74.   Memorandum of Conversation[1]

Washington, June 24, 1964, 10:30 a.m.

SUBJECT

Cyprus Problem

PARTICIPANTS

The U.S Side	*The Greek Side*
The President	Prime Minister Papandreou
The Under Secretary	Foreign Minister Costopoulos
Ambassador Labouisse	Alternate Minister of Coordination Andreas Papandreou
	Ambassador Matsas

The President welcomed the Prime Minister for a discussion of a matter which he knew was of deep concern to both of them. The President stated that he had no desire to impose our will on anyone; we have

[1] Source: Department of State, Ball Papers: Lot 74 D 272, Papandreou and Inonu Visits. Secret; Exdis–TUG. Drafted by Labouisse and approved in U on July 29 and in the White House on July 30. The meeting was held in the President's office.

no formula. However, he is worried that our friends differ among themselves, and he hopes very much that, rather than fighting, they can get together for talks which will lead to a solution.

The President referred to the recent threatened move by Turkey and the action he had taken in an effort to forestall it, saying that he was following the teaching of Isaiah: "Come let us reason together". The President had asked the Turks not to act without talking with us and with Greece. After an exchange of communications, Prime Minister Inonu had agreed to come to Washington for talks.

The President then went on to say that he had not presented to Inonu any formula or recommendation re a particular solution but that he had urged as strongly as possible that the Turks sit down and reason with the people of Greece. The President stressed that statesmen should get together and reason. He had told Inonu that if the Turks would agree to talk with the Greeks, the United States would provide the arrangements and facilities, including an outstanding American citizen, Mr. Dean Acheson, to assist.

The President said that he knew that Prime Minister Papandreou felt very strongly in the matter of Cyprus—that he knew the Prime Minister's viewpoint, and that Papandreou felt justified in it. The President added, however, that he hoped very much that Mr. Papandreou would agree that discussions be held with the Turks. He specified that he was not proposing talks on the Prime Minister or even Foreign Minister levels, but rather between duly authorized representatives of the two countries. He felt that the meetings should be secret and should be held in the immediate future, and he suggested they be held with the assistance of Dean Acheson at Camp David. The Prime Minister indicated that he had a high regard for Mr. Acheson.

The President went on to say that the Secretary General of the UN wanted the United States to help, in fact, he was anxious for us to do it within the spirit of the UN. There was no proposal to go around the UN.

The President said to Papandreou that he had told Inonu that he wanted history to remember him as a statesman who would reason and not as a warrior. While Inonu had accepted this line of argument, the President did not know how long Inonu could keep his people behind him.

If the Prime Minister of Greece could designate someone who has his confidence who could meet with the Turkish representative and Mr. Acheson, President Johnson was sure that this could be arranged very quickly. There was everything to gain and nothing to lose by trying to reason. The alternative could be very bad and bloody, and we would want no part of it; we cannot be in a position of fighting our allies. The President went on to say that we have exercised our very best efforts to prevent a disaster. He pointed out that anyone can start a war, but confidence, patience and wisdom were needed to prevent one. He said, therefore, he wanted to have meetings started during the next week and he was sure that all people would welcome this. He emphasized that he was not asking that anyone yield any right, but only that they try to reason.

The President then referred to the vote which had just taken place on the foreign aid bill[2] and said that he could lead the American people if the people think he is doing all possible to prevent bloodshed and work with the UN. But the people are worried about growing tensions between Greece and Turkey and they do not want this to continue. He was sure that if we three try to reason this matter out, it will help a great deal.

He said to Papandreou that if the latter would cooperate and search for peace, he will have the approbation of the UN and of the people of this country; the alternative is too horrible to contemplate. If we cannot cooperate in this search for peace, the President will have to tell the American people what to expect, and he added again we cannot be in a position of fighting an ally. Under the circumstances, the President said what we want to ask is that talks be held in search of a solution and we do not think that this is an unreasonable request. He expressed the hope that before July 4 he could get Inonu to designate a representative and Papandreou to do likewise. They, with Mr. Acheson, could explore the roads to a solution.

The President continued that, with the help of Mr. Acheson, we can develop plans which will help both our allies down the years and he then referred to the need for economic development of both countries instead of wasting their resources. The President ended by saying that if the American representative recommends a plan for promoting peace and prosperity, he was sure the American people would follow along.

The Prime Minister then spoke. He said that we were before a very critical situation and we needed to avoid war. He wanted to explore what was the best procedure, for he thought that there was confusion between what we called absolute and relative questions.

He said that the two world wars could have been prevented if the leaders of those times had acted properly. He said that for this reason he expressed great appreciation for President Johnson's interest in the Cyprus matter.

On the question of procedure, Papandreou asserted that the procedure suggested by President Johnson would lead to war—"if an understanding does not come about through Mr. Acheson, war will result". He also asserted that we all have a common aim of avoiding war and this was why he could not accept the viewpoint put forward by Mr. Stikker

---

[2] On June 10, the House of Representatives passed H.R. 11380, the 1965 Foreign Aid Appropriations bill, by a vote of 230 to 175. The bill authorized a total of $2 billion in assistance.

that when an issue is between two members of NATO, NATO must be neutral. Since the arms of the NATO powers are for use against the enemy, is it possible that NATO would permit their use against an ally?

Papandreou stated that the Greeks have responsibility for bringing about peace on the island by influencing the Greek Cypriots; the Turks have a similar responsibility with respect to the Turkish Cypriots. This, he said, was his first point: differences should be settled only through peaceful means.

Papandreou went on to say that as the points of view between Turkey and Greece differed so widely, nothing could be expected from the meeting proposed by the President and consequently the extremists on both sides would contend that there was nothing to do but to fight. "When the presupposition is that no war will take place, we can then talk with safety."

Papandreou said that he was prepared to go personally to Cyprus to insure calm and then there would be no excuse for a Turkish landing.

The Prime Minister asserted that he was not thinking just as a leader of Greece but as a leader belonging to a country of the Free World. This led him to the discussion of intervention, saying there were two arguments to be discussed—one legal and one substantive. On the legal side, the right of intervention had been lost when Cyprus entered the UN— there was no longer any basis for intervention. On the substantive side, there was an argument that both the Turks and Greeks must be satisfied. This, he alleged, was false. "Turkey does not lose anything. A century ago it sold Cyprus, so what valid right does it have?" He argued that security was the only basis for negotiation and he agreed that Turkey must be offered security. This, he said, is why he had put forward "NATOfication" as the most desirable solution of the Cyprus problem.

He alluded to other possible solutions, saying that in the case of partition, the non-Turkish part of the island would become Communist.

Concerning the possibility of Greece giving up something to Turkey as part of a solution, Papandreou said that Greece wanted nothing in Cyprus—its position was "merely that through democratic principles the majority can rule and the minority can be protected." He put the question "if Greece does not take anything, why should Greece give?" He asserted that the question of enosis was a matter for the Cypriots; that self-determination would be good for Cyprus and for the Free World.

Returning to the proposal for a meeting, Papandreou said he was afraid that a confrontation of the two points of view at the present time would lead to war. Instead of this confrontation, talks should be carried on by the Mediator and, meanwhile, peace on the island should be maintained in order to avoid provocation.

Papandreou then repeated his argument that NATO should not permit NATO-furnished arms to be used by either Turkey or Greece to fight one another.

Papandreou concluded by expressing the view that if the meeting should be held with Mr. Acheson, the latter would have to report no agreement at the end of ten days.

President Johnson asked why Mr. Acheson would have to report no agreement if the two parties entered the discussions in good faith.

Mr. Ball interjected here to say that we cannot be sure that the Turks will not move. He suggested that we explore this whole matter further at luncheon.

75.   Memorandum of Conversation[1]

Washington, June 24, 1964, 12:30 p.m.

SUBJECT

Cyprus Situation and Greek-Turkish Relations

PARTICIPANTS

United States
The Under Secretary
Dean Acheson, Former Secretary of State
Robert McNamara, Secretary of Defense
Maxwell Taylor, Chairman, Joint Chiefs of Staff
Phillips Talbot, Assistant Secretary, NEA
Ambassador Henry Labouisse
John D. Jernegan, Deputy Assistant Secretary, NEA
George S. Springsteen, Special Assistant to the Under Secretary

Greece
Prime Minister Papandreou
Foreign Minister Costopoulos
Andreas Papandreou, Minister Alternate of Economic Coordination
Ambassador Alexander A. Matsas

Under Secretary Ball referred to President Johnson's proposal of that morning that Greek and Turkish representatives meet quietly with Dean Acheson to try to arrive at some agreement on the main issues in

---

[1] Source: Department of State, Central Files, POL 23–8 CYP. Secret; Exdis. Drafted by Greene and approved in U on August 10. The meeting was held aboard the Presidential yacht S.S. *Sequoia* on the Potomac River.

the Cyprus crisis.[2] In making this suggestion, the President did not intend that the U.S. replace the UN mediator. Rather, the mediator himself had realized he had come to an impasse and asked us to use our good offices. The U.S. agrees with the Prime Minister's remark that a breakdown of these proposed talks would lead to a dangerous situation, but we are also convinced that serious danger exists now, and so negotiations are essential.

Mr. Ball continued that there are two elements in the problem: (1) to negotiate a just solution and (2) to do so in a way which will prevent irresponsible forces from taking over Cyprus. He said Greece and Turkey are thinking along the same lines; and so now is the time to talk about procedures which serve everyone's interests. Mr. Ball added that the day before the Americans had taken a strong line with Turkish Prime Minister Inonu. Turkey now recognizes that a new basis for Cyprus must be negotiated.

The Prime Minister commented that the first requirement is security on Cyprus. Greece is trying to establish security; Turkey must try also. He said the Cypriots must then have an opportunity to exercise self-determination. Under any final arrangements, there would of course be guarantees for the Turk-Cypriots.

The Prime Minister said NATO needs a new principle: no member has the right to begin war against another. He continued that Turkey's former right of intervention is not valid now that Cyprus is covered by the UN Charter. If there is no danger to the Turk-Cypriot community, then Turkey's argument on the need to intervene collapses. As for solutions, Turkey suggests partition or federation, neither of which is anyone's interest, including Turkey's. The Prime Minister said partition would lead the non-Turkish part of the island into becoming another Cuba, and thus a grave danger to Turkey's security. The other proposal, federation, would lead to civil war. The Prime Minister concluded that the only possible solution is unrestricted independence. This would be followed by a plebiscite and enosis, a solution which is certainly in the free world's interests. Turkey would lose nothing and would in fact gain security. The Turkish-Cypriots would be protected just as are the Thracian Turks now. Prime Minister Papandreou said Greece would also be willing to offer international guarantees for the Turkish minority. The Cyprus crisis had now moved into the context of East-West rivalries, and the Prime Minister said he could not always exclude contacts by Makarios with the USSR.

Mr. Ball replied that he must question the Prime Minister's statement that NATO should oppose war between two members. He said he

---

[2] See Document 74.

was certain that no NATO country would oppose Turkey if it tried to enforce its treaty rights on Cyprus. As for the United States, the President had said in the morning we would not fight an ally in a situation as complicated as this. The Under Secretary said we will not interpose the Sixth Fleet. The U.S. would certainly attempt to dissuade Turkey, but not by the use of force. With this background, he concluded, it is obvious that the talks as suggested by President Johnson are essential to avert danger and permit the mediator to get on with his work.

Prime Minister Papandreou said that this line of thinking leaves no conclusion but war. In a conflict between the old agreements and unrestricted independence, there is no bridge. Sooner or later Turkey will go to war, although he said he would be happy if his pessimism were shown to be unfounded. Turkey is too weak now to bridge this gap, and so there is no need for the Prime Minister to meet with Inonu. Rather the better approach would be to wait for the mediator's report. Perhaps by the process of elimination and with the passage of time, we may find a way. For the moment, the Prime Minister said he thought Greece and Turkey should undertake a reconnaissance to see whether future negotiations are possible; if so, then the real talks might begin.

The Under Secretary said it would be a mistake to limit action to keeping the peace on Cyprus while awaiting the mediator's report. We would only be deceiving ourselves, because if there is no progress, we could not expect the GOT to restrain the activist forces in Turkey.

Mr. Ball continued that what the Prime Minister suggests is an exploration—that is, a Greek representative, Professor Erim of Turkey, and Mr. Acheson would meet to explore quietly the possibilities of some kind of action and to narrow the differences between the two sides. During that interval, Turkey would attempt to keep the Turk-Cypriots quiet. We would certainly fear the consequences should we have to tell Prime Minister Inonu that, despite his desisting from military action, we had been unable to arrange any useful alternative.

Prime Minister Papandreou repeated that the GOG would be willing to begin exploratory talks with Turkey. If there appeared to be room for talks he would then appoint someone for real negotiations, but given the present positions of the two Governments, there is little point at present of undertaking actual negotiations. Even though Greece and Turkey may be close now, there must first be cautious preliminary contact.

On Mr. Ball's invitation Mr. Acheson commented that in insisting that there be peace on Cyprus before serious negotiations, the Prime Minister was raising the old chicken-egg question. He asked whether any pacification is possible until the views of Turkey and Greece are closer than they are now. Mr Acheson said no solution can fully satisfy both parties, but what is important is maintaining peace. He said the Prime Minister speaks of principles and theory, but as Mr. Acheson grows older, he believes more and more that general principles do not decide specific cases. The Prime Minister's suggestion would place the talks in too narrow a framework. There must be more room for flexibility.

The Prime Minister replied that in this case the principle comes from a concrete case on which he had generalized. The point is, he said, that if the impression is given that negotiations are underway and they then fail, there would certainly be trouble. So there must be a reconnaissance first. He said he defended the principle of self-determination. If he did not, the Greek-Cypriots would follow their own way, and he could not influence them. If the United States thinks negotiations are possible, does it have an opinion about a final solution?

The Under Secretary replied that Prime Minister Inonu had asked a similar question and Mr. Ball's answer now would be the same: any USG-sponsored solution would be condemned to failure. But in the course of Mr. Acheson's talks he could evoke certain points of view, and he might then be able to say that A is better than B. Mr. Ball turned to self-determination, saying that the USG had long advanced such an approach to international problems, but, in looking at Cyprus, there are a number of elements of which self-determination is only one. He said Mr. Acheson would try to identify all of the elements on each side. If we do not do something, America's influence over the GOT would rapidly dissipate, and the consequences could be terrifying. Mr. McNamara and General Taylor are here to discuss these possible consequences.

The Prime Minister said the GOG has great esteem for Mr. Acheson and accepts in principle his offer to make contacts on both sides. If, after these contacts, Mr. Acheson thinks actual negotiations would be useful, then the Prime Minister would appoint a representative.

Mr. Acheson said there are several elements immediately obvious. One is that of prestige and dignity. No solution can humiliate either side; nor can it be a complete victory for either side. Secondly, is the question of security, which concerns Turkey more than Greece. Therefore, the GOG should be sympathetic on this issue. Next come the people of Cyprus. The Prime Minister has said this element is more important to Greece, but actually it is also important to Turkey.

Prime Minister Papandreou said he was glad Mr. Acheson had included the Cypriot people in his listing. The greatest weight must be given to that element—its rights to a majority decision and its right to appeal to the UN. He said he also agreed that the security element is more significant for Turkey. He continued, however, that Mr. Acheson must be aware that the Greek starting position for any negotiations is unrestricted independence for Cyprus.

Mr. Ball commented that this would be a negotiation beginning with the conclusion and, therefore, would not be a negotiation at all.

Mr. Acheson said the purpose of two-party negotiations is not to take an unchangeable stand, but rather to see what can be accomplished. If the GOG sticks to its position, the GOT will not change its views about the binding validity of the present treaties and Turkey's resulting right of intervention.

Prime Minister Papandreou insisted that there is no alternative to unrestricted independence. Mr. Ball replied that he agrees the present system on Cyprus has not worked. We must search for others. There are dangerous forces at work, and we must be practical; as the President said during the morning meeting, the USG cannot make moral judgements on this crisis. We are in a grey area in which neither Cypriot community has met 20th Century moral standards. The only choice is a compromise solution.

The Prime Minister concluded that he had expressed his views and heard those of the Americans. He would give his reply to their proposals before leaving Washington.[3]

---

[3] For text of the joint communiqué issued on June 25 by President Johnson and Prime Minister Papandreou, see *American Foreign Policy: Current Documents, 1964*, pp. 582–583.

---

76.   Memorandum of Conversation[1]

New York, June 26, 1964.

SUBJECT

Cyprus

PARTICIPANTS

U Thant, Secretary General of the UN
Mr. Tuomioja, UN Mediator

George W. Ball, Under Secretary of State
Adlai E. Stevenson, U.S. Representative to the UN
Charles W. Yost, U.S. Deputy Permanent Representative to the UN
Phillips Talbot, Assistant Secretary of State for Near East and South Asian Affairs
Harlan Cleveland, Assistant Secretary of State for International Organization Affairs

---

[1] Source: Department of State, Ball Papers: Lot 74 D 272, Memcons Other Than Visits. Secret; Exdis–TUG. Drafted by Cleveland and Yost and approved in U on June 29.

I.

In morning session with the UN Mediator Tuomioja, Under Secretary Ball and Ambassador Stevenson (with Ambassador Yost, Assistant Secretary Talbot and Assistant Secretary Cleveland) outlined upshot of Washington conversations with Prime Minister Inonu and Papandreou, and asked whether Mr. Tuomioja would be prepared to ask Greek and Turkish Governments to appoint representatives to assist him, ask the United States to provide someone to help, and arrange private Greek-Turkish talks as part of the UN mediation framework.

Mr. Tuomioja said he personally considered this "a practical approach", but as "UN man", he had to consider following angles and discuss them with the Secretary General:

(a) He saw no difficulty in his asking Greek and Turkish Governments provide representatives to assist him in finding a permanent solution.

(b) He thought something would have to be done to cut the Cypriots in. He was clear they should not be in the Greek-Turkish meetings as such, but should perhaps be available somewhere nearby so that Mr. Tuomioja could keep in consultation with the Government of Cyprus. Mr. Tuomioja made clear he regarded this as window dressing at this stage.

(c) He did not like Camp David as a site, preferring somewhere in Switzerland. Recognizing that Geneva is quite accessible to daily contact with the press, he mentioned Lausanne or Evian as possibilities.

(d) He found most difficulty with his designating an American to help him or asking the United States Government to do so. He clearly thought this would produce considerable political heat from the Russians, Cypriots and others, and wanted to consider with the Secretary General how much of this kind of heat the United Nations could properly take.

On the substance of the solution, he said in his opinion "only basis is enosis", with whatever compensation is necessary to make it palatable to the Turks. But he also commented that the "Makarios solution", which he defined as unrestricted independence leading rapidly to enosis, would not be so bad.

He was not surprised to learn that the Turks were relatively easy to deal with in Washington, while the Greeks were making difficulties. The Turks are in "very weak" position, unless they play their ultimate card. The Greeks naturally believe that the United States will prevent the Turks playing that card; counting on the United States, therefore the Greeks feel that they "have it their own way."

II.

A meeting of the same Americans with the Secretary General (also Bunche and Rolz-Bennett) followed:

The Under Secretary opened with a summary of the events since February as the United States sees them, stressing the Turkish threats, and Turkish "bitterness and frustration" when dissuaded from action by the United States. The United States had decided we could help best by having the Greeks and Turks get together with Mr. Dean Acheson at a private retreat such as Camp David.

The Turks had agreed, but the Greeks evidently found difficulties with this proposition. Papandreou had made strong domestic commitments that he would not talk with the Turks under US pressure; and the Greeks anyway think time is on their side. Mr. Ball said the United States had made clear we would not fight an ally ("You couldn't sink Turkish ships," commented U Thant); the Under Secretary added that our influence in Ankara might prove a wasting asset.

At the end of the Papandreou discussions in Washington, Mr. Ball said, the Greeks agreed that they would do anything the Mediator asks them to do, including designating representatives or even meeting jointly with Mr. Acheson if the Mediator requests it. Mr. Ball then reported on our conversation with Tuomioja. The Secretary General said Tuomioja had also meanwhile reported to him.

The points the Secretary General made in reply were these:

(a) The UN Mediator is competent to adopt whatever procedures he wishes, but asked the Secretary General for political advice on US suggestions.

(b) The Secretary General and Tuomioja have agreed that it would be useful to ask Greek and Turkish Governments to provide representatives to assist in finding a permanent solution.

(c) The resulting discussions should probably be in Geneva rather than in the United States.

(d) The Secretary General thought that any formula for designating Mr. Acheson as counsel to the UN Mediator would create difficulties under the Security Council Resolution of March 4th.

(e) The Secretary General's counterproposal was that Tuomioja would invite the Turks and the Greeks to designate representatives to meet with him in or near Geneva, on the understanding that Tuomioja was also free to consult with a representative of the United States (Dean Acheson). Mr. Acheson could be close by and in frequent touch with the Mediator as conversations proceeded.

The Under Secretary said in his judgment the contribution of the United States would not be worth anything on this basis, and a lengthy discussion followed.

The Secretary General made clear that he did believe "the United States is in the best position to contribute to a peaceful solution of this problem" and that it would be useful for the United States to be constructively related to the mediation process. But he was sure that if the United Nations served as cover for United States participation, it would make great difficulties for the Secretary General under the Security Council Resolution. His point was that the Security Council Resolution provides for appointment of a Mediator with the consent of all four governments concerned (Turkey, Greece, the United Kingdom and Cyprus). If Cyprus, or any of the others decided that the Mediator was operating in an unsatisfactory manner, and so declared to the Secretary General, U Thant said he would have no alternative but to terminate Tuomioja's services and get another mediator.

The Secretary General also argued that the presence of Acheson as a UN representative would increase likelihood Cypriots would want to be represented too and he predicted the Soviets would ask for a Security Council meeting to complain of manner in which the Secretary General was discharging his responsibility under March 4 Resolution. Some political risk was acceptable, but as Ralph Bunche put it, the risk was too high if the Mediator provided cover for a US operation. "Perhaps the mediator is expendable but the Secretary General is not."

In the course of this discussion, the Secretary General and Mr. Bunche came around to a somewhat more flexible proposal, under which Mr. Acheson, operating not as UN counsel but as a representative of the United States Government, would meet not only with Tuomioja but also with the Greeks and Turks, together or separately as seemed most useful. But such meetings would have to be worked out on spot with the Greeks and the Turks rather than taking place under the UN Mediator's direct sponsorship.

The Secretary General seemed not to share fully our sense of urgency in a quick solution, though Ralph Bunche commented at one point that the United Nations Force in Cyprus is in an increasingly untenable position, with the continuing inflow of arms and growing bitterness between the two ethnic groups.

In the course of discussions, the Under Secretary mentioned that the Mediator had made known to the Turks his personal view that a likely permanent solution was enosis with Greece. This was clearly news to both the Secretary General and Bunche, who said this had not been included in any report by the Mediator; they could fully understand the dangerous effect of such comments by a UN Mediator on sensitive Turkish nerves. The Under Secretary made clear that the United States has no position on an ultimate solution, but doubted that any straight enosis recommendation by the Mediator was a useful starting-point for the substantive discussions.

III.

After luncheon for Prime Minister Papandreou, the Secretary General informed Ambassador Yost of the substance of his conversation with the Prime Minister before lunch, as follows:

Papandreou had said he is entirely willing, if the UN Mediator so requests, to designate a Representative to meet with a Turkish Representative and with Tuomioja at any time. If meeting is to take place in New York, the Prime Minister would designate the Greek Permanent Representative to the UN, Ambassador Bitsios. The Secretary General replied that Tuomioja would be making his headquarters for the time being in Geneva and the meetings could be held there.

When the Secretary General raised question of the presence of a United States Representative at these meetings, Prime Minister Papandreou replied he would not wish a US Representative to be formally designated by Mr. Tuomioja as advisor or counsel or to take part in meetings of Greeks and Turks chaired by Mr. Tuomioja. When the Secretary General proposed, however, that Mr. Dean Acheson as US Representative might be available in Geneva, "even in next room or in next building", to meet separately with mediator, and with Greek and Turkish Representatives, in order assist in search for settlement, Prime Minister Papandreou replied that this would be entirely agreeable to him.

The Secretary General commented that this seemed to him a reasonable arrangement which should take account of our views and needs without risking the kinds of difficulties which he had outlined to us this morning. He added that Prime Minister Papandreou and Mr. Tuomioja were at that moment discussing details of the proposed arrangement.

Subsequently, Ambassador Yost called Mr. Tuomioja who said he had reached agreement with Prime Minister Papandreou along the lines the Secretary General had described, and would be addressing to the United States about July 6 an invitation to send a representative to Geneva to be available for consultation. He has in mind himself proceeding to Geneva from Cyprus July 4, and opening the meeting with Greeks and Turks early the following week. He would keep closely in touch with Mr. Acheson, and believed the Greeks and the Turks would do likewise.

He said he plans to hold conversations with the Greeks and the Turks at UN headquarters in Geneva (the Palais des Nations) but that meetings with Mr. Acheson might take place wherever convenient to all concerned. He was confident of his ability to carry on negotiations without undue press interference and did not contemplate any announcement to the press of the proposed Greek-Turkish talks until they actually begin. He did not intend before July 6 to address formal invitation to Greeks and Turks to meet with him.

Ambassador Yost emphasized the importance of extending an invitation to the Turks promptly so that they would know that the desired negotiations are about to commence and would hence be more likely to refrain from any hazardous action. Mr. Tuomioja saw the point and said that, after consultation with his UN colleagues, he would either address formal invitations to the Greeks and the Turks right away, or else would issue statement to the press announcing that he intends to extend such an invitation.

Comment: It is clear that the Secretary General cannot be pushed to provide United Nations sponsorship for mediation between the Greeks and the Turks essentially conducted by the United States. However, we must apply a sufficient proportion of US persuasion to a mediation process set up by the UN Mediator. Sine qua non is therefore that we make sure that all parties concerned at this stage (Greeks, Turks, SYG and Tuomioja) understand need for, and welcome, day-to-day discussions with US representative at or near the scene of mediation talks.

77.   Memorandum of Conversation[1]

New York, June 26, 1964, 6:30 p.m.

SUBJECT

Cyprus

PARTICIPANTS

Greek
His Excellency George Papandreou, Prime Minister of Greece
His Excellency Andreas Papandreou, Minister-alternate for Economic
    Coordination
His Excellency Alexander A. Matsas, Ambassador of Greece
Mr. John Sossides, Chef de Cabinet of the Prime Minister

United States
The Honorable George W. Ball, Under Secretary of State
The Honorable Henry R. Labouisse, American Ambassador to Greece
The Honorable Harlan Cleveland, Assistant Secretary of State for International
    Organization Affairs
The Honorable Phillips Talbot, Assistant Secretary of State for Near Eastern and
    South Asian Affairs

---

[1] Source: Department of State, Conference Files: Lot 74 D 272, CF 2417. Secret; Exdis–TUG. Drafted by Talbot and approved in U on July 11. The meeting was held at the Plaza Hotel.

Mr. Ball called on Prime Minister Papandreou to confirm and pull together the results of several discussions earlier in the day that had involved the Greek Prime Minister's party, the Secretary General of the United Nations, the United Nations Mediator, and Mr. Ball and his colleagues. The Prime Minister was extremely tired. Three hours earlier he had cancelled a talk at the Council on Foreign Relations. He was cheerful, however. He felt he had reached a "perfect understanding" with the mediator, and could leave the United States having overcome the "mood of dispute" that characterized his Washington talks. Nevertheless, when pressed on details of the proposed arrangements, he continued to resist firmly all suggestions that the Greek and United States Governments could, if necessary, agree together to involve an American representative in the Cyprus discussions.

Observing that the Prime Minister had had a busy day in New York, Mr. Ball asked how he now saw the situation. The Prime Minister replied that happily he and the mediator, Ambassador Tuomioja, had reached total agreement. The mediator would be in Geneva and Mr. Papandreou would name a representative to meet with him. After that the mediator would have the total initiative; whatever he asked, Mr. Papandreou would accept. The meeting with the Secretary General, on the other hand, had been rather more difficult. In passing, U Thant had said that all people were speaking to him today about Dean Acheson. The Secretary General believed an impression of conspiracy would develop if Mr. Acheson were brought directly into the negotiations.

Mr. Ball said that in considering possible arrangements we had been sensitive to the political problems of the Prime Minister. We wanted to see a satisfactory solution. As he understood the agreed plan, the mediator would invite Mr. Acheson to Geneva and suggest to the Greek and Turkish representatives who would be there that there be some talks with Mr. Acheson as well. The Prime Minister said the mediator had not told him Mr. Acheson would see the representatives independently of himself. Mr. Cleveland noted that we had understood from Ambassador Tuomioja that he would prefer not to have four-way meetings. The mediator would meet with representatives of Greece and Turkey, and he expected that Mr. Acheson would do so also. The Prime Minister said he had understood the essence of the mediator's position to be that at the first stage any meetings with Mr. Acheson should be bilateral and not with the Greeks and Turks present together. The Greek and Turkish representatives would not meet together unless their Governments specifically agreed on that. However, he respected totally the initiative of Mr. Tuomioja.

Mr. Ball said we probably had the basis for the beginning of some talks. Success would depend on the will of the parties. Knowing it would not be easy, we were prepared to be helpful in any way we could. The

Prime Minister expressed pleasure that we were now in agreement. He was also grateful for the initiative that had been taken by President Johnson. Greece needs peace, and for this it needs a final objective solution of the Cyprus dispute.

Mr. Ball commented that meanwhile we had received disturbing reports about conditions on the island itself. The Prime Minister replied that on those matters he would use all of his influence. We could count on that. He had told Mr. Tuomioja that as soon as the mediator's request arrived he would send a representative immediately to Geneva. The Prime Minister added that he was happy that we could meet today to show a change in the atmosphere to one of friendship and understanding rather than dispute.

The Prime Minister reiterated that so long as the mediator suggested a meeting between the Greek representative and Mr. Acheson it would be done. Mr. Ball concluded that this formula should help move things along if the parties so desired. Mr Talbot asked hypothetically what would be the situation if the mediator invited Mr. Acheson to Geneva but for one reason or another was shy about specifically asking the Greek and Turkish representatives to meet with him. There would be a general invitation but from what the Secretary General had said in the morning it was conceivable that the mediator would hesitate to make a formal request of the parties to meet with Mr. Acheson. Mr. Talbot said that if something like this should happen he assumed our two governments could work things out together. The Prime Minister replied that this would change the basic situation. It was essential that the mediator take the initiative. He could send a general invitation to all the parties. Just four men would be involved so there should be no mystery. It would need to be at the mediator's initiative, however.

Mr. Ball said that we understood the Prime Minister's approach. In a situation like this, of course, people must proceed pragmatically. We would have preferred a simpler situation, but we will work within the practical framework. As the President had said to the Prime Minister, we had been disappointed that we could not work out a more straightforward arrangement. Faced with the dangerous situation in Cyprus, however, we must do all we can. He could assure the Prime Minister that the United States would do everything possible to cooperate. As the Prime Minister had observed, Ambassador Labouisse was greatly trusted by the Secretary of State and the President and he could speak with an authoritative voice in discussing these matters with the Prime Minister. We would do what we could to get us all out of a very dangerous situation.

The Prime Minister once again thanked Mr. Ball, expressing his appreciation for the reception that had been given him in Washington, and confirmed that Ambassador Labouisse's many qualities made him a valuable cooperator in Athens. The discussion was left at that point.

THE ACHESON MEDIATION, JUNE–SEPTEMBER 1964

78. Telegram From the Mission to the United Nations to the Department of State[1]

New York, June 27, 1964, 3:25 p.m.

4651. Re: Cyprus. Stevenson, Cleveland and Yost had rather discouraging conversation with SYG this afternoon.

When told that Tuomioja had informed us he intended to dispatch invitation to USG to send representative to Geneva to be available during his conversations with Greek and Turkish representatives, SYG said he had never contemplated that Mediator would go so far and that it would be most unwise politically. He repeated what he had said yesterday that this might provoke withdrawal of confidence in Mediator by Cypriot Govt.

He was, however, prepared to advise Tuomioja that, if Acheson comes to Geneva during Greek-Turkish conversations, he would recommend to both parties that they meet separately or collectively with Acheson and express view US could make unique contribution to negotiations.

In course of conversation, SYG expanded somewhat on his conversation with Papandreou yesterday, reporting that PM, while prepared to have his representative meet with Turks and Mediator at latter's request, saw no real use in meeting since he thought both parties would merely repeat known positions. As far as Greece is concerned, he added, Cyprus is independent state and UN member, and its only obligation is to decide its future by democratic principles laid down in Charter. Turks must simply accept such settlement, although there can be NATO base on Cyprus with Turkish participation and international guarantees for Turkish minority.

It was left that Stevenson would communicate with SYG after he meets with Papandreou this evening and that, unless new complications appeared, Thant would communicate with Tuomioja in Helsinki, urging him to dispatch invitations to GOT and GOG promptly, to get meetings started as soon as possible, and advising him under circumstances described above, he should recommend parties meet with Acheson.

Incidentally, it was also mentioned that Galo Plaza has informed SYG he intends to leave Cyprus end of first week in July since he believes

---

[1] Source: Department of State, Central Files, POL 23–8 CYP. Secret; Immediate; Exdis–TUG.

there is nothing more he can do unless and until there is progress toward political settlement.

Stevenson

---

79.   Telegram From the Embassy in Cyprus to the Department of State[1]

Nicosia, June 29, 1964, 6 p.m.

1422. Re Deptel 978.[2] In hour-long conversation with President this morning we discussed number of subjects, principal among them the problem of Tylliria area and Grivas return. (Latter covered in separate telegram.)[3]

Conversation opened by my reference to recent Washington talks in which I followed point by point suggestions outlined reftel 978. I made special point of fact that my reason for bringing up subject of Tylliria was with reference to present delicate situation outlined to me by my old friend Galo Plaza and General Gyani. As in past I was again urging restraint and patience since any dramatic development might well bring on new Turkish move which we might not be in a position stop again.

In response Makarios said first of all we should not read too much into his statement to Associated Press.[4] His purpose had been to avoid possible adverse reaction to "expected failure" of Washington talks, hence his effort to play them down while at same time making clear that any decisions regarding future of Cyprus would have to be submitted to Cypriots and could not be result merely of talks between other countries. Said he quite understood US effort in context of over-all UNSYG attempt to find satisfactory solution but he wondered whether failure of Pres

---

[1] Source: Department of State, Central Files, POL 23–8 CYP. Secret; Priority; Exdis–TUG. Repeated to USUN.

[2] Telegram 978 to Nicosia, June 28, instructed Belcher to convey to Makarios the reality of the danger of a Turkish intervention and the likelihood that the United States would be unable to deter such action. (Ibid.)

[3] Telegram 1427 from Nicosia, June 30. (Ibid.)

[4] Apparent reference to Makarios' rejection of the U.S. offer to provide assistance to the U.N. Mediator.

Johnson's efforts had not perhaps left situation worse than it had been two weeks ago. I told him that although matter would be kept confidential for obvious reason we understood Mediator had some further thoughts regarding possibility of further consultations among parties concerned (I did not mention any US involvement and he would presumably be hearing from Tuomioja upon his return). Makarios went on to make surprise statement that in any bilateral talks that might develop with Turkey, Greek Government could only discuss solutions on the basis of enosis of Cyprus with Greece and that any solution other than enosis and/or complete independence could only be reached with participation of Cypriot representatives. (This would seem to explain Papandreou's refusal consider any possible divergences from these two principles.)

Archbishop said that both Plaza and Gyani had called to impress on him need for patience and restraint but said he had told them that although he would not use armed force that the status quo could not continue indefinitely. He said he had feeling UN would consider its job well done in next three months if it could say that not a shot had been fired. Naturally this was most commendable aim but without some progress on political front basic tensions at least on Greek side could hardly be reduced. Some change would have to come before the end of the year when economic and political pressures would be severe.

President went on to say he could understand our apprehension regarding the present tense situation particularly with regard to possible Turkish intervention and all that would imply. Said he could assure me that for their part Greek Cypriots would not use force unless attacked. They were however giving serious consideration to use of other pressures which he had enumerated to me previously and he again said that if freedom of movement not restored in presently Turkish-held areas, his govt would be forced to deny freedom of movement to Turkish Cypriots.

I expressed gratification at this indication that Greek Cypriot side would do nothing to create a new crisis through military action and I urged him to give very careful consideration to nature of other pressures which he might feel were required in order not to bring on new danger of Turkish intervention which this time we might find even more difficult if not impossible to prevent. Although I had made it quite clear that US could not contemplate hostilities with an ally over Cyprus problem I am not convinced that Archbishop has accepted this as cold fact of situation.

President was more relaxed than during last meeting and seemed much less militant in his declarations of need for progress on political front. Perhaps UN reps plus Greek Amb Delivanis plus our representations have had some effect.

Belcher

80.   Telegram From the Department of State to the Embassy in
      Greece[1]

Washington, July 1, 1964, 9:17 p.m.

6. For Chargé. Please deliver soonest following letter from President Johnson to Prime Minister:

"Dear Mr. Prime Minister:

I want to tell you again how glad I am that we had an opportunity to visit together and to exchange views on the critical problem of Cyprus. I know that the course of the discussion was not altogether easy for either of us, but I am sure that it is of great importance for those of us who bear the responsibility for government within the Western Alliance to talk honestly together on such grave matters. It is out of just such hard work together that we can ensure a high degree of understanding.

Over this last weekend I have been thinking some more about our conversation and about the problem of Cyprus, and I think it may be helpful for me to continue our discussion by sending this message to you as you return to Athens.

First of all, let me say that the last week has only strengthened my deep conviction that the problem of Cyprus grows more urgent and dangerous with every day that goes by. Until we can get serious negotiations started, we must recognize that time will not work on the side of peace. Right now we are coming near to the last hour. That is why I hope our two Governments can agree in the view that in this very dangerous situation it is absolutely essential that serious and searching talks should be started promptly.

I promise you that my conviction that we are at the edge of a crisis is not lightly formed. It rests on two powerful facts: the first is that passion on Cyprus is now intense on both sides, and the second, that the build-up of armaments on the Island continues. This is a condition which is bound to become increasingly explosive; indeed, the build-up of armaments on the Island is already dangerously close to the flash point. And even without an immediate explosion the belief that danger is steadily increasing could at any time create pressures for intervention in Turkey which may prove irresistible. Having prevented such intervention by most strenuous personal efforts last month, I know very well that there is a limit to what any of us can do from now on, to prevent the Turks from exercising rights which are very real indeed to them.

---

[1] Source: Department of State, Central Files, POL 23–8 CYP. Secret; Immediate; Exdis–TUG. Drafted by Bundy, cleared by Talbot, and approved by Ball. In a July 1 memorandum to the President, Bundy commented that Ball felt a letter to Papandreou was needed as a stern reminder of the dangers created by Papandreou's resistance to real negotiations. Bundy further commented: "Papandreou will not like this letter, any more than Inonu liked your letter of June 5. But that is not the point now." (Johnson Library, National Security File, Memos to the President—McGeorge Bundy, Vol. 6)

I see only one way in the world to turn the course of events away from this pathway toward disaster, and that is by a prompt and determined search by Greece and Turkey for a permanent political settlement. I recognize that such a joint effort will have some critics and opponents on all sides, and I recognize also the quite understandable belief of many in your country that all that is needed is that the majority of the people of Cyprus should be allowed to settle their own future. But let me urge with all the force I can, that it simply is not enough, in this most dangerous situation, to have a belief in the rightness of one's own argument. The pressures on Turkey for action are extremely strong, and they too derive from a deep conviction that Turkish rights are at stake.

As I said in our discussions, the United States most earnestly desires to be helpful in the search for a solution, but the United States does not seek to impose any outside view, or to take sides with one of its friends against another. Our conviction is that any successful solution must derive from the agreement of the parties and cannot be dictated or imposed from outside. But we shall be just as helpful as we can to both our friends, once a serious discussion begins.

Moved by my sense of the increasing danger of this question, let me say once again, as solemnly as possible, how much I hope that the Government of Greece will be able to join in a prompt and determined effort to seek through negotiation a lasting answer to this perilous problem. It is in this spirit that I hope your representative will be empowered to discuss all aspects of the Cyprus problem with the mediator and the Turkish representative. I hope also that his instructions may be so framed that our American representative will also be able to help in bringing about a settlement. In such discussions, neither side must insist that there is only one acceptable basis for discussion; both sides—and all of us who hope to be helpful—must approach these negotiations with a resolute determination to work out a peaceful answer.

Let me say again in closing that I fully recognize your responsibility not only to join in preserving peace but to uphold the principles of your Government and the rights of your people in accordance with your duty as the leader of Greece. You can be sure that the United States, in urging negotiation and in offering help to the mediator, intends no disregard whatever of the rights of Greeks and of Turks in their homelands and on Cyprus. My conviction is simple: that the real interests of the peoples and the real responsibilities of their leaders can be met if there is real negotiation—and that if there is not such negotiation, none of us can prevent a disaster for which all of us will be held accountable.

Sincerely, Lyndon B. Johnson"

Rusk

81.   Telegram From the Embassy in Greece to the Department of State[1]

Athens, July 2, 1964, 8 p.m.

18.   Ref: Deptel 06.[2] I transmitted President Johnson's letter to Pri-Min Papandreou today at 1 p.m. As I arrived Papandreou was conferring with Defense Minister Garoufalias and Cypriot leaders Georkatzis and Illiades who excused themselves, leaving us alone.

During reading of President's letter, PriMin's expression was serious even grim. After having read letter he commented, "more of the same." Everyone in Washington, he said, applied pressure on him to negotiate as though negotiation were the magic formula, but he had not heard one specific suggestion in Washington as to what he is to negotiate about, or what US would consider an acceptable solution. Because of danger of armed Turkish intervention, Greece is urged to make concessions. But what concessions is Greece to make, what rights are Turks giving up which require that they be compensated by Greece. Greece asks nothing from Cyprus. This is not basically a Greek-Turkish problem. There are questions of principle involved, one of which is independence, self-determination and integrity of Cyprus.

I am told, he said, that I must negotiate because if I do not negotiate the Turks will resort to armed intervention. The US has exhausted its efforts to restrain Turks and responsibility for the peace thus rests upon Greece. Mr. McNamara pointed out to me how powerful Turkish military forces are, but Greece cannot act under pressure of ultimatum. We did not accept an ultimatum from our enemies in 1940,[3] and it is very difficult for us to accept an ultimatum today from our friends. How can a nation (US) maintain its position as the leader of free world unless it has a policy? How can it fail to continue to support principle of self-determination? How can US fail to say to Turkey—or to Greece for that matter: "the arms which you possess are arms which we have given you for the purpose of self-defense. We (US) will not accept that our arms be used in an aggressive manner, risking the danger of war, perhaps a small war, but one which could escalate into a large war." How can Greece's NATO allies fail to tell the Turks that they do not accept aggressive actions which may precipitate a war. Greece can accept a political struggle; Greece can accept debate in the UN and in NATO; but Greece cannot accept a policy which justifies the use of force.

---

[1] Source: Department of State, Central Files, POL 23–8 CYP. Secret; Immediate; Exdis–TUG.

[2] Document 80.

[3] Reference is to the Greek Government rejection of an ultimatum from Italy.

Papandreou said de Gaulle had agreed that Cypriot right to self-determination must be respected and that Turkish threats of armed intervention were unacceptable. Papandreou gave no intimation that de Gaulle may have been alluding to right of both Greek and Turkish Cypriot communities to self-determination.

I replied GOG would be making a serious error in interpreting Washington's analysis of current situation as an ultimatum, and I asked whether he did not have feeling that although there may be serious differences of view regarding tactics, US and GOG were, in fact, moving in same general direction. Prime Minister did not answer directly, but excused himself for bluntness of his statement and promised that he would reply tomorrow (*sic*) to President's letter.[4]

I inquired whether press reports that Nikolareizis (Greek Ambassador to Belgrade) would be sent to Geneva were correct. He confirmed this and added that Nikolareizis arriving in Athens tomorrow to report to him prior to going to Geneva. I said that I was confident that Washington would be very much gratified by his decision to send such an experienced diplomat to Geneva.

Comment: Papandreou made no effort conceal his disappointment at failure Greek position evoke greater understanding and sympathy in Washington, as well as certain irritation at what he considers implied US threat to stand aside in event of new Turk decision intervene militarily. Papandreou's Washington visit has probably produced some bruises which will be slow in disappearing. Although he spoke with obvious [garble—agitation] he was not abusive or discourteous.

I think we should consider appointment Nikolareizis as gesture in our direction even though it may not presage immediate substantive changes in GOG position.

Anschuetz

---

[4] Papandreou replied to this letter on July 6, defending Greek policy. A copy of that letter is in the Johnson Library, National Security File, Memos to the President—McGeorge Bundy, Vol. 6.

82.   Memorandum for the Record[1]

Washington, July 7, 1964.

SUBJECT

NSC Meeting July 7, 1964 at 12 Noon on Cyprus

PARTICIPANTS

See Attached List[2]

Secretary Ball led off the discussion of Cyprus by telling the President he thought it would be useful to report to the NSC on a situation which was like a time bomb that could blow up any time in the next six weeks. His report largely reflected the State Department memorandum submitted prior to the meeting.[3]

One of the principal problems, he said, is irrationality on both sides. The Greeks figure time is on their side. They think they can work out a plebiscite followed by enosis simply by sitting tight. The threat of Turk invasion has roused their stubbornness and Athens seems blind to its long-range interest in conceding enough to Ankara to provide a basis for improved relations after a Cyprus settlement. The Turks, on the other hand, see their position being eroded day by day. They resent our having restrained them when chances for a successful invasion were best, and they are bitter over Greek and Cypriot disregard of the London–Zurich treaties. They see a political solution as the only alternative to exercising their right of intervention.

Pressures are building up, Mr. Ball went on. The Greeks have sent 4000 troops to the island (CIA believes 5–7000), in addition to their regular garrison there. The Turks, who have to put their men ashore at night from small boats, have sent perhaps 1000 in addition to their garrison. The Turks see the Greek buildup outrunning theirs and their hope of successful intervention vanishing. Meanwhile, General Grivas—a fanatic, fortunately anti-Communist—has taken over the Greek Cypriot forces and hopes to build an army of some 35,000 men. The Turks have a lurking fear that Grivas may overthrow Makarios suddenly and simply announce annexation of Cyprus to Greece. So the pressure on the Turks to act soon is increasing. Moreover, the Turks know of the Greek plan, if the situation drags on through the summer, to throw the whole question

---

[1] Source: Johnson Library, National Security File, NSC Meetings File, Vol. 2. Top Secret. Drafted by Harold H. Saunders.

[2] Not found.

[3] A memorandum entitled "Talking Paper for the Under Secretary at NSC Meeting," July 6, outlined the current situation in Cyprus and the options available to the United States. (Department of State, S/S–NSC Files: Lot 70 D 265, NSC Meeting July 7, 1964)

to the UN General Assembly where the Greeks are confident they will get a blessing for self-determination leading to enosis. On top of this, incidents could trigger Turk Cypriot rebellion or island-wide fighting at any time.

We are staking our bets of necessity on the Geneva talks, Mr. Ball continued. Acheson has arrived. The arrangements made for him there are not good but are the best we have been able to work out. He had his first talk with the UN Mediator yesterday and reports an atmosphere of pessimism. However, we hope his further discussions before talks with the Greeks and Turks begin early the week of 13 July may improve the atmosphere. Meanwhile, we are doing extensive contingency planning to limit the scope of a Greek-Turk war if the Turks invade and to keep bloodshed on Cyprus to a minimum. We are also considering how we should handle ourselves in the UN Security Council and how we might develop safehavens for refugees on the island. On 9 July we are holding a meeting here with the British and Canadians to see what pressure they can bring to bear on the Greeks. We are also studying seriously the problem of evacuating officials and tourists should war break out.

At that point the President broke in to ask how many Americans are in the area. Mr. Ball replied that there are about 250 on Cyprus, mostly with our communications facilities there. Since we went through an evacuation exercise earlier this year, he contemplates little difficulty there.[4] In Greece there are 5–6000 Americans and in Turkey 16–17,000. However, he felt that danger in the mainland countries of a severe anti-American reaction would not be great.

The President then asked whether Papandreou had replied to his letter (of 2 July).[5] Mr. Ball said the reply had just come in and that it was simply a pro forma reiteration of the Greek position and really did not take us anywhere.[6] The President said he wanted to see that letter as soon as possible.

There followed a detailed briefing by Gen. Burchinal on the military forces that would participate in any hostilities on Cyprus. The attached memorandum records the substance of this briefing.[7] Mr. Ball, at the end of the briefing, highlighted the fact that the Turk goal is limited to establishing a beachhead for bargaining purposes; the Turks do not want the kind of war that complete conquest would require. Mr. Ball also estimated that perhaps 20–25,000 villagers might be slaughtered once an invasion started. General Burchinal suggested that Turk air mastery

---

[4] In January 1964, the United States evacuated the families of officials working in Cyprus.

[5] See Document 80.

[6] See footnote 4, Document 81.

[7] Not found.

might prove some deterrent since Greek villages would be vulnerable. No one responded, but the feeling seemed to be that this would only increase the carnage.

The President summarized his understanding in these terms: The Turks have substantially greater forces than the Greeks in every respect; they could land and maintain a beachhead; and the Soviets would not intervene. General Burchinal confirmed the President's understanding, estimating Turk army superiority at 3–1 and air force at 4–1. [2-1/2 lines of source text not declassified]

Secretary McNamara elaborated on the President's last point, saying we didn't think the Soviets would intervene militarily but they would unquestionably try to make political hay out of any disorder on Cyprus. General Wheeler added that a prime Soviet objective is the fragmentation of NATO and any Greek-Turk hostilities would further that end.

The President moved on to the question of what our next steps might be and asked whether there is anything further we can do to prevent Turkish invasion and to assure the success of the Geneva talks. He pointed out that the Greeks didn't expect much to come of these talks and have shown a good deal of irritation at the way we treated them during Papandreou's visit here.

Mr. Ball felt that the President had seriously shaken Papandreou with his statement that the US would not militarily restrain a Turkish invasion. He felt we had gained some ground with the Greeks during that visit. Mr. Bundy felt less optimistic, noting Greek peevishness over the President's latest letter.

The President recalled that Papandreou had pressed for a US formula when he was here. Mr. Ball pointed out the pitfalls of providing one at the outset of discussions. He said that Mr. Acheson is well prepared to introduce the elements of such a formula in the course of the Geneva talks. However, if we presented a US solution in advance, he felt both parties would attack it and walk out. The President agreed.

Secretary McNamara brought up the desirability of using General Lemnitzer and the North Atlantic Council (NAC) to bring home to the Greek and Turk military that a clash between them would be suicidal. Mr. Ball said General Lemnitzer was bearish on this idea because he did not feel the Greek military had much influence over its political leaders. His previous talks with them had netted little.[8] However, the NAC will be meeting 8 July and we expect a strong Canadian challenge to the Greeks based on reports that Greek NATO units and matériel are now on Cyprus. Both Secretaries McNamara and Ball, however, favored

---

[8] See Document 5.

instructing General Lemnitzer to go ahead and tell the Turk and Greek military again what we have told the political leaders. While Papandreou seems to have absorbed the President's warning, the military leaders still apparently feel that we will stop a Turk invasion and that no move they make really risks a direct Greek-Turk confrontation.

The President asked General Wheeler whether we have taken into account the demands that a Turkish invasion would place on NATO. General Wheeler felt we had examined the consequences carefully. He was concerned particularly about how the Turks would receive a direct US rebuff. However, he did not feel Turkey would "fall into the Soviet Bloc." He felt the strength of Greek Communists made Greece potentially very unstable. Ultimately he saw both Greece and Turkey lost to NATO if hostilities were permitted to go on very long.

The Attorney General suggested another approach. He asked about the possibility of organizing an effort to explain to influential elements other than the military and government in Greece and Turkey what the situation would be if either country took the steps it is contemplating. In other words, would the Turks like the situation that would exist after they secured a beachhead on Cyprus—carnage in the Turk Cypriot villages, world opinion against them, Greece less willing than ever to negotiate a settlement? Would the Greeks welcome a Turk foothold on Cyprus, the economic disruption of a Greek-Turk war, possibly defeat of Greek forces? Wouldn't there be some deterrent effect in getting across to influential Greeks and Turks an objective analysis of the situation they will have to cope with if they don't negotiate now?

Mr. Bundy asked Mr. Ball whether we could not do this sort of thing through our embassies. He felt that embassy involvement might create a clearer view in Ankara and Athens of our concern. Mr. Ball felt that it would be very difficult to do anything of this kind publicly because of the irrational atmosphere in both capitals. Anything we do, he said, gives the appearance of our working for the other side. For instance, if we described the terrible consequences of a Greek-Turk war, the Greeks would simply ask why, then, we would refuse to stop a Turk invasion. [1-1/2 lines of source text not declassified]

When the President asked how much of the position we took in the Washington talks has "dribbled down to the Greek and Turk populace", Mr. Ball said that the average Greek thinks we're holding the gun of a Turk invasion at Greek heads to force a deal. The Turks feel that, because we restrained their invasion, we're pro-Greek. So the people have very stereotyped views of our position. In the current hysterical atmosphere, it is very difficult to put across a reasonable explanation of our goals.

Secretary McNamara asked whether we couldn't stimulate leading Greek citizens to brief their own press and make it more aware of the consequences of the present course of events. For instance, could we get

Onassis and others of his importance to explain the economic consequences of provoking a Greek-Turk war?[9] He did not feel we could do
this directly but felt perhaps Mr. McCone might have some suggestions
to offer.

The Attorney General said he did not see any objection to our being
associated with such an effort. He felt that we would be talking simply
about the facts of a potential situation, not about controversial positions.
Mr. Bundy asked Mr. Ball how painful it might be if such a campaign
came out of Paris—from NAC members and NATO officers there. Mr.
Ball agreed that the farther from Washington the better and pointed out
that the UN Secretary General could also do some of this if he would.

Mr. Bundy wrapped up this part of the discussion by suggesting to
the President that we draw up a program for mounting such a campaign
just to see what it looks like. The President instructed him to do so with
the help of the agencies involved.

Mr. Bundy then moved to the problem of how we get the Geneva
talks going. He felt that the Greeks could get what they wanted if they
would just sit down and talk and asked whether we shouldn't use this
argument with them. Secretary Ball said he had done just this during his
luncheon with Papandreou. However, he pointed out that it is difficult to
carry this argument much further than private conversations because
the Turks could easily construe it as a US-Greek deal.

Mr. McCone asked whether the real problem wasn't what the Turks
would get out of these talks rather than how we could satisfy the Greeks.
He said he hadn't seen any evidence of a formula that would meet Turk
needs. Mr. Ball said he felt we could put together a package which the
Turks would think pretty good if we could once get the two parties
together.

The President returned to the question of how we might bring pressure to bear on the two governments. He asked Mr. Wilson how seriously
concerned the people of each country are about what is going on. Mr.
Wilson responded that the people of Turkey particularly are frustrated
by their government's inability to act in the current situation and pointed
out the danger that such frustration would lead to impulsive action. He
did not feel, however, that the people had thought through the consequences of a Turkish invasion. He felt we could draw up a list of people in
Paris, Athens, and Ankara who might be useful in creating a more realistic view of the consequences of invasion.

Mr. Talbot brought the discussion back to Geneva by pointing out
that we can't count on the Greeks to act in their own best interests. We

---

[9] Documentation relating to subsequent contacts with Aristotle Onassis are in
Department of State, Central Files, POL 23–8, and ibid., Ball Papers: Lot 74 D 272, Cyprus
Miscellaneous and Cyprus: Proposed Solutions.

can't rely simply on a campaign to make people aware of the consequences of their action—especially when they are acting irrationally. Therefore, he felt our best hope was in pushing the negotiations in Geneva.

The President reacted by saying if we are to succeed there we will need more power than we have had to date. We did our best during the Washington talks to convince both Greeks and Turks to negotiate. Now we are going to make another approach to the Turk military in an effort to get them to throw their weight into the scales on the side of moderation. He saw no reason why we should not explore every way of getting a reasonable view of the situation across to important people in both countries.

In conclusion, the President outlined two courses of action: (a) our military in Paris would make clear to the Greek and Turk military what consequences they could anticipate if either nation moved militarily; (b) we should also draw up a plan for getting this understanding across to as many influential people in both countries as possible.[10]

With that the meeting adjourned.

---

[10] Efforts to make the consequences of military action clear were outlined in a July 8 memorandum from Talbot to Bundy. (Johnson Library, National Security File, Country File, Cyprus, Vol. 9)

---

83.   Telegram From the Mission in Geneva to the Department of State[1]

Geneva, July 11, 1964, 2 p.m.

92. From Acheson.[2] We had amicable hour and quarter meeting this morning with Erim and Alacam. I began by suggesting we consider Turkey's security needs with regard to Cyprus. I mentioned possibility Turkish base on Karpas Peninsula. Erim countered by putting forward Turkey's desired partition line, enclosing whole northern part of island

---

[1] Source: Department of State, Central Files, POL 23–8 CYP. Secret; Exdis.

[2] On July 4, the Department of State announced that Acheson would go to Geneva at the President's request to provide assistance in helping to resolve the Cyprus crisis. Acheson held his first meeting with Turkish representatives on July 9.

and went on to give us standard Turkish position: that first Turkish demand was implementation London–Zurich Agreements and that failing this Turkey could only consider partition or federalism. We tried to point out probable impracticality of achieving any of these.

I touched on probable great cost to Turkey and Turkish Cypriots of solution which Turks would have to impose by force. Erim then took new tack, saying that after all Turkey could let Greece effect enosis as fait accompli, without fighting Greece, but refuse to recognize it and maintain continuing pressures against Greece in hope situation would change for better. I expressed great doubts Turkey's position would improve under such circumstances.

Speaking next about Turkey's concern for welfare Turk-Cypriots we broached idea that this might be taken care of without partition and within context of enosis. For example, I said, there could be a Turkish base large enough to be safe haven for those Turks unwilling to live under Greek rule, while for the other Turks a special semi-autonomous regime could be set up. This might comprise one or more areas where Turks were in majority (such as strip from northern Nicosia to Kyrenia) which would be administered directly by Turkish local authorities: for those areas where Turks remained in minority, there might still be arrangement whereby a Turk-Cypriot authority would nevertheless control and administer local affairs of Turkish villagers.

Erim seemed intrigued with this idea and said he would like to think about it. He asked whether base–safe haven area would be sovereign Turkish territory, a part of Turkey. We stretched matter a bit and said yes. He then suggested it would be desirable for a Turkish military expert come here to discuss what would be needed on Cyprus to protect Turkey from military point of view. Proposed to send for General Sunalp. I raised no objection.[3]

Erim flatly admitted Turks were going to expel Greeks from Turkey at end six-month period following denunciation of treaty as reprisal for Greek policies toward Cypriots. He further strongly indicated that Patriarchate would also be expelled, even though Turk Government had nothing special against Athenagoros. I said that expulsion of Greeks was not sufficient lever to affect Cyprus question at present. It would be more sensible to keep this weapon in reserve to be used in reprisal if Greeks later failed live up to guarantees they might give Turk Cypriots.

When we were discussing Turkish security problem, Erim particularly pointed out location of Kastellorizon. I asked if Turkey's security would be improved if it had this island, and he said that it would. At

---

[3] In telegram 96 from Geneva, July 13, Acheson reported that he had put forward a scheme for a semi-autonomous Turkish area that would not require geographic division. (Department of State, Central Files, POL 23–8 CYP)

another juncture, Erim referred to remarks made to him while in Washington that possibly Greek islands of Lesvos, Samos or Kos might be ceded as compensation for Cyprus. We rather threw cold water on this. I do think, however, that his apparent interest in Kastellorizon may have some significance.

Expect to see Turks again early next week.

Tubby

---

84.   **Telegram From the Embassy in Greece to the Department of State[1]**

Athens, July 12, 1964, 3 p.m.

76. 1. I had long talk with FonMin Costopoulos yesterday on Cyprus situation.[2] Reviewing Washington talks, he said Greek side had been struck and disappointed by rigidity of US position. Greeks had hoped for some substantive response to Papandreou's proposals for a solution and were surprised that President and Washington officials "concentrated only on procedure without touching on substance." They had feeling of great pressure exerted to force face-to-face talks with Turks, whereas they had cautioned us ahead of time they would not do so under existing circumstances, and they wanted our ideas as to a substantive solution.

2. For my part, I explained again great disappointment in Washington over what appeared to us to be most rigid position of PriMin, going over much of ground covered in talks and stressing what to me seemed to be "unconditional surrender" nature of Papandreou's position.

3. During talk, Costopoulos acknowledged that there had been no pressure in Washington for Papandreou–Inonu meeting. (This has also been acknowledged by Andreas Papandreou in conversation with Embassy officer.)

4. Geneva talks. Although Costopoulos personally believes that Greco-Turkish talks could prove useful, he said that Papandreou still adamant against bilateral talks with the Turks so long as Turkish threat continues. "If either Turkey or the United States will remove that threat, such bilateral talks can be held."

---

[1] Source: Department of State, Central Files, POL 23–8 CYP. Secret; Priority; Exdis.
[2] Labouisse met with King Constantine the same day for discussions on Cyprus. He reported on this meeting in telegram 75 from Athens, July 12. (Ibid.)

5. I then questioned Costopoulos about Nicolareizis' instructions, saying I hoped very much that they were broad enough to permit frank discussions with Acheson. He replied that Nicolareizis' instructions included authorization to talk to Acheson, to exchange views with him and to report, but not to engage in "negotiations." Constopoulos said he would want to keep in closest touch with me as things developed in Geneva. We trust that Dept and Acheson will keep us fully informed to permit us to attempt to stimulate appropriate responses from GOG.

6. Grivas. Costopoulos believes Grivas is gaining control of irregular forces on island, and he observed that there had been no marked reaction either from the Turks or British about his presence there. He added that it was important to remember that Grivas is main hope against Communists and that Makarios had had to go along so far.

7. FonMin stated that there was no question of Grivas and Makarios acting together to establish enosis.

8. Greek troops. Costopoulos asserted figures about presence Greek troops in Cyprus greatly exaggerated. He admitted that some non-coms had gone to Cyprus in past months in effort gain control of irregulars (this stated to us some time ago by Papandreou). In addition, some 800 Greek soldiers of Cypriot extraction had gone to island—"lets call them deserters." Only others were about one thousand Greek-Cypriot students who recently returned to island as part of Grivas' following.

9. FonMin expressed irritation over Canadian criticism of Greeks, when Turks have infiltrated many more into Cyprus.

10. Suggested approach to solution. Costopoulos said that in conversation with de Gaulle, Greeks had taken same line as in Washington. But idea was developed during talks of some sort of "regionalism" on island—"something like Alsace." Costopoulos was vague as to who suggested this, but gave the impression it came from the Greek side. He was explicit in saying that de Gaulle supported this idea. I probed to find what exactly was intended by suggestion, but Costopoulos was not clear as to practical workings. His explanation was to effect that an arrangement might be worked out which would ensure Cypriot sovereignty of whole island (subject to later enosis), full protection of minorities and some "Alsatian-type regionalism" which was neither partition nor federalism. Although I am not at all certain as to the implications of this suggestion, it seems to me to be well worth exploration.

11. Costopolous repeated that territorial concessions were out of question, "except possibly something like Kastellorizon."

Recommend Dept pass foregoing Ankara and Acheson.

Labouisse

85.   Telegram From the Mission in Geneva to the Department of
       State[1]

Geneva, July 14, 1964, 10 p.m.

114.   From Acheson. Met with Greek rep Nikolareisis for more than
an hour this morning. I gave him fairly lengthy exposition of our informal ideas, prefacing my remarks by saying this should not be considered
an "American plan" but rather suggests ways we would like to explore
with all concerned. I spoke of the three Turkish requisites: national prestige, national security and welfare of Turkish-Cypriots. Also pointed out
no solution could be pleasing to both sides and anything agreed upon in
end likely to be displeasing to both. If this resulted in criticism directed at
me or US Government, we were prepared to accept it.

As I had previously done with Turk, I spoke of possibility that sovereign base area on Cyprus, for example Karpas Peninsula, might meet
minimum Turkish security requisites. Suggested this area should be
large enough to provide sort of safe haven for Turk-Cypriots in times of
communal disturbances.

I said it seemed to me that neither enosis by itself, nor double enosis
nor federalism would necessarily solve problem of securing welfare
Turk-Cypriots. Even under Turks own preferred solutions, there would
undoubtedly still remain Turkish minorities in Greek-ruled part of
island. I was inclined to dismiss double enosis or federalism in any case, I
said, because I saw no way to impose these arrangements on hostile
Greek-Cypriots.

Therefore, I had been thinking of arrangement within framework of
some sort of enosis which would give Turk-Cypriots assurance that not
only their lives but their property, business, and way of life would be
safeguarded. This might be done through a special arrangement, under
overall Greek sovereignty, which would take advantage of flexibility
inherent in Greek administrative system. Perhaps one or two small areas
on island, such as stretch north from Turkish quarter of Nicosia, might be
designated as Eparchis and given local self-rule under Turkish Eparch
who would, of course, be responsible to higher Greek authority. Another
form of local self-rule could be devised for Turks in rest of island, also
subject to overall Greek rule.

To ensure that Turks would feel confidence in arrangement of this
kind, I considered it necessary that there be some international authority,
possibly a UN commissioner of sort which had operated in Danzig and
Saar between World Wars I and II, empowered to receive and investigate

---

[1] Source: Department of State, Central Files, POL 23–8 CYP. Secret; Priority; Exdis.

complaints and make recommendations for corrective action. In turn, there could be right of appeal to International Court of Justice.

Nikolareisis listened intently, took notes and asked number of questions. His only real comment was that he feared his government's public position was pretty far from the sort of thing I had outlined. He pointed out that so far GOG talked publicly only about full independence with right of self-determination, not about enosis. I reminded him of my earlier comment that no solution would be fully agreeable to all parties. However, if Greece and Turkey could come to meeting of minds, we could then deal with the problem of how to get a solution accepted by Makarios and Cypriots generally. Jernegan suggested that at such time GOG should mobilize all its assets (propaganda and other) to create popular demand on island for enosis.

During our polite preliminary exchanges, Nikolareisis said that he had had a long talk yesterday with Mediator who had expressed pleasure at my presence here and had asked him to discuss matters with me. Nikolareisis asked that I get in touch with him whenever I wished. We agreed that each should feel free to talk to the other whenever he had anything to talk about, but I said I probably would want to give him time to report and get reaction from Athens on what I had said. He emphasized and I agreed that these talks should be kept extremely secret.

My impression is that Nikolareisis takes his function seriously and will do his best to convey our thoughts and relay those of GOG to us, but his attitude today certainly bears out previous word that he is not authorized at this point to negotiate. Real test will no doubt come when he gets Athens view on my remarks today. I certainly went rather farther in accepting enosis as good solution than, I believe, any of us has done previously. If anything will induce Papandreou to embark on meaningful dialogue, this should do it.

Tubby

86.   Telegram From the Mission in Geneva to the Department of State[1]

Geneva, July 15, 1964, 9 p.m.

132.   From Acheson. We met again with Turks this afternoon, and I handed them copies of piece of paper in reply to Erim's questions which he sent me following yesterday's talk.[2] My memorandum, text of which is being telegraphed separately,[3] contained in fair detail outline compromise plan which I had previously sketched orally to Turks and to Greeks. It also contained certain arguments in rebuttal of military objections raised yesterday by Sunalp.[4]

After reading paper carefully, Erim opened by saying he still considered that full partition, with space for all Turkish-Cypriots, was only satisfactory answer to problem. Failing that, no safeguards could protect Turk minority against long-term pressures which would be exerted by Greek majority. Once again cited case of Crete and added Western Thrace as examples proving that Greeks always found means to make life unendurable for Turkish minority.

He then said paper I had given him, nevertheless, provided "first sign of way out" he had seen. Questioning brought out that he meant that paper accepted principle of Turkish sovereignty on part of Cyprus. Once this was granted, Turks would have firm basis for claiming full area they would need to accommodate all Turk-Cypriots. They could show, as they had explained to me yesterday, that they were entitled to an area of the island proportionate to their percentage of its population and its present land ownership, plus their proportionate share of public lands which were not privately owned either by the Greeks or the Turks. This would approximate areas they had suggested in their partition schemes.

I responded that if Turks considered full partition was only possible solution, I would of course be willing to present this to Greek rep, but I had absolutely no hope of its acceptance.

There ensued somewhat confused exchange, during which Erim once fell back on his earlier thesis that he would rather see a Greek fait accompli, which Turkey would denounce and refuse to recognize and for which it would exact political and economic revenge, than acquiesce in solution which would not be permanent and would not protect Turk-

---

[1] Source: Department of State, Central Files, POL 23–8 CYP. Secret; Priority; Exdis.

[2] Not found.

[3] Telegram 129 from Geneva, July 15. (Department of State, Central Files, POL 23–8 CYP)

[4] Sunalp posed a series of military objections to Acheson's suggestion during a July 14 meeting. Acheson reported on these talks in telegram 117 from Geneva, July 14. (Ibid.)

ish-Cypriots. I countered that Turkey would lose tremendously by such an attitude and that consequences would also be extremely rough on Turkish-Cypriots. Sunalp joined in with strong words about how Turks were ready to die for national good, himself included, and implied that it really wouldn't mean too much if a lot more Turkish-Cypriots did get killed.

At this point Erim made a calming gesture and gave me to understand that perhaps after all there might be room for a little bargaining on the basis I had suggested. Possibly, he said, we could get the Greeks to expand area of Turkish base or, as he preferred to call it, "Turkish area" to point where it would accommodate substantial number of Turkish-Cypriots. Turkey could call this partition, while Greeks might call it something else. At any rate, Erim intimated he would go back to Ankara and see what reaction there would be. We could talk again next week.

I said I would do my best with Greeks but could guarantee nothing.

We agreed that if anything developed during Erim's absence we would communicate with each other through Embassy Ankara and Turkish Mission here. (Turk Perm Rep has been present at all our talks.)

Would appreciate any suggestions Department has and especially comments on paper I gave Erim. Unless otherwise instructed, I have in mind giving Greek rep a suitably modified version of it if initial reaction from Athens to our conversation yesterday seems to warrant it.[5]

Tubby

---

[5] In telegram 136 to Geneva, July 15, the Department of State noted the Sunalp's comments indicated less flexibility in the Turkish position than the United States had been led to believe. It requested that the Embassy in Ankara sound out the Inonu government on these issues. (Ibid.)

---

87.   Telegram From the Embassy in Greece to the Department of State[1]

Athens, July 19, 1964, 11 p.m.

116. 1. In hour's talk with Prime Minister this Sunday afternoon, he elaborated on urgency with which he viewed need for solution Cyprus

---

[1] Source: Department of State, Central Files, POL 23–8 CYP. Secret; Immediate; Exdis–TAG. Repeated to Geneva, Ankara, Nicosia, and London. Passed to the White House.

problem. He underlined that he wanted to facilitate Mr. Acheson's work as much as possible and pointed out that, to this end, he had in radio address last night for first time stated that security of Turkish state, as well as protection of Turkish minority, was subject for discussion. Nikolareizis had been called back from Geneva and he was seeing him in evening to give him instructions for his future meetings. He said Nikolareizis could have full and frank discussions with Acheson.[2]

2. Papandreou pointed proudly to new picture of President Johnson on his bookcase and stated he felt very sorry that he had put on appearance of stubbornness in Washington in countering proposed procedure for getting on with Cyprus problem. He said that he genuinely believed then, as he does now, that until adequate preparations undertaken direct talks would very likely lead to a breakdown and possibility of a clash. He recalled Turkish riots in Istanbul in 1955 as example of what Turks do when talks not going their way. He stressed with great earnestness that he wanted to avoid Greek-Turkish clash at all costs; "war was one hundred times more serious for Greece than for the U.S.," and it was for this reason that he wanted to get on with substance of problem rather than procedures. He had therefore been disappointed that there had been no conversation as to a solution in Washington and only the stress on sitting down for talks with the Turks. With Turkey's continued threats and rigid position, this was impossible under existing circumstances. However, talks now under way in Geneva were right approach in moving toward solution and GOG intent on facilitating them as matter of urgency. The need for urgency was that Makarios was moving closer to Soviets and Nasser and was making moves without consulting GOG. He hinted that if too much time elapsed a full independent Cyprus, under strong pressure from the East, might not opt for enosis.

3. As to a solution he reiterated that Turkish minority should be provided all guarantees necessary, including UN supervision—"whatever you want." For sake of Turkish security and meeting "national prestige" aspect of the problem, he stated Greece would agree to a conversion of British bases to NATO bases with Turkish troops and commander. From Kyprianou he had heard that both Wilson in the UK and certain HMG sources were prepared to consider this solution. He said UK could either retain sovereignty or relinquish it—in either event arrangements could be made for NATO take over under a Turkish Commander. This latter point (which could be provided for in agreement between parties), in Papandreou's mind, should meet fully any claim by Turkey on security or prestige grounds. Papandreou did not see any possibility for a Turkish sovereign area on the island. After all, London–Zurich Agree-

---

[2] The Embassy reported on Nikolareisis' meeting with Papandreou in telegram 126 from Athens, July 21. (Ibid.)

ments had only gotten Turkish troops onto the island; giving them a sovereign area now after nearly 100 years in which Turkey had no claim to sovereignty on the island, would be an unacceptable step for any Greek Government as well as for Cypriots. However, GOG would be prepared to turn over Kastellorizon as a base. (There was also hint that some other concession might be possible, but it was not spelled out.)

4. Papandreou touched on Greek troop increase on island, calling them volunteers and "tolerated deserters." He gave no figures but insisted that they were there to prevent violence, whether from within or without, but most importantly to check and control Makarios and other Greek-Cypriot military groups.

5. When I raised question of Makarios' harassing actions re materials for Turkish-Cypriot refugees, as well as Greek-Cypriot military moves in Temblos and Mansoura area, he stated that Makarios was being called to Athens July 26 and he would impress upon him how counterproductive these actions were in that they goaded the Turks.

6. Brewster's and my over-all impression was that Papandreou very anxious to get on with a prompt solution and that he was eager to see gap between Turk and Greek position closed as soon as possible in Geneva. He fully supported actions of both the UN Mediator and Acheson in their efforts to reach a solution. He stated Greeks and US must at all time talk like "relatives", because Makarios, USSR and especially UAR were now acting like "relatives." But he cautioned that ultimate solution must be generally acceptable to Cypriot people or else fighting could not be controlled. We consider that Papandreou seriously believes his suggestion set forth in paragraph 3 is as far as he can push Cypriots.

Labouisse

---

88.   **Telegram From the Mission in Geneva to the Department of State**[1]

Geneva, July 20, 1964, 8 p.m.

168. From Acheson. Erim and Sunalp reported to us this morning on their visit in Ankara, Erim discussing political aspects of problem and Sunalp expounding Turkish military point of view (although he wandered over into political elements at times).

---

[1] Source: Department of State, Central Files, POL 23–8 CYP. Secret; Exdis–TAG. Repeated to Athens, Ankara, London, and USUN.

Erim said he had given report to Prime Minister and Cabinet Thursday night. Reaction to this, as to his earlier reports on talks with me, had been one of disappointment. View of Turkish Government, he said, was that Greeks had no intention of making any concessions or negotiating seriously, because they believed that they would gain 100 percent of their objective by standing pat. Their military buildup on island would permit them to do this, defying threat of Turkish intervention, and to hold off until UNGA meets this fall, at which time they could either get two-thirds affirmative vote in support of their position for complete independence and self-determination or, if Turks took initiative, defeat any Turkish complaint against them. Meanwhile, there was continuing danger of Greek fait accompli bringing about enosis.

Erim said, however, that he had assured government of his belief in my good faith and that USG through me was making sincere effort to find way out. He thought I should be given chance to try. GOT accordingly had authorized him to return here and continue talks even though it shared his own pessimistic view of results to be expected. I thanked him for this tribute and assured him that I would not hold him here beyond moment when I became convinced there was no hope of agreement. Thought I might have good indications on this point when I next saw Greek rep after his return from Athens consultations. (Nikolareisis returned today and we have appointment to meet tomorrow at 17:00 local.) If I thought Greeks were clearly unwilling to continue discussions on basis offering some hope of success, I would feel obliged to tell Erim so.

I then asked whether they could tell me anything more specific about their consultations in Ankara. At this point Sunalp largely took over conversation. Said that Turk General Staff had been impressed by plan I had outlined in my memorandum (Mission tel)[2] and had given it very careful and sympathetic study. As he put it, they had looked at it "with their white glasses rather than their dark glasses". He produced map of Cyprus which he said showed some of results of this study. It showed three boundary lines corresponding to three possibilities I had suggested:

1. A line crossing Karpas Peninsula about 2/3 of way in from Cape;
2. A line from Peristeria village on north coast running across to Boghaz on south coast and in effect enclosing whole peninsula; and
3. A line running from just west of Karavas (north coast west of Kyrenia) irregularly southeast through Nicosia and on to Famagusta and paralleling but running north of main Nicosia–Famagusta road.

Sunalp called his first line "Greek line" and seemed to dismiss it without consideration. Second line he argued would still be "unsatisfac-

---

[2] See Document 86.

tory as giving Turkey too little territory and, from military point of view, too little maneuverability. Third line would enclose about 21 percent, 795 square miles of island area and would be acceptable from military point of view as well as providing minimum space for Turkish-Cypriots. This last boundary would give Turkey port of Kyrenia and also access to deep water port of Famagusta although this need not necessarily be Turkish port. They would be satisfied if it were NATO base, which Turkey could use in time of war.

Sunalp admitted that there were no great obstacles to construction of artificial port on Karpas Peninsula, provided we put up the money, and indicated a site around Boghaz as logical location. He also admitted construction of air strip was feasible but indicated as preferred site something in the neighborhood of village of Trikomo, which is outside second line. He continued to insist, however, on military necessity of having greater space for defensive maneuvering and argued that minimum Turkish military need would be for line taking in pass from north coast through Kyrenia range down to Lefkoniko as well as high part of ridge lying to west of that as far as Pentadaktylos Peak. This, he said, would give Turks flanking position against any enemy which might approach sovereign area across plain from southwest. Without it, Turk forces would be penned in narrow peninsula with no way of countering attack.

Sunalp and Erim were both somewhat vague in their justification for third line, and in course of conversation it became clear that they did not contend this was military necessity but rather was modification of double enosis proposal, based primarily on political considerations. Sunalp especially emphasized importance of holding Kyrenia as means of quick access to Turk-Cypriots in Nicosia in case of trouble. I got impression they probably would settle for boundary line which included pass north of Lefkoniko but stopped just west of it.

In course of conversation I raised question whether defense against major military attack from land was really important, suggesting that Turks themselves might well be able to forestall any such thing and in any case it seemed unlikely to occur. I got no satisfactory answer. I also indicated gently that I thought it would be very difficult to get Greek consideration of sort of thing they were proposing. At the end, however, I said I would not try at this time to discuss their presentation; first of all, I wanted to think about it and secondly I thought it would be a waste of time for them and for me to argue unless and until we found out that Greeks were willing to talk on basis I had suggested. I would be in touch with them again just as soon as I had anything new.[3]

---

[3] In telegram 166 from Geneva, July 20, Acheson further reported that during their conversation Sunalp had given a "'remarkably frank" outline of Turkish plans for intervention. (Department of State, Central Files, POL 23–8 CYP) In telegram 172 from Geneva, July 21, Acheson reported on Turkish views on the defensibility of a base area also developed during this meeting. (Ibid.)

After seeing Turks I had a talk with Mediator Tuomioja and summarized to him Turkish ideas. He had no particular comment. I told him I would be glad to meet with U Thant, who is back in Geneva, but would not want to take up his time unnecessarily. Tuomioja said he would report to SYG and let me know whether the latter wanted to see me.

Tubby

---

89.   Telegram From the Mission in Geneva to the Department of State[1]

Geneva, July 21, 1964, 8 p.m.

181. From: Acheson. One-hour discussion late this afternoon with Greek rep Nikolareisis may be summarized as follows:

1. He said he had been called back to Athens last Saturday and had gone expecting very negative reaction to suggestions I had put to him. He had long conversations with Prime Minister and Foreign Minister alone. Was pleased to find that they were determined to be forthcoming and conciliatory as possible. Papandreou had insisted on his great desire for peace and expressed appreciation of efforts I was making to avoid Greek-Turkish conflict. He had given him (Nikolareisis) reply to ideas I had thrown out, which PM thought really should be considered as tentative proposal rather than separate suggestions.

2. My proposal consisted of three parts: (a) minority rights for Turkish population of Cyprus; (b) international supervision of application of these rights; and (c) provision for Turkish national security. To these three points PM's reactions were:

(1) Although it would be difficult for Greece, with its excellent record of treatment of all its citizens, to give special privileges to minority on Cyprus, he nevertheless would be willing to grant substantially what I had suggested, even including two Turk-Cypriot administered Eparchis under Turk-Cypriot Eparchs, provided these latter were appointed from Athens and not by Ankara. He would also accept establishment special Turk-Cypriot courts.

---

[1] Source: Department of State, Central Files, POL 23–8 CYP. Secret; Priority; Exdis–TAG. Repeated to London, Athens, Ankara, and USUN.

(2) It would likewise be very hard to accept international supervision of this arrangement, but Papandreou was nevertheless willing to agree to type of UN presence I had outlined.

(3) Even though cession of Greek territory to foreign country would be extremely difficult to sell to Greek people, PM was prepared let Turkey have island of Kastellorizon as military base to protect its approaches. Question of sovereign Turkish base area on Cyprus, however, was another matter. Most he could contemplate in way of Turkish military presence on Cyprus would be a sharing of British base areas with Turkish forces, provided bases themselves remained entirely under British sovereignty.

3. I said that PM had indeed made genuine effort to bridge gap between Greece and Turkey and I was grateful for it. I thought this gave us real basis for continued discussion. In particular, I would now try to develop and give to parties in more concrete form ideas regarding character of minority regime and minority rights which I thought might be applied and which I had not tried to make precise in previous talks.

4. I said, however, that I should be less than frank if I did not express fears that Greek response on sovereign base question would fail to meet minimum Turkish demands.

Turks, in their conversations with me, had been arguing for a good deal more than I had proposed, whereas Greeks were not even accepting idea of Turkish sovereign area, regardless of how small. With regard to Papandreou suggestion that Turks might share British bases, I said I could not say definitely what Turkish reaction would be, since I had never put this idea to them. I doubted they would accept it, however. In any case, it was not useful for us to debate matter today since we did not even know whether British would be amenable. Nikolareisis commented that Papandreou and Costopoulos were now in London and he thought they would put the suggestion to British.[2] We agreed that we would await some report on London meetings before trying to go further along this particular line.

5. There followed considerable discussion of the Turkish sovereign base question. Nikolareisis was quite firm in expressing opinion that GOG could not accept it and that in any case Greek-Cypriots would never do so. He asserted it would be regarded both in Cyprus and in Greece as form of partition. Furthermore, it would "give Turks more than they had before" and would establish them in position to interfere in affairs of Cyprus in future. This would be perennial cause of trouble. I took issue with some of his argumentation, especially thesis that it would give Turkey more than she had before, but I shall not bother Department

---

[2] Papandreou visited London July 20–21. The Embassy reported on his talks at the Foreign Office in telegram 362 from London, July 22. (Ibid.)

with details. I admitted that question of sovereign base area might become breaking point which would make my efforts here useless, since I believed Turks felt just as strongly on their side as Nikolareisis said Greeks did on theirs. Nevertheless, I thought we could usefully continue our efforts and explore all aspects at least for a while longer.

I said I thought I should be as candid with Turks as I had been with Greeks and would therefore tell Erim and Sunalp substantially what Nikolareisis had conveyed to me. He agreed. Am seeing Turks again late tomorrow morning.[3]

Comment: At least we are still moving down the track, even though there is a very high hurdle between us and the finish line.

Tubby

---

[3] Acheson reported on discussions with the Turks and their initial response to the Greek suggestions in telegram 188 from Geneva, July 22. Noting that the Turks' basic demand was a sovereign base area, he commented: "It seems apparent that the hurdle of the Turkish sovereign base area is indeed very high." (Ibid.)

---

90.   Memorandum for the Greek Ambassador (Nikolareisis)[1]

Geneva, July 27, 1964.

After reflecting on the Prime Minister's message, I wish to repeat to you my deep appreciation of his constructive effort toward a fair settlement. I do not detract an iota of appreciation or admiration, in asking again for his understanding help. Though the gap has been narrowed, there still remains a gap. If both sides can find a way to help, it may be bridged. No one will understand the situation better than Your Excellency if I put it in Robert Browning's words:

"O, the little more, and how much it is!
The little less and what worlds away!"

---

[1] Source: Department of State, Central Files, POL 23–8 CYP. Secret; Exdis. Transmitted to the Department of State as an attachment to airgram A–44 from Geneva, July 27. There is no drafting information on the source text but presumably the memorandum was drafted by Acheson. The airgram indicates the memorandum was revised after discussions with Ambassador Nikolareisis and a copy was sent to the Embassy in Athens on July 27 for delivery to Prime Minister Papandreou.

The gap which from the Turkish point of view the Prime Minister's reaction to my suggestions leaves unbridged lies in the politico-military area. The protection of minorities seems in a fair way to being solved. If we look for a moment at the change in the Turkish position provided in the agreements of 1959–1960 to that contemplated by the Prime Minister's views on my suggestions, we can see what seems to them a serious deterioration in it.

May I summarize the Turkish views as follows:

When the Ottoman Empire ceded Cyprus to the British in 1878, it was ceded to a great naval power for the most part friendly to Turkey, except when in the two world wars Turkey made the same mistake as the Germans in miscalculating American intervention to change the relative military power of the embattled forces. So far as life on the island was concerned, the two ethnic groups lived peacefully together under British rule until the mid-1950s.

Under the settlement of 1959–1960, the island passed from the control of a world power to qualified independence under the guarantees and quasi-guardianship of three powers. Turkey and the Turkish Cypriots, to protect their relative interest, gained the following rights guaranteed by treaties:

1. A position in legislative and executive branches of the government for the Turkish Cypriots giving them veto power, the same right on questions of judicial interpretation of the constitution and separate courts for intra-Turkish Cypriot disputes.
2. A treaty right to maintain troops on the island.
3. A treaty right to reinforce those troops by intervention, after complying with specified procedures, and to use the troops if necessary to preserve the constitution, independence and territorial integrity of the island, as provided in the Treaty of Guarantee.

President Makarios maintains—and I am not here disputing the fact—that some of these provisions are "unworkable", and he is changing them unilaterally. Our present search is for a way to change them by agreement. Such a change by its very nature contemplates a diminution of the Turkish position from the present so-called "unworkable" one. The task is to gain mutual agreement to alteration by recognizing the essential elements of the various positions.

First: Turkish Position in the Government

The Greek and Cypriot views contemplate abolition of the veto power in the Government of the island as a whole. The Prime Minister has indicated a willingness to substitute for this a considerable degree of local self-government along the lines which I suggested and further spell out in an accompanying memorandum.[2] But while this is a happy con-

---

[2] Not printed.

tribution to protection of minorities under a constitutional system akin to that of Greece, it would not offer security against a change in the regime which would produce a communist government on the island. While we hope this is unlikely, it cannot be called absurd. This question requires further consideration.

Second: The Legal Position of Turkish Troops on Cyprus

This right is now established by the Treaty of Alliance. The troops are to form part of a tripartite headquarters on Cypriot territory to defend the independence and territorial integrity of Cyprus. The Prime Minister's proposal is to abolish this treaty right and—presumably by a new treaty, either a bilateral one with Britain, or a quadripartite one with Greece and Cyprus added—to have facilities provided by the British on one or both of their sovereign bases.

One sees at once—or if one does not, the Turkish representatives are quick to point it out—that by this exchange the Turks lose a right of military presence on the island which runs directly to them, and become instead tenants of the British. They point out that the British bases are already under attack in the Cyprus House of Representatives. Should the British come to believe that a change in their Middle Eastern commitments or other considerations might render the bases on Cyprus less necessary or desirable, the Turkish position as their tenants might be tenuous indeed. They also stress the difficulty of joint use of such small bases, even should the British be willing to consider it, and the complexity of the use of the rights ancillary to the bases provided the British under the Annex to the Declaration of the Government of the United Kingdom.

In this situation, I respectfully urge the Prime Minister to reconsider his position on a Turkish military presence on the island running directly to them. If the conception of a cession of sovereignty presents grave difficulty, is there another conception which might be more acceptable, such as a lease of an area, or the grant of administrative control, or something of the sort?

The Turks now have a right for their troops to be in Cyprus—and they are stationed in the heart of the island. The right to be in Cyprus, of course, carries with it a right to a location. The mere force of gravity requires it. Surely our imaginations are equal to adapting to a changed situation a new, stable and secure situs for the exercise of this military presence.

Third: The Interest, Right and Duty of Turkey to Share in Protecting and Maintaining a New Settlement

If the settlement provides for the continued independence of Cyprus, while keeping open the opportunity for the people of Cyprus to choose enosis, an agreed change in the present treaties would doubtless contain treaty assurances from Cyprus that in the meantime it would not enter into engagements with a foreign power permitting the use of its territory in a manner hostile to the interests of Britain, Greece or Turkey. Turkey, as well as Greece and Britain, would have a great interest in maintaining the new settlement. The granting of military or other facilities to unfriendly foreign powers would be contrary to the interests of the three powers mentioned above and would be inconsistent with a new settlement. Doubtless enosis would be a safeguard against this danger. But enosis is not a foregone conclusion and Turkey cannot be expected to rely on this alone. A Turkish legal military presence on the island would still be necessary for Turkish security.

These considerations underline the importance of what has been said about a proper, stable and secure location for this military presence.

91.   Telegram From the Mission in Geneva to the Department of State[1]

Geneva, July 27, 1964, 4 p.m.

223. From Acheson. We had go-around yesterday with Turks with Gen. Oberbeck from HQ US CINCEUR and Col. Gussie from Nicosia participating. I began by telling Erim I had made new approach to Greek rep to urge that Papandreou make greater effort to meet Turkish security need.[2] He thanked me. I mentioned that I still had no word as to whether British would be willing to share their base on Cyprus, as suggested by Greeks. Erim commented that this idea of using British bases not even within scope terms of reference given him and Sunalp by GOT; he was not prepared discuss it and hoped it would not be considered seriously. I said I had made clear to Nikolareisis my belief that bases would not do from Turkish point of view. I added that my military advisers (Oberbeck and Gussie) had agreed with Sunalp's arguments that sharing base would be very difficult and unsatisfactory.

At my suggestion, we then reviewed at considerable length and with considerable argumentation what Turkey's minimum needs might

---

[1] Source: Department of State, Central Files, POL 23–8 CYP. Secret; Exdis–TAG. Repeated to Athens, Ankara, London, and USUN.

[2] See Document 89.

be. Taking idea of base on Karpas Peninsula as basis for discussion, Sunalp explained that Turkey considered it had to have on Cyprus facilities and space for one division, 14,000 men, plus a port, an airfield and one squadron of aircraft. For this, he said, TGS considered even whole peninsula would be inadequate, primarily because of its narrowness and lack of [garble—space for dispersal?] and also because it would be bottleneck from which deployment would be difficult. It also lacked major terrain feature for defense.

Oberbeck and Gussie vigorously and ably took issue with this thesis, pointing out that area of more than 200 sq. miles comprised within peninsula was considerably more than we considered necessary for all peacetime purposes for one of our own larger divisions. Gussie stressed that in fact there was good road network on Cyprus and deployment from base of peninsula should be easy. On score of defensibility, our side made point that if major attack threatened Turks would clearly not sit on base awaiting it but rather would move out into other parts of island before attack took place. Apart from this Gussie pointed out that relatively small number of men should be able to hold peninsula until reinforcements arrived.

Sunalp countered with various arguments, including: (1) political situation might not permit Turkish deployment in advance of attack (e.g., allies had repeatedly prevented Turkey from moving against Cyprus during present crisis); (2) outlets for peninsula were not in fact satisfactory despite Gussie's assertion; and (3) because of location Cyprus, Turkish establishment there could not be regarded as being on normal peacetime basis; in Turkey, Turk Army units were always kept dispersed over a wide area because of imminent possibility of attack. Therefore, greater area was needed than would be required for American division in U.S.

At one time Oberbeck made point that if Turk military on Cyprus were threatened with major attack it was inconceivable that Turkey would be alone. To this Sunalp responded emotionally that Turkey's allies had done it no good since last December.

Debate went on for some time. Finally Sunalp asked Oberbeck to give his honest opinion from point of view of member Turkish General Staff as to whether with one division on Karpas Peninsula he could fulfill three missions I had suggested in my earlier memorandum:[3] (1) to deny island to an enemy as base of operations against Turkey; (2) to keep open approaches to ports of Mersin and Iskenderun; and (3) to provide guarantee against future mistreatment of Turk-Cypriots. Oberbeck replied flatly that he certainly could fulfill these three missions under circum-

---

[3] See Documents 86 and 88.

stances specified, and gave reasons. Sunalp's smiling rejoinder was that if Oberbeck were Turkish officer "he would be retired tomorrow". Col. Gussie intervened along same lines and also got himself "retired".

A couple of times I tried to get Turks to recognize that any arrangement would have to be compromise between what was ideal from military point of view and what was practical. I think Erim was probably fully conscious of this although he did not explicitly say so but Sunalp was stubborn to the last.

It is too soon to say what effect of all this may be; I think it was very useful exercise and probably impressed even Sunalp. Oberbeck, Gussie, Jernegan and I will meet again with Turks at lunch tomorrow.[4]

Tubby

---

[4] In telegram 241 from Geneva, July 28, Acheson reported that further discussions with the Turks had not yielded any progress. (Department of State, Central Files, POL 23–8 CYP)

---

92.   Telegram From the Mission in Geneva to the Department of State[1]

Geneva, July 28, 1964, 4 p.m.

236. From Acheson and Jernegan for Talbot. Ref: Deptel 244.[2] Your telegram raises question whether (a) Sunalp and Turks and (b) Greeks believe we are suggesting a Turkish right of intervention similar to that provided in present treaties. Taking "(b)" first Nikolareisis in candid talk yesterday raised this very question and asked a change in our memo pouched to you (Geneva's A–44)[3] to make clear that Turks military presence after enosis would be only to defend their own mainland and to help Greeks defend Cyprus against foreign attack. Before enosis Turkey would have additional right to prevent a change of regime that would

---

[1] Source: Department of State, Central Files, POL 23–8 CYP. Secret; Exdis–TAG.
[2] Telegram 244 to Geneva, July 25, requested that Acheson seek clarification of Turkish views regarding enosis and their rights of intervention in relation to the sovereign base question (Ibid.)
[3] Document 90.

bring about a Communist state on Cyprus. We are counting on Nikola-reisis and our memo to make this clear in Athens.

Turning to "(a)"–(Sunalp), he undoubtedly wants to use base for protection of Turkish minority, which is not conferred in haec verba by present treaties. His method of discussion is to confuse all desirable uses of base, jumping from one to another to avoid being cornered. With the able help of our General and Colonel we have pretty well got him pinned inside the Karpas Peninsula as a base for military purpose of housing and training a military force to protect Turkey and Cyprus from foreign foe. From there we will go on to limit his other desired purposes both before and after enosis; but always aware that whatever is said on paper, Turkish military presence will be a deterrent against abuse of the minority and will be used as a corrective if large-scale abuse should occur. Sunalp does not suffer from incapacity to understand our position but from unwillingness to accept it. We shall watch out, however, that we do not give him ground for a plausible claim that he misunderstands.

Tubby

93. Summary Record of the 536th Meeting of the National Security Council[1]

Washington, July 28, 1964.

[Here follows a report by Secretary Rusk on the OAS and Cuba.]

CYPRUS

At the request of the President, Under Secretary Ball summarized the current situation on Cyprus:

1. We put money in the bank with passing of every week without serious fighting on the island.

2. Progress is being made in Geneva negotiations being conducted by Dean Acheson. These talks are in their second round. Acheson has

---

[1] Source: Johnson Library, National Security File, NSC Meetings File, Vol. 2. Top Secret. Drafted by Bromley Smith. McCone's notes of the meeting are in Central Intelligence Agency, DCI Files: Job 80–B01285A, Meetings with LBJ, 1964.

managed to establish close relations with both the Greek and Turkish representatives. The talks will have to enter the third round before we know exactly how they will come out. The real problem consists of getting Makarios to accept an agreed Greek-Turkish solution.

3. We are using the NATO structure in an effort to gain some hold on the military buildup on the Island of both Greek and Turkish forces.

4. We are making a serious effort to build up the UN forces in Cyprus and prompt the UN officers there to act with firmness in holding down fighting.

5. Every effort is being made to play down the Geneva talks. Acheson is working quietly and without press attention. The talks are being carried on under the cover of the UN Mediator who is cooperating in this tactic. We have a moderately hopeful attitude toward the possibility of a solution of the problem.

McGeorge Bundy pointed out the importance of not letting the press know of our current optimism. It was agreed that no optimistic noises should be made to the press.

[Here follows discussion of Laos.]

Bromley Smith[2]

---

[2] Printed from a copy that bears this typed signature.

---

94.   Telegram From the Embassy in Greece to the Department of State[1]

Athens, July 29, 1964, 5 p.m.

163. DCM yesterday transmitted to FonMin Costopoulos second Acheson memorandum to Nikolareizis (Geneva 34 to Athens and Geneva's A–40 to Dept.)[2]

Costopoulos said Makarios had been apprised of contents Acheson memo to Nikolareizis regarding Turkish minority (Geneva's A–40 to Dept) and also of Turk demand for military base.

---

[1] Source: Department of State, Central Files, POL 23–8 CYP. Secret; Priority; Exdis–TAG. Repeated to Geneva for Acheson, Nicosia, and Ankara.

[2] Telegram 34 from Geneva to Athens was not found. Airgram A–40 transmitted the first draft of the memorandum (Document 90). (Department of State, Central Files, POL 23–8 CYP)

Makarios categorically opposed both proposals. (*Comment:* We rather suspect Makarios has actually been shown and perhaps given copy of first Acheson memo to Nikolareizis and cannot exclude possibility these documents may some day appear in press.)

Costopoulos said he personally also disappointed in proposals regarding Turkish minority which GOG considered unnecessarily complicated and constitute in effect cantonal arrangement. He noted that Makarios had agreed to issue "Bill of Rights" for Turkish minority and that if this were done some sort of international supervision of this bill of rights would be entirely acceptable to GOG.

Costopoulos mentioned his own ideas of seeking removal Turkish minority in exchange for Turkish military base on Cyprus (Embtel 147 to Dept, 33 to Geneva)[3] had not found favor with Papandreou who apparently considers this would be impracticable as well as inconsistent with excellent Greek record with regard to existing Turkish ethnic groups in Greece.

GOG concerned, he said, that concessions are being asked of GOG without any indication such concessions likely produce agreement with GOT acceptable to GOG. Nikolareizis will be instructed obtain clearer idea of what Turks actually prepared accept.

One of the most serious problems confronting GOG is fact Makarios would oppose any agreement between Greek and Turkish Govts providing for special civil organization for Turkish minority as well as Turk military base by asserting that such types of provisions would constitute only revision of London–Zurich Accords incompatible with completely independent Cyprus. Basically Makarios is opposed to enosis, but will not publicly admit it. Costopoulos did not assess possibility Makarios himself might be prepared make concessions to Turks on his own initiative in effort preempt GOG–GOT agreement, if by so doing he could preserve independent status of Cyprus.

Costopoulos, speaking very personally and confidentially, said he did not see how under these circumstances it was going to be possible to reach an agreement with Turks which would also be satisfactory to Govt of Cyprus. If agreement on basic issues could be reached by Turks and GOG, perhaps best tactical procedure would be as follows: simultaneous declaration by Greek and Cypriot Parliaments proclaiming enosis followed by plebiscite in Cyprus and possibly Greece ratifying this decision. After proclamation of enosis, Greek Govt would then be in position to honor agreements reached with Turks and US Govt as result of current negotiations. In Costopoulos' view such agreement would provide measures for guarantee of protection for Turkish ethnics as well as leased

---

[3] Dated July 26. (Ibid.)

Turk military base (sovereign base unacceptable) for period perhaps as long as 25 years. Base would be purely military, probably on Karpas Peninsula, limited in size, and without space required either for large number of Turkish troops or safe haven area for Turk ethnic civilians. If meeting of minds could be reached with GOT along foregoing lines perhaps prompt solution could be found before convening of UNGA and under circumstances which would avoid giving Makarios apparently valid justification publicly oppose enosis.

Comment: Obviously, Costopoulos' comments re possible GOG program involving understanding with GOT re possible lease base agreement and subsequent proclamation of enosis by Grk and Cypriot Parliaments extremely sensitive and should be tightly held pending further evolution of Greek attitude.

Labouisse

95.   Telegram From the Department of State to the Embassy in Greece[1]

Washington, July 30, 1964, 8:24 p.m.

165. Athens 170, 40 to Geneva.[2] Reuters story (Modiano) received prior to your telegram. Greek Ambassador was called in for explanation of leak.[3]

Talbot explained we cannot understand reasoning behind "confirmation" by Greek Government spokesman of "Acheson Plan". He noted Papandreou has insisted on essentiality absolute secrecy regarding talks. We understood his desire that information be held close so that various ideas could be discussed without governments having to take firm positions on one or another. Talbot assured Ambassador Matsas Mr.

---

[1] Source: Department of State, Central Files, POL 23–8 CYP. Secret; Priority; Exdis–TAG. Drafted by Bracken, cleared by Sisco and Talbot, and approved by Ball. Repeated to Ankara, London, Nicosia, USUN, and Geneva for Acheson.

[2] Telegram 170 from Athens, July 30, transmitted the text of the Greek press report outlining Acheson's proposals for a Cyprus settlement. (Ibid.)

[3] In telegram 265 from Geneva, July 30, Acheson expressed concern about the impact of press reports on the negotiations and stated that the Greeks had agreed to respond to inquiries with a "no comment." (Ibid.) In telegram 269 from Geneva, July 30, Acheson reported that the Turks were "disgusted" with the leak, which they blamed on the Greeks. (Ibid.)

Acheson has worked very closely with Mediator, has not pushed himself forward and that we have been fortunate so far in that press has not covered his activities. Talbot asked Matsas for his explanation. Ambassador said he was completely in dark.

Talbot said we had two problems: (1) how to answer press questions; and (2) what do we say to Turks. As Papandreou aware, talks have proceeded with candor and Mr. Acheson has reported back and forth to each representative. Fact that some of points mentioned in Reuters story have been reported to Turks and others not might arouse suspicions of Turks we are not playing fairly with them.

Matsas asked if there were a coherent plan. Talbot said a variety of ideas had been discussed but there was not a "plan". Matsas speculated that only first point "Union with Greece" would appeal to Greeks and other points, cession Kastellorizon, base, financial compensation, etc., would be detestable. Therefore he could not see it in GOG interest to leak this information. He surmised that since all of points at one time or another had been mentioned in press, Modiano had possibly read as "confirmation" a "no comment" reply by GOG official.

He proposed telephoning PM Papandreou for clarification and instructions. After talking to Papandreou Matsas reported that Prime Minister was very annoyed by the leak, indicating Greeks had endeavored to brief Cypriots on status of talks and Cypriots had talked too much. Prime Minister proposed to deny flatly that there was any such thing as "Acheson Plan".

Subsequently Matsas reported second telephone call with Papandreou, after latter had investigated Reuters story on Makarios' press conference. PM repeated his extreme annoyance and asked Ambassador convey to Department his sincere regret this had happened since he realized efforts at Geneva are being directed to fruitful results and this might be counterproductive.

No questions at noon briefing. Future queries will be answered: "Mr. Acheson has been discussing a whole range of ideas with Mediator, Greek and Turkish representatives. There is no such thing as an Acheson plan."

If Matsas had correctly reported Papandreou's regret and intention to deny along lines we are taking, we assume Nikolareizis will have early instructions on Mr. Acheson's memorandum and that exchanges will not be interrupted.

For Athens: Impress strongly on Papandreou our distress at possible deleterious effect this could have on talks in Geneva, and Mr. Acheson's efforts to help Mediator arrive at agreed settlement. We have understood and cooperated with Greek desire for secrecy because we recognize problem of domestic pressures on GOG as well as their difficulty in handling Makarios. The speed and forthcoming nature of Nikolareizis' next instructions will indeed be test of Papandreou's good faith and sincerity of his intentions to arrive at early negotiated settlement rather than "fait accompli" tack of Makarios, with all potential dangers of Turk resistance that approach implies. We understand Nikolareizis is returning Athens today. In order not to give Turkish public opinion leeway to suspect breakdown of talks and accelerate pressures by Turkish extremists, we hope he can return to Geneva earliest (certainly by Monday).

For Ankara: Drawing on above help Turks look at this in perspective. Mr. Acheson reports that Erim and Sunalp are calm about whole thing. Assure Turks that we hope that Makarios explosion will not have serious effect on negotiations.

As another sensitive period approaches when Turks might again think of intervention as their only alternative, we are dismayed at reports they might contemplate intervention by air bombardment. We recognize that neither Sunay nor Inonu has made such statement. However, we believe it useful if as opportunity arises you convey to appropriate quarters US position that we could not under any circumstances regard air bombardment as coming within purview of "action" contemplated under Article IV Treaty of Guarantee.

Rusk

---

96.   Telegram From the Embassy in Cyprus to the Department of State[1]

Nicosia, July 31, 1964, 3 p.m.

141. Nicholas Farmakis (protect source), former Greek ERE Deputy, here conducting survey for Greek opposition group (composed ERE political elements and Greek military) has given Embassy his views. Farmakis has talked with Greek Cypriot leaders and has traveled extensively throughout island inspecting defense sites.

Farmakis has deep misgivings re Cyprus situation which follow:

1. Makarios intends use military force obtain political solution. He intends increase pressures on Turks and then attack Turk strongholds. He will act within forty-five days. Makarios will by-pass UN mediation and introduce resolution UNGA obtain recognition de facto state.

---

[1] Source: Department of State, Central Files, POL 23–8 CYP. Secret; Priority. Repeated to Athens, Ankara, Cairo, Damascus, Geneva for Acheson, and London.

2. Makarios increasingly dependent upon Nasser. GOC has received UAR material and obtained Nasser's permission use UAR airfields by Greek Air Force defend Cyprus. Claims Papandreou "50 percent" in agreement. Added GOC endeavoring obtain support Syria Air Force and promise of Syrian attack Iskenderun event GOT attack.

3. Cypriots under direction regular Greek officers installing ground-to-air missiles near Nicosia. Farmakis has visited site and witnessed construction, but has not seen any missiles. He assumed they were shipped from Greece and were US origin. (This may reflect rumors we have heard other sources.)

In order prevent escalation problem, Farmakis intends recommend his colleagues that Makarios be deposed. Claims GOG being out-maneuvered. If Makarios able submit resolution UNGA Greece will face dilemma. In this event Papandreou cannot resist clamor support Makarios. Result will be further weakening Greek ties with West. He claimed Greece drifting toward neutralism and shifting its focus away from Communist threat. On July 27, for example, he informed Papandreou transferred 150 key army officers to provinces; and he afraid GOG will transfer Greek army officers sympathetic ouster Makarios from Cyprus unless action quickly initiated.

With regard Papandreou's position, Farmakis acknowledged Premier cannot be challenged at polls; and he does not wish participate any plan aimed removal Papandreou. Opposition group believes Papandreou will sanction Makarios removal if faced with threat of force by military elements. Farmakis indicated they would not, however, let Papandreou stand their way. Otherwise if situation continues civil war will occur Greece within year. Once Makarios removed enosis would be proclaimed. Farmakis said Turks would be given small part island to administer and he seemed unconcerned re Turk attitude.

Farmakis made low key pitch for US support. He emphasized Greece and United States had same interest in problem. Personally he would rather be "dead than red." Therefore, he favored action now. Added United States would be kept apprised, because United States would be expected offer its blessings.

Comment: We cannot judge extent plans described by Farmakis have progressed in Greece. We were impressed with deadly serious fashion which Farmakis revealed his views. If Farmakis' worries are based on fact, as he assured us, then Makarios with GOG being dragged along, has gone even further than we thought in playing brinkmanship game.[2]

Belcher

---

[2] In telegram 169 from Athens, August 4, the Embassy reported on further contacts with Farmakis and noted that his fellow conspirators included Nicos Sampson and Cypriot Minister of Labor Tassos Papadopoulos. (Ibid.)

97.   Telegram From the Embassy in Greece to the Department of State[1]

Athens, July 31, 1964, 9 p.m.

190. 1. I called on PriMin today at Kastri with Costopoulos, Sossides and Brewster present. We talked for about ninety minutes. PriMin received us in his bedroom (he has been in bed for several days with kidney trouble which apparently developed while on London trip). He immediately apologized profusely for unfortunate impression leak of "Acheson proposals" was bound to create. He attributed this leak entirely to Cypriots who had been here this week, with whom naturally he had had to discuss certain aspects of Geneva talks and to whom he had shown some papers but not all (he did not distinguish). He said he had just completed a call to Makarios in which he had expressed his deep indignation at this leak and at Makarios' most unfortunate press conference. He said he had come to conclusion this week that Makarios was "impossible to deal with" since he was completely intransigent on all points. He had "used" Greek press and all of this at expense of Greek Government which wants to maintain good relations with US. He had done the unforgivable by putting Greek Government in a position of looking soft and willing to bargain, whereas he (Makarios) was the hero standing up against the forces of the West. PriMin was convinced that Makarios was playing a completely "Nasser game" and wanted to set up an independent Cyprus "as an Arab state."

2. He then stated that, after this meeting with Makarios, he had concluded there was only one solution, "a dangerously simple one"—enosis must come promptly because there could be no interim period in which Cypriots had unfettered independence. It was important to follow this course in order to get rid of Makarios. Although Makarios is working against enosis, Papandreou believed if action is taken at early date it can be achieved. His proposal was that enosis be achieved by joint action of the Greek Cypriot and Greek Parliaments, while agreements could be reached within the "family group" (i.e., US, UK, Turkey, Greece) to provide for a bill of rights for the Turk minority and a NATO base with Turkish Commander granted by Greece to Turkey. He mentioned frequently that he, as PriMin, could not force concessions out of Makarios who thought he would win an independent Cyprus. Only way to be rid of this was to have Cyprus a part of Greece. Enosis with a NATO base should offer Turks security both for their minorities and strategically. A Cuba-type Cyprus under Makarios' aegis would certainly be dangerous for

---

[1] Source: Department of State, Central Files, POL 23–8 CYP. Secret; Priority; Exdis–TAG. Repeated to Geneva for Acheson, Nicosia, London, Ankara, and USUN.

Turkey and for us all. GOG would also be prepared to indemnify any Turk Cypriots who might wish to leave Cyprus, and hopefully there could be some economic aid provided Turkey which would help meet its problems. He said foregoing was in essence what he would put to Niko-lareizis who was arriving this evening for consultations, and which would in turn be passed on to Acheson.

3. Speaking personally, I stressed that I could not imagine Turks would accept such a proposal, even assuming that we all want to get rid of Makarios. The proposal did not take realistically into consideration the three basic factors which Turkish side considers essential to a solution. It was, in fact, asking Turks for complete and unconditional capitulation. After outlining some of events related to Makarios' visit, including his Nicosia departure statement that there could be no "agreed solution", the "complete identity of views" communiqué, and ending with Makarios' homecoming statement that Cyprus would have full support of Greek armed forces if attacked,[2] I said that, although I accepted his assurances re the Acheson story leak and his indignation at Makarios' press conference, [no?] Turks and few others would believe this was not Greek–Makarios maneuver. He denied this heatedly, and twice said that he now considered Makarios "an enemy."

4. I then pressed him on question of proposed appeal to UN on which he had apparently agreed a common line with Makarios. He replied that he agreed with Makarios on only three things: a) need to maintain peace on island (and here he said Makarios had promised him to take no military action of any importance without prior consultation); b) Greece would defend Cyprus if attacked; and c) Greece will support Cyprus in appeal to the General Assembly if no solution found. Papandreou repeated his urgent desire to reach solution before General Assembly meets, otherwise Makarios might gain his complete independence. If circumstances make appeal to Assembly necessary, Papandreou envisages that Cypriots would take initiative in trying to get resolution endorsing independence for Cyprus and right of its people to determine their own future. To this I responded that I knew of no authority whereby the UN could effectively take step which would nullify treaties entered into in good faith. I also pointed to questionable company he would be keeping and fact that, in interim, anything might happen and agreed that his proposal was "dangerously" simple. He acknowledged this, but said

---

[2] Text of the Makarios–Papandreou communiqué, announcing "absolute harmony of views" was transmitted in telegram 176 from Athens, July 30. (Ibid.) In telegram 187 from Athens, July 31, the Embassy commented on both Makarios' "self-assured" press conference and the bitterness of his comments about the "Acheson Plan." (Ibid.) In telegram 136 from Nicosia, July 31, the Embassy in Cyprus reported on Makarios' public statements upon his return. (Ibid.)

he saw no other course in view of intransigence of Makarios and strong public appeal of self-determination in Greece as well as Cyprus.

5. Conversation ended in friendly atmosphere, with Papandreou agreeing that next step was for him to give his instructions to Nikolareizis, who would continue talks in Geneva.[3]

Comment: Events of last few days lead us to believe that Papandreou is, in fact, fed to the teeth with Makarios and that he cannot draw any concessions from latter. Of course, this could all be Byzantine plot, but we are satisfied that only point Papandreou and Makarios have in common now is dedication to self-determination.

Many Greeks, including several officials, outspoken in their distaste for Makarios and his unreliability. However, the very strong and profound conviction among all Greeks that Cypriots should have right of self-determination is making them prisoner to Makarios' machinations and allows him, in name of what they all believe to be only just end, to call turn for Greeks. The "capital of Hellenism" is in Nicosia on this issue.

When I was pointing out to Papandreou the ways in which Greece was being "used", including giving military support to Makarios, Papandreou replied that he recognized this, but asked what would happen if Greece withdrew its support? He answered his own question by saying things would be even worse and there would be no control over possible military adventures; moreover, it would surely result in "others, particularly the UAR" giving more support "which has been promised."

Our reading of situation is that Papandreou sincerely wants to achieve enosis before matters go to the UNGA for he has come to believe it is only way to set aside Makarios and that latter is real stumbling block in all Western efforts to resolve Cyprus problem.

We realize Papandreou's present line is not compatible with Turkey's wishes, but if he cannot in fact deliver Makarios, it may well be only alternative which has a chance of being in Turkey's as well as our own interests. It may be possible in Geneva talks to pin Greeks down to specific understandings to meet some of Turk desires after enosis. However, in my opinion, we cannot expect agreement on sovereign base for Turks nor on full scale of special position for Turk-Cypriot minority envisaged in Acheson memo to Nikolareizis. Greeks consider this would lead to same type problems as exist under London–Zurich Accords.

Labouisse

---

[3] In telegram 192 from Athens, August 1, Labouisse reported that Costopoulos had assured him that Greece desired to continue bargaining at Geneva and that Nikolareisis would return shortly to the talks. Costopoulos also outlined Greek objections to the proposals made by Acheson. (Ibid.)

98.   Telegram From the Embassy in Turkey to the Department of State[1]

Ankara, August 1, 1964, 2 p.m.

191. Embtel 188[2] gives general account my conversation with Erkin yesterday re Cyprus. Following are points with specific reference Geneva conversations which require TAG transmission.

1. Erkin said that in his opinion cession of Karpas Peninsula was not enough. Would be impossible sell to Turkish people. Regarding territorial compensation elsewhere, GOT uninterested in acquiring territory in Western Europe, which apparently British idea. Re Kastellorizon, it so small that impossible consider as serious concession. These comments were made somewhat incidentally with Erkin making no attempt at outlining formula which could accept.

2. Erkin said he felt situation had developed to point where US and GOT should agree on solution, following which Acheson would endeavor convince GOG and GOG to convince GOC. I observed this not my understanding of modus operandi of Acheson who I thought had made clear that his first effort would be directed to attempting narrow area of difference between Turk and Greek viewpoints, following which consideration could be given to bridging gap by specific recommendations of our own. However, I assumed that whether this done would depend on degree of disparity of Turk and Greek views as established by current Geneva exchanges.

Erkin did not pursue further.

3. Erkin said he had heard from Erim that Acheson hoped get somewhere by end of next week. He hoped so because passage of time inimical to Turkey.

4. Referring to Athens leak as "despicable" and references of Makarios to Acheson as unpardonable, Erkin said this not first time however that there had been leak and referred to an unspecified article in *London Times* which he felt had been made privy to info furnished by British representative in Geneva. He observed this unfortunately falls within familiar pattern of British laxity in maintaining confidence and added this puts GOT and especially himself on spot when, having scrupulously adhered agreement maintain secrecy, others fail to do so with result that Turkish press demands know why press elsewhere given information of

---

[1] Source: Department of State, Central Files, POL 23–8 CYP. Secret; Exdis–TAG. Repeated to Athens, Nicosia, London, and Geneva for Acheson.

[2] Telegram 188 from Ankara, August 1, reported that Turkish positions were hardening as a result of Makarios' actions and that Erkin was again stressing the need for immediate action on Cyprus. (Ibid.)

vital importance to Turkey while Turk press kept in dark (only info in our records which might have bearing on this is London's 441 to Dept[3] which did not attribute anything to Acheson but did suggest rather assured awareness by *Times* of trend developments in Geneva).

I drew on Deptel 156[4] as authorized re Athens leak and Erkin appeared quite satisfied as far as our role concerned.

5. Finally, Erkin wanted know what we would be prepared do if Geneva talks broke down and to what extent GOT could count on our support. I replied would be difficult give specific answer to this question for simple reason that it based on hypothetical situation in which talks might end. Would depend on degree of progress made, analysis of resulting situation, etc., which are presently unknown. Erkin did not dispute this but did say he foresaw time approaching for some major decisions and he would ask us most earnestly to give subject serious consideration now.

Hare

---

[3] Telegram 441 from London, July 27, reported British press stories indicating a "more flexible" attitude on the part of Papandreou after his talks in London. (Ibid.)

[4] Telegram 156 to Ankara was sent for action to Athens as telegram 165, Document 95.

---

99.   Telegram From the Mission in Geneva to the Department of State[1]

Geneva, August 2, 1964, 11 a.m.

282. From Acheson for Ball, Finletter and Talbot. Reference: Deptel 291.[2] Our communications with you are better than telegraphic, they are telepathic. As indicated my telegram to Athens,[3] we too have been thinking of possibility skipping Cypriot full independence stage and going direct to enosis; we too saw dilemmas cited your telegram.

---

[1] Source: Department of State, Central Files, POL 23–8 CYP. Secret; Immediate; Nodis–TAG. Repeated to Athens, Ankara, and London.

[2] In telegram 291 to Geneva, August 1, Ball, reacting to Makarios' rejection of the "Acheson memorandum," outlined a suggested scenario for U.S. action and requested Acheson's comment. (Ibid.)

[3] Telegram 281 from Geneva, August 1. (Ibid.)

Following are our immediate comments, possibly to be followed by others later:

We would prefer to see next move in steps, rather than one big, desperate leap. Turks have been remarkably patient, but this can't last for length of time needed to work out whole scheme you outline unless in meantime they see something moving at least slightly in their direction. They have given quite a lot already, the Greeks hardly anything at all. I much doubt Turks would be responsive even to Ray Hare's eloquence so long as they have clear impression Greeks simply standing fast on extreme position.

I therefore hope Labouisse can induce Papandreou to send Nikolareisis back before mid-week with forthcoming proposals,[4] including long-term lease arrangement for at least part of Karpas Peninsula. Believe Turks would compromise for about time mentioned your telegram, and they might even accept shorter time period. These are things that could be bargained out, through me, or directly, if Greeks would once accept principle of Turkish base.

According to Nikolareisis, Papandreou accepted rest of my proposals and threw in Kastellorion to boot. It is important that Nikolareisis be empowered confirm this on his return. (Recent reports from Athens have cast serious doubt on sincerity of Papandreou's offer.)

If we can get these points accepted Athens, we can go to work full blast to work out agreement on substance of settlement.

As to method of putting agreement into effect, seems to me line to be explored is that of formulating some fairly vague announcement of agreement in principle which would say that understandings reached provide for safeguarding Turkish national security and welfare of Turkish Cypriots together with right of Cypriot self-determination and that both governments are satisfied on this. Then plebiscite or other action on enosis could be precipitated.

Realize this will call forth Makarios opposition and require very strong Greek propaganda effort together with use all available methods control His Beatitude, but if we don't approach enosis with at least this much assurance to Turks we risk overthrow of Inonu government and even Republican regime in Turkey. Fact is, procedural dilemma we face simply will not go away.

We are hesitant about proposed use of NATO because:

1. It would seem impossible to keep it secret, considering atmosphere and attitudes in Greece and number of governments who would know about it.

---

[4] In telegram 197 from Athens, August 2, the Embassy reported that Costopoulos had told Anschuetz that Nikolareisis would "probably" return to Geneva on Tuesday, August 9. (Ibid.)

2. If, or rather when, it becomes public knowledge, it will produce an array of Afro-Asian and SovBloc states, and probably also U Thant, in support of Makarios.

3. We doubt that NATO has any more or as much influence as US on Greeks, and we have already failed in massive frontal attack on Papandreou. As personal comment I would add that I couldn't predict where effort guided by Mike Pearson would end.

4. Finally, public NATO pressure on Greece if successful would have effect of change in Greek policy and position from one founded on Greek national interests to one adopted under duress applied by Anglo-Saxons. Could any democratic government stand this?

In short, I think we had better continue to try to play this big trout rather than risk everything by hauling on the line.[5]

Tubby

---

[5] In telegram 176 to Athens, July 30, Ball commented that he "accepted" the scenario outlined by Acheson and instructed Labouisse to ensure that Nikolareisis' instructions met the requirements of this plan. (Ibid.)

---

100.   Telegram From the Embassy in Greece to the Department of State[1]

Athens, August 3, 1964, 8 p.m.

200. Embtel 197 rpted Ankara 73; London 57; Geneva 58.[2] Costopoulos and Nikolareizis lunched with Anschuetz and me today. Conversation confirmed in general information Costopoulos gave Anschuetz yesterday as reported reftel; i.e., GOG determined continue negotiations, GOG will not retract any acceptances already made. Nikolareizis authorized propose only NATO base or Turkish participation British base. However, Costopoulos, in our presence, repeated instructions to Nikolareizis, explore without commitment implications of leased base arrangement.

---

[1] Source: Department of State, Central Files, POL 23–8 CYP. Secret; Exdis–TAG. Repeated to Ankara, London, and Geneva for Acheson.

[2] See footnote 4, Document 99.

Nikolareizis explained that Acheson proposals re Turk minority which Nikolareizis conveyed to Papandreou and Papandreou approved in principle, had been made purposely unspecific by Acheson in my effort stimulate examination of problem. Acheson memorandum this subject which was transmitted subsequently outlined much more comprehensive arrangement involving provisions which GOG could not accept for reasons which Embassy has previously reported. Greeks "accept principles outlined in general conversation but not proposed treatment in depth mentioned in memo."

Referring to Lausanne Treaty provisions for Tendos and Imbros, Costopoulos pointed out that (aside from fact Turks had not carried out provisions) situations were not parallel. Argument was that purpose Article 14 was to ensure that people on island, who mostly Greeks, should have local self-determination. Applying this to Cyprus, he contended that, even with current abnormal concentrations of Turkish population in certain sections of island, there is no single unit under present Cypriot administrative system in which Turks actually constitute majority. (We suggested this depended on how one drew the lines.) In those areas where Turks are temporarily most heavily concentrated, Costopoulos maintained economic factors alone would prevent continued existence these concentrations: i.e. Turkish farm lands and properties are in many cases remote from proprietors temporary abodes, while permanent installation in these areas of temporary concentrations could only be accomplished by dislocation long-term Greek residents.

Nevertheless, said Costopoulos, GOG perfectly prepared accept principles of Treaty Lausanne as applied to minority and would accept UN commissioners to supervise application these principles. GOG could not, however, accept arrangements which would in effect create and perpetuate barriers between communities. Nikolareizis will be prepared discuss this matter in depth with Acheson.

Discussion provisions for administration of Turkish Cypriots led directly into discussion of role of Turkish military contingent. Costopoulos reiterated his thesis that if indeed it were possible remove Turkish minority from island, it would then be possible to grant sovereign military base to Turkey. However, under special provisions for Turk ethnics outlined in Acheson memo, taken in conjunction with large sovereign military base, would only perpetuate and aggravate errors London/ Zurich Accords. He made it clear Greeks regard Turkish military justifications for base as spurious. Nikolareizis commented that Turkish demands for base area are larger than either one of the British bases which have at various periods accommodated between 5,000 and 30,000 men. Neither Costopoulos nor Nikolareizis denied, however, genuine necessity devise some means avoid humiliation of Turks.

Nikolareizis said he expects return Geneva August 5.

Comment: Today's conversation tends confirm but adds little new to our previous reports. Costopoulos has made it clear that in his mind a leased base not categorically excluded. His authority to Nikolareizis to explore possibility is made on his personal responsibility and not that of Prime Minister. I cannot determine, however, whether Costopoulos merely endeavoring preserve GOG negotiating position, or whether Papandreou is actually more unyielding on this issue. My surmise is that if agreement on other issues could be satisfactorily reached, Greeks might be induced to agree to leased base provided it were moderate in area and personnel. Greeks well aware that separate element of possible agreement can be evaluated only as part of total package.

Labouisse

---

101.   Telegram From the Mission in Geneva to the Department of State[1]

Geneva, August 4, 1964, 1 p.m.

296. From Acheson. Had interim sort of meeting with Turks this morning at my request for purpose of preparing them for bad news it seems probable Nikolareisis will be bringing from Athens. I told them I thought we were nearing moment of decision and would not have a great deal of time left to reach agreement. Prospects did not look very good to me. Although I did not know what sort of reply Nikolareisis would bring, I felt pretty sure it would not be satisfactory from Turkish point of view. At same time, I also felt pretty sure it would not necessarily be final Greek word.

Turks took this calmly and said it was really only what they had expected from beginning. Sunalp emphasized belief that Papandreou and Makarios were really working in partnership to play for time until they could achieve their common goal.

I then asked how much longer Erim felt he could continue conversation. I myself thought there was still some hope but apparently he did not. If that was case, was he still prepared to go on and for how long? He replied that would depend on me; he was ready to keep talking until I myself became convinced that case was hopeless. Implied that this conviction on my part would itself be help to Turkish position, just as he had

---

[1] Source: Department of State, Central Files, POL 23–8 CYP. Secret; Exdis–TAG. Received at 10:57 a.m. and repeated to Athens, Ankara, London, and USUN.

thought my endorsement for need of Turkish military presence on Cyprus had provided moral support which was useful even if no agreement reached with Greeks.

Comment: Conversation most amiable but rather discouraging.

Tubby

---

102.   Memorandum for the Record[1]

Washington, August 4, 1964.

SUBJECT

NSC Meeting, 4 August 1964, 12:30 p.m.

In attendance: The President, McNamara, Vance, Rusk, Ball, Robert F. Kennedy, Dillon, McGeorge Bundy, Carl Rowan, McCone

[Here follows discussion of Vietnam.]

2. *Ball on Cyprus:*

Makarios endeavoring to sabotage the Geneva meeting. Some pluses to this—not all negative. Greek negotiator returns to Geneva today and Papandreou plan for Enosis. Quiet deal with Turks. Leak would destroy effort—Turkish have leased from Greek Govt.

Time on our side.

Bundy—relations with Commies and Nasser.[2]

---

[1] Source: Central Intelligence Agency, DCI Files: Job 80–B01285A, Meetings with LBJ, 1964. No classification marking. Drafted by McCone on August 5.

[2] NSC Record of Action No. 2496, August 4, on this meeting reads: "Cyprus: Noted a briefing by Under Secretary of State Ball on the situation in Cyprus and the status of the current negotiations in Geneva." (Department of State, S/S–NSC Files: Lot 70 D 265) In a memorandum to Ball, August 4, Komer expressed surprise at the optimism that Ball had shown during the briefing. In an August 4 memorandum to the President, Komer noted that it was time to rethink the Cyprus problem since Makarios would leak any deal that Acheson worked out. (Both in the Johnson Library, National Security File, Country File, Cyprus, Vol. 11, Memos)

103.   Telegram From the Mission in Geneva to the Department of State[1]

Geneva, August 6, 1964, 2 p.m.

315. From Acheson. Had long and frustrating talk yesterday evening with Nikolareisis. Essence of message he brought back from Athens contained in three points:

1. My suggestions about safeguarding Turk-Cypriot rights, as set forth in memorandum of July 24th,[2] go too far and would perpetuate division between Greek and Turk communities. GOG considers objective should be to eliminate this difference so that all Cypriots could live together in peace and harmony.

2. Concession of sovereign area to Turkey is "out of the question". Greek Government renews offer of NATO base with Turkish troops and Commander. Nikolareisis additionally authorized to explore concrete elements which would be involved in leased base: such as area, purpose, length of lease, number of troops to be accommodated, etc., but not authorized make any commitment that GOG would agree to such lease.

3. Injection of Makarios into picture as result his latest visit to Athens and his public statements, makes it impossible for GOG to continue Geneva talks on basis independence for Cyprus. Talks on this basis would require collaboration of Makarios, who has made it clear he will not accept any negotiated settlement. Therefore, only way we can proceed is on basis that immediate result of talks will be enosis; on this assumption, GOG would be discussing through me disposition to be made of its own territory and thus not have to invite Makarios in.

Nikolareisis handed me memorandum evidently prepared in Athens on subject protection to Turkish minority. It largely rejected proposals set forth my memorandum July 24th. Said GOG could accept Lausanne-type guarantees and U.N. commissioner, provided latter's functions were "defined in detail". Also could accept appointment two Turk-Cypriot Eparchs but they must be on exactly same basis as Greek Eparchs and there must be no separate system of administration for Turks, even at Eparchy or village level. Central Turkish authority in Nicosia to look after special rights of Turks throughout island was unacceptable as producing form of partition and being "contrary to the reestablishment of good administration and peace in the island". Special Turkish courts could be accepted only for application personal status

---

[1] Source: Department of State, Central Files, POL 23–8 CYP. Secret; Exdis–TAG. Repeated to Athens and Ankara.

[2] Reference is presumably to Document 90.

law; in all other respects, Turks must be subject to ordinary, nonmixed courts.

I commented that this memorandum (copy being pouched)[3] was pretty bad. After some further discussion it appeared that there might still be room for clarification of my ideas and possible compromise. We therefore agreed to study this and talk about it again after we have had time for reflection.

The base question: I pointed out any Turkish force on island must have some physical location which would have to be granted to someone. This someone could not be NATO. Since it was not sovereign entity, therefore why not accept idea of long term lease to Turkey, which might conceivably act as trustee for NATO in interest of Greek-Turkish and general Western defense? I added this idea would be hard to sell to the Turks but I would try. Went on to indicate extent of what appeared to be present Turk minimum demands, i.e., whole of Karpas Peninsula plus north coast as far as Akanthou Pass north of Lefkoniko. Also mentioned their desire for port and airbase as well as problem which might arise if peninsula proved to have substantial population.

I then advanced idea that Turkish base on Cyprus (and minority protection as well) might be brought within the framework of larger Greek-Turkish joint structure similar to that in effect between U.S. and Canada. This could include joint defense board to discuss mutual problems of security in Eastern Mediterranean as well as a political, economic and social entity and perhaps other organs.

This would enable both Greece and Turkey to submerge their differences over Cyprus and resume friendly cooperation which was so important to them both. Nikolareisis did not comment specifically but seemed receptive to this idea.

We concluded discussion on base by my making appeal for GOG assurance it prepared to discuss lease in good faith so that I could have something solid to work on with Turks. Nikolareisis countered that on his part he needed something concrete as to what we had in mind. (I take it this means Papandreou unwilling to give him real authority without knowing beforehand order of magnitude of base area proposed and other characteristics of eventual arrangement.) Nikolareisis suggested starting from premise that Turks now have 650 men on island and would need base large enough only for that number. I said I thought Turks were thinking in considerably larger terms, on order of one division. We agreed to discuss this whole question further.

On matter of discussing enosis rather than Cypriot independence I said I was in entire accord; it was Papandreou—not I—who had kept saying that full and complete independence must be objective. Nikola-

---

[3] Transmitted to the Department of State in airgram A–63, August 7. (Ibid.)

reisis said would be helpful if I would put this strongly to Papandreou, possibly in letter. I said I thought this was dangerous, since letter might fall into wrong hands and I was already under grave suspicion as result Makarios' statements in Athens. Thought my position on enosis had already been made clear both here and by Labouisse in Athens. However, I could probably get Labouisse to make further oral communication.

Our real problem in discussing enosis, I said, arose from Turkish distrust of GOG and GOC. They seemed to believe that Makarios and Papandreou are in cahoots.[4] How could we prove to them case was otherwise? First of all, we must reach agreement on substance of what was to happen after enosis and secondly we must devise means to put this agreement into effect without bringing about collapse of Turkish Government. We must save Inonu, who was sole strong, moderate figure in Turkish regime. If enosis brought about without any public indication that Greece and Turkey had reached agreement safeguarding Turkey's minimum interest, GOT would certainly fall. Only way I could think of was to have very general statement issued after agreement reached and then quickly bring about enosis. But Papandreou would have to give more than he had up to now to persuade Turks to stand still.

Nikolareisis concluded conversation by assuring me Papandreou was very anxious to find solution, while I, on my part, renewed my appeal for greater Greek help in finding solution.[5]

Tubby

---

[4] Erkin expressed this view to Hare on August 3. The discussion was reported in telegram 202 from Ankara, August 4. (Ibid.)

[5] Acheson communicated the substance of this conversation to the Turks on the same day and reported their reaction in telegram 318 from Geneva, August 6. (Ibid.)

104.   Telegram From the Embassy in Turkey to the Department of State[1]

Ankara, August 7, 1964, noon.

212. Embtel 202.[2] Erkin asked me come in late yesterday to brief him on "anything you have received since we last talked", i.e. only two days before as reported reftel.

Since nothing had as yet been received in response his questions, I armed myself with such new information as was available regarding more favorable attitude of Makarios on freedom of movement of UN peace force and food distribution as reported by Nicosia and USUN, as well as our own efforts and those of UN in that regard. Also made inventory of current developments in other fields mutual interest including turning over second $40 million loan tranche, delivery of 104–G's and tanks under MAP, completion agreement for joint use Cigli airfield after prolonged negotiation, local currency assistance in building new labor union headquarters, imminent arrival of parachute jump training team, continuing efforts to obtain increased consortium assistance and satisfactory progress Turk parliamentary visit in U.S.

Contrary his wont, Erkin took notes on these items and then observed fundamental question remained what to do in rapidly deteriorating situation. He had lunched with Inonu who had asked him tell me situation grave as result such GOC acts as economic and physical blockade of Turks, obstructions to peace force in fulfilling mission, continuing armed attacks on Turks, breakdown of judiciary, territorial waters legislation, military secrets law, cutting of Turkish water supply and attempted removal Turk Cypriot Amb here in order replace by Turk Cypriot from Bonn and fill Bonn post with Greek. He said Inonu had asked him say that continued GOC aggression could result in Turk retaliation from air.

There ensued rather involved discussion in which I endeavored ascertain whether Erkin was talking about reaction from cumulative frustration or as result some new development. Using our relations with Soviet Union as example I pointed out that there had been recurrent situations over the years when cumulative friction had caused voices to be raised in advocacy of trial by arms but we had resisted this even at the time when we had atomic monopoly. Other examples abound; meeting

---

[1] Source: Department of State, Central Files, POL 23–8 CYP. Secret; Immediate; Exdis–TAG. Received at 7:08 a.m. and repeated to Athens, Nicosia, Geneva for Acheson, and London. Passed to the White House.

[2] See footnote 4, Document 103.

such problems is real test statesmanship and diplomacy. To give up is to shirk our job.

Also in such tense situation was important that GOT keep careful watch on actions of Turk Cypriots. I had just received several disquieting reports in this regard, one to effect that people of Ktima had wanted pay water bill but had been prevented by Turk "organization" and another indicating Turks responsible for fray involving UN forces in Nicosia (Nicosia's 175 to Dept).[3] In drawing attention to these, I realized that general pattern of incidents showed predominance of Greek Cypriot instigation but would be deplorable if in tense situation thus created spark would be supplied by some Turkish initiative. Regardless of how it might come about, it could be made to appear that it had been deliberately created to afford excuse for GOT retaliation.

This was stiff stuff but Erkin took it well, observing in latter connection he would get message off to Cyprus immediately to enjoin restraint on Turks.

Re occasion for retaliation, Erkin inquired what had President Johnson meant when he spoke in Washington talks of war as only last resort?[4] Also he already being asked why U.S. should feel warranted in taking such strong action in Vietnam (which he personally thought right) and at same time restrain GOT when it similarly inclined act in its own interest. To this he had no answer.

Conversation then turned again to type of incident which might cause GOT retaliate and Erkin mentioned, as he had in reftel, situation which could arise if Geneva talks fail and enosis carried out as purely Greek affair. Reference also made to danger of any substantial move to subdue Turks and indicated this was what Inonu especially had in mind when he warned of possible necessity of retaliation. Erkin renewed request for our views in this regard (to be borne in mind that, aside from real desire consult, these approaches could be cited as fulfilling our understanding re consultation in event decision taken retaliate in some way).

Broadening conversation, Erkin then expressed great concern re deteriorating relations with GOG, saying that, if Nikolareisis returned to Geneva with negative response, point of no return [would] have been reached between Greece and Turkey since action such as removal Greek forces from Bulgarian frontier to bolster strength versus Turks, illegal military build-ups in Dodecanese and intensive naval patrols from Mytilene to Rhodes would indicate that "Greece wants war". Wouldn't I agree?

---

[3] Telegram 175 from Nicosia, August 6, reported on exchanges of fire within the city of Nicosia. (Department of State, Central Files, POL 23–8 CYP)

[4] See Document 72.

I said definitely not. In first place would be completely irrational in view disparity between Greek and Turkish forces. Secondly, such information as I had indicated Greeks don't want war and that this feeling prevalent in Greek armed forces.

Erkin said this not assessment of GOT, citing public statements by Papandreou re readiness reply militarily and report Greek Amb in Nicosia had expressed opinion war inevitable. This why he was asking our views since moment may come when too late for USG to do anything. I said would submit to Dept but in meantime had considerable confidence in my own appraisal and felt GOT would be making serious mistake to proceed assumption Athens actually picking fight.

Erkin then brought up subject of Makarios, recalling that in previous conversation I had suggested would be mistake to assume that public professions of identity of view between Makarios and Papandreou accurately reflected basic relationship; also that I had suggested elements of opposition to Makarios on island as well. Relating to suggestions made in past to desirability of doing something to remove Makarios from picture, he said couldn't see how this could be done as result of Turk-Greek agreement but would rather have to precede agreement since seems Makarios still in position exert controlling influence on Athens. I said didn't wish get over my head in unauthorized discussion but one thing seemed obvious, which was that if Turkey and Greece should come to agreement on solution which would involve enosis in one way or another, role of Makarios would pretty much disappear. Obviously intrigued by even mention this subject, i.e. elimination of Makarios, Erkin said still felt difficult reach solution as long as Makarios remained in power and speculated on possible move by Grivas to replace him. I asked if there had been any contact by Grivas with GOT. Erkin said none; all that known is publicly announced intention of Grivas to promote enosis while saying steps would be taken safeguard Turkish community.

Erkin concluded conversation by making renewed appeal "to extract something from Washington" regarding views and intentions of USG since, if Geneva talks get nowhere, necessary devise alternatives for dealing with situation. Once again he wished emphasize gravity of situation as it is developing and to make clear he not talking under impulse of emotion but "coldly and solemnly".

While I was with Erkin he received telephone call from Deputy Prime Minister Satir who had just talked with Erim in Geneva who reported Acheson dissatisfied with proposals brought by Nikolareisis. Erkin's first reaction was to take this as indication of final break which he had predicted but I suggested Greeks adept at bargaining in old and established Near Eastern tradition where it is not first but "last price" that counts. Now not time throw in hand.

Was interesting that Erim's report was made to Satir, presumably acting on behalf of Inonu, rather than Erkin which would tend substantiate suggestion in reftel that Erkin–Erim relationship may be element in situation. However, would be mistake stress this unduly since believe what Erkin had to say was essentially what he very much had on his mind.

This tel being sent Immediate in view radio reports this morning of serious fighting in Mansura area, which is precisely type of development which could trigger Turk retaliation.[5]

Hare

---

[5] In telegram 223 from Athens, August 7, Labouisse "strongly endorsed" Hare's suggestions. (Department of State, Central Files, POL 23–8 CYP) In telegram 221 from Ankara, August 7, Hare reported that the Turkish Cabinet would meet at 10 p.m. to discuss events in Cyprus and that Erkin had promised to pass along a report to the Embassy. (Ibid.)

---

105. Telegram From the Department of State to the Embassy in Greece[1]

Washington, August 7, 1964, 12:50 p.m.

198. From Ball to Ambassadors. Ref: Ankara Critic One Repeated to you separately.[2]

For Athens:

You should approach GOG at highest level with following message:

1. They should do everything possible to prevent the GOC from reacting against Turk-Cypriot population or from attempting to destroy Turkish aircraft since either action could rapidly escalate dangerous situation.

2. GOG should avoid any reaction that could contribute to escalation or impede progress being made in Geneva.

3. GOG should discourage any move by GOC to bring this matter into Security Council since this again could lead only to exacerbation of relations and interference with possibility successful Geneva negotiations.

---

[1] Source: Department of State, Central Files, POL 23–8 CYP. Secret; Flash. Drafted and approved by Ball and cleared by Talbot and Sisco. Also sent to Ankara, Nicosia, London, USUN, and Geneva for Acheson.

[2] This telegram, August 7, reported that Turkish Foreign Minister Erkin had informed Hare that in response to hostile actions, his government had ordered a "demonstration" by the Turkish Air Force over Cyprus and that Greece had been informed of this decision. "Erkin made urgent plea for USG to do anything in its power to avoid disaster, saying that GOT wants above all else is to avoid spread of hostilities." (Ibid.)

4. We have told GOT that we strongly disapprove this demonstration and have cautioned them to take no further action that might heighten the danger of escalation.[3]

For Ankara:

We assume that by "demonstration" Turks intend only to fly planes over as they did on December 26 and that there will be no bombing. Please confirm this. Please also tell Erkin we are greatly disturbed by GOT decision. We are doing everything possible in relevant capitals to dampen reaction and prevent this from leading to escalation and disrupting the intensive efforts we have been making in Geneva.[4]

For Nicosia:

Please contact Thimayya and encourage him to do everything possible to prevent GOC reactions against Turk-Cypriot population. Suggest you do not inform GOC if this telegram arrives before air planes since that is not our responsibility and we do not wish to provide basis for any suspicion we are approving GOT action.[5]

Rusk

---

[3] In telegram 226 from Athens, August 7, Labouisse reported that Costopoulos had already urged Makarios to avoid any further provocation and, although treating the Turkish air raid as very serious, discounted the likelihood of armed intervention. (Ibid.)

[4] Upon receipt of telegram 221 from Ankara indicating that the Turkish "demonstration" would involve strafing and bombing, the Department of State instructed Hare in telegram 184, August 7, to request that the Turkish Government limit its action to a "flyover" and avoid any bloodshed. (Both ibid.)

[5] In telegram 197 from Nicosia, August 8, Belcher reported that, fearing the effects of a Turkish air attack, he had warned both U.N. and Cypriot Government officials of its likelihood, while urging upon them the need for an immediate cease-fire. (Ibid.) In telegram 109 to Nicosia, August 8, the Department of State noted: "Understand your reasoning behind your actions but nevertheless it is essential that we maintain confidential relationship with GOT." (Ibid.)

---

106. Telegram From the Mission in Geneva to the Department of State[1]

Geneva, August 7, 1964, 4 p.m.

325. From Acheson for Ball. We must begin prepare for last act of Geneva. Mediator plans to leave August 7 for Athens, Ankara, Nicosia, Athens, returning Geneva August 20, a veritable phantom Finn. Believes

---

[1] Source: Department of State, Central Files, POL 23–8 CYP. Secret; Nodis–TAG. Received at 2:14 p.m. and repeated to Ankara and Athens.

he should then urge on SYG that he (Tuomioja) make his final report if I am still stuck in mud. He will tell Greeks during visit to Athens his report will stress no change in present status Cyprus toward full independence and beyond is possible under UN Charter except by unanimous agreement signatories present treaties. Hence, if they want enosis now offered on silver platter they must pay comparatively small price to get Turkish agreement.

Believe we too should begin to make terminal noises, stating that if next round of talks produces no progress I shall go home to report and have no personal intention of returning. USG's future course not up to me.

Should like to give to Nikolareisis as personal opinion that under existing pressures and Makarios' present policies Turkish physical reaction inevitable, that I have urged restraint and will continue to do so, though knowing that advice is useless; furthermore, Turkish attitude quite understandable. Finally, that if USG asks, as it has done in past, my opinion on what our action should be in event Turkish move, I should give Lincoln's advice to Stanton (in view of Far East situation) "one war at a time." We are deeply involved on many fronts and Greeks and Turks are not only people with domestic political problems. Whether through UN or otherwise I would be against US military involvement in Cyprus.

Would also say to Greeks that if, as Nikolareisis suggested, move directly to enosis after understanding reached with Turks is contemplated, danger of popular upheaval Turkey could be overcome by announcement that Turkish forces would shortly arrive not as enemies but by prior agreement and to aid in orderly transition of Turkish Cypriots to enosis. They would thus transform greatest hazard in path of enosis to important asset. It also might even work, and help Inonu as suggested mytel 315.[2]

To Turks I would say that they know our advice that Cyprus not worth a war; we still believe that. But we would neither attempt to stop any military action by them, nor rescue them from the consequences of their action if any occurred. They would be entirely on their own.

To both I would say that, in UN, US would reenforce the Mediator's view that changes in status can only be recognized if accomplished by legal means.

So much for terminal noises.

Problem in reaching agreement lies primarily in Athens and primarily there with Papandreou. He has not made one attempt toward the agreement he could have and which would give him nine-tenths of all he hoped for. I cannot reach him because Nikolareisis is not wired for

---

[2] Document 103.

sound. Harry has got to get into the act with a baseball bat and make him see that he is risking everything by taking 100 percent negative attitude and not making one constructive suggestion. Specifically we want to get here some one with power at home authorized to work out a long-term lease of the peninsula—or any other place—without any more nagging restrictions than the British have and under some sort of organization like Canada–US Joint Defense Board. If no Greek can come here perhaps Harry ought to fly up secretly in military aircraft for talk with me and return to be a relaying station in Athens. God only knows what N says I say.

Impossible for Ray to do anything unless a Greek first comes here bearing a small gift or rather small downpayment on a rare bargain.

Tubby

107. Telegram From the Embassy in Cyprus to the Department of State[1]

Nicosia, August 7, 1964, 8:30 p.m.

192. At request Minister Interior, Thimayya and I went to see President urgently while he went to see Grivas. President in middle of Council of Ministers meeting which he broke off for hour-long discussion with us.

Thimayya made suggestion that President issue statement calling for cease-fire by Greeks on condition urgent negotiations be commenced at once for removal all posts both Greek Cypriot and Turk Cypriot in Mansoura area. President pointed out that this was similar to suggestion he had made some time ago and had even offered withdraw unilaterally if UN would take over Greek posts. UN had been unable do so but perhaps if both sides gave up posts outside villages UN could then maintain peace in area. Thimayya agreed this would be good idea and worth trying as last-ditch effort save situation from complete chaos. As we speaking of these matters word received of overflight reported previously and

[1] Source: Department of State, Central Files, POL 23–8 CYP. Confidential; Flash. Received at 3:13 p.m. and repeated to Athens, London, Paris for USRO, Geneva for Acheson, the White House, OSD, CIA, and JCS.

of fact villages of Alevgha and Selain Tou Appi had fallen to Greeks (according to Turk sources as told to UN). At same time President's secretary requested helicopter assistance in evacuating number seriously wounded Greek Cypriots from village Kato Pyrgos. All UN helicopters grounded due some mechanical fault and General offered ambulance.

President said he would contact Grivas (who still with Georkadjis at Athalassa command post) immediately and would go there to confer in view need for urgent communication facility only available at post.[2]

I offered send any message he wanted to Ankara for urgent transmission for GOT but pointed out that suggestion of bilateral withdrawal if not coupled with Greek cease-fire would have little effect. President said he would contact me as soon as he had conferred with Grivas, who is in command of operation.

General Thimayya pointed out communication difficulty in that his commander in area had been unable for past 36 hours contact any responsible Greek Cypriot. He expressed hope that communications from Athalassa command post might be more effective.

Belcher

---

[2] Telegram 194 from Nicosia, August 7, 11 p.m., transmitted the text of Georkadjis' report on the military situation in Cyprus. (Ibid.)

---

108. Telegram From the Department of State to the Embassy in Turkey[1]

Washington, August 7, 1964, 9:16 p.m.

193. Ankara's 223, 224 and 225.[2] While we are sorting out what happened today and implications for Geneva talks, NATO, and UN, you should make crystal clear to GOT our conviction further air action

---

[1] .Source: Department of State, Central Files, POL 23–8, CYP. Secret; Immediate; Exdis–TAG. Drafted and approved by Talbot and cleared by GTI, Cleveland, and Ball. Also sent to Athens and repeated to Nicosia, London, USUN, and Geneva for Acheson.

[2] Telegram 223 from Ankara, August 7, reported that Turkish aircraft had already left on their mission. (Ibid.) In telegram 224 from Ankara, August 7, Hare reported that Erkin said no bombing was planned in the overflight of Cyprus and that he would check into reports the jets had fired at targets. (Ibid.) In telegram 225 from Ankara, August 8, Hare reported that the Turks were concerned by reports that Mansoura had fallen to Greek Cypriot attacks and maintained that no Turkish aircraft had fired during the overflight. (Ibid.)

tomorrow would be major misfortune. We understand Thimayya exerting every energy to achieve effective cease fire and there are indications that Greek-Cypriots are becoming responsive to his proposals. Whereas Geneva talks admittedly have not yet found basis for GOG–GOT agreement, we have not at all believed Acheson has reached end of road. We fear today's events may have substantially increased roughness of diplomatic track; whether Acheson can salvage talks will be highly dependent on next actions taken by all parties. If any possibility of continuing Geneva talks is to remain, it is essential that there be no further military action.[3]

We have invested very great effort to pull our two allies back from abyss which yawns before them. We hold no brief for many Greek-Cypriot actions and have appreciated Turkish restraint. However, military action in midst of particularly delicate and significant diplomatic round in Geneva can only drive Greeks into an extreme position publicly as well as privately. It makes clarification and consideration of base question well nigh impossible this week as planned. Moreover, we disagree with Turkish estimate that Greeks will not react. As we have strongly urged restraint on Turks, so we are strongly urging restraint on Greeks.

For Athens: Follow up initial approach with Greeks and ensure they take measures to dampen reaction and particularly to get cease fire into effect.[4]

For Nicosia: Our ability to restrain Turks is obviously inter-related to Makarios willingness agree with Thimayya on cease fire. We should support his efforts actively in every appropriate way.[5]

Rusk

---

[3] In telegram 234 from Ankara, August 8, Hare reported that Erkin stated that the Turks had no plans for further demonstrations and wanted to continue talks at Geneva. (Ibid.)

[4] In telegram 235 from Athens, August 8, the Embassy reported Greek public statements calling for a cease-fire on the island. (Ibid.)

[5] In telegrams 202 and 210 from Nicosia, August 8, Belcher reported his efforts to secure a cease-fire. (Ibid.)

228 Foreign Relations, 1964–1968, Volume XVI

109. Telephone Conversation Between President Johnson and Secretary of Defense McNamara[1]

August 8, 1964, 8:35 a.m.

[Here follows discussion of an unrelated press statement.]

RSM: but, [we have] a very serious crisis brewing in Cyprus.

LBJ: Some of the reporters were quite critical about my coming down here last night.[2] One of these Navy chiefs told me—said, "Here's a war going on on two or three fronts here and he's walking off here to play for the weekend." Now, what's the best way to answer that?

RSM: Oh, I have seen no evidence of that at all up here and no reports on the tickers of anything like that.

LBJ: No. I just think they were visiting among themselves, but I may get a question along that line this morning. What do you think I ought to say? [pause] Hello?

RSM: Yes, I was just thinking. I think you could say that you were advised by the Secretary of State and the Secretary of Defense that there was no reason for your continued presence in Washington this weekend.

LBJ: Will you touch that base with Dean then?

RSM: Yes, sir, I will. Well, I know that he felt that way. I will call him, but he and I talked of this last night and we both agree. I'll call him and tell him.

LBJ: No, no. That's okay then. Now, what can this bring on as far as we're concerned in Cyprus?

RSM: Well, I just talked to George Ball two minutes ago about it, and it's his feeling—and I would certainly share it—that it would be wise to get Labouisse into Geneva[3] immediately to talk to Acheson. George had just finished a conversation with Acheson on the telephone,[4] hoping that possibly Acheson could make some proposal here, possibly an overt publicized proposal by the U.S. Government as to how the Greeks and the Turks might settle their differences. Unless something like that's done, it's very possible the whole place will go up in flames today.

LBJ: All right, then what do we do?

---

[1] Source: Johnson Library, Recordings and Transcripts, Recording of Telephone Conversation Between President Johnson and McNamara, August 8, 1964, 8:35 a.m., Tape 64.01, Side A, PNO 1. No classification marking. The President was in Texas; McNamara was in Washington. This transcript was prepared by the Office of the Historian specifically for this volume.

[2] The President had left Washington at 6:29 p.m. the previous night for the LBJ Ranch. (Ibid., President's Daily Diary)

[3] See Document 111.

[4] A memorandum of this conversation is in the Johnson Library, Ball Papers, Cyprus.

RSM: Well, the first thing to do is to get Labouisse up to Geneva so they can discuss this matter. I say it may go up in flames today, I should really say this weekend. I think we have, maybe, 12 to 48 hours here. So I'm getting an airplane down to Athens to take Labouisse to Geneva, and State is working on some kind of a proposal that might be made, really, along the lines that Acheson has already been proposing, which, in substance, was something that looked as though both the Turks and the Greeks might accept.

LBJ: Why is Labouisse going down there, because he's the Ambassador to Greece?

RSM: To advise on what the Turks, what the Greeks latest thinking is.

LBJ: What they might do?

RSM: Yes.

LBJ: Alright, now suppose—how does it go up in the flames. The Turks are bombing the island?

RSM: The Turkish planes, as you know, strafed one of the harbors yesterday.

LBJ: Yeah.

RSM: In response, it appears that the Greek Cypriots are attacking Turkish Cypriot towns on Cyprus today. And they have the force at hand to take those towns and destroy the Turkish Cypriots. The Turkish Government is in a state of panic at the moment. Erkin has talked to Hare,[5] our Ambassador, and expressed great fear as to what will happen. The Turkish Government just couldn't sit there and let the Turkish Cypriots on Cyprus be slaughtered. They'd be forced to respond. But they apparently ran this four-sortie attack, four-airplane attack, yesterday without having a clear-cut plan as to how they would respond to a Greek Cypriot response. It's a perfect illustration of starting something with too little force and without knowing what you're going do when the other side kicks back.

LBJ: Now, how could we be involved?

RSM: Well, I don't think we would be involved militarily, Mr. President. But I think that the diplomatic offense that George Ball has in mind is the way we should act.

LBJ: Alright.

[Here follows discussion of military operations in Southeast Asia.]

---

[5] See Document 104.

110. Telegram From the Embassy in Turkey to the Department of State[1]

Ankara, August 8, 1964, 1 p.m.

229. Had early morning session with Erkin prior his joining Cabinet meeting in which I drew on Nicosia's 199 to Dept[2] giving latest sitrep and status negots on UN taking over positions in Mansoura complex; Athens 226 to Dept[3] covering constructive recommendation by GOG to Nicosia; Athens 223 to Department[4] re lack Greek desire for war and probability that further bargaining could be useful in Geneva; Athens 227 to Dept[5] re instruction to Nicolareizis to continue talks with Acheson; and finally importance of avoiding further air action in order promote peace efforts in Nicosia and settlement efforts in Geneva as instructed Deptel 193.[6]

Erkin expressed appreciation and made following comments:

1) Said he would send message Turk Chargé Nicosia as requested by Thimayya but reiterated Turk approval was for withdrawal both sides from posts inside and outside villages affected and taking over by UN on status quo ante basis, e.g. Greeks should return Mansoura to Turks if occupied by them. He said this was point on which Ministers felt very strongly last night, with many insisting GOT should otherwise resort to bombing. Erkin said he would clarify again to Turk Chargé and hoped we might assist in Nicosia as occasion afforded. As matter stands Erkin fears Markarios seeking hold villages occupied in which case turning over higher land to UN and disarming villages would merely serve consolidate Greek Cypriot gains. However if there is complete mutuality of action GOT prepared agree.

2) Essential that attacks not now be launched against Kokkina such as made against Mansoura. This very important.

3) Erkin has impression casualties in Mansoura have been heavy and anxious obtain accurate info (would seem any info furnished on this or in similar cases might best be double-tracked through Turk Emb Nicosia).

4) GOT greatly concerned re situation Turks at Paphos where population being subjected excessive privation. Necessary obtain full info and that remedial steps be taken.

---

[1] Source: Department of State, Central Files, POL 23–8 CYP. Secret; Flash; Exdis–TAG. Repeated to USUN, Geneva for Acheson, Nicosia, Athens, DOD, CIA, and the White House.

[2] Dated August 8. (Ibid.)

[3] See footnote 3, Document 105.

[4] See footnote 5, Document 104.

[5] Dated August 7. (Department of State, Central Files, POL 23–8 CYP)

[6] Document 108.

5) GOT respects ability and diligent efforts of General Thimayya.

6) Inonu had hard time in Cabinet last night. Most of Ministers were demanding immediate and strong action, stressing that they represented will of people. Only advocates of moderation were Inonu, Erkin and General Sunay. Otherwise drastic decisions would have been taken last night since there was even opposition to recessing until this morning.

Believe info and thoughts which we were able feed Erkin before and during Cabinet meeting last night and again this morning have been very helpful to him in maintaining certain "one up-manship" with other Cabinet members and interesting to note that, whereas he has been avowed interventionist in recent weeks, he now appears be using influence in cause of moderation.

Since foregoing drafted have had second talk with Erkin giving details of new cease-fire proposal. Para numbered one therefore represents views which have subsequently been revised.

Hare

---

111.   Telephone Conversation Between President Johnson and the Under Secretary of State (Ball)[1]

August 9, 1964, 6:50 a.m.

LBJ: Yes?

GWB: Hello.

LBJ: Hello.

GWB: Hello, Mr. President. We've been watching the Cyprus situation all through the night. We thought we had it stabilized last night, but this morning the Turks resumed their air strikes using napalm and 750-pound bombs. They've got maybe 65 planes that they're using. And the Makarios government has just told our people in Nicosia that unless they stop within a half an hour, they're going to turn on the whole Turk

---

[1] Source: Johnson Library, Recordings and Transcripts, Recording of a Telephone Conversation Between President Johnson and Ball, August 9, 1964, 6:50 a.m., Tape 64.01, Side B, PNO 1. No classification marking. The President was at the LBJ Ranch in Texas; Ball was in Washington. This transcript was prepared by the Office of the Historian specifically for this volume.

Cypriot population on the island and attack them all over the island with just a general massacre.[2] Now, we've gotten the stiffest kind of notes—of messages—both to Makarios and to Inonu,[3] telling them they've got to stop immediately while this is all sorted out. But what I wanted to suggest was that I'm not at all sure that this thing is going to be held, and it may blow up within the next few hours into one of the bloodiest events we've seen in modern times, and I just wondered if your people shouldn't be making preparations so you could get back here fast if you have to do so.

LBJ: Alright.

GWB: Now, I may, if it's agreeable with you, I may have to use your name to Inonu in order to stop this. I don't think it will be necessary, but if we can't get them to stand down, I'd like to be—have authority to do it.

LBJ: Sure, sure. I wouldn't think it would do much good, though.

GWB: Well, I'm not sure. This is the one hope we've got to get this thing stopped before it turns into a general massacre. But these people are all so bloodthirsty there's just no telling. And the military may be out from under control, as far as Inonu is concerned, in Turkey which is the other matter that we don't know about.

LBJ: What did it look like last night?

GWB: Well, last night the bombing had been limited. And, actually, the attack had been limited. They didn't use bombs. They used only rockets and machine guns. And it looked as though the incident were closed. And this was the impression that the Turks gave. But the Greek Cypriots continued the fighting in these villages, apparently through the night, and that was enough to set—give the Turk military an excuse to go forward again today, and this time they're armored differently and with napalm and 750-pound bombs, it's become a very serious business. They've got a lot of the—a number of the villages are in flames, so that now the one recourse that Makarios has is to threaten to use the Turk Cypriots on the island—all hundred thousand of them—as his hostages and just massacre them unless this thing stops. So that we've gotten, as they say, the toughest messages to both sides. But whether they'll stop now with this bloodbath stuff, I can't tell. It's very questionable. So that the thing may be out of control. But, we're—doing my best. But in the meantime, I just have the feeling that someone—the way the world will look at it, that there ought to be preparations so you could move.

LBJ: I was planning to go to a funeral and come in immediately after the funeral in the middle of the afternoon.[4]

---

[2] See Document 113.

[3] See Document 108.

[4] The President attended the service for Mrs. Bess Beeman and departed for Washington at 3:15 p.m. (Johnson Library, President's Daily Diary)

GWB: Well, that may be alright if this doesn't get out of hand. But if it does, I would just want to raise the question with you as something to consider.

LBJ: Where's Dean?

GWB: He's on his way down now. I've been here all night. I've been in touch with him through the night.

LBJ: Bob's in town too.

GWB: Bob's in town; I've been in touch with him. And with Bus Wheeler and so on and so on.

LBJ: What are the possibilities—what else could we do?

GWB: Not much more, unless we wanted to intervene militarily, and I don't think anybody wants to do that. We're going to get the Sixth Fleet moved over closer, at least—just got a call in to Bob to talk to him about it now. We've got destroyers standing off Cyprus to take our own people off—there are about 350 Americans on the island—if it comes to that. But beyond that I don't know what we could do. The Security Council was in emergency session until 1:30 this morning but adjourned without coming to any decision. At that time, it looked as though the Turks were going to quit and this was an incident which we could then use to sort things out diplomatically. But the Turks have overplayed their hand and apparently the military may be out of control, so that it's going to be very hard to do anything. The Greek Cypriots called in or advised our fellow late last night, which was 2:30 o'clock over there, that they had asked the Soviet Union to intervene militarily.[5] Now, the Soviet Union hasn't done anything. I'm quite sure it isn't going to do anything other than to help them in the Security Council. But, we let—I let Moscow know right away last night, to put them on guard, and we'll have to watch this during the day, so we're alerting the fleets to be on guard.

LBJ: What'd we say to Moscow?

GWB: I just notified the Embassy there to find out everything they could, but we didn't want to take any strong line because there was no indication of any favorable response on Moscow's part.

LBJ: What do the British say?

GWB: Well, the British are in the position of taking orders from us. We're really getting nothing from them of a substantive kind, although we're keeping them on—of course, they've all gone away for a weekend over in London, as usual. Butler is out on an island somewhere, and I think Home is away from London, too. And they are partly inaccessible. But we're keeping the government informed, and, actually, I made use of

---

[5] In telegram 219 from Nicosia, August 9, received in the Department of State at 12:11 a.m., the Embassy reported that the Cyprus Government had requested Soviet military intervention. (Department of State, Central Files, POL 23–8 CYP)

the government planes last night to get them scrambled up off the island to have a look around to see what Turkish forces were in the vicinity. There's nothing, so far, of sea forces except about half a dozen destroyers that they have standing off. But there's no question that they're all loaded and ready to go as far as a land invasion is concerned. They've been making preparations for the last 24 hours, and this is a culmination of several weeks ago.

LBJ: What does Acheson say?

GWB: I talked to him last night[6] and he was fairly relaxed, but, of course, that was before this last attack. Now, I sent—I got a plane through Bob and sent Harry Labouisse up late last night to have a talk with Acheson so that Acheson, I mean Labouisse could come back to see Papandreou with a strong note from Acheson about the possibility of settling and the need to settle immediately. Labouisse is back in Athens now. The Greek Government so far has behaved quite well. Papandreou called on Makarios to stop the fighting last night but, apparently, without success. He has now summoned Grivas to come back to Athens. And it was our hope in the earlier hours this morning that he would work out some kind of a means of getting rid of Makarios so that this matter could be settled between the Greek and Turk Governments. But the Turks are overplaying their hand so badly that it may be very hard to put it back together now. But we'll keep working on it.

LBJ: Now what are the one or two possible alternatives? Our intervention would be one. You can rule that out. Any—what else?

GWB: I don't think from a military intervention point of view, there's anything that can be done because there's no United Nations force that could be gotten together for this purpose. Of course, if the Soviet Union—

LBJ: Well now, why not? Why not? Why couldn't the United Nations—why wouldn't that be something to at least pursue or hold out hope on?

GWB: Well, I think—

LBJ: you mean, just realistically, they don't have them, but couldn't we—?

GWB: They simply won't do it. That's all I mean. There are 6,000 UN troops in there now, but the orders that all the component governments have given to their own elements is that if an invasion should start, they would retire into the British bases and not stop it, because with 6,000 men they are not capable of stopping a Turkish invasion. And anyway, there isn't a one of the United Nations forces that's in there that's prepared to fight the Turks.

---

[6] A memorandum of this conversation is in the Johnson Library, Ball Papers, Cyprus.

LBJ: Well, is there any possibility that we could get the governments to agree to do that, and we could tell the Turks that we're going—that the United Nations is going to be fighting you if you don't stay away?

GWB: Well, realistically with the experience we've had in the UN of even getting the 6,000 and the nervous—the Canadians calling us every hour and saying they want to pull out, and the Swedes threatening to pull out, there's no member of the UN, I think, that's going to be willing to put up any forces against a Turkish invasion. I think the best bet there is just to use the biggest, the toughest leverage we have on the Turks. If we can't stop them, why we'll just have to cordon off the island and let the thing settle down itself. Because I don't think there's any way of putting outside forces between the Turks and the Greeks if they really get at it, without—I don't think there's anybody prepared to put forces into a situation like that.

LBJ: Well, UN intervention, our intervention—what else is conceivable?

GWB: On the military side, I think that the best thing we could do is to make sure that the Soviet Union doesn't do anything. But as far as trying to stop it, the only other way to stop it then is just to tell the Turk Government, which I already have, that they're going to be condemned in the eyes of the world by all civilized nations if they go ahead, in the face of the threat of a massacre, and precipitate it. And I've told the Government of Cyprus that if they go ahead with a massacre of this kind, they will be condemned as murderers by all civilized people. That we are working very hard with both governments—with the Turkish Government that gets the planes stood down. And if there's any civilian control left in the Turkish Government, I think we could probably do it. It's—but apart from that, there's no way we can stop this fighting because there's no available force that can go in and get in the middle of it. And, actually, for an outside force to come in—once this massacre starts, it's hopeless. I mean, if you had 50,000 men and put them in, you couldn't stop the bloodshed, because it's going on and it will go on in every little village all over the place. And a major force would only exacerbate it, actually, if they came in from outside. We just have to live through it and pick up the pieces. But it's a mess.

LBJ: Well, UN intervention, our intervention—I guess you've got to consider the likelihood of Soviet intervention, haven't you?

GWB: We've considered it very hard and we've looked at it very long and we don't think at all it's going to happen. But, nevertheless, we're going to try—we're going to get some fleet units up there just to be on guard if anything should occur. It would be very hard for them to intervene, almost impossible—except by air. They couldn't put enough ashore by submarine to do it and they can't get their—any naval units out there. They would just be exposing themselves in a way they never would. I don't think—they have told the Turks, within the last week, that if the Turks intervened they wouldn't do anything about it. And I don't, for a minute, think that they're going to respond to Makarios' call. We're going to take every prudent act to make sure that they don't, but I just don't see any serious possibility of it.

LBJ: Now, what are we waiting on to take our people off?

GWB: Well, I think we—

LBJ: Do we have the facilities there to do it now?

GWB: Yeah, We've got a destroyer standing offshore. We've got the airlifts all set up. The best way to evacuate them is by air. I'm—I hope that—we've got about a half an hour to play with here—and I hope that we won't have to pull them off in a wholesale way because it could even make the—it might trigger the thing. But they're pretty secure. I mean, it's as badly an exposed situation as it is [inaudible].

LBJ: Not very secure when you got 65 planes bombing an island, are you?

GWB: Well, we can get the Turks to stay away from our people, I think. They know where they are.

[Here follows discussion of military operations in Southeast Asia.]

112.   Telegram From the Embassy in Greece to the Department of State[1]

Athens, August 9, 1964, 2 p.m.

238. From Anschuetz. Have just seen Papandreou at his request. Costopoulos (Fon Affairs) and Garoufalias (Defense) also present.

Papandreou said GOG had received telephone call from Makarios demanding intervention of Greek aircraft to repel Turk bombings which resumed this morning. Papandreou alluded to his statement last night which he said constituted formal repudiation of Markarios' policy. Fighting has now stopped, however and Turkish action is putting GOG in untenable position. Whatever one might think of Makarios, he is

[1] Source: Department of State, Central Files, POL 23–8 CYP. Secret; Flash. Repeated to Ankara, Nicosia, Geneva for Acheson, Paris for USRO, London, USUN, DOD, CIA, and the White House.

apparently in the right in this instance, and public opinion in Greece and in Cyprus will not permit GOG stand aside indefinitely. Kyprianou had telephoned demanding formal declaration of GOG support by one thirty today failing which GOC would have no alternative but to seek help elsewhere. Papandreou appealed to USG halt Turkish attacks. Assured Papandreou USG was exerting its best efforts. Pointed out direct and immediate Soviet or UAR intervention seemed rather unlikely and requested assurance that GOG armed forces would not be engaged without further consultation with us. This assurance was given, but with insistence that next few hours would be extremely critical for GOG. I commented that awkward as is present position GOG, actual engagement Greek armed forces would be infinitely more serious.

Costopoulos said Grivas is returning within the hour. GOG at a loss understand how Kokkina–Mansoura affair had gotten out of control despite best efforts GOG. Garofoulias asserted no Greek nationals involved this affair.

All three Greeks were in rather emotional state. I assured them I would be in touch with them later today.

Labouisse

---

113.   **Telegram From the Embassy in Cyprus to the Embassy in Turkey**[1]

Nicosia, August 9, 1964, 3:30 p.m.

165. Just seen President in urgent last minute appeal to him, order cease-fire in order avoid further spread of violence. After making numerous points and expressing my real regret that we had not taken advantage of cease-fire which lasted almost 18 hours, I urged him in spite of reports which he had recounted of destruction of Greek villages as distinct from any military targets, make urgent announcement of cease-fire using whatever justification needed which would put GOC in best pos-

---

[1] Source: Department of State, Central Files, POL 23–8 CYP. Confidential; Flash. Repeated to the Department of State (where it was received at 9:58 a.m.), USUN, the White House, Geneva for Acheson, Athens, London, Paris for USRO, DOD, CIA, COMSIXTH-FLT, Istanbul, Beirut, and USDOCOSouth. The source text is the Department of State copy.

sible light. As he was saying "Do you think that Turks would stop if I did so?" aide came in to announce 2 further air strikes by 4 and 7 planes respectively on villages of Pamos and Kato Pyrgos setting center of towns afire. With this news President turned to me with hopeless shrug and said "What can I do?"

I suggested that he and his Ministers were putting USG in impossible position by using US as means of transmittal of "ultimatum" for two reasons (1) time element too short and (2) Turks unlikely respond this sort of threat. I urged him again in most urgent tones reconsider this terrible decision so fraught with dangers for his people.

I said I would do what I could but I was not at all hopeful that restrictions which he had placed on situation would make possible a favorable outcome. As he accompanied me to door I asked again regarding time limit and he indicated 1:30 GMT.

We at Nicosia recognize that if US successfully stops Turks on this occasion and in response this type ultimatum we will henceforth be held responsible for controlling Turks and subject this type of blackmail. However even so I believe we must make every conceivable effort obtain at least temporary cessation of bombing in order not to create holocaust on this island with all its ultimate consequences for our alliances not only in area but elsewhere.

Belcher

---

114.   Telegram From the Department of State to the Embassy in Greece[1]

Washington, August 9, 1964, 10:23 a.m.

224. For Ambassador from Ball. Please approach Papandreou urgently and make following points:

1. In spite of what GOC may have told him, they officially advised us last night that they were calling on the Soviet Union for military intervention; they confirmed this advice to the British Government. It is utterly essential that Papandreou concert with Grivas to insure that no Soviet, Egyptian or other armed forces be introduced into the island.

---

[1] Source: Department of State, Central Files, POL 23–8 CYP. Confidential; Flash; Exdis. Drafted and approved by Ball. Repeated to Ankara, Nicosia, London, Paris, USUN, and Geneva for Acheson.

2. The situation in Cyprus is on the verge of holocaust. Makarios has threatened a general massacre if the Turkish attacks do not stop. We are urgently trying to get the Turk planes to stand down and at the same time are pointing out to GOC that they will be regarded as murderers if they loose an attack on Turk Cypriot population generally.

3. Under these circumstances Papandreou must show his leadership by stopping the fighting on the island and getting Makarios under control. We will do all possible to stop the further Turkish offensive but Papandreou must get Grivas and his men in hand.

4. Above all Papandreou and Inonu must now promptly settle this matter along the lines of the Acheson proposals. There is no longer time for horse-trading or equivocation or passionate oratory. This is a time for calm heads, incisive action and rational leadership.

5. Tell Papandreou that all of us, including President Johnson, have greatly admired his restraint so far and the message that he sent to Makarios last night.[2] We must move on from there.

Rusk

[2] In his August 8 letter, Papandreou appealed to Makarios to cease Greek-Cypriot military operations.

115.   Telegram From the Embassy in Turkey to the Department of State[1]

Ankara, August 9, 1964, 7 p.m.

244. Deptel 201.[2] For Under Secretary Ball from Hare. Had appointment with Erkin immediately following receipt your telegram. Asked him what reaction had been to my asking them hold hand after receipt

[1] Source: Department of State, Central Files, POL 23–8 CYP. Secret; Flash. Received at 12:33 p.m. and passed to the White House, DOD, CIA, and USUN.
[2] Telegram 201 to Ankara, August 9, instructed Hare to "tell Inonu urgently that Turks have now made their point emphatically by military action. However, if they proceed further in the face of imminent warning of a general massacre, neither the US nor world opinion will condone this and they will have hurt their cause irreparably." (Ibid., POL 7 US/BALL)

your telephone call. He said has talked to Inonu who had said unable do so. I then asked see Inonu to deliver your message and Erkin and I went to his house together.

He was friendly but tough, saying every hour given Makarios is used for evil and he unwilling give him any more time. As for today didn't expect there would be much if any more air activity due to advanced hour. What he would agree to is to call off further air strikes if by tomorrow morning Makarios stops attacks at Kokkina and agrees to eventual withdrawal from area occupied by Greeks. This to be followed by agreement restore peace immediately on whole of island.

Inonu said felt confident this could be done if put to Makarios straight and hard. Time serves no purpose with him. Overnight will be time enough. He insisted on sunrise as expiration period put this over. I said couldn't see how this could possibly work since would give no time for exchange views in morning. In end he agreed I should see Erkin at nine o'clock tomorrow morning to determine where we stand. This was maximum I could wring out of him.[3]

He also said he convinced that if quiet restored in island Acheson should be able finish up in week.

He seemed think you and Acheson miraclemen. I said knew you damned good but would not want assignment he giving you tonight.

Longer telegram follows giving conversation in detail but this is guts.[4]

Will be available all night but suggest Flash telegrams preferable to telephone which usually pretty poor.

Hare

---

[3] The Department reported this to Nicosia in telegram 128 to Nicosia, August 9. It instructed Belcher to meet immediately with Makarios to secure a cease-fire. (Ibid.)

[4] Telegram 247 from Ankara, August 9. (Ibid.)

116.   **Telegram From the Embassy in Cyprus to the Department of State**[1]

Nicosia, August 9, 1964, 10:30 p.m.

240. Under Secretary from Belcher. Since I have seen Makarios only 15 minutes ago to deliver message as reported Embtel 239 and contained in Deptel 124[2] am now awaiting results this latest approach. Am loathe to hit him again with same issue complicated by new conditions apparently being imposed by Inonu. Furthermore, I feel I must consult with my British colleague who has been instrumental in obtaining two postponements of dire action previously planned by Greek Cypriots. British High Commissioner's approach and his messages to Ankara and to London spoke only of cease-fire in Kokkina for purpose of subsequent negotiations. Am seeing Bishop at once for this purpose and hopefully by the time I return we will have some indication GOC response to message from Security Council President. We still have a few hours in which to make ultimate pitch.

My own belief is that injection of conditions on top Security Council President's appeal might throw whole [garble] assuming there is chance of favorable reply from Makarios.[3]

Belcher

---

[1] Source: Department of State, Central Files, POL 23–8 CYP. Confidential; Flash. Received at 5:07 p.m. Also sent to Ankara and Athens and repeated to Geneva for Acheson, London, Paris for USRO, USUN, USDOCOSouth, JCS, OSD, DOD, JCS, and the White House.

[2] Telegram 239 from Nicosia, August 9, reported that the Ambassador had delivered a message from President Johnson. (Ibid.) The message, sent to Papandreou, Inonu, and Makarios, urged restraint on all parties and cooperation with the United Nations in its peacekeeping efforts. The text was transmitted in telegram 124 to Nicosia, August 9. (Ibid.)

[3] In telegram 121 to Nicosia, the Department reported that the Turkish Representative to the United Nations had indicated he would recommend that his government accept the Security Council appeal for a cease-fire. (Ibid.)

117.   Telegram From the Embassy in Greece to the Department of State[1]

Athens, August 9, 1964, midnight.

247. I delivered President Johnson's letter to Papandreou at seven thirty this evening.[2] Costopoulos and Anschuetz also present. Papandreou said he found the text excellent and was prepared to publish it.

Papandreou launched into a long analysis of the situation in Cyprus. GOG had an agreement with Makarios and Grivas that they were to indulge in no military operations except with the approval of the Greek Government. Both Makarios and Grivas violated that agreement. Makarios had probably planned the operation in the Mansoura area for some time, and Grivas was dragged along because he was attracted by the military advantages of eliminating the Turkish beachhead there. GOG had transmitted three messages to Cyprus with regard to fighting in this area. First was a telegraphic message Saturday morning August 7, the second a telephone call and last night the written message which was published (Embtel 235 to Department).[3] Last message was public repudiation of Makarios. Makarios' actions have demonstrated that it will be impossible to have a common or parallel policy with him.

Papandreou stated that Grivas had been offended by his messages and had said he would resign (Grivas tender of resignation confirmed by [*less than 1 line of source text not declassified*]).

Papandreou said that in light Makarios–Grivas action the Turks were right in staging their demonstration yesterday. Today with cease-fire of the Greek Cypriots, the situation is reversed and the Turkish attack without justification. If Turks will guarantee to discontinue their attacks, Greek Government will accept responsibility for maintaining cease-fire. (When asked if he could ensure this, he replied he believed he could.) Tonight may be a terrible night in Cyprus because the Cypriots consider they are abandoned. And it is reported that Georgatsis might organize some activity against Turk Cypriots. The only activity which the Greeks have taken today was what he called the theatrical demonstration of four planes which flew over Cyprus to reassure the Greek Cypriots.

If it is possible to obtain Turkish assurances to desist, both sides should accept authority of UNFICYP. Moreover, appeal of Chairman

---

[1] Source: Department of State, Central Files, POL 23–8 CYP. Secret; Immediate; Exdis–TAG. Received at 7:31 p.m. and repeated to Nicosia, Ankara, Geneva for Acheson, London, USUN, and Paris.

[2] See footnote 2, Document 116.

[3] Dated August 8. (Department of State, Central Files, POL 23–8 CYP)

Security Council[4] provides an additional basis for insisting upon a cease-fire. With a cease-fire Papandreou said it would be possible to move promptly toward a basic solution of the problem.

I seized on this to emphasize US conviction necessary to reach settlement all issues with Turks in shortest possible time.

I covered briefly my discussion with Acheson in Geneva. I took general line agreed with Acheson and will follow up tomorrow at another meeting with Prime Minister scheduled for noon.

It was clear to me that Papandreou prepared to accept some sort of lease arrangement although question of size, etc. will still pose problems. I believe he fully understands urgent need for agreed solution. As he was very tired and clearly showed strain of recent days, I told him that I would wait until our meeting tomorrow for full discussion.

I hope Geneva will send revisions of draft agreement in time for tomorrow's meeting.

Labouisse

---

[4] On August 9, the President of the U.N. Security Council appealed to Turkey to end the use of military force.

---

118.   Telegram From the Embassy in Turkey to the Department of State[1]

Ankara, August 10, 1964, noon.

254. For Under Secretary Ball from Hare. Saw Erkin nine o'clock and made presentation as instructed Dept 219.[2]

He was very upset, pointing out that key of Inonu provisions was for withdrawal of Greeks from Mansoura complex and restoration of status quo ante.

---

[1] Source: Department of State, Central Files, POL 27 CYP. Confidential; Flash. Received at 5:53 a.m. and repeated to Athens, Nicosia, USUN, Paris for USRO, London, Geneva for Acheson, and DOD. Passed to the White House and CIA.

[2] Telegram 219 to Ankara, August 9, outlined Security Council Resolution 193 (1964) on Cyprus and instructed the Embassy to underline to Turkish officials the resolution's evenhandedness and the need for Turkish restraint. (Ibid.) The resolution, sponsored by the United States and United Kingdom, was adopted on August 9 by vote of 9 to 0, with 2 abstentions (Czechoslovakia and the Soviet Union). For text, see *American Foreign Policy: Current Documents, 1964*, pp. 584–585.

Without such agreement, SC resolution would merely guarantee gains made by Greeks and he reluctant even submit such proposal for consideration of Cabinet. He felt we had let GOT down very badly. Also there had been no mention whatsoever re expediting Geneva negotiations.

I said felt Erkin looking at situation through wrong end of telescope. Inonu had mentioned four points: 1) cessation Greek attacks; 2) withdrawal by Greeks to position before attacks; 3) general peace in Cyprus; 4) speeding up Geneva talks. Security Council resolution covered points 1 and 3 and I knew for certainty that point 4 in train. This left only point 2, which obviously important from GOT viewpoint, but I saw nothing in resolution contrary to it. Possibly full knowledge of what took place either in New York or collaterally would reveal that progress made on this point of which I unaware. But in any event I saw no reason why subject couldn't be pursued and I would ask urgently for further guidance from Washington.

Meanwhile I gave him a copy of Cyprus "Gridiron" for Aug 8[3] indicating full understanding by USG on this point.

Erkin said would appreciate my doing so since pressure to continue aerial strikes very strong. TAF Commander Tansel had told Inonu last night that task could be completed in one more day and had made plea against holding up today. Inonu had refused but now would be put on spot by SC resolution giving Greeks all they want except possibly Kokkina and no info available re status there since no reports received since yesterday.

Foregoing summary of very rugged session in course of which I felt necessary draw on Deptel 222[4] to reinforce but even so I would hesitate say Turks will hold line unless we can give them something quickly to assure prompt Greek evacuation of territory occupied. Erkin said absolutely essential this point be covered by some political action for which we must assume responsibility of accomplishment, or Turks should be allowed complete job themselves. Previously we had persuaded GOT in advance to stop action it felt necessary but had then been unable correct situation; now we were suggesting they stop part way through and again we are not taking steps necessary to strike balance.

Hope I can have something pass Erkin on this as soon as possible since whole affair now seems dangling on this thread. Fact that Gridiron Aug 8 would indicate no policy difference with GOT on evacuation question is hopeful indicator.

---

[3] Not further identified.

[4] Telegram 222 to Ankara, August 10, stressed the need for Turkey to adhere to the Security Council resolution for a cease-fire. (Department of State, Central Files, POL 23–8 CYP)

Foregoing covers conversation as it took place and does not take into consideration reports of renewed Kokkina attacks covered Embtel 253,[5] which, if confirmed, could drastically change whole situation.

Hare

---

[5] Telegram 253 from Ankara reported that Erkin had information on two further Greek-Cypriot attacks on Turkish-Cypriot positions. (Ibid., POL 27 CYP)

---

119.   Memorandum for the Record[1]

Washington, August 10, 1964.

August 10, 1964, 12:35 PM—Meeting in Cabinet Room

PRESENT

The President, Secretaries Rusk, McNamara, Ball, Vance, Messrs. McCone, Wheeler, Reedy, McG. Bundy

For second item: William Bundy, John McNaughton

1. Cyprus

Secretary Ball reported briefly on the events of recent days and concluded with a report that a cease-fire appeared now to be accepted, although fragile and precarious. In this situation, he felt that the prospects for successful negotiations were somewhat less gloomy than they have been. He reported that Mr. Acheson in Geneva was encouraged, that the Greeks have adopted a serious negotiating position and had added a serious negotiator, Sossides, to the Geneva operation. In summary, Mr. Ball believed that we should press to make the cease-fire stick, and move forward with Mr. Acheson's negotiations. The President agreed with this position.

[Here follows discussion of Southeast Asia.]

McG. B.[2]

---

[1] Source: Johnson Library, National Security File, Files of McGeorge Bundy, Vol. 6. Top Secret. Drafted by Bundy on August 13.

[2] Printed from a copy that bears these typed initials.

120.   Telegram From the Embassy in Greece to the Department of State[1]

Athens, August 11, 1964, 2 p.m.

260. 1. At meeting with Papandreou and Costopoulos yesterday, I went over same general ground touched on in Sunday night meeting concerning Geneva conversations,[2] but in more detail. I again stressed that US Govt considered it essential we drive swiftly toward basic long-term solution; pointing to deadly serious prospects in event of failure; that Acheson considered Turks had moved very considerable distance from their original demands for partition or federation, but that we did not consider GOG had moved much from position of six weeks ago; that, while Acheson and Nikolareizis were on best of terms, Acheson did not feel latter had sufficient authority to move things forward, that there was too much tendency to explore in principle, and that there was apparently some failure of communications between Nikolareizis and Athens as witnessed by Nikolareizis' reported acceptance by Papandreou of Acheson's minorities proposal and GOG subsequent apparent reversal. The situation was much too dangerous to drift any longer in this way. We must get down to cases and work out practical arrangements this week. I suggested that Greeks were in way of obtaining large part of what they want provided they make reasonable concessions to meet Turks on questions of minority protection and military security which to them are very real. After going over main points of Acheson's memo for his August 10 talk with Nikolareizis,[3] the draft Defense Board "treaty" was translated to Papandreou by his son who had joined meeting.

2. Papandreou acknowledged that Nikolareizis' instructions had been to explore possible solution which was reason he had not been able be more forthcoming, but he agreed on need to move on urgently. His initial reaction to the Defense Board concept was that it was something for future, and that we should concentrate on key issues (a) treatment of minorities and (b) question of base. I replied that I was sure Acheson was not wedded to Defense Board concept as end in itself, but considered it as a proven and reasonable means for handling problems before us, adding that getting down to key issues was just what Acheson had been seeking to do and was pressing Greeks for now.

3. On base question, Papandreou clearly indicated acceptance of lease arrangement, ruling out concept of transformation of British bases

---

[1] Source: Department of State, Central Files, POL 27 CYP. Secret; Exdis–TAG. Received at 10:30 a.m. and repeated to USUN, Ankara, London, and Geneva for Acheson. Passed to the White House, DOD, and CIA.

[2] See Document 117.

[3] See footnote 2, Document 121.

as too complicated, etc. I urged that he react quickly to Acheson's proposals on this, adding that the twenty square kilometer suggestion was much too small to be considered. (He then discussed privately in Greek with Costopoulos size of present British bases.) When I alluded to Karpas Peninsula, Costopoulos asked what would happen to inhabitants. I said all this was matter for negotiation. (Incidently, I am told British base areas include previously existing villages.)

4. On minority rights, Papandreou made much the same noises as in past, agreeing to provide solid bill of human rights with UN supervision and rights of appeal to Hague Court. He said he would consider anything which did not smack either of federation or cantonments. Referring to my comments re Nikolareizis' transmission of his views, he said there had surely been mistake—"possibly Nikolareizis was being too agreeable." Papandreou said that Acheson memo on minorities although entitled enosis was in substance partition and federation. This was impossible for Cypriot people to accept and recent events did not make it easier. He said USG must remember that, even when Makarios is out of picture, the Cypriot people will have strong ideas which cannot be dismissed. He stressed point that often US fails to distinguish between Makarios and the will of the mass of people of island.

5. Conversation ended by his asking for copy of Defense Board treaty, saying that Sossides was expected back from Geneva in evening and that he would talk with him with view to pressing forward constructively. I shall follow up.

6. I also talked to King Constantine in general terms about urgent need for agreed solution which would take fully into consideration Turkey's military requirements and prestige, as well as protection of minorities rights. He agreed except concerning Turkey's argument re need of base for its military security. This was outmoded military concept, but he did agree that Turkey needed something for prestige reasons provided there was no disguised partition or federation. I said it was most important for GOG to be more flexible and forthcoming in Geneva talks, and he undertook to help in this direction. When I suggested that it might prove helpful in final analysis to get major opposition leadership committed to anything government agrees to, the King replied he was satisfied he could bring this about.

Labouisse

121. Telegram From the Embassy in Turkey to the Department of State[1]

Ankara, August 11, 1964, 6 p.m.

275. Geneva's 343 to Department, and last night's telecon with Under Secretary Ball.[2] Saw Erkin this afternoon and discussed Geneva situation and prospects as suggested.

Erkin said GOT definitely wants push ahead with talks and referred to stress on this point in Inonu's message to Papandreou, which Erkin said he had drafted himself (Embtel 273, repeated Geneva as 109).[3]

Re suggested treaty, Erkin didn't seem feel strongly one way or the other, observing that agreement on specifics has priority and inquiring if I had anything new to put forward in that regard. I said I didn't but stressed fact that Greek reps now showing disposition get down to brass tacks. This did not mean that margin of difference in substance had been decreased; far from it. But it did mean that for first time it may be possible really to come to grips with problem.

Regarding Erim, Erkin said he is now in Istanbul on several days leave as result preoccupation of GOT with Cyprus crisis but he is due back Thursday and should be returning to Geneva shortly thereafter. Erkin said he would certainly do his best go get Erim on his way as soon as possible.

Hare

---

[1] Source: Department of State, Central Files, POL 23–8 CYP. Secret; Immediate; Exdis–TAG. Received at 12:23 p.m. and repeated to Athens, London, and Geneva for Acheson. Passed to the White House, DOD, CIA, and USUN.

[2] In telegram 343 from Geneva, August 10, Acheson reported on two meetings with Greek representatives in which variants of a Turkish base lease agreement were discussed. (Ibid., POL 27 CYP) Memoranda of the two telephone conversations between Ball and Acheson are in the Johnson Library, Ball Papers, Telephone Conversations, Cyprus.

[3] Dated August 11. (Department of State, Central Files, POL 27 CYP) In his August 11 letter, Inonu wrote Papandreou suggesting they work together to reach a permanent solution to the Cyprus problem. In August 13 reply, Papandreou stated that Greece was ready to assist the U.N. Mediator in finding an agreed solution to a question.

122.   Telegram From the Mission in Geneva to the Department of State[1]

Geneva, August 13, 1964, 11 a.m.

364. From Acheson. Mission tel 356.[2] Nikolareisis came to see me last night, much relieved news he had received from Athens that Turks had agreed to cease overflights in Cyprus. He reported Sossides will return Geneva Friday bringing with him definite proposal for Turkish base, map, and at least outline of proposed plan for safeguarding minority under enosis. Said there were "currents in Athens" opposed to continuing along this line but that Prime Minister, Deputy PM Stephanopoulos, Sossides and (with reserves) Costopoulos were "on our side" and determined to go ahead. He said he was pleased Sossides is actively engaged in our affair, describing him as young, intelligent, enthusiastic and close to both PM and Deputy PM.

He commented that Inonu's message to Papandreou had been constructive and said he had urged Athens to give forthcoming reply.[3]

We gave Nikolareisis a revised memorandum on minority rights designed to help meet Greek objections to original proposals of July 24 [27]. Asked him not to send it to Athens until we had had opportunity to discuss it with him and Sossides in light of latest Greek ideas which Sossides was bringing. Copies of memorandum being pouched.[4]

For Department and Ankara only: (Ankara's 283 to Dept and Dept's 242 to Ankara.)[5] I think Hare's advice is good, and it is re-enforced by Nikolareisis who urges that we keep talks in our hands in Geneva and that I personally present Greek proposals to Turks. Accordingly, we shall await Erim's return to make new approach on that side.

Tubby

---

[1] Source: Department of State, Central Files, POL 27 CYP. Secret; Priority; Exdis–TAG. Repeated to Ankara, Athens, London, USUN, CIA, DOD, and the White House.

[2] Telegram 356 from Geneva, August 12, stressed the desirability of a Presidential statement designed to strengthen Inonu and Papandreou. (Ibid.)

[3] See footnote 3, Document 121.

[4] Transmitted in airgram A–86 from Geneva, August 14. (Department of State, Central Files, SOC 14 CYP)

[5] In telegram 283 from Ankara, August 12, Hare recommended that Acheson outline his proposals directly to Erim in Geneva rather than through the Embassy. (Ibid., POL 27 CYP) Telegram 242 to Ankara, August 12, transmitted the text of Makarios' letter to President Johnson. (Ibid.)

123.   Telegram From the Mission in Geneva to the Department of State[1]

Geneva, August 15, 1964, 4 p.m.

383. From Acheson. As I had anticipated, Turks took Greek counter proposal very hard, but they were even less flexible than I had hoped.

When we met at eleven this morning with Erim and Sunalp, I began by expounding fairly fully proposals which Nikolareisis and Sossides had outlined to me last night (Mission tel 382).[2] Showed them on map exactly where Greeks proposed Turkish base should be and gave them brief oral summary of proposals for protection of minority. Turks listened closely, had a few questions of fact, and Erim said European Commission on Human Rights would probably not be best organ from Turkish point of view because it did not have power to issue binding decisions. We said we saw no objection to use of ICJ or subsidiary body instead.

When I got through, both Erim and Sunalp made it very clear that Greek position was unacceptable. Erim pointed out proposal involved complete abandonment of London–Zurich Agreements, especially concept of separate Greek and Turkish communities in Cyprus. Turks had been willing to accept changes, in agreements, but only on condition that every change in favor of Greece was balanced by something for Turkey. No GOT, he said, could accept what Greeks were now proposing. Turkish people would not stand for it. GOT was already under heavy pressure from public opinion and army which considered it was not tough enough. It would not be realistic for him to discuss with me what Greeks had offered. In any case, he had authority from Ankara only to talk on basis of my own earlier proposals; anything else, he said, he would have to refer to Ankara, and he would do this with report I had just given him.

Erim went on to reiterate that my proposals were about the least Turkey could have considered. Sunalp interjected that Greek base suggestion was ridiculous and that Greeks were "being comic" in putting it forward. Erim emphasized that he was prepared to continue discussion on basis my suggestions provided Greeks would do likewise. If they did not, Turkey would have to make its own proposals. In this connection he gave us map of Cyprus showing four zones. First enclosed all of Karpas Peninsula and something more, which he said would be Turkish military base. Second enclosed area stretching from Famagusta

---

[1] Source: Department of State, Central Files, POL 27 CYP. Secret; Priority; Exdis–TAG. Repeated to Athens, Ankara, London, USUN, DOD, CIA, and the White House.

[2] Telegram 382 from Geneva, August 15, outlined Greek proposals for a Turkish base area leased for a period of 25 years. (Ibid.)

through northern Nicosia and up to north coast between Kyrenia and Lapithos; this, he said, would be Turkish territory but demilitarized. Third covered everything south and west of this line down to a line drawn along watershed from Pomos on coast of Tylliria through Mt. Olympus southwestward to coast at Petounda Point, between Larnaca and Limassol. This zone would be Greek but demilitarized. Fourth zone began from this line and covered rest of island, which he said would be Greek without limitation.

I commented this was merely another form of partition and left us where we were six weeks ago.

We had back-and-forth discussion for some time. I admitted Greeks had been slow to make proposals and had refused to accept my ideas. But what was the alternative to reaching agreement somewhere along their lines? I was convinced that there would very soon be a major fresh outbreak of violence on Cyprus. Sunalp agreed and said violence would come from Turkey too. "Then what?", I said. There would be a first-class mess. Suggested they should start from broad Greek-Turkish treaty I had put forward and thus get everything in far wider context. Erim said this was all very well but Turkey could not accept it if price was enosis. They could not trust Greece to keep any agreement, look at how quickly GOG had repudiated London–Zurich. It would be better for Turkey to stand on London–Zurich than to accept what Greeks were proposing.

I said if Cyprus case went to UNGA there would certainly be resolution calling for full and complete independence. Erim objected GA could not terminate treaties. I agreed but said nevertheless it would do so. Turkey would have to fight to block full Cypriot independence. To this, Erim replied it would be better for internal position GOT to accept independence under UN resolution than to go along with Greek proposition. He thought GA should be stopped, in any case, from ignoring Turkish rights, because it had recognized them by resolutions passed in 1957 and 1958. I pointed out GA would not be likely to be influenced by this. I added that Turkey could not afford to wait for Assembly to meet; major trouble in Cyprus would happen long before that. Sunalp said Turkey would intervene.

Throughout discussion I kept bearing down as strongly as I could on disastrous results of failure to reach agreement and inevitable consequent Greek-Turkish war. Turks repeatedly assured me they understood this and did not want war. Nevertheless, they were not afraid of war and did not see why they should be ones to make all concessions while Greeks made none. Sunalp commented that he hated war, having been in one (Korean) but also hated to see Turkey lose its rights and have its people suffer on Cyprus.

I observed that there was no way of telling where war would end; Russia might intervene. Turks should recognize that Makarios was like mad man whom Greeks could not stop. They had made grave mistake in giving him so much leeway. To this Sunalp remarked Turkey would have to pay for their mistake; I agreed but added that if Turkey made a grave mistake of its own in going to war it would have to pay for that too.

It seemed to me that the only alternatives left were violence and war on the one hand and acceptance of something like the Greek proposals on the other. The latter would at least get rid of Makarios. Turks should realize they could not get anything resembling partition from Greeks. Sunalp retorted that Greeks could not get enosis from Turkey. I said I realized it was tough decision for them to make, but there it was.

In conclusion, I asked Erim if he wanted me to tell Greeks that their offer of base at Cape Greco was totally unacceptable, or if he wanted to consult Ankara first. He said I should go ahead and tell them. Even with regard to whole Karpas Peninsula, GOT had rejected idea of leased base, and it would find present Greek proposal quite out of question. I said I would talk to Greeks again today and see Turks again tomorrow or Monday.

Tubby

---

124. Telegram From the Mission in Geneva to the Department of State[1]

Geneva, August 15, 1964, 7:30 p.m.

385. From Acheson. Ref: Mission tel 383.[2] Saw Greeks again this afternoon and gave them Turkish reaction to their counter proposal. I will not bother Dept with details, but I made it very clear that Turks considered proposal ridiculous and quite unacceptable and that they had said that they were prepared to talk only on basis of my proposals (by which they meant whole of Karpas Peninsula plus my original ideas of minority rights and safeguards) or on basis counter proposal of partition. To illustrate latter, I showed Greeks map Turks had given me this morning (para four reftel). Added Turks insisted that they would only consider sovereign base area, not lease, although I thought there was

---

[1] Source: Department of State, Central Files, POL 27 CYP. Secret; Priority; Exdis–TAG. Repeated to Ankara, Athens, London, USUN, DOD, CIA, and the White House.

[2] Document 123.

bare chance they might accept lease if terms and base area were satisfactory.

Essence of Greek reaction was that Turks clearly wanted more than military base, they wanted what was in effect form of partition. This Greece could never concede because it would be totally rejected by Greek people as well as by Cypriots. GOG would enlarge its Cape Greco offer if that were necessary from purely military point of view to accommodate adequate air and naval base, but it could not go beyond that.

We went round and round most of the old arguments about asserted Turkish unreasonableness, lack of Turkish right of intervention, domestic troubles of Papandreou, etc. I assured Nikolareisis and Sossides that I had done my best to convince Turks that they should take lesser of evils and accept something like what Greeks offer as better than war. However, I said, I did not believe I had made any impact. I feared we had come to end of rope. Greeks seemed to agree with me. They put forward no new suggestions and held out no hope that further consultation in Athens would bring anything forth.

We finally asked whether there was no chance at all of Greek Govt considering whole or part of Karpas Peninsula as Turkish base on long-term lease. Sossides thought there was no chance of granting anything more on that peninsula than could be offered in Cape Greco region. What Turks wanted, he said (and I agreed), was something resembling partition, which is a good deal more than would be needed for military base. GOG simply could not meet this.

Sossides went on that in these circumstances, with all hope gone in Geneva, GOG would have to drop its plans to work actively for enosis and would give full support to Makarios in his drive for full and complete independence. We questioned why this need be. He said Greece would have no basis for enosis campaign if there were no agreement with Turkey. If it staged coup d'etat, this would precipitate war with Turkey. We suggested war would probably come anyway, because Makarios would do things on Cyprus that would bring about Turkish intervention. Sossides, however, thought that if Makarios were relieved of his fear of negotiated settlement he would be willing to hold his hand on the island until General Assembly met, avoiding unbearable provocation of Turks, and would get his full independence endorsed by GA.

I suggested that Sossides should go back to Athens tomorrow and put to Papandreou two possible alternatives: (a) Greece should try to keep negotiations alive by agreeing to discuss Turkish area on Karpas Peninsula, or (b) it should abandon Geneva talks and concentrate on keeping Makarios quiet. Independent Cyprus under Makarios would be pretty bad, but it would probably be better than Greek-Turkish war. Sossides seemed to agree.

Comment: In light of today's meetings, I come to two pretty firm conclusions:

(a) Turks won't accept Greek proposals and there is no use talking about them further; on other hand, Turks will take my proposals as basis for discussion and will probably be flexible as to western boundary of Karpas Peninsula area although apparently inflexible on question of lease instead of sovereignty. (There is less than 50–50 chance they would talk about lease.)

(b) Greeks will probably not accept anything like whole of Karpas Peninsula for Turkey, if indeed they will accept any part of it, and will be inflexible re sovereignty issue.

This leaves us with not much of anywhere to go. Question is should we accept failure and look for best way to terminate talks, or should we try to continue until something happens on Cyprus to blow everything up? Argument for first course is that chance of avoiding violence and consequent Turkish intervention might be increased if Makarios knew Geneva talks were dead and he would probably get UNGA support for independence. Arguments for second course are simply good old bulldog spirit and chance miracle will happen.

In any event, I would not propose to leave Geneva before Mediator returns from his trip next Friday. I shall see him tonight or tomorrow morning to report. When we do leave, I would imagine best course would be for me to say nothing here and Dept simply to say that I am coming for consultation and that timing of my return to Geneva is uncertain.

Would be glad to have comments and reactions of addressees.

Tubby

---

125. Telegram From the Department of State to the Mission in Geneva[1]

Washington, August 15, 1964, 11:07 p.m.

418. For Acheson from Ball. To be delivered at 7:30 a.m. These are my night thoughts after reflecting on our teletype conversation this evening.[2]

---

[1] Source: Department of State, Central Files, POL 27 CYP. Secret; Immediate; Nodis–TAG. Drafted and approved by Ball.

[2] A transcript of this conversation is ibid., Ball Papers: Lot 74 D 272, Telephone Conversations, Cyprus Situation.

1. I am inclined to feel that we may have misread the emphasis in your 383.[3] The Turkish counter-proposal put forward by Erim seemed even more extreme than the original Turkish position. The saving aspect of Erim's presentation, which we may have overlooked, was a reaffirmation of GOT willingness to continue negotiations on basis your suggestions. A disturbing aspect was Sunalp's presence as a kind of military commissar and his assertiveness, which indicates that Turk military are a force threatening to become a discrete sovereignty not wholly under Inonu's control.

2. At this point, it seems essential to put leash on ebullient Turk military while moving at the same time to push a thoroughly scared Papandreou into serious negotiations on basis your proposals.

3. Hope of success would seem to imply that neither Greeks nor Turks take your proposals as a minimum which each must improve to satisfy its own requirements. If Turks accept leasehold rather than sovereignty then Greeks must exhibit territorial generosity. Whether Papandreou, who is both old and in bad health, could carry it off remains to be seen. But, in any event, Greeks must be told that your proposals remain the basis for negotiation since their counter-proposals have proved abortive.

4. The situation as of tonight seems precarious in the extreme. Even with luck we may be only four or five days away from an explosion. The signs pointing to this are the following:

a. The Turkish military have tasted blood. They are full of cockiness and apparently obsessed with the desire to finish the job they started last weekend. Their military plans are hair-raising since they would involve among other things taking out all airfields on the Greek mainland.

b. The Greeks will not be able to stand down again if the Turks move.

c. Makarios is putting increasing pressure on the embattled Turk-Cypriots, presumably to produce an act of provocation that will set in train events which can frustrate any settlement you achieve at Geneva.

d. The Turk-Cypriots are more than ever in a Gotterdammerung mood—particularly those squeezed between the Greek-Cypriots and the sea on the north coast.

5. We are still inclined to send Presidential messages both to Inonu and Papandreou. As we now see it the Inonu message would be stern but free from indignation.

6. We are not persuaded, however, that NATO Foreign Ministers' meeting offers merely "oratory". Both the Greeks and the Turks have military power today only because they are members of NATO. That military power was not provided for use against one another. By getting into an internecine war they are exposing the Southern NATO flank and

---

[3] Document 123.

inviting Soviet intervention. This was not the purpose for which NATO was designed. That point should be brought home to them. I think it might better be brought home by the NATO Foreign Ministers solemnly assembled than by the USG alone.

Rusk

126. Telegram From the Department of State to the Embassy in Greece[1]

Washington, August 16, 1964, 11:43 a.m.

306. Please deliver soonest following message from President to Prime Minister Papandreou:

Begin verbatim text.

Dear Mr. Prime Minister:

I have read with interest and appreciation your reply to Prime Minister Inonu's message.[2] Your readiness to look to the future and your sense of urgency about a negotiated solution are highly valued here.

I am sure you agree that nothing must interfere with the urgent business of achieving an agreement between Greece and Turkey. Yet today peace on Cyprus is precarious. Events could take the matter out of the hands of diplomacy at any moment. We know you are exercising your maximum influence and power on the Greek Cypriots in order to insure that they not provoke incidents in the days ahead. You and I both understand that if the Greek Cypriots renew their attacks or continue their present heavy pressure against the minority community, Turk Cypriots will call for assistance from Turkey and the situation might then become quite unmanageable.

I have followed with the keenest interest the discussions that Mr. Dean Acheson has been having in Geneva. No other question has taken so much of my own personal time and attention. I am pleased at the prog-

---

[1] Source: Department of State, Central Files, POL 27 CYP. Secret; Flash; Nodis–TAG. Drafted and approved by Rusk. Repeated to Ankara, London, and Geneva for Acheson. The President sent a parallel message to Prime Minister Inonu, transmitted in telegram 270 to Ankara, August 16. (Ibid.)

[2] See footnote 3, Document 121.

ress made on questions relating to the position of the minority community and on the principle of a Turkish base. The major remaining point appears to be the location and extent of the territory allocated for Turkish security arrangements.

I fully endorse Mr. Acheson's conclusion that the Karpas Peninsula has a special logic in that it protects the approaches to Iskenderun. In my view this consideration overrides the difficulty that some Greek Cypriots in that area might not wish to reside on a Turkish base even under a lease arrangement. In any case this should not be an insuperable problem particularly since the numbers affected would be small. I urge you to empower your representatives at Geneva to concentrate seriously on the Karpas location in this critical phase of the negotiations.

Let me say to you quite frankly that the United States is distressed to find it necessary to inject itself into the Cyprus problem. The three guarantor powers are all NATO allies, with responsible governments that should be able to find a solution without our taking a part. We are involved, however, because of our concern for NATO and our friendship for Greece and Turkey whose own relations have become so fragile.

I do not know what the next days may bring forth in this tragic situation. But I urge upon you and Mr. Inonu that war between Greece and Turkey must never be allowed to occur. Both of you have an utterly fundamental obligation to seek the counsel of NATO at the Foreign Ministers level before you become involved with each other in conflict. When France and Germany both became NATO partners, they put behind them a long history of conflict. Greece and Turkey have the same obligations.

The primary purpose of this message is to ask two things of you.

The first is to urge you to come to an agreement with Turkey on the basis of Mr. Acheson's suggestions. We must never suppose that the job of diplomacy is finished until an agreement is reached. An agreement between Greece and Turkey will not only avert a war between two NATO allies but will also provide an opportunity for the Greek and Cypriot peoples to combine their talents and energies to the greater good of Hellenism.

The second is that you continue to exert all your power and influence with the Greek Cypriots to maintain peace on the island. This includes securing their fullest cooperation with the United Nations and its forces as well as the lifting of blockades and obstructions that impair the ability of Turkish Cypriots to meet their daily requirements for food and other necessities.

Please be assured that I fully understand that you have very difficult political problems in your own country where feelings are at so high a pitch. I also understand your difficulties with Archbishop Makarios and other Greek Cypriots. But I am convinced that an agreement between you and Turkey is possible, that such an agreement could result in a definitive solution of the Cyprus problem and that this could be accomplished in such a way as to strengthen your NATO ties rather than destroy them.

You may be assured that I am making representations in other capitals and at the United Nations consistent with what I am now saying to you.

With personal good wishes

Sincerely yours,

End verbatim text.[3]

Rusk

---

[3] In telegram 317 from Athens, August 17, Labouisse reported he delivered the President's letter to Costopoulos who assured him that the Papandreou government would continue to negotiate in good faith at Geneva. (Ibid.)

---

127. Telegram From the Department of State to the Mission in Geneva[1]

Washington, August 16, 1964, 1:03 p.m.

426. For Acheson from Under Secretary Ball. In reflecting on our recent spate of communications, I wonder if you would agree that the scenario now looks like this:

1. Presidential letters as amended are going to Inonu and Papandreou today.[2] Papandreou letter should be at hand for review of situation in which Sossides is presumably engaged in Athens.

2. Hopefully UK will try to crank up Guarantor Powers' action to prevent Cypriot military involvement with Soviet Union.

3. Acheson to resume negotiations with Greeks as soon as Sossides returns—hopefully Monday or Tuesday.

4. If after Sossides returns negotiations still look on brink of failure, we would advise Papandreou and Inonu that we regard NATO Foreign Ministers' meeting as urgent next step.

---

[1] Source: Department of State, Central Files, POL 27 CYP. Secret; Flash; Exdis–TAG. Drafted and approved by Ball.

[2] See Document 126 and footnote 1 thereto.

5. Depending on response of Papandreou and Inonu, we would call Foreign Ministers' meeting at which we would make the points outlined in your teletype; namely,

(a) demand no US equipment used by either side.
(b) point regarding Section 5 NAT.
(c) advance concurrence by other NATO members that Greece and Turkey should delegate you to arbitrate remaining unagreed elements of settlement.

6. We would seek NATO support for Guarantor Powers démarche to Cyprus.

7. We wish to give further thought to emphasis on London–Zurich treaties before deciding whether they should be raised in NATO.[3]

Rusk

[3] The National Security Council discussed Cyprus at its August 17 meeting. According to notes prepared by McCone, Ball reported that the Turks had confirmed the cease-fire, that a "real break" had taken place between Greece and Turkey, that Grivas felt betrayed by the Greek Government, that Acheson was encouraged by events, and that Turkey appeared "amenable" to a deal. (Central Intelligence Agency, DCI Files: Job 80–B01285A, Meetings with LBJ, 1964)

128. Telegram From the Mission in Geneva to the Department of State[1]

Geneva, August 16, 1964, 6 p.m.

389. From Acheson. Lord Hood, Jernegan and I spent hour with Nikolareisis and Sossides early this afternoon and went over Turkish position carefully with them to make sure it was correctly understood.[2] (Mediator has told us last night that they seemed to have impression Turks had greatly hardened their attitude and were again insisting on full scale partition as basis discussion.) I made clear that Turks were perfectly willing to talk on basis of my proposals and that their partition was merely tactical counter to Greek proposals which Turks considered com-

[1] Source: Department of State, Central Files, POL 27 CYP. Secret; Priority; Exdis–TAG. Received at 5:47 p.m. and repeated to Athens, Ankara, London, USUN, DOD, CIA, and the White House.
[2] Acheson reported on his morning talks with the Turks in telegram 388 from Geneva, August 16. (Ibid.)

plete departure from line I had been taking and completely unaccept-able. Greeks said they fully understood this. I then told them Erim this morning had indicated willingness to discuss long term lease of Karpas Peninsula instead of cession of sovereignty, proposed [*provided*] conces-sions were made on Greek side in regard to area covered. Explained that Turks were insisting on substantial area—at least entire Peninsula—plus absolute freedom to do what they wanted on that area without restric-tions as to kind or number of troops or uses to which base might be put. Yesterday, I said, they had insisted they must also have full sovereignty, but today they had moved somewhat away from this.

I urged upon Greeks importance of giving this Turkish position seri-ous consideration and trying to come up with something that would meet it. Repeated points previously made about Turkish views on essen-tiality of quid pro quo for every change made in existing treaties and again reiterated need to accept as reality Turkish feelings about prestige and national honor. Greeks made usual reply about how difficult it would be to cede area of size Turks were demanding and how useless this was from military point of view. We went around this circle a couple of times. Sossides suggested it might be useful to get impartial commit-tee of military experts, or SACEUR himself, to arbitrate as to what area was really needed from NATO military point of view. I objected that Turks had political problem to consider as well as military and probably would not accept outside military arbitration. Also expressed doubt SACEUR would be willing undertake this duty. Sossides conceded that there was something in what I said and suggested that perhaps we could use military judgment only as starting point and then add on something to meet political problem. For example, he said, if SACEUR ruled that 25 square kilometers was enough, I could multiply this by 5 to take care of political factor.

My reply was that I thought we would do better to concentrate on what was needed to reach agreement and then bring in outside elements, such as military experts to dress up terms of settlement and give them rationale.

I told Greeks Washington was greatly disturbed by developments and would be making representation in Athens for great efforts to reach agreement and keep situation on Cyprus from blowing up. Emphasized again and again importance of keeping things quiet and keeping talks going by making some significant response to Turkish proposals, which were essentially mine. Both Nikolareisis and Sossides displayed serious doubt that GOG would consider anything like so large an area as Karpas Peninsula, but I got impression they might be somewhat impressed by my presentation and that Sossides was at least disposed to explore in Athens possibility of moving in that direction.

To my suggestion that since Mediator was no longer going to Athens today,[3] it might be well for him (Sossides) to stay on longer here, he replied that he thought it more necessary he should go back to Athens and give clear picture present state of affairs. We finally agreed this probably would be best course but urged that he come back as soon as possible, preferably by Tuesday. He planned to take 3:15 flight out of Geneva this afternoon and presumably he is on his way.

We had some discussion about effect of Mediator's illness on our talks here. Greeks were noncommittal, but at least did not say that Tuomioja's disappearance from scene would necessarily require discontinuance.

In connection with problem of preventing trouble in Cyprus, Sossides said there were two prerequisites from GOG point of view: (a) Turkish bombing and overflights must cease; and (b) expulsion of Greeks from Istanbul must be halted. We pointed out overflights had in fact ceased and said we were working on Turks about expulsions and likewise urging them to keep Turkish-Cypriots quiet. Told them we had reason to believe from authoritative source that recent *Soysal* statement that all Greeks would be expelled from Istanbul after September 15th was unauthorized and did not represent policy of Inonu and Erkin.

Tubby

---

[3] Tuomioja suffered a stroke on August 16 and died on September 9. In telegram 390 from Geneva, August 16, Acheson assessed the impact of the loss of the U.N. Mediator. (Ibid.) Secretary-General Thant designated Pier P. Spinelli to oversee Tuomioja's office on August 18, and designated Galo Plaza to succeed him as U.N. Mediator on Cyprus on September 16. He also announced that Carlos Alfredo Bernardes would replace Plaza Lasso as Special Representative of the U.N. Secretary-General in Cyprus as of September 25.

---

129.   Telegram From the Mission in Geneva to the Department of State[1]

Geneva, August 18, 1964, noon.

408. For Department only. For Ball from Acheson. Perhaps an explanation of the rationale of my No. 401[2] may be helpful. It attempts to combine lures linked to responsibilities, and threats to the bloody-

---

[1] Source: Department of State, Central Files, POL 27 CYP. Secret; Priority; Nodis–TAG.

[2] Telegram 401 from Geneva, August 17, outlined Acheson's scenario for achieving a quick settlement of the Cyprus issue once an accord between Greece and Turkey existed. (Ibid.)

minded linked with clear support for a specific settlement which both the GOG and GOT would, I believe, accept if the pressure of their public and military for extreme demands could be balanced by really effective outside pressure for moderation.

To accomplish this, my plan begins by assuring the Turks that we start from the joint premises that revision of existing treaties requires consent of the signatories and not merely a mob vote in the UNGA (the Turks set great store by this), and that revision by agreement is desirable, a view with which the Turks also agree.

The second idea is to relax the tension in Cyprus, restore for the benefit of Turkish Cypriots order and the necessities of life, and subject Makarios to a restraint which may end in his removal, by entrusting the task to the GOG, which can be held responsible. In return for this GOG is offered a prize which it greatly desires—i.e., NATO undertaking (which dilutes U.S. part in it) to restrain the Turks from intervening as long as the GOG maintains, or does the best anyone can to maintain, order and minimum just treatment of all in Cyprus. This plan offers the best chance of accomplishing the result sought and permits the Turks to accept Greek action on behalf of all guarantors as an acknowledgement of the validity of the Treaty of Guarantee. NATO's cover for the protection of Greek troops on this mission can be subsumed under Article 6 of NAT without unseemly stretching. Hence everyone gets something but has to pay for it and is threatened by trouble if assigned responsibility is refused or interference with others contemplated.

The proposal to make the Greeks responsible for preventing interference with the supply and rotation of the Turkish contingent is to end this unnecessary provocation and humiliation of Turkey by Makarios' flaunting of his denunciation of the treaties. It also puts pressure on the Greeks to accept their role as peacekeeper since, if they do not and Turks are fired upon when performing a treaty function in no way connected with intervention, Makarios will have fired the first shot and even the Russians will be hard pressed to find aggression in the Turks forcing the relief of their authorized contingent.

All these proposals are studded with deferential salaams to the U.N. so that U Thant and Thimayya can gracefully accept aid which they should regard as a gift from Heaven.

Acheson as arbitrator is your idea.

The gloss on the President's warning not to use NATO arms for unauthorized NATO purposes is to permit their use for authorized purposes on Cyprus. It also introduces a new reason for Sixth Fleet interposition, if desired, against improper intervention—i.e., blockade to permit search and seizure of unauthorized NATO weapons upon NATO, rather than purely American orders.

The last idea is merely to make things even. While bad boys will be prevented from fighting one another, good boys will be protected from attack or threat of force from USSR.

Tubby

---

130. Telegram From the Embassy in Cyprus to the Department of State[1]

Nicosia, August 18, 1964, 1:30 p.m.

338. After turning over President Johnson's message[2] for which Makarios expressed thanks we discussed food and water problems facing Turk Cypriots. I opened discussion by referring to fact world press beginning interpret GOC restrictions as designed pressure innocent people through deprivation bread and water and surely this was not record he wanted outside his country. Our ensuing discussion followed lines his talk with Plaza reported Embtels 328 and 335.[3] Makarios repeated commitments made to Plaza and said that this morning's meeting with UN reps would finalize arrangements. When I asked specifically whether kerosene would be provided today so Turks could bake bread he replied matter would be discussed and decided on today. In afterthought (which we have conveyed to Plaza) he said couldn't see why Turks should have kerosene while Greeks can't have land registry records or parcels in central post office (both in Turk quarter). I suggested it not only unfair equate these matters, but outside world would not understand actions preventing baking of bread as means forcing release

---

[1] Source: Department of State, Central Files, POL 27 CYP. Confidential; Priority. Repeated to London, Athens, USUN, Geneva for Acheson, and Paris for USRO.

[2] Johnson's August 14 reply to Makarios' August 9 appeal to restrain the Government of Turkey was transmitted in telegram 179 to Nicosia, August 14. In it, the President urged Makarios to cooperate with the United Nations in its efforts to restore peace in the region. (Ibid.) Makarios' letter is in the Johnson Library, National Security File, Special Head of State Correspondence, Cyprus—Makarios.

[3] In telegram 328 from Nicosia, August 17, Belcher reported that Plaza believed he had made progress in discussions with Makarios over the issue of resupply for Turkish Cypriot villages. (Ibid.) Telegram 335 from Nicosia, August 17, reported Makarios' uncompromising opposition to any solution arising from the Geneva talks. (Department of State, Central Files, POL 27 CYP)

of documents and mail. Surely the women, children and old folk should not suffer nor appear in eyes of world to be made to suffer in this fashion for decisions taken by their leaders.

Only new factor re Ktima water supply is assertion by President that when Greeks offered cancel all bills due if Turks agreed pay from now on, they refused (presumably on basis Constitution splits municipalities and therefore payments Turks can only be to own municipal authorities. It is for this reason they have refused to pay Greeks since 1960 Constitution went into effect).

I said we sincerely hoped GOC could make some immediate gesture which would give better press and also reduce tensions in Turk community and in Ankara. Said I hoped he was gauging very carefully how much economic pressure Turk Cypriots could take without explosion which could bring additional catastrophes to island.

With regard Geneva talks President had little to add to what other he told Plaza as reported Embtel 328. He did emphasize however that "Papandreou will accept anything I agree to but I don't necessarily accept any decision he may make." He added he felt State Department had got cart before horse in Geneva tactics and expressed continued resentment at being left out of discussions. I said he must realize we appreciated fact solution would have to be acceptable Greek Cypriots as well as others but that we also believed it necessary pave way by assisting Mediator in finding agreement between Greece and Turkey. No solution, whether saleable to Govt of Cyprus or not would work if other two disagreed. He was not convinced.

Meeting 11:30 this morning will show whether we are justified in limited optimism engendered by apparent changes which Archbishop has told Plaza (and me and Bishop) he will put into effect re freedom of movement and food and fuel supplies.[4]

Belcher

---

[4] In telegram 342 from Nicosia, August 18, Belcher reported that the United Nations and Cypriot Government had reached an agreement easing economic restrictions on Turkish Cypriots. (Ibid.)

131. Telegram From the Embassy in Greece to the Department of State[1]

Athens, August 18, 1964, 9 p.m.

337. 1. My talks with Papandreou of Sunday (Embtel 314)[2] and last night (Embtel 327)[3] reveal state of dejection and hopelessness of the GOG. They seem to have lost whatever sureness of footing they had. Papandreou's suggestion Sunday night of a Presidential declaration and his proposal last night for instant enosis with details to be worked out later had certainly not been thought through. He gave the impression casting about for some way out of his dilemma. He seems at the end of his tether (partly through his own fault) and he sees the US as his only hope. Although the Soviets had moved onto the scene when we met on Sunday, his main preoccupation then seemed to be his fear of another Turkish attack and the consequent involvement of Greece in a war with Turkey. Last night the Turkish threat seemed to preoccupy him less. He then had in mind Kyprianou's instructions to go to Moscow.[4] These instructions caused him to see Greece losing Cyprus to Soviet influence and the consequent failure of his own policies. He translated this failure into personal political defeat at the hands of the Communists who would be the only ones to gain by it.

2. Papandreou's reaction to the events of the last ten days has shown, not surprisingly, considerable emotion and some inconsistency. For example, while he was allegedly threatening Kyprianou with a parting of the ways in the event of a Soviet alliance, and was also in effect asking US and the Turks to accept his pledge of good faith in giving the Turks a fair deal in the event of enosis, he was at same time withdrawing the Greek elements from Sixth ATAF and LANDSOUTHEAST and presiding over a meeting of the Supreme Council of National Defense which decided to disengage, as necessary, military, naval and air units of the Greek forces now assigned to NATO. (Greek statement on this makes clear this was direct reaction to GOT withdrawal air defense units.)[5] We

---

[1] Source: Department of State, Central Files, POL 27 CYP. Secret; Immediate; Exdis–TAG. Repeated to Ankara, Nicosia, London, Paris for USRO, Geneva for Acheson, USUN, DOD, CIA, and the White House.

[2] Telegram 314 from Athens, August 16, reported the "mood of dark despair" of Papandreou. (Ibid.)

[3] Telegram 327 from Athens, August 18, reported Papandreou's concern regarding the entry of the Soviet Union into the diplomatic maneuverings over Cyprus. (Ibid.) On August 15, the Soviet Government issued a statement offering aid to Cyprus against foreign intervention, after a request from President Makarios. For text, see *American Foreign Policy: Current Documents, 1964*, pp. 586–587.

[4] Makarios' decision to send Kyprianou was revealed to the Greek Government on August 17.

[5] The Turkish withdrawal took place on August 17.

consider these Greek gestures unfortunate and untimely but not reversible until the general climate here improves.

Basic fact which recent events have driven home is that there can be no solution of the Cyprus problem which does not take into consideration will and emotions of Cypriot people. They cannot be by-passed or forced into line, and the Turkish air strikes are going to make it especially difficult to obtain agreement from the Cypriot people (regardless of Makarios) to any Turkish base on the island. Nevertheless, we continue to believe that we should make every effort to keep talks going in Geneva. Even though Mediator's illness has greatly complicated situation, as of the moment it appears that Greeks are still willing to try to narrow the gap separating them and Turks.

4. However, it is unhappy fact of life that Papandreou government is fundamentally weak, poorly organized for effective action, and short on talent. Papandreou himself by nature is long on words and short on deeds. It may be, in the end, because of this weakness and because of difficulties faced in obtaining any kind of Cypriot acquiescence, the US will have to accept the unhappy burden of being the guarantor of an "instant enosis" solution that leaves GOT/GOG final agreement to be hammered out at a later time. This might turn out to be the only way to forestall a Soviet intrusion on the island. This unpalatable position for the US, leaving us the target of the ill will of all the parties, should be adopted only in extremis.

Labouisse

---

132. **Memorandum From the President's Special Assistant for National Security Affairs (Bundy) and Robert Komer of the National Security Council Staff to President Johnson**[1]

Washington, August 18, 1964.

SUBJECT

Cyprus

This is the main topic for the NSC meeting tomorrow;[2] it is moving rapidly toward the point of decision. The Turk air attacks and now Soviet threats have brought the issue to a boil.

[1] Source: Johnson Library, National Security File, Memos to the President, McGeorge Bundy, Vol. 6. Secret.
[2] The National Security Council met at 1 p.m. on August 19, but no record was kept of the discussion. (Ibid., President's Daily Diary)

Whether or not the Soviets are serious, the Cypriots, Greeks, and Turks all seem to think so. The mood on the island has become violently anti-US and pro-Soviet, which makes the Acheson plan all the harder to achieve by agreement. Makarios may be playing with fire, but once again he has moved faster than Athens—or ourselves.

The one saving grace may be that Moscow's move is scaring Greece and Turkey into seeing reason. They may at last find a common interest in preventing Makarios and Moscow from coming out on top. But speed seems imperative if we are to push through a settlement by fiat before the Makarios–Moscow axis is firmed up.

I. *State seems to favor one more try at Geneva,* in hopes that Athens and Ankara may at last stop haggling and strike a bargain. In fact, their positions are not too far apart. The gut issue is how large a base the Turks get and whether it should be sovereign or on a long term lease. It's not clear that we have yet said everything we should to press Greeks and Turks once more, and we'll push this with Ball tomorrow.

II. *Should this fail, Acheson and Ball are thinking of a NATO pressure play to force a solution.* In essence Acheson himself would split the remaining difference between Greeks and Turks. We would then ask all the NATO powers to join us in: (a) telling Greeks and Turks to buy; (b) calling on Greece on behalf of Guarantor Powers to restrain Makarios; and (c) if this fails to maintain order, declaring that whatever violence may occur just be confined to the island.

To latter end, NATO would declare that: (a) No NATO-supplied arms could be used by Greece and Turkey against each other—if so, NATO will take measures to take back the arms and penalize the offender by denying him any more military aid; (b) the NATO powers would act under Article V to prevent Turk action against Greece or vice versa; and (c) if the Soviets intervened, NATO would move. This complex and ingenious plan raises several key questions:

A. *Granted that a NATO umbrella is desirable, can we get enough members to play?* Only a majority is technically needed, but if the Scandinavians or Low Countries balked, it would look thin. Would de Gaulle cause trouble? Would many insist on full explanation of the "Acheson award" or offer amendments?

B. *What are the consequences of taking the play away from the UN and giving it to NATO?* U Thant might be privately relieved, but can he publicly acquiesce? What about the SC resolutions?

C. *Do we want in effect to put the Sixth Fleet between Greeks and Turks if they seem to be going for each other?* This is what is called for, since we have the only power in the Eastern Mediterranean.

D. *Could Greece really enforce the terms on the Cypriots?* If Makarios smells a rat he'll appeal to the UN and to Moscow.

III. An alternative to bringing in NATO is Papandreou's scheme for *instant enosis.* He pleads that the only way to short-circuit the burgeoning

Nicosia/Moscow axis is to impose enosis now. Then the Greeks would make a deal with the Turks. We feel the Turks would never buy unless the terms are worked out beforehand. But if they can be, Papandreou's plan may be simpler and more direct than the NATO scheme—or perhaps the two can be combined so as to reinforce each other. If Greeks and Turks turned to NATO (knowing already what they'd get) we'd be home.

IV. The ultimate question is whether a Greek-Turk deal, assuming we could get one, can be imposed on the island. The evidence is quite inconclusive. Makarios has outmaneuvered the Greeks every time so far, and now he thinks he has Soviet backing. I think you will want to press George on this; the rest of us have not made much progress.

Finally, whatever road we take, we have all the ingredients of major crisis shortly. Makarios will try every trick he has, and the Soviets are now committed to make at least some trouble. Ball and Acheson must still carry the main load, but I think you'll want at least a daily report.

This is a brief summary, and I think it gives you what you need for tomorrow, but if you have time, the relevant cables are attached.[3]

R. W. Komer
McG. B.[4]

---

[3] Not attached. A handwritten note on the source text reads: "Geneva 401, 403; Athens 327; Embtel 327 Exdis."

[4] Printed from a copy that bears Komer's typed signature and Bundy's typed initials.

---

133.   Telegram From the Mission in Geneva to the Department of State[1]

Geneva, August 19, 1964, 9 p.m.

425. From Acheson. Ref: Nicosia 345 and Athens 343 to Dept.[2] Instant enosis, whether staged by Papandreou or by Grivas on his own, seems to us here to contain fatal flaw that Turks will not stand still for it or

---

[1] Source: Department of State, Central Files, POL 27 CYP. Secret; Flash; Exdis–TAG. Repeated to Nicosia, Athens, Ankara, London, DOD, CIA, and the White House.

[2] Telegram 345 from Nicosia analyzed intelligence information. (Ibid.) Telegram 343 from Athens, August 19, reported that Cyuprus had offered a lease on a 50-square mile base to Turkey after the completion of enosis. (Ibid.)

after it unless they have prior assurance from someone they trust that it will be quickly followed by settlement meeting their essential demands. What Grivas proposes to offer Turkey falls far short of this and so does what Papandreou has indicated he is willing to do up to now, although he has been distinctly more forthcoming than Grivas.

Furthermore, we have clear impression from Erim and Sunalp, with whom we had discussion this afternoon, that Turks do not trust either Papandreou or Grivas.[3] They regard Papandreou as deplorably weak and Grivas as bitterly anti-Turk.

Therefore, I think that coup d'etat in Cyprus at present time would appear to Turks as clear double-cross and that they would be most likely to blame us for putting up smoke screen of Geneva talks and leading them down the darkened path. Whether they would or would not, I should be extremely surprised if their response to coup were not immediate invasion with all consequences that that would have.

We may not be able to stop Grivas, but I think it would be unwise for us to connive with him unless he is willing to go whole way in granting rights to Turks. We should be able to deter Papandreou for present, and I think we ought to try to keep him on the Geneva path.

Tubby

---

[3] In telegram 426 from Geneva, August 19, Acheson reported that Erim had made clear his government's preference for dealing with other Greek political leaders. (Ibid.)

---

134.   Telegram From the Mission in Geneva to the Embassy in Greece[1]

Geneva, August 20, 1964, 2:30 p.m.

97. For Ambassador from Acheson. Ball asked me in telecon this a.m.[2] to send to you and him the following letter from me to Prime Minister Papandreou to be delivered by you, upon receipt of clearance from Washington, to Prime Minister and the King.

---

[1] Source: Department of State, Central Files, POL 27 CYP. Secret; Flash; Exdis–Tag. Also sent to the Department of State, where it was received at 10:44 a.m., and repeated to London and Ankara. Passed to the White House, DOD, CIA, and USUN. The source text is the Department of State copy.
[2] A transcript of the teleconference is ibid., Ball Papers: Lot 74 D 272, Telephone Conversations, Cyprus Situation.

Begin letter:

My Dear Prime Minister:

May I begin this letter by expressing deepest appreciation of the help you have given to our work here in Geneva by your own constant attention and thought and by permitting Mr. Sossides to join in our efforts.

Today the President has informed me of the urgency which he believes imminent Soviet involvement in the Cyprus problem has imparted to our work, and because of it has asked me to let you know our joint view that only a little while is left in which a settlement can be made and to give you my own views, which he has endorsed, of the general nature of the settlement which seems to me possible and fair. I know from our conversations with Mr. Sossides that you are impressed as we are here of the danger, which the Russian moves have intensified, that Cyprus will fall under Communist influence and of the far-reaching effects which this will have upon the political and power situation in the Eastern Mediterranean. I am sure we agree that the danger gives Turkey and Greece a common interest far transcending the exact lines on a map to be drawn in reaching an agreement. The problems presented to both sides in reaching a settlement are political and it is from that point of view that I approach them.

I am prepared to apply the utmost pressure and persuasion to get the Turks to give up any claim for sovereign territory on Cyprus, to reduce the dimensions of their requirements for a military base on the Karpas Peninsula and to settle the rights of minorities along the lines which I have discussed with Mr. Sossides and which I can translate into a draft to be available tomorrow. Specifically, I would urge the Turks to limit their plan to a lease for 50 years for that part of the Karpas Peninsula running from its northeasterly end to a line drawn north and south just west of Komi Kebir. I am persuaded from the study which I have made of the situation with the aid of military advisers that there is a sound military justification for such a base in the defense of the approaches to the Turkish mainland and in the defense of the base itself from surprise attack. It is quite possible that to draw the western line of this area as I have suggested would present a political problem to you at this time. This problem could be avoided by leaving the line undrawn, to be supplied after military study by the Supreme Allied Commander for Europe, with the assurance by the Government of Greece that if the line should be drawn as indicated it would be accepted. Indeed, the willingness of the Government of Greece to enter into such a settlement might be indicated to me without entering into any present direct commitment to the Government of Turkey. With this assurance I would do my best, and believe I could succeed, in obtaining the agreement of the Government of Turkey not to intervene to prevent or to demand prior intergovernmental agreement before the achievement of enosis between Greece and Cyprus.

Without something of this sort the Turks would surely believe themselves to be faced with having their treaty rights almost contemptuously destroyed and themselves faced with the alternatives of unconditional enosis or unconditional independence for a Cyprus under Communist domination.

What I have suggested will present the gravest difficulties for the leaders of both Greece and Turkey and for the peoples they lead. But I am confident that, in the face of imminent common peril, each nation can find unity at home in support of solutions which look beyond momentary controversy to the fundamental security and welfare of great Hellenic and Turkish states and support abroad by the grand alliance of free states against interference with their execution.

May I request, my dear Prime Minister, the early return to Geneva of Mr. Sossides to help us to this solution.

(Add whatever polite closure is appropriate.)[3]

Tubby

---

[3] In telegram 141 from Athens to Geneva, Labouisse reported that Acheson's letter to Papandreou had produced an "awkward personality situation" because of its failure to refer to the more senior Nikolareisis. (Ibid., Central Files, POL 27 CYP)

---

135. Telegram From the Department of State to the Embassy in Greece[1]

Washington, August 20, 1964, 1:18 p.m.

327. For Ambassador from Ball. The President now directs you to go ahead immediately with delivery of the Acheson letter as contained in Geneva's 97 to you.[2] In making your approach please have these points in mind:

1. If we cannot put this deal over right now the chances of success at a later date are slight. The interjection of the Soviet Union into this already tangled web of affairs will make the task almost hopeless.

---

[1] Source: Department of State, Central Files, POL 27 CYP. Secret; Flash; Exdis–TAG. Drafted and approved by Ball. Repeated to Ankara, London, and Geneva for Acheson.

[2] Document 134.

2. Acheson's solution is not a bargaining position. It is his decision that this is the minimum that can be given to the Turks without an explosion in Turkey which would have disastrous consequences for everyone. You must make this point sufficiently emphatic in order to overcome the mercantile instincts of your clients.

3. Time is really of the essence. That means now. We are talking in terms of a deal within 48 hours.

4. There are real advantages in a Greek decision today. The presence of Garoufoulias on the Island[3] should be helpful in making this work. Kyprianou has not yet left for Moscow. Any delay will change the picture to everyone's disadvantage.

5. It is not for us to tell the Greeks how to bring about instant enosis. You can say to the GOG that we have deliberately avoided any direct involvement with Grivas since we do not wish to interfere in the measures they may deem necessary to achieve the results.

6. Obviously this is not a deal Papandreou can carry off by himself. The King and military must also be aboard. Presumably the King will wish to have the ERE in line. A Greek national decision seems to us essential if we are to force this down the throat of the Turks which in any event will be very difficult.

7. If you find any disposition to further haggling you can tell the Greeks that we are putting this deal up to the Turks at the same time and we do not propose to haggle with them either.

8. What we are offering the Greeks after tremendous endeavors on our part is the possibility of avoiding a Communist take-over of the Island. Moreover, it is the opportunity to avoid setting in train a whole series of different events which in combination could result in the extension of Communist power over a very much larger area. This is a major decision directly affecting the future position of Greece itself. You cannot say this too emphatically.

9. From the time of Papandreou's visit here the Greeks have continually asked us what solution we propose. We have invested enormous time and effort in reaching this decision. This is it.

10. Yours is an epic assignment. We appreciate the difficulties but very large concerns hang on your success.

Good luck.

Rusk

---

[3] Garoufalias visited Cyprus on August 21.

136.   Telegram From the Embassy in Greece to the Department of State[1]

Athens, August 21, 1964, 2 a.m.

362. Have just returned from 10:30 p.m. meeting with PriMin at which Costopoulos, Andreas Papandreou and Sossides were present on Greek side. Anschuetz and Brewster accompanied me.

I opened discussion by recalling PriMin's urgent request for "instant enosis" and USG assistance; also my reservations that this could be accomplished without prior agreement on Turk demands. I said highest officials USG including President had concerned themselves with matter for past several days and had confirmed view that would be impossible proceed without prior understanding with GOT. After taking into account various developments in long history of matter, and in view urgent necessity reach immediate solution, Washington officials and Acheson had come up with proposal which went long way to meet Greek aspirations. We were by no means sure however that Turks could be persuaded to go along.

I then presented Acheson letter to Papandreou which Andreas Papandreou read in English and then translated into Greek. In submitting letter I made unvarnished presentation based inter alia on points Deptel 327 to Athens,[2] emphasizing that this proposed solution not a bargaining position and represents Acheson's and USG's best assessment of what might be made acceptable to Turks. I stressed particularly that a Greek national decision was essential to put solution across and underlined the fact that this solution offered the possibility of avoiding a Communist take-over of island and averting the extension of Communist power over a very much larger area including Greece itself.

PriMin acknowledged danger which Communist control of Cyprus would pose for Greece. After listening to the presentation attentively he explained that he must have a solution which can be rationally explained not only to his own people but also to the people of Cyprus and their "devilish leader Makarios." He confirmed offer Costopoulos had made to me two hours earlier that GOG prepared lease an area of 99 square miles on Karpas Peninsula. He added that if he had to deal only with Greek public opinion he could possibly have agreed to lease of roughly 200 square miles. However, in his struggle with Makarios he would be

---

[1] Source: Department of State, Central Files, POL 27 CYP. Secret; Flash; Nodis–TAG. Received at 10:20 p.m. on August 20 and repeated to Geneva for Acheson, Ankara, London, and Nicosia. Passed to the White House, DOD, CIA, and USUN.

[2] Document 135.

placed in a very difficult, and probably impossible, position if he granted Turks double the area of the two British bases.

I stressed again that the area delineated, which appeared to be not much more than 5 percent of land area of Cyprus, was absolute minimum which Acheson considers Turks might be willing to accept. We went over map a number of times showing where Turk demands had originally started and how they had been compressed.

At termination meeting Papandreou confirmed Sossides would leave for Geneva tomorrow carrying back Papandreou's answer to Acheson letter. I concluded by earnestly imploring PriMin to give this letter most serious consideration as a final offer inasmuch as it was Mr. Acheson's view, shared by entire USG including President, that this was best deal which could be obtained for Greece.

Comment: Greek side listened most attentively to entire proposal. Presentation I had made earlier in evening to Costopoulos had obviously had salutary effect. There was no detailed discussion of method of public presentation Acheson proposal if accepted, or of procedures in effecting enosis which I made clear we considered responsibility of GOG. However, when passage in letter re possible future determination of western boundary by SACEUR was reached, FonMin dryly commented in Greek to Papandreou, "That's the Vaseline." Although Papandreou made no comment it was apparent that he appreciated that he was confronted by a fundamental decision and that this decision must be made promptly. I believe he would sincerely like to meet Acheson proposal but has not yet resolved in his own mind how he can face Makarios and Cypriot opinion as well as his own potential supporters such as Grivas and Georkadzis.

Postscript: I threw everything at him but the glove. Goodnight for now.

Labouisse

---

137.   **Telegram From the Department of State to the Embassy in Greece**[1]

Washington, August 20, 1964, 11:36 p.m.

335. We have read your 362[2] with considerable dismay here. Despite what I know was a valiant effort on your part, it does not appear to us

---

[1] Source: Department of State, Central Files, POL 27 CYP. Secret; Flash; Exdis–TAG. Drafted and approved by Ball. Repeated to Ankara, London, and Geneva for Acheson.

[2] Document 136.

that Papandreou has understood the urgency of the situation or what great responsibility we are taking in offering him a solution to his otherwise insoluble problems. I believe it essential therefore that you see the King at the earliest possible hour today and make the following points:

1. What you are proposing is exactly what he asked [*less than 1 line of source text not declassified*]—our assurance that we would hold the Turks still if the GOG would move incisively to bring about instant enosis under terms that would give the Greeks 95 percent of what they want.

2. This is not an offer made cavalierly to be treated in a leisurely manner. We are at one minute to midnight. The GOG had better understand this. If the President is to continue to assume the responsibility for trying to keep peace in the Mediterranean and keep the Communists out, the GOG must do its part at this decisive moment.

We in Washington—including the President—will be profoundly shocked and disappointed if—after all our anguish and exertions—the GOG boggles at the leasing of 100 square miles of territory beyond the last Greek offer and thus permits Cyprus to pass under Communist control. (The total area of the Karpas base we are talking about amounts to 204 square miles.)[3]

4. If Papandreou cannot bite the bullet and act incisively, then the King must realize that a national decision is required and required immediately.[4]

5. Up to this point, the GOG has failed to come up with a single constructive suggestion that takes into account the realities of the situation. What we are offering is a way out of a catastrophic dilemma at little cost to Hellenism, either in territory or national pride. If this offer is not taken immediately, we see no alternative that offers anything but disaster.

6. Not only will our plan extricate Greece from great danger at minimal cost, but it will enable Greece at long last to achieve the historic objective of making Cyprus once and for all a part of Greece and making Athens the single capital of Hellenism.

7. There is no time for Sossides to return to Geneva for further talks with Acheson. We must have a prompt decision or the whole plan will fall apart. The proposal will leak—as knowledge of our efforts has con-

---

[3] In telegram 366 from Athens, August 21, Labouisse reported that Papandreou was ready to agree to a deal on Cyprus on the basis of Acheson's proposals, but it must include assurances from Turkey that it would cease the deportation of Greek minorities. (Department of State, Central Files, POL 27 CYP)

[4] In telegram 368 from Athens, August 21, Labouisse reported that he had met with the King who promised to attempt to secure support for a Cyprus deal from the ERE leadership. Constantine also noted the importance of Turkish agreement to cease pressures on Greeks in Istanbul and that Greek Cypriots living within a base area would not be forced to relocate. (Ibid.)

sistently leaked from Athens. Makarios will be put on guard. Grivas will be poisoned against the plan and his capabilities to achieve it will be undermined. Papandreou will once again find himself impotent.

8. We must have an answer today without waiting for Sossides' return to Geneva. The Turks have been alerted and Kyprianou may be on his way to Moscow at any hour. We cannot undertake to get the Turks into line if the Greeks procrastinate. This is the time to decide and to act and we are unlikely to have a second chance.[5]

Apart from your talk with the King, we would like comments on the following points:

1. We are puzzled by Papandreou's concern that he will not be able to explain the plan to Makarios. This seems incomprehensible to us since we had not assumed that such an explanation was ever contemplated. Obviously no plan that would possibly be acceptable to the GOT could ever be acceptable to Makarios.

2. We had assumed that the GOG would take measures to bypass Makarios and bring about instant enosis through whatever means they felt necessary. This seems to us the only possible way to effect a solution of this problem. If the GOG does not understand this, we fail to see how any solution can be effected.

Rusk

---

[5] In telegram 107 from Geneva to Athens, August 21, Acheson commented that while he did not believe the moment proper to extract further concessions from the Turks on either minorities or Cypriots living within a base area, he believed that such concessions would be forthcoming after an accord. (Ibid.)

---

138.   Telegram From the Mission in Geneva to the Department of State[1]

Geneva, August 21, 1964, 2 p.m.

445. From Acheson. Turks came to see me this morning to say they had reported proposal I put to them yesterday and already had "governmental decision" back from Ankara. Essence this answer was that

---

[1] Source: Department of State, Central Files, POL 27 CYP. Secret; Immediate; Exdis–TAG. Received at 11:01 a.m. and repeated to Ankara and Athens. Passed to the White House, DOD, CIA, and USUN.

Turkey had accepted initial proposals I made in Geneva but this was final, not bargaining position. What I had proposed yesterday was radical change involving abandonment of "principle" of sovereign area as well as basic principles of my plan for protection Turkish minority right. This Turkey could not accept.

I took strong exception to statement Turkey had accepted initial proposals. Told me they were acceptable "as basis for discussion". In my view, this meant discussion of all aspects, not merely that Turkey would accept my offer and try to get more. Erim said there must have been misunderstanding; Turkey would have been willing to discuss certain details, such as exact boundary of sovereign base area, but it was quite unable discuss idea of lease instead of sovereign possession.

I urged that Turks refrain from giving me at this time final rejection of latest proposal. They should wait and see what Greece did. It appeared GOG did not like my ideas any better than GOT. At least, Turkey might allow Greece to take onus for breakdown of talks.

Erim insisted, however, on going ahead, saying I could "use it or not." According to Ankara, he said, sovereign base area of adequate size would have been barely acceptable compensation to Turkey for enosis, but leased base could never be adequate conterpart. Turkey must be free on its base to do anything it wished in both civil and military fields. So far as minorities were concerned, my original proposal had been acceptable, but Greek counter proposal (which he implied I had adopted) was completely different. As he had already said, Turkish Government was not prepared to discuss basic changes. Since GOG had failed agree to my position, Turkey preferred no settlement at all.

He then began once again to talk about federalism, mentioning that USSR had never declared itself as opposed to this solution. Establishment of federal state on Cyprus would preserve Turkey's freedom of action, which would be lost once enosis took place. He went on to emphasize that it was impossible for Inonu to sell enosis to Turkish Parliament and people without sovereign base as counterpart.

At this point I read him excerpts from latest Ankara press summary which showed newspapers were talking about enosis as possible solution and pointing out dangers of self-determination for Cyprus in light of Soviet Cypriot rapprochement. They were pointing with alarm to danger of Russia achieving a Mediterranean Cuba. Greek press, I said, was taking somewhat similar line. This seemed to indicate to me that both Turkish and Greek opinion had realized we had entered a new phase.

As to federalism, I emphatically said this was not presently feasible alternative. Makarios simply would not accept it and he would have Soviet support.

With all the energy I could muster I tried to impress upon Erim that our only chance to save situation is now. This offer gave Turkey a great deal, even though I admitted it was not what GOT would like. There really wasn't all that difference between sovereignty and a lease. What had sovereignty meant in case of Britain and Cyprus? Possession between 1914 and 1960, less than the fifty years being offered Turkey. It would be incredible folly for GOT to turn down this last opportunity. Rejection would be disastrous for Turkey, for U.S., for Greece and for Cyprus. Turks should realize they can't get what they want without fighting. And that would bring down whole house of cards. I strongly hoped Greece and Turkey would not lose sight of their real national interest. They must not allow themselves to be blinded by wretched island of Cyprus to real Slav danger which threatened them both.

I summed up by saying that I had done everything I could. I had no more ideas. If my latest proposal were not accepted, I would be finished. Only thing I could do, and what I planned to do, would be to ask Amb. Hare to make final approach in Ankara to urge GOT to reconsider. (I said, however, I would not ask him to do this unless I heard that Greeks had accepted.)

Erim and Sunalp listened to this calmly, injecting occasionally repetitious remarks about Turkish inability to give more ground than I had asked them at first. Their only substantive suggestion was that we go back to validity of existing treaties and that U.S. and Turkey make new joint statement that these treaties must be respected. I said we had made our position in support of treaties clear ever since Inonu visit to Washington. Restatement in present circumstances would be futile.

At one point, Erim remarked that if there should be settlement between Greece and Turkey GOT would prefer to have all aspects of agreement made public at same time. We did not follow this up, but I assume he was referring to my earlier suggestion that agreement not be published, at least in full, until after enosis had been accomplished.

We parted amicably, with Sunalp remarking he would probably not see us again because he had received orders to take command of 29th Division at Erzerum. Erim said nothing about leaving Geneva.

Comment: Seems apparent that sovereignty is key issue in Turkish mind. With it, they can pretend to their people that they have achieved form of partition; without it they think this impossible. I got no reaction at all to my repeated warning about dangers of Soviet domination of Cyprus. Erim observed very calmly that if this happens "you will have your Cuba and we will have our Cyprus, each ruled by a man with a beard."

Tubby

139. Telegram From the Embassy in Cyprus to the Department of State[1]

Nicosia, August 21, 1964, 5 p.m.

357. Dept and other addressees already well aware views this post regarding impossibility any lasting peaceful solution involving Turkish base on island. From fragmentary info gleaned from various telegrams would appear we have now presented GOG fully approved USG plan which includes sizeable base on Karpas if not most of peninsula. At same time we are suddenly presented by GOG with "instant enosis" as only way Greeks can see out of present virtually impossible situation. At risk of being considered out of step feel I must observe that we are moving into almost hopeless dilemma and we cannot continue even for short period to ride both Geneva and (reluctantly but perhaps with no choice) "instant enosis" horses. Our reasoning is along following lines:

1. "Instant enosis" depends upon availability of reliable Greek troops for use in bringing it about and good discipline on part of Greek Cypriot armed elements.

2. Sovereign Turkish base not sellable here. Why should Greek Cypriots accept less than they think they will get at UNGA? And especially now that GOC has or thinks it has full Soviet backing? Greek army can hardly be expected to force base upon Cypriots who likely actively fight against it (Athens 353 to Dept).[2] Even leased base would be categorically refused by majority of Cypriots and certainly by their leadership including Georkadjis/Grivas. Therefore both crucial elements for imposed solution are lacking.

3. Turks believe we think Turkish base rather than NATO base can be imposed here if GOG agrees in Geneva. Therefore, it would seem that in Turkish eyes USG would be responsible if "instant enosis" did not result in establishment Turkish base.

4. Mood here is such that it not inconceivable Grivas et al. might go ahead with enosis anyway without our support and of course without any Turkish base. This will surely be terrible fait accompli for Turks to swallow after having held their hand on assumption that US would obtain them sizeable Karpas base.

Realize the foregoing obviously presents us with harsh choice. We feel here that possible solution could lie along lines our 345[3] but if deci-

---

[1] Source: Department of State, Central Files, POL 27 CYP. Secret; Immediate; Exdis–TAG. Received at 11:59 a.m. and repeated to Ankara, Athens, and Geneva for Acheson. Passed to the White House, DOD, CIA, and USUN.

[2] Telegram 353 from Athens, August 20, reported a discussion with the Greeks regarding Turkish base demands and indicated that the Greek Government had not yet taken a decision on the issue. (Ibid.)

[3] See footnote 2, Document 133.

sion made for higher policy reasons to give Turks territorial concession, we must be prepared for real bloodshed, rapid increase in Communist strength, to say nothing of possible Soviet intervention in more active form and at best, festering sore which will continue to torture our major alliance.[4]

Belcher

---

[4] In telegram 359 from Nicosia, August 21, Belcher advised the Department of State that "instant enosis" was impossible on terms that included a Turkish base. (Department of State, Central Files, POL 27 CYP) In telegram 206 to Nicosia, August 21, the Department of State instructed Belcher to avoid any statement to Greek or Cypriot officials that might suggest official doubts about the "instant enosis" with a Turkish base deal. (Ibid.)

---

140.   Telegram From the Embassy in Turkey to the Department of State[1]

Ankara, August 22, 1964, 3 p.m.

363. For Under Secretary Ball. Have just had two and half hours very difficult conversation with Inonu and Erkin in which I initially based presentation on summer negots to date in order establish extraordinary effort at highest level made by USG in this matter, following this by giving substance Ball telecon of last night[2] and delivering Acheson letter.[3]

To make long story short Inonu was obviously well primed and steadfastly insisted no agreement possible which did not provide for larger base area and full sovereignty, with especial emphasis on latter. He agreed however that this should not be considered as final decision but rather as exchange of views which he would report to Erim and I to

---

[1] Source: Department of State, Central Files, POL 27 CYP. Secret; Flash; Exdis–TAG. Received at 9:01 a.m. and repeated to Athens and Geneva for Acheson. Passed to the White House, DOD, CIA, and USUN.

[2] Following receipt of telegram 445 from Geneva (Document 138), Ball initiated a teleconference with Hare at 5:15 p.m. on August 21. Ball instructed Hare to press the Turks to settle on the basis of the Acheson proposals. (Department of State, Ball Papers: Lot 74 D 272, Telephone Conversations, Cyprus Situation) Hare reported that he requested a personal meeting with ailing Prime Minister Inonu in telegram 359 from Ankara, August 21. (Ibid., POL 27 CYP)

[3] Transmitted in telegram 112 to Ankara, August 22. In his letter, Acheson stressed the need for an immediate agreement on the basis of the proposal he had offered. (Ibid.)

Washington in order obtain reactions of USG. If our proposal unchanged he would submit to government for final decision but he made clear he would not support; to do so would end his political career. Limit to which he could go was original Acheson proposal.

It will probably take me several hours to try to patch this rather strange conversation together;[4] strange in sense that arguments advanced by Inonu, although having degree of cogency, did not give impression of indicating what he really had in mind.

As contrasted with Inonu's calm, Erkin's pressure seemed be running rather high. Said Turks always being asked make concessions; base proposal worthless; as Turk citizen support of proposal would constitute betrayal of his people; better let things go on as they are or even have enosis with no arrangement. Then and possibly with some significance he observed that in any event there now seemed be "light of hope for federation" and, when I asked him genesis of this idea, his first reaction was to say not result of consultation with Russians, which I had not suggested. Mention of same thing by Erim to Acheson (Geneva's 445 to Dept)[5] only yesterday may or may not be coincidental.

In sum, my talk was longer version of that between Acheson and Erim yesterday, with sovereignty and area of base given as striking point, but I am not at all sure that this was not used as excuse to get out from under whole thing, which in curious contrast with what appeared be inspired press build-up for something like what we finally proposed.

I of course used every gun at my disposal but Inonu had obviously entrenched himself well in advance and would give no ground beyond agreeing keep open for another round.

Hare

---

[4] In telegram 364 from Ankara, August 22, received at 12:56 p.m., Hare outlined in greater detail Inonu's objections to the Acheson proposals. (Ibid.)

[5] Document 138.

141. Telegram From the Mission in Geneva to the Department of State[1]

Geneva, August 22, 1964, 6 p.m.

461. From Acheson. Now that, despite heroic efforts by Labouisse and Hare, both Greece and Turkey have rejected the only remotely possible proposal, I recommend that we liquidate Geneva and try new policy outlined in following telegram.[2] I would say in both capitals that last Acheson proposal was final effort to reach agreement and no modification will improve its acceptability. It has now been rejected by both Greece and Turkey and deemed unenforceable on Greek-Cypriots. USG can make no further effort. It therefore considers Geneva talks concluded and will direct Acheson return to Washington. USG considers this turn of events most grave for all. It will continue to make every effort to prevent Cyprus from falling into Soviet orbit, but unfortunately it is now clear that this cannot be done by agreement between its two allies most concerned. USG will have to keep foremost in mind what is practical and what is in the interest of the entire Western world. USG would deeply regret any development which might lead either ally to believe that its interests had not been sufficiently safeguarded but it must be guided by the interest and purposes of the Alliance as a whole. It will continue the closest consultation with its allies.

I have already given the Department some thoughts on concrete actions we might now take (my tels 401, 408 and 439).[3] I am revising these in immediately following telegram in the light of the final developments.

Tubby

---

[1] Source: Department of State, Central Files, POL 27 CYP. Secret; Flash; Exdis–TAG. Received at 1:23 p.m. and repeated to Ankara, Athens, London, and USUN. Passed to the White House, DOD, and CIA.

[2] In telegram 462 from Geneva, August 22, Acheson recommended a policy of supporting Greece in an effort to neutralize Soviet influence over Makarios. (Ibid.)

[3] Telegram 408 is Document 129. Regarding telegram 401, see footnote 2 thereto. Telegram 439, August 20, is not printed. (Department of State, Central Files, POL 27 CYP)

142. Telegram From the Department of State to the Embassy in Greece[1]

Washington, August 22, 1964, 3:25 p.m.

347. For Ambassadors from Ball. Your 375.[2] We cannot accept the Greek Government's vacillation and you should make this point quite clear to them. The President has been advised that the GOG has accepted our proposal and we intend to proceed on that basis. We are using every possible means to bring about a Turkish agreement and we cannot accept any Greek second thoughts at this point.

I suggest, therefore, that in your next meeting with Papandreou you convey to him the deep sense of surprise felt in Washington by his apparent backsliding. You must continue to keep the pressure at the maximum until we get this whole business nailed down. So far as the United States Government is concerned this is a last major effort and we do not intend to see it fail. If it should break because of the lack of courage or determination on the part of the GOG we would have to make clear to the world where the responsibility lay.

We have been considering how to respond to the Greek request for guidance in handling the situation in Cyprus. You should alter or amend the following suggestion as you see fit.

With the approval of Papandreou and hopefully of Canellopoulos also, the King would send word to General Grivas that he wished to see him. He would then make the following points to General Grivas preferably speaking in the presence of Papandreou and Canellopoulos.

1. The Government has fully considered the USG proposal and believes that it should be carried out.

2. A quick solution through the American proposal is the only door still open of preventing the Communization of Cyprus without the practical certainty of a Turk attack.

3. The Americans have been making a substantial effort to help find a solution. They have assured the GOG that if enosis is immediately effected through a peaceful bargain with the Turks on the basis of the American proposal they would promptly provide substantial assistance for the rebuilding of Cyprus and the development of its resources.

In connection with this last point you may indicate that we would be prepared to undertake an aid program that could result in the reclaiming

---

[1] Source: Department of State, Central Files, POL 27 CYP. Secret; Flash; Exdis–TAG. Drafted and approved by Ball. Repeated to Ankara, London, and Geneva for Acheson.

[2] Telegram 375 from Athens, August 22, reported that as a result of Garoufalias' visit to Cyprus, the Greek Government was convinced that Makarios would reject any settlement involving cession of territory in the Karpas Peninsula to Turkey. (Ibid.)

of more land for Cyprus than would be included in the proposed Turkish base. How you should formulate that is for you to decide. We are reviewing the situation with the experts this afternoon and will forward you promptly some harder data as to the possibilities of desalination and soil reclamation.

What must be gotten across to General Grivas is that what the American proposal offers is an opportunity for him to fulfill his Dighenis role and thus reclaim Cyprus for Hellenism and save it from Communism to which Makarios is leading it. He would also secure for the people of Cyprus the chance to make their Island blossom like a rose.[3]

Rusk

---

[3] In telegram 379 from Athens, August 23, Labouisse endorsed the proposal for support of Greece made by Acheson as the best means of checking Soviet influence. (Ibid.)

---

143. Telegram From the Embassy in Greece to the Department of State[1]

Athens, August 22, 1964, 9 p.m.

378. Embtel 375.[2]

1. I told PriMin that statement that GOG did not consider itself in position carry out enosis on basis Acheson proposal came as shocking news on top of yesterday's confirmation that he was prepared to accept the Acheson proposals in principle and was drafting a letter along those lines. I said new situation confronted us with possible disaster.

2. PriMin acknowledged above, but appeared greatly distraught and genuinely disturbed over report on Grivas' position and atmosphere in Cyprus. PriMin added that although it was folly to risk war over question of the size of a base, he was not master over Greek Cypriot community as Inonu is over Turk Cypriots. He said he had been most sincere in his statements to me yesterday and day before and that he had and is

---

[1] Source: Department of State, Central Files, POL 27 CYP. Secret; Flash; Exdis–TAG. Received at 4:36 p.m. and repeated to Ankara, London, Nicosia, and Geneva. Passed to the White House, DOD, CIA, and USUN.

[2] Telegram 375 from Athens, August 22, reported that because of Cypriot resistance to a Turkish base area the Greek Government was in "total disarray" and unable to accept the Acheson proposal. (Ibid.)

acting in good faith; that Acheson proposal is acceptable to gov as way to avoid war and resolve Cyprus question, but that he is helpless because he could not impose this solution on the island. This was brought force-fully to light by Defense Minister's discussions in Cyprus. He finds him-self in a serious impasse and does not know where to turn.

3. He and Costopoulos asked several times for US guidance. Would it be desirable for government to state publicly that it accepted concept of Acheson plan but that Makarios turned it down? As result of such state-ment, Greece would, of course, have to withdraw its forces from Cyprus and leave the island to its fate. Both Papandreou and Costopoulos ques-tioned that this would be desirable course of action, as it would play more into Makarios' hands and drive him even closer to Moscow and Nasser. "But what can be done?"

4. Papandreou said only way out that he could see was proposal he had made to me on Monday (Embtel 327),[3] which would bring about instant enosis with no prior commitments, get rid of Makarios, cut out Soviets, and leave it to GOG to promise full safeguards (presumably along general lines Acheson proposal, with few relatively minor modifi-cations).

Comment: As indicated, we believe GOG was sincerely attracted Thursday night to Acheson plan as being solution basically in over-all Greek interest (Embtel 362)[4] but frankly stated their reservations regard-ing their capacity to make concessions regarding Turkish base. Yesterday morning Papandreou under intense US pressure took policy decision to accept US proposal in principle (Embtel 366)[5] although he continued express misgivings as to his ability to execute program. Today following Garoufalias' return from Cyprus, Papandreou's illusion GOG might have capability to execute program evaporated.

It was always the case that the prospective settlement with Cyprus had to be of a nature such that the Greeks could impose it, overcoming whatever resistance exists among the Greek Cypriots to the settlement. As events moved along, under our pressure the Greeks gave more and more ground, hoping that what they were conceding was not beyond their capability to deliver. In their anxiety to obtain settlement based on enosis, they got beyond their capability to deliver.

Labouisse

---

[3] See footnote 3, Document 131.
[4] Document 136.
[5] See footnote 3, Document 137.

144.   Telegram From the Department of State to the Mission in Geneva[1]

Washington, August 23, 1964, 2:10 p.m.

479. Geneva for Acheson. For Ambassadors. After a long telecon with Ray Hare early this morning[2] and the dubious result of his subsequent final try with Inonu,[3] I have reluctantly concluded that Geneva, as originally conceived, has run its course.

In order to salvage remaining possibilities, I ask your comments on the following new proposed course of action:

1. In Athens Labouisse would say to the GOG that it has proved impossible to persuade the Turks to accept anything less than the Karpas Peninsula Base and even that is doubtful on a leasehold basis.

2. However, we are not prepared to let conditions drift to the point where Cyprus becomes another Cuba, as will almost certainly be the case if the Makarios regime continues in control of an independent GOC.

3. We are, therefore, considering saying to the GOG that they should go forward with their plans to bring about enosis and that we will undertake to see that, if they bring it off with reasonable promptness, neither the Turks nor any outside power will intervene with military force.

4. The conditions of this offer are:

(a) The GOG must undertake, once enosis is concluded, to negotiate promptly and in good faith with the GOT regarding the mutual recision of the Treaties of Guarantee and Alliance.
(b) In the course of this negotiation, the GOG must undertake as a minimum to offer the Turks, in exchange for the abrogation of those treaties, two major concessions.
(c) The first is the assurance of minority rights to the Turk Cypriot population in the form developed by Dean Acheson.
(d) The second is an undertaking by the GOG to grant to the GOT a 50-year lease for a suitable area to be mutually agreed on with the advice of SHAPE.

5. While the GOG may be reluctant to agree now to negotiate these concessions in the absence of a simultaneous Turkish agreement, we can point out to them that without an understanding with the GOT a post-enosis Cyprus will face sticky problems. For example, it will be confronted with the presence of a Turkish garrison which the Turkish

---

[1] Source: Department of State, Central Files, POL 27 CYP. Secret; Flash; Nodis–TAG. Drafted and approved by Ball. Repeated to Athens, Ankara, and London.

[2] Initiated at 4 a.m. on August 23. (Ibid., Ball Papers: Lot 74 D 272, Telephone Conversations, Cyprus Situation)

[3] See Document 140.

Government will no doubt insist on maintaining under the Treaty of Alliance unless the juridical situation can be sorted out by agreement. The garrison, the rights claimed under Article 4 of the Treaty of Guarantee, and the unresolved status of other Treaty provisions can make relations very difficult. This is true even though the UN General Assembly might pass a resolution calling upon the Turks to relinquish these rights and get out.[4]

In Ankara we would propose to take the following actions:

(1) Hare would say to Inonu that he regrets that the GOT has not accepted our proposal and that Turkey will probably never be able to obtain as good a deal again.

(2) The USG, however, is not prepared to let Cyprus become another Cuba.

(3) We are advising the GOT, therefore, that we are encouraging the GOG to bring about enosis and propose to tell them that we will assure that this is achieved without outside intervention from any quarter.

(4) At the same time we are insisting, as a condition of this assurance to the GOG, that the Greek Government must agree as outlined in paragraph 4 above.

The advantage of this course of action from the point of view of the GOT is that it does not require the Turkish Government to agree to anything. It would merely accept notice of our statement that we expect it to stand down on Cyprus and that we propose again to concentrate on the great issues that bind Turkey to the Western Alliance. We should get some sense of the risks involved in giving the Greeks an assurance of Turkish standdown through General Porter's visit to Ankara in the next two or three days. I would like particularly to have Ray Hare's comments on this.[5]

In order to share these risks and at the same time give a firmer underpinning to the proposal, we might consider trying to associate the UKG as well as Germany and Italy with our action.

If we get an affirmative reply from the Greeks and implicit acquiescence from the Turks, you might wish to stop off in Rome, Bonn and London on your return to the US to try to get them on board.

Meanwhile, both Dean Rusk and I feel that it would be helpful if you could stay on in Geneva for some days more until we fully explore the possibilities of trying to work out an arrangement along the above lines. This would minimize the possibilities of a sudden sense of alarm result-

---

[4] In telegram 387 from Athens, August 24, Labouisse endorsed Acheson's proposal and stated that in order for Papandreou to carry out enosis successfully, he would have to be able to limit the commitments he had already made to Turkey. (Department of State, Central Files, POL 27 CYP)

[5] Hare's comments are in telegram 370 from Ankara, August 24. (Ibid.) In telegram 379 from Ankara, August 24, Porter reported that he would make an effort to convince the Turkish General Staff that the Karpas Peninsula was militarily sound for a base. (Ibid.)

ing from the conspicuous termination of the Geneva talks. Moreover, your departure at this point from Geneva might well encourage Makarios and the Greeks to take a more obstructionist stand. Your continued presence, on the other hand, could reinforce the general situation while both the Greeks and Turks are sorting out their final arrangements.[6]

In preparing the above suggestions we have obviously taken into account the Papandreou letter to Acheson (Athens 153 to Geneva)[7] which gives some encouragement to the course of action proposed.

I would greatly appreciate a reaction from all addressee posts regarding this proposal.[8]

Rusk

---

[6] In telegram 467 from Geneva, August 23, Acheson stated his readiness to stay as long as necessary to carry forward Ball's proposals. (Ibid.)

[7] Papandreou's letter was transmitted in telegram 381 from Athens (repeated to Geneva as 153), August 23. (Ibid.)

[8] In telegram 911 from London, August 24, Bruce registered his "deep misgivings" about Ball's proposals. (Ibid.)

---

145. Telegram From the Embassy in Greece to the Department of State[1]

Athens, August 24, 1964, 4 p.m.

388. 1. Before receiving Deptel 351,[2] I had informal talk last night with King Constantine, during which I reviewed sad state of affairs and stressed our grave disappointment and shock over inability of GOG to carry through on Acheson proposal. He told me he had talked with Garoufalias on his return from Cyprus and was satisfied that latter's report of situation on Cyprus was fair and objective. Makarios is extremely popular on island and his influence very great. King seemed convinced there would be serious public reaction, both in Cyprus and in Greece, if GOG sought to force Turkish base on Cypriots.

2. I asked whether Grivas could be stiffened by pressure from him and Greek army. He replied it was not question of trying persuade Gri-

---

[1] Source: Department of State, Central Files, POL 27 CYP. Secret; Immediate; Nodis–TAG. Repeated to Ankara, London, and Geneva for Acheson. Passed to the White House.

[2] Telegram 479 to Geneva (Document 144) was repeated to Athens as telegram 351.

vas to take tougher position versus Makarios, but rather, for reasons stated above, it was not in cards to overcome Makarios' influence just through force.

3. I spoke of Papandreou's letter to Acheson re a base.[3] The King thought Greek and Cypriot people could be brought to agree to one. However, he said questions he had asked me on Friday (Embtel 368)[4] were most pertinent. For example, he could not imagine granting Turkey base if mistreatment Istanbul Greeks continues. He also emphasized importance not forcing any population movements and continuation of normal traffic in base area. The King seemed to think smaller base on Karpas might be possible to sell on above conditions, but he was obviously not sure of himself.

Comment: The King appeared to be groping for something to save situation and was not thinking in terms of procedure or of how GOG could in fact go about arranging base. Although the young King is giving commendable attention to his country's Cyprus dilemma, there is no doubt his mind is somewhat diverted by prospect of his coming marriage.[5] Moreover, his ability to influence the action of his government is subject to severe, if not precisely defined, constitutional and practical limitations.

Labouisse

---

[3] See footnote 7, Document 144.

[4] See footnote 4, Document 137.

[5] King Constantine's marriage to Princess Anne Marie of Denmark was to take place September 18.

---

146.   Telegram From the Embassy in Greece to the Department of State[1]

Athens, August 25, 1964, 9:30 p.m.

405. Department may wish repeat to Nicosia. Embtel 399.[2]

1. Meeting with Papandreou took place at Kastri with his son, Andreas, and Dan Brewster present. Papandreou said Makarios coming

---

[1] Source: Department of State, Central Files, POL 27 CYP. Secret; Immediate; Exdis–TAG. Repeated to Ankara, London, and Geneva for Acheson. Passed to the White House, DOD, CIA, and USUN.

[2] Telegram 399 from Athens, August 25, reported that Papandreou had justified his press statement as a tactic needed to put himself in a position to deal forcefully with Makarios. (Ibid.)

at PriMin's invitation and that he would also see King before leaving this evening.

2. I then stated that I was finding it very hard to explain Greek policy on Cyprus to Washington. I referred to Papandreou's public statement last night regarding "complete accord" with Cyprus leadership, while at same time Kyprianou was saying there could be no base on the island[3] and Makarios telling Nicosia press Cyprus attitude on Soviet military aid remained unchanged. How did all this fit in with what PriMin had been telling me about his distaste for and differences with Makarios, etc.

3. Papandreou replied he was in death struggle with Makarios and had to make these tactical "moves." He referred to rest of his statement to effect there was no pressure and no agreed solution, adding there was surely no agreement in Geneva.

If he (Papandreou) had approval from us of his offer, then he could disagree with Makarios, hence, his statement that there is no agreed solution was accurate. He said he was in complete accord with Makarios in that Makarios is also claiming that he is for enosis following self-determination. Moreover, as long as there is a "spontaneous" Soviet offer to prevent Turkey from attacking Cyprus, he could not condemn Makarios for accepting this. I questioned whether the Soviet offer had been spontaneous in response to Makarios' appeals. I also recalled his statement to me of several days ago that, if Makarios should make an alliance with Soviets, there would be parting of ways.

4. Papandreou then reviewed briefly events of past weeks, saying Turkey threatened to attack and in fact had attacked the island, at which point allies did not stop it. Neither did Greece help nor could it help. With no one offering guarantees that Turkey would not attack, Papandreou's position was made extremely difficult vis-à-vis Makarios. He affirmed, however, that Greece would not change its foreign policy position, and if Makarios undertook any commitments to Soviets, he would withdraw Greek forces.

5. There was then some talk on what had been achieved at Geneva. According to PriMin, Sossides had asserted that Acheson (as late as last night) was greatly disappointed at fact Turks "who had originally accepted concept of leased-base had reverted to position of maintaining sovereign base was only solution." I corrected this misimpression, stating it was Acheson who had proposed leased base concept but that according our record, Turks had not as yet budged from their position that they required sovereign base area.

6. Andreas Papandreou then spoke of despicable manner in which press on Cyprus and in Athens were attacking Papandreou government

---

[3] Reported in telegram 398 from Athens, August 25. (Ibid.)

for even considering negotiated base. Papandreou's position on island was completely destroyed because Makarios was spreading word that Papandreou had betrayed Cypriot cause. PriMin then stated his tactics were to attempt to disarm Makarios.

7. Papandreou said he was going to talk to Makarios strongly and insist on following policy lines:

a) That there be no tie-ins with the Soviets or commitments made to them. He added he would make clear to Makarios that Greeks could not fight on side of USSR.
b) That there be peace on the island and no provocations.
c) That common aim would be enosis and not independence.

8. Papandreou asked that he be permitted to sum up his policy concerning Cyprus:

a) He preferred an agreed solution which would bring peace and lead to enosis and NATO-fication. That is why GOG participated in Geneva and Makarios did not.
b) Papandreou expected acceptable plan to be found at Geneva but this was not achieved.
c) Since bombings of Mansoura an agreement which would satisfy Turkish needs and be acceptable to Makarios and Cypriot people has become far more difficult to attain.
d) Although everyone on island is convinced there would be no base, he, Papandreou, took full responsibility for a base area size of British bases in his letter to Mr. Acheson (further proof that he differs with Makarios). He added unfortunately there has been no response to his proposal. He has been told that Turks are insisting on sovereignty of whatever base they might obtain and hence agreement impossible. He could not accept sovereign base. If Turks could accept his proposal he would be willing to struggle with Makarios.
e) Following "Geneva failure", he now faces situation without basis of Geneva talks. He would be more than delighted if coup d'etat for unconditional enosis would be achieved in which case Makarios would be his captive. Acheson has been informed of this and although Papandreou had no hopes that this could be accepted, it would be desirable. He was willing to eliminate Makarios.

9. He repeated again that he planned to stress with Makarios that there be no aggressive action on part of GOC and no provocations. GOG wishes wash its hands of responsibility in this area. Problem would then go to UNGA. If Turks attack because Geneva has failed, GOG will fight on side of Cyprus "but under flag of enosis and not of independence." As to Soviets, he emphasized he would demand that Makarios make no commitments.

He repeated that if he were to make any commitments, Greek army will leave Cyprus.

10. I stressed great importance of Papandreou making clear to Makarios today that, despite his statement of accord, Greeks would not

put up with further Makarios brinksmanship. I specified various areas which must be covered, including cooperation with UN on island, cessation of Greek-Cypriot attacks, discontinuance of economic blockades, permission for rotation Turk contingent. Papandreou said these were "details", but it very nearly got Greece into a war. I noted that frequently it was not general understanding but "details" which caused wars, and added that Makarios was trifling with peace in his tactics. If by a provocation the communities on Cyprus were to fight each other it would be Makarios' fault, yet because of PriMin's public statements of identity of views, he was permitting Makarios to determine Greek foreign policy and possibly, to involve Greece in war.

Papandreou agreed that Makarios trifling with peace, but asked what more could he do? He asserted that he could not make public statement against Makarios now. I replied that he could at least make it crystal clear to Makarios that he would have to go it alone if he did not conform to Greek wishes. Papandreou said he would make strong statement to Makarios against provocations.

12. Papandreou said he realized what a problem he had with Makarios and that he proposed to enhance Greek military forces on island to ensure pacification of island and to do whatever he could to enhance GOG influence on Cypriot press and public opinion. I said that something along these lines made sense to me, but that if he had in mind sending planes to Cyprus, this was something else again. This would not only be provocation to Turks, but would run counter to UN resolution. Papandreou's spontaneous reaction was "you want Greece to control island and yet you don't want airplanes delivered. If GOG does not send them, Makarios will say he will get them other places."

13. Meeting concluded with Prime Minister repeating that he was in death struggle with Makarios and that he hoped I would give him time to work things out with Makarios today and report to Washington after events of this afternoon.

14. In parting, I raised question of municipal elections, expressing view that if Athens found itself with an EDA Mayor in a fortnight, this would be very bad for Greek image. Papandreou stated that I could be assured there would be no Communist Mayor of Athens.

Comment: Main purpose of my call was to stiffen him up against Makarios and to let him know I was genuinely unhappy with his public stance. He appeared to us to be in trouble. Whether his tactics will work with the wily Archbishop remains to be seen.

Labouisse

147.   Telegram From the Mission in Geneva to the Department of State[1]

Geneva, August 26, 1964, noon.

482. For Ball from Acheson. Reference: Athens' 407 and 408 to Department.[2] I see nothing in King's statements to Labouisse or his message to President which warrants any optimism. Having balked at leased base in own name, Turks certainly will treat with contempt proposal that they have NATO base instead. Lease of base on Castellorizon will not make any difference. "Full guarantees" for Turkish minority on Cyprus is old story. Although I think Turks would probably settle for my revised minority proposals, they have never flatly said so and in any case sovereignty and size and location of base are key questions.

Fact that settlement on basis King's proposal would be Greek national solution and would involve negotiation rather than coup d'etat is undoubtedly important from Greek point of view but, I should say, totally irrelevant from viewpoint of GOT.

I would therefore reiterate my advice against giving USG agreement to instant enosis without prior agreement with Turks.[3]

Re Deptel 492 to Geneva,[4] I accept changes proposed in my letter to Papandreou but would like third sentence of your new third paragraph to read as follows: "However, as you know, the Government of Turkey is finding as much difficulty in accepting these proposals as you are, although it has not, as I understand it, finally rejected them." As implied by my comments above, I think there is no advantage in holding up delivery of letter (as instructed Deptel 364 to Athens).[5]

In mentioning "period of silence on our part", do you have in mind that Jernegan and I should simply sit in Geneva awaiting developments or that we should come home for consultation, thus emphasizing "shock treatment"?

Tubby

---

[1] Source: Department of State, Central Files, POL 27 CYP. Secret; Immediate; Nodis–TAG. Received at 9:22 a.m. and repeated to Ankara, Athens, and London. Passed to the White House.

[2] See footnote 2, Document 148.

[3] In telegram 503 to Geneva, August 26, Ball responded: "You can be assured that I have no intention of giving USG agreement to instant enosis without prior agreement with Turks. We are definitely off that ticket." (Department of State, Central Files, POL 27 CYP)

[4] In telegram 492, August 25, Ball explained that he wanted to allow both governments, but especially Papandreou, to ruminate over the proposals they had rejected and suggested changes to a proposed letter from Acheson. (Ibid.)

[5] Telegram 364 to Athens, August 25, instructed Labouisse to hold up delivery of Acheson's letter. (Ibid.)

148.   Telegram From the Embassy in Greece to the Department of State[1]

Athens, August 26, 1964, 3 p.m.

411. DCM called on Costopoulos in effort obtain [garble] considerations lying behind King's letter to President Johnson (Embtel 407).[2] Costopoulos said GOG would be prepared to assume obligation of negotiating NATO base after enosis. In fact, there could probably be two bases, one on Karpas Peninsula of about 50 square miles and one in Cape Greco area of about 50 square miles, totalling approximately area existing British bases. He referred also to base on Kastellorizon. Papandreou probably prepared make this undertaking in writing. Costopoulos made it quite clear he had little confidence in Makarios' sincerity.

DCM commented information regarding location and dimensions of bases indispensable to permit USG evaluate King's proposal and that a written undertaking on the part of Papandreou to this effect would be essential to add element of reality to situation.

Next step would be to request Grivas come to Athens, possibly tomorrow, to obtain his concurrence, at least in principle. Costopoulos implied question of precise area and location of NATO base, or bases, might not be specifically discussed with Makarios or Grivas. This aspect of solution would be undertaken only by GOG as an obligation to be discharged after enosis. GOG would, however, say publicly at time enosis proposed and Greek and Cypriot Parliaments convoked, that GOG would be prepared grant NATO base and that Makarios had concurred.

Costopoulos confided to DCM on "top secret" basis, that Kyprianou and Georkadjis had agreed to support a GOG push for enosis when the appropriate circumstances have been created. This apparently included agreement to principle of NATO base and willingness denounce Makarios in event his defection. Meanwhile some additional 500 military, "not fighters, mostly technicians" (sic), were being sent to Cyprus and other unspecified measures being taken strengthen GOG position there.

DCM pushed Costopoulos hard regarding current status of Cypriot/Soviet negotiations. Costopoulos was very vague, but after further interrogation said one of principal reasons for Makarios' visit to Cairo

[1] Source: Department of State, Central Files, POL 27 CYP. Secret; Flash; Nodis–TAG. Received at 11:07 a.m. and repeated to Ankara, London, Geneva for Acheson, and Nicosia. Passed to the White House.

[2] Telegram 407 from Athens, August 26, reported that the King had won Makarios' agreement to the creation of a NATO base on Cyprus following enosis, and government and opposition agreement in Greece for the lease of a base on Kastellorizon to Turkey. (Ibid.) The text of the King's message to President Johnson was transmitted in telegram 408 from Athens, August 26. (Ibid.)

tomorrow is to make arrangements for basing of "the 15 planes" which Makarios is endeavoring to have delivered as soon as possible. Although Costopoulos declined to be precise, DCM came away with impression planes presumably of Soviet origin might be available within next week or so, and that they would be piloted ostensibly by Cypriots but actually by Greek civilians. (*Comment*: Garoufalias once argued that use Greek civilian pilots would provide GOG with best possible control if Makarios insisted planes be made available to GOG.)

Comment: Costopoulos explanation leaves much to be desired, and DCM tells me FonMin obviously did not appear prepared to talk of matter in any detail. I have asked to see PriMin. If GOG prepared screw up its courage, give us assurances in writing along lines King's proposal but with more detail, and force issue with Makarios, King's proposal probably worth serious consideration by GOT, UK and USG. GOG (assuming Grivas backing) may have in mind possibility using alleged Makarios "commitment" as justification for public break with him.

Labouisse

---

149. Telegram From the Embassy in Greece to the Department of State[1]

Athens, August 27, 1964, 10 p.m.

435. Deptel 378.[2]

1. While hesitating further to delay delivery of President's message to King, I feel that President Johnson should be aware that I continue to entertain the gravest doubts about the wisdom of his proposing that Greeks now make concessions beyond those suggested by Acheson. The following expansion of reasons set forth in Embtel 424[3] deserves most serious consideration:

A. In involving himself in a successful effort to push Makarios further than Papandreou had been able on the question of a base, the King

---

[1] Source: Department of State, Central Files, POL 27 CYP. Secret; Flash; Exdis–TAG. Repeated to Geneva for Acheson, Ankara, London, and the White House. Passed to DOD and CIA.

[2] Telegram 378 to Athens, August 27, contained the revisions to the text of a letter to King Constantine. (Ibid.) The original text of the letter was transmitted in telegram 366 to Athens, August 26. (Ibid.)

[3] Telegram 424 from Athens, August 27, outlined suggested changes to the Presidential message. (Ibid.)

also involved himself in a delicate constitutional issue. You will appreciate that the govt has seemed reluctant to discuss his proposal with us and may be sitting back to see what results will flow from the King's "meddling." The King will be plunged into profound embarrassment vis-à-vis the govt if one of his first real efforts in diplomacy results in his getting a tougher line from the President than the US has so far put to the govt. This will considerably damage the King's prestige (which Papandreou may well wish to do) and make him less willing in the future to try to be helpful.

B. The rap on the King's knuckles is exaggerated by the inconsistency between what the President now would be proposing and Acheson's characterization of his less demanding proposals as "fair" (his letter of August 20)[4] and as "equitable, realistic and reasonable arrangements" (his letter of August 26).[5] Moreover, Acheson has told the GOG that the Turks have not finally rejected his proposals.

C. If it is to be our policy to push the Greeks for concessions beyond those which Mr. Acheson was proposing, this policy, it seems to me, should be put first to the govt rather than the King.

D. I strongly recommend that if the President wants to include the paragraph in question, it be rephrased to read as follows:

"After all, that part of the Karpas Peninsula which Mr. Acheson proposed for a Turkish base is only a little more than 5 percent of the area of Cyprus. This would not appear in any serious way to derogate from the great benefits that would flow to the Greek peoples from the accession of Cyprus to the territory of the Hellenese." (This re-phrasing eliminates the reference to a larger area than was proposed by Acheson and the reference to the granting of the area in perpetuity to the Turkish Government.)[6]

Labouisse

---

[4] See Document 134.

[5] The Acheson letter of August 26 was transmitted to the Department of State as an attachment to airgram A–166 from Athens, August 29. (Department of State, Central Files, POL 27 CYP)

[6] In telegram 385 to Athens, August 27, the Department of State approved further modifications in the President's letter to King Constantine. (Ibid.) In telegram 449 from Athens, August 28, Labouisse reported that he had delivered the message. A copy of the letter is ibid., Ball Papers: Lot 74 D 272, Cyprus–Miscellaneous.

150.   Summary Notes of the 542d Meeting of the National Security Council[1]

Washington, September 1, 1964, 12:45–1:15 p.m.

Global Briefing–Cyprus

[Here follows McCone's briefing.]

Under Secretary Ball: With respect to Cyprus, the Geneva phase of the negotiations is over. Two months have been spent in narrowing the gap between the Greeks and the Turks and defining their differences. There are two reasons for the failure of the Acheson talks at Geneva:

1. The weakness of the Greek Government which was unwilling to move in and take over in Cyprus, and
2. The Turks' insistence on having a sovereign base on the island, which in effect, meant partition. The Greeks insisted on leasing an area to the Turks; hence, Enosis.

We should not despair of a Greek reply to President Johnson's letter[2] which may indicate the Greeks are prepared to give way, thus permitting continuation of bargaining.

The UN Secretary General's press conference was not helpful in that he said that the Cyprus Government had to be a party to any deal between Greece and Turkey.

There are two timebombs in the situation:

1. The rotation of Turkish troops on the island which will take place within the next few days.
2. The cessation of the rights of 10,000 Greeks living in Turkey, which will undoubtedly cause trouble.

A Tamaya report on Cyprus is impartial and gives a true picture of the situation. It cites the heavy pressure of Greek Cypriots on the Turkish Cypriots.

[Here follows Secretary Rusk's briefing.]

Bromley Smith

---

[1] Source: Johnson Library, National Security File, NSC Meetings File, Vol. 3. Top Secret/Sensitive; For the President Only. Drafted by Smith.

[2] King Constantine's September 3 reply to the President's August 28 message stated that Greece could not accept the Acheson proposals. (Ibid., Country File, Greece, Presidential Correspondence)

151.   Telegram From the Embassy in Greece to the Department of State[1]

Athens, September 2, 1964, 8:30 p.m.

471. Costopoulos told me at lunch he had just come from small Cabinet meeting which considered report made by Garoufalias following his return early this morning from overnight visit to Nicosia.

Costopoulos said (presumably on basis Garoufalias' report) that:

A. Makarios had not succeeded in obtaining UAR airfield facilities.

B. Nasser had promised provide certain unspecified type war materials, presumably obsolescent British equipment for most part.

C. Makarios insists Kyprianou visit Moscow shortly. Costopoulos interpreted this as indication Soviets proving somewhat shy in discussion with Cypriots. GOG has no specific information regarding negotiations with Soviets including question of planes.

D. Kyprianou coming to Athens tomorrow and may request see me. Costopoulos asserted Makarios had suggested calling on me at time his most recent visit here in order assure USG that he (Makarios) has no desire or intention fall into hands of Soviets.

E. Costopoulos said he thought Soviet motor torpedo boats had been delivered to Cypriots and that Greeks providing at least some elements of crews. He was not precise.

F. Makarios agreed to rotation Turk contingent (Embtel 470)[2] provided this done under supervision UNFICYP in order insure departing Turks genuinely soldiers (not non-combatant peasants) and that replacements not all officers.

I reviewed for Costopoulos our analysis of Turk legal position with regard right rotate its contingent, fact London/Zurich Accords could be changed only by mutual agreement (Deptel 400)[3] as well as our position on use MAP equipment (Deptel 403).[4] Costopoulos seemed well aware of US positions.

I also pointed out introduction military equipment into Cyprus from any source might produce violent Turk reaction and that USG would be constrained raise such action in Security Council as violation

---

[1] Source: Department of State, Central Files, POL 27 CYP. Secret; Immediate; Exdis–TAG. Repeated to Ankara, London, Nicosia, and USUN. Passed to the White House, DOD, and CIA.

[2] Telegram 470, September 2, reported on Greek efforts to disengage from Makarios. (Ibid.)

[3] Telegram 400 to Athens, August 30, outlined the legal basis for Turkey's right to a troop rotation. (Ibid.)

[4] Dated August 31. (Ibid.)

UN resolutions. Costopoulos accepted this statement with a faintly ironical smile, noting that this position was at variation with the personal advice Nikolareizis received from Acheson.

We had inconclusive discussion with regard to what likely occur in event Cyprus problem raised at UNGA as well as some discussion of status Greek citizens in Istanbul after September 16. Costopoulos mentioned GOG has discussed Istanbul situation with UN SYG with view to raising question in Security Council in near future.

I endeavored obtain from Costopoulos statement of how GOG sees evolution of Cyprus problem. Costopoulos answered it is important that new Mediator be appointed, that conditions for negotiations be restored and that tranquility be maintained on island. This would decrease tension and passion which in turn would enhance capability GOG gain acceptance on Cyprus of solution negotiated with Turks, provided Turks proved reasonable.

When pressed as to outlines of possible negotiated solution, Costopoulos pointedly referred to an article on Cyprus in August 27 issue of foreign report published by *Economist*. Without accepting responsibility for formula set forth in this article, he said that solution along these lines (with the exception of the removal of the Patriarchate from Istanbul) could be contemplated by GOG.

Plan set forth in *Economist* foreign report provides for enosis with protection of Turkish minority. Turkey would receive large scale economic development assistance, removal of Patriarchate to Mount Athos or Patmos, establishment of NATO base possibly on one of present British bases with Turk participation, transfer of Kastellorizon to Turkey and rectification of boundary between Greek and Turkish Thrace so that the railway line from Istanbul to Idirne would fall entirely within Turkish territory. I noted that aside from fact Turks unlikely to accept this proposal, interesting to note implied provisions that US would pick up substantial part of bill for Turkish economic development plan, and that British would provide military base. Costopoulos acknowledged I had not failed grasp essential elements this formula.

Costopoulos, in his indefatigable effort assure an appropriate future for Makarios today noted that Patriarchate of Alexandria likely to become vacant shortly. Although we both appreciated poetic aspect of this solution, neither Costopoulos nor I evidenced any optimism that Makarios would be irresistibly attracted by this opportunity.

Labouisse

152.   Telegram From the Department of State to the Embassy in Greece[1]

Washington, September 3, 1964, 8:37 p.m.

432. While we are continuing to seek a permanent solution of the Cyprus problem we have been giving further study as to how we can:

a. prevent deterioration in the relations between Greece and Turkey that may lead to a dangerous explosion;
b. create a climate in which we can prosecute a productive search for a permanent settlement; and
c. widen the scope of negotiations in order to get the discussion off dead center.

The first order of urgency is to bring about the relaxation of tensions on the Island and restore a more stable—if still uneasy—relation between the two communities.

The second is to prevent the Turks, Greeks, or Cypriots from setting in train a chain reaction of retaliation and counter-retaliation.

With these objectives in mind we are considering the floating of a possible arrangement between the GOT and GOG, aimed at a wide range of Greek-Turkish issues. Each side would explicitly recognize this arrangement as an effort to prepare the conditions in which a final settlement may be possible. Each side would agree to continue to search for such a settlement urgently and in good faith.

There would be several advantages to such an arrangement if it could be negotiated. If both sides complied, it could reduce the probability of an explosion. If the arrangement broke down because one side or the other proved unwilling or unable to carry out its share of the commitments, we would at least have isolated responsibility and made it easier to handle a major row in the Security Council.

Assumptions

The assumptions upon which we are suggesting the general lines of an arrangement are the following:

a. The GOG has sufficient military force under its control on the Island to enable it to assure that the peace is kept—if it has the will to do so. There are in the neighborhood of 10,000 Greek troops on the Island and in addition the 30,000 Greek Cypriot National Guard has been placed under the command of Greek officers.

---

[1] Source: Department of State, Central Files, POL 27 CYP. Secret; Immediate; Limdis. Drafted and approved by Ball and cleared by Jernegan. Also sent to Ankara, Paris for USRO, Nicosia, and London to deliver to Acheson at breakfast. Acheson left Geneva on September 2, stopped in London September 2–4, and returned to Washington on September 4.

b. The GOG would genuinely like to narrow the engagement of its own military forces in relation to the Cyprus problem. At the same time it would like assurance that the GOT will not intervene capriciously. (Support for this assumption implied in Costopoulos' suggestion to Labouisse, reported in Athens 470 [471] to Department.)[2]

c. The GOT would like to avoid the creation of a situation in which it feels compelled to intervene with military force. It would, therefore, welcome an arrangement that contributed to the quieting down of the Island and the improvement of the welfare and safety of the Turk-Cypriot population.

Main Lines of Arrangement

Commitments by GOG:

1. The GOG would use its best efforts to assure that the GOC did not interfere with the rights reserved to the GOT by the Treaties of Guarantee, Alliance and Establishment, including the right of the GOG [GOT] to rotate its garrison.

2. The GOG would undertake to assist the restoration of more normal conditions on the Island. It would use its best efforts to prevent the GOC from interfering with aid to Turk-Cypriots from outside organizations and agencies. It would assist in the rehabilitation and resettlement of Turk-Cypriot refugees. It would endeavor to end the economic blockade, etc.

3. The GOG would undertake not to provide military support to the GOC against Turkish action, except in case of an unprovoked attack by Turkey.

4. The GOG would undertake to prevent the GOC from seeking or obtaining military equipment or personnel or any other form of military assistance, from any nation not a party to the London–Zurich Agreements.

5. The GOG would refrain from any acts of discrimination or harassment against Turkish nationals living in Greek territory, including Western Thrace.

Commitments by Turkey:

1. The GOT would extend for at least an additional six months the special privileges granted to Greek nationals under the 1930 Treaty of Establishment, Commerce, and Navigation[3] and would undertake not to engage in any acts of discrimination or harassment against Greek nationals living in Turkey.

---

[2] Document 151.
[3] For text, see 124 LTS 371.

302 Foreign Relations, 1964–1968, Volume XVI

2. The GOT would undertake not to exercise its rights of military intervention under Article 4 of the Treaty of Guarantee unless the GOC were acting in such a manner as (a) to deprive the GOT of substantial rights accorded it under the London–Zurich arrangements or (b) to endanger the lives or welfare of the Turk-Cypriot population.

3. The GOT would use its best efforts to prevent the Turkish Cypriots from engaging in any provocatory acts.

4. The GOT would avoid any provocation against the Government of Greece, including interference with fishing rights, etc.

Method of Procedure

Obviously the points included above are merely suggestive of the general scope of an arrangement. Each point would necessarily have to be articulated and expanded through negotiation. Some points might have to be excluded and additional points added.

The development of such an arrangement could be approached through several possible ways. We might ask Brosio to undertake this through NATO channels since what is contemplated is an arrangement between two NATO members. Alternatively we might undertake the negotiation by asking the GOC and GOT to send representatives to meet with Mr. Acheson in Washington—or possibly Rome. Or we might have Embassy Athens first put the proposition to the GOG and—if that yielded promising results—have Hare follow through in Ankara.

In any event we are faced with a tight time schedule since several prospective actions are scheduled for the middle of the month. The termination of the special privileges accorded Greek nationals under the Treaty of Establishment will take place on September 17. The Security Council discussion of the extension of the UN Peacekeeping Force is scheduled for the second week in September. At the same time the Turkish Government has indicated that it may wish a Security Council review of the economic blockade.

Each of these actions may contribute to a deterioration in Greek-Turkish relations. Taken together their cumulative effect could be serious.

We would appreciate your prompt reactions to these very preliminary suggestions. We shall look forward to reviewing them with Mr. Acheson upon his return to Washington.[4]

Rusk

---

[4] In telegram 475 from Ankara, September 5, Hare commented that the suggested proposals would help get through a difficult situation "while a permanent solution being sought," and offered some specific revisions. (Department of State, Central Files, POL 27 CYP)

153.   **Telegram From the Embassy in Greece to the Department of State**[1]

Athens, September 4, 1964, 3 p.m.

483. King Constantine asked me to see him Thursday afternoon. He handed me a letter to President Johnson, text of which being sent in immediately following telegram.[2] We then talked for more than an hour about the Cyprus situation.

The King expressed his great sorrow and disappointment that the President has not found it possible to support lines suggested in the King's message of August 25[3] as they had seemed to him only way out of the mess. He supposed, however, there was nothing President could do under circumstances. King said that even though Makarios has since come out against any base on Cyprus, he felt he could still hold him to his word re NATO base.

King asked how it would be possible to "trap Makarios", whom he branded as an impossible scoundrel. I replied that it seemed to me largely matter for GOG to find some means of controlling him, pointing out that part of trouble resulted from Papandreou's public support of Makarios to such an extent that his government had gradually worked itself into Makarios' pocket. I said it essential that calm be restored and harassments stopped, going into such points as rotation Turkish contingent, blockade, full support of UN. The King agreed and said he thought his government was doing all possible now on this score. I suggested there was much GOG could yet do without increasing Greek forces in Cyprus, and went over Acheson's suggestions to Sossides as well as points made by Belcher in Nicosia's 304 to Athens,[4] adding that I personally could get no sense that there was yet a line of command on Greek side. The King carefully listened to these comments and I believe took them to heart and will use his influence with government.

The King then reverted to matter of finding a solution, asking what could possibly be done. I said here again that much depended on ability and courage of government to take things in hand. He did not disagree, but reacted as do all Greeks by saying there are definite limits to Greece's ability to persuade Cypriots. He was afraid the USG did not comprehend

---

[1] Source: Department of State, Central Files, POL 27 CYP. Secret; Priority; Exdis. Repeated to London and Ankara.

[2] Telegram 484 from Athens, September 4. The letter requested deferral of any further initiatives to secure settlement in order to alleviate tensions. (Ibid.)

[3] See footnote 2, Document 148.

[4] Telegram 304 from Nicosia to Athens, September 2, suggested actions that would increase Greek control over the Cypriot Government. (Department of State, Central Files, POL 27 CYP)

this point nor the fact that Turkey had no justification for having separate position on island provided rights of minorities protected. I again went over arguments in Deptel 400[5] (which, incidentally, we have been using for some time in our conversations here but which usually fall on deaf ears), concluding that if Makarios continued his insistence on no compromises it seemed to me Greece faced a dismal outlook.

The conversation was friendly and intimate. At one time the King asked smilingly whether I wanted him to get rid of Papandreou. In same vein I asked whether he could if he wanted to. He replied he could not do so now.

He is deeply and genuinely troubled about Cypriot situation which is also having its serious and alarming repercussions in the country, economically, politically and psychologically. He would like very much to find a way to "trap Makarios" but he appears convinced that Turkish threats and air action have served to strengthen Makarios' position.

In my talk with the King, as with the PriMin, FonMin, Deputy PriMin, and with other Greek leaders, I have been following the line that, whereas we are still most interested in helping to find way out, their responsibility for doing so rests largely with the Greek Government. I believe that psychologically this, plus the general deterioration mentioned in preceding paragraph, is beginning to have an effect. However, I have grave doubts that the Greeks will ever be able to change the attitude of the Cypriot people sufficiently to meet the demands of the Turks.

Labouisse

_____

[5] See footnote 3, Document 151.

_____

154.   Telegram From the Embassy in Cyprus to the Department of State[1]

Nicosia, September 4, 1964, 7:30 p.m.

448. We had just completed drafting following telegram when we received Deptel 240.[2] Believe that it, if taken with Embtel 431[3] (Notal) provides lines of action which are complementary to those proposed in 240.

_____

[1] Source: Department of State, Central Files, POL 27 CYP. Secret; Immediate; Exdis. Repeated to Ankara, Athens, London, USUN, and Paris for USRO. Passed to the White House, DOD, and CIA.

[2] Telegram 432 to Athens (Document 152) was repeated to Nicosia as telegram 240.

[3] Telegram 431 from Nicosia, September 2, noted concern regarding the declining influence of the Greek Government over Makarios and suggested means by which Greece could improve its leverage. (Department of State, Central Files, POL 27 CYP)

Suspension of Geneva negotiations and GOG–GOC communiqué announcing agreement of two governments to take Cyprus problem to UNGA has led us to explore among ourselves ways and means whereby lid could be kept on situation here while at same time doing something to impede present rapid drift to left. We still believe that some variety of "instant enosis" before UNGA along lines proposed Embtel 174[4] and 345[5] would be course of action most in US interest. However if, as it appears from here, Turkish agreement to "instant enosis" cannot be obtained on terms which would assure successful operation, we think that determined effort by USG of sort we are proposing could be valid second-best policy. This policy would have as its objectives keeping the peace on island, preventing Communist domination and producing for the post UNGA period a more rational and internationally responsible attitude on part of Cyprus leadership. Presumably enosis would still be our ultimate solution to Cyprus problem but none of our proposed lines of action would appear to stand in way of that goal.

Keep the peace. Basic assumption upon which whole policy is based is, of course, that Turks do not invade Cyprus during this period. This means that on island provocations to them are held to a minimum. At moment, as USUN's 589 to Dept[6] expressed very well, two most inflammatory issues are troop rotation and economic blockade. These show some chance of being alleviated or fuzzed over but there will be other difficulties which will immediately arise. We foresee no basic change prior UNGA in present impasse which manifests itself in virtual absence intercommunal area travel, continuing Greek Cypriot pressure aimed at stimulating defection among Turks to end de facto separate entity, lack of all direct official Cypriot Greek/Turk contact and steady deterioration Turkish Cypriot living conditions.

On food and living condition for Turks we can see no new or imaginative alternative to unremitting and coordinated pressure on GOC at all levels by USG through Embassy here, UNSYG through his representative on island and other interested governments. All of us are engaged in this now but are seeking ways improve coordination. (Galo Plaza's modest successes in raising blockade indicate that he should be kept on if at all possible.) We would also try direct world press attention more sharply at pressures on Turks. At same time, we would continue (as now in our weekly luncheon meetings with leaders) to try to prevent Turkish Cypriots from creating their own provocations by over-exaggerating their plight.

On military side of keeping the peace, believe that continued UNFI-CYP presence with hopefully wider or at least more discretionary pow-

[4] Dated August 5. (Ibid., POL 23–8 CYP)
[5] Dated August 19. (Ibid, POL 27 CYP)
[6] Dated September 1. (Ibid.)

ers remains important. However, determining factor will be degree of restraint GOG can exert through its forces here and through Grivas. We have made proposals in Embtel 431 (Notal) for strengthening GOG hand in Cyprus and would hope that these could be pursued actively.

Political action in Cyprus. The West still retains certain basic assets in its competition with Communist forces for Cyprus. These are: ideological affinity of Greek Cypriot people with the West growing out of their age-old yearning to return to Mother Greece, a Western country; fear of a Communist take-over on part of business, educated, and professional groups who, while they lack political strength, have some if dwindling influence; presence substantial number Greek troops, loyal, well-disciplined and anti-Communist, Greek Cypriot National Guard as yet not extensively penetrated by Communists; several Ministers and General Grivas who are anti-Communist and oppose Makarios' policy on this subject. In addition, USG has worked with non-Communist nationalist Greek Cypriot organizations in fields of labor, youth, veterans affairs, farmer unions and certain newspapers.

Unfortunately, due sharp anti-US hysteria which prevails in Cyprus today because of what Greek Cypriots believe to be US pro-Turk policy we are precluded from taking full advantage of contacts in anti-Communist forces listed above. There are two possibilities which occur to us to get out of box we are in:

(1) [less than 1 line of source text not declassified] seek take advantage of contacts with certain carefully selected key figures on only grounds possible under present circumstances, namely by privately indicating that USG fully supports concept of enosis with NATO base and is working covertly now and will be openly later to bring this about, and

(2) Assess and support anti-Communist programs through Greek Embassy (perhaps using Greek Embassy Political Counselor proposed Embtel 431 Notal).

Number one has serious risks in our opinion since it could lead to leaks with bad Turkish reaction thereto and increased pressure for overt commitment to enosis. Therefore after consideration we strongly prefer number two.

Meanwhile as far as possible we would try to establish appearance of business as usual. Fulbright and other student exchange programs would be carried forward as if there were no question that Cyprus was going to emerge on Western side from present difficulties, trade promotion activities and contacts in economic community would be pursued with same principle in mind, our aid program would be continued along lines set forth Embtel Toaid 45.[7]

Other random suggestions are that:

---

[7] Not found.

(a) Greek language VOA broadcasts should be increased in number of hours. We have noted that Greek Cypriots are indefatigable radio listeners and great comparers of news broadcasts.

(b) Greek American associations could be utilized as means keeping some American lines open into Greek Cypriot community. Aside from limited objective of Embtel 443[8] Notal believe real effort in "people to people" type program would pay dividends; scholarships to village boys to American farm school at Thessaloniki; direct contact with moribund Cyprus American Academic Assn as an agent on island; support of sports clubs along lines one-shot deal arranged through Eugene Rossides; community to community program; visits here by prominent Greek Americans traveling in Greece or general area, etc, etc.

In interim before UNGA, image of US as pro-Turk would tend to grow due to Greek Cypriot propaganda campaign and open Soviet support of GOC position. There is little we can do except attempt to present impression of strength, calm and faith in eventual mutually satisfactory Cyprus solution; here on island we will avoid air of impatience in such official contacts as remain since this is inevitably taken as sign of exasperation at "failure" of Geneva talks and "frenzy" to achieve "NATO" settlement prior to UNGA.

Additionally I would hope be able establish more meaningful relationship with President than has been possible in recent months about which we will submit further comments septel.

Most difficult to handle big problem remains that of Soviet penetration and, of that problem, most dangerous aspect is Makarios tendency to try to play US off against Soviet Union (Embtel 441[9] provides very good example of how GOC naively thinks it can do this). We know Soviet game here is receiving close attention from Dept so will only suggest that somehow US should put Soviet themselves on notice through diplomatic channels that Cyprus is in Western sphere of influence and that further Soviet penetration into this area will not be tolerated.

Belcher

---

[8] Telegram 443 from Nicosia, September 4, suggested a U.S.-Greek effort to dissuade Makarios from sending Kyprianou to Moscow. (Department of State, Central Files, POL 27 CYP)

[9] Telegram 441 from Nicosia, September 3, reported on Belcher's presentation to Kyprianou on the issue of the Moscow trip. (Ibid.)

155.   Memorandum for the Record[1]

Washington, September 8, 1964.

The principal subject for discussion at the President's luncheon today was Cyprus. Those present with the President were: Secretary Rusk, Secretary McNamara, Under Secretary Ball, Mr. Dean Acheson,[2] and myself.

Acheson and Ball revealed their agreement on the conviction that the only solution now would be a fait accompli in which the Turks would move to occupy the Karpas peninsula, triggering an instant enosis under Greek leadership, with a consequent supercession of Makarios. Acheson in particular emphasized that no negotiated solution was possible because of the weakness of Papandreou and the strength and intractability of Makarios. On the other hand, a program of indefinite delay could only strengthen the hand of Makarios and increase the danger that an eventual Turkish explosion would be both violent and undirected.

A number of questions were raised by the President. What would happen to the Turks on the island? Mr. Ball answered that he would expect most of them to stay and that, with luck, bloodshed would be limited. The President asked whether the Greeks would follow this scenario and whether they could control the Greek Cypriots. Ball and Acheson pointed out that there already exists between Athens and Nicosia agreement to move to instant enosis if the Turks move against the island. They expected that this agreement would probably be carried out.

The Secretary of State asked whether Makarios would appeal to Moscow instead of to Athens. Mr. Ball thought he would not, and he said the appeal would not be answered in any serious way. I asked what would trigger the Turkish action, and Acheson answered that nearly anything would serve. The most immediate possibility was the refusal of troop rotation.

The President summarized by saying that Mr. Acheson's argument appeared to be that we must expect a resort to action in one way or another, and that the choice was whether it should be messy and destructive or controlled and eventually productive, in accordance with a plan. Mr. Acheson agreed with this definition of the problem. He indicated that in his discussions with a Turkish military leader the Turks had shown that there was a great Turkish interest in such a plan and that the Turks would do their best to execute it with a minimum use of American

---

[1] Source: Johnson Library, National Security File, Memos to the President—McGeorge Bundy, Vol. 6. Secret. Drafted by Bundy.

[2] Acheson returned to the United States on September 4.

weapons and a minimum resort to those kinds of force—like air bombing—which were internationally unpopular.

Mr. Ball pointed out that it would be impossible to warn the Greeks of any planned Turkish action because of the danger of leaks to Nicosia. He also noted that the British would be troubled about this plan because of the status of Cyprus as a Commonwealth state. Mr. Acheson remarked that this might be true for Butler, but that Mountbatten would be friendly and that the British bases would be protected under this plan.

The President indicated his own doubt that the plan as put forward could in fact be neatly and tightly controlled, without risk of escalation. He thought that in particular the Greeks would be very likely to move with all their strength on the island against a Turkish lodgment, and he asked McNamara for a careful Joint Staff study of the problem. The President also noted that the next two months were not a good season for another war, and the question was raised whether it was essential to press along this road before November.[3] No definite answer was given, and it was agreed that Mr. Ball would prepare a more detailed staff study of the entire plan, to include both its military and political elements.

McG. B.[4]

---

[3] On September 11 at 10:45 a.m., Bundy telephoned Ball to discuss the meeting with the President: "Bundy wanted to know if he and Ball had the same sense of the President's feelings about it. Bundy said he got the impression that Acheson thought the President wanted to make sure nothing happens. Bundy did not read it this way. Ball did not either. Bundy read it, 'Don't make something happen out of your own energies.' Bundy thinks we need to be ready in case something does get hot. Ball agreed. Ball thought something might happen in connection with the mercy mission to Cyprus on Tuesday. Ball plans to go over this with Hare this morning. Hare has to be able to go back to Inonu and say that if you are bent on retaliation 'this is the way to do it'." (Johnson Library, Ball Papers, Telephone Conversations, Cyprus)

[4] Printed from a copy that bears these typed initials.

DISCUSSIONS ON CYPRUS, SEPTEMBER 1964–JUNE 1965

156. Telegram From the Embassy in Turkey to the Department of State[1]

Ankara, September 8, 1964, 6 p.m.

485. During past few days, Turkish political developments appear headed toward two brinks simultaneously: severe attack against Inonu and pressure for national coalition; and resurfacing xenophobia expressed in desire reorient Turkish foreign policy, including Turkish withdrawal from NATO.

To dump Inonu at this time is serious and could even be dangerous, but to go toward neutralism has even more serious implications. This double trend was almost inevitable outcome internal pressures and general mounting dissatisfaction as Cyprus situation continued degenerate and efforts promote solution failed materialize. Dissatisfaction appears fanning out two directions mentioned above. Interesting note dissatisfaction with Inonu almost stronger in RPP than in opposition. Latent world-wide dissatisfaction which chafes against foreign presence everywhere important factor second development. While xenophobia centering on U.S. presence and alliance, it is also being focused on NATO.

While these developments approaching respective brinks, maneuverability Inonu govt on both foreign and domestic issues is close to zero. Striking example is present strong Turkish opposition to enosis in any form expressed by PriMin's statement, "Declaration of enosis means war,"[2] banner headlined in Sept 7 *Cumhurieyt* (Ind) with notation battleground would not be confined to Cyprus. Few weeks ago there was cautious acceptance enosis if accompanied by suitable guarantees for GOT, by press, Parliamentary and academic contacts (Embtel 478).[3] At that time, enosis regarded as preferable alternative to independent Cyprus which, in Turkish eyes, tantamount establishment Mediterranean Cuba. Together with stiffening against any type of enosis is softening toward Soviet foreign policy initiated by Inonu speech to house Sept 3. Responsible pro-govt but left of center *Cumhuriyet* and *Milliyet* have played incorrectly Inonu's speech as emphasizing criticism of U.S. and support of

---

[1] Source: Department of State, Central Files, POL 27 CYP. Confidential. Repeated to Athens, Nicosia, London, Paris for USRO, and USUN.

[2] In a September 3 statement to the Grand National Assembly.

[3] Telegram 478, September 5, reported on the Turkish Parliament's special session on Cyprus. (Department of State, Central Files, POL 27 CYP)

Soviet Union. *Cumhuriyet* sub-headlined Sept 4, "PriMin, who states U.S. has placed wrong diagnosis on Cyprus problem, announced Soviet Union, itself a federal republic, would accept as suitable, federal administration for Cyprus."

Many extravagant statements being made concerning readiness, almost eagerness, to go to war over Cyprus. PriMin on Sept 6 declared "any decision outside our wishes renders war a necessity." This has been taken up by spokesmen smaller parties during Sept 7 Parliamentary debate (being reported separately), and by many Turk Cypriots, especially Denktash. Turk character, while not always quickly aroused, if once brought to state of combat readiness and eagerness, does not easily recede from this fever pitch. Many thoughtful Turks wondering why Inonu playing this game, feel it fraught with danger and could set Turkey back many years if armed conflict results.

In addition above, readjustment existing alliances also being advocated. JP source indicated to Embassy officer Aug 26 that group within RPP planning submit resolution to GNA request Turkish withdrawal from NATO. According this source, group within RPP sponsoring resolution headed by Deputies Feyzioglu and Kirca. In private conversation, Kirca has stated Turkey is approaching policy of neutralism, which is considered by some Turkish leaders as one most in Turkey's national interest. This view also supported by CNU group (Embtel 353).[4]

During RPP group meeting Sept 5 Inonu was subject to heavy attack for lack of decisive policy over Cyprus. Chief aim among rebel group within RPP headed by Feyzioglu appeared to be replacement present government with RPP/JP coalition which Feyzioglu would head. In past, Feyzioglu has made contacts with JP re such a coalition but reports from JP sources indicate JP leadership cool to latest Feyzioglu overture. During Sept 7 House debate, the RPNP, NP and NTP all spoke in favor of formation national coalition.

However, JP, while criticizing the government, did not reiterate its willingness, expressed as recently as a week ago, to take over the reins of government, and did not seem prepared to do so. Erim speech at House on behalf RPP appeared discredit opposition attacks and save day for RPP (being reported separately) but not clear whether sufficiently strong deterrent to exert definitive check on emotional impulse toward internal political change and reorientation of foreign alignment.

Hare

---

[4] Dated August 20. (Ibid.)

157. Telegram From the Embassy in Greece to the Department of State[1]

Athens, September 16, 1964, 4 p.m.

545. I called on Costopoulos this morning and explained that in Washington we had been engaged in general review of Cyprus situation.[2] I had come back with no specific new proposals, we still awaiting GOG response suggestions which we had made with regard to further initiatives under 1956 NAC resolution,[3] and that although we continue to be ready actively to assist in reaching solution, willingness find solution must come in first instance from parties directly involved. The horses have been led to water but have refused to drink.

GOC-Soviet negotiations. Costopoulos said he was afraid something serious might be developing, perhaps Cypriot efforts to extract Soviet guarantee in integrity of Cyprus. GOG would be tempted to break with Makarios on this issue, but would it be in Western interest to do so and to withdraw Greek forces presently on the island? I replied that much of present embarrassment of GOG is due to fact Makarios has always succeeded in obtaining implied Greek endorsement of Makarios' actions through continued reaffirmation of "complete identity of views" between the two governments. If GOG fails take strong public position in event creation of mutual GOC-USSR obligations, this fact would never be understood by Western opinion. GOG cannot avoid responsibility for taking firm line with Makarios during his visit here.

Costopoulos asserted that in recent conversation with Soviet Ambassador he had pointed out that a USSR-GOC agreement, quite aside from conflict with the provisions London–Zurich Accords, would probably cause serious difficulties at moment for consideration of Cyprus question by the UNGA. He said Kyprianou would probably request Secretary's reaction during his call on Friday to possible Soviet-GOC agreement. I assured Costopoulos that Kyprianou could anticipate a candid statement of our position.[4]

Istanbul situation. Costopoulos said prospect of large number of Greeks being forced to leave Istanbul in next few days has made almost impossible continuation of GOG efforts to improve understanding with GOT. He noted GOG will probably be forced raise this matter again in SC

---

[1] Source: Department of State, Central Files, POL 27 CYP. Secret; Priority. Repeated to Ankara, London, Nicosia, USUN, and Paris for USRO.

[2] Labouisse, Hare, and Belcher returned to the United States on September 10 and met with Secretary Rusk on September 12. No record of this meeting has been found.

[3] For text, see Department of State *Bulletin,* January 7, 1957, p. 17.

[4] See Document 159.

and that GOG cannot accept policy which seems to justify Turkish treatment Greek community in Istanbul because of Cypriot pressures on Turks which, as USG knows, GOG is attempting to eliminate. Approach reflected by USG unworthy US traditions and principles, and unfortunately Security Council discussions this problem have gone virtually unnoticed in American press. I took occasion to read virtually verbatim USUN's comments on Security Council debate last Friday (USUN 735 to Dept).[5]

Costopoulos asked me whether USG would be prepared make direct unilateral representation to GOT with regard to Istanbul situation expressing not only USG regret but also pointing up fact Turkish pressure in Istanbul is only discouraging Greek efforts reach some sort understanding with Turks. I said that I would transmit his request, but that he should understand that USG position had been stated by Mr. Stevenson. So long as GOG has never been able publicly disassociate itself from GOC policies, it is difficult not to relate Turk treatment Istanbul Greeks to Makarios treatment Turkish Cypriots. Costopoulos remonstrated that USG had been made fully aware of efforts which GOG has taken discourage provocatory measures on part of Makarios.

Brosio's mediation. Costopoulos alluded to fact Greek NAC Perm-Rep Palamas here and that Greek Ambassador to Ankara returning to join consultation. He reiterated that until now it has been Greek policy keep substance of Cyprus matter out of NATO forum, although question of precisely what aspects Greek-Turkish relations GOG would be prepared discuss in NAC now under review. He gave little intimation there is likely to be basic change in present policy, but said he would inform me results current deliberations. Although GOG cool to use 1956 resolution, GOG still prepared officially inform NATO SYG, in connection with his watching brief, as well as certain other interested NATO powers, of GOG intention not to provide support to Makarios in event of provocations.

However, Turkish threats vis-à-vis Istanbul Greeks make such GOG initiative difficult at this moment.

Economic blockade. Costopoulos was hopeful Makarios would, in fact, keep his promises with regard to elimination of economic blockade. Makarios has begun to realize that his policy runs directly counter to his hopes for sympathetic consideration Cyprus problem in UNGA. I commented that Washington has been disappointed by long series of Makarios' broken promises and is watching with great interest as well as reservation current efforts eliminate economic blockade.

---

[5] Telegram 735 from USUN, September 14, outlined the reasons that prompted the U.S. and other delegations to decline to link the issues of the Greek minority in Istanbul to the Cyprus blockade. (Department of State, Central Files, POL 27 CYP)

Troop rotation. GOG has raised question UN supervision of rotation Turk contingent with Thimayya and with U Thant. Costopoulos himself mentioned possibility of UN supervision to Turkish Ambassador who did not seem to be inclined take exception to this suggestion. It would be helpful, Costopoulos said, if U Thant would send a message to Makarios indicating UN willingness to supervise the rotation. No date for rotation has been discussed.

Comment: Local press has been widely speculating on new US solution for Cyprus. If GOG shared in this anticipation (even to small degree and notwithstanding previous Embassy warnings to contrary), this morning's session must have been disappointing and sobering for Costopoulos. I made it extremely clear US ability to be helpful could be based only on GOG's determination seek reasonable solution. Conjuncture of visits by Makarios, Palamas, Greek Ambassador to Turkey, Soviet-Cypriot negotiations, termination of Treaty of Establishment, etc., may possibly produce within next few days a clearer indication GOG policy.[6]

Labouisse

---

[6] In telegram 767 from USUN, September 16, the Mission reported a softening of the Cypriot position on troop rotation. (Ibid.)

---

158.   Telegram From the Embassy in Turkey to the Department of State[1]

Ankara, September 17, 1964, 5 p.m.

535. Saw Erkin late yesterday to give him reading on Washington talks as directed by Under Secretary, i.e. that situation had been given long, hard look; that time not ripe for new American initiative but necessary improve situation on island; that important Turk Cypriot leaders acting in such way as seem to be exploiting their compatriots. In so doing emphasized this not indicative any lessening interest in finding solution but concentration on immediate essentials which could smooth road to longer term objectives.

Erkin was not in particularly happy frame of mind, saying he had hoped we would be able come up with something new and definite. Fail-

---

[1] Source: Department of State, Central Files, POL 27 CYP. Secret; Priority. Repeated to London, Athens, Nicosia, Moscow, Paris for USRO, and USUN.

ure do so will make it necessary for GOT take strong measures itself and also leave field open to Soviets who are at this moment actively engaged in negotiations with Makarios. How is it they find it possible be so active and we unable do so? I said for simple reason that acting irresponsibly to cause mischief is always easy whereas acting responsibly for constructive purpose much more difficult. Repeated we not slackening effort; merely focusing attention on immediate objectives.

On other aspects of problem Erkin commented as follows:

1. He was not enthusiastic re initiative of Brosio but only specific criticism made was with reference to use of PermReps in role of "three wise men" rather than approaching at ministerial level.

2. Said he had just dictated reply to Costopoulos who had made plea through Turk Amb in Athens for holding up deportation of Istanbul Greeks and used as argument efforts GOG had made to resolve rotation problem. Erkin had said in reply that he had been able arrange postponement of four weeks but that he at loss understand use of rotation as argument since there had been no result.

3. Elaborating on foregoing, Erkin said GOG still seemed be operating on assumption that things going their way and unnecessary to do anything except let matters take their course. I demurred, saying that, although this might have been true sometime back, I was convinced that responsible officials in Athens now quite aware of danger of allowing Greek policy to be determined by Makarios and that this had been brought out with especial clarity in connection GOC flirtation with Soviets. It true that this changed attitude has not as yet produced strikingly obvious results but it is in right direction and should be understood. Erkin seemed interested but dubious.

4. GOT had consented somewhat reluctantly to appointment of Galo Plaza as Mediator but had immediately had reason regret decision when it had been learned that he had submitted report misrepresenting situation of Cypriot Turks which had been shown up in true light by subsequent report of General Thimayya.

5. There seems to be uncertainty as to when Cyprus question will come up in UNGA. If it goes into Political Committee later discussion likely but could be as soon as late November if it taken up in UNGA itself as question arising out of general debate.

Position of GOT will be that it still seeks federation but if there is question of enosis GOT will insist on double enosis. By same token, if proposal is for self-determination, GOT will insist on double-self-determination. GOT will definitely not accept UNGA resolution which would result in Greek-style enosis.

In this connection, Erkin observed only tangible result of Geneva talks was that U.S. and U.K. had promoted cause of enosis without being able obtain recognition of Turkish interests.

6. Concluding in same critical vein, Erkin revived complaint that, whereas USG not hesitant in initiating discussion with GOT in matters of interest to us, process often seems be one-way street because of our failure respond to requests for our views on matters of interest to GOT. As example, he referred to fact no reply received to his request for our reaction to Inonu speech (Embtel 470 and Deptel 386).[2]

Although sauce with which foregoing served up unduly vinegarish (please don't mention this to Turk Emb reps since difficulty caused when reported back here), substance believed be quite accurate reflection of Erkin's thoughts and attitude.[3]

Hare

---

[2] Telegram 470 from Ankara, September 4, and telegram 386 to Ankara, September 6. (Both ibid.)

[3] In telegram 440 to Ankara, September 18, the Department of State stressed the need for the Turkish Government to take steps, such as a pause in deportation of Greeks from Istanbul, to lowering tensions and prepare the Turkish public for a negotiated settlement of the Cyprus issue. (Ibid.)

---

159.   Memorandum of Conversation[1]

Washington, September 18, 1964.

MEMORANDUM OF CONVERSATION BETWEEN SECRETARY RUSK AND MR. KYPRIANOU, CYPRIOT FOREIGN MINISTER

After I had asked other colleagues to excuse us in order that I might have a private talk with Mr. Kyprianou,[2] he told me that it was necessary for him to go to Moscow because he did not wish to give offense to the Soviet Union in light of the fact that they had pressed President Makarios himself very hard to come to Moscow and he intimated (somewhat slyly)

---

[1] Source: Department of State, Ball Papers: Lot 74 D 272, Memcons Other Than Visits. Secret; Limit Distribution. Drafted by Rusk.

[2] Kyprianou visited Washington September 18 for talks on the Cyprus question. A memorandum of the other portions of his conversation with Rusk is ibid., Secretary's Memoranda of Conversation: Lot 65 D 330. A memorandum of his conversation with Assistant Secretary Talbot is ibid., Central Files, POL 23–8 CYP.

September 1964–June 1965   317

that he needed to be present to be sure that the Cypriot delegation in Moscow did not get off the track. He said that his purpose in going was to inform the Soviet Union that the ultimate object of Cypriot policy was union with Greece. He then asked me whether I did not think that if the Soviet Union and the United States both agreed to the union of Cyprus and Greece, this would ensure that Turkey would make no military moves.

I told him that whether he went to Moscow was his own affair but that I would urge upon him most solemnly that it would be a great mistake for Cyprus to abandon its position of non-alignment and find itself in a military or security arrangement with the Soviet Union. I said, very directly, that should such arrangements be in effect and there were trouble between the Warsaw Pact and NATO countries or between the United States and the Soviet Union, the result would simply be that Cyprus would be crushed. He tried to leave the impression that he expected nothing more than the unilateral declaration made by the Soviet Union in the Security Council yesterday to the effect that if Cyprus was attacked, the Soviet Union would defend Cyprus. I then told him that he could be sure that the Soviet Union would be playing a double or triple game in this situation since their object would be to stimulate difficulties for other people and tension between NATO allies. I pointed out the possibility that the Soviet Union might in fact stimulate Turkey to oppose enosis.

Mr. Kyprianou told me that upon his return to Nicosia from Moscow he would communicate very privately through Ambassador Belcher about his impressions of the Moscow visit.

Dean Rusk[3]

---

[3] Printed from a copy that bears this typed signature.

---

160.   Telegram From the Department of State to the Mission to the United Nations[1]

Washington, September 30, 1964, 4:03 p.m.

793. Request you see U Thant soonest and convey sense of great dismay which Dept feels at his statement to SC September 25.[2] From our

---

[1] Source: Department of State, Central Files, POL 27 CYP. Confidential; Limdis. Drafted by Buffum; cleared by Jernegan, Cleveland, and EUR; and approved by Ball. Repeated to Nicosia, Ankara, Athens, and London.

[2] For extracts (U.N. Doc. S/PV.1159), see *American Foreign Policy: Current Documents, 1964*, p. 595.

vantage point, he has not only given Greek Cypriots the victory that they sought in vain to achieve in a resolution but he has sacrificed fundamental prerogatives of office of SYG entrusted to him by GA. As he must well understand, efforts (instigated by Rolz-Bennett) to get reference in resolution to Makarios propaganda proposals contained his September 15 communication aborted because members refused to lend themselves to such partisan exercise.[3] US Del repeatedly indicated we would not support resolution which made explicit reference to Makarios proposals unless SYG's hand strengthened. Now we find SYG elevates and dignifies these proposals in his statement to SC and suggests UNFICYP commander cooperate with Makarios in seeking their implementation. Turks are obviously disturbed at this, and we do not blame them. At same time, SYG said nothing about his intention to ask Thimayya to discuss with parties concerned ways to implement para. 232 of his report.[4]

In addition, we are deeply disappointed that SYG retreated from his announced intention contained in para. 231 of his report to defray UNFICYP expenses from regular UN funds if voluntary contributions inadequate. We find it incomprehensible that SYG should retreat in face of opposition of the minority *non-contributors* to the UN on a principle involving fundamental authority of SYG and UN to undertake peacekeeping operations in an emergency. In doing so he has offered serious rebuff to *supporters* of a strong UN capable of acting when confronted by emergencies. In effect he has disavowed support by those who have spoken up in defense of SYG's competence to deal with unforeseen contingencies on his own authority. We note, for example, that Morocco spoke precisely to this point in debate.

Request you inform SYG in clear terms that USG deeply disappointed at this exercise. If this reflects attitude to be expected of him in confrontation which now approaching between the supporters and non-supporters of UN on Article 19, we are frank to say that we think he will preside over disintegration of UN as effective instrument for peacekeeping and will assure its transformation into nothing but a debating society.

Rusk

---

[3] Reference is to Resolution 194 (1964) (U.N. Doc. S/5987), adopted unanimously by the Security Council on September 25; for text, see ibid., p. 594. An extract of Makarios' September 15 message to Secretary-General Thant (U.N. Doc. S/5950/Add.2, Annex) is printed ibid., p. 593.

[4] The Secretary-General's report covered the period from June 8 to September 8; he submitted it to the Security Council on September 10 (U.N. Doc. S/5950 and Corr. 1). For extracts, see ibid., pp. 590–591.

161.   Telegram From the Embassy in Turkey to the Department of State[1]

Ankara, October 1, 1964, 1:16 p.m.

601. Embtel 596.[2] Made pre-arranged call on Erkin this morning for purpose general discussion.

As might have been expected he was very upset re recent turn of events affecting questions rotation and Cyprus road, saying he had just talked to Inonu and was at wit's end know what to do. Feeling in country is very strong and "pressures" (unspecified but presumably military) being exerted on govt. U Thant has turned out be just as bad as Makarios. GOT had been criticized before for using air force but they will do so again if necessary to effect rotation and be prepared "to fight it out".

I asked Erkin if he could clarify situation as he sees it. Following is distillation of what he had to say:

Rotation and opening Kyrenia Road are separate questions and must go ahead with first regardless of second. However, if we happened to be susceptible of simultaneous solution that would cause no problem.

As regards Kyrenia Road, both sides are agreed re Nicosia by-pass, Turks also agree that, with exception of Turk contingent and UNFICYP no armed forces would be allowed on road. Turks had agreed remove Turkish police against strong Cypriot Turk objection and Cypriot Turk armed forces would also not be allowed use (since this contrary to what we told yesterday, I managed get this repeated three times in effort avoid misunderstanding).

What GOT cannot stomach, however, and what it never agreed to in contacts with SYG was that Turk contingent could only use road without arms. GOT has given assurance that contingent would only use road for normal "requirements of service and liaison". It has also stated that contingent commander would maintain close contact and cooperation with UN commander. What further could reasonably be asked of GOT? After all there are limits to concessions and GOT cannot take action which would undermine integrity of a duly constituted military unit.

Emphasizing that contingent is only question as far as road concerned, Erkin asked that I communicate most urgently with Washington and seek its views with minimum delay since this could be most important in influencing current decision making here.

---

[1] Source: Department of State, Central Files, POL 27 CYP. Secret; Immediate. Also sent to USUN and repeated to Athens, Nicosia, and London. Passed to the White House, DOD, and CIA.

[2] Telegram 596 from Ankara, September 30, reported rising Turkish concern over the issue of troop rotation and the latest Turkish diplomatic efforts to deal with this issue. (Ibid.)

Comment: It will be noted that foregoing differs importantly from situation as presented yesterday by Turkemen in sense that it reduces problem to Turk contingent use of road by eliminating Cypriot Turk fighters, which in line with what Eralp presumably informed SYG in writing (Nicosia's 562 to Dept).[3] Would also constitute point which, according USUN's 926 to Dept,[4] is regarded as negotiable by Bunche.

How to reconcile difference between reftel and situation as postulated by Erkin is unclear. Hopefully, since Erkin had just gone over with Inonu, it represents a modification in position following report from Eralp and I believe we should proceed on that assumption, although confusion in this connection has been so great throughout that it is difficult know when on firm ground.

Would strongly recommend we take this opportunity flash something back here for communication to Erkin by tomorrow morning. This would serve two purposes; firstly, to capitalize on what could be settlement of rotation at time when pressure building up here to go off deep end; secondly, to give concrete evidence of our continuing interest in Cyprus problem at time when, despite full explanation, there is strong feeling here that we have abandoned Turks to their fate. In fact, Erkin made this pretty clear this morning and, although we cannot always pander to psychological reactions, I believe that in this case there is sufficient substance to it to justify recognition, especially since the context in which problem now raised would seem to be potentially constructive and not involve our getting into unduly deep water.[5]

Hare

_____

[3] Telegram 562 from Nicosia, September 30, transmitted the purported text of a Turkish note to the UNFICYP Commander on the rotation and Kyrenia Road problems. (Ibid.)

[4] Telegram 926 from USUN, September 30, reported on U.N. officials' discussions with Makarios over the rotation issue (Ibid.)

[5] Telegram 978 from USUN, October 5, reported that an agreement on control of the Kyrenia Road had been reached. (Ibid.)

_____

162.   Telegram From the Embassy in Cyprus to the Department of State[1]

Nicosia, October 6, 1964, 6 p.m.

585. As we have reported and as has been observed by USUN (USUN's 962 and 963 to Dept)[2] Makarios has apparently adopted policy

_____

[1] Source: Department of State, Central Files, POL 27 CYP. Secret; Priority; Limdis. Repeated to Ankara, Athens, London, and USUN.

[2] Both dated October 2. (Ibid.)

of "killing Turks with kindness" at least for period before UNGA. This Greek Cypriot policy combined with GOT's apparent willingness make major concessions on Kyrenia Road which in effect would mark beginning of disintegration entire Turkish Cypriot position on island (Embtel 578)[3] give us some reason to believe that our present policy is by and large proving successful on surface. However, it seems to us that any US policy which is confined merely to keeping lid on situation in Cyprus must be based on using time gained to obtain two results:

1. To bring GOT and Turkish Cypriots to accept concept of enosis with guarantees of rights for Turkish minority plus some face-saving gesture;

2. To bring GOC and other pro-Western elements on island into strong enough position vis-à-vis Makarios to enforce guarantees to Turkish minority and provide face-saving gesture to GOT.

Ankara, of course, is in best position to judge whether there has been any real give in GOT's attitude toward Cyprus recently. Although we still awaiting outcome current negotiations on Kyrenia Road this initial step in reducing GOT support of Turkish Cypriots appears to us as possible straw in wind and in line US overall policy and interests.

However, it is on GOG and pro-enosis Greek Cypriot side where there have been great slippages. While we are marking time there has been a noticeable decline in strength and influence of GOG and increasing momentum in the drift to the left. We have seen in past two weeks press campaigns which were inconceivable even on part of Communist papers three months ago. These have now reached point of Makarios inspired attacks on hitherto sacrosanct Grivas himself. Such attacks, of course, have as their real targets Greece and concept of enosis. There are reports of increasing conflicts between Greek officers and National Guard conscripts and good evidence that Makarios is working actively against Greek officers behind the scenes attempting to weaken their ability to influence developments here.

Makarios himself is becoming ever stronger with a popular base spread throughout all sectors on the island. To Cypriots of all types (and to many foreign observers) Archbishop seems incapable of making political errors, e.g. by skillful maneuvering over past two months he has eroded limits of what could be given GOT for prestige purposes from Turkish sovereign base on island, to Turkish share in NATO base separate from British sovereign bases, to Turkish participation in NATO base carved out of British bases, to present rapidly retreating possibility that Greek Cypriots would tacitly agree to undercover deal by GOG with GOT for NATO base in British area with modest Turkish presence after enosis.

---

[3] Dated October 3. (Ibid.)

Makarios, himself, of course is now talking in terms of no foreign bases on island at all and there is rapidly developing groundswell which, if unchecked, will produce almost united Greek Cypriot opposition to continued existence British bases to say nothing of any variety NATO base. Andreas Papandreou's remarks to *Le Monde*[4] might indicate Makarios has support for anti-base position in some GOG quarters as well. Greek Cypriots regard Makarios' negotiations with Moscow as complete success and now expect him to continue his victorious march through Cairo to General Assembly.

Meanwhile pro-enosis and anti-Communist elements who have usually been found around Grivas are falling apart. Their newspapers are unable to compete with pro-Makarios media. Their organization is weak and they have no significant political following aside perhaps from still remaining personal popularity of Grivas.

GOG recently made what in retrospect looks like ill-conceived and desperate gesture in sending Papandreou's personal emissary Delipetros to Cyprus.[5] Latter's heavy handed approach assured failure and served mainly to tarnish pro-enosis nationalists and deepen the gap between Makarios and GOG. As usual in contests of this sort Makarios has emerged even stronger than before.

What we are saying is the time for pro-Western solution of Cyprus problem seems definitely to be running out. Since viewed from here possibility of GOG–GOT accord on Cyprus looks dim, we do not see much hope of checking Makarios except by use of regular Greek troops on island and National Guard units which they control. Moreover because Makarios is having notable success in isolating Greek military further and further from mass of Greek Cypriots we cannot much longer count on successful action by them. Unless dramatic and decisive steps are taken very soon to reverse the trend, Cyprus will certainly become, after UNGA, an independent neutralist anti-Western island with a growing Communist element which could thereafter easily turn the island into Mediterranean Cuba.

In other channels we are making certain recommendations for actions US could take. However, nothing will work or should even be started until Turks are brought to recognize real danger they are running if they delay acceptance painful fact that only way out is enosis. If they move fast enough to withdraw their opposition to enosis, it is possible they can obtain some firm guarantees of rights for Turkish minority on

---

[4] Printed in the October 4–5 edition. The Embassy in Athens reported public reaction in telegram 665 from Athens, October 7. (Ibid.)

[5] A memorandum outlining Delipetros' activities in Cyprus is in the Johnson Library, National Security File, Files of Robert W. Komer, Cyprus.

island and some face-saver for GOT. If not, Cyprus will certainly become serious and immediate threat to Turkey's security.

Belcher

---

163. Telegram From the Embassy in Greece to the Department of State[1]

Athens, October 9, 1964, 9 p.m.

685. Re Deptel 609.[2] Cyprus. Basic Greek policy seems to be to continue build up Greek military and political capabilities on the island, to exercise all possible influence to reduce tensions (including overt collision between GOG and Makarios), and move ahead toward discussion of problem in the General Assembly. We find little indication of high level intention to take any initiatives in immediate future toward unseating Makarios. As reflected by recent press attack against Grivas and return of Delipetros from Nicosia to Athens, GOG efforts on island are producing obvious tensions and subterranean struggle between Makarios and GOG is now becoming apparent. Vigorous reaction by Makarios would seem imply GOG efforts have made or were about to make certain degree of progress.

While GOG has no illusions that debate in UNGA will of itself produce a solution, it assumes that the sentiments which it expects to be reflected and which are now being prepared in Cairo by Makarios will provide additional political restraint on Turks. GOG officials display considerable degree confidence in ability of Cypriots, strengthened by Greek personnel and equipment, effectively to deter Turkish military intervention. Although genuinely disturbed at prospect of increasing Soviet influence in Cyprus and in Mediterranean, GOG undoubtedly feels (as reflected in Andreas Papandreou's *Le Monde* interview) that introduction of Soviet factor serves not only as additional restraint on Turks but also possibly as useful element to force US and Britain to take more realistic view of situation.

---

[1] Source: Department of State, Central Files, POL 27 CYP. Secret; Priority; Limited Distribution. Repeated to Ankara, London, Nicosia, USUN, and Paris for USRO.

[2] Telegram 609 to Athens, October 8, requested an analysis of Greek efforts to gain influence with Makarios' civilian advisers. (Ibid.)

I do not believe Andreas Papandreou's statement, particularly regarding possible NATO base, reflects current views of GOG in general or of Stephanopoulos or Garoufalias in particular. (I do believe, despite Andreas' rather weak protestations when I discussed matter with him, that reportage probably reflects rather accurately his own orientation and unfortunately his influence with his father is a factor determining high-level GOG Cyprus policy.) There is no doubt, however, GOG and Greek public opinion feel deep-seated resentment at failure of NATO and US to make a categoric condemnation of Turkish aerial attack and use of NATO weapons. Both Costopoulos and Andreas Papandreou have spoken to me in this sense in last few days when I taxed them with Andreas' interview, and I am certain this is one of reasons GOG considers UN will provide more effective forum than NATO.

Lurking in minds of all high GOG officials is keen awareness that Cyprus solution would provide tremendous political prize to those individuals who bring it about. They are also aware potential entry of Makarios in Greek politics in event of enosis. Some Greeks believe (as Eralp appears to do, USUN 204 to Dept)[3] that Makarios not categorically opposed to enosis providing it is Makarios who brings about realization on his terms and is thereby in position to profit from his victory. Viewed from this perspective the issue becomes not only enosis, but whose enosis? In this context, Andreas Papandreou's reported opposition to possible Cyprus NATO base might be construed as effort to outflank Makarios on issue.

We find no evidence here that anyone is thinking of reexamining Acheson proposals and certainly not of improving previous Greek offer. Consensus seems rather to be, as Nicosia has pointed out, that evolution of situation has made it unrealistic to think in these terms and that in many respects, notwithstanding hazards of increasing Soviet influence, situation is evolving in manner generally favorable to Greek and Cypriot aspirations.

Sossides in recent conversation told DCM that if, however, US Government prepared in conjunction with British to stand the Turks down, GOG prepared utilize its military and political assets on island to precipitate enosis. This would mean US support for solution which could be politically acceptable in Cyprus—a solution which could withstand counterattack from Makarios. Sossides said under current circumstances this solution would require "unconditional enosis", protection of Turkish minority, and eventual conversion of British base into NATO base with Turkish participation. He estimated that, if this formula were accepted, GOG could precipitate enosis within a month or two. Sossides

---

[3] Telegram 204 from USUN to Athens, repeated to the Department of State as telegram 1039, October 8. (Ibid.)

is in touch with Grivas and participated in arranging Delipetros mission to Nicosia which was designed to strengthen GOG capabilities there in the press, radio, and among certain political personalities.

In contacts with other Greek officials in recent days, we have had no confirmation of Sossides' statements to DCM regarding present willingness GOG to move ahead in event US and UK prepared to support a solution providing for "unconditional" enosis and British base converted into NATO base. Prime Minister and Garoufalias have stated to DCM and me on several occasions in past that if US would support a solution which could be made politically acceptable on the island, Greek armed forces and Grivas would take measures forcibly to remove Makarios if necessary. We will seek new reading on their views.

Evidence seems clear GOG actively seeking extend its control on island a) in order deter Turk intervention which would lead to Greek-Turk war and b) in anticipation that situation might develop in which GOG assets could be effectively applied to bring about enosis.

As I see it there are two principal contingencies in which GOG would consider it feasible openly to challenge Makarios and attempt precipitate enosis: a) Cypriot involvement with bloc to degree which obviously approaches satellization, or b) US prepared support solution which GOG considers can be made politically acceptable on the island.

Have appointment with Papandreou for tomorrow morning in effort determine his analysis current situation and likely GOG course of action.[4]

Labouisse

---

[4] In telegram 639 from Athens, October 10, Labouisse reported that Papandreou was adopting a wait-and-see approach to the Cyprus question pending U.N. action and U.S. and British elections. (Ibid.)

164.   Memorandum of Conversation[1]

Washington, November 9, 1964.

SUBJECT

Cyprus

PARTICIPANTS

The Secretary
The Under Secretary
Phillips Talbot, Assistant Secretary, NEA
Harlan Cleveland, Assistant Secretary, IO
Gordon D. King, Officer-in-Charge, Cyprus Affairs

Mr. Galo Plaza, United Nations Mediator

The Secretary showed Mr. Galo Plaza a copy of the Turk-Soviet joint communiqué[2] and noted that the Soviets appear to have gone further in supporting the Turkish position on the inviolability of treaties than we had in the joint communiqué issued after the Inonu visit to Washington. The Secretary then noted that Cyprus Foreign Minister Kyprianou said when here some weeks ago before his Moscow visit that he would tell the Soviets point blank that the Greek-Cypriots want enosis eventually. The Secretary expressed the thought that the Soviet reaction to Kyprianou's statement together with the tone of the Turk-Soviet communiqué could be somewhat sobering for the Greek-Cypriots.

Mr. Galo Plaza said that it is important to know what type of enosis is being discussed since Makarios' definition is quite different from that of the Greeks. Plaza said that he had urged the Greek Government to sit down with Makarios and arrive at an agreed definition. He has the impression that Greece has pressed Makarios to arrive at such a definition with them, but that Makarios has successfully evaded an answer. Mr. Ball noted the former United States assumption that a strong pro-enosis line from Greece would arouse the latent enosis sentiment on the island and undercut Makarios, but he feels this is no longer possible. Galo Plaza agreed and said he considers Papandreou to be over confident regarding his ability to handle Makarios. He described Makarios as head and shoulders above any other Greek leader, in effect a "Mr. Cyprus" who was capable of running Greece as well. This was apparent from the beginning, Mr. Galo Plaza said, and had convinced him that he must work through Makarios and do nothing behind his back. Makarios told him the day before Tuomioja died that, even if the Geneva talks

---

[1] Source: Department of State, Central Files, POL 23–8 CYP. Secret; Exdis. Drafted by King and approved in S on November 20.

[2] Not found.

brought forth a proposed solution very much along the lines that Makarios himself wanted, he would still reject it since it was being applied
from outside. In line with his determination to work through Makarios,
Plaza noted that, as soon as he reached New York after his last round of
talks, he wrote the Archbishop a full report; and the Archbishop was
very flattered. Plaza said that he made the point with Markarios after the
Cairo Non-aligned Conference[3] that the Archbishop had to be flexible
since the Turk-Cypriots were cornered and he alone had room to maneuver; Makarios agreed. Earlier, Plaza explained, he had had a similar
experience with Makarios in connection with the economic blockade
after Kokkina–Mansoura. He told Makarios that it was not possible to
hold a people under siege in the twentieth century, and that he must call
the blockade off. The Archbishop then personally wrote his five-point
program to ease the economic blockade and offer amnesty to the Turks.
Makarios, Plaza noted, is always alone and all decisions are made on his
own. He now appears more flexible and realized that he has been very
lucky to date. He wants to attend the United Nations General Assembly,
but indicates that he will check with Plaza first before deciding to attend
and that he is willing to do whatever Plaza recommends is best for the
mediation. Plaza feels that Makarios wants to be the one to reach a settlement. He also feels, however, that if Makarios had from the beginning
exercised the good behavior he has shown in recent weeks, the problem
would long since been solved.

Galo Plaza explained that his own plans are to return tomorrow,
November 10, to Nicosia where he will have very concrete talks with
Makarios. He will then proceed to Ankara, Athens and London before
returning to New York in time for the opening of the General Assembly.
He had been thinking of making an interim report at that time, but has
given up the idea. Now he plans to report orally to the Secretary General
in January. The report, he feels, will reflect neither total agreement nor
total disagreement among the parties. It will contain his findings and his
recommendations for a solution.

Concerning Turkey and the Turk-Cypriots, Plaza noted that Inonu
and the Turkish leadership told him very firmly that they must find a
way out of the Cyprus problem, but that it must be on honorable
grounds. Inonu described Turkish objectives to Plaza as being, first, an
honorable way out, second, Turkish security and, third, the welfare of the
Turk-Cypriots, with the latter being much the weakest point as demonstrated by the Government of Turkey commitment on the Kyrenia road
without prior consultations with the Turk-Cypriots. Plaza said that
through most of his consultations to date he had done more listening

---

[3] The Conference of Heads of State or Government of Non-Aligned Countries was
held in Cairo October 5–10.

than talking except in Ankara where the Turks began speaking of separation of the two communities. Plaza said he told the Turks that he was completely opposed to any physical separation of the communities in a federation scheme and that he would not accept partition as a basis for discussion since he considered a Greek-Turkish border through Cyprus, with Greek-Turkish relations dependent on the unpredictable and volatile Cypriots, as completely unrealistic.

Plaza said he asked Inonu, and later the Athens Government, for views on an independent, non-aligned, demilitarized Cyprus. Both the Government of Turkey and Government of Greece said this would leave a weakened Cyprus which would be prey to many outsiders. The Turks, however, said that this would be acceptable from the point of view of their security. In answer to Mr. Talbot's inquiry, Plaza said that such an arrangement might be similar to the Austrian example and that it could, in fact, be based on an international agreement which would include the Soviets. The Turks, he noted, are definitely against instant enosis which would mean war with Greece. The British asked him why it should not be possible to bring about enosis by a takeover of the island by Grivas and the 10,000 Greek troops there. Plaza told them there was not a chance of this; Makarios has all the political power and could defeat any such move. Concerning enosis, Plaza noted, the United Nations itself could not write off a member state but could certainly accept such an arrangement if the countries concerned joined of their own accord.

The Secretary asked if it were far afield to think that the parties might start on the basis of the London/Zurich Agreements and proceed to amend them into something more workable. Plaza reacted negatively to this. He noted that both sides have now firmly rejected London/Zurich as a basis for the future and that the United Nations is trying to find a new basis for a political settlement; any attempt to return to London/Zurich would start the battle again.

Plaza re-emphasized that the Turks are weak in this dispute and would settle for much less than the goals they first spoke of. They must find an honorable way out, not for the fact of Turkish public opinion, but in order to satisfy the Turkish armed forces.

Galo Plaza noted that the Greeks have spoken of giving the Turks one of their small islands near Cyprus for a military base under a 50 year lease. The Greeks have also, he noted, spoken to the British about the possibility of one of the British bases on Cyprus being committed to NATO and shared with the Turks. Plaza checked this with the new British Government in London. The British did not reject the idea and, in fact, said that they are willing to go as far as necessary to reach a solution.

Mr. Cleveland asked if Galo Plaza's recommendations might include suggesting several alternative solutions to the Cypriot people in a referendum; he asked specifically if such alternative solutions could include enosis. Plaza said that it could since it would be the choice of the people and not a proposal by the United Nations.

The Secretary asked if the Turks might agree to participate with Greece in some sort of defense board concept. Plaza expressed doubt and noted that the Turks and Greeks have forces on the island now which show no evidence whatsoever of cooperation. He expressed the feeling that independence must come as the first step but that first Makarios and the Greeks must decide what they mean by enosis. Many complications lie ahead even before a firm definition can be reached.

The Secretary asked if Galo Plaza advised the United States Government to lie low for the present. Plaza stated that this was desirable to a point, but that United States was also needed with the Turks. When the Secretary pointed out that we have used much of our capital with the Turks through past intercession, Plaza expressed understanding but felt that efforts must be made to impress on Ankara the need to be realistic. He noted that they had first told him they must have population separation with the Turkish communities getting 30% of the land to correspond to their percentage of land ownership. Later Ankara dropped this to 20% and still later to a base area with enough space for some Turk-Cypriots in the event of another crisis.

Galo Plaza expressed the conviction that, with reference to the Turks, speed is important now because of Inonu's age. The Turks become nervous, he noted, whenever Inonu is ill since there is no one strong enough to make decisions if he goes.

The Secretary said that, if Turkey is trying to find a way out of the Cyprus dispute, it may find it earlier without any United States involvement. Inonu could be undermined if he appeared again to be responding to United States pressure. Furthermore, such pressure could cause an adverse reaction in the Turkish military.

Galo Plaza referred then to Geneva and said that the Acheson effort created the impression the United States and not the United Nations had the main initiative. Mr. Ball pointed out that the Geneva exercise did, however, deflate Turkish demands significantly. He noted further that we have suffered in our relations with Turkey because of their reaction to Geneva so that anything we do now could simply make it tougher for the United Nations. The Secretary observed in passing that since things change so rapidly these days, a 50 year lease on a base would seem long enough for an 80-year old Prime Minister. Plaza stressed the view that in any case a settlement involving base rights was not really satisfactory since bases are becoming anachronisms. He noted, however, that King Constantine said he had three times asked Makarios if he could accept the commitment of one of the British bases to NATO. Makarios did not reject this nor did the British. In response to the Secretary's question, Plaza said this could include Turkish soldiers and specifically the Turkish contingent on the base. He said this is an idea that he is trying to sell to the Turks. He hopes to persuade them that this is better than a sovereign base. It would appear not as a concession from Greece, but as something which the Turks themselves had won. In any case, he felt on the basis of his discussions with the Turks to date that they view their position more realistically than he had expected.

When Mr. Ball asked if the Cyprus Constitution required that if the British give up their bases they must be turned over to the Government of Cyprus, Plaza said that this would not complicate NATO-izing the base since it would in any case be done through Makarios.

The Secretary asked how the Department could best keep in touch with the Mediator. Plaza suggested that he could best continue his contacts through Ambassador Belcher. He noted, however, that he badly lacks intelligence reports and would appreciate assistance in this regard. The Secretary agreed that we could help provided the information was not passed to the Cypriots, Greeks or Turks. He cautioned also that we could not guarantee the accuracy of our reports.

In conclusion, Plaza stressed the importance of keeping the mediation effort within the United Nations as a United Nations initiative. He said the Americans are willing to take the blame and consequences of Geneva; he would take the blame for the mediation from now on. He realized that the United States is reluctant to press the Turks, but asked that we support him when the Turks ask our opinion of his approaches.

---

165.   Telegram From the Embassy in Greece to the Department of State[1]

Athens, November 19, 1964, 9 p.m.

888. Ambassador's statement Nov 18 emphatically denying U.S. involvement in resignation Andreas Papandreou (Embtel 875)[2] evoked immediate response from Prime Minister Papandreou, who late last night issued following statement: "I fully agree with statement of U.S. Ambassador. In fact, there was no U.S. Embassy intervention in matter of ministerial change. I, too, express my deep regret that such connection has been made. Besides, there could be no intervention."

---

[1] Source: Department of State, Central Files, POL 15–1 GREECE. Confidential. Repeated to Paris for USRO, Nicosia, and USDOCOSouth for Burris.

[2] Telegram 875 from Athens, November 19, reported the reaction to Andreas Papandreou's November 11 resignation. (Ibid.)

PriMin's statement seconding Ambassador's categorical rejection of charge of U.S. involvement in resignation was signal for cessation of govt press campaign against U.S.; most pro-govt papers today headline denials of U.S. intervention and except for pro-govt *Ethnos*, which initiated accusation, pro-govt papers imply denials have clarified situation and removed any doubts of U.S. complicity. Typical are headlines of sensational afternoon pro-govt papers *Ta Nea* and *Athinaiki*, both of which are usually critical of U.S.; *Athinaiki* headlines: "No U.S. Intervention in A. Papandreou's Resignation; Mr. Labouisse Expressed His Vivid Astonishment," while *Ta Nea* writes: "U.S. Not Involved." Unwilling to reverse itself completely, *Ethnos* suggests Labouisse denial was only "partly" supported by PriMin's statement, since PriMin said "U.S. Embassy" not involved in resignation, thus suggesting that other U.S. agencies may have played a part.

Opposition ERE press had field day at government expense on subject, with all ERE papers charging that PriMin was remiss in not rejecting charges earlier and that Ambassador's statement "forced" PriMin to denounce charges. Characteristic of ERE press is headline of influential *Kathimerini*: "U.S. Ambassador Labouisse amazed that resignation was associated with Cyprus settlement—PriMin was forced to share amazement," while conservative *Acropolis* headlines: "Severe reply from U.S. Ambassador Labouisse forced PriMin late last night to retract." *Acropolis* added: "U.S. Ambassador's statement was made when PriMin in his statement in Parliament virtually adopted and made official campaign of two Communist newspapers and of certain govt newspapers with personal ties with Andreas Papandreou against the Americans who were point blank accused of having exerted pressure for resignation of PriMin's son."

Comment: PriMin's failure during Parliamentary debate to denounce charges of U.S. intervention in his son's resignation—charges which he knew were patently false—is inexplicable. It is possible he was willing to go along with campaign that made his son appear as "victim" of foreign pressure, despite damage he knew it would do to U.S. prestige in Greece, in hope it would detract attention from real reasons for resignation. It is also possible that by billing Andreas as staunch defender of Greece's independent policies and as defender of Cyprus, the Papandreous hoped to build up Andreas' political appeal in country as well as within party where he was facing increasing antagonisms. In any event, Ambassador's statement clearly rejecting U.S. involvement forced PriMin to take stand on issue, which he did by issuing categorical, albeit tardy, denial. His delay in doing so, however, opened him and his govt to opposition charges that he was using charges of U.S. involvement as smokescreen for accusations of scandals involving his son.

While question of U.S. complicity now appears to be laid to rest as far as Greece is concerned, Archbishop Makarios has invited young Papandreou to visit Cyprus tomorrow. Very probably, Cypriots will attempt to foster myth that Andreas Papandreou fell victim to U.S. "pressure" as result his stand on Cyprus question, and undoubtedly Makarios and Cypriot press will play this for all it's worth.[3]

Labouisse

---

[3] The Embassy reported on possible causes of Andreas Papandreou's resignation in telegram 895 from Athens, November 20. (Ibid.)

---

166.   Telegram From the Embassy in Turkey to the Department of State[1]

Ankara, November 30, 1964, 4 p.m.

872. Embtel 860.[2] Although our Cyprus policy as recently re-stated by Assistant Secretary Talbot (Deptel 630),[3] has been not to favor particular solution but rather to lend support to any proposal that had prospect of acceptance, in fact our thinking and efforts during and even after Geneva discussions were oriented toward modified form of enosis as solution which held out best hope being definitive and of avoiding continuing trouble. However, review of recent developments in Cyprus situation indicates changes in several important factors which were previously determinants in our policy thinking.

First and most important is that both GOG and Makarios have in fact given up idea of "instant enosis", at least for the time being. Thus, while enosis with sufficient compensations for Turkey may still remain preferred US solution it retains little value as working concept in shorter run.

Furthermore, experience has shown us that no matter how much Papandreou continues talk about building up GOG position on island,

---

[1] Source: Department of State, Central Files, POL 27 CYP. Secret; Limdis. Repeated to Nicosia, Athens, Paris for USRO, London, USUN, and Moscow.

[2] Telegram 860, November 26, suggested delaying a U.S. response to questions raised by Foreign Minister Erkin. (Ibid.)

[3] Dated November 21. (Ibid.)

he has failed put GOG in position force enosis on Makarios or even accelerate pace of events. It now clear that on Greek side, Makarios and Makarios alone will call tune as to timing and nature of any significant steps toward enosis. This has obvious implications for our long-standing assumption that nub of problem was to get GOT and GOG talking, so that hopefully they could reach compromise agreement which Makarios would have no choice but accept. What has emerged, actually, is coincidence of GOT and GOC interest (though for different reasons and perhaps for short term only) in maintaining Cyprus' independence. Logically, this should lead Turks and Greek Cypriots talk together but neither side seems ready yet recognize this as tolerable alternative to present course of mutual hostility (Deptel 642).[4] In meanwhile, earlier open-mindedness of Turks to idea of modified enosis has changed. Unhappy denouement of Geneva talks and their aftermath have made even more acute feeling of Turks that they have been suffering unacceptable losses to their position and their prestige. As consequence enosis has again become dirty word for them, their whole attitude has stiffened and they have reverted to original position of federation, with partition relegated to automatic reaction if any overture made toward unilateral enosis.

Another change in policy background has to do with Soviets' role and influence. Will be recalled one of principal reasons for seeking urgently obtain agreement last summer on modified enosis formula was to abort growing Soviet influence in and over Cyprus and specifically to forestall Greek Cypriot mission to Moscow. In interval not only Greek Cypriots but Turks have been to Moscow. Although Russians may not have intended Moscow discussions give as much encouragement to Turks as latter reflect in conversations with US and others, nevertheless discussions and joint communiqué, at a minimum, created new element of uncertainty for Greeks and expectations for Turks. Thus, although does not appear have been any change in basic Soviet position, Soviets can now win kudos from both Greek Cypriots and Turks by taking public stance in favor of independence which per se no longer appears, in Turkish eyes at least, as pro-Makarios position.

Then, there is experience of Mediator himself. Despite Galo Plaza's inveterate optimism and political virtuosity, including close rapport with Makarios, his multiple conversations with all parties concerned have not resulted in any narrowing of gap (as Acheson's did) but instead have served reveal that gap greater than was thought. Measure of bleakness Galo Plaza's prospects is his decision defer submission his final report until after UNGA discussion of Cyprus item.

---

[4] Dated November 25. (Ibid.)

In addition all of foregoing we constrained adduce one parochial but nonetheless important consideration, which is continuing erosion of US political stock in Turkey. Given fact we have had no choice but sail on more or less straight line between Greek Scylla and Turk Charybdis, we had to expect growing disillusionment and despair on part of Turkish friends for our failure support them in position which they consider right and honorable. This mood has gradually given way to one of adapting themselves realistically to changed conditions but at same time seeking opportunities make them as favorable as possible to Turkey's needs, e.g., Erkin's Moscow visit and federation pitch made to Galo Plaza.

Put in summary form, the Cyprus question, as far as USG is concerned, has changed greatly in almost all of its aspects since we became actively concerned with it.

First, problem itself has changed as our immediate objective of preventing war between Greece and Turkey has essentially been accomplished. It is true that Turks still talk grimly of war with Greece if enosis should be carried out as a unilateral act but, as prospect of such action fades due to Greek second thoughts and Makarios having other ideas, likelihood of an armed clash recedes.

But unfortunately this does not get us out of woods since original major problem has now been replaced by series of others, which are perhaps of lesser magnitude individually but taken as a whole are not only immediately troublesome but could have important long term effects in the area and on our position in it. Turkey and Greece, on whose past cooperation so much depended, are now at daggers drawn and prospects are for further deterioration. Greece and Turkey who were model members of NATO, are now unhappy critics of that organization and partisans of non-alignment are raising voices. USG is under severe criticism in Nicosia, Athens and Ankara, which is unpleasant but bearable in its spleenish aspect but has serious implications as regards our specific national interests in Greece and Turkey which tend run parallel qualitatively but are considerably greater in Turkey quantitatively. Result is that problem which started out as primarily affecting others has now become one in which our own interests are directly involved and fact that war threat has receded should not leave us in doubt as to real situation.

In circumstances it would seem this time for re-evaluation in order determine whether policy evolved under other circumstances still holds good. If so, it should be consciously revalidated in terms which are explicable in light of present realities. If not, we should see what could be done by way of modification or substitution. In this re-examination cognizance should first be taken of fact that range of possibilities for settlement has been greatly reduced by exclusion of idea of early enosis, whether in unilateral, conditional or double form. This means scrapping Geneva concept and leaves independence, even though non-permanent, as single remaining solution with only question being determination of what kind of independence. As matters stand Makarios and Galo Plaza appear in agreement in principle if not in detail on an independent, unaligned, demilitarized Cyprus with certain minority right provisions for Turk Cypriots, and Papandreou's having pretty much chucked in his hand, is now taking position that anything that suits Makarios will go for him. This also would seem to be what Sovs would like since it would lead to pressure on British to give up their base rights and leave Turkey and Greece estranged and good for troubled waters fishing. This also coincides with Turkish policy to extent that it would block enosis but it leaves sharp cleavage on form which independence would take and it is on this narrowed but clearly defined gap that all the asperity and emotionalism which have characterized this problem in past are now concentrated in situation where both sides remain as deeply entrenched as ever in their positions with result that hope for agreed solution remains perhaps even more remote than before. In fact, Papandreou has categorically gone back to his original position of excluding all talks with Turks and there is no indication that Makarios, still confident of success without compromises will be any more flexible in future than in past.

It is for this reason that policy of advocating agreed solution, although having possible tactical advantages in situation where we (and also British) are at wits end act positively, is, following Geneva breakdown, dead-end street as far as Turks concerned and leads them endeavor induce US break log-jam by coming out in support of what they profess believe type of independence adapted to realities of situation. Unfortunately their nerves are pretty raw these days and they sometimes put their arguments in heavy handed form which is aggravating but this should not obscure fact that, regardless of form of presentation or our ability do something about it, this is normal approach in situation where Turks still deeply feel that something needs be done to redress imbalance but repeatedly stress that they would be open to compromise if real dialogue could be initiated.

This then is situation in which we find ourselves and in light of which review would seem in order. Should decision emerge from such study to give some form of support to principles of federation, we should realize that we might be backing horse that would never get far down track (Nicosia's 775 to Dept).[5] On other hand, there would be certain equity in making attempt since it would amount to giving Turk solution fair try as we did with enosis this past summer. It is foreseen, however, that it would be difficult to give type of general pig-in-poke endorsement of federation which Turks suggest. Furthermore, it would seem to be

---

[5] Telegram 775 from Nicosia, November 27, reported that a Cypriot federation could only be imposed by force. (Ibid.)

wishful thinking on part of Turks to assume that a word from US would cause Galo Plaza to retrim his sails and still more improbable that Soviets would fall in line (although, unlikely as it may be, sight should not be lost of possibility that they might take initiative themselves if this suited their purposes. After all in terms Soviet geopolitics Turkey easily remains at top of priority list). However, this does not alter fact that real imbalance exists, that Makarios has upper hand and that some concession by him is essential if matter is to be directed on more hopeful course. This observation is made in knowledge that current GOC policy is antithesis of this and that they too urging US abandon policy of neutrality (Nicosia's 789 to Dept),[6] which natural as far as GOC concerned but would make shambles of our relations here for simple reason that it would be directed to solution of greater rather than lesser imbalance in situation where our influence should presumably be directed to latter not only as matter simple justice but also in our own over-all interests. If USG, hopefully with assistance of Galo Plaza, could use influence to persuade GOC to undertake negotiations in spirit of sincere compromise there might be some hope. If not, all doors for helpful action prior UNGA would seem tightly shut since obvious GOT unable take initiative in absence some favorable indications in Nicosia or Athens.

Question currently posed, therefore, is whether we see any useful purpose could be served by putting renewed pressure on GOC primarily and GOG secondarily to take first step toward compromise solution and mutatis mutandis advise Turks as discreetly as possible of our views. In so doing, would be important make clear we not washing hands of Cyprus, that any limitations on our action are result of careful re-examination of facts and that we shall do our best be helpful as situation develops, especially in UNGA.

Incidentally, British Amb tells me Erkin approached him last Thursday in much same sense he had talked to me two days before (Embtel 856)[7] except that he included UK along with US, Soviets and Mediator in array which could push federation over goal line and focussed approach on immediately following visit of Mediator in London. German Amb told me he was also approached on same day by Bayulken and German support solicited on assumption that Galo Plaza left Ankara sympathetically disposed to federation idea.

Hare

---

[6] This reference is incorrect; the correct telegram has not been identified.
[7] Dated November 25. (Department of State, Central Files, POL 27 CYP))

167.   Telegram From the Embassy in Cyprus to the Department of State[1]

Nicosia, December 2, 1964, 2 p.m.

785. Ankara's 872 to Dept.[2] Reftel has again clearly described painful dilemma in which US finds itself namely that we cannot press forward on course which would provide permanent solution to Cyprus problem without at same time seriously damaging, if not destroying, our important relationship with Turkey. Since this is so, agree with Ambassador Hare that practical question now before us is what kind of independent Cyprus and is there anything US can or should do to shape this independence. Stating question another way is what kind of independent Cyprus can Turkey live with over next few years.

Our analysis of proposals reftel is based on following assumptions: 1) federation of Cyprus really means partition of Cyprus and therefore will require force to be imposed; 2) Makarios is in no mood to negotiate precisely because as reftel puts it he has upper hand and 3) US has very little leverage on Makarios and because of our proposed stand in UNGA we are likely to have even less influence.

Federation as envisaged by Turk-Cypriot leaders and we suppose by GOT is solution which might possibly be imposed temporarily at great cost by force of arms. Admittedly we have not yet got a definition of this all important word but before we go any further down this dangerous road we should know exactly what is in mind in Ankara. Geographic separation of most of two communities with boundaries cutting Famagusta and Nicosia and running west to Kokkina area is Turk Cypriot meaning. This is not merely a horse which can't go far down the track. It will stop any race which might possibly lead to an agreed solution through the efforts of the Mediator. Also worth noting again that Galo Plaza will need a lot of proselytizing on this one and obviously concept ought to be checked out thoroughly with him before we make any decision. We convinced there is no chance of selling this concept to Greek Cypriots generally or to Makarios in particular.

Since GOG has refused to agree to talk with GOT, possibility that Makarios who knows that he is master of Cypriot house would agree to talk with Turks would seem to be even more remote. As we have been regularly reporting and which reftel recognizes, Makarios and Greek Cypriots have preponderance of power, de facto control of government machinery, and strong determination to reach goal of "unfettered inde-

---

[1] Source: Department of State, Central Files, POL 27 CYP. Secret; Priority; Limdis. Repeated to Ankara, Athens, Paris for USRO, London, USUN, and Moscow.

[2] Document 166.

pendence." Makarios would react to suggestion to negotiate as another example of pressure to give up positions which he has already won over Turkish Cypriots. Therefore, not only would he refuse but if he follows past practice, would likely kick off another round of anti-US/NATO hysteria claiming foreign interference once again. Moreover, as long as GOC has indicated to Greek Cypriot public that answer to problem lies in resolution at UNGA, it would be politically impossible for GOC leadership to agree to undertake talks with GOC. In sum, we cannot detect any spirit of compromise here, at all. All shades of opinion, even those who deep down are for "instant enosis" at this stage of game agree with GOC public position that next step is UNGA and the best effort should be made there to obtain world consensus to invalidate treaties and resolution supporting unfettered independence and principle of self-determination.

GOC/Makarios current strategy is maintain facade of reasonableness combined with unilateral action of non-provocative nature. Meantime GOC proceeding step by step put into effect most of 13 points first promulgated year ago just prior to opening scene present tragedy. GOC already has accomplished de facto majority rule in Parliament, unified judiciary, abolished separate municipalities, and is considering new tax and measure to abolish Greek Communal Chamber. Such measures will continue to be applied between now and UNGA. After these "milestones" no matter what nature of resolution, Greeks here will probably promulgate new constitution providing framework for unitary state. The prospect is chilling for Turk Cypriots; they will be ignored and left to wither on vine like Arab refugees in Lebanon, Jordan and Gaza. At same time there is little likelihood that GOC will give new provocation to GOT to intervene.

Moreover, subsequent to UNGA and assuming GOC cannot get satisfaction in wording of resolution, we shall see not just continuation of series of faits accomplis establishing unitary state, but we shall also see accelerated leftward drift with all the trouble this means for USG installations and British bases. Therefore erosion of Western position, not to mention steady decay of Turkish Cypriot situation, both political and economic, to advantage only of Communists on island and elsewhere is something GOT must face. Turks (and we) must be prepared to live with this situation.

We must also recognize unhappy fact that except for our influence with GOG, US now has little influence on Makarios. Our modest aid programs are aimed chiefly at reestablishing some semblance of normality for Turkish community and to keep our foot in door while maintaining some momentum in Makarios' "peace offensive." They would have only marginal effect in getting GOC to do anything else. On other hand, GOC has relatively good leverage on us in shape of our communications facilities. After UNGA wherein we and UK will be villains of piece, GOC frustrations will be focused on US installations as most accessible target of vituperation and next on UK bases rather than on Turks (who strike back).

All these developments will involve no compensation to Turks and there will be no way of accurately measuring costly consequences to Alliance of which Turkey a vital link.

Under circumstances since we do not have means of persuading GOT to accept solution in best interests of Alliance, we must examine ways in which to ease burden for them. Perhaps as Galo Plaza and British seem to think, they will find UNGA educational experience and may emerge more malleable and thereby more susceptible to mediation effort, or failing that, when tempers have chance to cool they may be somewhat affected by realization US and West generally are losing on island. Even perhaps after dust settles and Turks can quietly come to realization that in fact there is no Turkish Cypriot position left on island, some face saving device can be devised where Turks bow to world opinion and to interests of Alliance in stemming leftward drift in Cyprus and perhaps also Greece. In meantime, if Turks, we and British can face sort of deterioration in all our positions described above, then we see the best intermediate policy for US as one of inaction combined with positive attempts to establish effective relationship with Makarios. If we do not choose even this path, then it is hard for us to see where we and Mediator can look further knowing that federation à la Turque is as much a casus belli for Greeks as enosis is for Turks.

This cable started out to be merely a somewhat strengthened reiteration of our previous commentary on hopelessness of selling peaceful federation here. We realize that Dept has in effect turned down (Deptel 403)[3] our previous proposals for inaction at UNGA and thus what we feel is best method for starting useful dialogue with Makarios (Embtel 674).[4] However since Ambassador Hare has argued cogently for new review of our Cyprus policy in light of GOT federation proposals we suggest that it might be appropriate to reconsider advantages of a policy of inaction at same time.

Belcher

---

[3] Dated November 17. (Department of State, Central Files, POL 27 CYP)
[4] Dated October 30. (Ibid.)

168.   Memorandum of Conversation[1]

SecDel/MC/12   New York, December 4, 1964, 4 p.m.

SECRETARY'S DELEGATION TO THE NINETEENTH SESSION
OF THE UNITED NATIONS GENERAL ASSEMBLY
New York, November 1964

SUBJECT

The Cyprus Problem

PARTICIPANTS

U.S.	Cyprus
The Secretary	Foreign Minister Kyprianou
John Baker, USUN	Zenon Rossides, Permanent UN Representative

During his December 4 talk with Foreign Minister Kyprianou, the Secretary asked him for his evaluation of Soviet policy. Kyprianou stated that when he was in Moscow at the end of September 1964,[2] the Soviet Deputy Foreign Minister, Kuznetzov, had told him that the Soviet Government prefers Cyprus to remain an independent state. Enosis would bring about the union of Cyprus with a member state of NATO. Kyprianou stated, however, that Kuznetzov had remarked that if the people of Cyprus want enosis (union with Greece), the Soviet Government would respect this preference.

Kyprianou stated that the Soviets had described to him the line which they were getting from the Turkish Government on federation. Kyprianou stated that he told the Soviets that this solution was out of the question completely. It was not a solution at all, he said—it would lead to partition.

Kyprianou observed that he did not see Khrushchev during his visit but that he had been introduced to Kosygin with whom he had a lengthy conversation. Kosygin was not yet then Prime Minister.[3]

The Soviets further told Kyprianou that they continued to regard the London treaties of Cyprus as unequal, exactly as Soviet Representative Fedorenko had stated in the Security Council.

Kyprianou remarked that he thought there was little change in the Soviet position on Cyprus except for the fact that they might be getting

---

[1] Source: Department of State, Secretary's Memoranda of Conversation: Lot 65 D 330. Confidential. Drafted by Baker and approved in S on December 10. The meeting was held at USUN. The source text is marked "Part II of II."

[2] Kyprianou visited Moscow September 26–October 1.

[3] Kosygin became Prime Minister on October 15, following the overthrow of Khrushchev.

closer to the Turks on the question of opposing Cypriot union with Greece. He believed that the Cypriots could still count on Soviet support on matters such as Cypriot independence, territorial integrity and sovereignty.

In response to the Secretary's question as to whether or not a General Assembly discussion of Cyprus would embitter the atmosphere, Kyprianou replied that the Assembly debate would help if it produced the right kind of resolution. Such a resolution might provide a way out of the problem of finding a solution to the Cyprus question. On the other hand, if the Assembly does not produce the right kind of resolution, the mediator's role would be frustrated or ended by "developments". Kyprianou later observed that if it were not for the tactical problem, the Cypriot Government could even suggest in the debate the inclusion in the resolution of statements on guarantees for the Turk Cypriots in order to make "the way out" easier for the Turkish Government with its own military people. Kyprianou remarked that in Turkey, public opinion does not exist.

The Secretary observed that the Security Council had noted the importance of an agreed solution to the Cyprus problem and remarked that the Assembly could not circumvent that.

Foreign Minister Kyprianou replied that by avoiding any mention of how the settlement will be brought about and by enunciating principles which would set the framework for a solution, the Assembly could play a useful role. Kyprianou stressed that he did not want anything in the Assembly resolution which would strengthen the veto which already is implicit in the agreed solution formula.

The Secretary observed that the trouble with enunciating principles of the Charter was that one can cite principles which clash. Kyprianou replied that "we like all articles of the Charter". He said the Government of Cyprus supports respect for treaties but not treaties or interpretations of treaties which are in contradiction with the Charter, which supersedes all treaties according to Article 103.

The Secretary asked what progress had been made on his suggestion of "killing the Turk Cypriots with kindness." Kyprianou observed that he had relayed to Makarios Secretary Rusk's advice in this regard.[4] He stressed that there had been progress in restoring normal conditions stating that in Limassol, Larnaca, and Famagusta things were entirely normal as far as free circulation was concerned and in Paphos conditions were improving, although there was still a problem of Turkish Cypriots being prevented by the Turk Cypriot leadership from returning to their homes. Kyprianou stressed that the central problem is in Nicosia "where the Turkish Army is."

---

[4] See Document 159.

Kyprianou described the new law on the judicial system and the makeup of the Supreme Court. He emphasized that Turkish judges were taking part in spite of the opposition of the Turkish Cypriot political leadership. He said he believed the judges had convinced the Government of Turkey that it was in the interest of the Turkish Cypriot people for these judges to participate in the new judicial system.

Kyprianou observed that the Government of Cyprus is trying to implement a new law unifying the municipalities.

He also observed that a small Armenian minority was suffering worse than either Greeks or Turks on Cyprus, stating that the Armenians suffered mainly at the hands of the Turks. Kyprianou stated that if the Turkish Cypriots would open up their communications and permit their people to move freely out of their sections of town and permit Greeks to move freely through them, it would be a big step toward the return to normalcy.

The Secretary asked what the economic balance sheet for 1964 of Cyprus would be. Kyprianou replied that exports had increased and imports had decreased, improving the balance of payments. The Secretary observed jestingly that perhaps there were some imports in 1964 that were not on the customs lists.

Ambassador Rossides asked the Secretary what would be useful in an Assembly resolution.

The Secretary stated that he felt that the process itself of discussing Cyprus in the Assembly was an inflammatory one, and stated that he was studying Article 33 of the Charter on whether or not it was wise to resort to the General Assembly with a problem of this kind.

The Secretary asked Kyprianou if his Government had any contacts with the Turks and their leaders. Kyprianou replied that there were none and that such contacts were very difficult. He observed that the mediator kept in touch with Turk Cypriot leaders. Kyprianou said that in London on his way to New York, he had heard a rumor that there would be some changes in the Turk Cypriot leadership on the island. This rumor suggested that certain Turk Cypriot leaders would be leaving the island and certain other ones coming in to take their places.

The Secretary inquired as to what possibility there was for the parties to the Cyprus dispute to "trade" and through a quid pro quo work out a solution. Kyprianou stated that the Cypriot bargaining position was weak. Cyprus had nothing to offer. All it can offer is guarantees to the minority. But it cannot offer part of Cyprus to Turkey, or "we'd all be hanged."

The Secretary observed that we did not see any solution now. Kyprianou stated that the Government of Cyprus does not see a solution either and was therefore not urging Galo Plaza to bring out a report before the General Assembly met. Galo Plaza was looking forward to the Assembly, he said, hoping it would assist his work.

Kyprianou then went over the primary Turkish Government sine qua nons in the Cyprus problem:

1) Rights of the Turkish Cypriots
2) Security
3) Prestige

He remarked that if the Cypriots were to be independent, they could not accept demilitarization of the island, unless the Turks did likewise.

If the solution were enosis, however, demilitarization could be involved. Foreign Minister Kyprianou observed that a UN guarantee could perhaps be obtained.

The Secretary asked what progress was being made internally with the Greek Cypriots on the shape of a solution. Kyprianou remarked that some Turks were amenable to an agreement, but without Turkish Government agreement, the Turkish leadership on the island would be unlikely to be agreeable. The Foreign Minister felt that the Turkish Cypriots for the most part, do not have a preference as to independence or enosis but are most interested in where they can get reliable guarantees of human rights. He thought that they would be happy to accept these if they involve some degree in autonomy and religion, culture, education, and personal status, combined with some Government financial assistance.

---

169. Telegram From the Department of State to the Embassy in Turkey[1]

Washington, December 29, 1964, 9:45 p.m.

722. Nihat Erim discussed Cyprus situation with Under Secretary December 29.[2] Ball said we see no solution in direction either enosis or double enosis. If progress appears possible toward independent Cyprus with protection of Turk minority, we should strive for this. Ball said we would do our best preserve sanctity of treaties in GA. He said he was

---

[1] Source: Department of State, Central Files, POL 27 CYP. Confidential. Drafted by Churchill, cleared by Talbot, and approved by Ball. Repeated to Athens, London, Nicosia, Paris for USRO, and USUN.

[2] A memorandum of their conversation is ibid.

assured that UK will support our position in GA. Since there is general agreement that present treaty system not working and since we hold to principle that treaties can be changed only by agreement, next step should be negotiations looking toward security of rights of Turk Cypriots in manner that does not impair sovereignty of an independent Cyprus.

Erim said he much comforted by position outlined by Under Secretary. In his view, adequate security for Turk Cypriots meant federal system with separated communities. Ball responded by repeating his views as indicated above. (In earlier conversations with Talbot and Jernegan, memcon being pouched, Erim had already heard difficulties we see in federation concept as means satisfying Turk needs.)[3]

Erim said island is quiet, but Makarios getting everything his way. Only obstacles to complete Makarios victory are continued separation Turkish community and strong points in Turkish hands. If Turk community accedes to proposals by Makarios or Galo Plaza to return to homes and give up strong points to UNFICYP, Makarios will have completed "fait accompli" and can claim no further problem exists. Erim said this assessment accounts for Turk refusal discuss Makarios proposals.

Erim said, after US stopped Turk invasion, Greeks sent 10,000 troops to island without public condemnation from US. Turk leaders might understand reasons, but impossible explain to Turkish people. Russians successfully exploiting situation with strong propaganda effort.

On next steps after GA, Under Secretary asked whether Erim thought UK might appropriately call for negotiating meeting. Erim said UK was reluctant become further involved but might make suggestion if requested by US. Ball said we would discuss this with British.

Rusk

---

[3] A memorandum of this conversation is ibid.

170.   Telegram From the Department of State to the Embassy in
         Greece[1]

Washington, January 22, 1965, 7:56 p.m.

946. Ref: Athens 1041 and 1071, Deptel 403 to Nicosia.[2] Para 1 Athens
1071 suggests that GOG misunderstands US views on question of
including reference to international treaties in any GA resolution on
Cyprus. Might be useful to set Costopoulos or Pilivakis straight next
time either raises Cyprus question.

As indicated Deptel 403 to Nicosia (rptd other addressees) US feels
strongly that GA should not interpret or modify international agreements or give moral sanction to their unilateral repudiation except in
accordance with agreement's abrogation clause if any. GA powers under
Article 14 to recommend measures for peaceful settlement of disputes
are to be interpreted consistently with Charter's objective of promoting
"respect for the obligations arising from treaties..." (Preamble). We feel
sure this view shared by large number UN member states.

It is not, however, our position that any resolution, regardless of its
terms, must inevitably contain paragraph affirming continued validity
of L/Z agreements. Whether US would advocate inclusion in any resolution on Cyprus of language specifically upholding legal validity of
Agreements will depend on circumstances, including question of
whether such resolution tended to call into question validity those
Agreements.

While as GOG knows, US holds L/Z Agreements still legally valid,
we do not consider them immutable. In fact, realities of situation make
clear they will have to be changed in some respects. However, any
changes in Agreements should be product of negotiations among parties.

FYI: We prefer not to tell GOG at this time whether Cypriot draft Res
would meet test outlined in foregoing. GA debate on Cyprus item still
some weeks off, and Cypriot Res in present form may, or may not, be an
active document when debate begins. However, as stressed in Deptel
403, Cairo type resolution would cast doubt on validity of Treaty Guar-

---

[1] Source: Department of State, Central Files, POL 27 CYP. Secret. Drafted by Moffitt;
cleared by Sisco, Buffum, GTI, and L/UNA; and approved by Jernegan. Repeated to
Ankara, London, Nicosia, USUN, and Paris for USRO.

[2] Telegram 1041 from Athens, January 8, reported Greek concern that U.S. insistence
on inviolability of treaties would strengthen Turkey's position in U.N. discussions. (Ibid.)
In telegram 1071 from Athens, January 15, Labouisse reported that he had repeated to Costopoulos that the United States was concerned about efforts to use the General Assembly to
undermine existing international agreements. (Ibid.) Regarding telegram 403 to Nicosia,
see footnote 3, Document 167.

antee and certain basic articles of Cyprus Constitution. Draft Res floated by Cyprus UN Del (USUN's A–857)[3] is stripped down version of Cairo Res and presents same problems in terms our position. Operative para 1 of Cyprus draft Res obviously intended imply that L/Z Agreements at variance with UN Charter and therefore invalid under Article 103 of Charter.

Operative para 2 of Cyprus draft would have GA call on "all states in conformity with their obligations under the Charter, and in particular Article 2, paragraphs 1 and 4 . . ." to refrain from threat or use of force or "intervention directed against Cyprus." This obviously included as challenge to Article 4 Treaty of Guarantee. End FYI.

Rusk

---

[3] Airgram A–57, January 7, summarized conversations with Cypriot and Turkish representatives on the issues involved in U.N. consideration of the Cyprus question. (Department of State, Central Files, POL 27 CYP)

---

171.   Telegram From the Embassy in Cyprus to the Department of State[1]

Nicosia, January 23, 1965, noon.

941. Paid routine call on President Friday.

After covering number of incidental items, raised problem of Cyprus issue in UNGA in view Article 19 problem. Said we would be interested knowing what GOC plans were for period after UN disposed of issue in General Assembly assuming voting problem settled. Makarios reminded me that he had always maintained that no matter what sort of resolution came out of General Assembly, whether good or bad from Greek Cypriot point of view, he realized UN had no capability for imposing whatever solution recommended. Therefore problem of future remained where it had always been—with people of Cyprus. Said he was giving serious consideration to promulgation of new Constitution (this is idea mentioned to me more than once by Clerides) which could be put forward on temporary ad referendum basis pending final approval by people as a whole. He observed that Turk Cypriots might or might not

---

[1] Source: Department of State, Central Files, POL 27 CYP. Confidential. Repeated to Athens, Ankara, USUN, London, and Paris for USRO.

accept Constitution at that time, but this made little difference to him under circumstances. Whatever happens at UN and whatever his decision may be regarding possible new Constitution Archbishop assured me he had no intention using further violence to impose Greek Cypriot will on Turks. He would give GOT no excuse for intervention and certainly had no intention of declaring enosis with Greece until he certain Greece understood possible consequences and prepared accept them. In his mind this ruled out enosis for time being since appeared be casus belli for GOT. When I pointed out that it all very well to govern under some new constitutional framework but that this did not provide for "normalization" and eradication of physical barriers now existing between two communities, Archbishop said that this matter was up to Turks. They were free as far as he concerned to stay as they were behind Green Line and within their ghettoes if they chose not to play part in life of state under new Constitution. Said he was following Secretary Rusk's good advice to Kyprianou given both in Washington and New York and would continue "peace offensive" expressing belief that in time more and more Turkish Cypriots would accept facts of life and return to normal existence. Makarios gave no indication he expected obtain favorable judgment in New York.

In view numerous press rumors of possibility GOC planning conversations with GOG or even with GOT, Makarios indicated he was not in favor of talks at this time since he feared they likely be unsuccessful and failure of talks to produce substantive progress might well only worsen situation. He would not be drawn out on question of possible trip to Athens but commented on my use of words "other interested parties" with reference to possible talks. With considerable emphasis Makarios said that as far as he concerned only interested parties to internal aspect of Cyprus disputes were two communities in Cyprus. Since Greek Cypriot community in majority they would determine fate of island, of course taking into account legitimate rights of Turk minority. Reiterated they had no intention using force in this connection but would rely on time being on their side. On several occasions he reiterated his ultimate aim for Cyprus was enosis but that as responsible leader and with Greek interests at heart he could not do anything which would be against the pursuit of this age-old aim of Greek Cypriots.

With regard Gromyko statement,[2] Makarios said this was further evidence that Soviets like all nations were pursuing own national interests and it quite obvious that there was much more at stake for them in Turkey than in Cyprus. Said he believed Soviets had decided against wholehearted support of Greek Cypriots and were now obviously inten-

---

[2] Reference is to the Soviet proposal for a "federal" form of government in Cyprus, made in an interview in *Izvestia,* January 21.

sively wooing Turks. Said he felt there something basically inconsistent in Gromyko statement with regard federation as possible solution. This would merely perpetuate divisions within island and make even more difficult achievement of ostensible Soviet aim of viable independent unitary state. Said it obvious that Soviets (as well as UAR) against enosis for own national interest, but by proposing solution which perpetuated divisions, Soviets at same time were creating system in which dream of enosis and "double-enosis" would continue be ultimate aim of both Greeks and Turks in island. Added he personally utterly opposed to federation concept and could not see how it could be applied in Cyprus in view of distribution of minority throughout island.

While President did not say so specifically, it was obvious he not too perturbed by nature Gromyko statement since it contained many words having great appeal to Greeks. Federation concept merely mentioned as one possibility and Greek reject this but cling to remainder of statement supporting territorial integrity, no foreign intervention and continued independence of island. From his response to my comment Gromyko's words would bolster Turks' spirits considerably, it was obvious that this made little difference to him. (President later issued following press statement: "The Soviet Foreign Minister's statement is open to various interpretations. In my view the Soviet Union supports, in the case of Cyprus, independence unfettered by treaties. But I cannot say that Moscow favors union of Cyprus with Greece.")

In response suggestion that there might be something on which to find basis for common ground in fact that we now found Soviets, Turks and, at least for near future, Greek Cypriots supporting concept of independent Cyprus, President commented that he found no room for compromise beyond providing Turks with rights and guarantees offered minorities in other states. If this could constitute common ground then there should be possibility of Turk Cypriot participation in life of country.

With regard extension of UNFICYP mandate President reiterated statement he made to Thimayya yesterday to effect he would rely on his advice as to needs but hoped could reduce numbers.

Comments and suggestions to follow.

Belcher

172. Telegram From the Department of State to the Embassy in Greece[1]

Washington, January 28, 1965, 1:05 p.m.

961. FYI. In separate conversations with Secretary and Under Secretary January 26, Turkish Foreign Minister Erkin reported that Greek UN delegation had been in touch twice recently (apparently within previous day or two) with member Turkish delegation. Greeks had frankly expressed their growing conviction that nothing leading toward Cyprus solution would come out of UNGA. Had proposed, therefore, that tripartite Greek-Turkish-Cypriot talks be arranged. In first conversation, Turk representative had suggested Greeks talk to Kyprianou about this. Second contact was made by chief Greek delegate Bitsios who reported Kyprianou was consulting Makarios for instructions.

Erkin seemed regard this as encouraging sign and to be quite ready undertake at least bilateral talks with GOG, provided they could be kept completely secret. He asked that USG speak to Greeks, without revealing his approach to us, to urge such talks. Both Secretary and Under Secretary endorsed bilateral negotiation, and Erkin was assured we would make approach to GOG.

When specifically queried about Turkish attitude toward tripartite talks, Erkin first expressed fear British would insist upon being included because of their worries about Cyprus bases. Ball said he thought British might be so relieved to have something going on which might lead to solution that they would not insist on taking part. Erkin later said that if Greek Cypriots included in discussions, Turkey would have to insist that representatives of Turkish Cypriots likewise be present. Again indicated his preference for initial talks with GOG alone.

Suggestion was made that there might be better chance of bringing Greeks to negotiating table if Turks indicated willingness to talk about all outstanding issues between Greece and Turkey, rather than Cyprus alone. Erkin balked at this, saying Cyprus was of overriding importance, but did suggest GOT would be willing sign undertaking with Greeks to settle other problems once agreement had been reached on Cyprus. Dept officer commented this, of course, was matter of tactics which hopefully Turks could work out in further preliminary contacts with GOG representatives.

Re substance of possible solution for Cyprus, Erkin once more spoke of federation as only logical way out, since modified enosis exemplified

---

[1] Source: Department of State, Central Files, POL 27 CYP. Secret; Priority; Exdis. Drafted and approved by Jernegan and cleared by Talbot, Bracken, Sisco, and Springsteen (U). Also sent to Ankara and repeated to London, Nicosia, and USUN.

in first Acheson Plan had proven unacceptable to Greeks. Insisted that physical separation of Greek and Turkey Cypriots would not be nearly so difficult as people asserted. More than half Turkish Cypriots were concentrated in area north of Nicosia. (Dept officer pointed out these people would need much greater area than they currently occupied if they were to support themselves permanently. Erkin agreed.) Turkey, he said, would not insist on forced transfer of all Greeks out of Turkish area or all Turks out of Greek area. It would undertake not to annex Turkish area to Turkey unless Greece took rest of island for Greece. We avoided any commitment to support federation, saying we still believed parties must work things out among themselves without outside intervention.

There was some discussion of UN Mediator's position, with Erkin reporting he had seen Galo Plaza January 25. Plaza had said he would make final round of capitals concerned after UNGA debate on Cyprus and then submit report. If it appeared debate was to be indefinitely postponed, he would make his rounds without waiting for it and submit report. It was agreed this line presented dangers and that Dept would try to talk things over in Washington in near future. It was also agreed, at Erkin's insistence, that nothing would be said to Mediator about possible Greek-Turkish talks. End FYI.

In light of foregoing but without revealing any knowledge of Greek approach to Turks or Erkin's approach to us on subject, please take earliest opportunity renew to Papandreou or Costopoulos our suggestion that direct, private negotiations between parties immediately concerned offer best hope of progress toward Cyprus settlement.[2] You may put forward as our view growing conviction that UNGA debate and whatever resolution may emerge from it is most unlikely move question any farther forward. In fact, we could not say with any real confidence at this moment that debate will even take place in near future in view of situation in GA. Therefore, it seems futile to lose time and possibly see situation deteriorate while waiting for something which has so little promise of positive results. We continue believe GOT desires talk to GOG, probably secretly at first, and hope GOG will make contact directly to explore this with Turks.

If Greeks insist on participation Cypriot Government in talks you should urge they keep open mind on this and not make it firm condition. Important thing is to get something started. From past experience we would judge both Greeks and Turks would prefer avoid public attention

---

[2] Telegram 1163 from Athens, February 2, reported that the Greek Government had responded to Turkish suggestions by encouraging dialogue between Greek Cypriots and Turkish Cypriots. Costopoulos added that a change in the Greek approach might be possible depending on future Turkish moves and the outcome of the General Assembly debate on Cyprus. (Ibid.)

to their contacts, and this would obviously be much more difficult if additional parties added to negotiations in early stages.

If it seems appropriate, you may say that we do not think it would be helpful to bring UN Mediator or other outsiders at this stage (including US) into picture. FYI. We think Turks distrust Plaza so much they would refuse even to begin if he were in any way involved.

On January 27 Ambassador Menemencioglu informed us Greek UN delegation again in touch with Turkish delegation with news that Makarios believes time not right for tripartite talks. Menemencioglu consequently feels chance for successful outcome of recent contacts remote. End FYI. Nevertheless, we believe you should proceed with above approach and point out to Greeks that some kind of bilateral talks even more essential if Makarios unwilling enter discussions at this time.

For Ankara: Our reading of developments in Nicosia suggests talks have better chance of evolving if GOT would exploit current sparkles of interest on part of Greek-Cypriots in talks with Ankara Turks. In any event it would help GOG exercise influence over Makarios (if that is Erkin's aim) if GOT would carry on facade of discussion with Makarios, even though it pins more hope on working out solution with GOG.

Ball

---

173.   Airgram From the Embassy in Greece to the Department of State[1]

A–605   Athens, January 29, 1965.

SUBJECT

Conversation with King Constantine

I met with King Constantine, at his request, on the afternoon of January 27. The King apparently had no special reason for asking me to see him, other than to exchange views on the general political and economic situation affecting Greece. The King observed that things were "in a mess" referring both to the internal Greek scene and to Cyprus.

Internal Political Problems

King Constantine remarked that there was much talk about the spread of communism within Greece, and while he thought there had

---

[1] Source: Department of State, Central Files, POL 15–1 GREECE. Secret; Priority; Limit Distribution. Drafted by Labouisse.

been some growth in the activity and boldness of the extreme left which caused him concern, he believed the press comment and other talk on the subject was exaggerated. I said that our observations led us to a similar conclusion although we agreed that the matter should be carefully watched.

Constantine then said that some people (unidentified) had wanted him to act against the Papandreou Government but he did not consider a move in this direction wise or practicable, at least at this time. There was no one on the scene who could replace Papandreou, as the latter still had a strong popular appeal among the Greek people. He went so far as to say that if he should try to unseat the Prime Minister now, Papandreou would "go into the streets."

The King then commented on the appointment of Tsirimokos as Minister of Interior. He recalled a meeting some time ago with Papandreou in which the latter had volunteered that he would never appoint Tsirimokos to the Interior Ministry.[2] Later, when the Prime Minister came to him to say that he wanted to make that very appointment, the King sought to elicit the reasons for Papandreou's change of heart, but he could obtain no satisfactory explanation except "political desirability." Constantine said that he tried to argue the Prime Minister out of making the appointment but that, although he felt the latter came close to giving in, he finally stood his ground saying that it would cause him to lose face if it should become known that he had given in to the King on this particular issue. Constantine observed to Papandreou that "if the King should happen to have a good idea once in a while there was no reason to reject it just because he was the King." But the Prime Minister stood firm and the appointment was made.

The King told me that he had initially considered standing up to Papandreou over the Tsirimokos appointment, forcing the Prime Minister's resignation. However, he sensed that a possible trap was being laid for him and he was not sufficiently sure that he could win if he stood his ground.

As he seemed to be desirous of some reaction from me on this, I observed that I could well understand the importance of his being reasonably sure of success before taking on the Prime Minister. I told him that I had been approached by persons suggesting that the King should unseat the government and that my reply had been that I thought the circumstances not propitious and that if the King acted prematurely he could do the regime irreparable harm. I went on to say that there might well come

---

[2] Elias Tsirimokos, former leader of the Democratic Union Party, was a critic of U.S. policies in Greece with ties to EDA. Labouisse reported on his discussions with Papandreou on the Tsirimokos appointment in telegram 1103 from Athens, January 21. (Ibid., POL US–GREECE) Tsirimokos became Minister of the Interior in February 1964.

a time when he would feel he must act, but I cautioned him not to do anything hastily. He agreed and then said that if Papandreou should "tamper with the Army as he has with the gendarmerie," he would definitely make this an issue and would call for the Prime Minister's resignation.

I inquired whether there were any indications that the Prime Minister is contemplating any such action against the Army Officer Corps, but the King did not think this was in the cards at the moment. He mentioned that Papandreou had at one point wanted to move Garoufalias from the Ministry of Defense to the Ministry of Coordination but both the King and Garoufalias had objected.

We then spoke of the deterioration of the general economic situation in Greece. The King's views coincided with those of the Embassy; namely, that whereas there has been some deterioration and will doubtless be more, a real disenchantment with Papandreou among the public because of failure of his economic policies will not be felt for some months at least. The King then observed that meanwhile the main problem was to maintain and strengthen the forces of law and order to offset possible increased boldness from the extreme left.

Concerning the opposition party ERE, the King said that it was holding together but that there was no outstanding leader who could inspire the people.

Cyprus

I asked the King what Grivas was doing in Athens, to which he replied that he was here to "seek more authority." Grivas apparently wishes more authority over the Greek forces in Cyprus and also is asking for some additional Greek officers to assist him with the Greek Cypriot forces. The King does not believe that the additional authority will be given him, but made no further comment about the additional officers.

Grivas had called on the King that morning and, during the conversation, Constantine asked Grivas whether Cyprus would accept the Acheson plan at this time. Grivas reportedly replied that although he personally was more receptive now than he had been, he could not persuade the Cypriot people "to go that far."

The King then went on to stress the point he has made during previous conversations with me that the deterioration of the situation in Greece was partly due to the continued Cyprus crisis and that it was most important that an early solution be found. I agreed, pointing out the various efforts we had made to encourage an agreed solution and repeating again our position concerning the necessity for the parties themselves to get together for talks. I told him that I saw no possibility of any solution coming from the UNGA debates, stressing the limitations of power in the General Assembly on this issue. He said that it was because he realized that nothing would probably come out of the General Assembly discussion that he thought other efforts should be made.

He then said that he was searching in his own mind for some possible way out of the impasse and went on to outline a proposal which was thoroughly confusing. He inquired what would happen if Makarios could be persuaded "to declare Cyprus independent, asking all troops to leave the island and saying that he would thereafter negotiate with the Turkish Government re one or two bases." Wen I looked somewhat surprised at this proposal, he hastened to add that if Makarios would not act along these lines, possibly Grivas could set him aside and he could make the declaration. He added that he of course realized that nothing like this could be done without US approval, tacit or otherwise. I said that the proposal struck me as quite impracticable: in the first place I understood that Cyprus was independent, and secondly, that I could not imagine the Turks being willing to withdraw their contingent from the island against some promise of future negotiations. I pointed out that this was a far cry from the Acheson plan of last August and that Turkey had even rejected that. Therefore, I did not believe this a saleable proposition. I tried to probe to find out whether or not there was something else the King had in mind, or whether some suggestion had been made to him by Grivas or others about the possibility of Grivas displacing Makarios, but the results were negative.

It appears possible, judging from other comments we have heard in recent days, that Grivas may have been entertaining thoughts of attempting a coup somewhat along these lines. However, as we have reported, it does not appear that the Government has been willing to go along with him. In recent talks with the Foreign Minister, he has been categoric in asserting that Greece will take no action to upset the present calm on the island.

Comment: The King is a young man of good will sincerely troubled by the political situation and eager to advance Greek interests. His enthusiasm, his desire to be helpful, his inexperience and the fact that he is naturally the target of many persons seeking to promote partisan interest make it especially important to weigh with caution his suggestions for action. Moreover, the narrower interest of the Crown as well as the broader interest of Greek internal political stability require that his initiatives be prudent and made only after mature reflection. During the first year of his reign, he has, on balance, handled himself with skill and with restraint. I shall continue to encourage him to act in this manner.

Henry R. Labouisse

174.   Telegram From the Embassy in Cyprus to the Department of State[1]

Nicosia, February 1, 1965, 3 p.m.

955. Deptel 495.[2] Bernardes has had very interesting meeting with Makarios. Latter confirmed that Sov Chargé has made it very clear that if enosis is GOC goal then "deal is off." If enosis is declared and Turks move in as they have threatened, then Sovs will stand aside; nor will they move if it is obvious that Turks take action as result of GOC attack against Turk Cypriots. Bernardes says Makarios told Satouchin that he could not specify GOC goals. Would appear that Sovs have indeed made clear to Makarios that he cannot count on them unless he prepared to deal enosis out of his future and they have at same time made clear what we have suspected all along: that they are quite pragmatic—as distinct from impression they made on gullible Cypriots—and would not get involved in nasty situation resulting from some GOC miscalculation.

There would seem to be no reason to doubt Makarios' statement to Bernardes. It confirms reports we have been getting and sending on to Dept in recent days and although Greeks here only now and then suffer from pragmatism, they and GOC must now realize that there is real trouble ahead in their attempts to use UNGA and supposed "open-ended" Soviet backing to achieve their aims. They may therefore be more amenable to negotiation than at any time in recent months. We have suggested this in recent cables,[3] but this is not to say that Makarios is now willing to accept dictation from Athens.

Which leads us to suggest that we should be very cautious indeed in proposing some new set of negotiations or talks (Deptel 495) between Greece and Turkey without being prepared to accept that the results may be abortive as the last time we did so. There is nothing that Makarios would like better than to have a chance now to burnish his somewhat, but not seriously, tarnished image a bit by appearing the super patriot again, as he did when he rejected Acheson Plan mark one once it was presented to him by Papandreou. In fact right now he needs another such chance in order to counter criticism that he had become too involved with the Soviets. As we have suggested, GOC–Makarios appear boxed in, and we should be careful not to give them opportunity get out.

We continue to believe that the time is ripe for some new initiative, whether or not along the lines of our suggestions, and that Plaza is our

---

[1] Source: Department of State, Central Files, POL 27 CYP. Secret; Priority; Exdis. Repeated to USUN, London, Athens, and Ankara.

[2] Telegram 495 to Nicosia was sent for action to Athens as telegram 961, Document 172.

[3] These suggestions were made in telegrams 945 from Nicosia, January 26, 947 from Nicosia, January 27, and 953 from Nicosia, January 29, all in Department of State, Central Files, POL 27 CYP.

best bet, despite real or imagined unhappiness on part of Turks with him (which USG might do something to counter). We are convinced however that no new game will be productive that deals Makarios out of the first hand. He is in charge here and he has made it unmistakably clear that there are no "parties concerned" with the internal problem as far as he is concerned, except the people of Cyprus, consisting of a Greek majority and a Turk minority. This position has international appeal and from viewpoint US interests whether he has the right to feel this way is immaterial: he is in a position to sabotage any bilateral agreement reached between Greece and Turkey and emerge stronger domestically than ever before, as he did after the last time he was dealt out of the game. Had we not better promote the Clerides position—i.e., GOG and Makarios talks to line up a possible mutually acceptable position which might then be negotiated by GOC and GOT, or by GOG and GOT. Our own feeling is that interests of settlement would be better served by direct negotiations between Makarios and GOT. Trouble with GOG handling joint position for GOC–GOG is that latter will always be vulnerable to Makarios if he thinks GOG is moving in wrong direction to detriment of Cyprus or if he sees some personal advantage in pulling rug. On other hand direct GOC–GOT negotiations based on joint GOC–GOG position would seem to have effect of multiplying pressures on Makarios while giving him important psychological (and political) incentive of appearing to be master of own fate.

Belcher

---

175.   Memorandum of Conversation[1]

Washington, February 4, 1965, 2:15 p.m.

SUBJECT

United States & Government of Cyprus Positions on the Cyprus Problem

PARTICIPANTS

United States:
The Acting Secretary
John D. Jernegan, Acting Assistant Secretary, NEA
Robert Anderson, U
Gordon D. King, Cyprus Affairs, NEA/GTI

Cypriot:
Foreign Minister Spyros Kyprianou
Ambassador Zenon Rossides

---

[1] Source: Johnson Library, National Security File, Country File, Cyprus, Vol. 16, Secret. Drafted by King and approved in U on February 16.

The Foreign Minister called on the Acting Secretary at his own request in order to exchange views on the Cyprus problem before his departure for Nicosia next week. During the hour long conversation, the following points emerged:

1. *Prospects for the UNGA.* Kyprianou expressed pessimism over prospects for the General Assembly. The Acting Secretary agreed that the chances for the General Assembly are not good, that it is likely to adjourn on or about Monday February 8, and that the adjournment may be for several weeks.[2] He inquired about the plans of the Government of Cyprus.

The Foreign Minister noted that the Government of Cyprus has been hoping for a General Assembly debate to strengthen its positions and that of the Mediator. With the likelihood of an adjournment, Kyprianou felt that it is now necessary for him to return to Cyprus for consultations.

2. *United States Position.* Kyprianou asked how the United States feels now about the Cyprus problem.

The Acting Secretary stated that there is no change in the United States position. The United States, he noted, has always hoped for a resolution of the problem through discussions. A solution cannot be reached otherwise. The United States has long been skeptical that the General Assembly debate would make a contribution to the settlement. The United States position regarding a settlement is the same, that the parties must work out a settlement themselves. We are not prepared to dictate the solution. We tried to help in Geneva and it did not work. We have no plans and no proposals.

The Foreign Minister rephrased his question, asking what, after the experiences of the past year, the United States sees as a solution. Negotiations, he stated, have been tried and failed and would be of no use now unless there were some hope for a settlement.

When Mr. Ball noted that no talks have been tried since last year in January in London, Kyprianou said that negotiations have been repeatedly tried over many years. But what, he pressed, is the United States view of a solution? The positions of the parties concerned are well known: the Turks favor federation; Cyprus wants unfettered independence, majority rule, and self-determination. Cyprus knows, he said, that the United States wants an agreed solution but does the United States have some advice on a solution?

Mr. Ball observed that he could only tell the Foreign Minister what he had told Erkin. The treaties are still on the books. No one denies that they are not very workable. When this is the case, the only thing to do is to

---

[2] The General Assembly recessed on February 8.

get together and talk. We told Turkey that we have no solution. Furthermore, a United States solution would not be useful. Because of the power and size of the United States, even if we made a proposal it would be taken as an attempt to coerce the parties concerned; so we refuse to make such a proposal. When we asked Mr. Acheson to offer advice to the Mediator, he was acting as an individual who put forward ideas which were not United States positions but were intended to move the parties toward agreement. He served as a catalyst. However, the effort did not work and is now academic. At present, there is nothing we can contribute by choosing a solution. On the contrary, we would be doing a disservice.

Mr. Jernegan stated that another facet is also important: countries which have made clear their views on a solution all have a direct national interest in the matter: the Greeks want enosis, the Soviets oppose enosis, the Turks want federation, etc. However, the United States by the nature of things is not directly concerned with any particular solution. We do not support enosis, nor do we condemn it. We do not support federation, nor do we condemn it. We want only to have peace and stability in the area.

The Foreign Minister insisted that there must, however, be a lasting solution. In order for it to be lasting, it must be acceptable to the majority of the Cyprus population. The majority does not want federation. Even a considerable number of Turk-Cypriots do not want to divide the island. But to say that all the parties concerned have a veto means that no solution is possible. In this context, the United States should press for the right solution. The United States cannot take a stand contrary to its principles. Others may do so, but not the United States. The situation only becomes more and more dangerous when the belief is accepted that the various parties have a veto. Turkey, for example, is not hurting because of the dispute. Neither for that matter is Greece. Therefore, they can afford to carry on and, as long as Turkey holds to its present course, no solution is possible.

3. *The Soviet Position.* Kyprianou said that it is wrong to believe that the Soviet position against enosis will make the Greeks or Greek-Cypriots anti-Soviet. They will instead again think it is the fault of the United States for not taking a firm stand. He asked why the United States is quiet over Turkey's approaches to the Soviet Union. When Mr. Ball pointed out that the United States did not object when the Government of Cyprus approached the Soviets, Kyprianou maintained that the Government of Cyprus quickly learned of the United States attitude through the American press. He said that, by contrast, even when Turkey withdrew from the MLF, there was no United States criticism. Mr. Jernegan pointed out that the change in Turk relations with the Soviets amounted to no more than a slight rapprochement to which the United States could not object.

The Foreign Minister said that the danger in this development is that it may lead to a competition between Turkey and Cyprus concerning the Soviets. If the tendency is to make the Soviets central to the dispute, each party may attempt to bid higher for Soviet support. Mr. Ball said there is no doubt that the Government of Turkey is willing to play up any kind of support it can get. However, he noted, the Turk-Soviet conversations, as the United States sees them, are not very far-reaching. We were surprised, in fact, at the Soviet statement regarding federation. Mr. Jernegan reiterated that the development is not a major element and expressed its primary importance as giving somewhat more encouragement to the Turks.

Kyprianou stated his belief that the Soviet position is simple. Moscow, he felt, supports the Government of Cyprus up to the point of enosis. If the Government of Cyprus says that it abandons enosis as an objective, the Soviets would be 100% on the Government of Cyprus side. Only here do Soviet interests coincide with Turkey's.

4. *Turkish Objectives.* The Foreign Minister maintained that in the long run it is not even in Turkey's interest to forget enosis. At present, he said, the Turks oppose everything Cyprus wants, but their basic interests would not prohibit enosis. He then professed to be puzzled as to Turkey's aims. He insisted that the Government of Cyprus really does not know, even though the Turks talk about federation and partition.

The Acting Secretary suggested that the Government of Cyprus ask them. Kyprianou hurriedly stated that the Mediator has been asking and cannot find out. He asked if it were prestige the Turks wanted, or land. He opined that the Turks know it is not possible to partition the island. He said that minority safeguards through the United Nations could be accepted in the Government of Cyprus. As far as East-West relations are concerned, Cyprus will choose enosis through self-determination and enosis will solve all problems. Therefore, he concluded, it is difficult to know what else Turkey could want.

Mr. Ball stated that, in a situation such as this, many deep emotional feelings, some rational, some not, are involved. Pride comes into the picture, national prestige, concern for the Turk-Cypriots, etc. It is very difficult to say that, objectively, the best interests of Turkey or Greece or Cyprus lie in a particular formula; this has been tried but is not what the parties concerned find acceptable. As far as Turkey's desires are concerned, Mr. Ball suggested that much depends on the manner in which a solution is worked out. Turkey might accept solution "A" at one time and not at another. He noted that, once last summer, there was a moment when it appeared Turkey might accept mere tokens to save its prestige, involving the lease of a small bit of land for a base, coupled with enosis. Mr. Ball said that he believes there is currently an enormous desire in

Turkey to get rid of this problem. It has been here a long time and has become a domestic liability for the Government of Turkey.

5. *Talks between the parties*. The Acting Secretary expressed the view that a quiet kind of conversation over a long period of time would be useful. He noted that talks could perhaps involve Cyprus, Greece and Turkey with someone from the Turk-Cypriot community and suggested that it would be far better to enter into discussions than to let the situation continue. Mr. Jernegan added that discussions should involve some kind of quiet contacts perhaps between the Government of Cyprus and the Government of Turkey, and should be secret bargaining sessions to discover if the first positions of the parties are final.

Mr. Ball expressed the opinion that Turkey's first position is not final. He argued that an undertaking to hold discussions would in itself be useful, even if it fails. Such discussions, he pointed out, should not be gone through quickly, and in the meantime it would help for reasonable stability to continue on the island.

The Foreign Minister contended that the Turk-Cypriots have been building their strength during this period of calm. The Acting Secretary responded that some new tensions have arisen and mentioned specifically President Makarios' election proposal and the upcoming Turkish contingent troop rotation problem. These, he said, could make the situation very rough, but nevertheless talks could be quietly entered into and quietly held between Cyprus and Turkey, or among Cyprus, Turkey and Greece.

Ambassador Rossides criticized the London–Zurich agreement and suggested that a real solution is one which will enable the Greek-Cypriots and Turk-Cypriots to live together. He argued that divisiveness must not be insisted on and predicted that, if Turkey does insist, again there will be trouble. Federation, he said, is all right in a situation where it is necessary to bring parts together into a whole, but in Cyprus federation would mean breaking up that which is already whole.

The Acting Secretary reiterated that the United States is not insisting on any particular solution, federation or otherwise, but feels that since the island is quiet now, this is a chance for profitable talks; they hold the only hope. Mr. Jernegan suggested that the Government of Cyprus might find a basis for satisfying the Turks without physical separation. Ambassador Rossides agreed. Mr. Ball suggested that such a possibility should not be excluded. He reiterated his thought that in a quiet atmosphere, over a period of time, Turkey might not stick to its original position. However, he stated, outsiders should stay out, including even the British. The Soviets should stay out as well, he added, and the United States.

Mr. Jernegan noted that the attitude of all the parties has changed in the last few months; it is now clear that anything which is acceptable to

Turkey and to the Greek-Cypriots would be acceptable to everyone else. Kyprianou objected that some differences between Turkey and the Turk-Cypriots are now apparent. He expressed the opinion that it would be helpful if agreement could be reached between Greece, Turkey and the United Kingdom to approve whatever the Greek-Cypriots and Turk-Cypriots would work out. Both Mr. Ball and Mr. Jernegan expressed strong doubts that either Turkey or the Turk-Cypriots would agree to such an arrangement; Mr. Jernegan added that, if the Government of Cyprus worked something out with the Turk-Cypriots, Turkey might possibly accept it after some study.

Mr. Ball emphasized that his advice to the Foreign Minister about entering into talks he had already given to the Turkish Government and that he would willingly give it to the Greek Government. The Foreign Minister stated that the Government of Cyprus' fear has always been and still is that it cannot get a lasting and proper solution if a country outside Cyprus has a veto. He termed this "always a mistake". During negotiations back in the 1950's, he contended, the matter could have remained a colonial issue but the United Kingdom brought in Greece and Turkey. Cyprus, he said, is now trying to overcome that mistake. The Government of Cyprus feels that if a solution were definitely in sight, it would welcome negotiations. However, it has reservations about abandoning principles when it knows that negotiations will fail.

The Acting Secretary reiterated that the only way to find out is to try. He stated that if one tries to solve the problem on the basis of abstractions, opposing abstractions cancel each other out. A good deal of pragmatism, he suggested, is the best approach; the best way to find a solution is to look for one and the best way to look for one is to talk.

6. *The Mediator.* The Foreign Minister remarked rather wistfully that if the Mediator's preferred solution were only known, talks might be more hopeful. Mr. Ball expressed doubt that the Mediator is in as good a position to look for a solution as the Government of Cyprus is. Mr. Jernegan pointed out that the Mediator working alone could be caught between strongly opposing positions, shuttling back and forth between the parties; under such circumstances, the talks might die. It would be better, Mr. Jernegan added, if the Government of Cyprus and the Turks talked together.

The Acting Secretary suggested further that the Mediator might be most useful if Cyprus and Turkey and Greece had representatives located somewhere with the Mediator on hand to help.

7. *Situation on the island.* Mr. Jernegan noted that two issues have revived tensions on the island, the Turk contingent rotation and the problem of another Red Crescent shipment. He expressed the view that the negative attitude of the Government of Cyprus on these matters could destroy the present relative calm. He questioned very seriously if this

Government of Cyprus action is worthwhile. Kyprianou described the second issue as a relatively minor one. The Government of Cyprus, he noted, has allowed all previous Red Crescent shipments in free even though everything in them was available on the island and Cypriot merchants were angry with the Government. As a result of Government of Cyprus leniency, this is tending to become an established practice. But with regard to the issue of the rotation, he said, a question of principle is involved. The Government of Cyprus questions the very presence of the contingent. The last time the Government of Cyprus agreed not to oppose rotation, it turned out that the Turks sent out 500 Turk-Cypriot students and brought in 500 Turkish soldiers. When Mr. Jernegan objected that there was United Nations supervision of the last rotation, the Foreign Minister insisted that the United Nations could not possibly tell whether or not such a thing happened. The Government of Cyprus, however, knows it as a fact and it makes the problem very difficult. Mr. Jernegan suggested a pragmatic view that even if true, it is a small matter compared to the obstacle the Government of Cyprus refusal raises to a final settlement.

---

176.   Telegram From the Embassy in Cyprus to the Department of State[1]

Nicosia, February 10, 1965, 10 a.m.

991. Deptel 518.[2] Saw Bernardes morning Feb 09 immediately after receiving reftel. He shares our assessment of troop rotation problem. He will see Makarios in next day or two and present strong oral démarche to Makarios which he will follow up with letter for the record. He does not recommend we use SYG yet since once having done so there is little left in our armory in event SYG turned down at this stage. Says he believes Greeks mistakenly thinking in terms of substantial quid pro quo. He has reports from N.Y. that Kyprianou had suggested to UNSYG that appropriate concession by Turks would be turning control of Kyrenia Road over to GOC. Bernardes described this as wildly improbable concession by Turks and indicative of Greek failure make any objective

---

[1] Source: Department of State, Central Files, POL 27 CYP. Confidential. Repeated to Athens, Ankara, USUN, Paris for USRO, and London.

[2] Telegram 518 to Nicosia, February 8, approved Belcher's proposal to meet with Plaza and Bernardes and urge them to make a "preemptive" appeal to all parties on the troop rotation issue. (Ibid.)

assessment of Turk position. When I outlined Aktulga's exposition of Turkish attitude toward rotation (Ankara's 1152 to Dept)[3] he agreed saying that he and his staff could not conceive of Turks making further concession on rotation question. Said he had already spoken to Makarios three times: once when he first knew of Turk request, again after hearing from Georkadjis that negative decision imminent, and again last Friday. Makarios had made it very clear at last meeting that he expected extract something further from Turks and also had mentioned Road. Bernardes had thought he had in mind some further relaxation of present restrictions on unarmed Greek use but word from New York mentioned above indicated they had grander ideas.

Bernardes believes Makarios will push this question to the limit despite fact that by doing so he is obviously not acting in accordance with SC resolution. Bernardes letter will refer to GOC action last November permitting rotation and will call upon him in terms SC resolution to make concession on rotation in order not further increase tensions. We do not believe this will elicit any favorable response at this time and that it will be necessary towards end of month to call on SYG for public appeal to Makarios to which he thinks Makarios at last moment will acquiesce. Bernardes pointed out that this time he certain Turks not bluffing when they say failure to rotate on time (by March 8) would require special legislation by Turk GNA. (Perhaps Ankara could comment on this.)

Will discuss this question with Plaza tomorrow afternoon and will discuss with UK and Canadian colleagues here to see if they perceive any utility in seeking additional instructions from their governments to make individual démarches to GOC in support of UN action.

As Dept aware I have already raised matter informally with Makarios and Araouzos, but there may be some additional mileage to be gained if I were to do so under instructions.[4]

Belcher

---

[3] Telegram 1152 from Ankara, February 6, reported that Turkey would neither make concessions nor enter into prolonged negotiations over the issue of troop rotation. (Ibid.)

[4] In telegram 526 to Nicosia, February 11, the Department of State declined to authorize another démarche to Makarios on the troop rotation issue, stating that it preferred to use the United Nations as a forum for dealing with this issue. (Ibid.)

177.   Telegram From the Embassy in Greece to the Department of State[1]

Athens, February 16, 1965, 8 p.m.

1227. Deptel 1032.[2] For Jernegan from Ambassador. I share your concern over indications that Grivas, Makarios, and GOG are working at cross purposes and offer following comments:

1. GOG–Grivas relation

As we have previously noted, Grivas is under clear directive from GOG to prevent any provocative actions by Greek Cypriot forces (Embtel 1177).[3] FonMin Costopoulos has told me Grivas was instructed during his recent visit to Athens to resist "another Mansoura"[4] and to use his efforts to maintain calm on island. Recent CAS reports also confirm Papandreou's and Costopoulos' advice to Grivas to maintain status quo. I also note Nicosia's 999 to Department[5] reports Greek Ambassador Alexandrakis informed Thimayya this past week that he had been requested to repeat GOG instructions to Grivas to take no action which would increase tension.

Important question remains, however, whether Grivas will act according GOG wishes or will become persuaded, as Embassy Nicosia fears (Nicosia's 992),[6] that new adventures may be worth the risk. Since Grivas' role or status on island has apparently never been clearly defined, it is difficult to know how much control GOG actually has over him. Greek General Staff members have always responded vaguely to our questions regarding their relationship to Grivas and to his calls at Greek Pentagon. They have emphasized, however, that he is individualistic, "stubborn mule from Cyprus." King Constantine has told me he understands Greek General Staff can influence Grivas but that latter is not subject General Staff's command. Costopoulos takes same line re fuzzy mil command channels, but considers Grivas will follow GOG policy guidance.

---

[1] Source: Department of State, Central Files, POL 27 CYP. Secret; Limited Distribution. Repeated to Ankara and Nicosia.

[2] Telegram 1032 to Athens, February 11, requested Labouisse's analysis of requirements for aiding Greece in keeping the security situation in Cyprus under control. (Ibid.)

[3] Telegram 1177 from Athens, February 6, reported Greek desire to keep the situation on Cyprus calm and Costopoulos' view that Makarios' stand on troop rotation was not "irrevocable." (Ibid.)

[4] Reference is to the fighting around this village in August 1964 that provoked Turkish air attacks and the subsequent crisis.

[5] Telegram 999, February 11, reported that UNFICYP officials had seen signs of Greek efforts to restrain Grivas. (Department of State, Central Files, POL 27 CYP)

[6] Telegram 922, February 10, reported UNFICYP concerns regarding arms build-up among Greek Cypriots. (Ibid.)

We recognize Grivas may be toying with idea of a coup d'etat to take Makarios out of the play and to create situation in which Cyprus Government would be actively pro-enosis and anti-Communist; such coup might put Papandreou in extremely awkward position domestically if Grivas were publicly to offer enosis and Papandreou were not in a position to respond for fear of Turkish reaction. There is also reason to suspect that Grivas actually proposed during his Athens visit that Makarios be set aside and was disappointed by what he considered to be lack of GOG policy on the Cyprus issue. Greek sources have been very discreet about Grivas' talks here. However, the King and today the Foreign Minister (contradicting his previous statement) told me General Staff making available some additional officers to Grivas to enable him strengthen command of Cyprus National Guard.

2. Cypriot elections and Turkish rotation

Costopoulos informed me that GOG was unaware of Makarios' plan for new elections and did not approve his statement on this subject. FonMin also confirmed to me today that Papandreou had spoken sternly to Kyprianou when he stopped here last week on return from New York and had urged him to avoid any actions likely to aggravate situation, and specifically, to refrain from holding elections, proclaiming new Constitution, and preventing rotation of Turkish force. Re latter, Costopoulos told me he suggested to Turk Chargé that rotation be under supervision Thimayya and that Turks had agreed.

Costopoulos hoped that, if Turks delay rotation short while, there would be no snags. He also said Plaza had agreed to try to help in persuading Makarios against changes in Constitution and to permit rotation.

3. GOG views on interim solution

To your question whether GOG appreciates problem of readjusting and adapting itself to prolongation of status quo, I think the answer is qualified yes. Soviet-Turkish rapprochement and postponement of UNGA debate have helped to make Greeks realize that unconditional enosis is out of question, although they still call for unfettered independence with right of self-determination. In these circumstances, GOG policy is to play for time, to avoid any incidents on island, and to await outcome of Plaza's efforts. Costopoulos this morning expressed opinion that Mediator's position was even more important in view postponement of UNGA. He observed, however, that when filed, his report would probably satisfy no one. Costopoulos also expressed hope Plaza would not file a final report in March, but would keep door open by simply submitting brief "temporary" report stating he had been unable find agreed solution and would be available for further talks. He will urge this on Plaza when he comes to Athens tomorrow and he believes Plaza may be willing extend his mediation efforts for some time to come. (This may well be wishful thinking.) Finally Costopoulos noted that there was little prospect of reaching agreed solution while political situation in Turkey in flux and until after Turk elections.

If Mediator, however, eventually outlined general plan for interim solution to problem and suggested talks, I think Greeks would find this face-saving way to get off hook of no negotiations—providing Plaza's recommendations did not rule out enosis at some future date. There are, I believe, elements in GOG that may still be considering whether current situation might permit a new effort to find solution roughly along lines of August 20 Acheson formula, although Karpas area would probably not be acceptable as leased base area. More and more Greeks realize they must break out of current impasse, and Papandreou himself, I believe, knows continuation of tension and uncertainty is heavy drain on Greek economic resources and also potential threat to longevity of his government.[7]

If some kind of interim arrangement must be made for an independent, demilitarized Cyprus, Papandreou will probably prefer that responsibility fall on Makarios and that Makarios conduct the negotiations. (This factor also explains in part Makarios' reluctance to talk to Turks.) In such an event, however, Papandreou will be increasingly vulnerable to attacks from the opposition asserting that he did not avail himself of his opportunities to assert his control over Makarios and to attempt to achieve at least a conditional enosis (subject to base rights, etc.).

In final analysis, what Papandreou could not accept, nor could any Greek leader, would be an agreement permanently forbidding enosis. In this respect, I believe the Greek position coincides with ours, i.e., enosis is the only solution which appears to hold out hope for lasting stability in the area.

Labouisse

---

[7] In telegram 1217 from Athens, February 13, the Embassy reported information that Papandreou believed the Cyprus issue had entered a new phase. (Ibid.)

178.   Telegram From the Department of State to the Embassy in the United Kingdom[1]

Washington, February 25, 1965, 6:25 p.m.

5342. Cyprus. Ref: Nicosia's 1030 and 1013 to Dept; Deptel 5269 to London; Deptel 511 to Nicosia, pouched London.[2] Dept officers discussed with British Embassy Counselor Trench Feb 24 apparent divergencies in US and UK attitude re Mediator's plans and nature of his proposed report. Following points were made to Trench:

1. Turks have pressed us several times to agree that Plaza should not submit report with recommendations; we committed ourselves to Turks to discourage submission of report.

2. Greeks also hold view that report would not be useful at this time.

3. We understood as of our last talks with British on subject in December that they also opposed submission substantive report.

4. Now, however, Plaza seems determined to submit report with recommendations which apparently weighted heavily in favor Greek Cypriot views.

5. We deeply concerned since we feel Turk reaction to such report may be dangerous.

6. We note at same time that UK and US views appear to be diverging; we concerned over differing UK–US assessments of Plaza's tactics and wish call to UK's attention.

7. We feel that Plaza may be giving UK one idea and US another as to what report would look like.

8. We also feel that among elements in Plaza's proposed solution, he is talking about demilitarization of island and not Republic; this appears to be one of matters which he may be making different noises about to UK and US.

9. We feel British should take measures to clarify Plaza's views on report before he commits himself to Makarios and leaves Nicosia to return to New York.

---

[1] Source: Department of State, Central Files, POL 27 CYP. Confidential. Drafted by King and Moffitt; cleared by GTI, BNA, IO, and UNP; and approved by Jernegan. Repeated to Nicosia, Athens, Ankara, and USUN.

[2] Telegram 1030, February 23, reported the views of Bishop and Plaza on the content of the U.N. Mediator's report. (Ibid.) In telegram 1013, February 17, Belcher reported that Plaza's views on the contents of his report had not changed. (Ibid.) In telegram 5269, the Department of State reported that the British Government had stressed the need for a constructive response to the Mediator's report in talks with Greek and Turkish representatives. (Ibid.) Telegram 511, February 6, reported on Ball's February 4 discussions with Plaza. (Ibid.) Plaza submitted his report to Secretary-General Thant on March 26; for extracts, see *American Foreign Policy: Current Documents, 1965*, pp. 505–510.

We queried Trench as to British attitude toward submission substantive report by mediator. Trench said he had little guidance on this but quoted from telegram on FonSec Stewart's statement to Greek and Turk Ambassadors, and Bottomley's statement to Cyprus HICOMer, on Feb 19 (Deptel 5269 to London) urging that parties exercise maximum restraint pending submission of mediator's report next month. Stewart's statement as read by Trench indicated British hope that Plaza report might contain new elements which could help toward settlement. Trench also stated that Cypriot HICOMer London had asked Bottomley whether British favored talks among parties. Bottomley had replied by letter to effect talks might be more meaningful after mediator's report submitted. From this it seems clear British at least reconciled to, if not in agreement on, submission report with recommendations for solution.

Trench said he would report conversation to London and give us HMG reaction when received. We hope this reaction will throw light on British thinking re wisdom of public report by mediator.[3]

Rusk

---

[3] In telegram 4203 from London, March 2, the Embassy reported that on the basis of discussions with the Foreign Office, Plaza still believed that Makarios was the key to a Cyprus solution and that the time had come for direct Greek Cypriot-Turkish Cypriot negotiations. (Ibid.)

---

179.   Telegram From the Department of State to the Embassy in Greece[1]

Washington, March 15, 1965, 8:30 p.m.

1161. Following report of conversation between Under Sec and Greek Amb. is based on uncleared memcon.[2] It is FYI, Noforn and subject to revision on review. Above caveat, however, does not affect portion of telegram requesting action by Embassy Athens.

Cyprus. Greek Ambassador called on Under Secretary Monday March 15 to respond to questions raised in March 12 conversation (Deptel 1048 to Athens).[3]

---

[1] Source: Department of State, Central Files, POL 27 CYP. Secret; Exdis. Drafted by Bracken, cleared by EUR, and approved by Talbot. Repeated to Ankara, London, Nicosia, USUN, and Paris for USRO.

[2] Not found.

[3] Telegram 1048 to Athens, March 12, reported on discussions between Ball and Greek Ambassador Matsas in which the Under Secretary outlined U.S. concern over Soviet armament of Cypriot forces and requested an explanation of the role of the Greek Government in these developments. (Department of State, Central Files, DEF 19–6 USSR–CYP)

Stated he was instructed to deliver GOG reply in form aide-mémoire (text per Athens 1359)[4] which he handed to Mr. Ball, suggesting it be read and discussed. Matsas was defensive throughout conversation and attempted justify in rambling fashion that Greece 1) had not acted contrary to best interests NATO, and 2) importation of military equipment by GOC was not something Greece had encouraged or could prohibit but derived from need of GOC to defend itself against Turkish threat.

Following main points and responses emerged during talk:

Under Secretary remarked Aide-Mémoire raised more questions than it answered. Several facts were obscure: for example who has been training in Alexandria and for how long. Our information indicated Greek officers had been sent in February. If training is completed in one month rather than three, it can only mean personnel were previously trained in Nike missiles. Whether personnel "released" or not, they had residual allegiance to GOG or Greek military and Greece had obligation to NATO. Matsas promised to request more information.

Ball reviewed our understanding of GOG efforts to bring stability to island by injection into defense apparatus of some 13,000 personnel, some of whom had been released from Greek services, and pointed out our tacit acceptance of this situation was predicated on assumption GOG could control situation, both provocations against Turk-Cypriot community causing local incidents, as well as such problems as rotation of Turk contingent. Importation of heavy hardware created provocatory situation. We do not know what Turkish reaction will be. Thimayya has reported to UN that some of missile equipment had arrived on island and it would not be long before Turks became aware of it.[5] Our point of view is simple. Situation has worsened. If there are advantages in having Greek forces engaged in Cyprus can we expect GOG to assume responsibility for maintenance of order and prevention of provocations? Matsas protested that GOG could not exercise complete control over GOC activities. Present degree of control has benefits for NATO since otherwise weaponry would be in hands of young EOKA men or raw recruits of Cyprus National Guard.

Talbot pointed out we have concerns at different levels, but related: (1) question military and intelligence people are asking—whether Greek forces sent to work with Soviets or Egyptians had been trained or had intelligence of Nike missiles since contacts brought about might provide

[4] Telegram 1359 from Athens, March 15, transmitted the text of a Greek note denying any involvement in arrangements for the supply and training of Cypriot forces with Soviet arms. (Ibid.)

[5] Belcher reported on Thimayya's views in telegram 1097 from Nicosia, March 14. (Ibid.)

opportunity for Soviets to acquire information on NATO forces or missile operations of NATO; and 2) our assumption that if NATO military
personnel, even though released, but subject to residual authority of
NATO government, come into contact with highly sophisticated Soviet
equipment, government concerned would discuss this with NATO. Matsas engaged in form and substance arguments. It was finally agreed form
might not be violated if personnel released from service but matter of
substance still important since training on Soviet equipment provided
opportunities for obtaining some knowledge of NATO equipment. Matsas comprehended security aspect and promised to seek further
explanation. He rephrased problem as need for GOG to persuade USG
whatever Greece has done has not been harmful to NATO interests. Mr.
Ball repeated we are not concerned with form but with larger considerations—that Greek personnel presumably owe allegiance to GOG, in
position of operating Soviet equipment, with Soviet training, and this
should be formally reported to NATO.

Talbot raised question of effect of recent shipments of heavy equipment on SC meeting March 17 and extension of mandate of UNFICYP.
He noted that in past SYG has taken position sovereign nation has right
to import arms for self defense but these heavy arms raise question
whether action is in accordance with earlier resolution. We do not know
what difficulties this will cause for SC meeting or who would be charged
with responsibility. Matsas said GOG could not be charged since it had
not told GOC to buy arms and had not been able to prevent. There was no
consensus on what might develop in UN as result recent shipments.

Under Secretary said we have been trying with enormous effort to
bring about some kind of settlement of this perpetual turmoil at some
cost to our interests since role of peacemaker is never easy. He supported
Mr. Talbot's statement of difficulties new situation has placed in way of
progress toward settlement and correctness of our assumption that in
light of our involvement so far we were entitled to more candor in connection with buildup than had been case.

Matsas asked for examples of what might be done to put situation in
perspective. Ball replied with statement of some possible immediate
steps: 1) arrange avoid having missiles emplaced, if erected put under
control of UNFICYP, and 2) further deliveries of heavy equipment, such
as 100 mm. guns, stopped; 3) rotation, that it take place without conditions in accordance with assurances we understand have been given.
Matsas said GOG did not have degree of control to stop deliveries, noting it would have had chance had there been no aerial aggression or no
Turkish threat. Ball noted that provocative nature of this equipment is
the real question, together with effect it has had on Archbishop's position, causing him to take harder, more inflexible line. Matsas said putting
weapons under UN control would certainly be resisted by GOC and

would require change in UN mandate. Under Secretary said it was matter of speech. They need not be controlled, they could be neutralized under UN.

Matsas queried whether there was any indication yet of Turkish reaction. Ball replied we had no idea, but there are number of reasons for avoiding stirring up Turks when we should be working to bring about settlement. He noted we had been encouraged by indication GOG in congratulating new Turkish PriMin had hinted willingness to talk. Matsas referred to Mediator's report, surmised it would contain suggestions for formal conference or other less formal way of consultations to move toward settlement and asked whether USG knew conclusions of Mediator. Talbot replied in negative.

Conversation concluded with Under Secretary's noting we would await more information from Matsas. Matsas indicated he would discuss further with Talbot on Tuesday.

For Athens: Aide-mémoire and Matsas' line indicate Greeks have not understood, and do not yet agree, with our assessment of unfortunate consequences particularly with regard to negotiations for settlement which introduction of missiles, AA guns and tanks has caused. Matsas indicated he did understand our NATO concern for security aspect. We do not want to chastize Greece; we do not doubt their sincerity and faithfulness as an ally. However we do believe you should follow up in Athens to convince Greeks it is in GOG's own best interests not to dwell on explanations of past but 1) to concentrate on estimate of difficulties facing us both in present situation and 2) to examine what each can do.

As Under Secretary and Talbot pointed out, we have spent enormous effort to improve chances for negotiation of settlement, something also of vital interest to Greece. Realistically we must analyze obstacles to negotiations brought about by present tense situation, caused by buildup together with Makarios' tougher line. Next we must examine ways and means of defusing situation. First step is neutralization of missiles. [*less than 1 line of source text not declassified*] reports continue indicate senior Air Force personnel are concerned with situation and are agonizing over fact missile hardware is arriving on island before crews are trained, with possibility Makarios might ask for Soviet crews. They therefore are more in tune with us on this point than GOG officials. Suggest some approach be made to them in your discretion if possible before Grivas' consultations to solicit their efforts in obtaining action on neutralization of missiles and some delay in future shipments mentioned by Under Secretary.[6]

Rusk

---

[6] In telegram 1101 from Nicosia, March 15, Belcher reported that the Greek Government had passed on the substance of U.S. protests on the introduction of Soviet arms to the Cypriot Government and that the Cypriot Minister of Defense had called the Embassy to complain about U.S. efforts to obstruct the acquisition of these arms. Belcher believed that this move was part of a Greek campaign to demonstrate its limited control over Cypriot actions. (Ibid., POL 27 CYP)

---

180.   **Telegram From the Embassy in Greece to the Department of State**[1]

Athens, March 16, 1965, 5 p.m.

1364. I called last night on PriMin Papandreou at his home in Kastri together with Anschuetz. The PriMin was in serious, almost grim, mood and seemed rather tired.

I immediately launched into discussion of Cyprus question and covered substantially same ground covered by Ball and Talbot yesterday with Matsas (Deptel 1161).[2] I said that although during latter part of February and first days of March, situation had seemed to be improving on island (for which I credited Papandreou's influence on Makarios and Grivas). In recent days things had taken serious turn for worse. There seemed to be two elements in this. First, increasingly hard line taken by Archbishop Makarios, as indicated by his restrictions on Turkish population, his refusal to cooperate with UNFICYP to reduce tensions in Famagusta, and his reported statement that his "peace offensive" had not yielded results with implication that therefore Archbishop would have to assume tougher line. Second aspect was introduction of Soviet heavy equipment including surface-to-air missiles into island, manned by Greeks trained in UAR. I pointed out introduction these missiles could be "straw that broke camel's back" with regard to GOT, taking into

---

[1] Source: Department of State, Central Files, POL 27 CYP. Secret; Immediate; Exdis. Repeated to Ankara, London, Nicosia, USUN, and Paris for USRO. Passed to the White House.
[2] Document 179.

account steady erosion Turk position as result Makarios policy of "faits accomplis." USG had been shocked that loyal NATO ally, Greece, without informing US or NATO, permitted its citizens to be trained in Soviet weapons. USG viewed this development with gravest concern, and we request GOG to exert all its influence on Makarios immediately to stop any further deliveries of SAMs and to seek means to dispose of or neutralize arms already delivered.

Papandreou first commented on "unacceptable" manner in which matter had been presented to Matsas. He said he realized Cyprus problem could involve question of war and peace between Greece and Turkey and possibly consequent escalation into confrontation between blocs. He reiterated that US had no more loyal ally than Greece and spoke with sincere regret of fact there had been series of misunderstandings between GOG and USG since he had come to power. He referred specifically to his inability to accept President Johnson's suggestion for direct talks with Inonu. Failure USG to take position on merits of Cyprus problem had unhappily permitted Moscow to inject itself dangerously into situation. His own invitation to Moscow was part Soviet disruptive policy. Although he had accepted invitation to Moscow he had interposed conditions with regard to timing and diplomatic preparation which would never be met. Internal divisions within country make it impossible for him to leave at this time and inasmuch as Soviet Union would never accept self-determination and enosis for Cyprus, diplomatic condition precedent for visit to Moscow will never be fulfilled. Reflecting obvious sensitivity to unfavorable reaction which might be created by his current domestic policy toward left, he reiterated his uncompromising opposition to Communism as well as his dedication to use of democratic measures to combat it. These measures he insisted require time and organization, but democratic approach is only one which holds ultimate hope for success.

PriMin then reverted to question SAMs and asserted delivery of SAMs do not constitute threat to GOT because they can be used only against aircraft and only in event of GOT aerial attack on Cyprus. Papandreou noted that last August Turks had been able to bomb island with impunity and that Cypriot Govt had legitimate right to seek defensive weapons. He observed it is much better that these missiles be in hands of Greeks, and not Russians, and thus could be controlled. He asked if I would prefer to have Russians man these weapons. In apparent effort vindicate participation Greeks, Papandreou noted that as result of training in use of SAMs, GOG now in possession of considerable technical data on these Soviet weapons which it would turn over to US. I noted USG had not been informed by GOG that it is in possession of such data but that we would welcome receipt of it. However, price is much too high and we would prefer not have secrets than see Greek soldiers trained by Soviets and Soviet missiles introduced into Cyprus.

Papandreou then turned to what he described as GOT's "threatening attitude." He asserted Turks are constantly threatening to bomb Cyprus which in turn justified Cypriots to seek defensive weapons. When I asked him provide instances such threats, he answered that aside from frequent declarations of GOT military figures, British MP Francis Noel-Baker, who had seen GOT PriMin one morning last week, had informed him that PriMin Urguplu had admitted that he could not control Turkish military which boasted that GOT Air Force needed only "seven minutes" to be over target on Cyprus.

PriMin continued that in view of these circumstances he could not logically tell Makarios to give up his defenses. It would be "illogical" for him to tell GOC that they must disarm themselves and only "pray" against Turkish attack. Papandreou then returned to his favorite theme, which he has repeated to me many times (cf. Embtel 314 August 16, 1964)[3] throughout Cyprus crisis: if US would only issue warning to both GOT and GOG against any military intervention in Cyprus, then he could assure US that there would be no further troubles on island itself. He himself could go there to establish GOG control over situation. PriMin spoke at some length on advantages to be gained from such "guarantee".

I answered that if GOT unwilling to give such pledge throughout past year it is most improbable that events now would induce them to do so. I contrasted Cypriot acquiring of SAMs as means to deter GOT attack to person who gets inoculation against disease only to find that inoculation itself provokes the disease. I stressed that GOT could consider Makarios' actions as attempted blackmail to which they would not submit, since GOT continues adhere their own interpretation of their rights under treaties.

I told Papandreou we would like certain specific information, which Under Secretary Ball had requested of Matsas and I had requested of Garoufalias, concerning arrangements made with UAR and/or USSR concerning training of Greeks to operate SAMs, number of SAMs, etc. GOG note (Embtel 1359)[4] had not been responsive in this regard. PriMin replied somewhat indignantly that as GOG note had stated, there were no agreements between GOG and UAR or USSR; PriMin said individuals involved were all retired personnel who had joined Cyprus forces of own accord. In fact he had only learned there were Greek personnel involved when present question arose. I noted I had been informed that GOG had recalled from US all those Greek technicians being trained in

---

[3] Not printed. (Department of State, Central Files, POL 27 CYP)
[4] See footnote 4, Document 179.

operation Nike–Hercules missiles in US immediately after completion of training instead of permitting them spend some extra time in US as has been custom. This led some observers surmise they might be recalled to replace those learning to operate Soviet SAMs. I added that I would like to discuss all of these aspects with DefMin Garoufalias. Papandreou said he would give DefMin instructions to supply me with all information I needed.

I then posed question to Papandreou as to what specific measures GOG could take re SAMs. Papandreou countered he was more than willing make every effort reduce tension but that it must be "joint effort." Therefore, he said, he would use all of his influence with Makarios and Grivas to prevent any further shipments of SAMs if US and/or GOT agreed to give guarantee against any future Turkish aerial attack on Cyprus except in case of serious provocation. He noted Grivas was coming to Athens and he would tell Grivas that he must obey instructions to refrain from aggressive actions and if he would not do that, he must resign.

I pointed out such GOT guarantee was highly unlikely. Consequently, question is whether PriMin would make necessary effort without this assurance. Reluctantly, PriMin said he would do all he could, even in absence of such guarantees. However, he concluded that he would be counselling "illogical" course, since he was asking Makarios to be "defenseless" in event of possible Turkish attacks.

Anschuetz asked if PriMin considered present situation might not be suitable moment to initiate direct GOG–GOT talks. Papandreou said policy of GOG is to not take any initiative prior to submission Mediator's report. He remains firmly attached to policy of maintaining peace on island pending eventual solution and says he will do all in power to that end.

Comment: Although interview was discouraging, I believe Papandreou and his govt will make sincere efforts to prevent escalation and, given some cooperation from Turkish side, to reduce tensions. Last night Papandreou limited himself to general assurances and provided no concrete commitments or precise information. Papandreou, of cource, attempted to bargain for cessation of shipments of Soviet anti-aircraft missiles to Cyprus and apparently saw controversy over SAMs as opportunity to present his favorite proposal for US "guarantee" that there be no outside military intervention in Cyprus. When he saw this was not possible, he agreed to exert his efforts to stop any further shipments, although it remains to be seen whether he can actually produce on this. His argument that Makarios and Cypriots may not be willing to follow his advice on this "illogical" line seems to me quite possible. Leaving Soviet equipment, emphasis on defensive nature of the missiles will have popular appeal here and on the island.

Although I feel that Papandreou and others with whom we have talked have come to realize very serious aspect of Greek involvement with Soviet SAMs they obviously find themselves in most serious dilemma and are hard put to work way out. Because of defensive nature of missiles and strong position Makarios and Grivas will doubtless take for their installation, it will not be easy. However, impotence of Papandreou's position, demonstrated once again, derives from knowledge he cannot control Makarios but must keep up pretense he is in control of situation, from his fear of taking a position which would compromise him vis-à-vis public opinion in Cyprus or in Greece, and fact that emotionally he is convinced Cyprus is justified in doing what it can to defend itself, notwithstanding reservations about methods employed to do so. On other hand, friction with USG and American public opinion deeply distresses him and he would sincerely like to be responsive to US requests.

I wish to stress to Department and others in Washington that final paragraph of Papandreou's reply to our démarche[5] is a sincere reflection of Greek feeling. In spite of all we have told Greeks over many months, they remain convinced that we pamper the Turks, reserving our condemnation for the Greeks.

To set the record straight (see para number 5 of Papandreou reply) FonMin Costopoulos did not tell me that members of active Greek military were training in UAR. He referred to "Greeks" or "Greek crews" as I recall. As Costopoulos may be called to task for going even that far and as he is undoubtedly very friendly to us, I made a point last night in my talk with Papandreou of minimizing Costopoulos' role as an informant. I stated that I had gone to see the FonMin because of the rumors I had heard from other sources; that, although the FonMin had acknowledged missiles were possibly on the way and that "Greeks" were training on them, he had not mentioned "regulars" but that we very naturally assumed those Greeks had been trained on Nikes and were part of Greece's armed services.

I intend continue press gravity of situation upon FonMin Costopoulos, DefMin Garoufalias and other high-ranking Greek officials at every opportunity.

Labouisse

---

[5] This paragraph stated that Greece had been and continued to be a "sincere and faithful ally" while Turkey, which had opened a "courtship" with the Soviet Union, had not attracted "any allied criticism which seems to be reserved as a prize of the steadfastness of Greece." (Greek aide-mémoire, March 14; Department of State, Central Files, POL 27 CYP)

181.   Telegram From the Department of State to the Embassy in Greece[1]

Washington, March 18, 1965, 9:44 p.m.

1179. For Labouisse. Your 1364.[2] If Papandreou interprets "guarantee" as some sort of assurance that the US will use all possible diplomatic means to prevent further "unprovoked" Turkish aggression and we could agree on meaning of "provocation", it might be possible to relieve Papandreou's worries somewhat on Turkish military threat. If GOG can prevent provocation, we and the Greeks would have more influence with Turks. Could Papandreou give us assurances GOG can prevent provocations for at least six month period, understanding this means: Rotation of Turkish contingent without conditions; no customs or import restrictions on Red Crescent shipments; no economic blockade on Turkish community; more cooperation with UNFICYP in working out piece by piece negotiations to prevent incipient incidents and bring about more freedom of movement? If Papandreou and other responsible elements of GOG guarantee they could keep status "unprovoked", we would be in position to go to Turks and obtain clarification of their assurances they will take no military action unless provoked and gain their agreement on "provocation". If you believe desirable you might respond to Papandreou's request using above line.[3]

Rusk

---

[1] Source: Department of State, Central Files, POL 27 CYP. Secret; Priority; Exdis. Drafted by Bracken, cleared by Talbot and U, and approved by Talbot.

[2] Document 180.

[3] In telegram 1187 to Athens, March 19, the Department of State instructed Labouisse to make "every effort" to ensure that Papandreou understood that a positive response to the Turk suggestion of direct talks would be critical in assisting U.S. efforts to reduce the threat from Turkey. (Department of State, Central Files, POL 27 CYP)

182.   Telegram From the Embassy in Turkey to the Department of State[1]

Ankara, March 19, 1965, midnight.

1376. Jernegan and I called on PriMin Urguplu this afternoon on what was intended to be essentially a courtesy call with additional thought that occasion might be used to do a little spade work on getting conversations started as suggested Deptel 1010,[2] and as my conversation with PriMin three days before had suggested that hopes from Turkish side looked quite promising (Embtel 1355).[3]

Accordingly, after usual exchange of amenities, Jernegan opened on modestly hopeful note that, after long and fruitless exchange of views through intermediaries and in view of various recent events which again spotlighting problem, it would seem that effort might be made to seek results by direct confrontation which had proved impossible of accomplishment by indirection.

PriMin listened attentively and then lowered boom—very hard.

Speaking from previously prepared notes he delivered himself as follows:

Time had come, he said, to stop talking of consulting parties and exchanges of views. Have now reached stage where views and advice are less than useful; situation much too serious. Determining factor is situation on island. Weapons, officers and men have been introduced on Cyprus allegedly for defense but actually for aggression against Turk Cypriots. If Turks attacked island, these could be used against Turk forces but real objective is Turk Cypriots.

Pointing to thick file of documents, Urguplu said that they contained messages of type being received daily describing dire plight of Turks on island. Also contained in file were other messages from Washington, United Nations, etc., conveying repetitive message to effect "we are not able restrain Makarios; you must be patient".

Furthermore, as far as UNFICYP concerned, its Commander admitted helplessness and only seemed be thinking of how evade trouble if it breaks out.

---

[1] Source: Department of State, Central Files, POL 27 CYP. Secret; Immediate; Noforn; Exdis. Repeated to Athens, Nicosia, Paris for USRO, USUN, and London. Passed to the White House.

[2] Telegram 1010 to Ankara, March 16, reported the build-up of Soviet arms in Cyprus. (Ibid.)

[3] Telegram 1355 from Ankara, March 17, reported on talks with Urguplu and Isik on Cyprus and the impact of the issue on Turkish politics and Greek-Turkish relations. (Ibid., POL 15–1 TUR)

In some unexplained way he seemed to think that some unidentified recent talk which Dept officer Churchill had with unnamed officer of Turk Emb in Washington served confirm this negativist attitude.

As consequence, situation has been reached when GOT can no longer be satisfied with "appeals and talk"; it must act. Turkish people believe their govt has left Turks in Cyprus to mercy of Makarios. GOT does not wish provoke an incident; for that reason needed supplies have not been sent in by force, but time has now come for decision and decision has in fact been taken in meeting of Security Council held today under Pres Gursel.

A brief outline of this decision had been given press (Embtel 1374)[4] but he would add following;

1) GOT intends warning GOG that, "if its inhuman actions do not stop in a very short time", it will have to intervene (in Cyprus). GOC will also be advised.

2) Date has been fixed for rotation. Permission will not be requested, treaty right will be exercised. If resistance is encountered, force will be used. All considerations have been taken into account re effects in Greece and elsewhere.

3) Other previous unimplemented decisions of Security Council will be carried into effect after study will be completed in several days.

Urguplu then said GOT wishes make clear that it considers GOG real "counterpart" in this affair, said it was from mainland that commanders, forces and "NATO equipment" had been sent to Cyprus.

This decision, said PriMin "is most regrettable" but Turkey has been left alone and isolated and time has come when it felt it necessary act on its own.

As regards Soviets, they had brought some relief (by political support) which GOT would prefer to have had come from its allies. Furthermore, GOT knows that in US, UK, France, etc., there is greater sympathy for Greece than Turkey. In so saying, Urguplu observed that he had served in the United States, had liked Americans and had worked for and believed in American-Turkish cooperation as Ambassador in Washington, but unfortunately he does not see same understanding on part of USG now. It was hard say this but must be frank.

There were many other angles of matter which might be discussed but preferable stick to essentials. Only hope is to stop "inhuman acts" and then negotiate.

With this said, he wanted to know what we are going to do. Were we going to make new appeals? Would we again be heard saying we had tried and failed? If we continue talk only in terms of advice, he saw no

---

[4] Telegram 1374, March 19, transmitted the text of a Turkish press release regarding a meeting of the Turkish National Security Council on the Cyprus issue. (Ibid., POL 27 CYP)

possibility of restraining Turk public and parties (*Note:* this somewhat elliptical but, like rest this message, based on almost verbatim notes drafted in sequitur without editing in order assure accuracy).

Urguplu said that same matter would be discussed tomorrow with political party leaders, including Inonu. On Monday Foreign Affairs Committees of both Houses would be similarly consulted (in secret) and on Tuesday would be put before Parliament in secret session. Thus far endorsement of policy has been unanimous and PriMin was confident that would be same with parties and Parliament. After this process completed Greek Govt would be officially informed.

Urguplu said foregoing was only being divulged to us. He regretted news was not good but this was not first time that situation faced which might result in war.

He concluded by saying that he had spoken with complete frankness. Still possible that there might be last drop of that reasonableness for which Greek ancestors known.

At this point Jernegan said there were several questions which he wished pose for clarification:

When would Greeks be informed? Reply: Following conclusion of consultations with parties and Parliament.

What kind of "inhuman acts" did PriMin have in mind? Our most recent reports indicated no notable deterioration. Reply: All kinds of harassments, economic restrictions, inability move freely, "everything, everything". For example, there were some 40 items on list of things Turk-Cypriots were not allowed to buy.

In saying that permission would not be asked for rotation, did that mean would not even inform GOC? Reply: GOC will be informed but may be at about same time rotation takes place. Galo-Plaza and U Thant had arranged for rotation toward end of month and then it would be.

How about awaiting Plaza report? Reply: Turkish people are mocking government for what is regarded as "wait and see" policy.

Not in form question but observation, Jernegan here said not correct to assert that friendship in U.S. greater for Greece than Turkey. True that there are many more Greeks in U.S. than Turks but Turkey greatly appreciated.

Jernegan also said that so-called support of Turkey by Soviet Union was hardly impressive; seemed just be lot of words with no commitment. We don't believe that Soviets really want a solution; just playing game. We could do same thing but would be harmful rather than helpful.

To this, Urguplu replied that he was happy to hear these words of friendship for Turkey. As regards Soviets, words may be vague but friends of Turkey not even prepared go that far. What's more, believes Turks understand Russians very well and we need have no reason for concern on that score. Jernegan said we did indeed understand this and it was for that reason that we had not been perturbed despite insistence in certain quarters that we should condemn GOT action to improve relations with USSR.

Jernegan then said he had noted that in my conversation with PriMin several days before, Urguplu had spoken somewhat hopefully of talks with Greeks.[5] Could not suggestion such talks be renewed in intended communication to Greeks? Reply: Situation has changed. Furthermore Greeks didn't reciprocate Turk indication of willingness talk (PriMin didn't explain nature these feelers but Bayulken later said he probably referred specifically to talks with Greek named Drossos who recently here in guise of newsman but was regarded as informal emissary). Also situation deteriorating so fast that will be too late for talks unless urgent action taken to redress situation. To this Jernegan said he had understood time would be given Greeks to take remedial action after delivery of notice. Urguplu said this correct but time would be short.

Once again Jernegan asked what would happen if Greeks prepared talk. Urguplu said would wait while and see what happens but made clear would not wait long. In any case, talks on basis enosis out of question. Jernegan said he felt sure GOG would not insist on this.

Finally, reverting to basics, Urguplu said wished make clear that if USG should seek intervene again as it did last year, results would be catastrophic for US-Turk relations. He wished stress this. Turks are patient people but there comes a time when they will act regardless of effect on mother, father, brother or son. It is not question of talking about what Turks can do with Greeks but of what U.S. can do. If we can do nothing, "events will follow their natural course".

Jernegan asked what PriMin had in mind that we could do. Urguplu said that was up to State Dept.

At this rather conclusive point conversation was cut short by announcement that Cabinet was assembled and awaiting PriMin.

At one point in conversation, I said that woven into the remarks of Urguplu I seemed to detect a certain suggestion of what might be termed impatience with USG of rather serious sort. If so, I wished recall that over the years and particularly since World War II U.S. and Turkey had established fine record of mutual effort in building up security strength of Turkey and also paving way for future development of internal strength. Many Americans and many Turks had contributed in this on basis of fundamental and enduring interests. Would be tragedy if Cyprus, which totally unrelated to this mutual effort, should be allowed affect basic relationship. Furthermore, in case of Cyprus itself, we had made unusual

---

[5] Reported in telegram 1355 from Ankara.

effort to be of assistance and fact problem had proved so intractable should not be charged unduly to us. As he had with Jernegan, Urguplu replied with right words but that was all.

Comment: Any similarity between this conversation and that of my talk with Urguplu of three days before would be that of night and day, or, to put it another way, practically all of the same points were covered in both conversations but in mirror-like reverse. It would be reassuring to discount this as being attributable to the temperamental reaction of an over-strained man such as we sometimes saw in Erkin or in a display of super-gamesmanship at which Inonu was adept, but this was seriously and ominously different.

This was not a man speaking for himself with the authority of high position but rather a man speaking under the impulsion of other forces over which he can exert little control. This is not, of course, the first crisis we have met in this wretched business but, serious as the others were, this one disturbs me the most for the reason that it seems to have developed a sudden head-long quality as distinct from previous crises where there was always an Inonu at the wheel who could be approached and could change course if he personally so decided.

Jernegan and I are having working lunch with FonMin Isik tomorrow and will see if we can find any rays of light in what is tonight very dark cloud.[6]

Hare

---

[6] In telegram 1378 from Ankara, March 20, Hare further commented that Urguplu had stressed that mounting public impatience with the Cyprus situation was reducing his margins for maneuver. (Department of State, Central Files, POL 27 CYP)

183.   Telegram From the Embassy in Greece to the Department of State[1]

Athens, March 21, 1965, 8 p.m.

1402. Re Deptel 1179.[2] I called on Prime Minister at his political office this noon at his request. Anschuetz accompanied me. FonMin Costopoulos, DefMin Garoufalias, UnderDefMin Papaconstantinou, and GOG Amb to Cyprus Alexandrakis were also present.

PriMin said he "agreed completely" with proposals contained in Deptel 1179 which I presented yesterday to Costopoulos (Embtel 1401)[3] suggesting that if GOG can give assurances that GOG can prevent provocations for at least six months, US would be in a position to go to Turks and obtain clarification of GOT assurance they will take no military action unless provoked. Papandreou said that he could give assurances "without reservations" to six month moratorium on provocation from Greek side. He said he had just spoken to Grivas, who agreed in principle. Garoufalias and Alexandrakis will leave for Cyprus this afternoon in effort to obtain agreement of Makarios on this. PriMin emphasized that although he agreed in principle with proposals, implementation must be completely honest with "no hidden aspects."

PriMin then went point by point over proposals.

1. Rotation of Turkish forces. GOG understands this to mean that no obstacles would be placed in face of rotation of Turks. However, he emphasized that unit must be composed of soldiers and must not constitute attempt to infiltrate Turkish officers. I asked if in accepting rotation PriMin meant that Greek side would not ask for exchange, or try to bargain. He answered yes.

2. No customs or import restrictions on Red Crescent shipments. PriMin said this unimportant matter and that GOG completely in agreement on condition that it be "honestly implemented."

3. Economic blockade. PriMin said this also "logical and reasonable".

4. More cooperation with UNFICYP. PM said of course.

5. GOG guarantee that so far as it was within its power situation on island would remain "unprovoked." PriMin said GOG agreed but with understanding that GOC is independent government. However, he assured me he would exert all possible influence on Makarios to accept this.

---

[1] Source: Department of State, Central Files, POL 27 CYP. Secret; Immediate; Exdis. Repeated to Ankara, Nicosia, London, and Paris for USRO. Passed to the White House, DOD, and CIA.

[2] Document 181.

[3] Telegram 1401, March 20, described a meeting in which Labouisse presented the proposals outlined in telegrams 1179 and 1187 (see footnote 3, Document 181) to Athens. (Department of State, Central Files, POL 27 CYP)

PM then said that US proposals had given him "great satisfaction" and that ideas "correspond to what we believe." At same time he asked that USG exert all its influence on GOT to accept same principles.

I pointed out to PriMin that Department's proposals were result of my meeting with him last Monday (Embtel 1364)[4] at which time he had asked for guarantee against Turkish attack. I recalled that while I had said a guarantee against military intervention was impossible, the USG is proposing that if PriMin can give assurances there will be no provocation from Greek side for six months then we would be able to use all our diplomatic power to obtain clarification and agreement from Turks against intervention. PriMin answered that he considered it essential to have harmonization of USG and GOG views, all other points being minor and can be worked out. He said he was sending Garoufalias, who has his complete confidence, to arrange matters with Grivas and Makarios. PriMin said that GOG wants peace and he believes that GOT does also. However, he fears that misunderstanding could cause conflict. For this reason he said this latest American initiative is "praiseworthy."

I then pointed out that proposals did not include certain points which were so obvious as to not need mentioning, such as GOG and GOC refraining from attack on Turkish contingent or proclaiming instant enosis. PriMin said "I give my guarantee on this" at which time Garoufalias interjected "unless you request it."

I said I wanted to be perfectly sure that we understood one another's positions clearly. I said that it was my understanding that the PM accepted completely the proposals contained in Deptel 1179. He said yes, on condition that proposals be "honestly applied."

I asked then if Makarios accepted proposals, to which PM replied that that is why he is sending Garoufalias to Nicosia. Garoufalias interjected that Grivas accepted proposals in principle although he wanted clarification of some details, but there remained question of Makarios, and that he hoped to have Makarios' answer when he returned, probably on Tuesday.

I then brought up question of Ambelikou and asked if Grivas is willing to accept UN control of position. Garoufalias answered that Grivas did not accept this but had counterproposed that UN forces be stationed there together with GOC forces. PriMin noted Grivas maintains it was Turks who started trouble by building road and then moving in platoon of troops. Therefore, Grivas insists that he remain in his position there but that UN force can join him. Grivas is reluctant to turn position over to UN because he claims that Turks built road even though UN was there. I pointed out that such a move by Grivas of turning over his positions to

---

[4] Document 180.

UN would be example of good faith and evidence of cooperation with UN that was needed.

Garoufalias then spoke at some length defending Grivas' position. He also asked us to inform Ambassador Belcher to ask Thimayya to be "more objective" re situation. He said Grivas believed there was tendency in UNFICYP of support for Turkish position because of what they believed was their "underdog" status.

I asked for more details on what FonMin told me yesterday about the Turks blocking the road between Nicosia and Limassol.

Garoufalias answered that Turks had not actually blockaded road as yet but had constructed block houses near it. I said Grivas should not take action on his own but should go to see Thimayya even if Turks move. He said Grivas would not take any initiative but it was essential that Thimayya do so. He said he would tell Thimayya and Grivas when he saw them to try and settle this and other questions.

Costopoulos asked me what I knew about press reports of GOT plans to deliver ultimatum to GOG. I said I did not know any details but I was aware that within GOT there are those advocating hard line and those following more conciliatory policy. I said thing of most immediate concern to Turks is the "inhuman treatment" of the Turkish Cypriots. For that reason, every measure must be taken not to provide examples of "inhuman treatment". PriMin said that as far as he knew everyone was free to move on the island and that there is no extreme hardship except for those in the Turkish created pockets.

When I left Amb Alexandrakis accompanied us to door, and I emphasized upon him once more necessity of avoiding incidents on island. I said that the Greeks are in incomparably stronger position and should be able to act with restraint toward any Turkish moves. Alexandrakis answered that while it is true Greek Cypriots are in top position on island itself, fact that Turkey is so close and constantly threatening attack makes Greeks underdogs as far as overall situation concerned.

Comment: Seriousness and importance with which Greeks view our proposals was highlighted by fact that Prime Minister had come into town on Sunday, contrary to custom, and had been holding conferences all morning with Grivas and high GOG officials before seeing me. I believe Papandreou genuinely pleased at Department's response which he considers is obviously a step toward reduction of GOT threat. Key question remains as to whether, assuming Makarios' acceptance in principle, GOG can enforce observance of conditions. Another factor of prime importance is that Turks refrain from sabre-rattling.

Labouisse

184.   Telegram From the Embassy in Greece to the Department of State[1]

Athens, March 26, 1965, 8 p.m.

1439. Jernegan and I called last night on Prime Minister pursuant invitation extended previous day. Costopoulos and Sossides were present as well as Anschuetz who accompanied us.

PriMin invited Jernegan open conversation. Jernegan replied PriMin might be interested in general impression which he had formed during his recent visit to Ankara. Jernegan reviewed current political situation in Turkey, determination GOT take more resolute position regarding deteriorating Turkish position on Cyprus, and desire new elements in GOT to improve their relationship with Turkish military. He noted there is no hysteria in Ankara but rather conviction that current situation could not be permitted continue. GOT recognizes possibility of war, tragic as it would be for Turks as well as Greeks, cannot be excluded. Jernegan emphasized GOT considers GOG real interlocutor regarding Cyprus problem and is therefore eager to initiate direct conversations with GOG.

PriMin expressed appreciation Jernegan's presentation. As a political leader himself he understood political and psychological problems which confront GOT. Pending final solution GOG attempting arrange provisional solution based on maintenance of peace and status quo on island which in turn would develop better climate between GOG and GOT. As result GOG initiative GOC has been forced accept rotation, abandon economic blockade and assure there will be no military provocations or operations. These conditions were forced on GOC after threat of break by GOG. Papandreou reverted to his basic argument that failure of bilateral talks would only aggravate problem and again expressed regret he had not been able accede last summer to President Johnson's request for direct talks.

Papandreou went on say that with submission Mediator's report period in which talks inadvisable is drawing to an end. However, he was at loss understand how Turks could justify such pressure for talks just on eve of Mediator's report. Following submission Mediator's report new discussions between GOG and USG would be in order.

Papandreou noted GOT proposes avoid talks with Makarios. In fact, Turkish Cypriots virtually do not exist as an effective economic or intellectual factor on island while Greek Cypriots exist both in numbers

---

[1] Source: Department of State, Central Files, POL 27 CYP. Secret; Immediate; Limdis. Repeated to Ankara, Nicosia, London, USUN, and Paris for USRO. Passed to the White House, DOD, and CIA.

and as a state. Turks assert GOG has an army in Cyprus, which is true to an extent. Greek military personnel were sent, however, to assist Cypriots who were faced with threats from Turkey at a time when Cypriots themselves had virtually no military resources and no control Makarios himself. Greek assistance to Cyprus is purely for defense, but now Turks again threaten because defense has been established. Some means must be found to break out of this vicious circle. Although GOG has moral and material force to impose its will if its demands are logical, Makarios is morally strong when he is threatened with attacks or with bombing. Since GOG has imposed its will on GOC to permit rotation, etc., Turks must now also demonstrate good faith by refraining from threats and thereby gain time to reach an understanding. War between Greece and Turkey is improbable but cannot be excluded, Papandreou said. If Turks want war they will have it because GOG cannot avoid it. However, he said, I am determined there will be 1) no pretext for war or 2) no misunderstanding which would constitute justification for war. War, if it comes, would probably not be limited. Bulgaria might move under pretext of protecting Greece while Tito would act to prevent Salonica from falling into hands of Bulgarians. I do not want historical responsibility for a war, he said, and I assure you that status quo will be maintained on the island and that there will be no pretext for war and no misunderstanding. With settlement of problem of rotation of contingent and guarantees against military provocation, dangerous aspects of problems have been eliminated. It is ridiculous consider minor economic issues as justification for actions which would cause war or peace to hang in balance. If Makarios takes any initiatives which would provoke military action, I will denounce him. I have told Makarios I will not follow him in such action and will not be led to war by him. After all, enosis will eventually be accomplished through union of Cyprus with Greece, not Greece with Cyprus.

Papandreou reiterated, as he had at our last meeting, that he regretted certain coolness which had developed in Greek-American relations as result of Cyprus. He hoped this ungrateful period will have passed without harm. Greece has been a sincere and loyal ally both in easy and difficult times and this will continue.

Costopoulos inquired whether in this pre-electoral period there is any real hope that concrete results could be anticipated from direct GOT–GOG relations. Jernegan suggested position GOT would certainly be easier if it could assert it had established contact with GOG. Urguplu is a man of good will and even Turk military do not want war, but they feel that time is working against them. Papandreou again warned that if discussions were undertaken which after a period of weeks or months were to reach an impasse, possibility of ultimate solution would become even more remote. Jernegan pointed out that if nothing happens, even on surface, GOG might within the same period of time find itself at point of no return vis-à-vis Turks. Papandreou insisted that indirect contacts through Acheson and Mediator had not produced an impasse, but that an impasse as result of direct conversations would be grave.

Papandreou asked toward what type final solution Turks seemed oriented. Jernegan said he had not come away from Ankara with any very clear impression. Turks seemed rather more preoccupied with concrete facts of current situation, although it had been made clear that enosis is totally excluded as a solution.

I alluded to Papandreou's earlier assurance that there would be no pretext or misunderstanding which could justify Turkish attack and that there would be no economic blockade or difficulties regarding Red Crescent supplies. I said frankly our discussions with Garoufalias had not produced this impression, that we believe GOT is restless particularly because of alleged oppressive measures against Turk community especially with regard to economic measures. Papandreou laughed and said Garoufalias was very tired after his long meeting with Makarios and Cypriot Cabinet. He reiterated his determination to impose on Makarios such measures as U Thant or United Nations would recommend in these matters.

Jernegan noted Tuluy, new Turkish Ambassador in Athens, is an extremely well qualified and able man. Consequently, it might be extremely useful if Costopoulos or PriMin could see him soon. Even though situation may not yet be mature enough to approach question of final solution, such contact would be of tremendous value in clearing away misunderstandings of fact regarding situation on the spot and thereby avoid any explosion.

I also urged GOG not just await Mediator's report in hope creating new situation but take immediate steps reduce misunderstanding and clear path for the future. Our talks with Garoufalias upon his return to Nicosia had not been encouraging and reports from Nicosia itself discouraging. While we have no information which leads us believe Turk community subjected to actual military threat, we are not at all confident GOC will take measures which will relieve economic pressures on Turks. In fact, according to some reports, ideas which I had discussed with PriMin in response to his suggestion and which he had accepted, had been presented in Nicosia as "American proposals" which GOC had turned down rather than alter its present policy. Position attributed to Makarios, that no flour could be included as part of Red Crescent supplies, hardly confirmed he is prepared cooperate for purpose reducing tension. It would be useful talk directly to Turks about such "details" which, small in themselves, are charged with explosive potentialities. Jernegan added it is much more important for GOG convince GOT it is sincerely endeavoring to reduce tensions than to attempt to convince USG.

Papandreou said that he would see Tuluy soon, possibly tomorrow,[2] and that he is prepared to tell him what he has told us. He acknowledged GOG policy may be misunderstood and said he is glad to have new persons of good will like Tuluy, Urguplu and Isik to deal with on Turkish side. Conversation with a diplomatic representative, such as Turkish Ambassador, is a natural and normal thing and would permit exchange of views without disclosing precisely what subjects were covered and without unduly exciting public speculation.

Comment: Meeting provided useful opportunity for Papandreou personally to restate directly to Jernegan line which he has been taking with us. It also afforded Papandreou with an excellent appraisal situation existing in Ankara. As indicated, Papandreou attempted to put best possible face on results of Garoufalias' efforts in Nicosia, as well as to reiterate his thesis, more than somewhat threadbare, that he could impose his authority in Nicosia in those cases where GOG position is morally unassailable. His efforts to discount importance of certain economic pressures being applied against Turk community suggests he does not in fact have much confidence in his ability to insure a complete relaxation in Makarios' policy in these regards. I am hopeful, however, GOG has been pushed to undertake serious contacts with Turkish Ambassador here. Incidentally, Tuluy has confirmed to me that Costopoulos had told him he wanted to see him often to discuss current matters (see Embtel 1401).[3]

Papandreou clung tenaciously to proposition that Mediator's report will provide basis for new assessment of situation and possibilities long-term solution. I am not confident he is yet prepared enter into bilateral conversations with regard to such final solution. Papandreou's comment that publication of Mediator's report should be the occasion for further discussion between USG and GOG lends weight our suspicion that he hopes induce USG again to become intermediary.

We are seeing Costopoulos and Garoufalias again tomorrow to pursue further with them results Garoufalias talks in Nicosia. Nicosia's 1150 and 1155 to Dept most useful.[4]

Labouisse

---

[2] Papandreou met with Tuluy on March 27. The Embassy reported on this meeting in telegram 1446 from Athens, March 27. (Ibid.)

[3] See footnote 3, Document 183.

[4] Telegram 1150, March 22, reported the Turkish Cypriots' need for supplies. Telegram 1151, March 26, commented on the Turkish Cypriot food supply. (Both in Department of State, Central Files, POL 27 CYP)

185.   Telegram From the Department of State to the Embassy in Cyprus[1]

Washington, March 26, 1965, 4:16 p.m.

620. Following is uncleared, FYI, Noforn and subject to revision upon review.

In hour and half conversation on March 24, Cypriot Foreign Minister Kyprianou reviewed recent Cyprus developments with Secretary, Under Secretary, Assistant Secretary Talbot. Meeting at Kyprianou's request.

Kyprianou said situation on island now relatively quiet. GOC seeks (1) to reduce tensions and return to normality; (2) agreement on minority rights for Turk-Cypriots. Current tensions caused by self-isolated Turk-Cypriots and their intimidation other Turk-Cypriots. Agreement on minority rights complicated by question of who are true Turk-Cypriot leaders. If there is any serious problem, it is minority rights; GOC prepared to discuss this.

Under Secretary reviewed recent talks in which we have been involved. Said GOG suggested US might seek agreement from Turkey that it not intervene on island for six months. Thus climate for negotiations might develop. GOG seemed enthusiastic about its suggestion and sent Garoufalias to Nicosia to discuss proposal. Now we hear Garoufalias has had no success in talks with GOC. Under Secretary said he wanted emphasize this Greek idea; we would cooperate by speaking to Turks only if Greece and Cyprus in agreement. What is needed is period of quiet in which parties immediately involved can talk.

Kyprianou commented GOC could never meet conditions for talks established by Turks since latter and self-imposed Turk-Cypriot blockade only causes current problems. [sic] Secretary and Under Secretary insisted there other problems such as arms buildup, relief supplies, refugee housing. Secretary said central problem that of Turk-Cypriot security.

Kyprianou replied to latter point saying he doubted Turkey only interested in Turk-Cypriot security. Partition remains final aim. Still GOC ready discuss minority rights which could be guaranteed by UN whether Cyprus remains independent or joins Greece. There could even be UN observers to oversee minority guarantees.

---

[1] Source: Department of State, Central Files, POL 27 CYP. Secret; Limdis. Drafted by Greene and cleared and approved by Talbot. Repeated to Ankara, Athens, London, USUN, and Paris for USRO.

Under Secretary said these thoughts worth exploring with GOT. Pointed out formation new Turkish Cabinet[2] might make explorations with it fruitful. If talks on that basis seemed impossible, then GOC should try another approach. Important point is to get talks started. But if GOC wants useful discussions, it must suspend actions which would hinder talks.

Secretary said thought had come to him which he had not explored with anyone. Present Turk-Cypriot and Greek-Cypriot officials elected to govern Cyprus, not to negotiate communal settlement. Perhaps communities could now hold new elections for sole purpose electing small number delegates to something like constitutional convention. Delegates could explore possibilities of interim arrangement and then during extended truce examine possible long term solutions.

Kyprianou said his immediate personal thought was that only GOC officials could represent Greek-Cypriot side, but elections might be held by Turk-Cypriots. However, how could GOC talk to Denktash, for example, without hurting real moderates like Ihsan Ali? How could Turk-Cypriots hold free elections when extremists intimidate moderates?

Talbot inquired about possible talks with GOT. Kyprianou thought discussions with Turk-Cypriots would be easier for GOC and perhaps for GOT also. Latter would certainly participate from behind curtain anyway. Asked whether Turks would be prepared to talk directly, Under Secretary replied we did not have Turkish proxy, but since Turks ready to talk to Greeks, they might also be ready talk to Greek-Cypriots. We know Turks sick of crisis.

Talbot said recent period has been one marked by waiting for developments such as UNGA debate, mediator's report. Latter expected within next few days, after which new phase will begin. This phase should be based on frank talks.

Kyprianou asked whether Cypriot-Turkish talks would be better than some between Greek-Cypriots and Turk-Cypriots. Under Secretary said we only interested in helping talks begin and precise composition of parties a secondary point. If talks began between Turk-Cypriots and Greek-Cypriots, they would probably eventually be expanded to include Greece and Turkey anyway. Important point is to begin talks and see how they go. It would be welcome initiative if Archbishop would inform Turkey he plans to initiate talks with Turk-Cypriots and, if there progress, Turkey and Greece should eventually join discussions. If Makarios did not want to make this approach directly, perhaps Athens could make it for him.

---

[2] On February 26, the Justice Party formed a coalition government headed by Prime Minister Suat Urguplu.

Kyprianou asked whether Turkey would accept such an approach. Under Secretary replied we do not know, but important point is to explore such ideas and see where talks might lead. Suggested recent assignment new ambassadors in Athens and Ankara might present useful opportunity. What we hope for is conversations. Immediately involved parties should determine precise procedures and USG would be helpful where possible.

Kyprianou concluded saying would wait for mediator's report and then determine what to do next.

During conversation there were several exchanges on two immediate problems:

Red Crescent supplies: Kyprianou said GOC could not extend free entry procedures since there ample supplies on island and businessmen would be hurt. ICRC had said latest customs free shipment should be last. Under Secretary said in this problem we faced with an immediate condition, not mere theory. Lawyers should be first to appreciate importance not being too legalistic. If GOC wants meaningful talks, it should suspend actions standing in way of those talks.

Ambelikou: Talbot said current situation seriously increases tension and asked why Greek-Cypriots could not withdraw as requested by UNFICYP. Kyprianou said UNFICYP had not acted when asked by GOC and so Greek-Cypriots must now take own action to counteract Turk-Cypriot moves. UN clearly in wrong at Ambelikou. Under Secretary said UN should be considered neutral force whose requests given special consideration.

Greek Ambassador informed Talbot March 25 that Kyprianou told him that US officials had not pointed to "perils of situation" and were not "alarmed". He was disturbed because this was counter to his reporting to Athens and his recommendations for action because of "critical phase". We suspect Kyprianou's remarks to him may have been ploy to resist GOG pressures. However Talbot told Matsas we would endeavor to clarify in Nicosia and Athens as appropriate.

Rusk

186.   Telegram From the Department of State to Secretary of State Rusk, at Tehran[1]

Washington, April 6, 1965, 9:54 p.m.

Tosec 16. Cyprus. From Ball. GOT stated publicly it considers Plaza's services at an end because he exceeded his mandate. Thant's letter in response strongly defended Plaza and report and called on Turks to reconsider position on Mediator.[2] His letter did not ask Turks to change attitude toward substance of Mediator's report.

Turks have replied to Thant with letter which we understand is somewhat conciliatory but does not rescind Turkish rejection Plaza; letter will not refer to report.[3]

Your discussion with Isik may provide an opportunity to bring the Turks nearer to reality. At the moment it is difficult to find any thread of rational strategy in their conduct. The purely negative position they have taken is not good enough. We have been trying to prevent public discussion of the report. However, by disqualifying Mediator and repeatedly threatening military action, Turks have opened the way for a GOC initiative for early SC debate on Cyprus issue. Moreover, they have weakened their position in that debate. Yet they will certainly ask our support and be bitter if they do not receive it.

Under these circumstances I think you should take a strong line with Isik. You should emphasize that Turkey is tearing itself apart over a situation that involves only 100,000 Turks and that the world is getting tired of stubborn inability of a handful of people to live together. We have made a great effort to assist Turkey to find an honorable solution. But Turkey's position does not improve with time.

We have made clear from the beginning that there was only one way to solve the Cyprus problem and that was by negotiation. This also is the burden of the Mediator's report. The Mediator suggests that negotiations start between the two communities on Cyprus. This may be impracticable but the GOT might still find some profit in announcing that it was advising the Turkish Community to begin such negotiations. This could put Makarios on the spot. Obviously, the GOT could provide

[1] Source: Department of State, Central Files, POL 27 CYP. Secret; Priority; Limdis. Drafted by Ball, King, and Bracken; cleared by IO; and approved by Jernegan and Ball. Repeated to Ankara, Athens, Nicosia, London, USUN, and Paris for USRO. Rusk was in Tehran April 6–9 for the CENTO Ministerial Meeting.

[2] For extracts of Plaza's report (U.N. Doc. S/6253), see *American Foreign Policy: Current Documents, 1965*, pp. 505–510. The Turkish letter to Thant and Thant's reply (U.N. Doc. S/6267) are summarized ibid., p. 510, footnote 36.

[3] U.N. Doc. S/6267/Add. 1, summarized in telegram 3950 from USUN, April 6. (Department of State, Central Files, POL 27 CYP)

competent men who could serve as advisors to the Turkish Community if such negotiations ever materialized.

If the GOT does not regard this formula as feasible, it might propose to negotiate directly with Makarios on behalf of the Turkish Community. This might be one way of forcing the hand of the GOG—compelling it to undertake negotiations with the GOT or risk losing its position in the situation.

USUN has expressed concern about the apparently aimless direction of Turkish actions and you may wish to raise one or more of the following questions:

1. If GOT expects our support, we think they owe us fuller explanation of what they are really driving at, expressed not in terms of ideal desiderata but of real possibilities in real world.

2. It not at all clear to us what GOT really expects to achieve through present course of action.

3. After Geneva experience, do Turks think GOG has capability of forcing Makarios to accept either partition or Federation?

4. Does GOT hope keep Cyprus problem on shelf for six months (beyond Turkish elections) meanwhile trying prevent status and welfare Turk-Cypriots from deteriorating?

5. We had understood GOT wanted protection for Turk-Cypriots and assurances against enosis; if Turks feel guarantees these two items insufficiently stated in report, what guarantees conceivably acceptable to other side would they propose?

6. If GOT continues along present course, we must assume question of Plaza report will come up for debate before UNSC very soon; how can US or other friends of Turkey be helpful unless we are fully informed re objectives present Turkish posture and actions?

You may wish also mention following elements in Plaza report which Turks might find positive and useable.

1. Debarring of enosis.

2. Demilitarization (genuinely demilitarized Cyprus would greatly reduce Turkey's security worries).

3. Human rights (Plaza's suggestions leave considerable room for GOT to maneuver, particularly in developing international institutional arrangements ultimately to replace London–Zurich).

4. Autonomy for Turk Cypriot community in communal affairs, specifically education, religion, and personal status.

5. Recognition of "hard fact" of distinctive character of two communities and that, without weakening unity of state, Turkish Cypriots should have "an equitable part in public life of country as whole."

6. UN role in settlement (UN assistance in demilitarization; UN safeguard of human rights; UN guarantee of final settlement terms).

Repeating to you USUN's 3840[4] which briefs principal features of Plaza report.

Ball

---

[4] Dated March 30. (Ibid.)

---

187. Telegram From the Embassy in Greece to the Department of State[1]

Athens, April 9, 1965, 7 p.m.

1519. Ambassador called last night on PriMin Papandreou and Fon-Min Costopoulos. DCM was also present. Bourguiba had just completed a 3-day official visit[2] and Papandreou was evidently tired from obligations involved in visit. Despite PriMin's weariness, he seemed relaxed.

Papandreou initiated discussion by having Costopoulos read text of GOG statement on Plaza report (Embtel 1517).[3] PriMin observed that there is basic "contradiction" in Mediator's report since it recognized right of self-determination but then suggested Cypriots should deny themselves that right because of threat from Turkey. Thus Plaza was in effect asking Cypriots to renounce rights guaranteed by UN Charter because of threat by one member of UN against another. GOG is, however, attempting mold its policy in harmony with Plaza report, since it is GOG view that Plaza should continue his role. There are two aspects to Cyprus question: first is need for provisional settlement and secondly final solution. Until now, GOG policy has been to wait for submission of Mediator's report. Now that report has been issued, basic question is what to do next.

In view of "vacuum" currently existing following publication of Plaza report, GOG would like to demonstrate "good will." GOG had "obliged" Makarios to give "real pacification" to Turk-Cypriots. First step is to begin negotiations between two communities on Cyprus. However, to do this Mediator must play role. Since Kuchuk would not

---

[1] Source: Department of State, Central Files, POL 27 CYP. Secret. Repeated to London, Paris for USRO, USUN, Ankara, Nicosia, and Geneva for Labouisse.

[2] April 5–8.

[3] Dated April 9. (Department of State, Central Files, POL 27 CYP)

respond to simple request to talk, Makarios will seek Plaza's assistance. Makarios, he continued, has had erroneous idea that Cyprus exists in isolation and consequently has assumed that by terrorizing Turk Cypriots they will submit. This, however, ignores fact that Turkish state and UN exist and since Makarios' "defeat" in his relations with Moscow Makarios no longer has courage to insist on his own policy.

Papandreou then referred to question of direct negotiations between Ankara and Athens. Papandreou observed that new Turk Ambassador, Tuluy, is "difficult" but that he has organized mind and could give intelligent answers "even when we disagree." He had told Tuluy that until now he had refused negotiations not because he is uncompromising, but because he has perhaps been "wise." Failure of direct negotiations could lead to rupture in relations between GOT and GOG. Even now time is "not yet ripe." Talks now would simply mean each side would air its views, with GOT advocating partition or federation and GOG supporting enosis. Result would be stalemate or even worse.

Rather than holding talks between GOG and GOT now on substance of problem, more meaningful step would be to "show our good will" and thus win time. Both sides must try to progress on day-by-day basis through maintenance of contact through diplomatic channels. Beginning will be by pacification in Cyprus "through total protection of Turkish minority." He had told Amb Tuluy time is necessary because there will be elections in Turkey in September or October and present GOT would find it difficult to make sacrifices immediately before elections. Thus, as GOG sees it, appropriate schedule is for negotiations now in Cyprus between two communities with help of Mediator to be followed by negotiations between Ankara and Athens after Turkish elections. Although Tuluy did not express agreement he said he would transmit these thoughts to his govt.

Question of final solution still remains, Papandreou acknowledged. From point of view of GOG it is not imperative find an immediate permanent solution since time is working for Greeks. Greeks control 98 percent of area of island and 98 percent of its military force. Situation cannot remain stationary, however, because (1) UNFICYP cannot continue forever and (2) Turkish restiveness cannot be indefinitely restrained. Plaza report had made it clear London and Zurich are unworkable and that there can be no federation and no partition. Therefore, there are only two possibilities for future of Cyprus: (1) completely independent Cyprus and (2) Cyprus as part of Greece—enosis. Put another way, choice is between "oriental" (pro-Soviet) Cyprus and "occidental" Cyprus, which through union with Greece would become part of NATO.

Papandreou then outlined GOT criteria in Cyprus solution. Basically, they are (1) protection of Turkish minority, which GOG was willing to guarantee, (2) security of Turkish state, which GOG could provide through Cyprus' membership in NATO, and (3) GOT prestige, which GOG is willing to "assure".

With regard GOT prestige, PriMin said settlement could be handled in such way it would seem to be Turkish victory. When Ambassador pressed Papandreou on what GOG could actually give which would meet demands of Turkish prestige, PriMin could only answer that "something" would be given, but that he did not know precisely what at present time.

Papandreou then reverted to practical steps which could be taken to ensure provisional tranquility. He said GOG wished collaborate with GOT for complete pacification of island and that he had repeated this to Amb Tuluy on previous evening during reception for Bourguiba. Even if GOT rejects Plaza report, GOG will seek to find way to bring about peace on island in conjunction with Turks. PriMin reiterated that GOG is working to create situation in which war would never arise as result Turkish "misunderstanding." If conflict came it would be only because Turks wanted it and not due to misunderstanding of Greek intentions. Papandreou referred to fact that Tuluy had given Costopoulos an aide-mémoire (Embtel 1454)[4] containing list of things GOT believes endangers Turk community on Cyprus. GOG is giving it serious attention in hope correcting most conditions to which GOT objects.

Ambassador referred to question of Soviet SAM's for Cyprus. Papandreou said this question is finished as far as GOG is concerned and that DefMin Garoufalias had given strict orders that no Greek be involved in any aspect of this program. When Ambassador pressed for information on what arrangements Makarios had made for training of Cypriot personnel and delivery of additional missiles, Papandreou disclaimed any knowledge. However, Costopoulos referred to rumor reported by Grivas that Egyptians considering training Cypriots in use of the missiles without knowledge of GOG. Costopoulos asserted he had instructed Greek Ambassador who had been in Athens during Kyprianou visit to inform GOC that if such thing happened, all agreements between Cyprus and GOG should be considered as terminated (*sic*).

Comment: Conversation provided additional evidence of GOG desire to work sincerely with GOT toward reduction of tension on Cyprus and to maintain continuing contact with Turkish Ambassador Tuluy to this end. Papandreou has had two conversations with Tuluy and Costopoulos at least three, including one this morning.

GOG seems confident of its ability to encourage a reduction of tension in the island. GOG also appreciates fact Plaza report represents substantial tactical advantage for Greek case which, accompanied by

[4] Dated April 4. (Ibid.)

decreasing tension on the island, might hopefully create a situation in which new efforts find solution could be fruitful. However, this calculation would collapse if Turks, aware that time is on Greek side and sensitive to increasingly less favorable position of Turkish case vis-à-vis world opinion, were to permit initiatives by Turkish community which might galvanize situation into new crisis.

Recent references in Athens press to Acheson plan as well as from Papandreou's formulation of final solution as choice between "oriental" or "occidental" Cyprus make it rather apparent that GOG hopes involve USG again in process finding solution. For time being at least, it appears our role here should be to encourage intensification GOT–GOG contacts in hope that in process certain general areas of understanding will eventually emerge which would provide valuable preparation for the time (perhaps after GOT elections) when GOT and GOG will feel they are in position to address problem of final solution on the merits.

Anschuetz

---

188.   Telegram From the Embassy in Iran to the Department of State[1]

Tehran, April 9, 1965, 1 p.m.

1104. Department please repeat to field as appropriate. Secretary in breakfast talk with Turkish Foreign Minister Isik this morning repeatedly emphasized that US would hope for and expect full consultations with NATO in advance of any military action Turkey might decide necessary to ensure physical safety and supply daily necessities Turkish community in Cyprus.

Isik said he was unable to give such assurance. Secretary then warned that in event GOT takes action without consultation Turkey would find itself isolated and this would spell disaster. Isik indicated he understood this point and insisted that GOT would take military action only if forced by circumstances to do so. He implied that such circum-

---

[1] Source: Department of State, Central Files, POL 27 CYP. Secret; Priority; Limdis. Repeated to Geneva. Secretary Rusk traveled to Geneva on April 9 to attend a meeting of U.S. Ambassadors to the Middle East.

stances might include (1) protracted threat to well being Turkish Cypriot community or (2) attempt by Makarios to bring about "juridical" fait accompli further diminishing rights of Turkish community. GOT, he said, would not take action impulsively.

Secretary pointed out that juridical innovations could always be changed by negotiations but Isik replied that GOI now has no other means than military action to oppose Greek Cypriot domination Turkish community.

Looking beyond Cyprus dispute to long-term objective of improvement relations between Turkey and Greece, Secretary asked Isik what role GOT would like to see us play. Isik's answer was that USG should seek to ascertain basic conditions sought by both sides, try to find a solution and then push both to agree. When US begins pushing Turks, provided solution be presented privately rather than in a public report, GOT will study US proposal "as carefully as possible." Secretary emphasized that USG has no independent view of Cyprus problem. Our objective has always been to help bring about a solution acceptable to parties to dispute.

Isik assured Secretary that GOT is "really interested" in talks with Greek Government if there is some prospect of concrete results. Isik feared that it would not be possible to preserve relations with GOG if urgent question of physical situation of Turkish Cypriot community is not settled within a "normal" period of time. If basic preconditions of (1) no territorial annexation and (2) no Greek Cypriot domination of Turkish community are acceptable to GOG, Isik felt there might be some hope that secret talks could lead to an agreed solution.

Foregoing is drawn from uncleared memcon, drafted after Secretary's departure for Geneva.[2]

Herz

---

[2] A memorandum of conversation is ibid.

189.   Telegram From the Department of State to the Embassy in Greece[1]

Washington, April 20, 1965, 9:54 p.m.

1342. We believe that efforts you have made so far to bring more reality to Greek consideration of possible elements of Cyprus solution should be accelerated.

One of points toward which GOG exhibits less comprehension, particularly since submission Plaza report, is unattainability of enosis without compensation to Turkey. This applies whether enosis sought in immediate future or over years as reportedly under consideration by Clerides.

Suggest you use occasion of your farewell talks with King, Papandreou, Costopoulos and others to help Greeks clarify in their own mind:

(1) Enosis cannot be achieved without compensation;
(2) If Greeks attempt enosis without prior arrangement with Turkey, there will be violent action by Turks. They have made this clear in public and private statements;
(3) Western alliance cannot be expected impose enosis or restrain Turk action while instant enosis attempted. Both Greece and Turkey are important to Western alliance and we could not (even if capable of doing so) try to help bring about enosis at expense of a frustrated Turkey who would surely then follow neutralist policies.

It seems to us that more realistic consideration by Greeks of above points would help Costopoulos in proposed initial talks with Isik on occasion NATO Ministerial, which we certainly hope will not be sabotaged by reported GOT actions against Istanbul Greeks.[2]

Rusk

---

[1] Source: Department of State, Central Files, POL 27 CYP. Secret; Limdis. Drafted by Bracken, cleared by EUR and Jernegan, and approved by Ball. Repeated to Ankara, London, USUN, Nicosia, and Paris for USRO.

[2] In telegram 1664 from Athens, May 7, Labouisse reported that he had made the points outlined in this telegram in calls on the King, Queen Frederika, Stephanopoulos, Costopoulos, Garoufalias, and Kanellopoulos. (Ibid.) The Ambassador left post on May 8.

190. Telegram From Secretary of State Rusk to the Department of State[1]

London, May 13, 1965, 1700Z.[2]

Secto 16. The Secretary's conversation at noon today with Costopoulos, Palamas and Pilavachi showed clearly that Greeks feel on very shaky ground in regard to proposed bilateral talks with Turks re Cyprus.[3] Main things worrying them seem to be:

A. Turkish insistence on talking about conditions for continued independence of Cyprus and reluctance to discuss enosis.[4] Costopoulos repeated point he had previously made to Ball that Greece had no right to negotiate about independence of island in absence of Makarios and that any attempt to do so would open way for Archbishop to sabotage whole operation. On this, we suggested talks might begin without any prior understanding as to their basis and that Greeks could take initiative to bring up enosis with compensation at very beginning, thus channelling further discussion in right track from their point of view. Costopoulos looked dubious and did not comment.

B. Greece does not feel it can undertake talks without some UN connection; Costopoulos thinks it important that "third person" at least have blessing of UNSYG even if he is selected by prior agreement by the GOG and GOT. Still thinks New York is best location and cannot accept Turkish idea of talks under NATO auspices. We asked whether Greeks had yet made suggestion about New York to Turks. Costopoulos said no and indicated he was hoping we would present this idea to Turks. Secretary asked why they could not sit down together and exchange ideas on their respective 1st, 2nd and 3rd choices for location and personalities to be involved; perhaps one of these sets would match. Costopoulos did not respond directly, merely reiterating difficulty of discussing anything but enosis in absence of Cypriot representative.

C. He fears Turks will be unwilling devote time necessary to work out solution this very difficult problem and that if there are any delays in course of talks Turks will charge bad faith and take action or make threats which will completely upset situation. Secretary emphasized that to prevent such actions or threats it was absolutely essential to have complete calm on island and full protection for Turkish-Cypriots. Costopoulos

---

[1] Source: Department of State, Central Files, POL 27 CYP. Secret. Repeated to Athens, Ankara, Nicosia, and Paris for USRO.

[2] Beginning in May 1965, the dates and transmission times of all incoming Department of State telegrams were in 6-figure date-time-groups. The "Z" refers to Greenwich Mean Time.

[3] Isik and Costopoulos met during the NATO meeting. Their discussions were reported in Secun 15 from London, May 11. (Ibid.)

[4] Reported in Secun 11 from London, May 11. (Ibid.)

rejoined it was equally necessary that Greeks and Patriarchate in Istanbul be protected, otherwise Greek public would explode. He urged that we use our influence to make this point understood in Ankara.

D. Costopoulos fears Turks want to make propaganda out of fact talks underway and might prematurely reveal substance of discussions. He emphasized that to prevent difficulties in Greece and above all sabotage by Makarios there must be absolute secrecy about substance, but he agreed it would probably be impossible to prevent public knowledge of fact talks themselves were underway. Secretary said he thought it should be possible to maintain secrecy on substance.

In course of discussion Secretary reiterated advice he had given Isik that above all contact must be maintained and participants must not be easily discouraged. Over a period of time new ideas might emerge. Assured Costopoulos that he believed Isik genuinely desired to keep things quiet on island, something which was essential to make lengthy talks possible.

Greeks mentioned Inonu press statement supporting present Turkish Cabinet in relation to Cyprus issue. Costopoulos himself volunteered that this seemed to show Turks really meant business. Secretary concurred.

Secretary asked about reaction to set of "agreed principles" we had submitted to them and to Turks.[5] Almost exactly as Isik had done yesterday,[6] Costopoulos replied most of points were acceptable but he felt there should be some additions. Also remarked that some points seemed in conflict with UNSC resolution of March 4. Secretary pointed out that if Greece and Turkey could agree on anything, they would certainly get unanimous endorsement from SC. Costopoulos asked whether our idea was that agreed principles should be published once understanding reached with Turks. Secretary said no, that idea was to give two parties a common basis to build on and enable them to launch negotiations on the easier rather than the most difficult issues. Jernegan suggested, however, that if agreement could be reached there would seem to be definite advantages in publishing, since a great many people in Greece and Turkey and elsewhere must be anxiously looking for signs of hope. Palamas replied problem would be adverse effect publication would have on Cyprus. Finally, Costopoulos suggested he could talk to Isik about principles tonight. Secretary agreed but said he did not think too much time should be spent on this at present moment since first essential was to get agreement on procedures.

With further reference to danger of violent action on either side, Costopoulos said we must keep in mind terribly important humanitari-

---

[5] Reported in Secto 2 from London, May 12. (Ibid.)
[6] Rusk reported on his conversation with Isik in Secto 9 from London, May 13. (Ibid.)

an aspect. If Turks attacked Cyprus whether by land or by bombing, Makarios would proceed to kill all Turkish-Cypriots and Turks would retaliate by killing all Greeks in Istanbul. Secretary again emphasized importance that there be complete calm on island. Costopoulos said during recent meetings in Athens Makarios had repeatedly promised GOG he would keep peace and abolish all measures directed against Turkish-Cypriots. He had also promised to refrain from initiating changes which would likely to provoke Turks: A) he will not carry out his plan to call new elections this summer when his present mandate runs out—instead he will continue in office without raising issue; B) he also agreed to refrain from appointing a pro-Greek Turkish-Cypriot minister, GOG having told him he must not bring a Quisling into his Cabinet.

Secretary suggested it might be useful for Turkish Ambassador Athens and Greek Ambassador-designate Ankara (both of whom are in London) get together this afternoon to see if they could smooth over some procedural difficulties before tonight's meeting. Costopoulos gave tentative endorsement to this.

Secretary asked if there was anything special USG could do to help negotiations along. Costopoulos indicated he did not want US participating, since that would be regarded in Greece and Cyprus as US interference and pressure. He made no concrete suggestion except to say that he hoped for continued close US interest and occasional help.

It was agreed that Pilavachi should meet with Jernegan tomorrow morning to report on how things go tonight. (Will be recalled Isik is seeing Secretary again tomorrow, at which time we can get Turkish version).[7]

Rusk

---

[7] Telegram 5519 from London, May 14, reported that Pilavachi stated that the Greek and Turkish Foreign Ministers had agreed on procedures for talks on Cyprus and provided details of concluding discussions between the Secretary and senior Greek and Turkish officials. (Ibid.)

191.   Telegram From the Department of State to the Embassy in Cyprus[1]

Washington, May 28, 1965, 6:20 p.m.

729. Embtel 1332.[2] What does Embassy believe is Archbishop's motivation in request for assistance in establishing GOC–GOT contact? Seems most likely he is intent on sabotaging GOT–GOG talks, thereby returning self to center stage. Recent reports from Nicosia and Athens indicate he strongly condemns Greco-Turkish dialogue, contending Cypriots must be allowed to decide future for themselves. Makarios knows Greeks want enosis with concessions while he obviously personally wants independence on his terms. He might figure best way achieving his goals would be to undercut Greeks by offering Turks independence which they find more palatable.

If he is sincere, he should consider having Kyprianou approach Eralp at coming session of UN or alternatively have Pelaghias or other FonMin official make approach through Turkish Embassy Nicosia. Considering fact USG strongly encouraged GOT–GOG talks, it would seem inappropriate at this time actively to aid in Makarios effort scuttle GOG effort. On other hand our position has always been Turks would some day have to talk to the Greek-Cypriots.

Makarios should also consider carefully impact his actions and statements over next several weeks on GOT's attitude toward him. For example, report he is "calling back" Galo Plaza has caused Turks to suspect more faits accomplis. Any GOC attempt try to have SC "endorse" or "approve" Plaza report, as recently rumored, would cause even further estrangement Ankara and Nicosia. If Makarios sees these as bargaining plays to increase pressure on Turks he is making same mistaken assessment Turks do when they threaten Greeks with force.[3]

For Ankara: Would appreciate reading on possible receptivity to Kyprianou approach and what if any effect it would have on bilateral talks.[4]

---

[1] Source: Department of State, Central Files, POL 27 CYP. Secret; Limdis–TOG. Drafted by McCaskill, cleared in GTI, and approved by Jernegan. Repeated to Athens, Ankara, London, USUN, and Paris for USRO.

[2] Telegram 1332 from Nicosia, May 28, reported Greek-Cypriot hints that they would resume a dialogue with the Turkish Government. (Ibid.)

[3] In telegram 1338 from Nicosia, May 30, the Embassy responded that Makarios' primary objective remained either participating in talks on Cyprus' future or derailing any bilateral discussions that might endanger his interests. (Ibid.)

[4] In telegram 1742 from Ankara, June 2, the Embassy responded that the Turks might be receptive to talks with Kyprianou although not at the expense of their dialogue with the Greeks. (Ibid.)

For Athens: Would appreciate reading on possible reaction GOG to Kyprianou approach to Eralp and particularly USG involvement this effort.[5]

Rusk

---

[5] In telegram 1772 from Athens, May 29, the Embassy responded that a Kyprianou approach to Erlap would raise "deepest suspicion" among the Greeks. (Ibid.)

---

192.   Telegram From the Embassy in Greece to the Department of State[1]

Athens, June 1, 1965, 1225Z.

1779. Andreas Papandreou came to see me last evening.

He said his father's conversation yesterday morning with Turk Ambassador Tuluy had gone well. Although understanding reached during Costopoulos–Isik talks in London provided that Greek Ambassador Sgourdeos would discuss possibilities Cyprus solution in Ankara with GOT, PriMin had moved directly into the matter with Tuluy. According to Andreas (who had not been present himself), PriMin followed very closely line which PriMin had outlined to me last week (Embtel 1754),[2] i.e.:

(A) GOG prepared to discuss enosis, immediate or deferred;
(B) GOG prepared to give consideration to any reasonable system of protection for Turk minority;
(C) GOT security interests much better preserved by inclusion Cyprus in NATO as result of enosis. GOG and GOT both confronted by Slav-Communist pressures and would continue to have common defense interests even if NATO ceased to function;
(D) Question of Turk prestige is problem to be dealt with although it is subjective and not susceptible satisfaction on basis of logic or of right. GOG prepared to discuss this matter in effort to find bearable concessions which might assuage Turkish prestige. Exact nature of what such concessions might be was apparently not discussed.

Although no specific conclusions were reached, PriMin was pleased with Tuluy's general reaction. Tuluy at one point proposed an Urguplu–

---

[1] Source: Department of State, Central Files, POL 27 CYP. Secret; Priority; Limdis; TOG. Repeated to Ankara and Nicosia.

[2] Telegram 1754 from Athens, May 26, reported a conversation with Prime Minister Papandreou in which he restated his basic positions. (Ibid.)

Papandreou meeting, to which Papandreou apparently replied that he is prepared to accept but wished to await prior measure of agreement.

I inquired whether any word had been received from MOD Garoufalias presently attending NATO Defense Ministers' meeting in Paris.

Andreas said Garoufalias had had conversation with his Turkish counterpart and had reported that latter seemed disposed to discuss question of enosis.

Andreas said he also wanted to apprise me of an important new development in Cyprus problem. On basis information he had received personally yesterday as well as information also received by Costopoulos two things are now clear:

(1) Makarios and GOC are not prepared to give any concessions to achieve enosis—"no British base, not even a pair of shoes". GOC will, however, mask its position by speaking loudly of unconditional enosis. Most Greek political leaders believe Makarios does not want enosis. This is a conclusion which he (Andreas) is coming to accept, but of which he is not yet irrevocably convinced since Makarios is a very clever politician. Although public opinion in Cyprus can be readily influenced, pro-enosis sentiment on the island is at the moment much less than it was six months ago.

(2) Makarios will call for Presidential elections by June 15.

I said I understood that Makarios had specifically promised during meeting of Crown Council not to take any action regarding elections unless his legal position were challenged by Turks (Embtel 1672).[3] Andreas confirmed this and said this had been recorded in minutes of meeting. However, Makarios is basically apprehensive that once his mandate has legally expired his position will depend to a large extent on attitude which GOG would adopt toward him and he does not wish to make himself vulnerable to possible pressure from GOG.

Andreas noted that Turkish reaction to elections might seriously jeopardize any prospect of successful GOT–GOG conversations and might even provoke military intervention by GOT.

Question of Makarios' policy was discussed yesterday during meeting of Cabinet Political Council (PriMin, Stephanopoulos, Costopoulos, Mitsotakis, Tsirimokos and himself. Garoufalias in Paris). During meeting PriMin declared his intention maintain present GOG course, to continue talks with Turks, and to break openly with Makarios if need be. PriMin transmitted long message to Makarios. Andreas acknowledged that in face this situation GOG might wish to accelerate discussions with GOT. In any event, he emphasized it is very important that substance

---

[3] Telegram 1672 from Athens, May 8, reported discussions at the Crown Council meeting on Cyprus. (Ibid.)

GOG–GOT conversations be kept highly confidential and protected from premature disclosure to Makarios.

Comment: Position attributed to Makarios by Andreas does not seem surprising as moment of serious GOG–GOT conversations approaches and in light Nicosia's recent reports including Belcher's conversation with Makarios.

Andreas' own position is, however, somewhat obscure. As Dept aware, Andreas is widely considered to have close and sympathetic relations with Makarios and to have played an important role in rejection of Acheson plan last summer.

In this connection Costopoulos commented to me recently that inasmuch as Andreas was also present during my conversation with PriMin on May 26 regarding GOG Cyprus policy, substance conversation had probably been reported to Makarios. In short, while I believe Andreas was factually accurate, I am not entirely certain whether he is basically supporting Makarios or GOG at this juncture.

Anschuetz

---

193.   Memorandum of Conversation[1]

Washington, June 10, 1965, 4:30 p.m.

SUBJECT

Cyprus

PARTICIPANTS

The Secretary
The Under Secretary
Phillips Talbot, Assistant Secretary NEA
Charles W. McCaskill, Officer-in-Charge, Cyprus Affairs, NEA/GTI

Cyprus Foreign Minister, Spyros Kyprianou
Ambassador Zenon Rossides, Embassy of Cyprus
Andreas Frangos, Counselor, Embassy of Cyprus

After an exchange of pleasantries, the Secretary informed Mr. Kyprianou that he hopes there will be no trouble in Cyprus since we have

---

[1] Source: Department of State, Central Files, POL 27 CYP. Secret. Drafted by McCaskill and approved in S and U on June 28.

enough trouble elsewhere. Mr. Kyprianou responded that he doesn't think there will be any. He continued that he expects the Security Council meeting to be very short and quiet. Kyprianou understands that the SYG favors a 6-month extension of UNFICYP; and while he sees some psychological disadvantage in such an extension—because people looking for a settlement will assume that nothing will be forthcoming for six months—on balance he feels that the advantages outweigh the disadvantages and that the 6-months extension will be passed.[2]

Kyprianou said that the GOC is doing its best to maintain peace. No major incidents have occurred for some months. The GOC has been trying to normalize the situation in Paphos, Limassol and Larnaca and things have been improving in those districts. The Limassol incident and other isolated incidents are accidents. There have been other isolated incidents instigated from the outside. In Limassol, the Turkish employees of Greek factories have been returning to work recently.

The Secretary asked about the economy of the island. Kyprianou said that it is not bad. Tourism has been off, but UNFICYP has taken up the slack in tourism. He said that when some people had suggested cutting down the numbers of UNFICYP, he had countered by saying that the number should remain the same since UNFICYP expenditures are important economically to Cyprus.

Mr. Kyprianou stated that the GOC has not objected to the Greek-Turkish dialogue despite its strong belief, as a matter of principle, that the Cypriots should be allowed to decide their future for themselves, and that no solution should come from the outside. Makarios does not object to the talks if the subject is enosis. If the subject is not enosis, however, the GOC does not see how Greece and Turkey can negotiate, since they cannot negotiate for an independent Cyprus. Cyprus itself would have to be brought into these discussions. After all, it is an independent country, recognized by the United Nations. Mr. Ball said that Foreign Minister Costopoulos had made the point to him in London that Greece could only discuss some form of enosis.

Kyprianou said the Greek Cypriots can never accept any solution involving any form of partition, whether outright partition or some settlement leading to partition. The reasons for this are twofold: 1) the Greek Cypriots feel very strongly against partition and 2) the presence of Turks in Cyprus would be the beginning of a new Cyprus problem. Continuous frictions resulting from partition or cession of any part of Cyprus would lead to other hostilities.

Kyprianou then asked if the Turks are really prepared to consider enosis. Mr. Ball and Mr. Talbot said the Turks apparently would consider

---

[2] U.N. Security Council Resolution 206 (1965), adopted unanimously on June 15, extended the mandate of the U.N. Peacekeeping Force in Cyprus for 6 months. For text of the resolution, see *American Foreign Policy: Current Documents, 1965*, pp. 512–513.

several solutions, including enosis. Kyprianou said the Greek Cypriots feel that enosis must take place but that it must be "outright union" of all Cyprus. What will satisfy Turkey, which needs compensation for reasons of prestige? The Cypriots have considered 1) strong guarantees for the minority, and 2) some form of demilitarization similar to that in the Dodecanese islands. The Greek Cypriots are looking for ideas so long as they do not involve territorial cession. He added that the Greek Cypriots regret that the Mediator is not continuing since he could fill the gaps which might occur, for example, if the Greco-Turkish talks break down.

The Foreign Minister said that Makarios had asked him to ask whether we are now willing to tell the GOC in confidence that we favor one solution or another, and then work with the GOC to implement that solution. If, for example, we favor enosis, talks outside the Greek-Turkish dialogue could be started. Since the Greeks and Turks are now discussing enosis among other things, GOC–USG talks would not be anything the other parties do not want. He remarked at this point that only enosis will provide a lasting solution, while all others will lead to other problems. The Secretary then asked if the GOC had had consultations with Turkey. Mr. Kyprianou replied that they had not.

The Secretary said the starting point must be that conditions on the island give diplomacy a chance. Nothing should be allowed to get in the way of talks. This goes further than just people killing each other, and extends to the whole situation. He wondered if diplomatic channels might quietly dig up clues for other settlements. He does not see any formal role for the US at this time and asked Mr. Ball what he thought. Mr. Ball replied that Mr. Kyprianou is asking that if we think of anything, we should discuss it with the GOC. Our experience has taught us that the US label has definite disadvantages to both sides. The Greeks and Turks in London both thought a US role would not be helpful at this time. Based on our experience, any American role would tend to impede acceptance rather than facilitate it. The Secretary added that our role had not produced much thus far.

Kyprianou said his suggestion is really that the GOC and the USG work together. He does not believe anything will come from the Greek-Turkish talks. The GOC believes that more would come from GOC–USG talks on the basis of a solution. If the solution is independence, there is not much the US can do. If the basis is outright enosis, the consultations would be helpful. Consultations would not commit or hurt anyone. Mr. Talbot raised the question whether talks with the Turks would be worthwhile. Kyprianou replied that no direct contacts between the GOC and the GOT or the GOG and the GOT will provide a formula. He said that he felt that GOC–USG informal consultations would be the only talks that would produce results.

The Secretary then said that the removal of Turkey's objection to enosis is of joint interest to both Greece and Cyprus. Has Cyprus discussed this fully with Greece? Kyprianou replied that it has but only up to a point, adding that if everybody was not in such a hurry for a settlement, things might be easier.

The Secretary said that he would like to point out that there is a difference between talks and negotiations. In preliminary talks, it has been useful oftentimes to have no agenda, with nothing listed and nothing excluded. In the course of this kind of discussion, a solution can sometimes be found. How would Kyprianou feel about this sort of approach? Kyprianou replied that such talks could be useful with us or the British. However, it is a question of the Turkish mentality, and the Turks are always ready to look with suspicion upon every Cypriot suggestion. The Secretary said that he did not necessarily mean GOC–GOT talks. He merely meant that oftentimes parties to a dispute are able to iron out differences through this informal type of meeting. He cited the Chamizal dispute with Mexico as an example, saying we had found a solution to a problem that had been in existence for fifty years through this approach. He cited as another example his talks with Gromyko in Berlin, when the informal talks actually revealed that there were no grounds for negotiations. He cited the technique as useful, however.

In answer to Mr. Kyprianou's suggestion, the Secretary said that channels of diplomacy between us are always open. We are always glad to hear any suggestions the Cypriots might have, and will pass along any ideas and suggestions we might have. He asked Mr. Ball if he had any ideas on this subject. Mr. Ball stated that he would like to give some thought to this to see what we might come up with. He asked when Mr. Kyprianou planned to leave New York, and said that he would get in touch with him before he leaves. The Secretary said again that what happens on the island is very important to a settlement. He said specifically that the removal of fear from the island is a basic ingredient to any settlement.

Kyprianou then said that the Archbishop had asked him to ask what objection the US had to missiles on Cyprus. (He said he could not use the word "objection" in public, but could do so in this meeting.) The missiles are defensive rather than offensive, he said. In view of this, what objections would we have. The Archbishop is under some domestic political pressures to bring them in, since everybody knows that the GOC has bought them.

The Secretary said that he would speak very frankly. The military advantages of this missile are not very great. Any low-flying plane could easily knock them out. On the other hand, the political disadvantages of bringing them in are very, very great. The Secretary said that the Archbishop should look at this from the very sophisticated military point of view and weigh this against the heavy political disadvantages.

Kyprianou then asked why objections arose if the missiles were not very dangerous. The Secretary replied that they are politically stimulating and they increase tensions. He could see no advantage at all for Cyprus to have these missiles. He said that he could not see how Cyprus could want union with a NATO country and have Soviet missiles. Mr. Ball then said that our original difficulties lay in having NATO trained personnel also being trained to man Soviet missiles, since it was possible that they would reveal information about NATO missiles which should not be revealed. He reiterated that politically it would be very bad and that tensions would be created by the missiles.

The Secretary said that this would also create some difficulty for us with Congress. He hoped Kyprianou would urge Makarios to look at this in the most sophisticated and detailed terms with regard to what the missiles mean to Cyprus militarily and politically.

POLITICAL CRISIS IN GREECE, JUNE–DECEMBER 1965

194. Telegram From the Embassy in Greece to the Department of State[1]

Athens, June 18, 1965, 1355Z.

1862. In past few weeks present govt has entered new phase of malaise which has afflicted it for at least six months. As result (1) dispute over "Aspida" organization[2] and presumed involvement of PriMin's son; (2) controversy over Public Power Corp (DEI) investigation which threatened to bring former PriMin Caramanlis and other former ERE ministers to trial; and (3) most recently, furor over alleged sabotage of military vehicles in Thrace (Embtel 1833),[3] question arises as to long-term prospects of Papandreou government.

PriMin Under Attack Within Party

Basically, govt is now paying for its accumulated mistakes over past year and half. PriMin's juggling act, of playing off one faction against another, which served him so well during early months in keeping party together, appears to be breaking down as party criticism of PriMin's leadership mounts. Pro-govt press, which was such valuable weapon in beating down periodic revolts which cropped up during 1964 is now increasingly critical of Papandreou. Cumulative resentment of Andreas and his activities is certainly a major cause of the problems which confront the PriMin.

Both left and right within Center Union are unhappy over PriMin's temporizing. Conservatives, always concerned over Papandreou's lenient attitude towards cooperation with left, are now disturbed at PriMin's acceptance of army's involvement in partisan politics. On the other hand, left wing of party, which has been increasingly critical of what it considers Papandreou's efforts to placate Palace, is now bitter at PriMin's decision to permit statute of limitations to be invoked in DEI case. Extreme left had been eagerly anticipating putting its old enemy, Constantine Caramanlis, in dock; however, PriMin's action, after building up leftist hopes since February, has snatched away this prospect at last moment. As pro-govt *Eleftheria* pointed out in last Sunday's editorial (Embtel 1847)[4] PriMin's handling of DEI case has been "neither straightforward, nor serious, nor brave."

---

[1] Source: Department of State, Central Files, POL 15 GREECE. Secret. Repeated to Paris for USRO, USDOCOSouth for Burris, Ankara, and Nicosia.

[2] A reputed conspiracy of left-wing officers within the Greek armed forces.

[3] Dated June 13. (Department of State, Central Files, POL 23–7 GREECE)

[4] Dated June 15. (Ibid., POL 15 GREECE)

Controversy Over Gen. Gennimatas

Important elements within party, including two leading pro-govt papers, *Eleftheria* and *To Vima,* are currently attacking PriMin for his failure to heed their demands to remove present Army Chief of Staff Gen. Gennimatas and to carry out general purge of so-called right-wing "junta." PriMin, however, reportedly promised Palace last Feb that he would make no changes in military high command before end of year (A–739, 3/16/65).[5] Moreover, *Eleftheria* editor Kokkas told Embassy officer that PriMin is indebted to Gennimatas for his help in keeping name of Andreas Papandreou out of Simos report on Aspida affair (A–1014, 6/12/65).[6] In view of dilemma posed by two opposing sets of pressures, Papandreou may choose rather characteristic way out by kicking Gennimatas upstairs to be chief of NGDS. Much depends on degree of pressure exerted by two papers; should it subside, Gennimatas could well remain on.

Antagonism of Army Towards Papandreou

Army, which from beginning has been unenthusiastic about Papandreou administration, is now widely disillusioned with his govt. First real jolt came with publication of so-called Operation Pericles plan in Feb, in which, much to distress of military leadership, PriMin used Lt. Gen Loukakis as his hatchet man in attempt to implicate army in exercise of partisan political activity in support of ERE 1961 electoral campaign (A–739). Now, "Aspida" case has further undermined PriMin's prestige with senior officers. Moreover, DefMin Garoufalias, who was considered conservative element in Cabinet, has demonstrated disappointing willingness to accommodate himself to some extent to PriMin game.

Rumors of Coup d'Etat

One feature present political climate is existence of rumors re possible army moves against Papandreou govt, fanned by extreme left. IntMin Tsirimokos this week told Emb officer he, too, was concerned about these rumors. While senior military officials have given no indication of such intentions, number of them have expressed concern in recent days about drift of current political situation. Retired Gen. Sakellariou, who was ousted last year as Army Chief of Staff, told Emb officers openly last week that it is essential Papandreou be "overthrown" before he drags country down to destruction. Certainly army leadership is strongly opposed to Andreas Papandreou, whom it regards as leftist sympathizer who might lead Greece out of Western camp if he ever came to power.

---

[5] Not printed. (Ibid., POL 14 GREECE)
[6] Not printed. (Ibid., POL 27 CYP)

Attitude of Palace

However, from all indications, talk of possible coup d'etat remains in rumor stage despite uneasiness it creates in political circles. Before military leadership would attempt such move, it would almost certainly seek Palace's approval. There are no indications, however, that King would be willing to go along with any extralegal solution at present time, despite the strong anti-Papandreou propaganda he is undoubtedly subject to from various rightwing sources. Palace was unquestionably upset by revelation of "Aspida" affair and involvement of PriMin's son (Embtel 1809).[7] Particularly disturbing to King was implication that "Aspida" represented essentially anti-monarchy element in armed forces which might be used at a critical moment by its leaders as an instrument of political and/or military pressure against throne. However, King is aware that Papandreou is still popular in the country, particularly in rural areas. King presumably aware of dangers to monarchy of a struggle at this time with PriMin who still has masses with him.

Possibility Some Ministers Might Withdraw Support

Possibility always exists that significant segment of party might suddenly withdraw its support of govt and thus bring about Papandreou's fall. Major obstacle to this action is continued popular support for Papandreou, general fear of new elections, and inability of various discordant elements within CU to agree on successor to PriMin. FinMin Mitsotakis is recognized as most dynamic in Cabinet but has disadvantage of bitter opposition of liberals in party, led by powerful *Vima* newspaper. More likely choice would be DePriMin Stephanopoulos, who while not highly regarded, has few real enemies and whose relatively advanced age makes him more acceptable to other ambitious leaders. Some observers believe such attempt might be made this fall, when Cabinet conflict over govt's economic policy, and particularly question of agricultural price supports, may well erupt. Anti- Papandreou forces in govt would prefer to act before PriMin could suddenly call for elections to secure new mandate while his popularity still holds. PriMin, of course, would not take revolt against him lying down, and would certainly press King for elections. In event King refused to proceed to elections, Papandreou might well go to streets to make his case.

Conclusion

In sum, uneasy atmosphere prevails in Greek political world. Opposition press, taking advantage of Papandreou's troubles, has stepped up intensity of its attacks. These attacks may well concentrate on Andreas Papandreou, who remains PriMin's most vulnerable point. In

---

[7] Dated June 7. (Ibid., POL 13–8 GREECE)

view of this strained atmosphere, further incidents involving army or national security, whether real or contrived, might set off train of events which could threaten Papandreou govt.

However, armed with his temporarily invulnerable position vis-à-vis Greek electorate and his undoubted political cunning, Papandreou will probably be able to sustain himself at least during summer months.

Anschuetz

---

195. Telegram From the Department of State to the Embassy in Greece[1]

Washington, June 19, 1965, 3:19 p.m.

1559. Ref.: Deptel 1545.[2] Matsas called on Talbot June 18 to report Isik–Sgourdeos talks not progressing well because of unacceptable Turkish territorial demands. (It was not clear whether he was speaking under instructions.)

Said after three sessions Isik still proposing in exchange enosis area equivalent 18–20 per cent Cyprus. Said area north of line from Dhidhimotikon to Bulgarian border had been discussed. Matsas described proposal as exorbitant and expansionist; GOG was coming to conclusion GOT not negotiating seriously on basis enosis, GOG might be forced renounce talks and suggest GOT continue discussions with Makarios on basis independence. Pointed out this would be unfortunate development with Bandung II and another UNGA session in offing.

To Talbot question whether GOG had presented any GOG counter-proposals, Matsas said none advanced. Turkish starting point too remote from anything GOG could sell Greek public. Claimed GOG started talks expecting GOT seeking face-saving formula, not expansionist acquisition. Claimed Turkish initial offer less forthcoming than last year. Talbot challenged this and reiterated line of Deptel 1545. As Talbot pressed need GOG counterproprosal, Matsas said Plaza report's recommendations

---

[1] Source: Department of State, Central Files, POL 27 CYP. Secret; Limdis; TOG. Drafted by Neil, cleared by Bracken, and approved by Talbot. Repeated to Ankara, London, and Nicosia.

[2] Telegram 1545 to Athens, June 16, instructed the Embassy to point out to the Greeks that Turkish territorial demands were extremely limited and more than compensated for by the land Greece would acquire through union with Cyprus. (Ibid.)

for independent Cyprus inhibited making substantial concessions to Turks for something which many assume will come about naturally.

Matsas inquired re Kyprianou meetings in Washington, and asked if armaments discussed. Talbot confirmed that they were and that we had said we would be unhappy to see them on Cyprus. Matsas asked whether Kyprianou had said there were missiles on Cyprus; Talbot replied no.

Comment: While Matsas raised specter of abandoning talks, his tactic apparently was to spur USG into pressuring Turks to lower ante similar to gambit Costopoulos used in reporting first meeting to Anschuetz (Athens 1801).[3]

Ref Embtel 1863,[4] this was first conversation with Greek Embassy officials during which 672 miles has been mentioned.

Detailed memcon by pouch.[5]

Rusk

---

[3] Telegram 1801, June 4, reported that Costopoulos had stated that Turkey was seeking territorial compensation in return for enosis. (Ibid.)

[4] Telegram 1863 from Athens, June 18, summarized press reports of alleged U.S. efforts to secure a compromise over Cyprus. (Ibid.)

[5] Not found.

---

196.   Telegram From the Embassy in Greece to the Department of State[1]

Athens, June 30, 1965, 1649Z.

1917. Confrontation between King and PriMin over question of military leadership remains distinct possibility although pressures for compromise on both sides are at work. Embassy has reliable information (Embtel 1880)[2] that King is disposed to make stand on question of retention of present Army Chief of Staff, and has apparently decided to either prevail upon Papandreou to accept this position or else demand Pri-

---

[1] Source: Department of State, Central Files, POL 15 GREECE. Confidential. Repeated to Ankara, Nicosia, Paris for USRO, and USDOCOSouth for Burris.

[2] Telegram 1880, June 23, reported a conversation with the Chief of the Royal Political Bureau, Choidas. (Ibid.)

Min's resignation. On other hand, both PriMin's personal secretary and his son Andreas have told U.S. officials in last few days that Papandreou is equally determined to remove Gennimatas and if King refuses, PriMin will resign.[3]

In event confrontation does occur, likely outcome would be resignation of PriMin and his replacement by other member of govt, possibly Deputy PriMin and MinCoord Stephanopoulos. Key question is whether Stephanopoulos or other political figure could secure sufficient number of votes from own party to form govt. Support of 99 ERE deputies is probable, since most anxious to bring down Papandreou and would likely be willing to support CU govt led by acceptable figure such as Stephanopoulos for limited time. However, if new vote unable to obtain minimum of 50–60 deputies from CU ranks, then elections would be in offing, despite fact that almost no one (with exception of Papandreou) would want them.

Dangerous aspect of current situation twofold: (1) If new election held, Papandreou would in all probability be returned with approximately same strength as at present, and could conceivably receive even stronger mandate. This would be heavy blow to King's prestige, particularly since Papandreou, supported by left, would possibly make monarchy an issue in elections. (2) If Stephanopoulos or other CU figure succeeded in forming new govt, Papandreou might go to streets to try bring down such govt. With leftist support, Papandreou would have capacity to provoke serious demonstrations throughout country. At this point army might intervene, fearing that stability of regime were being shaken.

Whatever outcome, confrontation at this time (while Papandreou still popular) and on issue of army leadership would appear to be unfortunate step both from point of view U.S. and Greek interests. Even opponents of Papandreou in both govt and opposition ranks believe timing is not right for challenge to PriMin. They maintain that in fall, when economic problems reach critical stage, PriMin's popularity will fall sharply, and challenge to his leadership will then come from within his own party, from Mitsotakis forces. However, these anti-Papandreou forces within party might be reluctant to line up with Palace against PriMin now. Deputies would not now relish facing alternatives of elections on one hand or participating in coalition supported by ERE on other.

Indications are that King, undoubtedly under influence of right-wing advisors, believes that his leadership of armed forces is being eroded by army's involvement in politics and by its penetration by forces

---

[3] Andreas Papandreou commented on his father's plan in a June 27 talk with Richard Barham, Officer in Charge of Greek Affairs, at the Department of State. A memorandum of their conversation is ibid., POL GREECE.

loyal to Papandreous (such as Aspida) rather than to throne. Therefore, King apparently is being persuaded that he must make stand now, rather than at later time, when his position might be weaker.

Embassy remains hopeful that head-on collision will be averted through realization by both sides that confrontation not in their best interests, and we are taking every opportunity to point out that confrontation would be damaging to nation's interests.

Anschuetz

---

197.   Telegram From the Embassy in Greece to the Department of State[1]

Athens, June 30, 1965, 1929Z.

1921. I called this morning on PriMin. Embassy Political Counselor and Sossides of PriMin's staff also present.

PriMin commenced by stressing that his aim is to bring internal peace to Greek political scene. He had achieved this in part by taking firm and moderate stand on question of referral Caramanlis to the courts (Embtels 1864, 1829)[2] although this had been unpopular step for him with many of his party.

Now he must face up to problem of taking politics out of the army. This means removing those within army who espoused cause of either right or left. He has therefore decided he must ask for MinDef Garoufalias' resignation within next few days and assume post himself. Garoufalias, in whom he has great trust and who would be highly competent in any other Ministerial post, is unhappily labeled as man of the Palace. Garoufalias strives to protect Palace interests but in order compensate Garoufalias does not act with appropriate vigor toward center elements who require discipline. His actions are constantly misjudged and he is thus no longer in position to do job necessary in keeping army free of politics.

Gennimatas, Chief of Staff, had also been labeled as a man of the King and was also unable to function effectively because he too is under

---

[1] Source: Department of State, Central Files, POL 13–8 GREECE. Secret; Limdis.

[2] Telegram 1864 from Athens, June 18, reported Parliament's decision to drop charges against Karamanlis. (Ibid., POL 15–2 GREECE) Telegram 1829 from Athens, June 10, reported Parliamentary discussion of the investigative report on the DEI case. (Ibid.)

fire from "the democratic elements". A new man is needed as Chief HAGS who would not be tarred with this brush and he, the past PriMin is going to advise the King that a change has to be made. He said he thought the King would agree to this change when he had presented his reasons for it.

I said frankly I am concerned at implications of confrontation between Palace and govt over question of military leadership. US interests in stability of Greece as well as our continuing contributions to Greek armed forces are basis legitimate interest in this question. I entirely agreed with PM that politics should be kept away from armed forces. While I agreed that govt, not King is responsible for policy determination, I am also aware that modern Greek history shows clearly that King has over period of time acquired a generally recognized interest in armed forces. Any severe shock to this delicate balance of powers could be dangerous and might even risk raising basic issue of regime. This would be tragic for Greece. For this reason I earnestly hope that a solution satisfactory to both parties could be found. I said that I am pleased PriMin will soon have occasion to see King in Corfu in connection with formalities following birth of Royal baby. This will provide opportunity for direct discussion and eliminate possible misunderstandings resulting from reliance on intermediaries. I expressed concern that departure of both Garoufalias and Gennimatas might create profound reaction in Palace and perhaps certain opposition circles.

PriMin bridled at inference his personal assumption of Defense portfolio could produce any anxiety. He was adamant that Gennimatas as a person would have to go but acknowledged that once agreement had been obtained to this move timing might be matter for negotiation.

Comment: Papandreou was in a very serious mood and showed a degree of stubbornness to my probing as to what the implications of the change in the military hierarchy might mean to the political fabric of Greece. He appears confident he can stand down King on this issue and will use the threat of resignation and elections in the event the King does not agree. He stated flatly no new government based on support of ERE could stand because it would be a travesty of will of people. He did not once mention Mitsotakis factor or allude to Kokkas attacks except indirectly, when he said his son Andreas is being blamed for all ills of Greece. He would not be surprised if they were to run out of issues to bomb him for, Andreas would be blamed for situation in Santo Domingo.

Garoufalias confided to me earlier this morning he did not intend to resign, that Papandreou would then ask King to sign decree revoking his (Garoufalias') appointment. If King refused, govt crisis would ensue and perhaps Garoufalias or Stephanopoulos would be requested to form government. This evening FonMin Costopoulos, a strong royalist, expressed concern that King would be in weak constitutional position if he refused to concur in Papandreou's assumption of Defense portfolio. According to Papandreou proposal Garoufalias would receive another portfolio. Houtas, present Minister Public Works and reliable from Palace point of view would replace Papaconstantinou as Deputy Min Def.

Anschuetz

198.   Telegram From the Embassy in Turkey to the Department of State[1]

Ankara, July 9, 1965, 1459Z.

33. Had long talk with Isik last night which began as review discussions on Cyprus but progressed into unexpectedly frank exchange on situation of Greek nationals in Istanbul and Patriarchate.

Re talks, Isik said dialogue continuing with Sgourdeos but getting nowhere. GOG still says it understands necessity for compensation to GOT if agreement to be reached on basis enosis but then says it has nothing to offer.

I asked what in circumstances they then had to talk about.

Isik replied this good question and answer is that, in effort keep talks going, he and Sgourdeos indulging in form of "mental gymnastics" which taking form not of real negotiations but of discussing various aspects of question on purely hypothetical basis. However, this type of shadow discussion could not go on indefinitely and, unless something more promising develops, he will have no alternative but to abandon idea of agreement on enosis and revert to settlement based on independence.

In painting this rather bleak picture, Isik again mentioned desirability of reaching agreement in order keep issue out of election campaign but did not press point as vigorously as he had before. However, this may have been more end of day fatigue than change of emphasis.

Isik took occasion once again express dissatisfaction with unfulfilled assurances of GOG to influence Makarios to improve situation of Turk Cypriots and said improvement in this respect remained essential

---

[1] Source: Department of State, Central Files, POL 27 CYP. Secret; Limdis; TOG. Repeated to Nicosia, Athens, London, and USUN.

to successful talks with GOG. He also referred to various statements and acts of Makarios which apparently designed impede talks but reemphasized that real problem is situation Turks on island.

This led to his observation that GOG attempting fan flames of situation of Greek nationals in Istanbul and draw analogy with that of Turk Cypriots, which obviously unreasonable since measures taken re Greeks are normal application of law such as is observed worldwide in situations where residence permits expire. If any analogy to be drawn it should be with Greeks of Turkish nationality whose status not in question.

I observed at this point that, without going into question of law, fact is that continuing eviction of Greeks from Istanbul lends itself to highly colored treatment with result that, rightly or wrongly, it does in fact have an impact in Greece similar to that of situation of Turk Cypriots here. Thus it is a practical problem which can affect progress of talks. Viewed purely pragmatically, could not something be done to alleviate this?

Isik hesitated and then said he did recognize this and had gone ultimate limit in trying do something but that action which would have effect of noncompliance with law would provoke reaction far more difficult than existing situation where various means can be used to modify application of law without actually voiding it. Isik added he had been frank in saying same thing to Sgourdeos since he believed only hope of successful outcome of negotiations was to lay cards on table.

He then added, as though thinking out loud, that perhaps just as well that presence of Greek nationals in Istanbul should be gradually liquidated since, viewed long term, it was constant irritant in Greco-Turk relations. Same could also be true of Patriarchate, especially if present incumbent continued to rely on political support of Greece and also to play international role by exchanging messages, gifts, etc. with heads of state in manner not consonant with his position as a prelate in Turkey. In situation where Turkey had abolished Caliphate as symbol of universal Islam, not permissible that Patriarchate should arrogate role to itself for which Caliph had been deposed.

Here again I intervened to suggest that, whereas this might be Turkish position, matter does not necessarily look same from outside where, although understood that Patriarch of Istanbul does not have same authority as Pope, he is nevertheless recognized as first among equals and thus not unnatural that he should be regarded at times as spokesman for Greek Orthodoxy. For instance, was trip of Patriarch to visit Pope at Jerusalem last year inappropriate?[2]

---

[2] The Pope and Partriarch met in Jerusalem January 5–6, 1964.

Isik admitted that distinction could perhaps be made where contacts were purely religious but he once again stressed that political connections which Patriarch has been maintaining are definitely improper in eyes of GOT and could lead to removal.

I might add that, in cases of both Greeks in Istanbul and Patriarchate, foregoing is my own distillation of long and frank discussion in course of which my probing evoked replies which Isik would hardly have volunteered. Views which he did express, however, even though on personal basis, would indicate that, as prospect of quid pro quo for enosis settlement fades, GOT will be taking harder look at alternatives.

Hare

199. Telegram From the Embassy in Greece to the Department of State[1]

Athens, July 9, 1965, 1725Z.

37. Incipient political crisis appears suddenly to have crystallized following letter from King to PriMin allegedly delivered last night by Chief Royal Political Bureau, Choidas, informing PriMin that King is prepared to receive him but not concur in the removal of DefMin Garoufalias or Army Chief of Staff Gennimatas (contents letter separately reported [less than 1 line of source text not declassified]). Apparently letter asserts, inter alia, King has always acted scrupulously within framework of his constitutional powers, and reproaches Papandreou not only for having failed to support the King, but for having permitted impression to grow that King is prepared to act extra-constitutionally. Existence of letter has not yet been publicly revealed, but may result in resignation of government.

Festering political situation which has developed as result of Palace and ERE alarm at alleged efforts of Papandreous and certain other Center Union elements to establish political control over the armed forces may well explode as result of this sudden action by King. According to some reports King has decided not to concur in any changes in leadership armed forces at this time, and is determined to push for showdown with PriMin and his son Andreas before what King regards as the cor-

---

[1] Source: Department of State, Central Files, POL 15–1 GREECE. Secret; Limdis.

ruption of the armed forces becomes more extensive and the position of EDA and extreme left even stronger. There have even been some rumors that King prepared to accept government under a military leader if satisfactory government, willing and able to confront demonstrations and strikes which Papandreous and left might foment, cannot be formed.

Embassy position has remained unchanged from that which we have taken ever since collision between King and PriMin first became real possibility. As reported in my conversations with Choidas (Embtel 1880)[2] and PriMin (Embtel 1921),[3] I have consistently expressed opinion that it should be possible for a compromise solution to be found which would permit persons mutually acceptable to PriMin and King to be named to the positions of DefMin and Chief of Staff of Army (subject to questions of timing) and that raising of the question of the regime would be tragedy for Greece from which ultimately only the Communists would profit. This position has naturally been received with a lack of enthusiasm by those elements on both sides who hoped to win the unqualified support of US.

Last night at dinner at which ERE leaders Kanellopoulos, Papaligouras, Tsatsos, Rallis and Theotakis were present, I reflected similar views. ERE leaders were highly emotional over current situation but revealed very little evidence they had carefully considered all implications of confrontation between King and PriMin at this time.

King has been isolated in Corfu presumably depending principally upon Queen Mother, his political advisor Choidas and his long-time confidant, Major Arnaoutis, as advisors and intermediaries. In extensive conversation with Choidas June 23 reported in Embtel 1880 I expressed serious reservations as to wisdom of direct collision between Papandreou and King under current circumstances. Since that time I have twice seen him socially. On each occasion he asserted he wished to talk with me again and promised to get in touch with me, but conspicuously failed to do so. I had also expressed my own opinion clearly to General Papathanassiades, Marshal of the Court, who asserted that he entirely agreed and that he had transmitted not only his own but my views to the King.

My present feeling is that the King has acted with imprudent haste and abruptness, thereby incurring serious risk to internal stability which might possibly have been avoided. If King's action results in establishment of relatively stable new government (presumably headed by a Center Union personality depending principally upon ERE support for its existence) without bringing EDA and the Papandreous even closer and

---

[2] See footnote 2, Document 196.
[3] Document 197.

without possible violence, he will have proved to be shrewder judge of the situation than I am prepared to hope.[4]

Anschuetz

---

[4] Telegram 48 from Athens, July 12, reported that during a meeting with the King, Papandreou offered a compromise that would remove Garoufalias but retain Gennimatas as Chief of Staff. The Embassy commented that the "key question now is whether PriMin will insist on holding Defense portfolio himself." (Department of State, Central Files, POL 15–1 GREECE) Intelligence cable TCDS/DB 315/02331–65, July 9, reported that on July 8, King Constantine expressed his determination to oust Papandreou. (Johnson Library, National Security File, Files of Robert W. Komer, 1965 Cabinet Crisis)

---

200. Telegram From the Embassy in Greece to the Department of State[1]

Athens, July 23, 1965.

123. Re Embtel 122.[2] Embassy's current position regarding solution present political crisis,[3] which we have coordinated [*less than 1 line of source text not declassified*], is as follows:

A) Situation has not developed to point where U.S. attitude might be decisive. Consequently we are endeavoring to maintain greatest possible discretion.

B) In circumstances where we felt it might be helpful, we have privately expressed view Novas solution which, though not very promising, at least has advantage some declared adherents, would not be prematurely abandoned.

C) With regard Stephanopoulos, we have noted this formula depends upon willingness of Stephanopoulos, certain other C.U. leaders, and particularly such newspapers as *Vima*, *Nea* and *Makedonia* to force acceptance this solution on Papandreou or proceed without him. Unless and until support these elements is definitely acquired it would

---

[1] Source: Department of State, Central Files, POL 15 GREECE. Secret; Priority. There is no time of transmission on the source text; the telegram was received at 5:27 p.m. on July 24.

[2] Telegram 122, July 24, reported that the political crisis in Greece was intensifying. (Ibid.)

[3] On July 15, following a clash with King Constantine over his desire to replace Minister of Defense Garoufalias with himself, Prime Minister Papandreou resigned. The King then nominated George Novas, a member of the Center Union, as Prime Minister.

be dangerous to abandon Novas. In principle we have no objection to Stephanopoulos or "Stephanopoulos plan", which in theory would preserve a wider measure of unity in C.U.

D) We have not demonstrated any enthusiasm for new effort to find compromise between King and Papandreou. This would probably leave Papandreou in even more powerful position in C.U. Moreover, it is highly unlikely King would consent. We recognize, however, Papandreou may yet emerge victor and that we may have to live with him. We are endeavoring avoid actions which might prejudice U.S. position in this eventuality.

Given incredibly sensitive political acoustics in Athens and virtuosity of Greek talent for misrepresentation and distortion, Embassy position is constant subject for local exploitation. For example: King has been quoted as saying I discouraged Stephanopoulos from forming or joining government following Papandreou resignation; rightist elements have charged that U.S. is no longer interested in fighting Communism; Andreas Papandreou told me he knows Americans are saying that he must go. This spectrum of commentary suggests that although our attempt not to become involved may not prove to be completely successful, the effort is at least a valiant one.[4]

Anschuetz

---

[4] In telegram 127 to Athens, July 31, the Department of State agreed that "discretion needed to avoid untimely involvement of American factor on eve arrival new Ambassador." (Department of State, Central Files, POL 15 GREECE)

---

201. Telegram From the Embassy in Greece to the Department of State[1]

Athens, August 10, 1965.

229. Choidas, Chief Royal Political Bureau, telephoned yesterday evening. He said he wanted me to know that even though CU party caucus yesterday afternoon had produced only 26 deputies who supported Stephanopoulos as against 116 who supported Papandreou, King was

---

[1] Source: Department of State, Central Files, POL 15 GREECE. Secret; Roger Channel. There is no time of transmission on the source text; the telegram was received at 5:23 p.m.

confident Stephanopoulos would continue his efforts. Stephanopoulos had assured King, through Choidas, that he would produce a solution. Palace hoped such solution would be Stephanopoulos' agreement to accept mandate himself. Embassy's good offices would be appreciated. King himself also commented to an American friend yesterday that he hoped Embassy could encourage Stephanopoulos to move forward.

Later in evening [*less than 1 line of source text not declassified*] and I received visit from CU Deputy Tsouderos. Tsouderos said he had just come from meeting at which Mitsotakis, Tsirimokos and Papapolitis were working very hard to persuade Stephanopoulos that it is essential he continue his effort. A word of encouragement from Embassy at this point could be extremely important. Tsouderos said there is increasing amount of disgust and unhappiness among 116 deputies who had supported Papandreou yesterday. Although it is not at all certain that all 26 who had supported Stephanopoulos yesterday would necessarily support him if he proceeded without formal support of CU, there is undoubtedly significant number of deputies who had supported Papandreou who would switch their allegiance if Stephanopoulos' determination to accept mandate and seek vote of confidence became clear.

I acknowledged that if Stephanopoulos solution failed, other possible solutions are certainly not very attractive. Stephanopoulos is now in awkward position to continue in light his public statements making acceptance of mandate contingent on approval of CU. Moreover, performance of Stephanopoulos' sponsor, Lambrakis, and his papers *Vima* and *Nea* have been extremely disappointing not to say ambiguous. Despite his professed private endorsement of Stephanopoulos plan, it seemed pretty clear Lambrakis had in fact done virtually nothing at the last minute to encourage those who might otherwise have been tempted support Stephanopoulos. Even though Stephanopoulos succeeded in forming govt and even though an additional thirty or forty CU deputies subsequently adhered to Stephanopoulos, serious situation would remain with Papandreous outside govt, resulting de facto popular front. Problem would be particularly awkward if powerful Lambrakis press continued support Papandreou. Nevertheless Stephanopoulos solution still seemed least unattractive and I hoped Stephanopoulos could be persuaded not to abandon his effort until it is certain he could not succeed. Tsouderos visited Stephanopoulos after having left us.

This morning I received a telephone call from Stephanopoulos. Asked him how he saw situation and whether he was prepared to continue his effort. He said he would inform King at noon today he could not under circumstances accept mandate. I commented it is obvious that solution must be found and asked whether he had any other ideas. He replied that he had, and that he would like to talk with me about them soon.

Comment: It was subsequently confirmed, as I surmised, that there were a number of other deputies in room when Stephanopoulos telephoned.

As reported above, I have within last 24 hours said to Tsouderos and clearly implied to Stephanopoulos himself that Stephanopoulos should persist in his efforts. Combined votes of ERE, Progressive Party, 25 votes of those who participated in Novas govt, and 26 votes of those who supported Stephanopoulos yesterday in CU caucus would be arithmetically sufficient to form a govt. Under these circumstances I considered Embassy should not withhold word of encouragement which might just possibly provoke necessary impetus to break current impasse and provide interim political solution. Situation had developed to point where issue apparently hung in balance and where cautious effort on our part justified.

[*less than 1 line of source text not declassified*] believes within limitations of resources currently available Embassy has provided maximum support to Novas and Stephanopoulos consistent with discretion which we have been endeavoring maintain. In light this situation I hope Dept will be in position to act affirmatively at appropriate moment on recommendations which I have made re PL 480 program.[2] Unfortunately, however, that moment has not yet arrived and may not for some days.

King acknowledged in private conversation with friend this evening that he is very much at a loss at this point. He had originally been led to believe Stephanopoulos could accumulate about 70 CU votes. Even after Papandreou's victory in CU caucus yesterday afternoon, King had clung to hope Stephanopoulos could be persuaded to accept the mandate.[3]

Anschuetz

---

[2] Not further identified.

[3] In telegram 164 to Athens, August 12, the Department of State responded: "Appreciate intense nature of pressure employed to force American involvement in crisis. However, believe response to any further approaches of type mentioned your 229 should be reiteration that ultimate solution will be healthier politically and more permanent if Greeks work it out without interference." (Department of State, Central Files, POL 15 GREECE)

202.   Telegram From the Embassy in Greece to the Department of State[1]

Athens, August 20, 1965, 1825Z.

279. As Greek political crisis enters its fifth week it is becoming increasingly clear that viable solution to present anomaly is nowhere in sight. Even if Tsirimokos' effort to form govt is successful—which does not seem too likely as of this writing—country must expect turmoil for months to come.[2] Whatever govt is formed under present circumstances will undoubtedly be an unstable one, with a razor-thin majority in Parl. If Tsirimokos does indeed secure vote of confidence next week, his contin-uation in power will be dependent on votes of an extremely disparate group, ranging from rightist ERE to his own centre-leftist followers, and will count for support upon such unpredictable personalities as Progres-sive leader Markezinis and EPEK head Papapolitis, any one of whom could suddenly pull rug out from under Tsirimokos govt by withdraw-ing support.

Even more serious in its effect on political stability is fact that former PriMin Papandreou and his followers will be touring country, beginning tomorrow, in effort to keep atmosphere as turbulent as possible. Contin-ued demonstrations both in Athens and in provinces are in prospect, creating conditions hardly conducive to serious deliberation by Parl in session. Although demonstrations have been frequent, few have been marked by violence. Eventually serious violence may take place, partic-ularly if Papandreou supporters feel their own strength ebbing. And of course if Papandreou takes to road ERE Party may consider it has to do likewise unless it wishes to leave field to Papandreou forces.

Unfortunately, this prospect of continued political instability comes at time when Greece is facing problems of major dimensions both on domestic and foreign fronts. Although Cyprus has been relatively quiet during first month of Greek political crisis, it is at least questionable whether it will continue to remain so in months ahead. Equally urgent are pressing economic problems, characterized by the continued fall in foreign exchange reserves and an increasing trade imbalance. Business confidence will undoubtedly be deeply shaken if prospects for eventual stable govt do not improve. A govt without a solid foundation—either in Parl or among general public—will hardly be in position to make firm (and probably unpopular) decisions in the coming months.

---

[1] Source: Department of State, Central Files, POL 15 GREECE. Confidential. Repeated to Ankara, Nicosia, Paris for James and Burns, and USDOCOSouth for Burris.

[2] On August 14, Tsirimokos withdrew from the Center Union. On August 18, King Constantine asked him to form a government. He took office on August 20 and was defeated in an August 28 vote of confidence by 135 to 159.

In addition to prospects for continued instability, two aspects of current crisis are particularly disturbing. First is that as result efforts to prevent extension Papandreou's influence into military and security forces, King had directly descended into political area with result that the "regime" issue has gradually arisen. And this despite repeated denials of Papandreou that there is any "question of monarchy" involved or that CU would raise it in future elections.[3] Anti-royalist sentiment is being continuously inflamed by such pro-Papandreou publications as powerful Lambrakis syndicate (*To Vima* and *Ta Nea*) which daily carry attacks on King. *Vima* for example recently carried editorial critical of King under heading: "Crown showing contempt for people." Slogans chanted and paraded by leftist-led demonstrators for Papandreou are becoming increasingly bold; although initially anti-monarchist slogans concentrated on Queen Mother ("the German woman must go"), in recent days they have included King himself. One banner in Aug 17 demonstrations read "people don't want you—take your mother and go." Thus, regardless of promises of Papandreou camp that they are not raising monarchist issue, in effect it has already been raised.

Second disturbing aspect is achievement of extreme left in making its catchwords the slogans of center through its collaboration "at the base" with followers of George Papandreou. For first time since bandit war Communists are no longer isolated but have succeeded in merging at popular level with much larger masses of center. It is difficult to determine what is Communist demonstration and what is not, since slogans have become virtually identical, except that Communists cleverly insert slogans peculiarly their own on such non-Greek topics as Vietnam, "imperialism," etc. While CU supporters provide bulk of demonstrators, Communists often provide leadership and hence are able to control demonstrations.

It seems clear that any long-term solution to current crisis must come through elections, however distasteful this may be to many quarters, including the Palace. As of now Crown maintains (quite rightly) that present climate is completely unsuitable for elections, and electoral campaign in current tense atmosphere would very probably be characterized by serious violence. Even more important from the Palace and conservative point of view, because current tide running in Papandreou's favor, former PriMin might well equal his 1964 feat of 53 per cent of popular vote. There are few serious politicians, even in his own party, who would welcome prospect of Papandreou returned with heavy popular vote (which he would consider vindication of his struggle with

---

[3] At a meeting with Embassy officials on August 25, Papandreou reiterated this assurance. (Telegram 304 from Athens, August 25; Department of State, Central Files, POL 15–1 GREECE)

King) and probably determined to punish those he considered responsible for his troubles in Palace, army, and his own party. Further, a Papandreou victory would not bring with it the tempering influence of more conservative leaders of party such as Costopoulos, Novas, Mitsotakis, etc. The influence of his left-leaning son Andreas in govt would undoubtedly be greater with so many of other major figures departed. Further, heavy vote in favor of Papandreou could only be interpreted as blow to King, despite Papandreou's denial that monarchy question would be involved; very possibly Papandreou would move to limit role and influence of Crown in Greek political life. Finally, return of Papandreous would probably increase unwholesome political tensions in military and security forces.

For these reasons, King, supported by ERE, Progressives and sizeable element of CU, strongly opposes elections, and would consider instability for indefinite period preferable to return of Papandreou. However, as unstable situation continues, pressure for elections from Papandreou will undoubtedly increase and idea might well gain support even among other elements (now opposed to elections) as only available means of clarifying situation.

Anschuetz

---

203. Editorial Note

During the period 1965–1967, senior U.S. policymakers, concerned that the return to power of George and Andreas Papandreou could open the door to the radicalization of Greek politics and permit the Communist Party to obtain influence in Greece, debated possible courses of action within the 303 Committee. (Concerning the role of the 303 Committee, see Note on U.S. Covert Actions and Counter-Insurgency Programs, page XXXI.) Some officials in the Johnson administration believed that the United States should take active steps to strengthen a moderate regime as well as weaken the political base of the Papandreous, leaders of the Center Union Party. The President's Special Assistant for National Security Affairs McGeorge Bundy opposed such a course of action. He contended that reporting on the situation in Greece did not bear out such apprehensions and that political lines were not clearly drawn. The 303 Committee first tabled the issue and later, upon considering it a second time and not reaching a decision, referred the matter to Secretary of State Dean Rusk. Rusk rejected such a program because he believed the security risk outweighed any possible gains that could be achieved. Ultimately, the Johnson administration endorsed no such programs for Greece.

204.   Telegram From the Embassy in Greece to the Department of State[1]

Athens, September 5, 1965.

369. [7 *paragraphs (2 pages) of source text not declassified*]

[*8 lines of source text not declassified*] Embassy has concluded George Papandreou's return to power should be avoided if this can be done without a direct and open confrontation with him. George Papandreou at this moment commands wide popular support among Greek people. This popularity has temporarily been raised to artificial levels in current crisis by Papandreou's clever exploitation of latent hostility towards the Monarchy. I am keenly aware that inasmuch as we may have to deal with Papandreou again in future, utmost discretion and avoidance of open hostility toward him are essential.

Andreas' motives are difficult to present categorically. In my assessment, based on half dozen extensive conversations with him, Andreas is neutralist, ambitious, amoral, and emotionally unstable. Although conclusive proof has not yet been adduced I believe Andreas is probably a leader in Aspida and that he hopes eventually to achieve a measure of control in army which would be exercised as decisive element in Greek political life.

In his view the weight of the American position in Greece, political and military, is an obstacle to "independent" foreign and domestic Greek policy which he advocates. I believe Andreas would seek significantly to reduce Greek military expenses, would progressively remove Greece from close NATO alignment, look increasingly toward Soviet bloc both as growing market for Greek products (30 per cent of Greek exports now find their way to the Soviet bloc) and as source of aid to fill gap created by decline in Western aid (U.S., OECD, NATO defense support). His natural ally in implementing such a policy is extreme Left and Communists. Explanation of his dubious role in Cyprus issue and his opposition to an active enosis policy may lie in his desire to avoid a position which would be offensive to Soviet Union and Communist elements to whom he seems to be looking for support in other areas. Under these circumstances, it is of great importance to obtain better measure Andreas' relationship Communists and extreme Left, determine sources and magnitude his financial resources, and circumscribe to extent possible his political power, actual and potential.

---

[1] Source: Department of State, Central Files, POL 15 GREECE. Secret; Limdis; Roger Channel. There is no time of transmission on the source text; the telegram was received at 10:48 a.m.

432 Foreign Relations, 1964–1968, Volume XVI

Greece is small, poor country in strategic area of world. Gradual elimination of Western economic aid, reduction of East-West tensions, increased trade between Greece and the bloc, frustration over the Cyprus situation, and current political impasse with its implication for viability of regime itself have all combined create movement of new dimensions in postwar Greek political life. This situation presents new opportunities for Soviet bloc and perhaps other unfriendly forces such as Gaullist France and Red China. Objective evidence such as organization of public manifestations, program of personal threats and intimidation, and rumors regarding substantial funds available to Andreas clearly suggests Communists are not standing aside. Kostopoulos and Zolotas have both recently mentioned to me that drachmae resources of Western European banks have mysteriously evaporated.

Changing factors in international political life have also reduced somewhat weight of American influence here. We recognize precisely because American influence is slowly declining it must be exercised with increasing caution and discretion. [13 *lines of source text not declassified*][2]

Anschuetz

---

[2] [*text not declassified*]

---

205. Memorandum From Albert Carter of the Bureau of Intelligence and Research to the Assistant Secretary of State for Near Eastern and South Asian Affairs (Talbot)

Washington, September 10, 1965.

[Source: Department of State, INR Files, 303 Committee Records, Greece, 1965–1967. Secret. 1 page of source text not declassified.]

206.   **Telegram From the Embassy in Greece to the Department of State**[1]

Athens, September 17, 1965, 1525Z.

450. In brief private exchange last night following dinner which King Constantine gave in honor of Astronauts Cooper and Conrad, King referred to current political situation.

King said it imperative Stephanopoulos succeed in effort form govt although it is not yet quite clear whether Stephanopoulos has in fact obtained assurances of six or seven additional votes necessary to obtain majority. He suggested that if Embassy had any influence such influence could be terribly important in present circumstances. If current effort to form govt fails it is difficult to know what to do next.

King recognized that even though Stephanopoulos were to receive vote of confidence, one could not predict how long his govt would last. It is of greatest importance that new govt not be formed on basis of a commitment to hold elections notwithstanding fact elections must eventually be held. It would be most unfortunate if elections were held now on basis of who is right and who is wrong. Important thing is to form govt of ostensibly indefinite duration thereby eliminating prospects of early election which provide Papandreou with hold over substantial number of his deputies. When activities of left have been controlled, electoral system changed, and appropriate situation had been created, quick decision could be taken to hold new elections. King expressed opinion elections should be held under proportional system. Although proportional system might strengthen hands of Communists, Communists would be clearly visible and power of Papandreou would also be reduced.

I observed that we had always recognized that whatever government might be formed from present Parliament should be regarded as evolutionary, and agree with him that elections must eventually be held. I added I was particularly pleased that records of Crown Council meeting just published had clearly established fact King had informed Papandreou on night of Papandreou's resignation that he was prepared to give Papandreou Defense portfolio as soon as Aspida investigation had been concluded and that he was also prepared to accept Stephanopoulos or any other CU deputy as DefMin pending completion of investigation.

Comment: King did not specify what remedy he might seek in event current effort to form government fails nor did he specifically exclude extra-Parliamentary solution. Nevertheless I found reassuring his reservations regarding durability of a govt formed from present Parliament

---

[1] Source: Department of State, Central Files, POL 15 GREECE. Secert; Limdis.

and recognition of necessity for elections when appropriate conditions had been created.

Anschuetz

207. Memorandum of Conversation[1]

Washington, September 24, 1965.

SUBJECT

Cyprus

PARTICIPANTS

Hasan Isik, Turkish Foreign Minister
Ambassador Turgut Menemencioglu, Turkish Embassy
Haluk Bayulken, Director General, Ministry of Foreign Affairs
Ilter Turkmen, Chairman for Policy Planning, Ministry of Foreign Affairs

The Under Secretary
Raymond A. Hare, Assistant Secretary for NEA
George T. Churchill, Officer-in-Charge, Turkish Affairs

Isik opened the discussion on Cyprus with the observation that the governmental crisis in Greece had brought efforts to settle the Cyprus question to a standstill. Even with Papandreou in office, there had been only a slim chance of reaching a mutual understanding; now there is no reason to hope for progress. He said he had just spoken with the Greek Ambassador (to the United Nations)[2] who said his government was trying to find a solution. However, it was clear that even with the good intentions of Greek officials, the situation in Greece was not conducive for a settlement. At the same time, Isik said, time is running out. It would be unfortunate if Cyprus developed along the same lines as Kashmir. We must act promptly to prevent this. He said he realizes the United States

---

[1] Source: Department of State, Central Files, POL 27 CYP. Confidential. Drafted by Churchill and approved in U on October 4. Isik was in the United States to attend the U.N. General Assembly meeting. According to telegram 279 to Ankara, September 25, this meeting was "essentially a probing session by Hare" to determine Turkish plans for the post-General Assembly discussions on Cyprus. (Ibid.) Hare left Ankara on August 27 and was appointed Assistant Secretary of State for Near Eastern and South Asian Affairs on September 11.

[2] Alexis Liatis.

Government wants to help find a solution, but it would be helpful to know what the United States now proposes to do.

Mr. Ball agreed that the present situation in Greece complicates the problem. Any Greek Government for the foreseeable future will be working with a very narrow margin and will not be in a strong position to negotiate. It was the presumption at London that any Greek Government would have to negotiate on the basis of enosis with compensation to Turkey. A weak government in Athens, such as we can expect for some time, would be unable to cede territory. This does make the prospect for settlement very difficult. If we accept the premise that Greece can only negotiate on the basis of enosis, we would have to examine the alternatives. One of these is negotiations between the Turkish Government and the Government of Cyprus, although we recognize this presents difficulties for the Turks, and is, therefore, an unlikely avenue.

Being frank, Mr. Ball said it is very difficult to say what the United States might be able to do under these circumstances. We want to see some kind of agreed solution, which is the only kind that could be permanent. Even if we were in a position to bring about a settlement by force, it would be unlikely to be a permanent solution. We had hoped a period of calm on the island would allow an evolution toward some kind of solution. This apparently has not happened. However, Mr. Ball said, we are not entirely clear as to what is happening on the island, or what shape Makarios' ambitions are taking. He said he would be interested in Mr. Isik's assessment of the situation and his suggestions as to what the United States might usefully do.

Isik responded that the United States must do its best to avoid a settlement that would not be satisfactory to Turkey. This was the most important element. Makarios is moving continuously toward his objectives. He is always trying to create unrest. Now Makarios is offering to improve the living conditions of the Turkish refugees. This seems a good sign on the surface, but is really only another attempt to maneuver the Turkish Cypriots into accepting the status of a minority. The Turkish community rejects these blandishments, but individuals, of course, are only human. The Turks have been living under conditions of hardship for a long time, and Makarios' offer will undermine morale in the community. Isik said that Makarios' action on the electoral law showed clearly what his real intentions are. But Turkey cannot accept further faits accomplis. We must find a way, he said, to prevent a further deterioration of the situation. If Makarios feels he can act, he will continue to move along his present path, and this will prove disastrous. Security lies in preventing Makarios from acting.

Isik went on to say that Turkey's relations with Greece could not be improved unless the Cyprus problem could be resolved. Turkey and Greece have implicitly agreed to avoid either enosis or partition, unless as part of a negotiated settlement. Annexation by Greece at this point would result in a direct confrontation.

Mr. Ball said we had made clear to Makarios on a number of occasions that we objected to unilateral revision of the London/Zurich Agreements, and we would continue to do so. We have also pointed out to him that if he proceeded with constitutional revisions, this would be a course of action unacceptable to the entire international community and a source of danger. It has been our feeling, Mr. Ball said, that Makarios has been more cautious after this warning. Isik responded that his actions were cautious but continuous.

Isik confessed that his Government was at a loss as to how to act under present circumstances. He said he was studying the situation carefully, and was interested in discovering what Turkey and the United States might do together. Mr. Ball assured Isik that the United States was prepared to do anything possible to facilitate a solution.

On the question of Cyprus in the United Nations General Assembly, Bayulken commented on the assignment of this issue to the First (Political) Committee. The Committee, he said, would determine when the issue would come up before the Assembly. He said the Turkish Government was working for a "procedural" (non-substantive) resolution. He felt that at least some of the unaligned countries would support such a resolution, although certain of these countries might feel themselves bound by the previous Cairo Conference resolution on Cyprus.[3] The upcoming Afro-Asian Conference in Algiers on October 28 might also affect the situation. A non-substantive resolution might be backed by NATO and other key countries. The attitude of India and the UAR is still unknown. Bayulken felt the chances for a non-substantive resolution were about fifty-fifty at present, but that strong support from the United States and the Latin American countries would ensure success, or at least prevent a resolution favoring Makarios. The danger, Bayulken pointed out, is that a resolution might be passed which would seem harmless but could be read by the Greek-Cypriots as a victory. If this were to happen, it would ruin any chance of working out a solution to the Cyprus problem.

Mr. Ball agreed with this assessment and said he would speak personally with Ambassador Yost in New York on this subject.

---

[3] The Conference of Heads of State or Government of Non-Aligned Countries, held in Cairo October 5–10, 1964, issued a declaration that, among other things, called for the "unrestricted and unfettered" sovereignty and independence of Cyprus. For extracts of the declaration, see *American Foreign Policy: Current Documents, 1964*, pp. 691–698.

208.   Telegram From the Embassy in Greece to the Department of State[1]

Athens, October 19, 1965, 1530Z.

645. Ref: Embtel 597.[2] In past week Embassy has intensively reviewed present political and economic dynamics in Greece and possible instruments available to mitigate adverse trends. While picture has many uncertainties and while indeed our information has many gaps, I have reached following current conclusions:

1.   Strains on Greek political fabric are more severe today than at any time since recovery from civil war and may not be containable. With far right and, more aggressively, far left nibbling at edges, fractured center is enmeshed in uncompromising power struggle between foxy old Papandreou and those former colleagues who have dared oppose him and son Andreas. As result, Greece is now weakly governed. Nor is any substantially stronger government in prospect.

2.   Ultimately, this struggle of center forces must be taken to electorate. There is substance, however, in fears held by opponents of Papandreous that election campaign in present tense atmosphere would undermine if not destroy effectiveness of Greek political center for years to come and open field to left-right dichotomy of sort Greece has so calamitously experienced before.

3.   Key to avoiding that prospect in next few months is ability of present government or one like it to muster support of workable majority of Deputies when Parliament reconvenes November 15. With current 152–148 edge tenuously based on alliance of ambitious rivals brought together by common opposition to Papandreou and to immediate elections, it will not be easy for Stephanopoulos to overcome timidity of other Deputies who are said to want to bolt Papandreou but to fear they would be dead ducks if he succeeded forcing early elections. Outcome depends on confidence current government can generate in its survivability.

4.   Meanwhile Greece is sliding into sharp double-headed economic strains, on which Embassy has commented in series of recent messages. On international payments front, firm fiscal management, emphasis on import substitutes (e.g., in meat production) and other measures should in long run stand good chance of restoring favorable payments balance on which remarkable Greek development has rested since currency reform of 1953. However, trend of declining reserves in

---

[1] Source: Department of State, Central Files, POL 2 GREECE. Secret; Limdis.

[2] Telegram 597, October 6, transmitted general comments on the Greek aid request. (Ibid., AID 4 GREECE)

relation to external obligations probably cannot be corrected this year by measures GOG capable of taking. Serious payments difficulties loom just ahead. I am assured these could gravely undermine confidence of drachma if GOG unable to find necessary financial resources or if accompanied by political turbulence here.

5.   Condition of domestic economy also causing anxiety as fiscal stringency becomes acute. Seeds of trouble lie in some long-term factors, but are accentuated by uncovered costs of Papandreou economic and social programs and by very large wheat surplus produced by past year's good weather and high subsidies. Administrative immobility reflecting political paralysis of recent months has also had effect. GOG has already cut back capital development program and may shortly have to interrupt work or at least payments on some ongoing projects unless new resources found. While economy still looks reasonably good to ordinary man, it is in fact highly vulnerable to economic and psychological shocks.

6.   GOG defense policies and foreign policies do not at present time show signs of deterioration similar to those evident on domestic political and economic fronts. Greece continues to waffle weakly on Cyprus question, but that is old story. A new Cyprus crisis this fall would of course further complicate domestic situation here.

7.   In sum, Greece faces imminent and heavy pressures on stability and progress achieved in past dozen years. Among limiting and hardly satisfactory political alternatives available, I now believe these pressures would best be resisted by continuation for some months of centrist government without Papandreous. Even if Papandreous should be returned to power in elections sometime in 1966, government then headed by them might be less unsettling to Greece and to our relations with Greece than if they were to ride into office on today's emotional tides.

8.   As indicated above, I believe there is small hope of averting political crisis unless measures taken to contain worst of economic strains. GOG has already committed itself to some difficult steps, e.g., its decision to substitute 100,000 tons of wheat for imported corn feed. Officials tell us GOG is cranking up to take other steps (Embtel 644),[3] but within life expectancy of present GOG these at best will be ameliorative rather than corrective. Effectiveness of such measures may in fact depend, as GOG argues, on Greece's ability to get some external assistance. I believe any such aid at this stage should be precisely focussed on immediate fiscal and economic problems. Its object would be to get prompt economic effect and to indicate continued sympathetic interest in Greece. It would thus improve psychological climate in which Stephanopoulos government struggling to meet most urgent problems, but if

---

[3] Dated October 19. (Ibid., AID (US) 15–11 GREECE)

well handled would not cost us influence with successors if Stephano-poulos govt should subsequently be overthrown. Ensuing paragraphs discuss possibilities and identify those I recommend.

9. To ease balance of payment strains, neither imports nor exports look amenable to constructive manipulation in short term. GOG has focussed on getting USAID program loan as tidiest instrument among available levers to meet combined problem of international payments, drachma shortage in investment budget, and psychic requirement to avert slump in confidence of traders and money market. Greeks have considered but, as Department knows, strongly resisted drawing IMF tranche on grounds it would have reverse psychological impact. (Zolo-tas says IMF staff agrees.) I am not sure they have yet looked hard enough at possibility of getting relief this winter through arrangements with Exim, World Bank or OECD consortium. In view of urgency of problem, Embassy urging GOG to explore all possibilities, not just US program loan, and to apply any measure of discipline permitted by exigencies of situation. I do not yet see how GOG can overcome short-term payments crunch and would welcome Dept's suggestions.

10. To meet growing shortage of drachmae available for upcoming commitments, GOG can choose one or mixture of several courses: mora-torium on new capital works and slow-down of current capital budget projects, cut in military outlays, or negotiations of new drachma-gener-ating loans. Naturally it is looking to latter, though capital works will also be slowed.

11. On particular problem of grain production and needs, GOG is progressing with plans for handling a considerable part of its wheat sur-plus by designating 150,000 tons for distribution in mountain villages, 1,000,000 tons for poultry and livestock feeding, and remainder for sale abroad. Ultimately several hundred thousand tons likely be sold to for-eign buyers, with good chance that bloc countries will take substantial part. Best estimate of Ag Attaché is that GOG cannot in any circum-stances succeed in coming year in displacing as much as 100,000 tons of corn with wheat for feed. Thus in Embassy's judgement GOG will re-quire 200,000 tons of imported corn to meet needs of starch, poultry and cattle producers.

12. Taking all factors into account, I recommend following USG decisions as urgent next steps to help limit risks of major political or eco-nomic turbulence this winter and to encourage constructive trends with-out assuming responsibility for costs of mistaken past Greek policies:

A. As sole practical economic gesture at this time, to offer 150,000 tons of corn by PL 480 sale Title IV plus 50,000 tons under "usual market-ing" to meet full requirements of starch industry and about one half requirements of poultry and livestock producers heretofore met by corn. Details of suggested agreement spelled out in separate telegram. This action if taken promptly would help GOG hold down payments deficit and meet substantial part of producers' demands for traditional feedgrains while forcing Greeks to start adapting to soft wheat as feedgrain. It would hopefully be read as sign of continued US belief in and encouragement of Greece. To produce maximum political and economic effect I urge that such agreement be concluded or intention to conclude such agreement be announced before convening of Parliament on November 13.

B. To examine carefully with GOG all likely sources of prompt international financial assistance other than USAID loans and to support reasonable Greek requests of prospective lenders.

C. To begin consideration of direct US concessional loans, with expectation decision could be made as situation evolves further in coming weeks.

D. To postpone consideration of Greek feelers for invitation to PriMin to visit Washington until we see situation after Parliament reconvenes and after UNGA considers Cyprus (unless, as now seems highly unlikely, Greeks in meantime come up with new ideas on Cyprus that we would wish to discuss with them).

E. To tidy up certain requests we have pending with Greeks. With agreement for VOA Gamma site now confirmed by Stephanopoulos government, top priority is settling marathon joint-use land issue. To avoid further encroachments and other difficulties, I strongly recommend we request GOG promptly expropriate these lands with costs to be borne by USG. Acquisition of additional 27 acres for use for personnel housing at USAF base at Heraklion is also pressing need. By acting promptly we can profit from present readiness GOG to be accommodating and at same time US dollar payments involved in these transactions would provide additional foreign exchange for Greek reserves.

Talbot

209.   Telegram From the Department of State to the Embassy in Greece[1]

Washington, October 21, 1965, 7:05 p.m.

457. Cyprus: Athens 647; Ankara's 454.[2] As a result of Greek-Turkish contacts at UN, and more settled governmental situations both Athens and Ankara, more attention being focused on Cyprus issue.

Although Isik professed acceptance no result of dialogue with GOG during talks Washington (Deptels 278 and 279 to Ankara),[3] in recent conversations Ankara he has emphasized need to recommence (Embtel 454). Greeks have implied further discussions enosis not practicable because GOG unable in near future commit itself to compensations satisfactory to GOT, but there are indications GOG still desires further consideration enosis. Both Athens and Ankara seem to be jockeying around re resumption dialogue for reasons perhaps associated respective tactics at UNGA.

We believe some action might be desirable to clear atmosphere or nudge parties into further consideration settlement possibilities and action need not await playing out UNGA discussions. This is important since it appears extension mandate UNFICYP (due discussion around Dec. 15) likely be difficult if there has not been forward movement on solution discussions.

Ambassadors should seek opportunity make following points:

1. In Athens: Urge GOG to resume Sgourdaios–Isik talks. No progress toward settlement seems possible until Athens has cleared atmosphere by making some sort of counter-proposal to the initial enosis discussions. Notwithstanding comments contained Embtel 647, if Greeks can reopen meaningful dialogue and present counter-proposal, way might be opened to further progress in this and other fields. By showing willingness continue talks, GOG would prove to world it in fact desires settle Cyprus question and Turk charge Greeks not interested in talking about settlement would be blunted. Reaction to "Turkish black-

---

[1] Source: Department of State, Central Files, POL 27 CYP. Secret; Priority. Drafted by McCaskill and Bracken, cleared by UNP and GTI, and approved by Hare. Also sent to Ankara, Nicosia, London, and USUN.

[2] Telegram 647 from Athens, October 19, reported press reaction to Urguplu's statement on the possibility of attacks on Greek property in Turkey. (Ibid.) Telegram 454 from Ankara, October 16, reported Turkish concern about the latest Greek statements on Cyprus. (Ibid.)

[3] Telegram 278, September 25, reported the Ball–Isik conversation (see Document 207). Regarding telegram 279 to Ankara, see footnote 1, Document 207.

mail" might have been expected, but we would hope GOG would not over-react to recent Urguplu remarks.[4]

2. In Ankara: Being careful to avoid giving Turks impression we engaged in joint planning, Ambassador might draw on materials furnished so far in effort to stimulate Foreign Ministry's consideration various alternatives, as purely intellectual exercise. While suggestion made to Isik in Washington that GOT should consider bringing GOC into talks elicited no enthusiasm, we should explore whether new government might be able to face up to fact that sooner or later GOT must communicate in some way with GOC if independence is to be discussed.[5]

3. In Nicosia: We appreciate comments contained Embtel 172,[6] which will be taken into consideration in formulation of Dept's next steps.

Rusk

---

[4] In telegram 711 from Athens, November 3, Talbot reported that with a new government formed, Prime Minister Stephanopoulos was hoping to resume talks with Turkey and was awaiting signs from Turkey of a willingness to talk. (Department of State, Central Files, POL 27 CYP)

[5] In telegram 476 from Ankara, October 22, Hart reported that he had talked with Isik who had outlined the Turkish positions on Cyprus in detail and indicated that Turkish participation in further talks would depend on the outcome of the General Assembly discussion of Cyprus. (Ibid.)

[6] In telegram 172 from Nicosia, October 5, the Embassy supported the idea of expanding talks among the parties involved in the dispute. (Ibid.)

---

210.   Telegram From the Embassy in Turkey to the Department of State[1]

Ankara, October 22, 1965.

472. Refs: Embtels 416, 452, 454; Deptels 278, 279; Nicosia's 172 to Dept.[2] Proposals re Cyprus Issue.

---

[1] Source: Department of State, Central Files, POL 27 CYP. Confidential; Priority. Repeated to Athens, Nicosia, London, USUN, The Hague, Paris for USRO, Istanbul, Izmir, and Adana. There is no time of transmission on the source text; the telegram was received at 9:46 a.m.

[2] Telegram 416 from Ankara, October 9, reported on a conversation with Isik. (Ibid.) Telegram 452 from Ankara has not been found. Telegram 454 from Ankara is summarized in footnote 2, Document 209. Regarding telegrams 278 and 279 to Ankara, see footnote 3, Document 209. Telegram 172 from Nicosia is summarized in footnote 6, Document 209.

Embassy has reviewed Cyprus question in context of Demirel's victory,[3] FonMin Isik's earlier discussion in US re Cyprus, and remarks of Turkish officials during Ambassador's initial calls. We have also taken into account helpful suggestions contained in Nicosia's 172 to Dept and attitude of Greek Government as reported by Embassy Athens. Against this background, it seems to us that major elements in current situation are following:

1. It is improbable that bilateral Greek-Turkish talks will be resumed before UNGA Cyprus debate despite Turkish efforts to renew discussions.

2. Turks believe they have commitment from us to support procedural resolution at UN. Even assuming US as well as possible Soviet support, Turks are concerned that majority of GA will approve substantive resolution, perhaps including reference to "self determination" for endorsement of Galo Plaza report.

3. Looking beyond UNGA vote, over which Turks have limited control, indications are that Demirel is anxious to try to achieve early resolution of Cyprus question so that he can devote his attention to Turkey's domestic problems. Compared with predecessor coalition government, he will head strongest Turkish Government since 1950's and thus will possess somewhat greater margin of flexibility. However, area of maneuver open to Demirel will remain small because he perforce will operate within familiar framework of Turkish national interests and also be ever sensitive to question of Turkey's prestige.

4. In contrast to greater political stability in Turkey, Stephanopoulos government's future seems doubtful. From our perspective, in view heightened Greek-Turkish tension which will probably intensify during UNGA debate, it seems probable that in immediate future no Greek Government will be able to consider new initiatives re Cyprus which would require any concession. Consequently, enosis-Greek territorial compensation formula appears shelved.

5. On Cyprus itself, Makarios' internal position apparently remains strong despite possibly weaker international position as reflected in August UNSC action and Soviet shift in direction of Turkey. Archbishop appears even less subject to Athens' influence than before, fact which Turks would now be willing to concede, and he remains determined to block any externally imposed solution.

6. Given political situation in three countries directly involved, and prospect of residual bitterness after UNGA vote, US initiative probably will be required to move Cyprus issue off dead center.

_____

[3] In the October 1965 elections, Demirel's Justice Party won 52.9 percent of the popular vote and 240 seats in the Grand National Assembly.

On basis Isik's conversations in Washington and Ambassador's discussions here with Isik and Bayulken, it is clear that Turks are still anxious to engage us in some type of joint planning, although they have no specific proposals in mind.

In order partially to meet Turkish desire without actually becoming involved in joint planning, they believe some merit in our exchanging views with GOT on informal basis. We might begin by reviewing with Turks various alternative proposals, including those which have been considered before, with objective of determining parameters of Turkish position. To create atmosphere of mutual confidence it would be advisable to hold talks in secrecy while making clear to Turks that no commitments on our part were involved during preliminary exchanges.

In this connection, we believe conversations with Turks should begin by explaining alternatives rather than on basis of US-drafted general outline of reasonable proposal (Nicosia's 172 to Dept), but we should be prepared put forward such an outline if talks evolve in fruitful direction. Talks should begin in Ankara on bilateral basis because it is highly unlikely that Turks would be willing to agree to Nicosia as focus of talks involving Archbishop, UK HICOM, Greek, Turkish and US Embassies. In addition to Turkish belief that Cyprus issue should be resolved primarily between Ankara and Athens, Turks would fear their interests would not be properly protected in Nicosia where they would be represented only by chargé, who would be operating in Greek-Cypriot dominated environment, subject to influence by unreliable Turkish-Cypriot community, and out of direct control of Ankara.

Parallel with informal talks in Ankara, we might wish to consider similar noncommittal bilateral exchanges in Athens and Nicosia, informing all three governments that we were carrying on informal exploratory talks in other capitals but that US did not view its role as mediatory one. Instead, our task would be to try to determine whether there was any possibility of forward motion on Cyprus issue by talking independently to parties involved.

Depending on progress made in talks in Ankara (and possibly Athens and Nicosia), we could decide whether there was any prospect for direct negotiation between interested governments in light of prevailing circumstances. It might, for instance, be desirable to encourage resumption of Athens–Ankara dialogue building upon conversations which US had previously undertaken with two governments. At that point, it could also be decided how and when Makarios might be brought into picture. We are inclined to agree with Embassy Nicosia's view that Makarios should be brought into discussions in early stage so that he does not remain aloof only to sabotage ultimate solution. Turks would remain skittish about including Archbishop in any discussions but their final attitude would hinge upon prospects of satisfactory settlement, rather than upon principle involved, and they might be willing to include Makarios if apparent that weak Greek Government could not deliver. Throughout proposed preliminary discussions with Turks (and possibly with others), we would remain alert to desirability of injecting third party into discussions at appropriate time. This could be done by again calling for UN intervention. Despite Turks' unhappy experience with Galo Plaza, or possibly through Acheson type arrangement.

Comments requested.

Foregoing thoughts are put forward on tentative basis to elicit reaction of Department and other interested posts. During stopover in Athens as well as at The Hague, Ambassador plans to discuss some of these ideas with Ambassador Talbot. If Ambassador Belcher or Department have any preliminary reactions, their comments could be forwarded to The Hague.[4]

Foregoing drafted prior to receipt of Deptel 342.[5]

Hart

---

[4] In telegram 209 from Nicosia, October 25, Belcher endorsed the approach outlined by Hart, adding that the United States needed to begin planning for its role in negotiations, and that a role had to be found for Makarios. (Department of State, Central Files, POL 27 CYP)

[5] Telegram 457 to Athens (Document 209) was also sent to Ankara as telegram 342.

---

211. Telegram From the Embassy in Turkey to the Department of State[1]

Ankara, November 3, 1965, 1635Z.

514. Deptel 362.[2] I saw SecGen Bayulken Nov 2 to inform him generally of my contact in Athens and in The Hague on Cyprus question and to tell him about Dept's instructions to Ankara and USUN regarding handling Cyprus item in UNGA.[3] Turkmen also participated in meeting.

---

[1] Source: Department of State, Central Files, POL 27 CYP. Confidential. Repeated to USUN, London, Paris for USRO, Athens, Nicosia, Istanbul, Izmir, and Adana.

[2] Telegram 362 to Ankara, October 30, provided instructions for a discussion with Turkish authorities about consideration of Cyprus at the General Assembly. (Ibid.)

[3] The U.N. General Assembly considered the Cyprus question at its 20th session. The First Committee considered the question during 10 meetings December 11–17.

Reporting on my conversation with Mr. Ball at The Hague, I said Under Secretary had reaffirmed US intention to support procedural resolution on Cyprus. Under Secretary had stated that, in his judgment, UN was not the place in which seek change in treaties. Treaties should be reviewed and renegotiated by parties involved; otherwise, agreed solution unlikely. Mr. Ball also had reiterated view that US is prepared to support any settlement of Cyprus problem which Turkey and Greece can negotiate bilaterally and get Makarios to accept. I explained that my stopover visit in Athens had given me opportunity to talk with Ambassador Talbot whose position was similar to mine in that both were in process of settling in and obtaining briefings from our respective staffs. While neither of us was therefore yet in position to speak with much local experience, we found it very useful to explore all aspects of Cyprus problem. In this connection, I emphasized that Embassy staffs in Athens and Ankara were of one mind in their desire to seek constructive solution to Cyprus question and that we did not have separate approaches to problem. (I did not go into any details of my Athens discussions.)

I then told Bayulken our UN Mission had been instructed to discuss with Turkish Del plans for handling Cyprus item in UNGA. Tactical matters re handling Cyprus question would have to be left to these New York delegations but I wanted FonOff to be aware of instructions sent out delegation. After I had drawn on relevant portions reftel, Bayulken expressed gratitude for being filled in on my talks in Athens and The Hague and for reaffirmation of strong U.S. support for Turkish approach. Line of joint action which U.S. envisaged at UN seemed well designed to avoid complications which might result from unsatisfactory resolution. In particular, Turks appreciated U.S. desire to work closely with Turkish Delegation in seeking passage of procedural resolution which, he hoped, would prepare the way for subsequent Greek-Turkish bilateral talks. He was grateful U.S. would work to prevent any reference to Galo Plaza report because inclusion such reference would be heralded as victory for Makarios.

In ensuing conversation, Bayulken and Turkmen made following specific requests for U.S. cooperation and support in our joint efforts to obtain satisfactory procedural resolution.

1. In addition to expressed U.S. willingness to work particularly with WE and LA Delegations to avoid endorsement Galo Plaza report, GOT hoped U.S. would exert similar efforts with other friendly countries.

2. U.S. might wish to take somewhat stronger line re Galo Plaza report than statement that we considered UN endorsement of report as "undesirable". For example, U.S. might emphasize that reference to report might lead to "serious complications" in terms ultimate settlement Cyprus question.

3. It would be helpful if U.S. could keep in close contact with U.K. Delegation because Turks somewhat worried about firmness of British position. GOT had received memorandum from British regarding UNGA handling of Cyprus issue which, although otherwise satisfactory, contained reference to Galo Plaza report—a reference which perhaps was included because of Galo Plaza's favorable comments re British bases. On the other hand, British had not mentioned Galo Plaza report in discussions of Cyprus in NATO Council. GOT hoped U.S. could persuade British to drop all reference to this report.

4. In his annual report,[4] U Thant referred to Galo Plaza report as forming "reasonable basis" for settlement. Turks considered such statement prejudicial and felt SYG should have remained neutral. In addition, they had received reports U Thant had been in touch with Ghanaians re possible Ghanaian initiative and they were also concerned that U Thant was being adversely influenced on Cyprus issue by senior officials in Secretariat. Consequently, it would be helpful if U. S. could express its views on Galo Plaza report to SYG as well.

Bayulken said that when he was recently in New York with former FonMin Isik their appraisal of prospects for satisfactory Cyprus resolution was rather bright. However, one could never be certain about firmness of number of UN delegations because probably more than one-half of delegations had luxury of "playing" with their instructions. Turks believed compromise resolution would ultimately prevail in New York and would pave way for future Athens–Ankara talks but initially they needed to introduce their own substantive resolution for tactical reasons and because of Turkish public opinion.

GOT possessed no definite information regarding timing or substance of Cypriot substantive resolution. Presumption was that it would be similar to earlier Cairo resolution in calling for "unfettered independence" for Cyprus and, in addition, endorsement of Galo Plaza report. GOT could not accept any resolution which suggested that enosis was possible now or in future, that Turkish Cypriots had minority status, or that Galo Plaza report should form basis for Cyprus settlement. They had been informed that way was being paved for introduction by a nonaligned country of satisfactory procedural resolution but cooperation between our two delegations was most important. On basis information I had conveyed to him re instructions to our delegations in New York, he would ask Turkish PermRep Eralp to coordinate his activities and tactics closely with U.S. Del.

---

[4] For extracts, see *American Foreign Policy: Current Documents, 1965*, pp. 515–518.

Bayulken went on to assure me that Cyprus section of PriMin Demirel's forthcoming policy statement had been drafted with great care and was quite moderate despite "vilification" campaign against Turkey in Greece. Turks did not wish disturb prospects of talks between two countries and, consequently, statement drafted for Demirel was balanced one which left way open for resumption Athens–Ankara dialogue. I replied that I was glad to hear this because attitude in Greece, as reflected in press, was that Turks were putting pressure on Greeks particularly in Istanbul. Bayulken commented that there was nothing new in Istanbul situation and that question of Greek citizens there was being handled routinely. He concluded by expressing opinion that Demirel government planned to pursue moderate policy toward Greece but its ability to do so would depend upon actions of Cyprus and Greece. Efforts of Greek Government to exploit religion for political purposes were not helpful in this regard.

Hart

212.   Telegram From the Embassy in Turkey to the Department of State[1]

Ankara, November 24, 1965, 1444Z.

598. USUN's 52; Deptel 429.[2] PriMin Demirel called me in November 24 to discuss Cyprus question in UNGA as well as MAP levels for Turkey (latter subject reported separately).[3] Acting FonMin Sukan, Acting FonMin SYG Binkaya and Soylemez of Cyprus Bureau also present during Cyprus portion of discussion.

In response to my opening comment that PriMin looked well and seemed to have enjoyed election campaign, Demirel said he had enjoyed it indeed, so much so that he wished campaign were still going on. When

---

[1] Source: Department of State, Central Files, POL 27 CYP. Confidential. Repeated to USUN, Athens, Nicosia, London, and Paris for USRO.

[2] Telegram 52 from USUN to Ankara, November 20, provided comments on the draft resolutions presented at the United Nations. (Ibid.) Telegram 429 to Ankara, October 13, reported that Turkey appeared ready to pursue bilateral talks with Greece on Cyprus. (Ibid.)

[3] Telegram 603 from Ankara, November 26. (Ibid., DEF TUR)

I left, anteroom and outer hall were crowded with well-wishers who, I was told, had been coming to Demirel's office on daily basis to shake his hand and congratulate him on electoral success.

Demirel said he wanted to talk to me because Turkish Government very concerned over 24-nation resolution re Cyprus.[4] He regretted such resolution had been tabled but task now was to block it because resolution would endanger peaceful solution of Cyprus issue. PriMin said he hoped that USG would use its influence to block this resolution and that USG would help garner support for Afghan-Iraqi resolution.[5]

I told PriMin I had read text of both resolutions and understood Afghan-Iraqi resolution had precedence. I also had observed obvious flaws in 24-nation resolution. As PriMin aware, U.S. was supporting GOT in seeking adoption of procedural resolution and I was certain that our two delegations in New York were in close touch in pursuit this objective. While I had no concrete suggestions, it seemed to me it might be possible to make certain adaptations in the Afghan-Iraqi resolution which would draw support from 24-nation proposal. However, tactics could best be handled in New York.

In response my inquiry as to whether he had received any report re support for Afghan-Iraqi resolution, Demirel replied in negative, adding he hoped to receive information soon. His main concern was that 24-nation resolution not pass because resolution was in violation UN Charter and existing agreements. I recalled we had previously informed GOT we did not consider UN appropriate place to change agreements between parties and reaffirmed that our respective delegations in New York would be in close contact. Demirel said he understood this was case but wished Turkish Government's views to be known directly through me as well as through Turkish UN delegation, and he was confident U.S. would not fail to assist Turkey in heading off 24-nation resolution. I replied that within framework of our common objectives, PriMin could be assured two delegations would be working together for procedural resolution.

Turning other aspects Cyprus problem, Demirel said GOT desired Famagusta settlement as soon as possible. In particular Turks wanted high school returned so that students [garble—could begin?] classes. He also referred to Javits visit,[6] reaffirming that roofing and window material was needed for houses for 6,000 Turk Cypriot [garble] otherwise

---

[4] On November 18, 24 nations (later joined by 7 more) submitted a draft resolution to the U.N. General Assembly on the Cyprus question. (U.N. Doc. A/C.1/L.342/Rev.1 and Add. 1–3) The draft resolution was adopted on December 18 as Resolution 2077 (XX); see footnote 3, Document 217.

[5] U.N. Doc. A/C.1/L.341.

[6] Senator Jacob Javits, Chairman of the NATO Parliamentarians Economic Committee, visited Ankara November 15–17 for meetings concerning possible Greek-Turkish economic cooperation.

faced prospect of spending winter in tents, with consequent problems for Turkish public opinion.[7]

Hart

---

[7] In telegram 2249 from USUN, November 25, the Mission commented that the Embassy should tell the Turkish Government that the United States would not sponsor its proposed resolution, judging that this approach would only complicate the Cyprus situation. (Department of State, Central Files, POL 27 CYP) The Turkish draft resolution is U.N. Doc. A/C.1/L.336.

---

213. Editorial Note

On November 29, 1965, King Constantine wrote to President Johnson requesting immediate U.S. economic assistance to deal with the "grave state of the Greek economy." The King cited a serious deterioration of the economy in the "last months" and expressed concern that a continuation of economic troubles when linked to "repercussions of a psychological and more general nature" could lead to a full-scale crisis that would undermine the social stability of Greece. The King also noted the readiness of his government to undertake drastic financial stabilization measures, but argued they would not be sufficient without U.S. assistance. (Department of State, Central Files, POL 15–1 GREECE) In a December 19 reply, President Johnson stated that while U.S. interests in Greece were undiminished, U.S. capacity to provide financial assistance was limited. (Johnson Library, National Security File, Presidential Correspondence, Greece, King Constantine)

214.   Airgram From the Embassy in Greece to the Department of State[1]

A–369   Athens, November 30, 1965.

SUBJECT

Andreas Papandreou's Comments on Current Greek Situation

On November 23, 1965, an Embassy officer and his wife attended a small dinner at the home of Mr. and Mrs. Richard Westebbe. The only other guests were Mr. and Mrs. Andreas Papandreou and Center Union Deputy Nikolaos Kountouris, an enthusiastic Papandreou supporter. Upon extending the invitation to the Embassy officer, Westebbe clearly implied that the evening had been specifically arranged to provide young Papandreou with an opportunity to explain and justify his position to an American official. Papandreou's comments during the course of the wide-ranging five-hour conversation were as follows:

Greek Economy:

Admittedly, Greece's present economic difficulties stem in some measure from mistakes made by the Center Union Government while it was in power. Chief among these are the tax reductions sponsored by former Finance Minister Konstantine Mitsotakis, which have cost the government some 1,200,000,000 drachmae in lost revenues. These tax reductions were instituted against the strong recommendations, in writing, of Andreas Papandreou. A second factor was the failure to obtain economic assistance through the Consortium. Particularly disappointing in this regard was the fact that the French, after offering a $25 million credit, imposed severe conditions and set exorbitant prices for locomotives, machinery, etc., which the Greeks wanted.

Despite these difficulties, Greece's economic problems would now be well on the way to solution had the Center Union Government remained in power. When the Center Union was replaced in mid-July, Andreas Papandreou was on the verge of consummating arrangements for the floating of a long-term, low-interest bond issue through commercial banks in West Germany, which probably could have put the Greek economy "over the hump" and on the road to healthy growth.

The present government is incapable of coping with the economic situation for a number of reasons. The individual ministers are not cooperating, and few of them are professionally competent; public confi-

---

[1] Source: Department of State, Central Files, POL 2 GREECE. Confidential. Drafted by Maury and approved by Vigderman.

dence has been severely shaken as a result of political and economic instability and uncertainty; the problem of agricultural surpluses is being badly mismanaged; and strikes and disruptive labor unrest will probably have a serious effect.

In the latter connection, labor problems during the period of the Papandreou government were kept to a minimum because labor leaders realized the government understood and sympathized with their position, and it was possible for members of the government—particularly Andreas Papandreou himself—to persuade the trade unions to refrain from strikes. Andreas could do this because the union leaders trusted him, and he in turn fully understood their problems. There is no one in the present government who enjoys this kind of relationship with the trade union movement.

Political Conditions:

Because of the foregoing economic conditions, internal divisions, and lack of public confidence, the Stefanopoulos Government cannot long survive—certainly not for more than a few months. If elections were held today, the Center Union would get perhaps 60% of the popular vote, ERE no more than 30%, and the "traitors" (Stefanopoulos supporters) a bare 10%. The EDA vote would be negligible—maybe 5%—because the Center Union would win the support of all but a very small Communist hard core within EDA.

The overwhelming and durable political strength of the Center Union, as presently constituted and oriented, stems from four basic issues which preoccupy the electorate:

a. The need for social and economic reform.
b. The necessity to restore civil liberties and restrain the arbitrary and oppressive activities of the police.
c. Keen national "sensitivity" regarding certain infringements on Greek sovereignty.
d. A strong and mounting resentment against recent activities of the Palace.

Item c above—the "sensitivity" regarding sovereignty—is something the Americans should understand. It stems from the widespread feeling that through its participation in NATO, Greece has surrendered certain elements of national independence. Although it is recognized that NATO served a useful purpose initially, in more recent years Greece's membership in NATO has entailed some loss of autonomy in such matters as the selection and assignment of senior officers (concerning which subtle pressures have been applied by the U.S. and perhaps other major NATO powers); the organization, training and equipment of the Greek armed forces; and Greece's military deployments and commitments. While NATO in some form must be preserved, the pride and sensitivities of smaller powers must be taken more into account. Simply because Greece is not as powerful as some other NATO members does not mean that she is not as sensitive as they where matters of sovereignty are concerned. The Greek attitude is much the same as that currently being expressed by de Gaulle, whose position has wide appeal in Greece.

The question of the Palace is another extremely important factor. Public resentment again the King's recent "interference" in political affairs has now reached massive proportions. Andreas and other Center Union politicians have noted in their recent travels a significant change in this regard. Whereas prior to last July there was considerable anti-monarchist sentiment, it was usually expressed by the man in the street in such terms as: "When will King Constantine abdicate and go to Denmark?" Now the question is more likely to be: "When will Constantine be brought to trial for his crimes?" Until recently it had been the popular assumption that the young King's misdeeds were the result of the influence of his mother, but now it is becoming clear that he is acting on his own responsibility and should be held accountable accordingly.

The King should realize that his position can only be saved by the Center Union Party, without which the political situation would become increasingly polarized between right and left, with the left by far the stronger faction and heavily committed to the abolition of the monarchy. If a plebiscite were held today on the regime issue, the anti-monarchists would draw some 70 to 80% of the vote.

Any effort to frustrate the continuation of the "peaceful revolution" which the Center Union, under the elder Papandreou, was in the process of carrying out will have dangerous consequences. "Progressive and democratic" forces in the country are on the march in quest of a more modern and liberal order and will not long tolerate efforts to obstruct their progress. In addition to popular internal pressures, there is another reason why "undemocratic" regimes such as the present Stefanopoulos government cannot survive. This is the presence on Greece's northern frontiers of powerful neighbors who are "not indifferent" to developments in Greece. The United States should not assume that Greece exists in a vacuum, or that the U.S. can freely and unilaterally manipulate the Greek political situation without creating "reactions" in other quarters.

It is the firm view of the overwhelming majority of the Greek people that the U.S. is aligned with the extreme right, the Palace, and the military. This may not be entirely true, especially at the moment, but it is nevertheless a deeply held belief and there is evidence to support it. For example, it is assumed that articles last summer in the *New York Times* by C.L. Sulzberger, highly critical of Andreas Papandreou and his father, were a fair reflection of the U.S. view and were probably inspired by U.S. officials.[2]

---

[2] *The New York Times,* July 28 and August 4, 6, and 8, 1965.

Reporting Officer's Comments: Throughout the evening Andreas, who dominated the conversation, was amiable, responsive to questions, and apparently intent on giving an impression of candor. He professed to welcome an opportunity for a frank exposition of his views which, he implied, had sometimes been misunderstood in American official circles. He said he knew he had been accused of having been a leftist and even a Marxist, but in fact he considered himself neither a rightist nor a leftist but a professional economist, now a politician, who tried to approach all political and economic problems analytically and objectively. His conversation was lucid and his points were well organized. In fact, he gave the impression that some of his remarks may have been planned or rehearsed in advance.

Throughout the evening Kountouris dutifully echoed Andreas' main points. Mrs. Papandreou was generally noncommittal. Westebbe tried to play the role of mediator, sometimes siding with Andreas and sometimes defending the American position.

For the Ambassador:
Alfred G. Vigderman
Counselor of Embassy for Political Affairs

215.   Memorandum of Conversation[1]

Washington, December 1, 1965.

SUBJECT

Turkish-United States Relations; Vietnam

PARTICIPANTS

Mr. Ihsan Sabri Caglayangil, Turkish Foreign Minister
Mr. Haluk Bayulken, Director General, Foreign Office
Mr. Ilter Turkmen, Director, Policy Planning, Foreign Office
Ambassador Turgut Menemencioglu, Turkish Ambassador

The Secretary
The Under Secretary
Raymond A. Hare, Assistant Secretary for NEA
William B. Buffum, IO
George T. Churchill, Officer-in-Charge, Turkish Affairs

---

[1] Source: Johnson Library, National Security File, Country File, Turkey, Vol. 1. Confidential. Drafted by Churchill and approved in S and U on December 16.

After an exchange of courtesies had established a cordial atmosphere, Caglayangil opened the discussion (Bayulken translating) with a statement of the new Government's emphasis on strengthening relations with the United States and the West. He mentioned that the Justice Party had received a substantial majority which would permit a stable government for the next four years. There has been a tendency in Turkey, made possible by increased freedom of the press, toward a more neutral foreign policy and toward leftism. The result of the recent elections indicates, however, that the great majority of Turkish people do not approve of tendencies that would take Turkey away from its traditional policies or, in the guise of social justice, move the country to the far left. The Justice Party won on the basis of a clear platform, and the people of Turkey have defined their leadership and the policies they want to have followed.

Caglayangil said that the democratic system has many opportunities but also has some inherent disadvantages. The Turkish Government, Caglayangil went on, has decided to make every effort to preserve and improve United States-Turkish relations. He is sure the United States will do its part to ensure that the relationship is not harmed by these (leftist) tendencies. If the relationship is not to be damaged, both countries must keep these tendencies in perspective.

The Secretary said he was encouraged that the Turkish people had made such a clear-cut decision, and that there was a good prospect for a political continuum. He said the new Government need have no doubt about our concern for Turkish stability and well-being. This was a stable concern, as it was based on our own self-interest and on our commitments, which we value and intend to honor.

PL 480

Caglayangil said he would be grateful if something could be done to accelerate work on a new surplus agreement, as progress was now very slow. Mr. Churchill explained that a rather technical discussion was going on within the United States Government to determine what commodities might be delivered, and also on the question of export restrictions. Since the Turkish Government had indicated it wanted export restrictions eliminated or reduced in the new agreement, we were trying to determine what flexibility might be allowed under the legislation.

The Secretary said he would involve himself personally in this matter. He said he was seeing Secretary Freeman December 3.[2] The Secretary added that the surplus situation in the United States was changing. We don't have the same stockpile as before. Wheat has dropped, and rice is in short supply. We will continue to take into account the needs of other

---

[2] No record of the meeting has been found.

countries, but the changing supply situation will affect what we can do in the future with PL 480.

Military Assistance

Caglayangil said he knows that the concerned authorities in the United States have the whole military assistance problem under review, but he wanted to stress Turkey's need for all-weather aircraft and Hawk missiles.

The Secretary responded that we planned to give substantial support for Turkey's military program. However, there are a couple of difficulties that arise, both attributable to Vietnam: (a) the problem of appropriations—our "bank balance" is overdrawn because of Vietnam; and (b) the question of types of equipment available. We are in a war in Vietnam and cannot be entirely sure where it will lead. This means we cannot clearly determine what our own equipment requirements will be, and thus what will be available for others. The Secretary said he did not mean this as a negative response, but only as an indication of the complications involved.

Economic Situation

Caglayangil stressed the importance the new Government places on planned development and the achievement of a self-sustaining economy through self-help. He was sure the United States would do everything possible to help achieve these goals. The Secretary said we were encouraged by development results in Turkey so far. He urged that the Turkish Government extend its own diplomacy to the limit in talking to other Consortium members. He said we would, of course, continue to do our part, but our approaches to the UK, FRG, and others may carry less weight than the Turks' own efforts, since we are pressing these countries all the time on so many issues.

NATO

According to Caglayangil, Turkey participates in NATO in the sincere belief that this organization has been successful in achieving its primary missions in the past and will continue to be useful in the future. Developments within NATO should be participated in by all member countries. It is the Turkish Government position that a directoire should not be formed within NATO.

USSR Relations

Caglayangil stated that the Turkish Government is interested in establishing good neighbor relations with the Soviet Union, according to the principles laid down by Ataturk. However, Turks do not forget that Turkey has been at war with the Russians thirteen times in the past. Since every war sets a country back fifty years in economic development,

Caglayangil said, Russia bears a large responsibility for Turkey's present underdeveloped state. The emphasis in Turk-USSR relations will be on the development of trade. The Secretary said we do not object to our allies having normal relations with the USSR. Specifically, we support the idea of Turkey's normalizing relations with Russia. However, the USSR could conceivably cause difficulties again in the future. If relations again become abnormal because of Russian pressure, we would share Turkey's interest in restoring the situation.

Cyprus

Caglayangil identified two phases of the Cyprus problem: (a) the immediate issues in the UNGA, and (b) the substantive problem of finding an ultimate solution. On the UNGA phase, Caglayangil said that if the "Cypriot" resolution drafted by 24 United Nations members were accepted, it would give encouragement to the Greek Cypriots and will ensure Makarios' freedom of action for further faits accomplis. Although the present Turkish Government is firmly in power, it does have a responsibility to the Turkish public and cannot ignore public opinion, especially in an issue of national importance, such as Cyprus. Caglayangil said that the adversary in this instance (the Cypriot Government) has an ever-changing policy. Now they are for full independence; but last month they were for enosis. They talk about human rights, but deprive the Turkish community of every right and treat them as rebels. Therefore, Caglayangil said, the Turkish Government is concerned that any resolution which might look like a political victory for the adversary might bring about disastrous consequences. Despite Turkey's desire for restraint, it might prove necessary to act, in the face of the Greek-Cypriot attitude.

Caglayangil continued that even if a procedural resolution is adopted in the United Nations, the problem of finding an ultimate solution remains. After the UN debate, Caglayangil said, he hoped Turks and Americans could join to search out the alternatives, to look at each one and to find the best, so that an optimum solution could be worked out.

Mr. Buffum agreed that the 24 member draft resolution was not acceptable, and said we were working for a procedural resolution. On the longer range aspect, the Secretary said the Cyprus question is full of agony for everybody. If it could be settled without us, we would be very happy. Our basket is already full! However, we are prepared to be helpful, and we would be glad to have a serious discussion in depth if the Turks would find it helpful.

Responding to the Secretary's query about possibilities for resumed Greek-Turkish talks, Caglayangil said the Turkish Government had always favored bilateral talks, but he was not sure about the Greek Government. There are indications that the Greeks may want to resume, but there is no way of knowing when or how they plan to start. Tsirimokos came to a Turkish cocktail party in New York and talked to Caglayangil for a few minutes, but showed no inclination to talk substance. The Secretary said he would talk to Tsirimokos in Washington next week and would explore this question again in Paris at the NATO Ministerial. Mr. Ball commented that the Greek-Turkish talks were first started as a result of the NATO Ministerial in May, and that perhaps they could be revived at the December meeting.

[Here follows discussion of Vietnam.]

216.   Memorandum of Conversation[1]

Washington, December 8, 1965, 12:30 p.m.

SUBJECT

Cyprus Issue

PARTICIPANTS

The Secretary
Elias Tsirimokos, Deputy Prime Minister and Foreign Minister of Greece
Alexander A. Matsas, Ambassador of Greece
Marcos Economides, Executive Secretary, Greek Foreign Ministry
Constantaine Panayotacos, Counselor, Embassy of Greece
William B. Buffum, Deputy Assistant Secretary, IO
Katherine W. Bracken, Director, GTI
Richard W. Barham, OIC, Greek Affairs
A. Tumayan, Interpreter

In the December 8 meeting between the Secretary and Greek Deputy Prime Minister Tsirimokos the Cyprus issue came up briefly in the beginning in connection with Mr. Tsirimokos' remarks about being reluctant to go to the NATO meeting until the Cyprus debate in the UNGA was concluded. He declared in this regard that his side was prepared to meet the Turks at any time to discuss Cyprus, but the Turks seemed to be making threats and, in general, waging a war of nerves. He did not understand their reasons for doing this but it was having an adverse effect on public opinion in Greece. In response to a query from the Secretary, Mr.

---

[1] Source: Department of State, Central Files, POL 27 CYP. Confidential. Drafted by Barham and approved in S on December 21. The source text is marked "Part II of II."

Tsirimokos said the Greek Parliament would be in session in case there should be talks soon.

Tsirimokos asked the Secretary for his comments on a Cyprus UN resolution. The Secretary referred this to Mr. Buffum who explained that we believe a procedural resolution would be desirable and that the Afghan-Iraqi resolution comes near to meeting our viewpoint, though it has some obvious defects; for example, we would not like to see a call for "new" mediation which might change the thrust of the earlier Security Council resolution.

Tsirimokis stated that, in his view, a UN resolution alone would not bring a final solution to the problem but could have an important influence on future negotiations by the way it was worded. At the moment each side had its own text which it felt strongly partisan about, but behind the texts there were ulterior motives. The idea of new mediation represented Turkish opposition to the person of Galo Plaza. Tsirimokos asserted that he favored mediation but had no preference as far as the person of the mediator was concerned. He noted that, since there was a Security Council resolution which clearly provided for mediation, the Secretary General could change the mediator for reasons of illness or other reasons and this did not constitute new mediation. Tsirimokos went on to say that UN mediation rather than being an obstacle to successful negotiations provided the framework within which negotiations ought to take place. Certain things at times had their own mystique and this was the case with the UN at the moment; if the UN was either sponsoring or guiding mediation this would create a favorable situation.

Commenting further on the text of a resolution Tsirimokos gave the opinion that preference for the Afghan-Iraqi text was not justified because it tries to avoid mediation and so many amendments are needed that it comes very close to the Cypriot one. For example: In their text, the Afghans have put many of the Turkish slogans. They refer to "negotiations" and "mediation" whereas what we must have is negotiation within mediation. They refer to "two communities", another Turkish slogan. They could refer instead to "the Cypriot people", without mentioning majority or minority, or they could refer to "all elements of the Cypriot people" without using either the Cypriot or Turkish wording. Tsirimokos noted that all texts pay lip service to the principles of the UN Charter but if the text states general principles and the principle of continued mediation, then it is the Cypriot text rather than the Afghan one. Tsirimokos said he had arrived at the above views after close study of all proposed texts.

The Secretary asked if any effort was being made by a combined drafting committee to come up with an agreed resolution, to which Tsirimokos replied that he did not think so.

The Secretary noted that in the context of this problem each princi-ple of the UN Charter carries a great deal of weight. The language of prin-ciples becomes complicated, however, and, because of varying interpretations, the UN has great difficulty in settling issues based on principle. In the long run, the Secretary added, this issue will be solved not by votes but by contacts between the governments concerned. He asked Tsirimokos in this regard whether continued mediation would help or hinder bilateral talks. The Deputy Prime Minister asserted that it would facilitate talks and would also make it easier for the Greeks to influence the Cypriots in favor of an agreement.

Mr. Tsirimokos told the Secretary that Greece would like to see the U.S. and other western countries adopt a neutral attitude and not fight for one side or the other, especially where two allies are involved. The Secretary remarked facetiously that he was pleased to hear this for he had been waiting twenty years for a foreign minister to say the U.S. should be "non-aligned" in a regional dispute. More seriously, he assured the Deputy Prime Minister that this was a situation where the U.S. could not take sides. He said, however, the word "neutrality" does not apply in this case because it has a connotation of indifference whereas we are passionately interested in a settlement of the Cyprus issue. Tsirimokos, who seemed pleased, said he understood.

---

217. Telegram From the Embassy in Turkey to the Department of State[1]

Ankara, December 20, 1965, 1614Z.

685. Ref: Embtel 683.[2] Cyprus. NATUS. Following is Embassy's pre-liminary assessment of effect of UNGA Cyprus vote[3] on Turkish Govern-ment and Turkish political and public opinion.

1. GA vote marks major diplomatic defeat for Turkey which has been preparing for this test for more than year. In anticipation debate

---

[1] Source: Department of State, Central Files, POL 27 CYP. Confidential. Repeated to USUN, Nicosia, Athens, London, Paris, Istanbul, Izmir, and Adana.

[2] Telegram 683 from Ankara, December 20, reported press reaction to Turkey's defeat at the United Nations. (Ibid.)

[3] Resolution 2077 (XX) passed on December 18 by a vote of 47 (including Greece and Cyprus) in favor, 5 opposed (including the United States and Turkey), and 54 abstentions (including the Soviet Union). The resolution called for respect of the sovereignty, unity, independence, and territorial integrity of Cyprus. For text, see *American Foreign Policy: Current Documents, 1965*, p. 521.

would occur in 19th GA, Turks dispatched good-will missions to Africa, Arab countries, Eastern Europe, Far East and Latin America as part of concerted GOT policy of broadening its international relationships. Turk officials realistically recognized difficulties of explaining their Cyprus policy in Afro-Asian world and in Latin America, where many countries have minority problems and where resolutions calling for "independence" and "sovereignty" and eschewing "intervention" evoke favorable response. Also recognized local Greek communities would be able to exert influence on policies some governments. However, magnitude of Turkish defeat has come as great surprise, particularly fact GOT failed obtain support of any non-aligned Afro-Asian countries or any LAs and was deserted by all its NATO partners except US.

2. Most serious substantive aspect of GA action for Turks is language in 31-nation resolution calling upon nations to desist from intervention in Cyprus, thus undermining GOT's fundamental argument its intervention rights are guaranteed by London–Zurich Agreements. While statements of Demirel and Caglayangil emphasize that GOT does not consider resolution binding, fact remains majority of those voting supported Cypriot view that this aspect of treaties is void. Consequently, GA resolution represents additional restraint on its policies which GOT must weigh in considering next steps re Cyprus, particularly if it continues seek improve its relations with Afro-Asian countries.

3. US-Turkish bilateral relations have been strengthened by strong US support for GOT, as demonstrated by warm statements of appreciation by Foreign Minister Caglayangil and Acting Secretary General Binkaya (USUN 84; Embtel 679).[4] Over weekend number of Turks, both civilian and military, voiced gratitude for US support. However, inability of US to influence other UN members, coupled with RPP and TLP attempts to cast suspicion on US motives (reftel) may partially offset current reinforcement of US-Turkish bilateral relations.

Furthermore, failure of any other NATO country to support Turkey will provide additional ammunition for those who question value of NATO Alliance.

4. Outside government circles, Cyprus vote has provided opposition with exploitable issue and Inonu's statement is clear signal that RPP during forthcoming GNA debate will charge Demirel government with gross mishandling of Turkey's case in New York. In this effort, RPP will benefit from its earlier decision not to permit RPP Deputies to become members of Turkey's UN Delegation and can count on support TLP.

RPP and TLP attacks in GNA will be reinforced by opposition press which is already highlighting dimensions of Turkish defeat while ignor-

---

[4] Both dated December 18. (Department of State, Central Files, POL 27 CYP)

ing fact no Turkish Government could have achieved much greater success. Theme of TLP and anti-American elements in RPP will be that Turkey's defeat attributable primarily to bankruptcy of GOT's alignment policy. Secondary theme, in which almost all opposition elements can join, will be ineptness with which unsophisticated Demirel government handles foreign affairs. Elements in press will also seek to twist US support for Turkey as example of back-stage deal by US, as allegation already advanced by RPP propagandist Cihat Baban in party organ *Ulus* (reftel). Efforts of parliamentary opposition to convert adverse GA vote into major domestic political issue may be supplemented by use of student demonstrations.

5. Embassy's preliminary conclusion is that while GA vote has been major setback for new Demirel government, it can ride out current storm by continuing to reject resolution, by pointing out government's policies essentially same as predecessor government's, including third coalition, and by emphasizing anomalous nature of vote. Foreign Ministry officials are already publicly stressing fact that more than one-half of those voting either voted against resolution or abstained. Privately they making point that majority of pro-Cypriot votes came from African nations with limited influence in world affairs and with no direct responsibility for problems of Eastern Mediterranean.

Major unanswered questions are effect of resolution on ultimate settlement of Cyprus dispute and on future direction Turkish foreign policy. US support for [garble] resolution was based on premise substantive resolution would hinder progress toward ultimate solution to problem. This judgment remains sound although it is too early to determine degree to which GA action will set back prospect of negotiations between parties directly involved. Much will depend upon how Makarios decides to exploit limited, tactical advantage achieved at UN. It is also premature to assess longer-term effect of GA vote on Turkish foreign policy other than to say that GA defeat may cause GOT to review some of basic considerations underlying its current policies.

Hart

CONTINUING DISCUSSIONS OF A CYPRUS SOLUTION, JANUARY–OCTOBER 1966

218. Telegram From the Embassy in Greece to the Department of State[1]

Athens, January 11, 1966, 1731Z.

1054. Ref: Deptel 744.[2]

1. We believe Tsirimokos had two main objectives in mind when he proposed mediation proceed under SYG aegis. Maintenance of UN cover for any talks on Cyprus is important for Stephanopoulos govt, just as it was for Papandreou, who had systematically drummed into mind of Greek public that UN path was only traversible course towards just solution of Cyprus problem. Will be recalled that GOG last May felt compelled to justify its agreement to begin its dialogue with GOT with argument that it was simply following suggestion of Plaza who had recommended talks among parties to dispute.

2. Second, Tsirimokos probably concluded that one sensible way out of cul-de-sac created by Plaza's resignation[3] would be for SYG himself to assume Mediator's mantle. To find someone else would be difficult and could lead to repetition of situation which has culminated in Plaza resignation. We doubt Tsirimokos expects that SYG would take up active role as Mediator, at least not initially. Rather, Thant could simply state that under mandate of March '64 SC resolution, he was placing himself and Secretariat at disposal of parties concerned for whatever ways they considered appropriate for assisting them in finding early solution to problem. Tsirimokos would not object to participation member SYG in mediation (Embtel 1055).[4]

3. Re para two Nicosia's 342,[5] we see merit in parcelling out Cyprus problem into [garble] elements in order to discover where points of flexibility may exist. But it may be difficult to mount the scheme organizationally, particularly considering sensitivities of participants to each separate negotiation. We believe it might be preferable first to await results of GOG soundings in Ankara regarding resumption of dialogue.

---

[1] Source: Department of State, Central Files, POL 27 CYP. Confidential. Repeated to Ankara, Nicosia, and USUN.

[2] Telegram 744 to Athens, January 10, requested an analysis of Tsirimokos' proposal for the resumption of U.N. mediation. (Ibid.)

[3] Galo Plaza resigned on December 22, 1965.

[4] Dated January 11. (Department of State, Central Files, POL 27 CYP)

[5] Dated January 8. (Ibid.)

Tsirimokos is aware, as we all are, that Makarios cannot be ignored, but he is rightfully fearful that Makarios and Cyprus press will seek to torpedo talks before they have any chance of success. It seems to us that we should concentrate our efforts now in stressing to GOG importance of avoiding imposition of preconditions to future dialogue with GOT (Embtel 1055). We might also suggest to GOT that it accept UNSYG cover for talks and that it be as forthcoming as possible with Greeks on resumption of dialogue.[6]

Talbot

---

[6] In telegram 576 to Ankara, the Department of State reported that Menemencioglu had stated that the Turkish Government strongly opposed the idea of resumed U.N. mediation. (Ibid.)

---

219. Telegram From the Embassy in Cyprus to the Department of State[1]

Nicosia, January 24, 1966, 0545Z.

367. NATUS. Ankara's 819 to Dept; Embtel 364.[2]

1. We agree with Ankara's 819 that general framework for solution should consist of enosis with compensations to Turkey in some form. However, we have serious doubts about anyone getting Makarios to agree to serve up sufficient compensations here on the island to enable GOT to regard solution as double enosis. Unless outside parties ready to impose double enosis concept on Greek Cypriots most we might be able persuade GOC accept would be GOT military presence in one of UK sovereign areas. Of course, [garble—no?] indication now that GOC would consider even this much compensation. In addition to enosis with compensations we believe solution should also include some form of non-federation-federation. (Embtel 953 to Dept, dated Jan 2, 1965)[3] Our talks here on island with various parties lead us to believe that neither Greeks nor Turk Cypriots are adamantly opposed to concepts set forth in that

---

[1] Source: Department of State, Central Files, POL 27 CYP. Confidential. Repeated to USUN, London, Paris, Athens, and Ankara.

[2] Telegram 819 from Ankara, January 20, suggested a U.S. approach to the forthcoming talks with the British on Cyprus. (Ibid.) Telegram 364 from Nicosia, January 21, endorsed these proposals but noted that neither the Cypriot nor Greek Government appeared ready to negotiate .(Ibid.)

[3] Not printed. (Ibid.)

cable. This makes non-federation-federation perhaps best starting point for negotiations.

2. Believe that one way of getting around enosis problem would be to come up with some formula for postponing decision. This might be along following lines: parties would agree that although other elements of settlement would come into effect immediately question of enosis would be delayed until end of pre-established period, say five years. At that time people of Cyprus voting as whole and not by community would hold plebiscite under UN supervision. They would be asked to consider whether they favored continued independence or enosis with Greece, but it would be agreed in advance that none of rights given Turk Cypriots in other parts of settlement or arrangements preserving these rights would be changed no matter which way vote went. During five year period international financial assistance would be given to both Greek and Turkish Cypriots to leave island if they so chose or to resettle elsewhere on island itself. (Last concept would have to be worked out carefully to avoid it being cloak for partition.) Also during period UN would maintain fairly large observer force which would assist UN Commissioner for Human Rights. At end of period and after plebiscite Turk Cypriots only would be asked to vote on whether or not they wished such Commission and Observer Force to continue.

3. We realize that this suggestion means continuation of enosis issue for several years but think it might be easier for Turks to accept than immediate enosis even with compensation, thus perhaps lowering price of latter. Furthermore, pro-enosists here becoming discredited and considerably weaker than at various times previously during Cyprus crisis and there is now very little pressure which can be brought to bear on Archbishop to accept enosis with compensations. As long as Makarios is around he will determine island's basic attitude towards enosis and Greek Cypriots overwhelmingly accept his tactical approach of obtaining unfettered self-determination first.

4. On short range approaches believe that in addition to measures suggested Ankara's 819 we might consider seriously idea para 5 Deptel 1765 to USUN,[4] of having Bernardes center his operations in Nicosia and deal with GOG and GOT through respective Embassies. With his low visibility Bernardes could "mediate" without trappings of formal mediation, facilitate GOG and GOT "dialogue" without either formally having to agree to such and expand Turk and Greek Cypriot talks on daily problems into wider elements of overall settlement without attracting undue attention. In fact, Bernardes already has opportunities in daily diplomatic round here to make moves along these lines, but because of

---

[4] In telegram 1765 to USUN, January 21, the Department of State provided guidance for dealing with diplomatic inquiries about the U.S. position on U.N. mediation. (Ibid.)

his mandate and temperament is extremely cautious and presumably would need some push from SYG. Best of all, perhaps, using Bernardes in this way would give us chance to monitor and even guide course of talks (Embtel 351).[5]

5. In any case we think that emphasis on obtaining "mediation" and "mediator" somewhat misplaced in context realities Cyprus situation. [garble] is that mediation implies partial effort by Mediator and our guess is that as Tuomioja and Galo Plaza before him Bernardes would end up with same general conclusions as Plaza report. In light of this we would cast Bernardes in role para 4, rather than as new Mediator. However he thought he could get parties to talk with each other through him we agree with Ankara that US–UK "external initiatives" will be necessary to reach final agreement.

Cross

---

[5] Dated January 24. (Ibid., STR 10 VIET N)

---

220. Telegram From the Department of State to the Mission to the United Nations[1]

Washington, January 29, 1966, 6:54 p.m.

1813. NATUS. Cyprus mediation. Ref: USUN's 3297.[2]

1. Dept concurs in response you made to Rolz-Bennett re undesirability involving Soviets directly in any effort mediate Cyprus dispute or any joint action with Soviets in promoting or guaranteeing solution. We have always viewed Cyprus question as of primary concern to West and NATO and Soviet position on question as opportunistic effort to weaken NATO ties in eastern Mediterranean. Request you continue discourage SYG from pursuing Big Four guarantee idea and convey this position to UKUN.

2. Seems to us that any suggestion of international guarantee for ultimate Cyprus solution is premature. What is needed at this time to

---

[1] Source: Department of State, Central Files, POL 27–14 CYP/UN. Secret; Limdis. Drafted by Moffitt; cleared by UNP, GTI, and Hare; and approved by Sisco. Repeated to Athens, Ankara, Nicosia, London, and Paris.

[2] Telegram 3297, January 26, reported that the Secretary-General was seeking U.S. views about a four-power guarantee of an independent Cyprus. (Ibid.)

move Cyprus problem off dead center is resumption active UN mediation effort directed to finding elements on which agreement might be reached. While not prepared at this stage to rule out any proposal for solution, Dept tends to agree that, to obtain GOT acceptance of any formula, it may be necessary to continue prohibition against enosis at least for time. If this proves be case, however, continued exclusion of enosis would be only one element in any package which it might be possible to develop. For example, future status of Turk Cypriots in independent Cyprus would be critical. We feel that finding these elements is first order of business.

3. We hope therefore SYG will act soon on resumption mediation and believe, as indicated Deptel 1765,[3] expansion Bernardes role offers best prospect for agreement on new mediation. Believe would be useful try to influence SYG in this direction prior Rolz-Bennett's departure.

4. Despite parties' statements in GA, we do not agree with SYG and Rolz-Bennett conclusion that an independent Cyprus is "common thread" running through position of parties; GOG, while it may not be optimistic about achieving enosis, clearly hopes that unfettered independence for Cyprus would ultimately lead to union with Greece.

Rusk

---

[3] See footnote 4, Document 219.

---

221. **Telegram From the Embassy in Turkey to the Department of State[1]**

Ankara, January 28, 1966, 1652Z.

858. NATUS. Embtel 841.[2] FonMin Caglayangil summoned me to his residence Jan 28 for first exploratory talk on elements of possible solution to Cyprus problem. Turkmen from FonOff Cyprus Bureau also attended. FonMin said he had wanted to see me before leaving for RCD meeting in Pakistan and hoped to see me upon return. Meanwhile he

---

[1] Source: Department of State, Central Files, POL 27 CYP. Confidential. Received at 8:09 a.m. on January 31 and repeated to London, Paris, Athens, Nicosia, EUCOM and USDOCOSouth for POLAD, Istanbul, Izmir, and Adana.

[2] Telegram 841 from Ankara, January 26, reported that a statement by Caglayangil comparing Cyprus and Austria did not represent any change in Turkey's position. (Ibid.)

wished express Turkish desire to find logical, just solution acceptable to all parties and give us Turk aims and viewpoints:

First: Turkey wants to study what initiatives are possible in UN, how to evaluate present situation, what are mediation prospects, how would Greeks and Greek Cypriots act.

Secondly: Turkey interested in what are available alternatives in seeking basis for settlement satisfactory to all. Legally, London–Zurich treaties are valid, GOT agrees, however, that treaties not eternal but maintains that principles continue exist. Principles on which Turkey must insist re Cyprus are: (A) no unilateral annexation; (B) acknowledgement of existence of two communities; (C) no domination of one community by the other; and (D) both communities must participate in administration.

Turkey can negotiate on alternatives (federation, cantonal system) but not on basic principles. In answer to my questions, FonMin said he did not wish to go into details of cantonal or other system, all of which can be studied later. Could include "municipal autonomy" or other features. FonMin continued GOT has no complaint against treaties but it is Greeks and Greek Cypriots who want to amend them. Let them make proposals. Turkey is willing to amend treaty provisions if proposed alternative solution at variance with treaty but acceptable to all parties because it is logical and just. Our aim is to find such alternative.

I asked FonMin if he had adopted independent Cyprus as basis of solution and was no longer considering double enosis formula such as Acheson plan. He replied double enosis does not injure principles outlined above. Any solution including double enosis, federation, cantonal government, a base (by which, I believe, he meant Turk base on Cyprus), might fit in with principles.

I said US not committed to any particular solution, nor did it even have a favorite one. We only desired an agreed and permanent one. Asked FonMin whether two communities had co-existed without much irritation under Ottoman and British rule. He replied they had never lived together without irritation and conflict, but problems always of local nature until possibility of enosis and independence gave rise to increased conflict. Noted that it useful to discuss Cyprus problem now before situation heats up again, referred to GOT interest in own economic development and to Cyprus issue hanging over GOT like Sword of Damocles. Said Turk-Greek bilateral relations must be improved and added, after Turkmen's intervention, that these relations cannot improve outside context of Cyprus problem. Observed that Turkey had raised no claim on Dodecanese, but Greek unilateral annexation of Cyprus would upset Turk-Greek balance established by Treaty of Lausanne, and Turkey would be strategically surrounded.

Re UN mediation, FonMin said he had no personality in mind. Voiced strong opinion that institution of mediation should be one in which Mediator seeks find middle ground and bring opposing parties together. Said Mediator could not also be arbitrator and judge, like Galo Plaza. I raised as my personal idea possibility of Bernardes discreetly expanding his activities and functions on Cyprus without benefit of official nomination or publicity. FonMin said only that GOT did not want Mediator with preconceived ideas. Turkmen commented that Latin Americans do not have feel for European problems and tend see things in Latin American context. Probably thinking of Bernardes as well as Galo Plaza, he added that person who had been engrossed in island scene might not see larger Turk-Greek picture. FonMin said this problem would not arise if European were Mediator. Then he warned that enosis by force or apparent independence views of eventual enosis would not be peaceful solution but would lead to guerrilla warfare, sabotage, etc.

FonMin remarked that UK Ambassador told him of his return to London for consultation on Cyprus with FonOff and colleagues from Athens and Nicosia. FonMin said he thought UK would then consult with us and hoped that US and UK not reach any firm position without consulting Turkey. I replied that any US–UK consultations that might occur would certainly be exploratory. He then asked whether it true that US Ambassadors in Athens and Nicosia had made proposals re Cyprus to respective governments. I said I sure they could not have done so because US has no solution to propose on Cyprus issue.

Comment follows by septel.

Hart

---

222. Telegram From the Embassy in Turkey to the Department of State[1]

Ankara, February 3, 1966, 1440Z.

885. NATUS. USUN's 3340 to Dept, Deptel 629.[2] Embassy shares Department's views contained Deptel 629, especially paragraph 4. Nev-

---

[1] Source: Department of State, Central Files, POL 27 CYP. Secret; Limdis. Repeated to Athens, Nicosia, London, Paris, USUN, Izmir, Istanbul, and Adana.

[2] Telegram 3340 from USUN reported that the Secretary-General had been apprised of preliminary negative U.S. response to his four-power guarantee proposal. (Ibid.) Telegram 629 to Ankara was sent for action to USUN as telegram 1813, Document 220.

ertheless Department may find Embassy's estimate of Turk views useful supplement. We believe four-power guarantee of Cyprus independence (and against enosis and partition) would not be feasible or desirable from Turkish point of view. Principal reasons are:

1. GOT still not inclined to place great trust in USSR. Despite past disappointment in US and UK and recent efforts toward Turk-USSR normalization of relations, GOT continues regard USSR as more friendly to Greece and Cyprus than to Turkey;

2. Turkey is committed to position against unilateral enosis but not necessarily against partition or double enosis (Embtel 858);[3]

3. Turkey is concerned about its strategic position vis-à-vis Greeks and Greek Cypriots whom Turks tend regard as one enemy, not two. Therefore, in event Cyprus is annexed to Greece, or if Turks lost foothold in Cyprus represented by their 650 men contingent and Makarios becomes undisputed lord of island, resulting Greek strategic envelopment of Turkey (as Turks prone to see it) constitutes situation which Fon-Min said was unacceptable.

4. Nature of guarantee and rights of Turk Cypriot community within independent Cyprus more important in Turk view than guarantee of independence for Cyprus. SYG and Rolz-Bennett arguments do not seem take account of future role of Turk Cypriot community in independent Cyprus.

Hart

---

[3] Document 221.

---

223. Telegram From the Embassy in Greece to the Department of State[1]

Athens, February 5, 1966, 1125Z.

1163. NATUS.

1. GOG–Makarios communiqué (Embtel 1154)[2] which climaxed week of discussions shows how far present GOG anxious to avoid cleav-

---

[1] Source: Department of State, Central Files, POL 27 CYP. Confidential. Repeated to Ankara, Nicosia, London, Paris for Crawford and James, USDOCOSouth for Freshman, and USUN.

[2] Dated February 3. (Ibid.)

age with Archbishop over any part of current Makarios doctrine for Cyprus.

2. Theodoropoulos (FonOff) volunteered to us that communiqué was "too long" (by which he likely meant it to be understood that so much detail in communiqué led to spelling out of positions issue by issue which would make future negotiations difficult). He said current tight identity of views between Makarios and GOG was victory for diplomacy of Tsirimokos because it had patched up outstanding differences between Athens and Nicosia. In this connection, Theodoropoulos recalled that Archbishop had been cool to current GOG and in particular to Stephanopoulos because latter on record in Parliamentary speech in course of which Stephanopoulos suggested "dark forces" had obstructed adoption of Acheson plan. This had led Makarios to refrain from congratulating Stephanopoulos on his elevation to Prime Minister last September.

3. GOG public position on future discussions with Turks has certainly been getting appreciably less flexible in the last month. Tsirimokos at reception this week honoring Makarios said, "We agree on basic principle that Cyprus problem is not problem of negotiations and haggling between Greece and Turkey. Cyprus problem is basically and mainly, if not exclusively, despite its impact on Greek-Turkish relations, a problem of self-determination, independence and sovereignty of people of Cyprus. It is up to them to decide their future and their fate."

4. This contrasts with Tsirimokos remarks in Parliament and to the Ambassador (Embtel 1005)[3] last December when he indicated a much more flexible view on propriety and utility of Greek-Turkish talks.

5. Theodoropoulos reiterated that if Turks want to talk about enosis, Turks and Greeks are competent for such discussions since problem then is addition of territory to Greek soil. But discussions which have to do with the regime on the island as an independent state principally concern Republic of Cyprus and cannot therefore be conducted without Makarios' participation as principal. GOG would be happy to see GOT consult with Makarios re administration of island but GOG will not discuss such questions separately with Turks.

6. In contrast to rigor of above, FonMin Tsirimokos told me in predinner conversation two nights ago that he counts good Greek-Turkish relations as extremely important and hopes some agreement could be reached in area of a specific guarantee of independence of Cyprus for ten years. He thought rights of Turk Cypriots could be worked out, preferably on basis that enjoyment their rights be assured by international (presumably UN) mechanism rather than by Greek-Turkish joint or separate arrangements. He believed agreement along these lines would do

---

[3] Dated December 30, 1965. (Ibid.)

away with any purpose to continued presence of Greek and Turkish contingents on the island. He agreed with me that Turks would consider such an arrangement only on such justification as that Turkey had succeeded in barring enosis for fixed period, at end of which Turks could presumably be in a stronger position to attract world support for justice of Turk views. Tsirimokos concluded that he did not believe in official negotiation on these points, but suggested obliquely possibility that "your people in Ankara" (meaning US Emb) could smoke out whether Turks interested in arrangements sketched out above.

7. Discussion of defense questions between GOG and Makarios said to have resulted in decision that Greek General Staff would study defense of Cyprus with view to possible reduction of forces. We have no direct confirmation, and Tsirimokos (for public consumption) announced yesterday that "under present conditions, GOG did not intend to reduce its military forces in Cyprus."

8. Theodoropoulos reports three candidates are under active consideration as new GOG Ambassador to Ankara but "snags" have developed with respect to each candidate. Hopes this personnel placement problem will be ironed out soon.

Comment: For domestic political reasons GOG wanted to succeed in making Makarios visit occasion for doing away with impression of divergency of views between Makarios and GOG. This impulse, we believe, will continue to inhibit GOG in taking initiatives to re-start dialogue with Turks except if specific and stated purpose is solution involving enosis. Greeks keep pointing out that nothing in Turk attitude so far suggests to GOG that more generalized dialogue likely to have fruitful outcome.

Talbot

---

224. Telegram From the Embassy in Turkey to the Department of State[1]

Ankara, February 21, 1966, 1513Z.

965. NATUS. Ref: Deptel 711, Embtels 949, 966.[2] Cyprus. After delineating background and noting questions to be resolved in US-Turk rela-

---

[1] Source: Department of State, Central Files, POL 27 CYP. Confidential. Repeated to Athens, Nicosia, London, USUN, Paris, EUCOM and USDOCOSouth for POLAD, Istanbul, Izmir, and Adana.

[2] Telegram 711 to Ankara, February 17, provided instructions for discussions with Caglayangil. (Ibid.) Telegram 949 from Ankara, February 17, requested guidance for this meeting. (Ibid.) Telegram 966 from Ankara, February 21, reported Caglayangil's discussion of the domestic "background" to Turkey's foreign policy positions. (Ibid.)

tions, FonMin Caglayangil told Ambassador US and Turkey should work on one or several alternatives. Best alternative should be selected and both countries should then direct efforts to achieve it. He suggested he, FonOff SecGen Bayulken and Cyprus Bureau Chief Turkmen should participate on Turkish side and Ambassador and one member Embassy staff on US side. He would devote as much time as he could to these meetings although he might not be able to attend every one.

FonMin observed that Cyprus should not be considered separate question outside context of US-Turk relations. Cyprus situation now static but cannot be left thus. Cyprus was sore point for Greece as well as Turkey because all three had other problems, especially economic, to which they could more effectively devote their energies. Furthermore, GOT had to consider continuing difficult situation of Turk-Cypriot community. Turkey convinced question must be solved by means of negotiation, and US had important role to play. US should therefore be active now and try to help solve problem before it reached another acute crisis. FonMin pressed for exchange of views and information with us and for dispassionate ("outside-looking in") evaluation of Cyprus alternatives. If US-Turk agreement on best alternative reached, US would then, he hoped, use its influence to achieve results.

Ambassador replied we could begin exchange of views anytime. He noted big difference in Greek and Turkish positions on approaches to problem of Cyprus. However, it seemed to us that there was still room for maneuver and negotiation between Greek and Turkish positions. Ambassador observed that first Turkish principle was opposition to any unilateral enosis (Embtel 858).[3] Then he continued along lines para 3 Deptel 711.[4] FonMin made no substantive comment, and Ambassador continued along lines para 1 Deptel 711. FonMin agreed continuation of UNFICYP of great importance.

In reply to Ambassador's question, FonMin had nothing new to add on Rolz-Bennett's visit (Embtel 952).[5] He said perhaps Rolz-Bennett's report to SYG would form basis for SYG to explain to Security Council that mediation will not work under present circumstances. Perhaps, FonMin continued, SC can take new decision on mediation, for example, establish team of three mediators. In any event GOT told Rolz-Bennett that Turkey ready for mediation so long as functions of Mediator agreed upon ahead of time to preclude Mediator becoming arbitrator and promoting publicly his personal views.

---

[3] Document 221.

[4] This paragraph discussed Greece's position on Cyprus.

[5] Telegram 952 from Ankara, February 18, reported Rolz-Bennett's visit to Ankara. (Department of State, Central Files, POL 27 CYP) Rolz-Bennett visited Ankara, Athens, and Nicosia February 9–19.

Discussion concluded with FonMin saying he would be in touch concerning further talks on Cyprus.

Hart

---

225.   Field Information Report[1]

[*document number not declassified*]   Athens, March 7, 1966.

COUNTRY

   Greece

SUBJECT

   Rightist Greek Military Conspiratorial Group

DATE OF INFO

   August 1965–23 February 1966

PLACE & DATE ACQ

   [*less than 1 line of source text not declassified*] (24 February 1966)

SOURCE

   [*1-1/2 lines of source text not declassified*] information has been fairly reliable

1.   In late 1963 and early 1964 a group of rightist Greek Army colonels (reported at that time as the military conspiratorial group) organized to stage a military coup if Georgios Papandreou accepted support from the United Democratic Left (EDA). After Papandreou's election, the group was dispersed by transfers to Cyprus and northern Greece. Those officers have now completed their tours in these areas and are gradually returning to key command positions in Athens through the help of Lt. Colonel Georgios Vagenas, Director of the Greek Army General Staff (GAGS) office dealing with assignments.

2.   Although Vagenas is not a member of the military conspiratorial group, he is friendly with many of its members and is influenced by Lt. Col. Georgios Papadopoulos, who is now with the First Army in Larissa, and Lt. Col. Dimitrios Stamatelopoulos, both of whom are competing for

---

[1] Source: Department of State, Athens Post Files: Lot 71 A 2420, POL 15 GVT. Secret; Noforn; Controlled Dissem.

the leadership of the group now being revived. Col. Ioannis Lazaris, Director of the Chief of GAGS office and reportedly well thought of by the Palace, is also influenced by Stamatelopoulos. Lazaris is also a key man in the placement of officers.

3. The following members of the military conspiratorial group have recently returned to key positions in the Athens area:

a. Lt. Col. Kostas Papadopoulos, brother of Georgios, has been assigned as commander of the Dionysios Battalion since early February 1966;
b. Lt. Col. Dimitrios Stamatelopoulos, commander of the Agia Paraskevi Battalion since mid-October 1965;
c. Lt. Col. Antonios Mexis, expected soon to take a battalion command in the Athens area;
d. Lt. Col. Ioannis Ledis, Director of Military Police with headquarters in GAGS;
e. Lt. Col. Dimitrios Ioannides, expected soon to take a battalion command in the Athens area;
f. Lt. Col. Theodoros Patsouros, expected soon to take a communications command function in Athens;
g. Lt. Col. Michail Roufogalis, temporarily assigned on 23 February 66 to head the Security Office of the Greek Central Intelligence Service (KYP), is expected to move to "A" Branch of KYP.[2]
h. Lt. Col. Antonios Lekkas, expected soon to take a key command in the Athens area.

Ladas, Ioannides, Patsouros, Lekas, and even Kostas Papadopoulos, who is at odds with his brother, are supporters of Stamatelopoulos. Roufogalis is close to Papadopoulos, but Stamatelopoulos is trying to win his confidence.

4. Just before the Center Union (EK) 16 February 1966 rally in Athens, Lt. Colonel Georgios Papadopoulos came to Athens to contact military colonels in the event a coup was deemed necessary to thwart mob violence instigated by EDA or by Georgios Papandreou at the rally. Papadopoulos told his military contacts that Lt. General Grigorios Spandidakis, Chief of GAGS, had summoned him to Athens.[3,4]

---

[2] *Field Comment:* A Greek security official reported in late February that Roufogalis will act in Papadopoulos' stead while the latter is in Larissa. [Footnote in the source text.]

[3] *Source Comment:* Spandidakis is generally aware of the rightist military conspiratorial group but believes that it is more in line with his thinking relative to military intervention if necessary; i.e., that the King would rule through martial law. He therefore condones many of the transfers taking place now. [Footnote in the source text.]

[4] *Field Comment:* [1-1/2 lines of source text not declassified] Papadopoulos [less than 1 line of source text not declassified] that he had come to Athens to determine what type of support the army could expect from the police in the event there was trouble during the 16 February rally. If the crowds decided to march against the Palace or Parliament, Papadopoulos [less than 1 line of source text not declassified] that the army would take over. Papadopoulos also [less than 1 line of source text not declassified] that there were only "precautionary plans" [1-1/2 lines of source text not declassified]. [Footnote in the source text.]

5. The aims of this rightist group are to counter or avert leftist infiltration of the government and the military. Its fears that an uprising similar to that which occurred in the Greek Forces in the Middle East during World War II were increased with the discovery of another military conspiratorial group, Aspida, which the rightist group believes was inspired by the neutralist trend oriented by Center Union (EK) Deputy Andreas Papandreou. As a result of the strenuous efforts by former Chief of KYP, Lt. General (retired) Alexandros Natsinas to have a *Reader's Digest* article on Brazil, "The Country that Saved Itself", translated and widely distributed in Greece, the group saw a parallel between the situation in Greece under the Papandreous and the situation created in Brazil by the Joao Belchior Marques Goulart regime. It identifies itself with the thinking and policy of the Brazilian military junta.

6. The group has been divided since 1963, when Stamatelopoulos felt that Papadopoulos was willing to sacrifice competence and integrity for political expediency by his aid to certain officers to obtain key KYP positions and other command positions. Papadopoulos' actions were in response to political pressures and his desire to placate General Natsinas, then his superior, who was too closely identified with the National Radical Union (ERE). Stamatelopoulos' faction preferred not to align itself with any political party. Papadopoulos has used Natsinas and Nikolaos Farmakis, a former ERE deputy noted for his extreme rightist convictions, as contacts to rightist politicians. The key factor now joining the Papadopoulos and Stamatelopoulos factions is their common desire to neutralize the power of any officers who have any connections with AS-PIDA. Emphasis is now being placed on identifying these officers who continue to occupy secondary posts within the military commands of Athens and who are in a position to learn of the group's activities. The tempo of replacement of these officers is expected to increase during March 1966. As a figurehead, the Stamatelopoulos group tends to favor Major General (retired) Georgios Ballas.

7. Stamatelopoulos' faction has contact with the Palace through one of the King's aides, Lt. Colonel Dimitrios Zagorianakos. The King's personal secretary Major Michail Armaoutis does not have Stamatelopoulos' confidence. Stamatelopoulos feels that if the King opts for extra-constitutional military activity, the King would prefer martial law with rule by decree—a situation which Papadopoulos and the higher military commanders (particularly Spandidakis, Lt. General Christos Papedatos, and other generals hand-picked by Lt. General (retired) Konstantinos Dovas, former Chief of the King's Military Household) would be inclined to accept. Stamatelopoulos' faction prefers a military junta which would allow the King very few prerogatives; this faction blames the Palace for the political instability, starting with the fall of former Prime Minister Konstantinos Karamanlis in 1963.

226.   Telegram From the Embassy in Cyprus to the Department of State[1]

Nicosia, March 22, 1966, 1135Z.

438. NATUS. Athens 1379 to Dept; Athens 1388 to Dept.[2]

1. Aside from its effect on Greek politics (reftels) current acute phase of Makarios–Grivas feud represents danger to peace and stability on island. We believe there are dangers inherent in Grivas "victory", i.e., unequivocal control over forces of Greek side on Cyprus especially National Guard.

2. From US viewpoint Grivas' initial appearance on island in June 1964 had some utility, mainly in organizing and disciplining National Guard and disbanding or absorbing armed bands of Lyssarides and Sampson, etc. These purposes were largely accomplished by end of ' 64 but since that time Grivas presence here has had disruptive effect on developments. It is not clear how much collusion or tacit agreement existed between Makarios and Grivas at critical moments such as Famagusta last November or Ambelikou earlier but obviously Grivas did not exert restraining influence and consensus was that both were Grivas doing. On political side his followers constitute most intractable (even though they are anti-Communist) group on island. They are against anything except enosis now and likely continue to be adamantly opposed to any compromise solution.

3. Earlier when "instant enosis" was actively being considered as possible solution perhaps Grivas had value as man who could be relied upon take effective action on island, theory being that he had necessary prestige with Greek Cypriots and could hold island briefly until GOG assumed administrative control. None of various schemes floated on island at that time envisaged him as ruler of Cyprus for more than few hours or days, it being well understood that except for Makarios' alleged opposition to enosis there existed no real complaints against his government for corruption or mal-administration. Now "instant enosis" followed by immediate appearance of GOG is unthinkable because of inevitable Turkish reaction. At same time Grivas continues to remain at center, in eyes of Cypriots at least, of opposition to Makarios and possibility will always exist that Grivas, if he had wherewithal in shape of armed forces at his disposal would become exasperated with Greek Cyp-

---

[1] Source: Department of State, Central Files, POL 27 CYP. Secret; Priority. Repeated to Athens, London, USUN, Paris, USDOCOSouth, and Ankara.

[2] Telegram 1379 from Athens, March 20, discussed the problem created by Grivas' presence on Cyprus. (Ibid.) Telegram 1388 from Athens, March 21, analyzed the impact of the Makarios–Grivas struggle on Greek politics. (Ibid.)

riots over trivial or personal reasons and attempt coup d'etat, unilaterally declaring enosis with ominous consequences or even more
idiotically attack Turk Cypriots. Furthermore, having given him this
facility GOG would be hard put to disengage from Grivas' actions and
thus would also bear brunt of Turkish response. (One wonders, under
circumstances, what Stephanopoulos could have thought would be end
result of ill-advised move in appointing Grivas supremo in Cyprus.)

4. We are inclined to say that best result of this confrontation now
leading to Makarios–Grivas showdown would be to neutralize Grivas
by giving him only nominal authority and aiming at his eventual withdrawal from island under face-saving circumstances. This could be
achieved by leaving Grivas in command Greek units and appointing
someone stature Gennimatas as National Guard commander who
would be more stable cooperative individual understanding dangers to
Greece and Cyprus of precipitate action against Turk Cypriots or in
respect to enosis. We suggest that if occasion presents itself Embassy
Athens if appropriate might express opinions along these lines as soon as
possible to GOG officials perhaps including Bitsios in Palace.

Belcher

---

227.   **Telegram From the Embassy in Turkey to the Department of
State**[1]

Ankara, April 6, 1966, 1547Z.

1203. Embtel 1121.[2] NATUS. Cyprus. At luncheon which I gave for
FonMin Caglayangil April 5, Political Counselor summarized impres-
sions of four day trip to Cyprus and subsequent conversations in Athens.
This provided opportunity for us to explore Foreign Minister's views on
Cyprus situation and Turk attitude toward possible solution.

Political Counselor summarized impressions of Cyprus as follows:

A. Apparent that Turk Cypriot leaders both in Nicosia and other
parts of Cyprus were determined to do utmost to protect Turk Cypriot
population and defend its rights.

---

[1] Source: Department of State, Central Files, POL 27 CYP. Confidential. Repeated to
USUN, Athens, Nicosia, London, Paris, Adana, Izmir, and Istanbul.
[2] Telegram 1121 from Ankara, March 22, reported the latest Turkish positions on the
Cyprus issue and the recent Greek-Turkish exchanges. (Ibid.)

B. Greek Cypriot area of control seemed to be developing normally in economic terms, in contrast to evidence of restrictions and limitation on Turk Cypriot construction, travel, economic development, etc.

C. Over long run, Makarios has interest in at least maintaining status quo because he will thereby strengthen his position and contribute to continuing erosion Turk Cypriot position on island.

D. Turk Cypriots hold limited cards on Cyprus. They do not have enough bargaining power to offset Makarios' efforts to whittle away their rights and position.

In informal personal discussion in Athens among Embassy representatives from Nicosia, Athens, and Ankara, three possible approaches to Cyprus problem were aired.

1. Continuation of existing situation. While this seemed in line with Makarios' wishes and might be acceptable to Greeks, continuation of existing situation could not be regarded as satisfactory by Turk Cypriots or by GOT.

2. Reconsideration of Acheson plans which might still contain some useful elements which were worthy of negotiation among parties concerned.

3. Modus vivendi with provision for deferred settlement, in ten years time, for example. Language would have to finesse ultimate settlement of issues of enosis and partition, and stress would be on protection of Turk Cypriot physical security in intervening period. Variable elements would include future of Greek troops on Cyprus, status of Greek and Turkish contingents, role of UNFICYP, various types of administrative, judicial and police arrangements for Turk Cypriots, and possibility of UN or other international organ to guarantee security Turk Cypriot community.

FonMin replied in several installments as follows:

1. Prior to becoming FonMin, he had reached conclusion that because two communities could not live together, only solution was partition or federation. However, seems unlikely such solution could be attained at present time.

2. In GOT view, it was also apparent Greek Govt was weak and not in position to make decisive commitment re future of Cyprus. For this reason GOT agreed that modus vivendi, if it could be achieved, followed by interim period leading to final settlement might be possible way of approaching Cyprus problem.

3. Continuation of status quo was out of question since GOT had made it clear that this, in itself, was form of fait accompli. Lack of settlement might provoke some Greek Cypriot elements to take action against Turk Cypriots which would compel intervention of Turk armed forces. On other hand, Turk Cypriots, beleaguered and frustrated by status quo,

might themselves instigate incident which would incite Greek Cypriot reaction and thereby trigger Turk intervention.

4. Neither Turks nor Turk Cypriots had any faith in Makarios' interest in security of Turk Cypriots. GOT would therefore find it impossible to agree to withdraw Turk military contingent prior to final solution.

5. FonMin stressed instability in Eastern Mediterranean which would continue to exist, in absence of progress toward settlement, with all that this instability means to NATO. Suggested that NATO had important stake in guarantees for Turk Cypriot security and noted sadly that lip service which NATO paid to London–Zurich agreements was of little use to Turk Cypriots.

6. Turks considered that basic principles of London–Zurich agreements were still valid and must be incorporated in any new agreements although they were willing to accept modifications and adjustments in LZ to reflect current situation. Any settlement, even of interim nature, must be in accord with honor and dignity of Turkey.

In reply to FonMin's question re contact with Greek FonOff, Pol Counselor mentioned talk with Theodoropoulos April 2. In general terms latter had personally expressed positive interest in approach toward modus vivendi now with provision for deferred settlement.

Hart

---

228.   Telegram from the Embassy in Cyprus to the Department of State[1]

Nicosia, April 7, 1966, 1525Z.

469. NATUS.

1. Conversation with Bernardes yesterday indicates continued impasse here with regard his taking any new initiative within context his extended mandate.[2]

2. His most recent conversation with Makarios showed, if anything, a hardening of Greek Cypriot position with regard any further

---

[1] Source: Department of State, Central Files, POL 27 CYP. Confidential. Repeated to London, USUN, Paris, Athens, and Ankara.

[2] On March 4, Secretary-General Thant informed the Security Council that he was broadening Bernardes' responsibilities by authorizing him to employ his good offices and to approach the parties in order to achieve discussions at any level. (U.N. Doc. S/7180)

concessions to Turkish Cypriots living in enclaves. He said Archbishop had warned him that in making any proposals under extended mandate he should bear in mind that Greek position based on concept of unitary state and any proposals out of line with this concept would be automatically rejected by Greeks.

3. In discussing question of any conversations with appropriate representatives Turkish Cypriot community, Makarios has made clear that he not prepared authorize conversations unless Turkish Cypriot side included representatives of dissident Turkish Cypriot elements, i.e. specifically Dr. Ishan Ali. Bernardes commented that this proviso was new and obviously completely unacceptable to Turkish Cypriots. He went on to say, in his view, there was no "will" on part of Greek Cypriots to enter conversations and as matter of fact Archbishop had pointed out that if Turkish Cypriots willing now to sit down to discuss future, in three months time they would be even more willing. In meantime, Archbishop said he prepared wait matter out and reiterated old theme of letting Turks die on vine in their enclaves.

4. Bernardes said his attempts to point out need for some progress prior to June force renewal apparently fell on deaf ears although he continues to believe Makarios would be worried if force were reduced by more than half. Bernardes believes Greek Cypriot leadership being deluded by own propaganda that Turkish Cypriots on verge of collapse. He (and Embassy) have been at some pains to attempt moderate this belief on the part of Greek Cypriots but apparently with little success.

5. As further indication that Greeks in no mood make further compromises in "return to normalcy" Bernardes pointed out that they had substantially changed signals on question of Land Registry Office. Clerides had originally told UN to negotiate on basis of books being in UN custody and on this basis his staff appeared be making progress. A few weeks ago, however, Greeks changed position and now insisting that books come under GOC custody with only supervisory role for UN. It must have been obvious to Greeks that Turks would never accept on this basis.

6. Needless to say Bernardes discouraged by lack of progress here and while not seeing any great potential good in travel to Athens and Ankara, he is now considering attempting use his influence there late this month or early May.

7. *Comment:* Unfortunately our recent conversations with Greek and Turkish Cypriots did not give me any grounds for optimism or encouragement in my comments to Bernardes.

Belcher

229.   Telegram From the Embassy in Greece to the Embassy in Turkey[1]

Athens, April 20, 1966, 1830Z.

379. Cyprus.

1. Turkish aide-mémoire[2] rightly pinpoints continuing Greek and Greek-Cypriot conviction that time is definitely on their side as important reason for lack of forward movement on Cyprus issue. Present weak GOG is aware of certain dangers in permitting situation to rest as it is, but sees these dangers outweighed by risk to its own survival in granting any major concessions in return for what whole Greek political spectrum has accepted as only truly viable solution, i.e., enosis. Except for those few who talk of grasping nettle to arrest deteriorating Greek-Turkish relations, tendency of Greeks is to continue trying to keep island quiet and to play for time.

2. Implicit Turkish ultimatum would unquestionably anger Greeks. We assume GOG would deny GOC is restricting freedom of movement of Turkish-Cypriots and insist Turkish-Cypriot leaders are in fact themselves preventing their brethren from leaving enclaves and returning to their villages. Regarding other "inhuman" restrictions, Greeks would presumably contend that these are properly matters for discussion between two communities under aegis of Bernardes. GOG would also point to Turkish "inhuman" actions against Greeks of Istanbul, most of whom have been forced to leave during past two years. Finally, I believe GOG would insist (as it regularly and ruefully reminds us) that, however willing it might be to help ease restrictions on Turkish-Cypriots, its influence over Makarios is definitely limited and it is Archbishop who would have final say.

3. If Turks should begin move toward direct actions on island, even in so humanitarian a cause as aide-mémoire adumbrates, Greeks would of course go screaming to United Nations and USG to stop attack on sovereign nation.

4. I assume that Turks in their deep frustration over recent developments on Cyprus now see tactical advantage in involving USG in morass of internal problems on island at moment when they have also opened question of U.S. military facilities for discussion. As U.S. has long asserted and as aide-mémoire now underscores, responsible parties

---

[1] Source: Department of State, Central Files, POL 27 CYP. Secret; Priority. Repeated to the Department of State, USUN, EUCOM for POLAD, Nicosia, London, Istanbul, Izmir, and Adana. The source text is the Department of State copy. Passed to the White House and USIA.

[2] Transmitted in Secto 5 from Ankara, April 19. (Ibid.)

would indeed do well to press on with alleviating conditions of Turk-Cypriots. This would be true even though, as Ambassador Belcher may comment, GOT assertions about inhuman restrictions on Turk-Cypriots are not necessarily to be accepted at face value. However, I doubt USG, with its limited leverage on Makarios, can help situation by getting overly involved in details of Turk-Cypriot conditions. Would not prospective Bernades tour of capitals offer opportunity we can urge Turks to grasp for impressing on parties the seriousness with which GOT regards restraints against Turk Cypriots?

5.   Fundamentally, I see no present course open to USG other than continuing to press for direct talks among parties. With departure of Tsirimokos[3] and prospect that Stephanopoulos will win vote of confidence and appoint less difficult FonMin, we can hope for more active Greek effort to ease tensions with Turkey (though not, so far as I yet see, at material cost to what Greeks consider to be their interests). In this connection, we here interpret Grivas–Makarios conflict as at least in part reflecting intention of certain elements—e.g. Stephanopoulos, Costopoulos, Markezinis—to retain position on island which could in appropriate circumstances permit Athens to enforce on Nicosia an agreement which might have been reached between GOG and GOT. Though clearly not willing eschew enosis forever and thus blocked so long as Turks publicly insist on prior exclusion of enosis, Greeks may edge toward serious discussions if Turks are really disposed to find a solution. Presumably these talks would include consideration of ways of protecting Turk-Cypriots as part either of final settlement or of interim agreement that would include postponement for some years of decision on Cypriot independence, enosis, or partition.

6.   Prospects for injecting realism into Greek-Turkish talks would be enhanced if Turks could be persuaded also to talk directly with Makarios regime and to permit direct talks between Makarios and Turkish-Cypriots. Recognizing how vigorously GOT has resisted opening those channels, I nevertheless believe we should push this idea.

7.   If Greek political scene quiets down somewhat after current confidence debate, we here will do all in our power to rub Greek noses in realities of Turkish frustrations. At same time, I hope USG can make clear to GOT that threat of force applied unilaterally to provision Turkish-Cypriots would bring us all to a dire state.

Talbot

---

[3] Tsirimokos resigned as Vice President of the Council of Ministers and Foreign Ministers on April 11.

230.   Memorandum of Conversation[1]

US/MC/3   Ankara, April 22, 1966, 8:30 a.m.

PARTICIPANTS

United States	Turkey
The Secretary of State	Prime Minister Suleyman Demirel
Ambassador Parker T. Hart	Foreign Minister Ihsan Caglayangil
Asst. Secretary Raymond Hare	Haluk Bayulken, Turk Foreign Ministry
Robert S. Dillon, Second Secretary,	Ilter Turkmen, Turk Foreign Ministry
American Embassy	Sukru Elekdag, Turk Foreign Ministry

SUBJECT

Cyprus

Foreign Minister Caglayangil opened the conversation by telling Secretary Rusk that he was pleased to have an opportunity to talk about problems of mutual interest and particularly wanted to discuss Cyprus and the aide-mémoire which the GOT has recently delivered on the subject to the USG. The same aid-mémoire had also been sent to HMG but to no one else.[2]

Secretary Rusk replied that he wanted to stress that his remarks on the aide-mémoire would be strictly preliminary and that there would be an official reply after he had had an opportunity to discuss it with the President. The Secretary assured Caglayangil that the USG shared his concern about the situation of the Turkish Cypriots. He hoped that the GOT would make a full démarche on the subject to the UNSYG.

The Foreign Minister then alluded to the recent appointment of a Greek Cypriot as Minister of Agriculture on the island as another example of the Makarios technique. He stressed that the difficulty in talking with Makarios or in presenting the Turk demand for "normalization of conditions" for the Turk Cypriots (contained in the aide-mémoire) to the UN would be that Makarios would say let them go back to their villages. This, of course, would not be normalization because the Turk Cypriots would remain under pressure; what the Turks have in mind is equalization of living conditions for the Turk Cypriots within their present enclaves.

The Secretary indicated that he understood the point, but asked if that were an obstacle in going to the UNSYG. Bayulken, SYG of the Turk-

---

[1] Source: Department of State, Central Files, POL 27 CYP. Secret; Exdis. Drafted by Dillon and approved in S on May 6. The meeting was held at the Foreign Minister's residence. Secretary Rusk was in Ankara April 19–22 to attend the CENTO Ministerial Council Meeting.

[2] The Embassy in Ankara commented on the Turkish aide-mémoire in telegram 1346, April 26. (Ibid.)

ish Foreign Ministry, interjected "no—we can make a démarche and wait awhile." The Secretary then asked the GOT position on Turkish participation in the Cypriot Government. For example, at one time the UNSYG had offered some guarantees in connection with Turk participation in the government.

Caglayangil then replied that Turk participation in the Cypriot Government was a good step toward normalization and would be a part of a modus vivendi which the Turks could accept. However, the prospects for such participation looked dim. The aide-mémoire was addressed to the idea that the Turks must have the same conditions in their sectors as the Greeks have in theirs. If the two communities were living under the same conditions then time would cease to be a factor working in favor of the Greek Cypriots.

The Secretary said that the USG accepted the central idea of normalization. Furthermore, the Foreign Minister was correct in saying that Makarios would reply, "if the Turks want normalization, let them go back to their villages." Makarios would not want any steps taken that would represent de facto partition.

The Foreign Minister said that he had two very important points that he wished to emphasize: (1) the Greek Government was weak, which offers easy opportunity for Makarios to engage in provocations; (2) the Turk community was weakening; particularly its morale was weak. It also might engage in provocations. The GOT, USG and "even a reasonable Greek Government" were concerned with other important problems and would want to avoid provocations. However, Makarios, the Greek Cypriots and the Turk community would not be bound by the same sense of responsibility.

The Secretary said that he believed that the governments involved did not want to inflame the situation; therefore, it behooved all to be patient and diligent in seeking solutions to the problem.

The Foreign Minister replied that the GOT was the last one to whom patience needed to be recommended. He felt the GOT record was clear and that it had been extremely patient. He emphasized that the aide-mémoire did not represent a new GOT decision nor was it in preparation for a move (the implication was a military move). However, the GOT wished to raise some of the difficult questions involved. These were also questions that in some manner had to be answered for Turkish public opinion. For instance, what should Turkey do in case of new massacres? In case of an attack on the Turkish contingent? In case of the withdrawal of the UN forces which could lead to the events suggested in the first two questions? For how long can the Turkish community be left in its exposed position?

Without waiting for a reply, he continued that he wanted to reemphasize a point that he had already made to the Secretary. "Why is the

U.S. in the Cyprus problem at all? It is not a signatory power to the treaty of guarantee. However, Cyprus has in fact become a very important factor in Turkish-American relations. There was an outbreak of violence on the island in 1963. Turkey could have intervened. At a time when there were no opposing forces on the island and an intervention could have been successful, relatively bloodless, and could have prevented the terrible things that subsequently happened to the Turkish community, why did we not intervene? The answer is that the U.S. did not want us to do so. For example, the Johnson letter was an obstacle and we are still under an obligation to reply to public opinion in Turkey to the question why we did not use this right of intervention guaranteed by the treaty."

The Secretary replied that the problem to the U.S. had not been a question of treaty rights but a question of a war between Greece and Turkey. The U.S. position had been that the serious consequences of such an event to the NATO alliance must be considered.

The Foreign Minister said that he had given the same answer to the Turkish Parliament. However, this did not change the situation that the treaties had been violated. Furthermore, in any appeal to NATO the answer was a foregone conclusion, do nothing. Under the treaties a solution to this type of problem was already provided. Greece and the UK were committed as was Turkey to intervene to prevent violence. The real solution should have been tripartite action to protect the communities and to enforce the treaties. This had not happened because neither the UK nor Greece was willing to live up to treaty obligations. He also wanted to clarify that the GOT did not hold treaties to be permanent and that Turkey was prepared to negotiate changes as needed. He ended by emphasizing again the great pressure of public opinion on the GOT as regards a satisfactory solution to Cyprus.

The Secretary said that he wanted to thank the Foreign Minister for understanding that the U.S. did not invent the Cyprus problem. He hoped that it was also understood that it was because of our friendship with Turkey that we had become involved. However, he wanted to say frankly that Turkey must not allow this problem to become the central issue of our bilateral relations. Around the world there were 25 such problems e.g., India–Pakistan, Indonesia–Malaysia, etc. If in each case these specific problems were to be made the central issue of our own bilateral relations with the countries involved, we would be given a burden we could not carry. "You would make us your satellite and we cannot be a satellite. This is the kind of situation that would drive us into isolation."

The Foreign Minister thanked the Secretary for his frankness. He said that the present Turkish Government did not start to make Cyprus the central issue. He did not want to discuss internal Turkish politics, but when this government came to power, Cyprus had been made the central issue between the U.S. and Turkey by the previous government. At any rate, the GOT was now saying that if present conditions on the island continue, it must take initiative. It has prepared an aide-mémoire with a specific list of conditions to which the Turks object. The GOT wants the U.S. to come forward and say yes, the Turks are right. Human rights, etc., are being violated. This sort of stance would help the problem of Turkish-American relationships.

The Secretary answered that he had personally spent much time with the Greeks, Greek Cypriots and other parties on the problem of the Turkish Cypriots. President Johnson had also. A moment ago the Foreign Minister had raised a series of difficult questions. The Secretary wanted to emphasize that what we all wanted was to prevent the situations that gave rise to those questions. In other words, the questions were so difficult to answer that one must prevent the questions from having to be asked.

At this point Prime Minister Demirel entered the conversation, saying, "We accept the fact that you have very difficult worldwide problems but we are saying that here in this country, Cyprus is the hot issue from which none of us can escape. The events on the island have been inhuman, cruel, and against human rights. Why is the U.S. connected with Cyprus? It was not a party to the Cyprus agreements. Those agreements contained a procedure for solving the kind of dispute that arose in December 1963. That procedure was three party intervention. This did not occur for the reasons we discussed. Now the agreements have been violated several times. Makarios has said there are no agreements. The USG has said 'no' to the use of the guarantees contained in the treaties. We understand that the U.S. position was based on its concern that there be no war between Greece and Turkey. We are an independent country. Perhaps we should have gone ahead anyhow. However, that's all behind us. As it appears to Turkish public opinion, you do not want us to use the agreements. But why did you react so strongly to the prospect of our intervention and then do nothing when the Greeks sent 15,000 troops to the island? Cyprus is almost under Greek occupation. Why was there no reaction to this? Perhaps there is no need to discuss this point but you must understand that it is a factor. It is for this reason in the eyes of Turkish public opinion you have responsibilities. Now our Foreign Minister is saying that the issue may flare up again. This is no threat. There are responsible governments in Turkey. However, if something happens again—public opinion will demand action. If anything happens, it will be difficult to keep peace although we want to keep the peace and it is clearly to the advantage of the Turks that there be peace in this part of the world. If the UN force withdraws leaving 10,000 Greek troops on Cyprus, what happens if shooting starts? We want you to influence

Makarios and the Greek Government to see that nothing happens. We cannot always be the ones to give."

The Foreign Minister said he wanted to make another point—because of Cyprus the Turkish army was constantly on the alert and had been distracted from its NATO mission. Another point to be remembered was that in the NATO Council the Greek Foreign Minister had said categorically there were no Greek forces on Cyprus. Now, however, Makarios, Grivas and the Greek Government were engaged in a public dispute about the function of the force, its command, etc., and there was no further pretense it did not exist.

Bayulken interjected to say that the Greeks had used the excuse that Turkey was on the point of invasion, which was not true. He also wished to emphasize, returning to the aide-mémoire, that the GOT must have a pipeline to the Turk Cypriot force supply. This was part of normalization. Furthermore, if something should flare up on the island, then what? Would there be another letter from the US? If the Turks should react, and if there were a threat from the outside, would Turkey get NATO help?

The Secretary replied that it was important to discuss this kind of situation within NATO. He then asked for Turkish views on the UN force. The Foreign Minister replied that it must continue and that an improvement in the manner in which it carried out its function was an important factor for the improvement of the condition of the Turks.

The Secretary asked the GOT's view of the Russian position. For instance, he had heard rumors that the Russians had told Makarios that they would send no more arms. The Foreign Minister replied that the Russians accepted the principle of two separate communities on the island and accepted the idea of a federal constitution. Their other condition, however, was no outside intervention. In his opinion, if the Turks and their allies were able to come up with a solution, there would be no Russian interference.

Secretary Rusk then commented that there was at present a very weak Greek Government and asked if the GOT entertained any hope that a future GOG would be strong enough to make an agreement on Cyprus. Prime Minister Demirel replied that he expected no stronger Greek Government at any time in the future. If the Greeks were to go to elections, Cyprus would be an issue. Subsequently, a Greek Government would have even less flexibility. He wished to emphasize that his party, although it could have, had not used Cyprus as an issue in the October elections.

The Secretary then said that it had been a valuable chance to discuss the aide-mémoire. In Washington he would be discussing it again with the President following which there would be an answer.

Demirel said he wanted to emphasize his belief in Turkish-American friendship and his regret that the Cyprus issue had become a trap for this friendship. It was clear that Turkish public opinion felt that if Cyprus could not be solved by the guarantor powers, it should be solved within the NATO alliance.

The Secretary ended the Cyprus discussion by promising, "We will do our best."

231. Telegram From the Embassy in Greece to the Department of State[1]

Athens, May 6, 1966, 1135Z.

1652. NATUS Info.

1. I invited PriMin Stephanopoulos to lunch at residence May 4 to meet AsstSec Hare.

2. Regarding Cyprus, PriMin said GOG sincerely desired to resume friendly relations with Turkey and to find solution to Cyprus question. He said that in his meeting with Turkish Amb Tuluy he had emphasized this point, and in addition assured GOT that (1) GOG would not accept coup d'etat by Makarios on island and (2) GOG renounced use of force as means of settling dispute. PriMin added that he hoped GOT would also declare itself along same lines.

3. Initial question, PriMin continued, was how to begin talks. One major problem was Makarios: if talks were held in secret and he learned of them—which he probably would—then he would denounce them as "betrayal" of Cyprus cause; whereas if Makarios were informed in advance of them, he would undoubtedly "torpedo" them. King, he said, had suggested that talks be undertaken without knowledge of Makarios, but PriMin commented that he doubted that this would be possible, particularly in view of many connections Makarios has here. PriMin observed that Makarios could count on support of opposition (Papandreou) and Communists in Greece, as well as certain elements of right-wing press whom he has "bought." PriMin then posed question, asking what we thought would be best approach. AsstSec Hare replied that he agreed it would be extremely difficult to keep such talks secret.

4. Another problem, Stephanopoulos continued, was "level" on which talks should be held i.e., whether at Ambassadorial, Ministerial,

---

[1] Source: Department of State, Central Files, POL 27 CYP. Confidential. Repeated to Ankara, Nicosia, London, Paris for Crawford and James, USUN, and USDOCOSouth for Freshman.

or even "higher" level. Should talks be held at higher level and not succeed, it could be disastrous. AsstSec Hare asked if PriMin had confidence that both GOG Amb Delivanis in Ankara and GOT Amb Tuluy in Athens had "necessary contacts" to carry out this task. PriMin replied that as far as Delivanis is concerned, he has complete confidence that Amb shares fully views of GOG on Cyprus problem: as to his abilities, only time would tell. Tuluy seems genuinely to want to find solution to Cyprus crisis, Stephanopoulos said.

5. PriMin then talked of possible final solution. Enosis, he pointed out, would be best for all concerned, since an independent Makarios could be dangerous element in area, due to his connections with the non-aligned nations. However, if GOT insisted, perhaps question could be put off for "three to five years," at end of which time plebiscite could be held to determine will of Cypriot people. Possible solution, he continued, would be changing of one of British bases into NATO base, in which GOT could participate: GOT could even represent this base as their own to Turkish public. British, he continued, have indicated they would be willing to discuss giving up one of their bases if by such means solution could be found to Cyprus problem.

6. PriMin then asked for U.S. views on problem. AsstSec Hare said he had found during his recent visit to Ankara[2] that GOT is most anxious to settle Cypriot problem as quickly as possible so that it can face up to economic problems confronting country. However, opposition would not let govt alone on Cyprus question, thus forcing it to devote considerable time and effort to this problem. However, AsstSec Hare said his visits to both Athens and Ankara had indicated there was sincere desire on both sides to find early solution to Cyprus question. Perhaps for first time, AsstSec Hare said, psychological climate in both countries is similar, and this should facilitate moving ahead on problem. When Stephanopoulos complained about Turkish "threats" to invade Cyprus, which he said made his own position more difficult with Makarios and Greek opposition, Sec noted that Demirel also had problem with his own opposition, and that "threats" should be seen in this light.

7. *Comment:* As in our previous talk (Embtel 1589)[3] PriMin impressed me with his sincere desire to restore good relations with Turks and get discussions underway, although Greeks still preoccupied with mechanics of initiating talks. Further, there appears to be growing inclination to accept idea of putting issue "on ice" for period of up to five years, although in Greek view such a delay in settlement would need to

---

[2] As part of the U.S. Delegation to the CENTO Ministerial Council Meeting April 19–22.

[3] Telegram 1589, April 26, reported Stephanopoulos' assessment of the prospects for his government and his views on the Cyprus situation. (Department of State, Central Files, POL GREECE–US)

be coupled with some provision that at end of period would enable Cypriots to opt for enosis. Despite his good intentions, however, it is apparent that PriMin is hesitant to move forcefully lest he give opposition and Makarios opportunity to attack him.

Talbot

232. Telegram From the Embassy in Turkey to the Department of State[1]

Ankara, May 14, 1966, 1150Z.

1441. NATUS Info. Cyprus. Embtels 1429, 1421, 1346 and Secto five (Notal).[2] Reviewing recent developments, Embassy does not believe Bernardes' visit has had much effect on Turks. They have been conscious of his limited ability to improve conditions of Turk Cypriots and have never expressed much enthusiasm about his expanded instructions. They are also aware of negative US position on SYG's four-power guarantee proposal.[3] Furthermore, while pressing forward toward bilateral talks with Greece, GOT apparently does not foresee much hope in outcome of such talks unless some means is devised to move Makarios.

We believe GOT recognizes that attitude of Makarios is key to any Cyprus solution. We also believe that GOT sees need to use all available means to apply pressure on Makarios. Accordingly, this would call for rather far-flung GOT approach to problem which is foreshadowed in Turk aide-mémoire.

Following would seem to be included in this policy:

A. Bilateral talks with Greece on final solution. If it agreed that final solution currently impractical, negotiations would turn to modus vivendi. Since Turks believe realistically that even modus vivendi, or interim arrangement, would require elaborate, lengthy negotiation process, they have focused on more immediate question of welfare and security of

---

[1] Source: Department of State, Central Files, POL 27 CYP. Secret; Priority. Repeated to Athens, Nicosia, London, USUN, Paris for Crawford and James, EUCOM for POLAD, USDOCOSouth for Freshman, Istanbul, Izmir, and Adana.

[2] Telegram 1429 from Ankara, May 12, reported Turkish reaction to a Greek aide-mémoire on Cyprus. (Ibid.) Telegram 1421 from Ankara, May 11, reported on Bernardes' May 9–11 talks with Turkish officials. (Ibid.) Regarding telegram 1346 from Ankara, see footnote 2, Document 230. Regarding Secto 5 from Ankara, see footnote 2, Document 229.

[3] See footnote 2, Document 220.

Turk Cypriots. They have furthermore weighed in with aide-mémoire for maximum effect.

B. GOT will not exclude any reasonable proposal coming from any direction. This means it will not automatically reject Bernardes' proposal, or more specifically SYG's four-power UNSC guarantee, or mediation, or role by NATO powers, etc.

C. Aide-mémoire clearly sets forth Turk position to US and UK. It refers to GOT's "new assessment of the problem" and offers to consult with respective governments. It therefore invites the two governments to take active role in situation. If they should refuse, the GOT could always assert it had consulted US and UK.

D. Use of somewhat threatening tone in aide-mémoire is not only attributable to GOT frustration and its increasingly weakening position on Cyprus. It seems also designed to spark activity in other quarters (like US) to bring pressure to bear on GOG and GOC to adopt reasonable and forthcoming posture.

E. Recent military and naval exercises by Turk armed forces seem designed to enhance credibility of eventual Turk unilateral action. They may feel need to stress to outside world that second Presidential letter to Turkish PriMin[4] will not sidetrack GOT plans.

F. GOT also wishes to expose insincerity of Makarios in his stress of independent Cyprus at UN while pursuing pro-enosis line at least in communiqué signed in Athens and in "permission" to Athens to discuss enosis with Turkey in his absence.

G. Deadline for bringing political discussion to some kind of conclusion has probably not been established by GOT but instead depends on developments. It is unlikely, however, that GOT would allow situation to drag on into late fall or winter without action on its part unless it were persuaded that signs of progress and diplomatic activity justified delaying deadline.

H. As completely last resort, we are convinced GOT is prepared to undertake unilateral action to assist welfare and security of Turk Cypriots. In first instance, such action might well be non-military but would be supported by military units if any interference occurred.

While taking foregoing into account, we should also bear in mind that US reply to aide-mémoire along bland lines of UK reply would be negatively received by GOT. Instead we would recommend US reply along following lines:

1. As follow-up to Secretary's remarks to reporters at Ankara airport upon departure from CENTO meeting (Deptel 323 to Nicosia, 1082

---

[4] Not found.

to Ankara)[5] we should express sympathy for welfare of Turk Cypriots and convey our willingness to explore their needs with GOT. We should also indicate our willingness to discuss the means whereby these needs could be satisfied.

2. We should urge GOT to take advantage of apparent GOG willingness to negotiate outstanding issues. We would hope to keep in close touch with GOT on status of these talks.

3. We should include in our reply specific statement that we are willing in principle to do what we can to assist in promoting settlement between Turkey and Greece. We should add that timing of any such assistance would naturally depend on the attitude of negotiating parties and on our view whether we could usefully contribute to settlement.

4. We would consider desirable for the GOT to consider possibility of agreeing to reciprocal freedom of movement for Turk Cypriot and Greek Cypriot civilians to and from each other's areas of control.

5. We would have to state frankly that we believe military action by Turkey in regard to Cyprus would be unprofitable for Turkey and unlikely to improve the prospects for satisfactory settlement.

We strongly support continuation of UNFICYP as long as situation requires it and provided other nations assist in its maintenance. We would, however, point out that climate for continuation of UNFICYP at an adequate level may rapidly worsen in the absence of evidence of sincere negotiation efforts.

Point 4 above probes somewhat into Turk intentions as decided at COM meeting in Beirut (Beirut's 1074).[6] Caglayangil's busy schedule did not afford Ambassador suitable occasion to probe, but recent discussion with Turkmen suggests GOT below Caglayangil level not yet willing to show flexibility on question of reciprocal freedom of movement (Embtel 1429). Ambassador will probe this matter with Caglayangil at earliest opportunity.

In addition to other considerations, we believe we must call attention to fact that in Turkey we are dealing with moderate [illegible] party government essentially friendly to us. Not only immediate question relating to bilateral defense agreements but also shape of future relations with this government and with Turks may be affected by tone and nature of our reply. Equally important to GOT will be US attitude toward lending helping hand in negotiations with Greeks or in latter stage when Makarios must inevitably enter picture. Essentially US position should be friendly and forthcoming as possible and should avoid placing

[5] This telegram, May 11, informed the Embassies that the Department of State was reviewing proposals that would improve the welfare of the Turkish Cypriot community. (Department of State, Central Files, CENTO 3 TUR–CAN)

[6] Telegram 1079 from Beirut, May 1, reported on discussions of the Turkish aide-mémoire at the U.S. Chiefs of Mission meeting. (Ibid., POL 27 CYP)

unrealistic hopes on GOT–GOG bilaterals or give impression of "passing the buck" to UN. Latter particularly important since UN not regarded here as capable of developing constructive solutions to Cyprus problem in keeping with Turk national interests.

Re timing of US reply to aide-mémoire, we inclined to believe it could be delivered to FonMin upon his return to Ankara from present travels (Brussels May 14, RCD meeting in Tehran May 18 to 23, and official visit to Baghdad about May 24 to 26). Even so, FonMin might be unavailable since he is up for reelection to Senate and election day is June 5, just before Brussels Ministerial Meeting which he expects to attend. Nevertheless, on assumption that his Senate seat is safe and that he will be available here last week in May, we believe US reply should be ready for delivery at that time.[7]

Hart

---

[7] Telegram 547 from Nicosia, May 17, recommended that the United States avoid involvement in issues such as the conditions of the Turkish Cypriot minority and urge the Turks to adopt a policy of insisting on total freedom of movement on the island. (Ibid.)

---

233. Telegram From the Department of State to the Embassy in Turkey[1]

Washington, May 31, 1966, 5:57 p.m.

1152. Ref.: Ankara's 1441; Nicosia's 547.[2]

1. Turkish Aide-Mémoire represents clever diplomatic move to (1) involve U.S. more deeply in Cyprus problem, in direction of improving welfare Turk Cyps and perpetuating Turkish enclaves, or failing that, (2 clear way for Turkish ultimatum backed by real threat of limited military action. This presents us with dilemma in replying, since either forthcoming or cool response would lead us in undesirable direction.

2. Turkish move appears to have been based on assumption even interim political settlement unlikely in near future. We somewhat more optimistic regarding possibility interim "modus vivendi" arising from

---

[1] Source: Department of State, Central Files, POL 27 CYP. Secret. Drafted by Churchill, cleared by GTI and L, and approved by Davies. Also sent to Athens, Nicosia, London, and USUN.

[2] See Document 232 and footnote 7 thereto.

planned Greek-Turkish talks, with possible assist from USG. We, there-fore, believe it logical and beneficial put off dilemma posed by Aide-Mémoire by postponing (rather than intensifying or refusing) discussion with Turks on ways improve welfare Turk community and continuance UNFICYP. This approach implies we must take hard look our position, if Greek-Turkish talks fail.

3. Except for general wording on avoiding actions that would dis-turb talks, we agree Nicosia's 547 that response should not include direct reference to unfortunate consequences Turkish military action.

4. With above in mind we propose respond to Turks with following Aide-Mémoire:

5. "The United States Government greatly appreciates the Turkish Government's past willingness to consult on problems involving Cyprus and is gratified to be given the opportunity to comment on the Turkish Government's current thinking regarding this subject as set forth in its Aide-Mémoire of April 19. As the Turkish Government is aware, the United States Government has followed the Cyprus problem closely since December 1963, and shares the Turkish Government's pro-found concern that this issue continues to be a source of friction in the Eastern Mediterranean.

6. "The United States Government is aware that even though the conditions existing during the first year after the outbreak of the present crisis appear to have been ameliorated somewhat, the Turkish Cypriots still live under circumstances which are abnormal and regrettable. The United States Government sympathizes with those who have suffered hardships as a result of the unsettled conditions on the island and has done what it could to improve the welfare of the Turkish Cypriots by donating relief supplies to the Turkish community and by offering other assistance. The United States Government shall continue to seek ways in which it can be of further help, pending a settlement of the fundamental political problem that will permit a stable, secure life for the people of Cyprus.

7. "The United States Government is closely following and encour-aging the efforts of the UN Secretary-General's personal representative, Ambassador Bernardes, to bring about improved conditions on the is-land. The United States Government welcomed the decision of the United Nations Secretary-General to enlarge the terms of reference of his Special Representative, and hopes that this broadened mandate will open opportunities for such improvement.

8. "The United States Government notes the importance which the Government of Turkey has attached to the role of the UN in Cyprus and its relationship to the security and welfare of the Turkish community on the island. The United States has consistently supported the peacekeep-ing efforts of UNFICYP since that force was established in March 1964. It

notes with satisfaction that the Turkish Government also recognizes the role which UNFICYP has played in the maintenance of peace and order. The United States Government shares the Turkish Government's belief that a UN presence must be maintained on the island and to this end the United States is prepared to cooperate in supporting the UN peacekeeping effort in Cyprus. However, as the Aide-Mémoire of the Turkish Government properly notes, many countries have become reluctant to continue their contributions to UNFICYP in the absence of significant progress on the underlying political issues.

9. "Since receipt of the Aide-Mémoire of April 19, 1966, the USG has been advised of the intention of the Turkish and Greek Governments to resume talks on this subject. In the opinion of the USG this must be considered a most encouraging development which will permit consideration of the means of achieving a settlement leading to stability in Cyprus. The United States Government would like to keep in close touch with the Turkish Government on the status of these discussions.

10. "While these talks are in progress, it would clearly be desirable to avoid statements or actions that might in any way impair the still tenuous links of communication among the parties involved. However, if the forthcoming discussions should fail to have the hoped-for result, the United States Government would wish to discuss further with the Turkish Government the matters raised in the Turkish Government's Aide-Mémoire".

11. Comments requested ASAP.[3]

Ball

---

[3] The addressees endorsed the language of the document in telegrams 1540 from Ankara, June 3; 581 from Nicosia, June 1; 5749 from London, June 1; 5106 from USUN, June 1; and 1787 from Athens, June 1. (All ibid.) The final text of the memorandum was transmitted to Secretary Rusk for delivery to Foreign Minister Caglayangil in Tosec 97 to Brussels, June 6. (Ibid.)

234.   Telegram From the Embassy in Cyprus to the Department of State[1]

Nicosia, June 1, 1966, 1015Z.

582. NATUS Info. Ref Embtel 579.[2]

1. Talked with FonMin on problem of rising tensions and Bernardes proposals to defuse number problems by trading new relief ship for Turk Cypriot concessions. Kyprianou said he not meeting Bernardes until Saturday to discuss but his first reaction was this was non-starter. He parroted Archbishop's remarks of some months ago that GOC not prepared facilitate Turk aim of perpetuating de facto partition by making life simpler and more comfortable for Turkish Cypriots in enclaves.

2. With regard new tougher policy vis-à-vis Turkish Cypriots he was adamant in assessment that govt must take some action against Turkish Cypriot provocations. Claimed their aim in Bey Keuy, Chattos, Trepimeni, Knodhara area was consolidation of new enclave and GOC would not permit it. Asserted this was GOC policy and not merely some idee fixe of Grivas. Despite dangers of action there was a point beyond which GOC could not go in permitting Turkish Cypriots enlarge or further strengthen their perimeters. It was UNFICYP job, which they not doing, to prevent, but failing that GOC must take necessary steps. He did not accept my arguments that increased pressure on community in general only served strengthen control of Turkish Cypriot leadership and we dropped matter by agreeing that our assessments disagreed.

3. *Comment:* Believe situation can only be defused by additional outside efforts both in Athens, as suggested reftel, as well as through continued support of UNFICYP efforts which so far unavailing. Have informed UK HICOMer along lines reftel and foregoing. He is informing London and will see what he can do to help in Athens as well as here.[3]

Belcher

---

[1] Source: Department of State, Central Files, POL 27 CYP. Secret. Repeated to London, USUN, Paris, Athens, and Ankara.

[2] Telegram 579 from Nicosia, May 31, reported a hardening of the Cypriot Government position on treatment of the Turkish Cypriots. (Ibid.)

[3] In telegram 351 to Nicosia, June 1, the Department of State stated its agreement with the need for diplomatic action by Greece to defuse the tense situation on Cyprus and authorized a démarche by Ambassador Talbot in Athens. (Ibid.)

235.   Telegram From the Embassy in Greece to the Department of State[1]

Athens, July 22, 1966, 1800Z.

365. Dept repeat further as desired.

1. At Luncheon today PriMin briefed me on process [*progress?*] of Greek-Turkish dialogue to date.

2. His impression is that GOT (meaning Demirel, Caglayangil and some around them) are serious about reaching accommodation with Greece in order concentrate on economic questions but that "forces" beyond their control frustrate attempts to proceed. He characterized atmosphere as one of serious intent but where both parties are fearful of next step in belief increasing number pressures desiring sabotage discussions will win out and that interrupted discussions will mean serious setback for both Athens and Ankara. He identified as forces in Turkey limiting GOT maneuver press and the military. He cited sequence of recent events on Imvros and Tenedos as basis Greek assessment split in Turkish intentions re dialogue.

3. He said GOT representatives visiting Imvros lately have told Greeks there that Turkish Government would like to straighten out situation, but cannot in view fact Turkish National Security Council has decided militarize Imvros and expropriate property. Turkish press now playing up Greek "colonizing intentions" re islands and citing Greek concern as example Greek imperialism (megali idhea). Stephanopoulos reports Toumbas now of opinion that he does not see how GOG domestically can withstand any more press play re "persecutions" on Imvros and suggested time had come to refuse extension residence permits of Turk nationals (particulary on Rhodes) who come under expired 1930 Treaty of Establishment, even though he, Toumbas, believes dialogue is important and would like to see it continue.

4. Stephanopoulos of course lamented fact Turkish tactics (particularly extremist anti-dialogue forces) are only playing into Makarios' hand. He repeatedly professed sincere determination withdraw Greek forces from Cyprus if some arrangement could be reached for demilitarization and some form Turkish assurance and suspension military action. He said fact Greek forces on island are hostages in hands of Makarios is source deepest concern to responsible members his government. Makarios indicates lack of concern should his actions lead to Greek-Turkish military confrontation on island. According PriMin,

---

[1] Source: Department of State, Central Files, POL 27 CYP. Secret; Exdis. Repeated to Ankara and Nicosia.

Archbishop thinks he can undermine current Greek Government by lending support to ERE leader Canellopoulos who, because of his complex regarding Karamanlis and his desire to strengthen his own position as head of party, wants early elections. Makarios is making funds available to new Athenian daily *Eleftheros Cosmos* which is scheduled to begin publishing next week and which is expected to support views of Makarios on Cyprus and of Canellopoulos on domestic issues. (However, Canellopoulos can bring down government at any moment on domestic issues before recess committee, without depending on Cyprus question.)

5. PriMin says next stage dialogue is Turkish expression their views on Greek suggestions for definitive solution involving demilitarization of Cyprus, conversion of UK base into NATO or multipartite base with Greek and Turkish participation, plus liberal minority rights for Turkish-Cypriots. Stephanopoulos suggested now would be appropriate time for American intervention to convince Turks to consider carefully how GOT can help keep dialogue alive.

6. PriMin also mentioned possibility of provisional arrangement including demilitarization, conversion of UK base into NATO or multipartite base with Turk and Greek participation, minority rights, plus plebiscite after five years. If Turks would agree to plebiscite, PriMin said, he thought GOG could persuade or somehow get Makarios to return exclusively to his ecclesiastical functions. Key feature of this scheme would be GOT's giving up right of intervention in Cyprus under Article 4. In any case, PriMin added, some Greek-Turkish agreement is essential before GOG can act to control Makarios.

7. *Comment:* I do not believe we have yet reached point where it would be advisable for U.S. to weigh in with either side regarding substance of dialogue, particularly since according Stephanopoulos GOT has not responded to Greek ideas for definitive solution. I am very much concerned, however, that elements opposing dialogue may shortly be successful in spoiling atmosphere for talks. Measures against Greeks on Tenedos and Imvros are receiving increasing attention in Greek press and helping elements here who do not wish talks to succeed. I would much welcome Embassy Ankara's comments on what PriMin alleged is situation in Turkey, particularly with reference to Demirel government's relation to Turkish military and latter's attitude towards dialogue.[2]

Talbot

---

[2] In telegram 433 from Ankara, July 27, the Embassy reported that the Turkish Government favored dialogue. (Ibid.)

236.   Telegram From the Embassy in Greece to the Department of State[1]

Athens, August 11, 1966, 3:36 p.m.

713. At my request, I called on George Papandreou on August 5 for his views on current political situation. He was obviously braced to make more specific comments than on some earlier occasions.

1. Papandreou described Greece today as at critical stage. He said there are two roads it can follow. Present course would lead to catastrophe—other to normality. Queen Frederika, former ERE PriMin Pipinelis and former DefMin Garoufalias are urging King on first course. Queen Frederika is exploiting King's sense of honor (filotima) to hold him to present catastrophic course. Present course if pursued will bring dictatorship and revolution, which would be Communist-led but supported by many non-Communists, as occurred during EAM period and guerrilla war of 1946–49.

2. Papandreou said both he and King had taken opposing positions in past and both should now forget past and look to future. Neither can renounce all past stands. In his July 23 speech, he had spoken sternly about past, but in conciliatory tone about future. King could break current impasse by making gesture of reconciliation with people in form of declaration calling for elections and confirming his desire to see smooth operation of democratic government in Greece, free and honest elections, and constitution observed. He, Papandreou, would support this.

3. Papandreou said basic issue for Constantine was and is control of army. Army should be national, not belong to any party. Former DefMin Garoufalias had made a mistake by identifying himself with the Palace because he wanted to become PriMin. Papandreou could assure King that, if there were elections and he came to power, he would appoint as DefMin someone in whom both had confidence. Neither he nor Constantine wants to see organizations in army of IDEA and Aspida type. However, King wants an army loyal to him personally.

4. Papandreou commented that people speak of splinters in the Center Party. This is not true. He alone controls party. Center policy is his policy. But if he should "leave," he cannot guarantee that this will be the case.

5. Papandreou then made his main pitch. What is needed at present critical moment is help by Americans. US could use influence to help King see need for abandoning road leading to dictatorship. Action on American side would not be considered intervention. Dictatorship could

---

[1] Source: Department of State, Athens Post Files: Lot 71 A 2420, POL 15. Secret; Limdis. Drafted by Talbot, Bracken, Day, and Anschuetz.

cause chaotic situation which could have serious repercussions outside Greece (unrest in Balkans; free hand to Turkey to intervene in Cyprus). Successful functioning of democracies is in US interest all over world. It is logical for US to speak on this point to save Greece from civil war.

6. In response to my question, Papandreou said he has had no contact with Palace. Someone needs to convey his views to the King, someone outside invidious Psychiko circle (meaning Queen Mother and her confidantes). If he (Papandreou) attempted to convey this kind of feeling, it would be interpreted as compromising his position, and both sides would suffer. Gesture to be effective must be spontaneous initiative on part of King. It must not appear that there are secret agreements. Papandreou added he had not heretofore intimated these thoughts to anyone, not even to his friends.

7. I remarked that some feel rapprochement between himself and King is being impeded by public statements of younger CU elements. Papandreou acknowledged there are some "eager for applause who have found that anti-monarchist statements bring this applause. Today they say these things for demagogic reasons; if allowed to continue, they only become persuaded." Longer present course continues bitterer are public emotions, even though demonstrations may become fewer.

8. I asked whether he expects monarchy to be electoral issue. Papandreou replied that election declaration by King could bury the issue. Campaign would then be fought mainly "between parties" of which there are really only two: ERE and Center. Except for EDA, foreign policy would not be an issue. Papandreou added that his own position is well known, i.e. Greece belongs to Western Alliance but should cultivate economic and cultural relations with East.

9. Papandreou denied that EDA has succeeded in confusing issue whether popular front exists between CU and EDA. His position of not cooperating with EDA is well known and he holds to it. Questioned about kind of electoral law he favored, Papandreou said it makes no difference whether simple or reinforced proportional system used. He wanted only return to normality. Regarding a person who could head an interim government, he quipped Greece already has an interim government with Stephanopoulos. Who heads a government, whether Kanellopoulos or Zolotas, is not significant. Important point is need for statement regarding free and honest elections.

Comment:

1. If he means it, Papandreou's suggestion that King could have voice in selection of DefMin in any future Papandreou government represents shift from his earlier position. It was ostensibly on this issue that Papandreou broke with King in July 1965. That he should now propose a "mutually acceptable" DefMin suggests he currently sees himself caught in dilemma between aggressive harshness of positions taken by his son Andreas and continuing opposition to elections by Palace and other ele-

ments who fear what Andreas would do to Greece. There are some qualified observers who believe that in recent weeks George Papandreou has
indeed (as he stated to me) become seriously concerned for the political
future of Greece and who assert that his remarks on July 23 and his
approving comments on the August 6 Mavros open letter to the King (see
Weeka #32 August 13)[2] must be interpreted as a deliberate effort to separate himself from more violent statements of Andreas.

2. Papandreou looked alert and seemingly now in good health.
Nonetheless, several times he showed his awareness time remaining for
his active political leadership may be short. Though he repeatedly
asserted he now controls all elements of party, I inferred that he realizes
this is no longer true, particularly with regard to his son Andreas. This
could account for his expressed desire to re-establish communications
(on his own terms) with King while he is still in charge.

3. Papandreou has various means, other than the American
Embassy, by which he can communicate his views to King. He may well
see certain tactical advantage in trying to involve us in kind of middle-
position between Kastri and Palace. He also is undoubtedly aware that,
during course two conversations with Andreas in recent weeks,[3] DCM
urged Andreas (with obvious lack of success) to soften his attack on Palace in order help create conditions which would advance possibilities for
inevitable elections. My conversation with George Papandreou might
have been regarded by him as opportunity to get American influence
actively in support of early elections.

4. At appropriate early occasion I propose to inform Palace of
Papandreou proposal, but without comment.[4] Palace, like Embassy, will
not fail to have most serious reservations because of discrepancy
between George Papandreou's comments to me and statements of
Andreas Papandreou whose speeches over weekend were even more
acerbic and aggressive toward King and more inflammatory in revolutionary tone. Nevertheless, I would hope Palace would find in Papandreou's remarks to me encouragement to establish dialogue directly
with Papandreou through its own channels.

5. However, over and above the question of George Papandreou's
sincerity and his willingness and ability to disengage himself from
Andreas' policies, the Palace is faced with a more fundamental dilemma.
This dilemma is whether Greek national interests and the particular
interests of Palace would be better served a) by indefinitely postponing
elections, notwithstanding increasingly vicious attacks of Andreas and

---

[2] Not printed. (Ibid., Central Files, POL 2–1 GREECE)

[3] No record of these conversations has been found.

[4] Talbot informed the Palace of Papandreou's views in a meeting with Ambassador
Bitsios, Chief of the Royal Protocol Office, on August 18. He reported his talk with Bitsios in
telegram 868 from Athens, August 22. (Department of State, Central Files, POL GREECE)

risk of aggravation of question of the regime, in the hope that George Papandreou will disappear as an active political force and that CU will then fragment or b) by accelerating elections before position of Andreas in CU can be further consolidated and while the moderate elements in CU, presumably including George Papandreou, still have an important position. Ironically, increasing violence of Andreas may in fact precipitate elections before Andreas will have been able to achieve effective control of the CU.

Talbot

---

237. Telegram From the Embassy in Greece to the Department of State[1]

Athens, September 15, 1966, 1455Z.

1343. Following on my talks with Ambassador Hart last week and private luncheon Tuesday with Greek Prime Minister I have following comments on Greek-Turkish dialogue and possible U.S. involvement:

1.   Comparison of Stephanopoulos report to me of GOG and GOT positions (Athens 1293)[2] with that given the Secretary by Caglayangil would indicate that, unless Turks still not revealing their full hand to us, either (1) Greeks are confused as to substance of GOT position or (2) to encourage U.S. involvement they are deliberately portraying gap in positions as narrower than it really is. I believe it would be helpful to probe further in September 17 meeting with Toumbas for confirmation Turks are actually considering enosis, even though "loose" as reported in para 3 of Athens 1293.

2.   First task may be to clarify communication between two sides rather than more direct participation, particularly if Caglayangil's statement in para 1 State 46636[3] implies Turkey intends to view U.S. support for Turkish position as touchstone U.S.-Turkish relations. Further discussions while FonMins at UNGA might elucidate this.

---

[1] Source: Department of State, Central Files, POL 27 CYP. Secret; Exdis. Repeated to Ankara and Nicosia.

[2] Telegram 1293 from Athens, September 13, reported Stephanopoulos' belief that dialogue with Turkey had reached a point that might require U.S. mediation. (Ibid.)

[3] Telegram 46636, September 13, reported on talks between Rusk and Caglayangil on Cyprus. (Ibid., POL TUR–US)

3.   Revelations volunteered so far give inadequate basis for judging utility of U.S. re-entry into negotiations along lines GOG is about to propose. My net impression, however, is that Greece and Turkey have not yet exhausted their maneuvering room in current dialogue. It would follow that they should be pushed to try harder to reach a settlement. Our basket is already pretty full and they have at least as much interest as we in peace in Eastern Mediterranean. In any event U.S. ability to exert influence toward settlement would depend on what U.S. would be prepared to do or not to do to bring Turkish position nearer to conditions that could be imposed on Greece and Greek Cypriots.

4.   However, since demise of Stephanopoulos government could bring Greek-Turkish negotiatons to grinding halt, we have interest in seeing dialogue move as rapidly as possible. It may be long time before we again see combination as constructively committed to resolution of Greek-Turkish difficulties as are Demirel–Caglayangil and Stephanopoulos–Toumbas. Also, it would be brash to forecast how much longer extraordinary secrecy so far maintained in dialogue can continue. When leaks start, public reactions could build up rapidly. For these reasons, I hope we can be in position to offer assistance such as Ambassador Bunker's services on very short notice if two parties demonstrate willingness to take his suggestions seriously.

5.   I gather Caglayangil may involve U.S. assistance for interim solution. In considering whether there would be opportunity for constructive U.S. action along this line, we should keep in mind several factors: (1) status quo (including presence UNFICYP) is almost impossible to freeze precisely. Negotiating interim solution would therefore involve some of same compromises regarding internal structure as would permanent settlement; (2) unless basic revisions of Zurich–London could be agreed upon as basis of interim solution, which seems unlikely, Treaty of Guarantee and possibility of Turkish intervention under Article IV would continue to exacerbate Greek-Turkish relations; (3) under interim solution Cyprus would presumably remain independent, in which case Greeks are convinced Ankara would have to address itself to Nicosia rather than Athens and negotiate with Makarios. GOG considers interim solution just as difficult to negotiate as permanent one. I would tend to agree.

6.   Nor am I sanguine about peaceful prospects of solution of "unfettered" independence. In that event, Cyprus would seem likely immediately to become cockpit of international struggle. Soviets and non-aligneds would develop sudden vested interest in preserving Cyprus as uncommitted country outside NATO area. Simultaneously Greeks (with or without government inspiration or support) would undoubtedly mount strident, intensive campaign for quick referendum to bring enosis. Presumably Turks would regard such Greek actions as

betrayal of understanding, and might reserve right to counteract. In one case we could be confronted with serious derogation of Western interests in Cyprus area; in other, with sharpened bitterness between Turkey and Greece. "Unfettered" independence with prior implicit Turkish acquiescence in enosis campaign would be a different thing, and might be workable compromise.

7.   With reference to Stephanopoulos report that Greeks and Turks are discussing disposition of Dhekelia base area, this at least is progress over 1964 Karpas Peninsula debate which if raised now would in my opinion be non-starter. Question of nature of Turkish rights in base area would be closely related to issue of demilitarization of Cyprus along Dodecanese lines. A Turkish military base on a demilitarized island would seem anomalous, though Turks would presumably find restriction to Dhekelia less attractive if rest of island were within Greek active border defense zone. It may be that Dhekelia issue can be resolved only within context of an Acheson-style Greek-Turkish defense board, a device by which defense needs of Cyprus could be reduced to proper proportions.

As to form of enosis, we here have been pondering idea of commonwealth along Puerto Rican line. From Greek (and U.S.) point of view this would have serious deficiency of leaving Makarios in saddle internally while making Greece responsible to Turks and rest of world for policy pursued in Cyprus. Nonetheless, if idea of enosis is still shocker to Turks, commonwealth theme might be worth examining by both parties despite Greek resistance to getting committed to anything short of full enosis.

9.   I advance these random thoughts at this time on assumption Department will in immediate future be intensively considering next steps.[4]

Talbot

---

[4] In telegram 48821, September 16, the Department of State commented that while the Turkish Government might not have totally ruled out a dialogue on enosis, the Greek Government should avoid raising the issue. (Ibid., POL 27 CYP)

238.   Telegram From the Embassy in Turkey to the Department of State[1]

Ankara, September 16, 1966, 1532Z.

1426. Ref: State 46636; Athens 1343 and 1293.[2] Cyprus.

1. In light Secretary's conversation with Caglayangil and in anticipation his forthcoming meeting with Toumbas, I am putting down these thoughts to clarify a few points in hope this message may be useful to Secretary before meeting with Toumbas.

2. It seems agreed among us (Athens, Nicosia and Dept) that present Turk-Greek dialogue offers best hope for permanent settlement of Cyprus issue for some time to come. We also recognize that sincerity of both sides and secrecy of talks are good omen. Our fear lest dialogue fail if Greek Government should fall encourages me to believe that USG should use available time to make concerted effort to contribute to success of present negotiations.

3. I realize that we have been well burned before in trying to mediate Cyprus problem and are therefore reluctant to let ourselves be dragged into the middle.

4. In present circumstances, we are also handicapped by lack of knowledge. We have some idea of Greek proposals and of Greek attitude toward Turkish reactions. We do not have any idea of Turkish proposals nor specific Turkish attitude to Greek proposals nor of Nicosia's likely attitude to either side's position. We really do not know how close or far apart the two sides are on any issue.

5. We should probably recognize that our decision to intervene in Turk-Greek negotiations may well be based less on careful assessment that we can help bridge relatively narrow gap in two sides' respective positions than on sheer hunch and on feeling that we cannot turn down plea for help from two NATO allies who come to us as fair and impartial friend after having virtually exhausted their own resources.

6. If Caglayangil and Toumbas meet in New York at end of September, their meeting should give us important indication whether talks losing momentum. Despite certain urgency, I would recommend that we await results of that meeting and evaluation of subsequent situation by respective Foreign Ministers before taking any steps (known to parties) to help out dialogue.

---

[1] Source: Department of State, Central Files, POL 27 CYP. Secret; Exdis. Repeated to Athens, London, Nicosia, and USUN.

[2] Regarding telegram 46636, see footnote 3, Document 237. Telegram 1343 is Document 237; regarding telegram 1293, see footnote 2 thereto.

7. If after that meeting both Foreign Ministers agree on U.S. taking active role in dialogue, I believe that will be propitious time for offering services of experienced figure like Ambassador Bunker. In regard to Makarios we should focus hard on any suggestion Embassy Nicosia may have which could help us neutralize his talent for upsetting applecart.[3]

8. On balance, time is approaching when we shall have to take risk of more active involvement if we are seriously concerned about alternatives to peaceful accommodation. Attitude of Turks and Greeks in this dialogue since June gives me some ground for optimism that we may be able to help them, and Cypriots, to find some way out on Cyprus issue. I therefore wish to reaffirm line expressed by Secretary to Caglayangil that we are prepared to seize opportunity for constructive action.

9. I will have more to say later on detail of various proposals.

Hart

---

[3] In telegram 410 from Nicosia, September 19, Belcher commented that Makarios might prove more amenable to talks as a result of the perception that time was favoring the plans of the Turkish Cypriots. (Department of State, Central Files, POL 27 CYP)

---

239.   Telegram From the Department of State to the Embassy in Greece[1]

Washington, September 19, 1966, 4:58 p.m.

49718. Greek Foreign Minister Talks—Cyprus, September 17.

1. Following summary FYI only and Noforn. It is uncleared and subject to amendment upon review of memcon.[2]

2. Greek Foreign Minister, speaking on Cyprus issue, said he believed strongly in Greek-Turk dialogue and tensions in Greek-Turk relations had relaxed. It essential to seek permanent solution which would not have in it germ of new difficulties. Greek position based on three principles: 1) protection of prestige of Turkey, 2) granting of most advanced and generous type of minority guarantees, 3) guarantee of

---

[1] Source: Department of State, Central Files, POL 27 CYP. Secret; Limdis. Drafted by Brewster and approved by Rockwell. Repeated to Ankara, London, Nicosia, and USUN.
[2] Not found.

Turk security. Agreement of course extremely difficult to reach and there were those in Greece, Turkey and on Cyprus who did not want solution and want to torpedo dialogue. GOG is not only trying to solve Cyprus issue but to settle whole range of Greek-Turk problems. Package offered by Greeks covers 1) Cyprus solution, 2) bilateral treaty of alliance within NATO framework, 3) commercial and industrial relations, 4) fisheries, 5) tourism, 6) cultural relations. He added, without going into detail, that final solution should take form of "some kind of enosis." Independence raised all dangers of Cuba-like Cyprus.

3. Soviets, he is convinced, oppose solution and as example he noted that Soviet Chargé on Cyprus had expressed view that "opinion poll" be taken on question of enosis among young people who had not participated in 1950 plebiscite. Soviets obviously hope exploit expected shift in sentiment which Toumbas said was not anti-Greek but anti-West. A nation of only five hundred thousand cannot avoid falling into sphere of influence of one of great powers if independent.

4. Toumbas stated Greek and Turk representatives holding another meeting this week. Foreign Minister added he neither optimistic nor pessimistic about outcome of dialogue but wanted to continue to hope for best. He asked if Greek efforts fail and there is breakdown in talks, what would US consider doing procedurally? He had in mind good offices.

5. Secretary thanked Foreign Minister for report. He was encouraged to see talks being carried on seriously and privately. He thought Greeks had achieved one very important thing which USG esteemed highly, namely creating atmosphere of restraint. He noted Turk Foreign Minister had said his Greek colleague dealing on this subject in serious and responsible way. Secretary urged dialogue continue and not be broken off, since consequences of failure would be very serious. Utmost patience and determination were required and if talks did not succeed today there is always tomorrow. Cyprus question of interest not only to Greece, Turkey and Cyprus but to all of NATO and USG. USG had used its good offices in past and had suffered many bruises from this endeavor. Therefore we do not want to rush in. Secretary then made three points: 1) every possible effort should be made to maintain peace on island; 2) Greeks and Turks should exert maximum effort to work towards solution, 3) if there are ways in which US might be of help, we would be glad to give it most serious consideration. Secretary added he was not sure we had expertise or miraculous formula to solve Cyprus problem and that roots of problem go back into history to before birth of US as a nation. He believed strongly that those who had to live with results of solution should be ones to find it and he had complete respect for GOG efforts in this regard.

6. At end of meeting Secretary stated he hoped to see Foreign Minister again in New York, particularly if there were any future develop-

ments on Cyprus issue. Secretary noted that not having pressed for details concerning dialogue was through no lack of interest in problem but because we feel private conversations are most fruitful.

Ball

---

240. Telegram From the Embassy in Turkey to the Department of State[1]

Ankara, October 6, 1966, 0627Z.

1740. Cyprus. Ref: Ankara 1426.[2]

1. Tenor of speeches of FonMin Caglayangil and Toumbas before UNGA and their further contacts in New York have diminished sense of urgency about what U.S. role should be in event of break of Turk-Greek talks. Nevertheless, it may be useful for Embassy to record certain current impressions.

2. In reviewing messages re Turk-Greek talks, Embassy is struck by fact that only solid information has been provided by high Greek sources to Embassy Athens. We must remain cautious however lest these sources without malice aforethought may have misrepresented Turkish positions.

3. We also assume that both Greek and Turk positions at outset are superficially irreconcilable. We would therefore not wish to encourage idea that initial Greek positions may eventually be acceptable to Turkey or that initial Turk positions are unalterable.

4. We are inclined to believe, for example, that Turkish Government would be in deep trouble if it accepted full enosis of Cyprus with Greece and participation in NATO base, as suggested by Stephanopoulos (para 4 Athens 1293).[3] If Turks are to hold sovereignty over base area and can obtain nearly complete demilitarization of island outside base area, GOT might be interested. However, we note Greek PriMin rejected this (para 2 Athens 1293).

---

[1] Source: Department of State, Central Files, POL 27 CYP. Secret; Exdis. Repeated to Athens, London, and Nicosia.

[2] Document 238.

[3] See footnote 2, Document 237.

5. When Caglayangil told Secretary enosis would be "difficult proposition" (State 46636),[4] it may have been form of politeness to avoid appearing rigid. On other hand, Turks have long been favorable to idea of double enosis but reject unilateral enosis. Adjective qualifying enosis is important.

6. FonMin may also have in mind interim solution which would freeze status quo with aim perhaps of preventing Makarios from undertaking new initiatives pending further negotiations on permanent settlement. While we are aware of problems involved, interim solution might provide for certain Turk and Greek steps to ease tension and increase mutual confidence during period that Cyprus still remains independent state. It might not go so far as to take up Cyprus constitutional-legal problems and might therefore be easier to negotiate than permanent settlement.

7. Yet another possibility in which we see benefit is "limited accord" which in itself resolves nothing but has merit of maintaining suitable atmosphere for difficult negotiations. Such accord might provide for continued secrecy of talks, agreement on attitude toward press, immediate consultation on new bilateral and Cyprus issues vital to each side, periodic high-level meetings of political leaders, etc.

8. In reviewing various ideas ranging from "unfettered independence" to double enosis to commonwealth and condominium, we must take into account Turkish four principles. Any permanent solution must be susceptible of being interpreted as fulfilling more or less these four principles. These were described by FonMin in Ankara 858 of January 28[5] in slightly different terms from those used by FonOff SecGen in Ankara 1394 of September 15.[6]

A. No domination of one community by the other. Permanent solution probably must grant Turk Cypriots broad rights to administer themselves, at least approaching what they now have within enclaves.

B. No unilateral modification of London–Zurich treaties. Permanent solution must acknowledge this point even in process of throwing treaties to the winds and establishing new constitutional-legal framework which would still give Turk Cypriots role in central administration.

C. No unilateral enosis. Permanent solution must include turning over to Turkey some land in compensation for enosis. Turk-Greek negotiators may have to bargain hard on which piece of land (Evros River area, Aegean offshore island, Karpas Peninsula, Dhekelia base etc.) should be turned over on what basis (Turk sovereignty, joint Turk-Greek

---

[4] See footnote 3, Document 237.

[5] Document 221.

[6] Telegram 1394 from Ankara reported that Turkey would not comment on the substance of the talks with Greece. (Department of State, Central Files, POL 27 CYP)

sovereignty, long-term lease from Greece to Turkey, temporary NATO arrangement, etc.).

D. Maintenance of the balance established by Lausanne Treaty. This suggests that developments on Cyprus are of strategic interest to Turkey and position of Turk Cypriot community cannot be ignored.

9. For time being, we have no special formula to suggest. In absence of precise knowledge as to Turkish position, we believe we should merely continue stressing that it is to Greek and Turkish advantage to push talks toward settlement. As stated above we see no danger at present of an imminent breakdown and are therefore reluctant to speculate too far afield on possible compromise formulas for settlement.

Hart

241. Airgram From the Embassy in Greece to the Department of State[1]

A–196   Athens, October 8, 1966.

SUBJECT

    Ambassador's Conversation with George and Andreas Papandreou,
      September 29, 1966

SUMMARY

At a luncheon at Kastri at which I was the only guest, George and Andreas Papandreou were at pains to get across three messages. The first was that the CU will not make a popular front with the Communist-line EDA and cannot do so because of policy disagreements over legalization of the Communist Party of Greece, return to Greece of refugees from the guerrilla war, Greek membership in NATO, and the national democratic political character of the Center Union. Secondly, they asserted that Greece under a Papandreou Government would remain a staunch ally of NATO and the West, though—to use Andreas' words—Greece would insist that its voice be heard more than in the past. Andreas expressed his

---

[1] Source: Department of State, Central Files, POL GREECE–US. Secret. Drafted by Talbot and approved by Bracken.

admiration for Turkish diplomacy as the way for a small country to project its views in the councils of powers. Third, the Papandreous proposed that the King install a service government which would (a) be set up with non-political personalities agreed upon by the Center Union and ERE, (b) gain a vote of confidence for a restricted period and for the restricted purpose of adopting an electoral law (presumably by the simple proportional system), and (c) be in power for long enough to adopt the electoral law before the beginning of the 45-day period provided by the constitution for the holding of elections. The Papandreous thought that this procedure, based on a precedent established in 1958 with the Georgakopoulos Government, would add "a few weeks" to the life of the service government. For the first time in my discussions with George Papandreou, he ruled out the possibility of an interim ERE government and emphasized that only a "service government" of non-political personalities would be acceptable.

[Here follows a detailed report of the discussion.]

Talbot

---

242.   **Telegram From the Embassy in Turkey to the Department of State**[1]

Ankara, October 22, 1966, 1127Z.

2061. Cyprus.

1. During course of long private conversation Oct 21 FonMin Caglayangil brought up his last private talk with Secretary Rusk in Washington,[2] during which he stated he had told Secretary that while GOT had little confidence in results, it was continuing its secret bilateral conversations with Greece on Cyprus. Since that talk there had been no real closing of gap in basic views. Toumbas, despite his good will and very correct and sincere attitude, was shying away from the bases [garble] durable and final solution. Politics of Greece restricted him and he appeared intent on gaining time in view of Greece's internal concerns.

---

[1] Source: Department of State, Central Files, POL 27 CYP. Secret; Priority; Exdis. Repeated to Nicosia, Athens, and London.

[2] See footnote 3, Document 237.

Greeks in general were insisting on enosis which could not be accepted by Turkish opposition, which was "cruel" and would say that if enosis was to be solution it could have yielded that concession to Greece itself, when in power. "Form of enosis was not Turkish affair" Caglayangil said and apparently Greeks had to have some form of enosis. As matter of fact, bilateral Greek-Turk talks had not yet included any discussion of enosis or political ties of Cyprus. Each side had at once identified "unacceptable" proposals and by mutual consent these had been set aside and dialogue focused on such matters as demilitarization of island, rights of Turk Cypriots and a base to guard Turkish community. GOT had recently insisted that Greece set forth its definite opinion on one vital element: a statute for Turkish forces on the island. If Greece could clarify its position on this matter dialogue could be continued, but GOT had no hope that this could be done. If dialogue should produce no results (and in a short time Turkey would know) this would constitute a rupture.

2. Recalling breakfast meeting with Secretary Rusk at Ankara in April,[3] Caglayangil referred to Turkish aide-mémoire in which it made clear (and in accompanying conversation) that some "normalization" and "equalization" of Turk-Cypriot position on island must be undertaken. Disparity in rights between the two communities was totally objectionable and unfair. While Greeks were free to come and go everywhere on island, Turks were subjected to harassments, restrictions, assaults, and blockades. It was not humane. Secretary Rusk had agreed with Caglayangil in private portion of Washington meeting that there must be some normalization and avoidance of restriction on human rights. Now winter was approaching and situation could not be allowed to go on. If GOT were in position to tell Turk Cypriots that everything would be settled in six months and they should therefore be patient, that would be one thing. But Turkey could not give such assurance. If it should come to point where GOT had to demand from Makarios removal of restrictions imposed on Turk Cypriot community then GOT could be obliged to act to ensure compliance.

3. In response to my request for clarification status of dialogue, Caglayangil confirmed dialogue not ruptured but continuing as of now. If Greek reply to Turkish request regarding a base for Turkish troop presence on Cyprus "approached" Turkish point of view there would be possibility of further contact, for example, between Caglayangil and Toumbas. If not, there was no utility in prolonging dialogue.

4. There ensued long discussion, during which I emphasized first and foremost importance of continuing this dialogue and not having rupture. I said we estimate that present GOG while fragile was best govt in Greece foreseeable at present in its attitude toward Cyprus problem. I

---

[3] See Document 230.

asked whether he had given thought to possibility of keeping talks in some status of continuation despite lack of progress and perhaps in establishing something like "hot line" to be used with Athens if events on Cyprus became serious. Caglayangil responded that he had, but there must be condition that there be some improvement in Cyprus situation. He agreed it would be most undesirable to "declare" that there had been rupture of the talks. It might even trigger fall of present Greek Govt. However, there continued in Cyprus harassments, inability of Turk Cypriots to cultivate their lands, to circulate freely, and he stressed time and again need for assurance that Turkish aid to Turk Cypriots could get through to people. Toumbas had agreed with him on this. GOT "had no desire to arm Turk Cypriots". Arms had been too long held by both sides and shootings were chronic and irresponsible on both sides. What he objected to most was inequality of treatment. I said it had been my impression, and I felt I had received every important communication sent to Washington by our Embassy in Nicosia, that situation, while far from "normal" was nevertheless distinctly better than it had been few months ago.

There had been recent postal agreement. He nodded. Little by little and very painfully I thought some of elements in situation were being diminished. I asked whether in view of this situation on island could justify breaking off dialogue. Caglayangil seemed to agree, but then backed away to say situation not basically improved. He referred to sudden blockadings of Turk Cypriots under blanket accusation they were responsible for forest fires or explosions. He said GOT had issued most categoric instructions to Turk Cypriots not to fall into provocations. As regards explosions and shootings, he knew they occurred sporadically and were started by both sides. "For all I know", he said, "Turks may be to blame for an explosion but Greeks should not without awaiting investigation and under general influence of prejudice declare publicly Turk Cypriots to blame and then blockade some Turk Cypriot community. This is inhuman."

5. Caglayangil volunteered GOT not trying to rush final solution. GOT understood that "right now" Greece could not talk about partition and "right now" Turkey could not talk about enosis. As far as Turkey was concerned conversations could go on for another year or two years, or a modus vivendi worked out if situation on island could be made to improve, but this situation had had profound repercussions on Turkish public opinion. I then asked whether I could define his position as this: "If there could be some real sign in improvement in situation on Cyprus this would help him in justifying prolongation of dialogue." He agreed.

6. I then said that he had referred to free access of Turks to their lands. One very important point which concerned me was whether Turk Cypriot leadership would permit Turk Cypriots to circulate freely to and

from enclaves if Greek Cypriots permitted it. I had been disturbed over stories that Turk Cypriot judges had been activtely dissuaded by local Turk authorities from resuming their positions on bench. Caglayangil made clear it was Turk Cypriot community not Turkish Government that dissuaded them and that judges did not wish to return. I said it very important to know whether, if Greek Cypriots dropped restrictions on movement of Turks, e.g. to return to their own lands (to which I understand they had been invited by GOC anyway), they would be permitted to do so and not prevented. Caglayangil replied that he could give me fullest assurance on this point. I said I proposed to relay this to Washington and he said, "Please do."

7. When I asked Caglayangil specifically what he was suggesting we do, he again referred to private conversation with Secretary and said he had been "greatly encouraged" that Secretary had agreed with him that improvement of Turk Cypriot situation must somehow be found. GOT needed assurance that Turk Cypriots would have access to port facilities, that they could build some decent housing, that Turk relief could get through. He was very concerned that if he had no alternative but to demand from Makarios lifting of restrictions confrontation would take place from which Turkey [garble] not possibly back down. There was "question of prestige of a country of 31 million against this small island."

8. As we had carried on this conversation for well over an hour out of total conversation of two and one-half hours, I said I would like to mull all this over and come back to see him soon.

9. *Comment:*

"Procedural agreement" does not appear sufficient in itself to stop GOT–Makarios confrontation if GOG–GOT dialogue lapses, even if not declared ruptured. Caglayangil obviously in dilemma over his posture on Cyprus problem on eve opening of Parliament and expected opposition probes and heckling. I think it clear he wants to declare dialogue still on. He needs badly evidences of clear improvement Turk-Cypriot situation and hopes Washington can back Athens in pressuring Govt of Cyprus.

Hart

BREAKDOWN OF CONSTITUTIONAL GOVERNMENT IN GREECE, NOVEMBER 1966–APRIL 1967

243. Memorandum of Conversation[1]

Tatoi, Greece, November 2, 1966.

PARTICIPANTS

>His Majesty King Constantine
>The Honorable Phillips Talbot

In taking my leave of the King before Washington consultation, I mentioned the prospective visits to Athens of several U.S. Congressional groups. The King said he would particularly like to see Senator Javits and might even challenge him to a tennis match.

The King said he understood Admiral Toumbas had told me about current Greek-Turkish negotiations on Cyprus and had said the time might be approaching when it would be important for the U.S. to exercise some moderating influence on Turkey. I commented that I had asked the Foreign Minister whether he had any particular issue or timing in mind and he had replied not at present. I added that I had gained the impression from the Prime Minister in a separate conversation that the key sticking point seemed to be the status of the Dhekelia sovereign base area. The King said this was his understanding. I asked whether he would expect the negotiations to break down over such an issue as a Turkish base versus a NATO base with Turkish participation. "Absolutely within this room," he replied, "I have told the Government they can't let that be the final breaking point. It wouldn't work to have obtained 95% and stick on the last 5%". However, he went on, Greece could not accept the present Turkish demand for a Turkish sovereign base combined with demilitarization of the Greek part of the island. One of these two elements would have to be modified. He hoped that the Turks could be persuaded to accept a lease status in Dhekelia. I noted that this might be exceptionally difficult if the Turkish mood continued anything like it was in 1964 when Acheson got nowhere in his effort to persuade the Turks that in today's volatile world a long-term lease is just as good as sovereignty. The King commented that in any case the two governments were still negotiating on this point. The heartening fact was

---

[1] Source: Department of State, Greek Desk Files: Lot 69 D 15, Briefing Book Greece, 1966. Secret; Nodis. Drafted by Talbot. The meeting was held at the Palace at Tatoi.

that both governments seemed now to be showing a sense of urgency. That was new.

If the negotiators should reach an agreement, the King foresaw that the problem for Greece would be how to get a national decision and then, of course, how to deal with "the Priest." I commented that I had supposed that the Archbishop could be dealt with much more successfully in the context of a Greek-Turkish settlement than when Greece and Turkey were at odds. The King repeated that a Turkish base on Cyprus would be a very difficult thing to make Makarios swallow. On the Greek side, he said, the question was whether Papandreou could be brought along. In any case, the present government could not carry the burden of a settlement alone; the decision would have to be put up to all the parties. If each party were forced to make its stand known to the public, even the "Old Man" (Papandreou) might pause before rejecting it. However, this would not be an easy matter to get over and if worse came to worst Greece would at least show the Turks which elements in Greek political life had sabotaged the settlement.

The King asked whether I thought the British would go along with cession of Dhekelia. He had understood that in the end they would. I said this was also my impression; I had in fact been somewhat worried for fear the British financial crisis might cause a premature movement by London, such as an announcement of future withdrawals similar to that made on Aden, which would reduce the base area's bargaining importance in the Greek-Turk negotiations. The King said he would try to find an opportunity to caution some people in London about the delicacy of the present situation when he goes there next week.

"And just as soon as the Cyprus issue is settled," the King added with a twinkling eye, "I'll make an official visit to the United States." I said that he would be most welcome at that time, and that I agreed there were good reasons for not planning such a trip while the issue is unresolved.

The King had little to add to the comments he had made to me on October 27 about the Greek domestic situation.[2] He expressed himself as very well pleased at the way things had gone in Thessaloniki. The Prime Minister had also been pleased, he said, with his reception in Macedonian villages. Things seemed relatively quiet in the country and if in fact there should be a Cyprus settlement it ought to be possible to move to elections very quickly. I noted that people such as Markezinis felt that elections in the context of a Cyprus settlement would have a different and much healthier flavor than otherwise. The King agreed that in those

---

[2] A memorandum of Talbot's October 27 conversation with the King is ibid. The King gave his opinions on government press subsidies, Karamanlis, and the Aspida affair.

circumstances public attention could be turned away from the issue unfortunately now so prominent.

The King commented that he had been to the Greek Pentagon for a military briefing and that the projections for 1970–71 showed serious if not critical shortfalls in the Hellenic military proficiency. The projected military assistance program was just not adequate to meet the needs, though he assumed that once Vietnam was settled the prospects might improve. I replied that Vietnam is certainly an important factor in our overall defense posture, but that Congressional attitudes and growing Greek capabilities also have to be considered. On the first, I noted that for reasons good or bad the trend line of military aid, like that of economic aid, is going down. In addition, particular Congressional sensitivity has grown over the military assistance programs to countries seemingly on collision courses with their neighbors. The India–Pakistan war had, of course, stimulated adverse Congressional reactions, but the problems of military assistance to Arab countries and Israel and to Greece and Turkey had also been featured in last year's Congressional hearings. However, a Greek-Turkish rapprochement might ameliorate that situation. "Yes," the King responded, "that's another reason we must get a settlement with Turkey."

The King said he would be back in Greece on November 16.

---

244.   Telegram From the Embassy in Cyprus to the Department of State [1]

Nicosia, November 21, 1966, 1325Z.

705. 1. During meeting with Archbishop today he gave me same story he had given Hunt Nicosia 689[2] re his meeting with Stephanopoulos. Using most emphatic Greek, Makarios said there was absolutely no possibility now or in future that he would agree to establishment of Turkish base in Cyprus whether sovereign or leased. When I asked him whether he felt same way about possible NATO base in which Turks could participate as part of multilateral force along with Greeks and perhaps others, he said this was different matter and he did not object to con-

---

[1] Source: Department of State, Central Files, POL 27 CYP. Confidential; Limdis. Repeated to Ankara, Athens, and London.

[2] Telegram 689, November 18, reported a Makarios–Stephanopolous discussion of the issue of a Turkish base. (Ibid.)

cept. He expressed doubt, however, that Turks would accept such proposal if GOG made it in connection with dialogue. (According to Finnish Ambassador who called today Archbishop made same statement to General Martola during recent meeting.)

2. Makarios reiterated well-known view that by mid-December "we should know where we stand" with regard to dialogue and he asked me whether I had any news as to present status. I replied in negative suggesting that probable meeting between Toumbas and Caglayangil in Paris might have some results which would become known to him.

3. *Comment:* While we have had numerous influential Greek Cypriots express acceptance of NATO base concept, this is first time any of us in diplomatic corps or in UNFICYP have heard direct from Archbishop that he would not be opposed to a NATO base as part of an enosis solution.

Belcher

---

245.   Field Information Report[1]

[*document number not declassified*]   Athens, December 20, 1966.

COUNTRY

   Greece

SUBJECT

   Leadership of rightist Greek military conspiratorial group

DATE OF INFO

   13 December 1966

PLACE & DATE ACQ

   [*less than 1 line of source text not declassified*]/15 December 66

SOURCE

   [*1-1/2 lines of source text not declassified*] Information on this group has been fairly
   reliable.

---

[1] Source: Department of State, Athens Post Files: Lot 71 A 2420, POL 15 GOVT. Secret; No Foreign Dissem/Controlled Dissem.

1. The leadership of the rightist military conspiratorial group met secretly on 13 December 1966 at the home of one of its members, Lieutenant Colonel Ioannis Ladas. This leadership, now loosely referred to as the "Revolutionary Council," is composed of the following military officers—2 3

> A. Lieutenant Colonel Georgios Papadopoulos
> B. Lieutenant Colonel Ioannis Ladas
> C. Lieutenant Colonel Dimitrios Stamatelopoulos
> D. Lieutenant Colonel Dimitrios Ioannidis
> E. Lieutenant Colonel Ioannis Lekkas
> F. Lieutenant Colonel Mihail Roufogalis
> G. Lieutenant Colonel Ioannis Mexis
> H. One or two other offiers unknown to source, one of whom is either a Brigadier or Major General, but whose name source did not know.3

2. The group discussed the current political situation, but did not make a decision concerning the establishment of a dictatorship. The merits of selecting a single leader for the group was also discussed but it was finally decided to leave the direction of the group in the hands of the Council as a whole for the time being. The group's members also stated that they would continue their efforts to remove or isolate leftist and other unreliable persons from the Greek Army.

3. Roufogalis is suspected by some members of the group of reporting on its activities to the Deputy Chief of the Greek Central Intelligence Service /KYP/, Brigadier General Emmanouil Zacharakis, because the latter was responsible for the recent assignment of Roufogalis to a senior position within KYP.

---

[2] *Field Comment—[document number not declassified]* reported the continued concern over the political situation of the rightist Greek military conspiratorial group, which has been in existence since late 1963. One of the group's leaders, Lieutenant Colonel Georgios Papadopoulos, stated on 22 November that if the political situation continues to deteriorate at the present rate, drastic action, i.e., dictatorship, will be needed. [Footnote in the source text. The document is dated December 13. (Central Intelligence Agency, History Staff Files)]

[3] *Field Comment—*All of the persons named in para 1 were previously reported by the same source *[document number not declassified]*/7 March 1966/ as being members of the conspiratorial group. However, the leadership grouping was not referred to as a "Revolutionary Council" at that time. Concerning the unidentified General officer referred to in the same paragraph, source reported *[document number not declassified]*/October 1964/ that a Brigadier General Stamatios Skliros was a member of the group. [Footnote in the source text. The first document is printed as Document 225; the second has not been found.]

246. Telegram From the Embassy in Greece to the Department of State[1]

Athens, December 24, 1966, 1527Z.

3093. 1. Former Foreign Minister Toumbas[2] told me last evening he had returned from Paris strongly heartened by tone and apparent progress achieved in his extended discussions with Caglayangil. For first time he felt optimistic that Greek-Turkish agreement could be reached by careful negotiation. Believing that Turks anxious to settle and get rid of Cyprus issue, he had telephoned Caglayangil in Ankara when Stephanopoulos government fell to assure him Greece continues equally eager to settle issue.

2. As described by Toumbas, he and Caglayangil started Paris meeting with each side putting down in writing the basic principles underlying its position. As anticipated, this exercise resulted in reaffirmation of Turkish insistence on condominium or an independent Cyprus while Greece stood firmly for enosis. However, once the record had been made he and Caglayangil went on in oral discussions for another 10 hours in the course of which Caglayangil proved not only willing but apparently anxious to explore doctrine of enosis and what it would mean for Turk Cypriots and for Turkey. In their discussion of enosis, Toumbas discerned no issue that seemed likely to become a final sticking point except question of a Turkish base area on island. Caglayangil had insisted that Turkey would need to obtain sovereignty over Dhekelia base area. Toumbas had tried to persuade him that in practical terms a lease for a number of years would be just as valuable as sovereignty and also that Turkish needs could be equally well served by an arrangement that put Dhekelia under a NATO umbrella with Turkish, Greek, British and perhaps other participation. Although they did not reach accord on this point, Toumbas did not believe it had brought them to the breaking point. On contrary, he felt optimistic that with skillful negotiation agreement could be reached even on this question.

3. Toumbas said he had returned to Greece with the impression that Turks would definitely be prepared to make a deal on basis of enosis once base question resolved. He described mood of conversation as forthright and friendly throughout. On arrival in Athens he had reported this to Stephanopoulos and had predicted that agreement with Turkey was within reach provided that Makarios should not be brought into the

---

[1] Source: Department of State, Central Files, POL 27 CYP. Secret; Priority; Exdis. Repeated to Ankara, Nicosia, London, and Paris.

[2] Prime Minister Stephanopoulos resigned on December 21 following the withdrawal of ERE support.

picture until the Athens–Ankara settlement was final. He had also given press conference—though without divulging details of talks—to correct false impression in Greek press that Paris talks had ended in near collapse of dialogue.

4. Toumbas said he would make similar reports to new Prime Minister Paraskevopoulos and to the King. Except to them, he said, he would not reveal the contents of his talks to anyone so that secrecy of dialogue and its future prospects could be protected.

Talbot

---

247.   **Telegram From the Embassy in Greece to the Department of State**[1]

Athens, January 18, 1967, 1634Z.

3439. NATUS Info.

1. When I made initial call on Prime Minister Paraskevopoulos today I found Cyprus issue at top of his mind. He said GOG trying to persuade Makarios not to distribute Czech arms, and may call for U.S. assistance. He now preparing communication to go to Makarios within few days and would decide on next steps after getting Archbishop's reply.[2] I responded that we also much concerned, as we have made clear in Nicosia and New York where as his government knows, we have been pressing for effective UN action to defuse issue.

2. He reiterated his desire and intention to resume dialogue with Turks, if Turks willing, but in response to my question said he had not yet completed discussion with leaders of major parties on how far his government could go in dialogue. I reminded him that USG had not sponsored any particular plan as best solution for Cyprus, but had repeatedly made clear its strong belief that peace in Eastern Mediterranean can be

---

[1] Source: Department of State, Central Files, POL 27 CYP. Confidential. Repeated to Ankara, Nicosia, London, and Paris.

[2] On December 13, 1966, Secretary-General Thant reported that the Cypriot Government had confirmed the importation from Czechoslovakia of a quantity of arms to be distributed to the Cyprus Police. (U.N. Doc. S/7611/Add.1) Makarios agreed to delay issuing the arms for 2 months.

secured only when Greece and Turkey have settled their problems. As in Arab–Israel and India–Pakistan disputes, I said, time seems to be on no one's side. All would suffer greatly if continuing failure to achieve solution should some day result in an explosion. He insisted that he fully agrees, and that his strong ambition is to move vigorously in direction of settlement with Turkey while he is Prime Minister.

3.   Prime Minister said he thought time probably not ripe for Greek Crown Council to meet on Cyprus, but he would be examining this question also with party leaders.

Comment: Political realities here make it clear that Paraskevopoulos can move only as far with Turkey as Kanellopoulos and George Papandreou will permit. I have no fresh reading on Papandreou's private views, but Kanellopoulos told me later today that he favors continuation of dialogue by Paraskevopoulos government. He expressed himself as persuaded that settlement with Turkey can be obtained only if both major Greek parties agree on terms. For that reason he believes present period as propitious as any other for negotiations since both parties support Paraskevopoulos during current interim. At same time he showed himself still bearish on chances of getting agreement, since he sees enosis as only basis Greek parties can accept and professes to be unable to discover what sort of compensation to Turkey could be devised that would be both payable by Greeks and acceptable to Turks. Kanellopoulos favors early meeting of Crown Council to get briefing on dialogue, though presumably not to set guidelines for its continuation (Ankara's 3361).[3]

Talbot

---

[3] Telegram 3361 from Ankara, January 16, summarized press reports that the Turkish Government was unwilling to deal with a caretaker government in Greece without the endorsement of the Crown Council. (Ibid.)

248.   Telegram From the Department of State to the Embassy in Turkey[1]

Washington, January 20, 1967, 7:54 p.m.

122819. NATUS. State 118498.[2]

1. Your talk with GOG Amb Delivanis (Ankara 3420)[3] as well as Amb. Talbot's conversation with new GOG PriMin (Athens 3439)[4] has demonstrated GOG determination to resume dialogue and, if possible, reach agreement on Cyprus problem. We are impressed by persistence and sincerity with which GOG appears to be pursuing this objective, and consider GOG recognition that recent bellicose statements in GOT Parliament are designed for domestic consumption as further evidence their sincerity.

2. As we perceive current situation, existence of Paraskevopoulos Government offers opportunity for move forward on Cyprus issue. Main obstacle on Greek side would be potential opposition of George Papandreou and his CU party to any settlement which could be regarded as sacrificing Greek interests (and since any conceivable settlement will involve Greek concessions, such "sacrifices" will not be hard to identify). However, since Papandreou has reasonable expectation of returning to power in May elections, he is well aware of potentially destructive impact of Cyprus issue on his popularity and existence his government and thus has every reason to wish it out of way before he assumes office. As CU leader has said to Amb. Talbot in past, Cyprus crisis was his greatest worry during his 16 months in office, and preoccupation with this question prevented him from carrying out his domestic policy which was closest to his heart. If Paraskevopoulos Govt. were able to reach Cyprus settlement on terms representing something less than complete success for Greek side, Papandreou could presumably acquiesce, since he would not bear main responsibility for lack of total victory and would be freed of this potential burden when and if he took office. Further he would probably not begrudge current government credit for positive aspects of Cyprus settlement, since Paraskevopoulos and his ministers are "non-political" personalities and hence not his political rivals.

---

[1] Source: Department of State, Central Files, POL 27 CYP. Secret. Drafted by Owens, cleared in NEA, and approved by Handley. Repeated to Athens, Nicosia, London, and Paris.

[2] Telegram 118498 to Ankara, January 13, reported that Kohler reiterated to the Turkish Ambassador the U.S. belief that the Greek-Turkish dialogue held out the best hope for a Cyprus settlement and urged the Turks to press forward with discussions. (Ibid.)

[3] Telegram 3420 from Ankara, January 19, reported talks between Hart and Ambassador Delivanis on the Greek position in the Cyprus talks. (Ibid.)

[4] Document 247.

3. We recognize there is no way of preventing certain elements on Greek political scene, notably Andreas Papandreou forces and crypto-Communist EDA party, from attacking efforts to achieve Cyprus settlement on any realistic terms. Younger Papandreou has shown his willingness in past to take irresponsible line on this national issue when he considered it politically profitable. Nevertheless, we think that on balance it is possible that sufficient support from among party leaders—necessarily including G. Papandreou—could be mustered to approve a Cyprus settlement which would then be ratified by Crown Council. Powerful plus factor is determination of King Constantine to settle Cyprus problem as quickly as possible, and we would count on King to exert pressure on political leaders to this end.

4. In light of this assessment you should seek early opportunity to discuss with Caglayangil our analysis Greek situation, and our belief that Greeks mean business on resuming dialogue and working towards final settlement. While GOT skepticism about current GOG ability to reach and implement real agreement is understandable in view of past disappointments with various Greek governments, this should not deter GOT from seizing what appears to be opportunity to make significant progress on explosive Cyprus question. At very least it would halt deterioration in Greek-Turkish relations which has taken place since importation of Czech arms into island and fall of Stephanopoulos Government, and reestablish hot line between Athens and Ankara which would be most helpful in event of further crisis.[5]

Rusk

[5] In telegram 3476 from Ankara, Hart reported that he had transmitted the substance of the Department's instructions to Caglayangil. (Department of State, Central Files, POL 27 CYP)

---

249.   Telegram From the Department of State to the Embassy in Turkey[1]

Washington, January 25, 1967, 1:43 p.m.

124890. NATUS. Subj: Cyprus. Following is FYI Noforn subject to revision upon review summary uncleared Secretary–Turk Ambassador

[1] Source: Department of State, Central Files, POL 27 CYP. Confidential; Priority; Noforn. Drafted by Draper; cleared in IO, NEA and S/S; and approved by Rockwell. Repeated to USUN, Athens, Nicosia, London, and Paris.

Esenbel Memcon Jan. 24th re Cyprus.[2] Other subjects discussed reported septel.

1.   Turk Ambassador Esenbel said Cyprus and Czech arms problem was one of three major subjects on which Prime Minister Demirel had asked him convey GOT views to Secretary. GOT wanted Czech arms placed under continuous UN custody, considered "control" measures offered through U Thant–Makarios agreement unsatisfactory, did not trust Makarios, and lacked confidence in Greek capacities to deal with him. Turkish people, he added, were puzzled and frustrated in looking at Cyprus issue, and although they basically tended to trust U.S., had been disappointed in past U.S. attitudes. This was situation which leftists exploited.

2.   Demirel, he said, might be compelled carry out openly and unapologetically measures such as airdrop of weapons to Turk Cypriots if Czech arms distributed, although he hoped to avoid it. With Cyprus problem one never knew what would happen. Sooner a real solution was found, the better. Nevertheless, GOT entertained doubts caretaker GOG could negotiate seriously in resumed dialogue.

3.   Secretary said U.S. had not invented Cyprus problem, U.S. not guarantor power, yet it concerned us deeply. Requested Esenbel to convey personal, private message to Caglayangil urging that Turk-Greek dialogue be resumed. Secretary said earlier dialogue had revealed that both governments had responsible, serious attitude. Caglayangil should not despair of present GOG. Present attitude in Athens appeared good, he said, and he suggested such non-political government might possess advantages over successor government in seeking constructive solution in which Greek compromises would be necessary. Asked his personal comment be passed Caglayangil that little to lose and possibly something to gain in resumed dialogue.

4.   Secretary said he personally convinced GOG did not know of arms deal, and noted GOG actions to prevent distribution had been timely. Secretary viewed U Thant–Makarios arrangement as retreat for Makarios. Abuse of agreement would permit UN, U.S. and others to move in vigorously. We are working hard in UN and Nicosia to tighten agreement, but U Thant had accomplished something. In urging U.S. to exert still greater pressures, GOT was giving U.S. credit for more leverage than we posessed. We cannot deliver on Makarios, he concluded, any more than Turks can.

Rusk

---

[2] Not found.

250.   Telegram From the Embassy in Greece to the Department of State [1]

Athens, January 26, 1967, 1330Z.

3550. NATUS Info. Cyprus.

1. In luncheon conversation January 25 George Papandreou seemed to me to be in good spirits, more sure of himself and more durable over several hours conversation than I have seen him in past year. He gave the impression of a man who has gained electoral opportunity he had long sought, and who intends to control his party despite pressures from his son Andreas. His political comments being quoted by airgram.[2]

He also made following comments on Cyprus question.

2. He is not aware of substance of Athens–Ankara discussions. PriMin Paraskevopoulos is scheduled to brief him in next several days regarding dialogue so far. Presumably PriMin Papandreou and Kanellopoulos to work out a consensus with Paraskevopoulos on what the two parties will support with regard to continuation of dialogue before May elections.

3. Based on his reading of press reports, he does not believe dialogue has progressed at all or has accomplished anything beyond relieving tensions between Athens and Ankara while talks have continued. He suspects dialogue in this case has been pseudonym for two monologues. He would be pleased if Paraskevopoulos could report otherwise to him. He has no objection to continuation of dialogue if he, Kanellopoulos and Paraskevopoulos agree among themselves and with the Turks on meaning and intent of dialogue.

4. If his assumption regarding lack of progress on dialogue is correct, he does not see possibility for arriving at agreed solution for present and therefore believes it necessary to agree with Turks to suspend attempts to reach final settlement for some time until situation has become more relaxed.

5. His reasoning for inability to agree is as follows: (1) enosis: Turkey will not agree unless there are territorial compensations, either in Cyprus or in Greece (Thrace and islands) which Cypriot or Greek people are unable to accept even though a government might desire to make the concessions; (2) double enosis: this is equally unacceptable because of resistance of Greek Cypriots to territorial concession this implies; (3) independence: Turks insist on restricted independence of Zurich–Lon-

---

[1] Source: Department of State, Central Files, POL 27 CYP. Confidential; Priority. Repeated to Nicosia, Ankara, Paris, London, and USUN.

[2] Airgram A–400 from Athens, January 26. (Ibid., POL 14 GREECE)

don type which again is unacceptable to Greeks because it precludes opportunity for opting for union with Greece after 5, 10 or 20 years.

6. If this is case, Greeks and Turkey should work to agree not on final settlement but on measures to keep situation on island under control. In this context he sees need for Crown Council with participation of Makarios. His reasoning for inclusion Makarios is that otherwise Greeks will make decision and Makarios will assume role of judging whether decision is proper. Roles should be reversed. Makarios should participate in Crown Council discussions and his forecast of coming events, Cyprus initiatives, etc. should be made part of record, and discussed and whatever consensus possible between Greeks and Makarios recorded. This is only way, in Papandreou's view, to "control" Makarios initiatives. He kept returning to what he considers greatest problem of moment on Cyprus—state of enmity between Makarios and Grivas and constant suspicions of former that Grivas is about to pull coup against him. Because of this, Makarios considers every small act in terms of suspicion and insecurity for his personal position. He thus lashes out in various ways, all for wrong reason. If one could solve current "Grivas problem" one would have better chance of agreeing with Makarios on course of action precluding initiatives of faits accomplis which only provoke Turks.

Talbot

---

251. Memorandum of Conversation[1]

Athens, January 28, 1967.

SUBJECT

Conversation with Dimitrios Bitsios

PARTICIPANTS

Mr. Dimitrios Bitsios, Chief of the Royal Cabinet
Mr. John Maury, First Secretary

1. I had a one-hour private conversation with Dimitrios Bitsios following a dinner at the home of Mr. and Mrs. Angelos Kanellopoulos on January 28. I gained the impression that Bitsios deliberately sought me out to raise some of the matters noted below.

---

[1] Source: Department of State, Greek Desk Files: Lot 69 D 553, Andreas Papandreou. Confidential. Drafted by Maury on February 1.

2. He began by commenting on the recent activities of Andreas Papandreou and his friends, remarking particularly upon what he interpreted as their use of the Aspida trials to amplify their electoral campaign themes.[2] Bitsios went on to say that it now seemed perfectly clear that Andreas was serving the purposes of the Communists and the Soviets, and that it was thus hard to explain the apparent American reluctance to face this fact. He added that reluctance of the Embassy to become involved in internal political controversy between the "national" parties was fully understood and accepted; but that if the U.S. was serious about resisting Soviet aggrandizement and internal Communist subversion, it should certainly be serious about countering the activities of Andreas.

3. I responded that we may all have our suspicions about Andreas, but I was aware of no solid evidence of collaboration between him and the Soviets. I said that if such evidence existed we would be much interested in it. Bitsios admitted that there was no "direct" evidence, but he felt the "circumstantial" evidence was conclusive. He said he had no doubt that Andreas was receiving generous financial support from Moscow and from the KKE. When asked for details Bitsios said that money was probably being provided through Greek business firms who had lucrative contracts with the Soviets, and who, as a quid pro quo, were forced to contribute to Andreas' coffers. Bitsios went on to reiterate that everything that Andreas had said and done demonstrated his sympathy with Communist and Soviet aims and his hostility to constitutional government in Greece and to Western unity.

4. Bitsios then asked what I thought the U.S. reaction would be if the "situation" required resort to "extreme measures." I said if he were speaking of unconstitutional measures, I was confident that U.S. reaction would be extremely unfavorable. I pointed out that:

a. It is our general observation around the world that unconstitutional measures rarely solve knotty political problems, and once such a course is embarked upon it is difficult to turn back.

b. Whatever we may suspect of Andreas' motives and affiliations, there is still no proof of active Communist or Soviet connections.

c. However Andreas may look to us from the perspective of Athens, the fact remains that in the U.S. and perhaps in serveral other Western countries, he has influential admirers in intellectual, political and academic circles.

I added that there was the further question of whether a dictatorship could be effectively imposed in the face of the kind of strikes, violence

---

[2] An October 1, 1966, report on Aspida had charged Andreas Papandreou with involvement. On January 26, the court martial trying the officers accused of participating in Aspida went into secret session. The Center Union attacked this decision as a violation of the rights of the accused and as an effort by the Greek Government to cover the weakness of its case.

and general resistance measures with which Andreas might react. Bitsios said that if a dictatorshiop were decided upon, "Andreas would not be around." In response to my further question, Bitsios said that for the present the loyalty of the army could be relied upon to support a temporary dictatorship, but a few years hence "it might be too late."

5. I then asked Bitsios under what conditions the situation might call for "such drastic measures." He replied that action would have to be taken, if at all, before rather than after elections. (It was not clear whether he referred to the next election or some future election from which Andreas might appear likely to emerge with an absolute majority.)

6. I reiterated that whatever justification might be found here for an unconstitutional solution, I saw no way in which it could be justified in the eyes of the American public, press or political leaders. I said that if Andreas was the threat that many believed him to be, it was difficult to see why influential and responsible Greeks did not work more vigorously against him. Bitsios agreed, deploring the lack of leadership in ERE and among moderate elements in the Center.

7. I asked Bitsios' views about the possible return of former Prime Minister Karamanlis. He replied that he felt this was urgently needed "at the proper time" but was not clear on just when this would be. He did, however, go out of his way to emphasize that there is "absolutely no foundation" for rumors that Karamanlis' return would not be welcomed by the Palace. In response to Bitsios' question, I said the nationalist elements seemed much in need of leadership, vitality and unity; but whether Karamanlis' return now would help to fill these needs was a question he could answer better than I.

252.   Telegram From the Department of State to the Embassy in Cyprus[1]

Washington, February 1, 1967, 9:18 p.m.

129683. NATUS.

1. Following, based on uncleared memcon of Secretary's meeting with Cypriot Ambassador Rossides on February 2, is FYI Noforn and subject to revision upon review.[2]

---

[1] Source: Department of State, Central Files, POL 27 CYP. Confidential; Immediate. Drafted by Wood, cleared by UNP and NEA, and approved by Rockwell. Repeated to Ankara, Athens, USUN, London, and Paris.

[2] In telegram 129862, February 2, the Department informed the Embassy that this telegram was a full and complete report of the discussion and that no memorandum of conversation would be prepared (Ibid.)

2. Rossides, citing Caglayangil remarks of January 6 (Ankara's 3249)[3] and other evidence, made opening statement which he summed up by saying Turkey insists on an impossible solution (partition) by the use of force (invasion). Turkey should be discouraged from the use of force, in his opinion, by the US.

3. Secretary replied, in our view situation had been relatively calm on the Island and efforts were being made to reach a solution when everyone was surprised by the importation of arms. Those arms could only have one purpose: to use against the Turkish Cypriots. He inquired about arrangements with the Secretary General and said he had heard some arms had been distributed for training.

4. Rossides said arms not intended for use against Turk Cypriots "because we have sufficient arms." He insisted on new rationalization: arms for police who have paramilitary duties in defense of Island.

5. He claimed in discussions with SecGen latter had suggested small arms distributed at end February, but not heavy arms which to be kept locked and inspected. Makarios had replied we won't distribute arms of either type "for time being."

6. Secretary said defense Cyprus depends on good sense of Greece and Turkey, on the efforts of the UN and on the support of nations interested in peace such as the US. Arms imported by Cyprus would not have major effect in case of invasion. Fact they came in surreptitiously made very unfortunate impression, especially if police already had enough arms. He asked if it wise for Rossides to ask US to seek assurances from Turks without being able give US assurances on how arms would be used. He emphasized GOT concerned about attack on Turk Cypriots for whatever reason or pretext.

7. Rossides said there was no sign of GOC attack on Turk Cypriots.

8. Secretary inquired about SAM missiles. Suggested they were junk and should be left where they were.

9. Rossides speaking personally suggested "balance" whereby GOC would abandon missiles and import no arms in return for which no invasion from Turkey.

10. Secretary said GOC not having taken US into confidence originally now wanted US go to GOT not knowing what might be done on Cyprus tomorrow. Secretary asked if arms import had been discussed with GOG or UN Commander.

11. Rossides said not to his knowledge. This sovereign matter. Many previous arms imports not discussed.

---

[3] Telegram 3249 from Ankara, January 7, reported Caglayangil's statement to Parliament that Turkey retained its full right to military intervention in Cyprus. (Ibid.)

12. Wood raised SC Resolution of 4 March 64 (S/5575)[4] and gave document to Rossides who read aloud para 1: "... all member States ... to refrain from any action or threat of action likely to worsen the situation in the sovereign Republic of Cyprus ..."

13. Rossides suggested since US opposed use force it should oppose use force by GOT. Secretary replied US equally against use force against Turkish community.

14. Secretary emphasized that he had participated in discussions of Cyprus for some years. There had been many suggestions about what US should do. Henceforth he intended to ask each nation separately how it could contribute towards keeping the peace.

15. Rossides said GOC would leave arms alone for time being, perhaps for some time, but if necessity arose would have to use them sooner. GOC had right use arms.

16. Secretary said nations have many rights which they do not exercise in interest avoiding international danger.

17. Campbell (IO) later tried pin Rossides down on circumstances under which arms would be distributed. Rossides refused to say.

Rusk

---

[4] Reference is to Security Council Resolution 186; see *American Foreign Policy: Current Documents, 1964*, pp. 566–567.

---

253.   Telegram From the Embassy in Turkey to the Department of State[1]

Ankara, February 3, 1967, 0945Z.

3698. NATUS. Cyprus.

1. Summary: During meeting Feb 2 I raised Cyprus matter with FonMin Caglayangil, who said GOT would not accept fait accompli of Czech arms under Makarios control. GOT had taken very clear decision that if arms were not placed under UN custody, it would "by one means or another" send equal number of arms to Cyprus to restore balance. Caglayangil said GOT fully aware that armed clash on Cyprus might result. Also stated GOT would not resume dialogue with Greece until

---

[1] Source: Department of State, Central Files, POL 27 CYP. Secret; Priority. Repeated to Athens, London, Nicosia, Paris, Prague, USUN, Adana, Izmir, and Istanbul.

arms question settled to its satisfaction. (Elekdag and Turkmen also present.)

2. Details: I began by explaining that US takes problem of Czech arms very seriously and is concerned lest situation develop to a dangerous point. We are making constant and unremitting efforts at UN, Nicosia and Athens to obtain tightest possible arrangements to guard against distribution of Czech arms and felt we were making some progress. We have never altered our view that all parties including UNSYG should seek to obtain UN custody of arms but so far results have been negative. We have therefore concentrated on tightening specifics of UNSYG–Makarios arrangements. Mentioned particularly Ambassador Belcher's efforts with Makarios and that Secretary had talked with Rossides (without giving substance).[2]

3. In sober tones, Caglayangil said SC resolution of March 4, 1964 provides that no one should undertake action which would worsen situation on island. At moment negotiations were started to find peaceful solution to problem, Czechoslovakia permitted arms to be sent to Cyprus. Czechs should not have done this, nor should Makarios. But there was general belief that all faits accomplis of Makarios end successfully and other countries believe Turkey must eventually accept them. FonMin underscored that GOT cannot accept fait accompli. Concerning Czech arms, GOT decision very clear. If arms were not turned over to UN custody, GOT would send equal number of arms to island to restore balance. "We have taken necessary decisions and will implement them." FonMin continued that no one could expect nation of 32 million to accept faits accomplis endlessly. Repeated that if arms not placed under UN custody, Turkey would send arms by any means possible. This did not necessarily mean Turkey would "intervene" on Cyprus but Turkey would abide by its decision. (This statement not further explained.) Noted that UNSYG was responsible for implementation of SC resolution. Asked rhetorically why UNSYG had [not?] called Czechs to account for shipping arms. Asked why he did not now insist on US [UN?] custody. US had made representations to UNSYG and so had Turkey but UNSYG resisted démarches.

4. I said Secretary and our Missions at New York and Nicosia were all heavily engaged in tightening up arrangements for control over arms. I thought we were slowly gaining some ground. We would continue to work to prevent distribution of arms for indefinite period, however long that may be. Stressed that US not being half-hearted about this.

---

[2] See Document 252. Belcher's February 3 meeting with Makarios was apparently moved to February 4. Telegram 1109 from Nicosia, February 6, reported that at that meeting Makarios told Belcher he intended to begin the distribution of Czech arms on a phased basis beginning in late February. (Department of State, Central Files, POL 27 CYP)

5. FonMin replied that whatever the effectiveness of inspection and control measures, "nothing less than UN custody would satisfy Turkey." Effectiveness of control system would not satisfy Turkey either from point of view of measures taken or from point of view of its prestige. To my question whether this meant Turkey would not be satisfied even if control were completely effective, Turkmen replied (and FonMin confirmed after returning from phone call) that Turks could not understand how any system could be effective if Makarios retained custody and warehouse keys.

6. FonMin remarked that Turk Ambassador at Athens told by Greek Government that it too wanted UN custody of arms. FonMin noted Makarios does not have "effective power" on island but Grivas has it. Greek Government talks about UN custody but fails to use influence and pressure on Grivas to obtain effective control. If UNSYG would insist on UN custody, this would have effect on GOG attitude and policy. Furthermore, GOT convinced Makarios could respond to U Thant's pressures, if exerted, without losing face.

7. I said our information was that no arms had been generally distributed as yet. FonMin disagreed saying their information indicated one shipment had been unloaded and was now at Nicosia. This was shipment everyone focussed on controlling. But another shipment believed to have arrived week later and was moved elsewhere on island, and distribution of arms from this shipment had occurred. FonMin pointed out that in any case it was against nature of Makarios and pattern of his behavior to have arms and not to use them.

8. I said we would continue applying pressure on UNSYG and Makarios on basis that only by means of such continuous efforts would we move them little by little. Ambassador Talbot in Greece had also weighed in with new Greek leaders against arms distribution.

9. I noted Turk press reports about possible arms airdrop. Said Embassy Nicosia's clear assessment of effect such action was that Grivas would react immediately without waiting for Athens' instructions and that results of clash could spread unpredictably. Parenthetically, also noted MinInt Georkadjis admission that GOG not informed in advance about arrival of Czech arms.

10. Emphatically, Caglayangil said GOT had already accepted that if it dropped arms in Cyprus it would not be an "excursion" but "warfare". Raising his voice, he said no Greek political party would have courage to accept sacrifice in Greece for Cyprus. But government of technicians could do so. Instead GOG is not sincere and fails to hold Grivas under its orders. Greek politicians and Makarios are aggravating situation on island. Hellenic General Staff also government unto itself. In fact, four govts existed in Greece today: army, dynasty, GOG and opposition. Turkmen noted that several higher ranking Foreign Office members

(Christopoulos, Rendis, Sgourdeos among others) had requested leave at same time in protest against Makarios.

11. I urged continuation Turk-Greek dialogue and Turkmen interjected by asking "who speaks for Greek Govt." I asked if Turk Ambassador had not seen Paraskevopoulos. Reply was he had not. I said presumably he was point at which all parts of GOG could be pulled together. Furthermore, I convinced King was seriously and sincerely in favor of constructive dialogue. Turkmen wondered whether fall of Stephanopoulos government was not fait accompli directed against King. Caglayangil commented it had often been said that Turkey had made previous threats about landings on Cyprus. Perhaps people had been lulled into false security because landings did not take place. Turkey did not want to threaten or increase tension but situation was intolerable. If it was question of prestige for GOC and GOG, it was also question of prestige for GOT and Turk Cypriots were in danger.

12. To my question as to prospects of resuming dialogue, FonMin replied firmly "not before arms matter settled. It would be ridiculous." He asked if it was not ludicrous to talk with Greece about peaceful settlement while Makarios plans how to use arms under his custody. Besides, FonMin added, if Greece cannot use its influence effectively re UN custody of arms, how can Greeks be expected convince Makarios to accept results of dialogue.

13. I replied it was my understanding conditions in Cyprus were quiet at this time. I then stressed utility of dialogue as means of communication between two govts and opportunity for secret talks. I said if Makarios had intended to upset dialogue he would have succeeded if it were not now resumed. Had new GOG expressed willingness resume talks at point where they had been interrupted by fall of GOT? Caglayangil twice side-stepped answering this. He wondered with whom GOT could possibly talk and Turkmen observed that Greek Crown Council had not even been able to decide to meet. Both major party leaders had expressed reservations re GOG negotiating powers in dialogue. I said resumption of dialogue would help us all and especially at UN. But Caglayangil repeated that Turkey would not resume dialogue before Czech arms were placed under UN custody and again said would be "ridiculous" for it to do so. I ended by saying US working for peace in Cyprus and I hoped this would be kept in mind.

14. As rather an anti-climax and prompting by Turkmen, Caglayangil then mentioned completely unacceptable conditions GOC trying to impose on next Turk troop rotation (March). No conditions whatever would be accepted and rotation would proceed backed by all necessary force. He also referred to Turk-GOC impasse over exit permit for Coskun and asked that US Govt make démarche to GOC to obtain permit. I said I would transmit this request.

15. *Comment:* At no time did FonMin mention any deadline within which Czech arms would have to be under UN custody. On Feb 3 Fon-Min and Turkmen both travel to Italy for 3-day visit. Unlikely therefore that Turks would undertake any diplomatic (or military) action before FonMin returns. No sign of military crank-up is observable as of now. Nevertheless, Turks clearly losing patience with attitude present GOG and are convinced only hard line will move things forward. It possible they may plan to run arms in as secretly as possible but will use overt methods if necessary to deliver or in response to further GOC provocation, such as release Czech arms or interference with rotation Turk army contingent.[3]

Hart

---

[3] In telegram 131270, February 3, the Department of State instructed the Embassy to inform the Turkish Government of its concern over any efforts to supply arms to the Turkish Cypriots and to urge the Turks to make their concerns about arms supply known to the Greek Government. (Ibid.) Hart reported his démarche in telegram 3735 from Ankara, February 4. (Ibid.)

---

254. Telegram From the Embassy in Greece to the Department of State [1]

Athens, February 10, 1967, 1530Z.

3802. NATUS Info. Cyprus

1.   Discussions we have had in past few days with persons who participated in Crown Council on Cyprus held Feb 6 have disclosed that Makarios reassured Council on basis his personal knowledge that US would intervene at appropriate moment as mediator to settle problem, enforce negotiations, and could be counted on to prevent Turks from taking any military action. This disconcerting information comes from serveral sources, as detailed below.

2.   I met with ex-FonMin Toumbas Feb 8 at his request. He said he wishes brief me on Crown Council, which he considered of interest to USG. According Toumbas, Makarios took strenuous objection to resumption dialogue, which he considers futile endeavor. When Toumbas asked Makarios if he could offer alternative to dialogue in view

---

[1] Source: Department of State, Central Files, POL 27 CYP. Secret; Priority; Limdis. Repeated to Ankara, London, Nicosia, Paris, USUN, and Naples for USDOCOSouth.

deadlock reached with Cyprus issue, Archbishop replied he had good reason believe US would intervene as mediator at appropriate moment and start negotiations in which US, Greece, Turkey and Cyprus would participate, probably under aegis U Thant or some other well-known personality. Archbishop was vague and mysterious on this point, but he gave Council impression some American had whispered to him that that would be case. Toumbas stated he did not believe Archbishop was referring to American Ambassador Nicosia or any other senior officer of Embassy Nicosia, but he wondered whether an American possibly of junior rank might not have whispered something to that effect to Makarios in Nicosia. Toumbas asked me if I could confirm this. I replied in negative and assured him position my government had been made very clear to all parties concerned on number of occasions.

3.   Toumbas said he pointed out to Makarios with firmness that Greece's foreign policy could not be based on mere assumptions but on facts only. Archbishop reiterated his belief that US would intervene at appropriate time. Toumbas commented that one good result of Council was that all political leaders present agreed on policy to be followed. Furthermore, after hearing Makarios they became convinced he does not want enosis. I asked if it could be taken for granted that Makarios is now fully acquainted with all phases dialogue. Toumbas replied that full text synopsis (three pages) of minutes of dialogue, signed by Caglayangil and himself, had been read to Archbishop and that note to this effect had been made in minutes Crown Council.

4.   Toumbas continued that he is worried about maintenance peace in Mediterranean and involvement his country as well as repercussions on Greece's allies. He is not convinced Paraskevopoulos government is in position handle problem effectively. Though he considers Economu-Gouras intelligent and able diplomat, he feels Gouras will be at disadvantage when he meets with his Turkish colleague. He will not be able to speak as equal to equal. With responsible politician at head FonMin, situation would be different. Toumbas at this point gave example of how a politician can assume responsibility in critical situation. He said that at time he was discussing Czech arms question with Caglayangil and NATO he had not hesitated to send telegram to Greek Amb Nicosia instructing him to return to Athens if Makarios did not comply with obligations he had accepted in connection Czech arms. It had been only after Alexandrakis had shown this telegram to Makarios that latter realized how serious situation could become if he failed comply with prior agreement.

5.   I told Toumbas I shared his anxiety, particularly in view fact I have been hearing from Greek friends that they do not doubt USG will intervene in case Turkey should decide attack. I added that from such assumptions, miscalculations and frustration could very well result, pre-

cipitating an extremely serious situation. It would then be impossible to make the Greeks believe that the US had given prior warning that it would not be able play again the role which Greeks apparently expect of it. Toumbas said he fully agreed.

6. DCM elicited following from Progressive Party leader Markezinis, who also participated in Council. Principal results Council were: (a) unanimous agreement dialogue should continue; (b) agreement to proposition that enosis can only be achieved if some sort compensation (undetermined) is given Turkey in exchange (although not specifically agreed, consensus was that this compensation could not be territorial); and (c) agreement that GOG could offer NATO base with Turkish participation to be located on an existing British base, presumably Dhekelia. Makarios apparently pointed out that this would be decision of GOG after enosis. According Markezinis, debate was dominated largely by Makarios and himself. At one point Makarios implied that because of his close relations with certain American sources (unidentified) he is in position know that Turks are bluffing and that the Americans, already preoccupied with Vietnam, would never permit Turks to resort to another military action which would produce crisis in this part of world. Markezinis feels that, despite apparent unanimity achieved as result Crown Council, Makarios and perhaps others have already begun undermine situation. Belief exists in some Greek military quarters that the Americans will, in last analysis, prevent any resort to force by Turks.

7. Feb 9 I had long meeting with former PriMin Stephanopoulos, also a Council participant. He expressed anxiety because Makarios had come out strongly against resumption dialogue. In effort convince Archbishop Greek political leaders had used argument resumed dialogue would serve only to elucidate certain obscure points in dialogue carried on by previous government. Makarios' view was that talks with Turks are futile since he is determined not to offer anything in exchange for enosis, or for guarantee of continued independence, and therefore continuing dialogue would only cause Turks to believe Greeks and Cypriots are worried and afraid, with result Turks would be even more demanding. In support his negative attitude on dialogue Makarios displayed to Council paper in English, which bore no signature but which he alleged he had received from an American source. This paper gave him assurance that if Turks decided launch an attack they would be stopped by us. Under these circumstances Makarios took position that situation should be allowed remain more or less as is. Turks are confined to small pockets and are subject severe economic hemorrhage, whereas rest of Cyprus is prospering economically. At this point Stephanopoulos said he remarked it may well be so with Cyprus, which is receiving considerable aid from Greece and UK, but it is not case with Greece. Turning to George Papandreou and Kanellopoulos, Stephanopoulos made point that they,

who both hope govern Greece soon, [garble—must?] think not only of what helping Cyprus is now costing Greece but also of what sacrifices will be required in order fill in gaps in Greek economy. Stephanopoulos also reminded Council that General Tsolakas had said earlier to group that in case Turkish attack immediate defense requirements of country would amount to two hundred million dollars. Turning then to Makarios, Stephanopoulos remarked that in these circumstances should enosis be achieved a flourishing Cyprus would not receive much benefit from mother country, which would be in poverty. There can be no happiness in Cyprus if there is none in Greece.

8.   On question Czech arms Makarios told Council he did not anticipate violent reaction on part Turks. As evidence he cited call on him by American Ambassador Nicosia three days before arrival of arms via Yugoslavia. He knew their types and numbers. According Stephanopoulos' account, Makarios quoted Ambassador Belcher to effect that if arms were not distributed at once and if provocations by Greek Cypriots were avoided, Turks would not react strongly. I expressed strong doubt that any American official could have made such a statement. On contrary, I said, USG efforts have consistently been directed to getting Czech arms under effective UN supervision. Stephanopoulos continued that at this point in their exchange he reminded Archbishop that his government had first learned of Czech arms from Turks, who in turn may have received information from Americans. In any event, former PriMin continued, so far as he concerned Turks had protested very strongly and whole incident had left GOG exposed in eyes international public opinion. Turks were no longer content to threaten merely to supply their compatriots with additional arms but had even asked that Czech arms be reexported from Cyprus. Archbishop responded vaguely that he had probably forgotten to inform GOG about these arms when he had been in Athens in November 1966.

9.   In face Makarios' insistence that dialogue not be resumed, Stephanopoulos suggested to King during an interval in Council session (Paraskevopoulos was present) that it might be well to tell Makarios that if he did not agree with Greek political leaders on resumption dialogue it might become necessary alter instructions of Greek forces in Cyprus. King and Paraskevopoulos agreed to this tactic and it was decided PriMin would break news to Makarios. All three, however, first sought opinion of Kanellopoulos, who, on hearing proposal, threw up his hands and said, "Never, never, we can never say that to Makarios." Idea was at once abandoned. It was finally decided PriMin would issue statement to press that Crown Council had unanimously decided resume dialogue. Stephanopoulos commented that Makarios had very reluctantly gone along.

10. What had come out clearly in Council discussion, Stephanopoulos said, was that both Panpandreou and Kanellopoulos had committed themselves to accept no solution to Cyprus issue that was not acceptable to Makarios. This left Stephanopoulos deeply troubled. On this basis, what future could the dialogue have?

11. Stephanopoulos asked me if paper produced at Council by Makarios could be of American origin. I expressed strongest doubts. I added that I shared his anxiety, for situation as explosive as present one could easily get out of control. Dialogue had virtue that talking is better than doing nothing. I asked if idea of a NATO base had come up in Crown Council. Stephanopoulos said that whereas this idea had originally been proposed by Makarios, he is now clearly uninterested in this solution.

12. Stephanopoulos said he would be seeing King within 24 hours and asked if he might tell him what, in my opinion, USG would do in case Turkish attack. I replied that I doubt that at present anyone can answer that question. We would expect to weigh in with countries concerned in attempt to avert calamity to themselves and Alliance. Matter would also come up immediately in UNSC, which would obviously try to stop fighting. But it is difficult to determine if that could be accomplished in situation where a country has decided to resort to arms in defense its national interests. But it would be risky in extreme to pursue a policy based on assumption US or UN efforts would be successful. Experience has shown, I continued, how difficult it is for USG, UN or anybody else to stop two nations from bringing to a climax an issue which they have failed to solve at less heated levels. I cited India–Pakistan and Israel–Arab states as examples. As for Cyprus, should fighting ever break out a very grave factor which US and NATO would have to consider would be Soviet reactions. Would Soviet Union limit its responses to propaganda field or act in other ways as well? I hope I conveyed to Stephanopoulos the impression that we would always be interested and concerned but that Greece could never count on the Sixth Fleet's being at its beck and call if because of Makarios' intransigence it failed to negotiate seriously toward an understanding with Turkey.

Talbot

255.   Telegram From the Embassy in Greece to the Department of State[1]

Athens, February 11, 1967.

3805. After intensive review of all considerations that we can evaluate here, I have concurred in [*less than 1 line of source text not declassified*] recommendation that authority be sought for limited covert political action in connection with forthcoming Greek elections.

In contrast to earlier programs which focused on EDA, purpose would be to restrict dimensions of power base being built by Andreas Papandreou, by encouraging support for certain competitive elements [*less than 1 line of source text not declassified*]. Details of action program will be presented to Department [*less than 1 line of source text not declassified*].

I have come to this recommendation reluctantly. Basically, it is for Greeks who believe their country benefits from close ties with West including United States to generate enough political energy to oppose effectively those who would lead Greece down more dangerous trails. It would be unhealthy for even our best friends here to depend overly long on American crutch. However, at this moment following considerations are to my mind compelling:

1.   Though forthcoming Greek elections will ostensibly be struggle among pro-Western indigenous nationalist parties, important successes by Andreas could set off policy shifts away from traditional firm alliance with West.

To my knowledge younger Papandreou is not under Communist Party discipline. He has adopted and is vigorously promoting many EDA policies, however. Significance is that he gives respectable centrist cover to advancement of Communist policies. Moreover, his public commitment to these policies has become so complete that EDA and his personal supporters from left will have effective grip on him should he attain high office after elections. American interests in Greece would be vulnerable to substantial erosion in such an atmosphere.

2.   These elections come at crucial moment in Andreas' career. They constitute his first major bid for power, at moment when age and weakness of his father open way for succession. If Andreas is set back at this juncture, others with different orientation may improve their chances to take leadership of Center Union. Also, assuming May elections may be inconclusive and followed soon by second elections which (as in 1963/64) would strengthen and confirm political trends identified in

---

[1] Source: Department of State, Central Files, POL 15 GREECE. Secret; Roger Channel. There is no time of transmission on the source text; the telegram was received at 10:41 a.m. For additional information on U.S. views on the Greek political situation in early 1967, see Alexis Papakhelas, *The Rape of Greek Democracy: The American Factor, 1947–1967* [*O Viasmos Tis Ellenikis Demokratias: O Amerikanos Paragon, 1947–1967*], pp. 276–281.

May, setbacks in these elections could seriously undermine Andreas' base for takeover effort in second elections. Conversely, successes in May would strengthen Andreas' claim to succeed his father, his position within the party, and prospects of dominating government after second elections.

3. Upsurge of Andreas' strength is deepening dichotomy in Greek public life to degree his incipient success might set off rightist counterrevolutionary attempts with prospectively adverse consequences for Greece and for the Alliance. What we don't need in NATO now is a Greek military dictatorship.

4. Greek political interests opposing Andreas are unquestionably now in a majority but are also in disarray. They seem incapable or at least unprepared for job that should be theirs of cutting Andreas down to size.

5. At this moment Communist-directed EDA faces decision whether to seek strengthened Parliamentary position by fielding a full slate or to throw support of its center-left elements to Andreas. From our viewpoint, former course would be preferable even if it brought EDA more Parliamentary seats. Center Union and other parties would then find it essential to oppose Communist-line minority. Should Andreas gain strong position with EDA assistance, however, not only would Communist Party leverage on Andreas be strengthened but Center Union would become more ambivalent between EDA and national parties.

6. My recommendation presupposes that United States has interest in maintenance in power of a Greek Government, of whatever party, that is committed to continued close and broad relations with United States, and that Andreas is the most immediate and prospectively potent factor opposing this relationship. [1-1/2 lines of source text not declassified] U.S. policy needs also to demonstrate sympathetic American support for Greek progress and stability. This has become more difficult at stage when economic assistance has been phased out, military assistance is being phased down more rapidly than either government had foreseen, and unresolved Greek-Turkish differences put strains on Greek-American as well as on Turkish-American relations. Best long-term answer will be found in maintaining variety of active if inexpensive cooperative and contact programs during this transitional period when, rightly or wrongly, Greeks still have not got over sense of dependence on United States developed during past two decades and look to U.S. to push them into doing what they know they should. Suggestions for overt programs being forwarded separately.[2]

Talbot

---

[2] Not found.

256.   Telegram From the Embassy in Greece to the Department of State[1]

Athens, February 13, 1967, 1550Z.

3819. NATUS Info. From Ambassadors Belcher, Hart and Talbot.

1.   In meeting on USS *America* February 12 and 13 we have focussed on implications for US policy for Greek-Turkish dialogue and of contingent confrontations over Czech arms and Turkish troop rotation.

2.   On dialogue, we all believe Greeks and Turks should be pressed to resume talks urgently and to stretch hard for prompt agreement. Present juncture, while full of difficulties, also offers opportunities unlikely soon to recur. It is significant that Greek Crown Council has committed Greek political leaders, at least temporarily, to acceptance of Toumbas–Caglayangil protocol worked out in Paris in December and also to continuation of dialogue, and that Makarios for moment also committed to this course, however reluctantly. Stresses of Greek politics including Makarios machinations could soon unravel current unified position, resulting possibly in new opposition to dialogue in Greece and in Cyprus and in enhanced prospects of trouble over Czech arms, rotation of troops or other areas. In short, failure to achieve settlement in very near future could make life more difficult for all concerned.

3.   On parameters of possible settlement, Greek leaks to Embassy Athens suggest that protocol may include considerations of possible arrangements for protection of Turk Cypriots from mistreatment by majority community. Comments Toumbas has made imply he and Caglayangil may also have laid base for some status of island which would bring it under Greek sovereignty though with certain semi-autonomous fiscal, economic, administrative and political institutions. At any rate, we believe resolution of differences over status of Turk Cypriots and over some sort of commonwealth scheme should be manageable.

4.   If our sketchy information valid, Paris protocol seems also to point way toward "NATO base" as means of giving Turkey some locus standi on island to compensate for island's basic attachment to Greece. If Turkey willing to accept concept of a NATO base—whatever that is—in present British sovereign base area of Dhekelia, we believe modalities should be negotiable. They could include continued British sovereignty, transfer of present Greek and Turkish contingents into base area and possible addition of other NATO facilities or national units. In this solution, presumably rest of Cyprus would be demilitarized along lines of Dodecanese.

---

[1] Source: Department of State, Central Files, POL 27 CYP. Secret; Limdis. Repeated to Ankara, Nicosia, London, and Paris.

5. Whether Turkey would be prepared to move quickly toward settlement within these parameters is unclear to us. If so, we estimate present Greek Government with support of Palace and acquiescence of major political leaders could negotiate effectively, subject to ratification of any agreement by Crown Council and then by Parliament. If Turkey should stand on insistence that Turkish sovereign base should be established on Cyprus, then we estimate that present Greek Government would have neither authority nor support in Greece or in Cyprus to proceed with negotiations. Effective Greek-Turkish contact would then presumably be broken off at least until after next Greek elections. Since Greek political climate at that time could be less conducive to solutions based on NATO interests (see recent Andreas Papandreou speeches), we would anticipate that arena of action could shift to more direct Turkey–Cyprus confrontations. Indeed, even with progress in dialogue and almost certainly in absence of progress, coming weeks may bring serious Turkey–Cyrpus difficulties.

6. Following difficulties, now with us, are assessed as follows:

A. Czech arms: Turkey will continue to press SYG and others for UN custody but will probably settle for SYG understanding if GOC position as expressed by Rossides is made reasonably tight. However, in event distribution significant number light arms GOT would be forced to take some action to answer domestic Turk criticism that it is accepting another Makarios fait accompli. It would probably call for session of UNSC to establish that distribution contravenes 4 March 1964 SC resolution. Presumably would get some support. Minor arms infiltration might later be undertaken by Turks. This might not amount to much as it would be operationally difficult but could help to bolster GOT's internal position vis-à-vis TGS and Parliament. Only as later or last resort would GOT attempt arms drop since, as Caglayangil has said, this would mean war on island. (Rationale: GOT aware that issuance of small arms is not sufficient to justify act of war against GOC in eyes world opinion. Having devoted much diplomatic effort over past year to winning friends, GOT is therefore likely, if GOC does not push distribution soon or rapidly, to use all diplomatic and UN channels to find redress. If these fail GOT will have to take some action for domestic reasons. A graduated series of military steps intended to galvanize favorable action in UN seems most likely. We can only speculate what these steps might be.)

B. Rotation: This is potentially most serious problem in immediate future. GOT has made clear it is not accepting GOC conditions set forth aide-mémoire.[2] Furthermore in letter to Turk contingent commander, Chief of Staff has told him if rotation opposed Turkey "will use force."

---

[2] Transmitted as an attachment to airgram A–137 from Nicosia, February 6. (Ibid.)

If no agreement reached through UNFICYP good offices by March 31 we have assumed unarmed troops on Turk transport would not immediately attempt disembark at Famagusta but rather link up with force which usually alerted by GOT in Mersin/Iskenderun area in conjunction periodic rotations. GOT would probably then make immediate appeal to UNSC to arrange for rotation as provided by treaty and if this not accomplished, would "shoot her way in."

7.   Decision to inject Turkish military into either Czech arms or rotation issue would probably mean some sort of graduated action—demonstration flights, selected target bombings, followed if ultimately necessary by air drop of men and supplies and "full scale" invasion. Air drop would require full scale follow-up since we convinced GOC and Grivas would order attack.

8.   We note that troop rotation scheduled for day before EOKA day observance and four days before Sunay due in Washington. We assume therefore that failure of parties to reach accommodation would create high tensions and that Turkish reaction might be delayed briefly so Sunay could put problem personally to USG.

9.   In order defuse rotation issue believe we should push UN and SYG to find acceptable compromise but should not ourselves as yet get into act directly with either party. However, at some point fairly soon seems advisable approach Makarios making clear to him his views on US intervention as expressed Crown Council utterly wrong (and contrary to what Embassy Nicosia has been saying all along). Belcher would point out that US [garble] would be warned in time to try prevent start of hostilities even though we would as in past make every effort through diplomatic channels.

10. In view above, Ambassadors Hart and Talbot propose subject to Department's approval to seek opportunities in next few days to explore with leading members of host governments prospects of rapidly resuming dialogue. We would informally encourage them to proceed urgently. Without interjecting ourselves into substance of dialogue, we also propose to touch lightly on such topics as possible commonwealth idea. Ambassador Belcher will talk with Makarios and selected Cabinet Ministers re Czech arms and rotation in context of US policy on intervention and at same time will attempt impress upon them fact that present is new opportunity to make progress toward solution.

Talbot

257.   Telegram From the Embassy in Greece to the Department of State [1]

Athens, February 16, 1967, 1430Z.

3874. Cyprus. NATUS Info. A good deal of familiar ground was covered in seven hour discussion of Cyprus today with Prime Minister Paraskevopoulos.

He also opened up some new terrain, however, particularly on resumption of dialogue and on base question.

When Prime Minister said he ready resume dialogue immediately and couldn't understand why Turks delaying, I replied we believe major misunderstanding must have developed between Greeks and Turks.

It is our impression Turks consider they have not received GOG assurances of willingness to resume dialogue at point where interrupted by fall of Stephanopoulos government. Paraskevopoulos replied flatly that he had told GOT and had announced to Greek Parliament his willingness to do just that. I asked if this meant GOG prepared to talk on basis of full faith and credence in Toumbas–Caglayangil discussions. He replied that since no agreement had been reached it was a question of continuing from point at which it had broken off and that GOG is ready and eager to pick up dialogue even today from point at which it was interrupted in December. He reminded me that Toumbas and Caglayangil had agreed to meet again soon. That is exactly what his government wishes to do.

Paraskevopoulos showed some reluctance to resume dialogue with Turkish Ambassador Athens [2] (or, presumably, Greek Ambassador Ankara). He suggested Bonn as site where Greek and Turkish Ambassadors are both able men and enjoy good relations. He would be ready to instruct his Ambassador to Bonn immediately, he said, if this agreeable to Turks.

After suggesting that GOG would want to clear up apparent misunderstanding with GOT I asked if it would be helpful for me to inform my colleague in Ankara of Paraskevopoulos government's position on resuming dialogue so that if appropriate Ambassador Hart might advise GOT of our understanding of Greek position. PriMin immediately agreed, and asked our help in getting Turks to respond quickly.

These comments were made in context of exchange between us on value and importance of reactivating dialogue promptly. Paraskevopou-

---

[1] Source: Department of State, Central Files, POL 27 CYP. Secret; Limdis. Repeated to Ankara, Nicosia, London, and Paris.

[2] In telegram 3869, February 17, Talbot reported on Tuluy's perplexity about Greek intentions. Talbot stated that he had assured Tuluy that, based on talks with Paraskevopoulos, Greece wanted to continue the dialogue. (Ibid.)

los asserted that his government is well positioned for serious discussions with Turks since Crown Council has given it all-party mandate to proceed.

On substance of dialogue, Paraskevopoulos said that at point Toumbas dropped out Turkey had proposed to Greece that a Turkish military base be established on Cyprus as quid pro quo for enosis. (I did not understand clearly, nor perhaps does Paraskevopoulos, whether Turks had actually agreed that a base would compensate them for straight enosis, or for something less jarring to their ears, such as Greek-Cyprus federation or commonwealth, or whether enosis bridge had not been crossed.) Turks had not indicated extent or nature of base, but were awaiting Greek reply on acceptability of concept. Obviously, Prime Minister said, reply could only be given when dialogue reactivated.

After lengthy review of dangers embedded in Cyprus issue, Paraskevopoulos then made pitch United States support of NATO base idea. He argued that a Turkish military base could guarantee only permanency of tensions that have already so gravely damaged life on island. In contrast, NATO base with Turkish presence along with Greek, British, American and possibly other national components would give all possible protection to security of southern Turkey. It would also help normalize living conditions in rest of island. Prime Minister expressed hope that logic of NATO base would commend itself to Turks. He also expressed certainty that with settlement of base issue other problems such as guarantees for minority community on island could be solved. If base question left unresolved, he said, explosive potentials on island could damage not only Greek and Turk interests but those of Western Alliance since Soviets obviously eager to turn Cyprus into Mediterranean Cuba.

I responded that we have indeed [been] long aware of explosive possibilities both on island and between Greece and Turkey. As Prime Minister knows, United States is not supporting any particular plan for solution of Cyprus issue. We believe parties must reach solution by agreement, and I could say confidently that U.S. would support any agreed solution. We have supported dialogue so strongly, I said, because only hope lies in their direct and common search for accommodation with which each can live. Moreover, as demonstrated more than once during Toumbas period, commitment to dialogue of high officials in Athens and Ankara enables them to communicate directly when dangers emerge on such related subjects as might arise this spring over Czech arms, fortification programs, or the next Turkish rotation. Commenting that some people seem to believe Eastern Mediterranean could live without solving this problem because at last moment United States would somehow prevent explosions, I said that situation obviously not that simplistic. Indeed, I was under instructions to remind Prime Minister that United States had made no undertaking to intervene and that it would be quite dangerous to make any assumption regarding future U.S. position in this regard. He said he understood.

Describing Crown Council meeting to me, Prime Minister said Greek political leaders had started out in considerable disagreement. After eight hours of hard discussion, they had come to virtually full agreement. Makarios strongly opposed political leaders' views, but came around after two more hours so Prime Minister could accurately announce unanimity of views. He took obvious pride in noting that unanimity had been achieved this time even though it has been quite rare not only in course of Cyprus issue but in Greek political history generally. I commented that this another reason to proceed with all speed toward agreement with Turkey, lest unusual unanimity of support for his course be eroded with passage of time. He heartily concurred, and again asked that we help to get the Turks agreement to immediate resumption of dialogue.

Comment:

I believe Ambassador Hart could appropriately mention to GOT that in view apparent confusion we had checked with Greek PriMin, who had confirmed GOG readiness to resume dialogue at point it broke off.[3]

With each high-level conversation here I am becoming more convinced that Greece is preparing to call upon U.S. to persuade Turkey to accept formula consisting basically of a NATO base in Dhekelia and protection of minorities according to best international practices as compensation for substance of enosis. In any case, I avoided probing further on content of understanding between Greece and Turkey in order not to encourage request for further U.S. involvement at this stage.[4]

Talbot

---

[3] In telegram 3977 from Ankara, February 18, Hart reported that he had passed on Talbot's report to the Turkish Government. (Ibid.)

[4] In telegram 3893 from Athens, February 17, Talbot further reported that the Prime Minister also stated that Makarios had confirmed that he would not distribute the Czech arms and added that armored cars were among the Czech weapons. (Ibid.)

258.   Telegram From the Department of State to the Embassy in Greece[1]

Washington, March 3, 1967, 8:27 p.m.

148939. NATUS. Joint State/Defense cable. Subject: Considerations of NATO Presence on Cyprus. Ref: State 97095.[2]

1. Prior to suspension in December Greek-Turkish dialogue on Cyprus included consideration of base on Cyprus as compensation to Turkey for enosis. Reftel explored possibility of a "NATO base" on Cyprus in very general terms as part of a Cyprus solution. Responses at that time indicated that:

a. While a NATO peacekeeping force on Cyprus was not considered advisable, a NATO presence such as a headquarters, command, airfield, port or support base (possibly for AMF) might provide a Turkish and/or multinational military presence on the Island that could satisfy the Turks in the interests of reaching a solution to the problem.

b. The major problems to overcome are the possible opposition of Makarios, the Turkish stand against enosis and the requirement for guarantee of the rights of Turkish Cypriots.

c. The Turks (according to Ambassador Hart) might be willing to accept enosis provided the right formula could be found. This formula must include Turkish troops on the Island under a Turkish-dominated joint or NATO base at Dhekelia and guarantee of Turkish Cypriot rights by the UN.

d. Other NATO nations might go along with such an idea if it becomes a critical factor in a solution. Subsequently, the situation has been altered: (1) Recently the Greek Crown Council (including Makarios) agreed to accept NATO base concept after enosis, and (2) the problems of troop rotations, fortifications, and Czech arms have increased tensions. In order to provide some ideas for further consideration, a closer look at the possibility of utilizing NATO in a Cyprus solution appears necessary, even though we have no assurance this will satisfy the Turks who were "offered more" during 1964 Acheson effort.

2. General concepts in para 3 below might be developed in an attempt to accommodate Turkish-Greek requirements. Their consider-

---

[1] Source: Department of State, Central Files, POL 27 CYP. Secret; Noforn; Priority; Exdis. Drafted by Smith; cleared by NEA, EUR/RPM, OSD, JCS, and L; and approved by Rockwell. Also sent to Ankara, Nicosia, London, Paris, USCINCEUR, and Naples for USDOCOSouth and repeated to Rome and USUN.

[2] Telegram 97095, December 6, requested the views of concerned posts regarding the possibility of creating a NATO base area on Cyprus with a Turkish contingent attached to it. (Ibid., DEF 15 CYP)

ation along with response to questions in para 4 is requested. These ideas are entirely exploratory, are aimed at providing plausible NATO role for continued presence of Turkish forces on Cyprus, and represent an expansion of the ideas contained reftel. The US would not initiate or advocate them but would propose them discreetly to the Greeks and/or Turks for their use or sponsorship if NATO base idea proves feasible. They do not represent a US position. These concepts presuppose enosis, adequate guarantees of the rights of Turkish Cypriots, demilitarization of the Island less the SBA bases and the retention of a UN presence on Cyprus as observers. Additionally, all parties involved must accept and have valid assurance of fulfillment of all conditions in advance of execution.

3. The following are listed as possible concepts for utilizing NATO forces on Cyprus at the Dhekelia Base:

a. A Greek-Turkish joint command with the possible addition of UK forces as an extension of LANDSOUTHEAST with a mission of planning and training ground forces. The forces assigned would be from those now on Cyprus.

b. A headquarters and/or exercise base for units of the AMF or other NATO force. The same Greek, Turkish and UK forces as in 3a, above, would be based at Dhekelia as a permanent nucleus force with the addition of limited numbers or representatives of nations providing forces to the AMF as a part of the staff.

4. The questions listed are issues that should be considered and answered in connection with the above concepts:

a. What is the probable reaction of host nations to these ideas at this time?

b. Should sovereignty of Dhekelia be retained by UK?

c. Who should the commander and vice commander of such a force be and should these positions be rotated among the nations involved?

d. Should there be an honorary base commanding officer (Turkish) in addition to the force commander to enlarge the number of prestige positions?

e. Should the size of the Greek, Turkish and UK forces be limited in size to possibly a battalion each?

f. Should the Greeks and Turks contribute to the cost of such a concept particularly in view each spends over $10 million annually on Cyprus?

g. Should other NATO nations contribute towards financing, and to what degree?

h. Would participation by the Turks, by having a military force on Cyprus and a degree of command, satisfy their requirements?

6. Your comments on these ideas and questions are requested by March 10. This material should be closely held. NATO base concept

should not be discussed with SYG Brosio at this time. However we realize necessity discuss base concept with Brosio at appropriate stage.[3]

Rusk

---

[3] In telegram 4344 from Ankara, March 10, the Embassy commented that Turkey remained very guarded about its positions, and no Turkish official had ever suggested a willingness to accept enosis in exchange for participation in a NATO base on Cyprus. (Ibid.)

---

259.   Minutes of Meeting of the 303 Committee[1]

Washington, March 8, 1967.

[Here follows discussion of unrelated topics.]

4. *Covert Political Action re May 1967 Greek National Elections.*

a. Mr. Rostow and Ambassador Kohler indicated they had definite reservations but were anxious to hear the arguments. Mr. Vance had earlier registered reservations.

b. [*1 line of source text not declassified*] the major arguments for a U.S. role in the elections were contained in Ambassador Talbot's cable (Athens 3805) dated 11 February 1967.[2]

c. [*1-1/2 lines of source text not declassified*] whereas the U.S. participation could not guarantee the winner it certainly would have an impact. [*less than 1 line of source text not declassified*] Andreas Papandreou had been observed for a sufficient period to realistically place him in a camp definitely hostile to U.S. interests. Andreas Papandreou was driving very hard while other candidates were, at best, lethargic.

d. Mr. Rostow wondered if we weren't approaching this type of 1967 election on a momentum started in the fifties. We had assets, techniques and money, and we could perform almost by rote. Was the threat that great? Ambassador Kohler felt that the papers had not made the election issues entirely clear. Was it not possible that we were attributing more potential to Andreas than he deserved?

---

[1] Source: Johnson Library, National Security File, Intelligence File, Greek Coup, 1967. Secret; Eyes Only.

[2] Document 255.

e. At this point, Mr. Rostow was called to a meeting with the Secretaries of State and Defense, and it was agreed to resume discussion of the proposal on Monday, 13 March 1967, at 1600.[3]

---

[3] See Document 261.

---

260.   Intelligence Information Cable[1]

[*document number not declassified*]   Athens, March 9, 1967.

COUNTRY

Greece

DOI

15 February through 8 March 1967

SUBJECT

Increased Activity of Group Advocating Dictatorship

ACQ

[*less than 1 line of source text not declassified*] (8 March 1967) Field [*document number not declassified*]

SOURCE

[*1-1/2 lines of source text not declassified*] source has provided generally reliable information on Greek military affairs for several years. He obtained this information from Spandidakis and Mitsakos.

1. Summary: On 6 March 1967, Chief of the Greek Army General Staff (GAGS) Lieutenant General Grigorios Spandidakis stated that within the past ten days various key officers have been on unofficial alert status, the first step in implementing "Ierax (Hawk) Number Two." Spandidakis also said that since 15 February, 30 to 35 trusted middle-grade officers have been transferred to the Athens Military Command. Major General (Retired) Petros Mitsakos stated that Air Vice-Marshal Georgios Antonakos has ordered Chief of Air Force Security Lieutenant

---

[1] Source: Central Intelligence Agency, DDI Files, Intelligence Information Cables. Secret; No Foreign Dissem/Controlled Dissem/No Dissem Abroad.

Colonel Ilias Tsasakos to keep in daily contact with key Air Force officers, all of whom have been briefed on the general objectives of "Ierax Number Two" and their specific duties in connection with it.

2. Spandidakis stated on 6 March 1967 that within the past ten days various key officers have been on unofficial alert status, the first step in implementing "Ierax (Hawk) Number Two". *(Field comment:* According to Spandidakis, "Ierax Number Two" is a plan for the military take-over of Greece contingent upon the occurrence of another political crisis. In the event such a crisis occurs, the plan outlines the role of key military units which would be involved in the take-over. See [*doucment number not declassified*] (TDCSDB–315/03301–66)[2] for additional details on this contingency plan). This unofficial alert status involves maintaining daily contact with Spandidakis and a "fairly high state of readiness for action in the units involved." Spandidakis stated that the above is due to Palace uneasiness over the present situation. Key officers on unofficial alert status are GAGS G–2 Brigadier General Pavourgias Pangorgias, Commander of the 9th Division, Major General Sotirios Liarkkos, Commander of the 8th Division, Brigadier General Stamatios Syliros, and GAGS G–3 Chief Lieutenant Colonel Georgios Papadopoulos. Lesser officers involved are director of Spandidakis' office Lieutenant Colonel Ioannis Lazaris, and Chief G–2 Athens Military Command Captain Konstantinos Kotinis.

3. Spandidakis also stated that since 15 February, 30 to 35 trusted middle-grade officers have been transferred to the Athens Military Command. Kotinis was in this category.

4. Mitsakos stated on 7 March that Antonakos, acting under the orders of King Constantine's personal secretary, Major Mihail Arnaoutis [*document number not declassified*] (TDCSDB–315/03301–66) ordered Tsasakos to keep in daily contact with key Air Force security officers, all of whom have been briefed on the general objectives of "Ierax Number Two" and their specific duties in connection with it. (*Source comment:* The above action amounts to a low-key alert.)

5. Field dissem State Army Navy Air EUCOM CINCSOUTH (personal) CINCUSNAVEUR CINCMEAFSA USAREUR USAFE (also sent Paris, London, Rome).

---

[2] Not found.

261.   Memorandum for the Record[1]

Washington, March 13, 1967.

SUBJECT

Minutes of the Meeting of the 303 Committee, 13 March 1967

PRESENT

Mr. Rostow, Ambassador Kohler, and Admiral Taylor
Mr. Vance was absent in hospital
[1 *line of source text not declassified*]

Covert Political Action re May 1967 Greek National Elections.

a. The meeting interrupted on 8 March 1967 (see minutes dated 10 March 1967)[2] continued with the members asking [*less than 1 line of source text not declassified*] a series of detailed questions regarding the Greek elections. Mr. Vance, still unable to attend, advised by telephone that he was opposed to the proposal unless there was an overwhelming conviction on the part of the other principals that the United States must participate.

b. [*less than 1 line of source text not declassified*] the strong appeal of Andreas Papandreou to discontented youth. [*less than 1 line of source text not declassified*] there was a heavy trend toward urbanization of the youth drifting away from rural areas.

c. When Mr. Rostow suggested that there were other examples of leftists settling down after an election, he mentioned Betancourt in Latin America.

d. [*less than 1 line of source text not declassified*] one of the principal factors making Andreas Papandreou a distinct threat was his percolating animosity to the United States which was unlikely to change. [1 *line of source text not declassified*] if it looked likely that Andreas was moving closer to victory, the monarchy and the military could well suspend the constitution and take over. The military was estimated as being loyal to the king.

e. Ambassador Kohler stated that there were divided counsels in State and that he should talk to the Secretary.

f. Mr. Rostow summed up both sides of the case: the well stated recommendation of the country team versus the risks of disclosure at a ticklish time and the consequences of not participating at this time.

---

[1] Source: Johnson Library, National Security File, Intelligence File, Greek Coup, 1967. Secret; Eyes Only. Drafted by Jessup on March 16. Copies were sent to Kohler, Vance, and Helms.

[2] Document 259.

g. [4-1/2 lines of source text not declassified]

h. The principals decided that Ambassador Kohler would take the matter up with Secretary Rusk, and if the latter felt the proposal was vital, Mr. Rostow would discuss the matter with higher authority.

i. On 14 March, Ambassador Kohler reported by memorandum that he had discussed the project with the Secretary and that "He comes down negative. In the Greek case, he believes the possible political gain is outweighed by the security risks. He commented that if the dual-national Greek-Americans are concerned about the prospects and if $200–$300,000 will make the difference, they should have no trouble raising that sum themselves without involving the United States Government."

Peter Jessup

---

262.   **Memorandum of Conversation**[1]

Athens, March 17, 1967.

PARTICIPANTS

George Papandreou, Leader of EK Party
The Honorable Phillips Talbot, U.S. Ambassador to Greece
H. Daniel Brewster, Country Director, Greece, State Department
John G. Day, Political Officer, Embassy

We called on EK leader George Papandreou today at his Kastri home and found him mentally alert and in seemingly good health.

Papandreou began by apologizing for his son's, Andreas, recent speech before the Foreign Press Association (A–463 of March 7).[2] Unfortunately, he said, "Andreas tries to be a Kennedy and a Fulbright" in the wrong setting. Papandreou called our attention to his brief statement after Andreas' speech in which he repeated that the foreign policy of the EK remains unchanged. He added that, specfically, he does not share

---

[1] Source: Department of State, Central Files, POL 12–6 GREECE. Confidential. Drafted by Day and approved by Bracken. Transmitted as enclosure 1 to airgram A–491 from Athens, March 22.

[2] Not printed. (Ibid., POL 6 GREECE)

Andreas' view concerning American interference in the internal affairs of Greece. In the past, particularly during the period of the late Ambassador Peurifoy, there was open intervention by the U.S., but in recent times, especially since the arrival of Ambassador Talbot, there has been no such interference. (Ambassador Labouisse once mentioned to him that CIA in Greece was not completely under his control). The EK leader added that he intended, during a UPI press interview this Sunday, to deny the existence of any U.S. intervention in the recent past. [Q: "Were there interventions by U.S. in the internal policy of Greece? A: Unfortunately there was—in the past. And in such an unprovoked way that they caused the disappointment of our People. During the last period however, as far as I know at least, the United States Embassy made no intervention. And it never encouraged deviation".][3] (This quotation appeared in the UPI interview published March 19.)

Turning to the current political situation, Papandreou candidly admitted that he knew beforehand of the plan to topple the Stephanopoulos Government and to form the present transitional government. In fact, Paraskevopoulos as Prime Minister was his choice. Papandreou also admitted that he had promised the King not only to support Paraskevopoulos but also to back the simple proportional electoral system. Even though this system is contrary to the interests of the EK and is opposed by many EK deputies, he agreed to vote for it to promote the return of political "normality".

He predicted that all EK deputies will vote for it out of respect for him as leader of the party. He also commented that ERE leader Kanellopoulos had acted as a real statesman during the past several months.

Papandreou expressed grave concern over the current activities of the "junta". In response to the Ambassador's question, he named Garoufalias, Pipinellis, and (retired) General Dovas as members of the junta. It also includes other retired generals and deputies who fear elections. The "president" of the junta, Papandreou added, is probably Queen Frederika.

The EK leader expressed fear that the junta might try to upset the plan for elections and to create the conditions for a dictatorship by arresting Andreas for the Aspida affair just as soon as Parliament is dissolved and he no longer is protected by his immunity as a deputy. If he were arrested, Papandreou continued, there would be no elections. There would surely be demonstrations and protests, and Andreas would become "a hero and a martyr". In fact, the elder Papandreou added, Andreas would like nothing better than to be arrested.

The best way to avoid this danger and to ensure the holding of elections would be the granting of an amnesty for the Aspida affair. This is

---

[3] Brackets in the source text.

exactly what he told Bitsios, the King's political advisor, during a conversation at Kastri yesterday. He also said to Bitsios that the EK could not publicly ask for an amnesty because "we are the accused"; the King, however, should take the "initiative" in granting it. Papandreou admitted to Bitsios that some EK politicians and deputies would point to an amnesty by the King as proof that the Palace was guilty on July 15, 1965, and that Aspida was merely a conspiracy against the EK. Though he could not prevent the press from expressing its views, Papandreou stated that he would publicly say that the granting of an amnesty was an act to promote political normality and that he would use his influence to try to persuade the EK papers to follow the same line.

Papandreou also warned Bitsios that a dictatorship would be a disaster not only for Greece but also for the monarchy. King Constantine would soon find that he was no longer master of the situation and that, on the contrary, he was a captive of the dictator, just as the King became a captive of John Metaxas in the 1930's.

According to Papandreou, the King should take a long-range view of developments and should be less concerned over the words of Andreas. He should realize that "it is deeds, not words that count". Papandreou asserted that, despite Andreas' line, he, George Papandreou, is the leader of the party. Evidence of this was the vote for the Paraskevopoulos Government when Andreas disagreed, but eventually accepted the decision of his father to support the new government. In a revealing remark, the elder Papandreou told us that he would have expelled Andreas from the party for his general behavior if Andreas were not his son.

Returning to the King, Papandreou argued that the young monarch should not be worried about the elections because he was given assurances that there would be no "popular front" between EDA and the EK and that he would not raise a regime question. (Papandreou commented that he strongly believes that the institution of the monarchy is necessary in Greece.) Even if Andreas should break away from the EK and take 30, 40, or even 50 deputies with him and cooperate with 20 or 30 EDA deputies, he would still only have less than a third of Parliament and he would not be able to change Greece's foreign policy. Therefore, according to the EK leader, the King should not be so worried over Andreas' attacks.

Finally, referring once more to the junta, Papandreou expressed the hope that the Ambassador would use his influence in favor of an amnesty for Aspida. Papandreou obviously had in mind the Ambassador's speaking to the King.

(Athen's 42494[4] reported Papandreou's comments on Cyprus.)

---

[4] Dated March 18. (Department of State, Central Files, POL 27 CYP)

263.   **Telegram From the Department of State to the Embassy in Greece**[1]

Washington, March 21, 1967, 4:51 p.m.

159364. NATUS Info. Ref: (A) Ankara's 4448; (b) Athens' 4249, para 4; (C) EKN 1398; (D) Nicosia's 1338.[2]

1.   Now that dialogue may be resumed (ref A), GOG and GOT have moved one more step and achieved useful precedent: GOT willing continue dialogue with a new GOG. It is no longer limited to relations of two men, Toumbas and Caglayangil.

2.   Next problem would appear to be an agenda. Dept concerned that after rehashing NATO base concept, GOT may be tempted pull out on grounds there nothing further discuss. In view imminence Greek elections a Cyprus solution now seems unlikely. Alternatively GOG and GOT might be discreetly encouraged again open question reducing size Greek and, later, Turk military forces on Island:

   a.   In view Grivas' intransigent behavior and such incidents as Bozkurt removal and Kophinou[3] Dept no longer persuaded Greek or Turk forces are a stabilizing influence.
   b.   Stabilizing force should be UNFICYP.
   c.   Since solution not now in sight we face problem that supporting and contributing nations likely during coming months take further actions reduce UNFICYP. It would only be possible reduce UNFICYP and maintain its viability if size Greek and Turkish forces on Island reduced.
   d.   Reduction forces, no matter how gradual, would give all concerned some sense of progress which has been lacking in Cyprus.
   e.   Would save GOG and GOT money neither can afford.
   f.   Would facilitate UN rep. Tafall's efforts on Cyprus to achieve greater freedom of movement for population. (See below)[4]
   g.   Atmosphere may be ripe. George Papandreou has raised subject (ref B) in Athens and position Turk military elements appears to have been weakened as result Kuneralp's findings during his visit (ref C). If

---

[1] Source: Department of State, Central Files, POL 27 CYP. Secret. Drafted by Wood and McCaskill, cleared by NEA and UNP, and approved by Rockwell. Also sent to Ankara and Nicosia and repeated to London, Paris, and USUN.

[2] Telegram 4448 from Ankara, March 15, reported Turkish confirmation that the dialogue with Greece would resume. (Ibid.) Telegram 4249 from Athens, March 18, reported George Papandreou's views on Cyprus. (Ibid.) EKN 1398 has not been found. Telegram 1338 from Nicosia reported Makarios' readiness to reduce military pressure on the Turkish Cypriots. (Ibid.)

[3] Reference is to armed clashes between Makarios' forces and Turkish Cypriot military formations.

[4] After Bernardes' departure from Cyprus on January 5, Pier P. Spinelli acted as the Special Representative of the Secretary-General in Cyprus until February 20, when Bibiano F. Osorio-Tafall took up the function. Secretary-General Thant announced Osorio-Tafall's appointment on January 26.

Papandreou comes into power after elections, his Government could continue dialogue on this subject.

3. On basis above Dept requests views Ambassadors Talbot and Hart on possibility they suggest as appropriate occasions may arise that GOG and GOT may wish consider how agreement on gradual troop reduction might be worked out. Realize such negotiations likely be long and difficult, but they would keep dialogue alive and would be in good cause.

4. Meanwhile request Ambassador Belcher continue lend his support as appropriate to Tafall's efforts secure greater freedom circulation by reducing check points and fortifications. We are encouraged by Archbishop's current views (ref D). We believe this is local and complex issue better handled on spot by UN and GOG who understand issues than it would be by GOG and GOT, although they certainly could lend useful, general support.

5. Negotiations on Cyprus to this end would:

a. Reduce tensions on Island which have increased in past decade.
b. Complement any progress that GOG and GOT might make on troop removal.
c. Constitute step toward eventual talks between Greek and Turk Cypriots under UN auspices.
d. Eventually hamper Grivas' braggadocio.

6. In general since time again out of joint for Cyprus solution would seem wise if GOG and GOT could discuss troop reduction, and issue for which they have primary responsibility, while UNFICYP, GOC and eventually Turkish community deal with local issue of freedom of movement which would not detract from importance dialogue and might complement it.

7. Addressees' views welcome.[5]

Katzenbach

---

[5] In telegram 1388 from Nicosia, March 27, the Embassy suggested that troop reductions include both Greek and Turkish Cypriot forces as well as Greek and Turkish troops and that Grivas' removal would facilitate a reduction of tensions. (Ibid.) In telegram 4565 from Ankara, March 23, the Embassy reported that Turkey might react favorably to proposed troop reduction talks. (Ibid.) In telegram 4340 from Athens, March 24, Talbot analyzed the difficulties Greece would face in a troop reduction negotiation and its likely reluctance to enter into talks. (Ibid.)

264. Telegram From the Embassy in Greece to the Department of State[1]

Athens, March 24, 1967, 1315Z.

4335. NATUS.

1. During past few days there has been flurry of rumors in press and elsewhere regarding fall of Paraskevopoulos government and postponement of elections. These stories have now been partly discredited, however, by (A) statements of both George Papandreou and Kanellopoulos reaffirming their support of Paraskevopoulos and reexpressing their belief in need for return of political normality through elections in May; (B) Parliament's approval in principle of simple proportional electoral bill; and (C) statement by government day before yesterday saying it "is certain of its stability which is guaranteed by confidence of two large parties supporting it". Most leading personalities now seem either to want early elections or to be reluctantly reconciled to seeing them held.

2. There is still, however, an active rightist group which is reportedly seeking to upset Paraskevopoulos and to postpone elections through formation of government, even if this government could not obtain vote of confidence in Parliament. Reports vary, but persons usually mentioned as favoring this extreme course are: former ERE PriMin Pipinellis, *Electheros Kosmos* publisher Kostantopoulos, former DefMin Garoufalias, former Public Security Minister Apostolakos, former ERE Deputy Farmakis and Queen Mother Frederika who, according to George Papandreou, is leader of "junta". There have been conflicting reports whether Major Arnaoutis, King's private secretary, is also an adherent of this group. CAS has also reported that Lt. General Spandidakis, Chief of Greek Army General Staff, has recently acted to prepare for implementation of Ierax (Hawk) 2, an alleged plan for military control of Greece contingent upon occurrence of another political crisis.

3. In our view, a plan probably does exist for certain actions by military in event of a dictatorship, but there is no evidence that army leadership is actually plotting to create conditions leading to deviation from Constitution. On contrary, we hold to opinion that military would not seek independently to impose a dictatorship: but it would support a dictatorship if King decided in favor of such a regime. (Also see USDOA message 0345 March 67.)[2]

4. Though it is not clear how well integrated civilian side of "junta" is or how determined it is to upset path to elections, its members all seem

---

[1] Source: Department of State, Central Files, POL 15 GREECE. Secret; Priority. Repeated to Ankara, Nicosia, Paris, Thessaloniki, USDOCOSouth for Freshman, and USCINCEUR for POLAD.
[2] Not found.

to be united, however, by fear that elections in May, particularly under Paraskevopoulos government, would result in EK's obtaining at least plurality of votes and in Andreas Papandreou's being the dominant voice in new government. There are several ways by which they could try to topple present government and create situation leading to postponement of elections. One, they could create some incident, e.g. arrest of Andreas Papandreou following dissolution of Parliament, that might produce all kinds of pyrotechnics providing pretext for postponing elections. Similar result might be achieved if government acted flagrantly in favor of ERE during electoral campaign, e.g. actions by gendarmerie and TEA (Home Guard) forces. Another possibility would be to try to persuade Paraskevopoulos himself to resign on pretext his government was under irreconcilable ERE and EK pressures on how it should behave during campaign.

5.   In certain quarters, Progressive Party leader Markezinis has been mentioned as likely choice for mandate if government fell. Theory would be for Markezinis to appear in Parliament for vote of confidence for specified period, perhaps six months, to conclude Aspida affair, seek settlement of Cyprus problem, make certain reforms in economic field, etc. Supporters of Markezinis believe he could obtain vote of confidence, even though he does not enjoy wide popularity, because Deputies would realize choice was either Markezinis or dictatorial regime. Markezinis might be able to gain support of EK or part of it for a short postponement of elections, if he could assure George Papandreou that an amnesty of Aspida affair would be forthcoming.

6.   Key and still uncertain element in current picture, however, is attitude of King. We know that King was initially pleased by smooth transition from Stephanopoulos to Paraskevopoulos and by prospect of extricating himself, through elections, from vulnerable position in which he found himself after July 1965. Recently, however, the King has reportedly been dismayed by George Papandreou's failure to control his son and King has begun to have second thoughts on wisdom of holding elections in May and of permitting EK, and, particularly, Andreas Papandreou to emerge as leading political force. King has undoubtedly been under strong pressure from rightists, including possibly his mother, to alter his stand towards present transitional government and elections. On other hand, he has also been warned by George Papandreou, through Palace political advisor, Bitsios, that any deviation from Constitution could be catastrophic both for country and for monarchy (A–491).[3]

7.   In our view, any effort by Palace and by Right to postpone elections could play right into hands of Andreas Papandreou and Left, unless it were carefully engineered to avoid appearance of direct

---

[3] See footnote 1, Document 262.

involvement by King. This, however, would be extremely difficult to accomplish. Even more dangerous would be establishment of a dictatorship—a view that we have expressed to many Greek personalities, including King, over past several months. On balance, we are inclined to believe that our assessment of political situation as reflected in A–432[4] is still essentially valid and that King, despite pressures by Right, wishes to avoid extremism. CAS and DATT concur in this message.

Talbot

---

[4] Dated February 11. (Department of State, Central Files, POL 2 GREECE)

---

265.   Letter From the Ambassador to Greece (Talbot) to the Country Director for Greece (Brewster)[1]

Athens, March 30, 1967.

Dear Dan:

As the attached memo of conversation shows,[2] the King last night confirmed our suspicion that Greece is entering a new political stage. He represented himself as deadly serious in concluding that he cannot afford to risk the destruction of free Greece by permitting Andreas Papandreou to come to power. From that conclusion, if he should hold to it, there naturally would flow decisions ranging on the extreme. At least for now the King's thinking has been narrowed to the question of whether he can stop Andreas by constitutional (or relatively constitutional) means or will be forced outside the Constitution into an extraparliamentary government.

Perhaps optimistically, I do not regard the dialogue on his major premise as yet closed. Last night, with the Paraskevopoulos Government aparently falling round his head and with the near future even murkier than it had looked 24 hours earlier, the King seemed little interested in any general discussion of the proposition. Indeed, it is hard for us to

---

[1] Source: Washington National Records Center, RG 84, Athens Post Files: Lot 75 A 02, Greek Desk–Bracken–Brewster. Secret; Exdis.

[2] Not found.

argue that Greece under the Andreas that has emerged in the past year would be either a liberal democracy or firmly oriented toward the West. The signs increasingly point in another direction.

You will note that I raised enough questions to keep the door open for a later presentation of views of American Andreas-watchers. We in the Embassy will, and perhaps you in Washington can, get to work immediately on a commentary on the King's major premise.

On his minor premise, i.e., that, however reluctantly, he might need to move to an extra-parliamentary government, I used a similar approach. My questions in this area were directed only toward prag-matic aspects: what kind and strength of opposition would be generated and how repressive would such a regime have to become? You'll recall that in earlier talks I had emphasized to the King our generally repug-nant attitude toward dictatorships, citing our foot-dragging in recogniz-ing the new Argentine regime. He is sufficiently aware of the general American posture so that I saw little point in going over the same ground last evening.

What we need to do now is to prepare a response which can be pre-sented to the King as the view of the United States Government. I am sure that, like us, you will ponder seriously the King's request for assurance of United States support of moves he may feel forced to take. Nor will it be easy to frame a reply, since our record in dealing with extra-parlia-mentary regimes covers the broadest possible spectrum of cases, ranging from the Communist coups d'etat of the 1940's through Pakistan in 1958 and Turkey in 1960 to the rash of authoritarian takeovers spreading across Africa in the 1960's—not to mention Latin America. We shall of course work urgently on a draft for consideration by Washington. Natu-rally, the essential decisions must be made at your end.

As to the question of persuading George Papandreou to give Andreas a one-way ticket out of Greece, it is such a gloriously simple idea that I could wish it were not wholly impractical. If you have any thoughts that would moderate our sense that we can't do anything about this one, please do let me know right away.

A word about timing: in this fast-breaking situation crucial deci-sions could be made almost any night in the next dozen. As of this moment (when we don't yet know the outcome of the EK–ERE con-frontation over immunities), however, it still seems more likely that the King will try to stick to the parliamentary track as long as he can until he is finally persuaded that if elections are held the Andreas forces are headed for an EK majority. Today I don't know whether the critical moment will come in mid-May or a further interim period will carry Greece through the summer and into the autumn.

In any case, until the signals become clearer I believe the King's request must be treated with the utmost urgency. Unless we learn over the weekend that a more extended time-frame will be available to us, I would hope that you can get instructions to me early in the coming week. Knowing what a demand this puts upon you, I pondered sending all this by telegram. Since pouch delivery should be very prompt, however, I concluded you would be in a better position to proceed by having the whole story at once.

As I say to my colleagues here: Well, chaps, we're in it now!

With best wishes,

Yours sincerely,

Phillips Talbot[3]

---

[3] Printed from a copy that bears this typed signataure.

---

266.   Memorandum of Conversation[1]

Washington, April 3, 1967, 5 p.m.

SUBJECT

> NATO and the East-West Détente; The Middle East; Cyprus; U.S.-Turkish Relations; and Viet-Nam

PARTICIPANTS

> Cevdet Sunay, President of Turkey[2]
> Ihsan Sabri Caglayangil, Foreign Minister of Turkey
>
> Lyndon B. Johnson, President of the United States
> Dean Rusk, Secretary of State of the United States

The two presidents met at 5:00 PM at the White House for the first of two substantive meetings during President Sunay's state visit. After an initial exchange of courtesies, the Turkish President discussed at length, from prepared notes, Turkey's position on NATO and the East-West détente; the Middle East; Cyprus; U.S.-Turkish relations; and Viet-Nam.

---

[1] Source: Johnson Library, National Security File, Country File, Turkey, Memoranda, Vol. 1. Secret. Drafted by Howison. The meeting was held at the White House.

[2] Sunay visited Washington April 3–5. For texts of statements regarding the visit, see *Public Papers of the Presidents of the United States: Lyndon B. Johnson, 1967,* Book I, pp. 412–414, 418–421, and 425–426.

Sunay's Presentation

NATO—Turkey seeks national security in NATO. No sacrifice would be too great to raise Turkey's military strength to the required level. NATO was an important force for world peace. Sunay was concerned about the effects of France's attitude. Political rather than military devices would do most to strengthen NATO. Equality among member nations was one need.

Turkey's position at this juncture was critical. Turks "appreciated and respected" United States commitments to Turkey, but the entire Southeastern flank would collapse if Turkey could not hold out until help arrived. Turkey's forces were being kept strong. Soviet aims and aspirations remained unchanged. If NATO collapsed, countries bordering the Soviet Union could not resist.

Lately some East European countries had begun to pursue their separate national interests. In the atmosphere of détente, Turkish relations with Romania, Bulgaria, and the Soviet Union had begun to improve, but Turkey had no illusions. The basic guiding principle in Turkish foreign policy remained "fulfillment of commitments to allies."

The Middle East—Conflicts among the Arabs were matters of concern. The Arab-Israeli question remained unsolved, and now there was the question of Aden. As a result of the Soviet factor, this situation was becoming more delicate.

North Africa was not a bright spot. In December, Bourguiba had told him that Tunisia sought United States assistance in view of Soviet military assistance to Algeria and Egypt.

India-Pakistan disputes produced many difficulties. Pakistan was very disappointed not to have American aid. The Pakistanis had right on their side in the Kashmir dispute; they should be helped to settle it, to prevent their turning to Red China. India would then be able to extend Western influence to Burma and elslewhere. If Iran could strengthen its armed forces, peace and security in that area would prevail.

Cyprus—Good Greek-Turkish relations, within the alliance to which both belonged, were vital for regional security. The Cyprus question must be settled peacefully before these relations are damaged further. The Turks had been patient, but Greece still wanted to annex the island. Cyprus was now a question of national pride in Greece. In Sunay's view, solution would only be possible through mutual concessions. The gap between the communities on the island was deep; it would be difficult for them to co-exist peacefully. He suggested (a) in Turkish majority areas, Turks should be granted municipal autonomy, (b) Cyprus should be demilitarized, and (c) Turkish troops should be permitted to stay there as a guarantee of Turkish interests.

The Turks had recognized sincerity and understanding on the Greek side during the recent dialogue, but no agreement had been reached. The

Greeks could only talk about annexation. The Greeks maintained that independence meant increasing Communist influence and decreasing mainland influence.

In the Turkish view, these arguments did not justify enosis. Greek forces have de facto control on the island today, but a solution to the problem should be possible with the help of the allies. He suggested a Turkish-Greek condominium putting an end to Cypriot independence.

Sunay reflected concern about political instability in Greece and urged that Czech arms on the island be at the "disposal" of the UN. He implied that Turkey would be willing to resume the dialogue with the Greeks when the Greek political situation permitted. The sufferings of the Turkish community on the island were a result of Makarios' "Byzantine tactics." Makarios must be made to see reason.

Perhaps the U.S. could help bring this about. "Turkey expects the utmost help from the United States."

U.S.-Turkish Relations—There was real identity of interests and policies between the two countries. Their fortunes were inseparable. Turks would never forget 1947 and the Truman Doctrine. Sentiment had entered the equation, and had been an emotional shock to the Turks when the U.S. disappointed them on the Cyprus issue. Turkey had rushed to help in Korea, and had expected the U.S. to reciprocate. Our "intervention" had provoked strong criticism and charges that Turkey's foreign policy had produced a loss of freedom of action.

The present Turkish regime wished to eliminate these wrong views. The enemies of our friendship were merely a noisy minority. We hoped his visit would aid in producing a consensus in support of Turkish-American cooperation.

Viet-Nam—President Sunay recognized the wisdom of President Johnson's efforts in Viet-Nam for the preservation of world peace. Our policy was similar to our Eastern European policy of 1947. Sunay thought there could be no purely military solution to the problem. Under these circumstances, the Turks followed closely our efforts toward a peaceful settlement.

President Johnson's Response

President Johnson thanked President Sunay for an enjoyable and constructive presentation. He hoped that when the Viet-Nam conflict is finally settled, people will think we did the right thing as they now think we did the right thing in 1947 by aiding Turkey under the Truman Doctrine. Fighting aggression anywhere is costly in dollars and lives, but worth it.

He was aware of strong Turkish feelings about Cyprus and mentioned the United States initiative to avert a Turkish invasion, to which the Turks had reacted. We were in full sympathy with the Turkish community in Cyprus and would help to see their security guaranteed. He was encouraged by Sunay's stress on the need for a peaceful solution. Just as he regretted that peace in Viet-Nam was so elusive, he regretted that no Cyprus solution had been found.

The President noted that the topics discussed by Sunay would be discussed one by one between Mr. Rusk and Mr. Caglayangil on April 4.[3]

The President believed the benefits derived from some $5 billion in aid to Turkey since 1947 had been mutual. This aid was a reflection of the American people's attitudes toward Turkey. While there might be some anti-American feelings in Turkey, there are strong pro-Turkish feelings here.

---

[3] The Department of State reported to Ankara on these talks in telegram 168638, April 4. (Department of State, Central Files, POL 27 CYP)

---

267.   Telegram From the Department of State to the Embassy in Greece[1]

Washington, April 3, 1967, 8:14 p.m.

167844. For Ambassador from Rockwell.

1. Your two letters received over weekend[2] and given very careful study. You are to be highly commended for manner in which you handled first session with King. We hope that there will be continuing dialogue. Gratified in meanwhile to see that King has offered mandate to Canellopoulos thus providing time for political parties themselves to work their way out of impasse. We concur with points you propose to make orally (ref March 31 letter). We recommend that points one, two and four be made strongly and in whatever detail you consider advisable at time.

2. We would be inclined to warn more strongly against possible constitutional deviation. Depth of Greek feeling against such a move should be more carefully weighed by King. Andreas as "martyr" with Lambrakis machine standing fully behind him would be very formidable opponent. As matter of principle, of course, U.S. would be opposed to extra-parliamentary move. You should stress point that U.S. reaction to

---

[1] Source: Department of State, Central Files, POL 15 GREECE. Secret; Immediate; Exdis. Drafted by Brewster and Owens and approved by Rockwell.
[2] Talbot's March 30 letter is Document 265. The letter of March 31 has not been found.

such move cannot be determined in advance but would depend on circumstances at time.

3. Finally, strong statements along lines paras 6 and 7 most desirable. We are glad that lines of communication are open to you and hope that King will feel free to communicate directly with you whenever he wishes to discuss his problems.

4. Letter follows.

Rusk

---

268.   Telegram From the Embassy in Greece to the Department of State[1]

Athens, April 8, 1967, 2340Z.

4573. 1. In our view, decision to give mandate and right to dissolve Parliament to Kanellopoulos is most important move young King has made since he ascended to throne three years ago.[2] It may prove to be his worst. Admittedly, King's choices were limited once he had decided that he could not risk a Center Union majority victory in the elections and once Paraskevopoulos Govt was upset.[3] Whether ERE's unyielding stand on admendment of electoral law was part of a pre-arranged plan by Palace and Right to overthrow Paraskevopoulous and to provide ground for formation of an ERE Govt, as alleged by Andreas Papandreou and *Eleftheria*, is highly debatable. In any case, if Paraskevopoulos Govt had not fallen over amendment issue, we believe another way would probably have soon been found by hard-core ERE and Palace to bring it down. ERE press and Kanellopoulos have argued that King had

---

[1] Source: Department of State, Athens Post Files: Lot 72 A 5030, POL 15. Secret; Priority. Drafted by Talbot and Day. The date-time-group was obtained from the copy in Department of State, Central Files, POL 15 GREECE.

[2] The King asked Kanellopoulos on April 3 to form a government to take the country through elections. In telegram 4569 from Athens, April 7, Talbot reported that he had pressed the new Prime Minister for an indication of what action he would take in the event of a Papandreou victory in the May elections. Talbot noted that his "prodding" led Kanellopoulos to declare that "the Greek nation would never be delivered to the communists or to Andreas Papandreou. It would be saved for real democracy." (Ibid.)

[3] Following a disagreement over an amendment to the proposed electoral law designed to extend the parliamentary immunity of Andreas Papandreou, the Center Union announced its decision to withdraw its support of the Paraskevopoulos government, which resigned on March 30.

no alternative but to grant him mandate when George Papandreou refused invitation to meeting to discuss ecumenical-type govt. King knew, of course, that Papandreou was opposed to idea of an ecumenical govt, and even if meeting had been held, chances were party leaders could not agree.

2.   By granting mandate to Kanellopoulos, King has openly committed himself to ERE which probably has support of between 35% to 40% of population. This is obviously narrow ground on which to base his future. (King has undoubtedly hoped that FDK and Progressives would vote for Kanellopoulos for sake of electoral bill and that their support would give to government appearance of broader base.) No only has King provoked EDA and EK, both moderates and Andreas Papandreou supporters, but he also has deeply embittered Progressive and FDK deputies who feel they have been left in lurch after they came to King's rescue in July 1965. They have now unhappy choice of either voting for ERE Govt or going to elections under an electoral system which is to their disadvantage. Stephanopoulos has bitterly remarked to us that FDK and probably Tsirimokos and Progressives will abstain if Kanellopoulos Govt conducts elections.

3.   For time being, George Papandreou seems to be following cautious policy, despite his strong criticism of King and Kanellopoulos and his warning of a "revolution." We have impression that both Papandreous are frightened by present situation, Andreas because of possibility of his arrest and imprisonment and George because of chance of postponement of elections and constitutional deviation. EK leader still seems to believe that, notwithstanding ERE Govt, his party will gain at least plurality in elections. Therefore, he has shown no interest in Mitsotakis' proposal that EK, FDK, etc. announce that they will abstain from elections. Panpandreou might change his mind, however, if he became convinced that elections would be rigged to make ERE first party. His attitude would undoubtedly be different if Andreas was arrested prior to elections.

4.   Hope of ERE has undoubtedly been that right of dissolution would be sufficient weapon to persuade smaller parties to support Govt and that psychological and material benefits of office would give party a significant advantage in electoral campaign. Though PriMin has spoken confidently of an ERE victory, he would probably not be unduly disappointed if his party emerged as close second to EK. We believe hard-core ERE ministers, on other hand, would be willing to proceed to elections only if they were certain of ERE's achieving first place. They would argue that if EK won plurality, it could form govt with EDA support and that this possibility could not be risked. Therefore, we fear that ERE will soon realize that 45 days is not enough time to change situation appreciably

and that effort will be made to find a pretext to postpone elections, if necessary, through a deviation from constitution.

5. It is difficult to convey gloom over future developments which exists in political circles. Especially dismaying is present deep lack of trust between political leaders themselves as well as notably between King and both Papandreous and also between King and Stephanopoulos and Markezinis. Latter two, who believe King deliberately deceived them recently and who despise Kanellopoulos personally, seem to feel no sense of responsibility to try to help avoid collision course on which country is now heading. In our view, there are basically two options (a) for King and ERE to push ahead to elections in late May despite opposition of all other parties; or (b) for King to try to promote formation of inter-party government. Situation might still be salvaged if Kanellopoulos could be persuaded to step aside and to give up his right to dissolve Parliament and if ERE, FDK and Progressives could agree on inter-party govt. Everyone agrees, however, that hour is late.

Talbot

269.   Telegram From the Embassy in Greece to the Department of State[1]

Athens, April 9, 1967, 1426Z.

4574. Basing myself on State 167844[2] and NEA/GRK letter dated April 3,[3] I gave King Constantine five-part answer Saturday evening to his question of March 29 whether he could count on United States support should he be forced to undertake a constitutional deviation. I reassured him of continuing United States interest at highest level in Greece's difficult situation. I said we share his concern over policies that might be adopted by government with Andreas Papandreou as leading figure but believe certain restraints could operate to keep such a government from at least some of extreme measures Andreas now advocating. I expressed our agreement with the King's hopes that current difficulties can be overcome through parliamentary processes. I stated the inability of USG to

---

[1] Source: Department of State, Central Files, POL 15 GREECE. Secret; Priority; Exdis.
[2] Document 267.
[3] Not found.

give advance assurances of support to King and noted our traditional opposition to dictatorial solutions to constitutional crises. They are wrong in principle and rarely work yet create many new difficulties. A dictatorship in Greece might cause short-term upheavals, leading to more repressive measures, and to coalescence of opposition forces which in turn could be penetrated and dominated by international Communist agents. Adverse international reactions would not be limited to the Communist apparatus but would include supporters of democracy. Considerable criticism could be expected in United States. Finally, I restated as a guiding principle of United States in Eastern Mediterranean our policy to encourage progress and stability in Greece and to maintain close relations with Greece.

The King responded with thanks, but felt many questions remained unanswered. His own key question about risks inherent in a Papandreou victory related to control of the armed forces. He anticipated that a Papandreou government would move rapidly to retire or transfer officers loyal to the King and move Papandreou adherents into positions of trust, thus effectively ending the King's control of armed forces. This would destroy his ability to keep Greece free and attached to West. He asked whether this is what United States wished.

In response to my prodding the King conceded that constitutional crisis might arise as early as coming week. Kanellopoulos government is scheduled to appear before Parliament and will probably have to dissolve it for lack of vote of confidence. I asked whether this could immediately precipitate question of arresting Andreas Papandreou. King said it could, though no decision to arrest him has been made. Consequences of his arrest should it occur could raise issue whether elections would have to be postponed and Greece ruled for a period by a government without parliamentary sanction.

The King estimated that next critical moment could come in mid-May if ERE party had by then failed to develop electoral lead which Kanellopoulos but few others expect it to achieve. At that point the King would have to decide whether to let elections proceed. At that point also he would want American assurances. Most important of these, he said, would be assurances that Greece would continue to be protected against its northern neighbors, that U.S. would help keep Turkey from taking advantage in Cyprus of Greece's difficulties, that USG would help American public and other countries understand need to stabilize Greek situation and protect Greece from Communist penetration of sort that almost succeeded in the 1940's, and that economic assistance would be available to enable the new government to meet basic problems of Greek economy. He asked whether he could get further clarification of USG position.

I emphasized that in other situations, such as in Argentina, where extra-constitutional governments had been imposed, American actions had been different from what he had in mind. I repeated that USG would watch situation closely, but discouraged him from expecting further statement of American position at this time.

It was clear that young King believes his throne and Greece's attachment to the West to be at stake in this crisis. He has concluded that only near miracle can save him from final choice of yielding his country to Papandreou, or establishing a dictatorship either before or just after elections scheduled in May. More clearly than in any previous conversation, he expressed his dependence on United States for general support. I would anticipate his continuing to ask for American reassurances, with ever shorter deadlines as the scheduled electoral date approaches.

Memcon being pouched.

Comment: We share King's fear that events in Greece approaching climax. In recent days we have found little if any taste for compromise in any quarter. Should government decide to arrest Andreas Papandreou after dissolution of Parliament, as hard-liners urging, country could be thrown into crisis. For moment, however, most likely course is continuation of Kanellopoulos government and active political campaigning until mid-May. Embassy recommendations of USG actions that could be helpful will follow as situation evolves.

Talbot

---

270. **Telegram From the Embassy in Greece to the Department of State**[1]

Athens, April 13, 1967, 2300Z.

4650. 1. My expectation is that Kanellopoulos government, acting on decree by King, will disolve Parliament tonight or tomorrow and will announce elections May 28. This situation follows several days of intense efforts, primarily by FDK elements, to gain approval of concept of an ecumenical government. It also follows period of largely unsuccessful

[1] Source: Department of State, Central Files, POL 15 GREECE. Secret; Immediate; Limdis. Repeated to Ankara, Nicosia, Brussels for POLAD SHAPE, Paris, USDOCOSouth for Freshman, USCINCEUR for POLAD, and Thessaloniki. Passed to the White House and USIA.

efforts by ERE to obtain FDK and Progressive Party support of Kanello-poulos government. Both King and ERE obviously miscalculated in their estimate that two smaller national parties would give PriMin vote of confidence for sake of simple proportional electoral law.

2.   FDK view, as expressed to Embassy by Mitsotakis and *Eleftheria* publisher Kokkas, has been that ERE government would inevitably lead to dictatorship prior to elections and that only way to avoid this disaster would be for King to make final effort to form ecumenical government to pass electoral bill and to postpone elections until 1968. FDK theory has been that Papandreou would probably refuse initially to participate in ecumenical government and that ERE, FDK, and Progressives would then be in better position to form coalition government. Neither ERE nor Papandreou, however, was receptive to FDK proposal. ERE was naturally reluctant to give up fruits of office and to admit defeat, and Papandreou argued that ecumenical government would be an unworkable political "monstrosity." FDK proposal was also weakened when Papandreou reportedly enticed six or seven FDK deputies away from party by promise they would be eventually re-admitted to Center Union. Votes of these six or seven, plus 122 of EK and 22 of EDA, could thus make it virtually impossible for coalition of other parties to win vote of confidence in house of 300.

3.   Having seen Markezinis, Stephanopoulos, and Kanellopoulos in past few days, I called on George Papandreou today and found him, like other leaders, in self-righteous, unyielding mood. EK leader asserted that King had made major blunder by giving mandate to Kanellopoulos and that he has now ceased to be King of all Hellenes. "He is now King of ERE," and must suffer fate of any party leader. Papandreou made repeatedly clear that, if Parliament is dissolved and country is led to elections by ERE government, it will no longer be just Andreas, but all of EK including himself who will be conducting anti-monarchial campaign. Elder Papandreou also warned that if dictatorship occurs, he will wage civil war. In his view, only exodus from present crisis would be for King to name service government of common confidence to conduct free and honest elections. Such a government could be given an ecumenical flavor by having each party designate a Minister without portfolio as an observer. Otherwise Papandreou made no concession to idea of ecumenical government.

4.   This evening King's political advisor Bitsios visited me to pass on latest thinking of Palace. Part of Bitsios' presentation was detailed account of how George Papandreou had repeatedly broken his promises to King between December when Paraskevopoulos government was formed and late March. EK leader had specifically failed to live up to his written promise to expel Andreas if latter deviated from party line and attacked monarchy. Turning to today's developments, Bitsios reported

that, following careful consideration by King, Palace intermediary was authorized this afternoon to make following proposal to Papandreou: formation of ecumenical government under non-politician of common confidence with Cabinet representation from all parties to pass simple electoral bill and to conduct elections May 28, provided two largest parties, i.e., ERE and EK, would make written promise to cooperate in a post-electoral government for 6, 8 or 10 months.

5. Later this evening Bitsios telephoned me that Papandreou had not only rejected this proposal but had also made "threats." (These, I presume, were same threats he had expressed earlier today to me regarding anti-monarchical campaign, etc.) Bitsios added that PriMin has been informed of Papandreou's response and that he will be in touch with King later tonight. In my and my colleagues view, King's last minute approach to Papandreou was not really serious effort to find another solution, since he could hardly have expected Papandreou to sign paper promising to cooperate with ERE after elections. Even if elder Papandreou had accepted, Andreas would surely have disagreed and would probably have broken away from party.

6. All this gives only highlights of recent fast-moving events which will be reported in detail later and which have been characterized by blunders, miscalculations, distrust and stubbornness on all sides. In last few days, insatiable vivacity of Greeks for quarreling among themselves seems to have triumphed over their traditional knack for producing compromises.

Talbot

---

271. Telegram From the Embaasy in Greece to the Department of State[1]

Athens, April 14, 1967, 0001Z.

4651. Personal for the Secretary from Ambassador.

1. I regret to report time has come to hoist urgent storm signals from Greece. Through multiple blunders of past fortnight instability endemic since July 1965 has deteriorated into imminent danger of first-class mess leading country to brutal choice between dictatorship and

---

[1] Source: Department of State, Central Files, POL 15 GREECE. Secret; Priority.

Andreas Papandreou-led attacks on monarch and probably Greece's foreign alignment.

2.   Our reporting has supplied details and, I hope, has adequately signalled threat to U.S. interests. In summary, Greek failure to find acceptable solution to 21-month political impasse has led principal players not to try harder but to dig deeper into inflexibly polarized positions. With King and one party (ERE) now aligned against rest of political field, traditional instruments of power—Palace, armed forces, conservative political and economic interests—find themselves ranged against all centrists as well as leftist elements, undoubtedly representing majority of population, who in turn act increasingly frustrated, angry, anti-monarchical and probably anti-Alliance.

3.   PriMin Kanellopoulos as well as Papandreous and apparently bulk of voting population still want election May 28, but nobody can expect these to be ordinary elections. In relatively free elections under existing electoral system, Papandreous predicted to come in probably with clear majority and at least as leading party, depending on popular groundswell and also largely on how much strength Communist-line EDA diverts from its own candidates to Andreas-supported centrists.

4.   This wouldn't be too bad if George Papandreou would emerge as boss. At age 80, however, he's lost biological race to his son Andreas, only other leader of vigor now in party, and a government with Andreas either as backstage manager or at helm would—as we evaluate thrust of his campaign—transform military high command into a party-controlled instrument and thus effectively break authority of King and traditional influentials in this country. United States would not necessarily find that and various domestic programs projected by Andreas so damaging except that they would give him springboard for foreign policies that sound like a Mediterranean Bhutto's. Comfortable and satisfactory Greek-U.S. relationship of past 20 years would inescapably yield to kinds of strains we are experiencing not only in Pakistan but in too many other countries. By all signs visible here, Russians would not be slow to take advantage.

5.   Fearing such consequences of adverse election results next month, coteries in Palace, armed forces and ERE are evidently building up steam for "constitutional deviation," meaning dictatorship. They would hope to set things straight by period of firm rule and control of radicals. While their script is unclear, we presume that after dissolution of Parliament, and probably in May if election prospects then look unfavorable to them, current ERE government would be transformed into an emergency government with, initially, civilian Ministers backed up by armed forces under orders of King. Whether difficulties in enforcing order and meeting national problems would subsequently lead to direct

army takeover is hard to perceive, as is method by which authoritarian rule would later make way for resumption of democratic government.

6.   How to escape both Scylla and Charybdis? The King muffed best chance ten days ago when he failed to get smaller parties opposing Papandreous (FDK and Progressives) into governing combine with ERE. With Karamanlis, the "authentic" ERE leader, still in Paris, I am not sure even most powerful effort by King would have brought Kanellopoulos and small parties under same roof; at any rate, his milder efforts failed.

7.   Since then, extremely limited remaining options have been intensively explored. We are told tonight that no nourishment has been found in any of possible alternatives to present course.

8.   It now appears that Greece will proceed toward elections May 28 with King hoping ERE can garner enough support to hold Center Union to plurality. This result, still possible though not now probable, would be acceptable solution. It would enable King to insist on post-electoral coalition government excluding EDA and excluding Andreas from sensitive security ministries.

9.   This is result I believe we should next encourage diplomatically and with whatever resources can be made available to us. Although it will open us to charge of consorting with rightwing, that is preferable to visible alternatives.

10.   If ERE campaign falters under Center Union attacks on it and on King leaving prospect in mid-May of clear Center Union majority, then I believe dictatorship can be avoided if at all only by very heavy American pressures on Palace, armed forces and rightist politicians. From here I cannot judge what would be domestic US reaction to dictatorship in Greece, though I suppose it would produce new attacks (generated in part by anti-Royalist Greek-Americans) on administration's alleged support of rightwing, militaristic, monarchical regimes and would deepen difficulties encountered by military assistance program on Capitol Hill. In any case, efforts cited earlier in this message would set Greece far back domestically and internationally and in end might not save either monarchy or Western orientation, though immediate foreign policy of authoritarian regime would presumably be pro-US.

11.   As you know, King and Kanellopoulos have told me Greece "will not" be delivered to Andreas Papandreou. Nonetheless, we must consider this possibility if we are to oppose dictatorship. My own view is that key question—to which I have no present answer—is whether basic Greek institutions can withstand shock of Andreas' takeover attempts so that further elections could be assured after couple of years or so. Based on his past record of executive performance, I believe Greek people would then reject him and excesses of his fiscal and administrative policies. In these circumstances we could live for a while with his abrasive if not defiant policies. However, Andreas strikes me as capable in adver-

sity of dismantling traditional Greek institutions and policies if he is permitted to do so and to lead country even deeper into Nasserist posture.

12. Whole picture has many imponderables, of course. Questions that cannot now be answered but could vitally affect situation include such as when and how Karamanlis will return to Greek scene, when George Papandreou will disappear and effect of this on his party, and whether some new leader capable of challenging Andreas will emerge.

13. As any US action in this situation would need to be speedy and decisive, I should like to discuss issues personally with you and others before crunch comes. For this purpose I may ask soon to come to Washington for few days.

14. Meanwhile we have been urging conciliation and compromise on party leaders (though whether they have been listening is another question) and, as detailed in recent reports, in recent talks with King I have stated with increasing plainness our views of dangers in situation.

15. Sorry to burden you with this lengthy message, but despite your other preoccupations I fear you need now to be specifically informed on looming dangers here.

Talbot

272. Telegram From the Department of State to the Embassy in Greece[1]

Washington, April 20, 1967, 6:51 p.m.

179151. For Ambassador from Battle.

1. We have studied closely your recent messages describing the grave situation in Greece and dilemma facing King of (1) imposing dictatorship or (2) permitting CU to assume power following next elections with possible far-reaching consequences for Greece and its relations with US. We have pondered carefully question of what, if any, steps USG might take to meet situation and propose following formula for your consideration and comment.

2. We are working on assumption Papandreou's chief fear at present time is arrest of his son Andreas for alleged membership in Aspida

---

[1] Source: Department of State, Central Files, POL 15 GREECE. Secret; Immediate; Exdis. Drafted by Owens and Brewster, cleared by Rockwell and Katzenbach, and approved by Battle.

conspiracy. Arrest of Andreas could easily touch off violent demonstrations which in turn would be met by extreme repressive measures by government and possible imposition of dictatorship. On other hand, King's deepest fear is that if Papandreous win elections, Center Union will move immediately to strip King of his power by major shakeup in military forces and intelligence setup, with eventual aim of undermining and perhaps eliminating monarchy. Concurrent to this is general concern that younger Papandreou would move Greece away from Western Alliance.

3. Proposed scenario would be that you call on George Papandreou at earliest oppurtunity, and inform him on instructions that USG deeply concerned at present rift in Greek body politic and increasing polarization due to extreme positions being taken by both sides. You would emphasize that we have great stake in future of Greece as result of major US investment in men, money, and matériel dating from 1947. We consider prosperous Greece is essential to Western Alliance. USG is fully aware of Papandreou's devotion to democracy, his long history of anti-Communism, and his dedication to welfare of his country.

4. You could add that as we view situation, cooling off of highly charged political atmosphere could result from an agreement on both sides to moderate language in public statements and speeches. (This would seem to be particularly important at present juncture, since elder Papandreou is about to make one of his two major speeches this Sunday in Thessaloniki. Extremist remarks on that occasion would set unfortunate tone for entire campaign and might increase tensions, already dangerously high, to breaking point.)

5. To meet problem outlined para 2 we would propose compromise based on iron-clad assurances from both sides. Our formula would envision assurance from King to G. Papandreou that Andreas Papandreou would not be arrested, in return for following two concessions from Papandreou, on assumption he wins May 28 elections: (1) that he appoint only persons of "mutual confidence" to sensitive positions of Foreign Affairs and Defense and (2) that he not carry out widespread shakeup in armed forces leadership. FYI, these two assurances from Papandreou would appear to be minimum concessions acceptable to King to stay his hand from imposing dictatorship in event CU wins majority in elections. End FYI.

6. You should attempt to induce George Papandreou to put such a compromise formula forward to Palace on his own. If he will not see King but asks you to help, you could serve as "honest broker" and convey compromise proposal to King.

7. None of elements in proposed formula is sacrosanct and we leave it to you to modify them according to prevailing conditions there. If you perceive major objection to recommended action, we would wel-

come countersuggestions from you. However we feel time is of essence in view of fast-moving developments in Greece, including Papandreou's opening speech this weekend and indications that government may be moving to arrest Andreas Papandreou. If latter happens, it may be too late to play constructive role in this deteriorating situation.

8.   Would appreciate your comments urgently as to wisdom forego-ing proposal. Please include your thoughts re dangers, charges US med-dling in internal situation. Also comment on possibility approach being made through CAS or unofficial channel.

9.   Take no action in absence further instructions.

Rusk

THE MILITARY COUP IN GREECE AND THE INITIAL U.S. RESPONSE, APRIL–SEPTEMBER 1967

273. Telegram From the Embassy in Greece to the Department of State[1]

Athens, April 21, 1967, 1123Z.

4753. This is Country Team message.

1. On basis still fragmentary information I have formed tentative impression that coup was triggered this morning by small army group not including High Command, King or civilian political leaders. Service Chiefs of Staff, faced with question of whether they would cooperate, all appear to be joined and to be actively participating in planning next steps. Military command seems united and now fully committed to coup. King also appears no longer to fear possible arrest as he did when Defense Attaché talked with him at 0415 local time[2] but rather to have joined with military leadership in considering where to go next. Presumably he was asked about military leadership and all have emphasized their fidelity to King and to NATO.

2. We have been told most members of Kanellopoulos government in protective custody. Andreas Papandreou reported in local military prison.

3. Because we had heard rumors that some political prisoners might suffer harm, I had Chief JUSMAGG and Defense Attaché call on General Papadatos to convey messages any such actions would greatly increase complications of already complicated situation.

4. So far as we know, Athens, Thessaloniki, Crete and all other parts of the country are quiet now.

5. I see no present indication of resistance to the coup.[3]

Talbot

---

[1] Source: Department of State, Central Files, POL 23–9 GREECE. Secret; Flash. Received at 6:33 a.m. and passed to the White House, DOD, CIA, USIA, and NSA at 6:55 a.m.

[2] Telegram 4746 from Athens, April 21, reported that the Defense Attaché had called Tatoi Palace at approximately 5 a.m. to "find out what was going on." King Constantine answered that he had no clear idea of what was happening, adding: "They are headed this way for me. Get word to Sixth Fleet. Get word to Washington and have them send your army in." (Ibid.)

[3] In a memorandum for the President, April 21, Rostow outlined the fragmentary evidence available and commented that "the immediate question is what we say. At some point, I feel we should express regret—even if softly—that democratic process has been suspended." (Johnson Library, National Security File, Country File, Greece, Vol. 2)

274.   Telegram From the Embassy in Greece to the Department of State[1]

Athens, April 21, 1967, 1610Z.

4769. 1. Margaret Papandreou's father, Mr. Chant, and her friend Mrs. Schacter, came into the Embassy for the second time today and were received by Amb.[2]

2. They referred to fact Article 18 of Constitution (which forbids executions for political crimes) and fact rumors exist that some of political prisoners might be disposed of before morning. Under these circumstances they, as well as Margaret, are acutely apprehensive about Andreas' fate. They also referred to fact that Margaret and her children are American citizens and inquired whether Ambassador was in position to give any particular guidance concerning their actions.

3. Amb said Emb had been following situation as closely as we could but that our information still extremely limited by inaccessibility of persons involved, fact telephonic communications had been cut, and that circulation in city had been prohibited. He informed them he had already conveyed to Greek military (Athens 4753)[3] his conviction that bloodshed and violence would not only have most unfortunate implications for evolution of the Greek situation but could be expected produce serious repercussions outside of Greece, especially in US. Amb. observed we had been informed that King had not in fact signed emergency decree suspending certain articles of Constitution and that as far as we aware meeting between King and senior military officers still continuing. This suggests to us serious disagreement does in fact exist.

4. Chant and Schacter appeared highly skeptical that coup may have been staged without King's approval. Chant commented if Andreas were executed there would without question be revolution in which many people would lose their lives. He said that in light seriousness situation Margaret believed some word of admonition from Pres. Johnson would be appropriate.

5. Ambassador expressed sympathy for their anxieties regarding personal safety of Andreas. He again assured them US has and would by every means discourage Greek military leaders from any resort to violence or bloodshed and to an appreciation of serious damage which

---

[1] Source: Department of State, Central Files, POL 23–9 GREECE. Confidential. Received at 12:36 p.m.

[2] Telegram 4740 from Athens, April 21, reported that Mrs. Papandreou, her son George, her father, and another person had come to the Embassy to report the seizure of Andreas and George Papandreou. (Ibid.)

[3] Document 273.

would result both within Greece and in Greece's relations with other countries.

6. *Comment:* Ambassador has in fact instructed all official American representatives seeking establish contact on various levels with Greek military to emphasize that bloodshed will make an already tragically complicated situation infinitely more so.[4]

Talbot

---

[4] In telegram 4841 from Athens, April 23, the Embassy reported it had "made numerous inquiries to determine welfare of both Papandreous" and to ensure they were unharmed. It was also ready to "extend protection" to the Papandreou family although it did not believe such action would be necessary. (Department of State, Central Files, POL 29 GREECE)

---

275.   Telegram From the Embassy in Greece to the Department of State[1]

Athens, April 21, 1967, 2030Z.

4787. 1. King Constantine, blazingly angry, has just told me that neither he nor General officers control Greek army tonight. "Incredibly stupid ultra-rightwing bastards, having gained control of tanks, have brought disaster to Greece," he said.

2. According to King, government which he swore in tonight was forced upon him after five-hour rough session with coup leaders during which he had wrung sole concession that it be headed by civilian.[2] King believes Spandidakis generally aware of plan and easily agreed to go along with three officers who mounted coup (presumably those reported separately).[3] King said he had contemplated shooting perpetra-

---

[1] Source: Department of State, Central Files, POL 23–9 GREECE. Secret; Flash; Limdis. Repeated to USCINCEUR, USDOCOSouth, the Secretary of Defense, and DIA. Received at 3:59 p.m. and passed to the White House, DOD, CIA, USIA, and NSA at 4:16 p.m. Rostow forwarded the substance of this telegram to the President at 6:30 p.m. in a memorandum. (Johnson Library, National Security File, Country File, Greece, Vol. 2)

[2] King Constantine subsequently provided Talbot with a detailed account of his meetings with the coup plotters. Talbot reported this discussion in telegram 4794 from Athens, April 22. (Department of State, Central Files, POL 23–9 GREECE)

[3] Probably a reference to telegram 4767 from Athens, April 21. (Ibid.)

tors when they came to Palace to be sworn in tonight, but concluded this would be worthless gesture as his Palace then surrounded by tanks loyal to them.

3. King is unsure of next developments. He asked how long it would take helicopters to reach Tatoi to evacuate his family if needed. He also asked whether any possibility U.S. Marines could be landed in Greece if necessary to help him and Generals reassert their control over armed forces. He expressed view Greek troops would not fire at U.S. Marines.

4. King also asked if I could make strongest démarche to his new government to insist that it not only maintain order and protect civilians who have been arrested but also strictly follow orders of King. He proposed that I say "U.S. will hold King responsible for actions of this government and government responsible to King."

5. At King's request we have arranged and will attempt to maintain emergency communications directly with Royal Palace at Tatoi.

6. I have just talked with General Spandidakis and Nick Farmarkis, now his aide, and have obtained immediate appointment with new Prime Minister. I will assert that I am speaking on instructions and state we look to the government to maintain order, we insist that they open up communications for stranded Americans and call strongly upon government to restore normal life as rapidly as possible. With all force we call upon government to protect detainees from physical harm, and I will assert that United States, which gives Greece much assistance, will watch developments minutely. I will also express our support for role of King as Chief of State.

7. Important to hold King's comments closely at this time.

Talbot

---

276. **Telegram From the Embassy in Greece to the Department of State**[1]

Athens, April 21, 1967, 2330Z.

4792. 1. By mutual request, I called 2200 local time on PriMin Kollias at his office in presence of Vice Premier and Def. Min. Gen. Spandidakis.

---

[1] Source: Department of State, Central Files, POL 23–9 GREECE. Secret; Flash. Repeated to the Secretary of Defense, DIA, USCINCEUR, and USDOCOSouth. Received at 7:07 p.m. and passed to the White House, CIA, DOD, USIA, and NSA at 7:10 p.m.

2. In introductory comment, PriMin asserted that today's developments were prompted by grave Communist threat to Greece and by decision of army to thwart this threat. Army has established complete control throughout country without any bloodshed. PriMin emphasized that purpose of his government is to protect freedoms of all Greeks and to restore normality as soon as possible.

3. Gen Spandidakis broke in to report, as we knew, that telephone communications have been restored and other communications would return to normal tomorrow. In response to my question regarding well-being of people arrested today, Spandidakis stated former PriMin Kanellopoulos, Papaligouras, and other people in ERE govt would be released tonight immediately after our conversation or at latest Saturday morning. He said that George Papandreou, but not Andreas, would also be released, although he did not specify when. Spandidakis assured me that none of detainees would be physically harmed.

4. I told PriMin that, acting on instructions from my government[2] I must state (a) that we were deeply distressed by today's developments, including the use of American-furnished equipment to overthrow the constitutional government of Greece, and (b) that we will look to government to maintain order, open communications to stranded Americans, and restore normal life as rapidly as possible. Spandidakis reported that communications will be restored by tomorrow.

5. Gen. Eaton, who was with me, and I also expressed great concern over use of American-supplied equipment in today's coup. PriMin responded that he was also sorry that use was made of this matériel, but that action was absolutely essential in view of Communist threat. By Communist, he explained that he meant not only those who belong to extreme left but also those who "sympathize" with them. (In latter category he undoubtedly was thinking of Andreas.) PriMin asserted that, had military not acted, another Viet-Nam might have occurred in Greece and country might have fallen in Iron Curtain abyss. Neither Spandidakis nor PriMin was precise in explaining what exactly had happened to trigger coup.

6. I responded that I hoped (a) that if army was instrument of coup it would plainly be under control of senior military leaders not of junior officers, and (b) that new government would be completely loyal to and

---

[2] In telegram 180319 to Athens, April 21, the Department of State approved the approach outlined by Talbot in telegram 4787 from Athens, Document 275. The telegram contained an estimate that U.S. helicopters could evacuate the Royal family within 36 hours of a request. It further instructed Talbot to disabuse the King of any notion of a U.S. military intervention, adding that it was "alarmed" by the tenor of Constantine's report to Talbot: "Admittedly he is not calling all the shots but riding herd on this faction of the Greek army and political spectrum would not seem to hold nearly the same dangers as he would have faced had an Aspida-type military team moved in." (Department of State, Central Files, POL 23 GREECE)

responsive to orders of King. PriMin and Spandidakis both alleged that government is devoted to King and strong supporter of NATO. They expressed hope that GOG, as in past, could count on support of US.

7. Asked about calling of Parliament into session, PriMin told me that Parliament could not meet until elections were held and that latter depended on developments. In any case, he hoped that normal conditions would soon be restored and that elections could be conducted at an early time.

8. Observing both Kollias and Spandidakis tonight, I was confirmed in my impression that PriMin is merely front-man and that real power rests with military. Question is which military.[3]

Talbot

---

[3] In an April 22 memorandum to the President, Rostow noted that continued U.S. silence on events in Athens, a position that Secretary Rusk had chosen, was creating major difficulties for the "Administration's posture before the intellectual and liberal communities in the U.S." Rostow nonetheless argued that for the present the United States should refrain from a public statement. (Johnson Library, National Security File, Country File, Greece, Vol. 2)

---

277.   Telegram From the Embassy in Greece to the Department of State[1]

Athens, April 22, 1967, 0015Z.

4795. I now recommend:

(1) That for present we continue fairly starchy posture toward new Greek Government but still stay in touch with it and not burn bridges by threatening cutoff of aid and other drastic measures unless government's performance in next few days is rough and rotten.

(2) That I attempt to stay in closest possible communication with King and that we rapidly canvass steps which could strengthen his hand, since King likely can prove principal focus for restoring normalcy. While I do not now expect situation to require emergency evacuation of Royal family, urgent response to King's request on helicopters would be practically and psychologically valuable.[2]

---

[1] Source: Department of State, Central Files, POL 23–9 GREECE. Secret; Immediate; Limdis. Received at 7:38 p.m. on April 21 and passed to the White House, CIA, DOD, NSA, and USIA at 7:50 p.m.

[2] See footnote 2, Document 276.

(3) That our public and press posture reveal our regret and our distaste for process of changing governments by military coups but also reflect a certain slowness to pass moral judgments since there remain so many gaps in our understanding of what has happened and why.[3]

Talbot

---

[3] In telegram 4797 from Athens, April 22, Talbot commented: "So far as I perceive we have now completed reportage of the day of the rape of Greek democracy. I am certain that Greece will long rue this day's events, whose long range effects are hard to foresee." (Department of State, Central Files, POL 23–9 GREECE) Talbot's comments were reported to the President in an April 22 memorandum from Rostow. (Johnson Library, National Security File, Country File, Greece, Vol. 2)

---

278. Telegram From the Department of State to the Embassy in Greece[1]

Washington, April 22, 1967, 1:44 p.m.

180648. For Ambassador.

1. In fast-moving situation facing King and yourself, we recognize we unable to give close and current guidance. However, following are basic points which we believe should govern King's actions and which we suggest you convey to him as opinion USG:

(a) We believe it essential that the King remain in Greece.

(b) We believe he should not depart from Greece except under duress.

(c) We think that his position vis-à-vis the military officers controlling the government is stronger than he appears to think and that he should use what we consider to be their considerable need for him to extract from them the maximum concessions.

(d) We think that his efforts vis-à-vis the coup officers should be toward reaching a compromise of type which will make it clear to Greek people that King has not capitulated but has forced military leaders to make significant concessions. We are not informed as to what other points may be at issue between King and the governing military group except the questions of suspension of articles of Constitution and the

---

[1] Source: Department of State, Central Files, POL 23–9 GREECE. Secret; Flash. Drafted by Rockwell and approved by Battle.

martial law decree. But there must be other matters, such as ratio of civilian vs. military in Cabinet, which could be used as bargaining points to off-set concessions which for example might be made regarding martial law decree. Latter concessions might involve limiting decree to specified time and moderating provisions calling for extreme restrictions on civil liberties.

(e) If King is concerned about safety his wife and would feel better if she could go somewhere else, we would be willing to help in this. We believe it would be preferable for her not to leave Greek soil.

(f) Finally, while we recognize that decision as to capitulation vs. resistance must be made by King alone, it is our view that if he capitulates he will have lost all opportunity for leadership. This does not mean that he may not have to compromise on some issues while showing his own stamp on the situation as he forces others to compromise, we would hope in as visible a manner as possible.[2]

Rusk

---

[2] In telegram 4836 from Athens, April 22, Talbot reported that the Embassy had tried to maintain contact in the last 24 hours with new regime "in order to exercise what influence we have toward more constructive second phase of coup than now appears probable unless coup group abandons its thuggery." He also reported Embassy contacts with Nikos Farmakis and Lieutenant General Spandidakis. (Ibid.)

---

279. Telegram From the Embassy in Greece to the Department of State[1]

Athens, April 23, 1967.

4856. 1. Sixty hours after coup Embassy estimates that new authoritarian government is solidly in control. Key is unity of army. New command appointments and military moods discerned by attachés and JUSMAGG strengthen belief that no significant opposition exists to present control of armed forces.

---

[1] Source: Department of State, Central Files, POL 23–9 GREECE. Secret; Immediate; Limdis. The time of transmission on the source text is illegible; the telegram was received at 3:29 p.m. Repeated to CINCEUR, USDOCOSouth, the Secretary of Defense, JCS, and DIA. Passed to the White House, DOD, CIA, USIA, and NSA.

2. Chances of countercoup, never bright, have sunk hour by hour and now seem virtually nil. King, whose surprise at and opposition to coup is becoming increasingly widely recognized here, presumably is also recognizing coup as fait accompli.

3. Coup is revolutionary. Its central core—Papadopoulos, described as the top theoretician; Patakos, the top executive; and Makerezos—are limited, politically inexperienced, tough-minded, no-nonsense types setting out to "purify" Greek political, social and economic life. Their manifesto sounds like Ayub in 1958. Also like 1958 model Ayub, they declare themselves thousand percent pro-American and are urgently seeking any hint of American understanding of what they're doing. With or without it, they know they must succeed or lose their heads.

4. If military coup in this NATO country has demolished liberal political reputation of Greece, oddly enough failure of coup—once attempted—would have been even greater disaster. Coup effort pushed aside political moderates and conservatives (as represented by Kanello-poulos government and its supporters) who were duped not by their enemies but by group with roughly similar anxieties about strong leftist trends in Greece. Had coup failed, carrying conservatives and moderates down with it, only beneficiaries would have been far leftist segment of Greek political life. Greece would then have surely gone where rightists fear Andreas Papandreou was taking it.

5. While it is early to judge causes of coup, personality and policies of Andreas Papandreou may be prime reason Greece today is under dictatorship. King, moderate centrists and moderate conservatives had all been opposing ultra-rightist convictions that only the army could safeguard Greece from Communism. Andreas' style and the thrust of his threats to the Greek "establishment", particularly the armed forces, were alien to normal to-ing and fro-ing of Greek political life. Because they exceeded bounds of Greek political tolerance and therefore induced deepest distrust in rightist quarters especially the army, Andreas lost chance to move Greece in directions he favored.

6. These thoughts are historical footnotes. Question is what direction to take next. Until now Embassy has indicated readiness to stay in communication with new government and top military leadership but has coldly pointed out American reaction to overthrow of parliamentary government of a NATO ally by military establishment trained and equipped by Americans. We have been all but rude to Spandidakis and others in cross-examining their assertions that they and other properly constituted commanders are actually in control of army. Without predicting what policy lines United States might adopt we have spelled out possible consequences in short words. We have made sure arrival of Sixth Fleet task force group in Greek waters has not gone unnoticed by

top people. If we haven't educated the mule, at least we have given it those knocks required to get its attention.[2]

7. Now that we have its attention, what do we say? From our vantage point here, what is essential is to get Greece pointed again in direction of some kind of government with consent of governed. Obviously this government is not about to yield power to a political government. Therefore, question is one of transitional arrangements. One possibility is, for example, Vietnam pattern: a pledge by new government to proceed toward election of a constituent assembly which in turn would produce revised constitution subject to plebiscite. Another idea is establishment by fiat of a national constitutional council consisting of eminent jurists and others of unquestioned integrity and stature. Whatever the mechanism, avowed steps toward restoration of constitutional rule would give promise of way out from present dictatorial deadend.

8. There are fragmentary indications that new government is hunting for some such course. It badly needs cooperation and participation of responsible conservatives, at least. Latter (of whom former Foreign Minister Averoff and Bank of Greece Deputy John Pesmazoglu have already expressed their anxieties to me) could contribute to solution. Moreover, declaration of definite constitutional course by this government would enable King to identify himself with specific constructive purposes and thus bring him back into tolerable relationship with army and public life. This would also help to justify in eyes of American public opinion USG cooperation with coup government.

9. While maintaining stiffish attitude toward present government for time being, I propose unless Department objects to stimulate exploration of above ideas with key members of new government and with others who may be in a position to influence this regime. I also propose to suggest it to King as line worth considering to break current impasse.[3]

Talbot

---

[2] In telegram 4901 from Athens, April 24, the Embassy reported "deep distress" on the part of the coup leaders to the "negative reaction" of the United States to their actions, and concern about possible employment of the Sixth Fleet against them. It also reported that the new government was "absolutely determined" to fulfill its goals. (Ibid.)

[3] In telegram 181282 to Athens, April 24, the Department of State informed Talbot that military aid shipments to Greece would be discontinued for the time being and that "In sum, we should follow a policy of watchful waiting, and an attitude of coolness towards new govt while encouraging King vigorously to support move towards more viable government." (Ibid.)

280.   Telegram From the Department of State to the Embassy in Greece[1]

Washington, April 24, 1967, 8:47 p.m.

181462. Your 4898.[2]

1. We concur in continuation normal working relations with GOC at sub-ministerial level and that JUSMAG should pursue its normal contacts except for forward planning. We query need for long range planning at the moment and suggest that reluctance to engage in this might be advantageous tactic for us at this time.

2. We also concur that we like the King will need a modus vivendi with this Government but believe that establishment of ours should await establishment of his.

3. With regard to high level contacts we believe that for the moment these should be restricted to purpose of gathering information rather than for substantive discussion of future course GOG.

4. We entirely concur in your suggestions as to points we might put forward as basis our willingness to work with this regime but believe that we should hold off on going to bargaining table for moment, leaving it to King to press for broadening basis of Government. We hope that he will work to decrease extensive security measures now in force and continue encourage men of stature and ability to come into Government.

5. We anticipate increasing Congressional and public disapproval of association with this regime, to say nothing of collaboration with it, and that its use of MAP equipment in staging coup will be particularly sore point.

Katzenbach

---

[1] Source: Department of State, Central Files, POL 15 GREECE. Secret; Limdis; Noforn. Drafted by Rockwell, cleared by Katzenbach, and approved by Battle. Repeated to Bonn for Secretary Rusk as Tosec 26.

[2] Telegram 4898 from Athens, April 24, requested guidance on policy toward the Greek regime and outlined the Embassy's views on that policy. (Ibid.)

281.   Telegram From the Embassy in Greece to the Department of State[1]

Athens, April 25, 1967, 2300Z.

4942. 1. During 75-minute conversation at Tatoi this evening King Constantine appeared under considerably less strain than I had seen him at any time since coup. He thought meetings with Cabinet members yesterday had gone well. My net impression is that he is moving rapidly to adjust his relations with coup government and has moderate expectations of gradually regaining leadership of army and government.

2. According to his account, meeting with Cabinet group Monday evening went very satisfactorily. After berating coup instigators once again for having moved without his knowledge, he had told them: "Now you have done it and you are here. Now you must not fail." Patakos had replied that coup had already succeeded. King's response was that "not at all. You have succeeded in taking country, but unless you succeed in running it you have brought Greece to final disaster." He had then lectured them on need to get expert advice on economic and other problems and act constructively and effectively. Cabinet members had repeatedly insisted on their loyalty to King. In response to his repeated questions, they had also insisted that army is loyal him.

3. King said he had pressed Cabinet hard on need to demonstrate to Greece's allies that its goal is resumption of constitutional government. Drawing on points discussed earlier between him and me,[2] he had told them that government must promptly set up some sort of constitution-drafting committee to prepare revised constitution that would be examined by government and then subjected to national plebiscite, after which elections could be held under new constitution. To his great satisfaction, they had agreed to announce this program. He had therefore consented to attend Cabinet meeting Wednesday at which he believed major item of business would be promulgation of new constitution-making process.

4. I commented that main problem might be to obtain domestic and foreign credibility. It would be easy to announce such a scheme, but who would believe it? Perhaps Royal decree could be issued, committing both King and government to fixed process. King said he would pursue this line Wednesday.

---

[1] Source: Department of State, Central Files, POL 23–9 GREECE. Secret; Immediate; Limdis; Noforn. Repeated to Bonn for Secretary Rusk, USCINCEUR, USDOCOSouth, the Secretary of Defense, JCS, DIA, and London. Passed to the White House, DOD, USIA, CIA, and NSA.

[2] Talbot reported on discussions with the King regarding treatment of the junta in telegram 4840 from Athens, April 23. (Ibid.)

5. I told King our main problem at moment is what sort of relations to have with coup government. While question of recognition does not arise, we remain exceedingly uncomfortable at having Greek ally under military dictatorship. Embassy is showing this discomfort in cool and reserved posture. Obviously, Americans would find it extremely difficult during this period to deliver tanks and similar major weaponry to regime which has used American-made tanks to overthrow established government. He would understand that this would have to be our posture until Greek Government itself sorts out its purposes and programs. Perhaps our rather stiff posture might even help him re-establish his Kingly position with this regime.

6. King agreed, adding that he hoped we would not get such an inflexible position that we could not respond if this government should demonstrate its readiness to return to constitutional rule. I commented that given public and congressional opinion, this was a risk, but that unless this government reached that state there was no prospect that American reserve would melt. King said he understood.

7. King said he had finally faced Cabinet with protracted question of unsigned decree declaring martial law and suspending certain articles of the Constitution. He had told Cabinet that government had acted without his signature, that he saw no sense in signing decree now and did not propose to do so. There had been no visible reaction, so he thought he probably had gotten away with this issue.

8. However, they insisted (Athens 4934)[3] that his secretary, Major Arnaoutis, go abroad and he had agreed. This left him without staff. I suggested that anyone in his position needed some confidant, and expressed the hope that he would find someone who could effectively replace Ambassador Bitsios (who cravenly resigned at height of crisis) and Major Arnaoutis.

9. King said Cabinet members had told him government greatly needs his support and that public increasingly anxious because of stories he not in accord with regime. They asked him to show himself at Easter eve religious ceremonies next Saturday night and to take part in traditional egg-cracking frivolities in army barracks. He said this depended on whether army is truly loyal to him. He would reserve decision for some days until he could get better reading. They professed army absolutely loyal to King even though they and army commanders had acted without his knowledge last Friday morning, "but only to protect you, Your Majesty."

---

[3] Telegram 4934, April 25, reported on a meeting between the King and Colonel Papadopoulos and summarized the King's comments on the meeting and recent developments in the military. (Ibid.)

10. King said these are people inexperienced in government who include some really stupid types such as Farmakis, but that it now becomes his role to gain their confidence, persuade them that he is not plotting a counter-coup, get time to work on country's serious problems, and gradually reassert his authority. I commented that this is sort of program that would require his continuing to follow delicate path of neither embracing nor breaking with coup group, and taking advantage of their need of him at early stages to extract all vital concessions. He replied that he is type who gets giddy on tightrope but he will try.

11. I noted that since first night of coup I had not been in touch with Ministers of new government but that Prime Minister Kollias had summoned me for Wednesday morning. I said I was asking instructions (Athens 4941).[4] He expressed hope I could talk with Prime Minister to reinforce King's line before Cabinet meeting.[5]

12. I mentioned that Sixth Fleet task group is still in Aegean Sea though it has other chores. If situation easing, did he think it might be on its way? King replied that while government's true intentions may take two or three weeks to come out, he now is confident he and his family will stay in Greece. He would have no objection to departure of task group, though he would hope it could come back rapidly if situation should deteriorate. I said that we keep task groups always in Mediterranean, which isn't such huge sea after all.

Talbot

---

[4] Telegram 4941, April 25, requested permission to respond favorably to Prime Minister Kollias' request for a meeting. (Ibid.)

[5] In telegram 182277 to Athens, April 25, the Department of State replied: "We have no objection to your seeing Kollias. Suggest you take this opportunity to ask regarding welfare of political prisoners and newspaper owners." (Ibid.)

282.   Telegram From the Embassy in Greece to the Department of State[1]

Athens, April 28, 1967, 2015Z.

5016. 1. At his request[2] I rendezvoused today with Brigadier Patakos, Minister of Interior. We met at the home of JUSMAGG officer with whom Patakos was associated at Fort Knox in early 1950's and has worked in recent months on questions related to armor training center which Patakos commanded. Initially somewhat reserved but later open, Patakos quickly expressed pro-American attitudes and identified his American connections. These include siblings in Sioux City, Iowa and Salt Lake City and two nephews who are officers in US Army, one a major in DOD/ASCI and the other a dental officer in Vietnam.

2. Patakos impressed me along lines we have heard him described. As military operator, precise and effective executive, who insists he is in a revolutionary movement but is himself no long-haired revolutionary theorist. Like other coup leaders, he had been working almost without sleep for a week, but was alert and energetic throughout our conversation. After leaving me, he was to meet King at Tatoi.

3. After somewhat slow conversational start, I proposed we might proceed by his commenting on questions that face USG as it attempts to understand what happened in Greece and to sort out its policy in relation to new situation. He would understand events of past week in Greece had come as great shock to us, and that in interest of looking to future it would be well to be frank and specific. Patakos agreed. He neither requested nor got any assurance about U.S. policy. In answering my questions, he commented on purposes of revolution, plans for constitution-writing, current status of detainees, and intentions toward political prisoners. He repeatedly referred to what has happened as "the revolution" and to present GOG as "the revolutionary government." He exuded confidence that revolution is irreversible fact, whether or not US finally accepts proffered hand of friendship. With consolidation effected, he emphasized current task is to look forward to running government and returning to constitutional rule.

4. Patakaos assured me he sincerely desires friendship of America. He would be our friend even if we were not his. New GOG had not made deep or broad plans prior to the coup but had acted primarily to save sit-

---

[1] Source: Department of State, Central Files, POL 15 GREECE. Secret; Priority. Repeated to Ankara, London, Nicosia, USCINCEUR, and the Secretary of Defense. Passed to the White House, CIA, DOD, NSA, and USIA.

[2] Talbot reported the request and sought authorization for a meeting in telegram 4984 from Athens, April 27. The Department of State gave authorization in telegram 183174 to Athens, April 27. (Both ibid., POL 23–9 GREECE)

uation in Greece which leaders felt was rapidly deteriorating. Now they are studying and planning to rectify all shortcomings they had earlier suspected. They had not known all specifics before, but now with opportunity to look into Ministries and other facets of government, they feel able to develop concrete programs. Demagogues had split the Greek people into factions and lawbreakers such as robbers and murderers could be found on the streets. Greeks had even seen individual biting ear of a policy official. Revolution has tried to unite country and cleanse Greek life. In his own Ministry he had found civil servants sitting all day doing nothing except drinking coffee. Now, like military, they have daily planning conferences at 7 a.m. New government wishes to be more responsive to public needs, and to bring tranquility to the people. It should restore their confidence in economic and political facets of Greek life.

5. We wasted little time on military aspects of takeover. As to ways in which his group will move to next phase of governmental operations, he had studied problems Ayub and Turkish military leaders had faced in managing government after their military takeovers, and would draw on their experience while adding essentially Greek approaches. With confidence born of one week's experience, he felt sure new GOG could operate Greece's official establishment much more effectively than had its predecessors.

6. I asked about role of King. He reaffirmed that King had known nothing about coup. He could not be a revolutionary, and therefore was kept out until it fait accompli. King remains as head of state and head of army, though not responsible for appointment of persons in government. (I do not feel remarks I was able to draw from Patakos fully illuminates what role new GOG expects to permit King to play. My tentative conclusion is that Patakos, like most traditional Greek politicians, views throne as useful unifying symbol, so long as King doesn't interfere too much in their affairs. This aspect will bear further watching.)

7. As to constitutional status, Patakos said Constitution has not been suspended. He stated flatly GOG will shortly set up constitution commission of eminent jurists who will determine what sort of Constitution Greece should have. They will draw on experience of other states, such as US. They will examine why Greece's affairs sank so low under existing constitution and what changes would be necessary to prevent repetition. Proposed revisions, or new Constitution, will be submitted to government and thence to plebiscite. Once adopted, new Constitution would provide framework for new elections. I asked how long this process would take. He did not know, would not guess, and declined to be drawn into comment on my speculation that it might take anything from a few months to a few years. I asked when constitution-making process would be announced. He said as soon as possible, which he defined as within

596   Foreign Relations, 1964–1968, Volume XVI

next few days. I commented that this would be of considerable interest to my country, a nation deeply devoted to democracy, which after military takeovers in such countries as Pakistan, Turkey and South Vietnam had unfailingly and vigorously encouraged existing authorities to take steps that would lead their people back to constitutional and representative rule. Patakos said he understood this. Process could start quickly in Greece.

8. I asked about situation of detainees. Patakos was carrying a folder which he opened to reveal exact statistics and certain names that he was about to report to King. (He asked me not to transmit these to Washington until he had had chance to present them to King and Prime Minister. To help establish basis for continuing relations, we will telephone him tomorrow to get his approval for transmission of following statistics to Washington.) According to Patakos, up to April 26, 6,500 prisoners had been taken into custody and 1,701 subsequently released, leaving 5,437 still in custody. Of those, 1,558 had already been installed in camps on Island of Yioura and 1,727 were now being shipped in that direction by boat, leaving 2,152 still in detention on mainland. Some of these latter would be sent to camps being constructed on Yioura and on island of Makronisi.

9. For ease in handling, detainees being classified in three categories, "A","B," and "C". Investigation of these people does not look to misdeeds of long ago, presumably during the Communist war of 1946–49, but rather to their current records. Persons in "A" category would be quickly releasable if nothing adverse found. In "B" category are persons not easily determined to be releasable but also not well-known Communists or anarchists. These persons will be examined to determine whether they should be put in "A" or "C" categories. In "C" category are those individuals who are initially regarded as dangerous. If investigation proves otherwise, some of these too could be released. Others will be "instructed" and "re-educated" to become good citizens.

10. In addition, Patakos spoke of 25 "special class" detainees in Athens, 33 others in provinces, and 4 in "special economic class." These are being held in hotels or at home under guard. (Names he mentioned being transmitted separately.)[3]

11. Patakos said Andreas Papandreou is detained for two reasons. First, on charges of involvement in Aspida conspiracy, he is being investigated by public prosecutor (this confirms our understanding that GOG has decided to bring Andreas to civil trial on Aspida charges, which as we understand it could bring maximum sentence of 28 years). He is also being held because of his declarations that he would cause revolution. Patakos would not say that Andreas would be tried on these second

---

[3] In telegram 5016 from Athens, April 28. (Ibid.)

charges. His summary response to my several questions was that Andreas would be held in detention until they could be satisfied that he would not attempt revolution. I concluded that GOG is thinking of dealing with Andreas on civil charges unless he gets disagreeable in which case he could be court martialed on second set of charges.

12. As to others, Patakos said Mitsotakis has now declared he is "with" government but leaders of revolution unconvinced.[4] He did not name economic detainees, but did not dissent when I said we had heard these include Professor Stratis Andreadis, Chairman of the Ionian Popular Bank and other financial and industrial institutions, and Bank's general manager. Patakos said heavy bank withdrawals on first days after coup had stopped suddenly when a few bankers detained.

13. In response to my further questions, Patakos answered specifically that regime intends to kill no one. All such rumors, including recent stories of planned execution of Glazos (Athens 5013)[5] are false. He warned however that saboteurs would be dealt with severely—whatever that means.

14. Patakos summarized by restating strong desire to work closely with Americans. Whether that possible or not he said, success of revolution is sure.[6] He expressed satisfaction at direct contact with me, and hoped we could continue to meet and deal frankly with new problems that might arise.

Talbot

---

[4] Telegram 4969 from Athens, April 26, reported that in his initial contact with a U.S. Government official Patakos had explained that the junta feared Mitsotakis would lead an insurrection in Crete. Patakos added that Mitsotakis had shown hostility to the new regime, but, as a fellow Cretan, he would try to secure his release. (Ibid.)

[5] Not found.

[6] In the conversation summarized in footnote 4 above, Patakos concluded: "Just remember, we are with you whether you want us or not." This comment was reported to Secretary Rusk in an April 27 memorandum from Battle. (Ibid.)

---

283. Telegram From the Department of State to the Embassy in Greece[1]

Washington, May 2, 1967, 7:47 p.m.

186592. For Ambassador from Battle.

---

[1] Source: Department of State, Central Files, POL GREECE. Secret; Limdis. Drafted by Rockwell, cleared in NEA, and approved by Battle.

1. Would appreciate receiving your early views on where we go from here with new GOG, and how fast.

2. There is feeling here that King seems to be giving way too rapidly in his relationship with new regime and that perhaps he should be withholding more cards at this time in order be able ensure meaningful concessions.

3. There is also concern lest pressures within Greece for us to enter into normal relationship with regime result in our moving in that direction without having gained anything in return. We feel we must not permit our leverage to be dissipated thus.

4. Regime has made a number of appropriate statements with regard to its desire that Greece return to a constitutional situation but the timing of this development is of course left imprecise.

5. Meanwhile hostile pressures against the GOG are building up abroad and in this country, with urgent reference to the fate of political detainees but also based on a profound distaste for the coup regime.

6. Although we have spoken in general terms to the new leaders about need to lift restrictions on civil liberties and to establish goal of returning to constitutional normalcy, we have been precise so far only with regard to detained political figures. We have been pondering whether we should seek to pin regime down to a definite blueprint of political steps in direction of normalcy and if so what this blueprint should be and how soon we should put it forward. The price would probably have to be the relaxation of our restrictions on military aid and the commencement of normal relations with the GOG, with the resultant disadvantages for the U.S. image. We would of course have to satisfy ourselves that the regime meant what it said and that real progress in the direction indicated was likely.

7. We wonder whether it would be a good idea for you to discuss this whole question with the King in order to obtain his views. At same time you might wish to intimate that from the tactical point of view it might be better if the King should move more slowly in reaching an accommodation with government leaders.

8. It has also been suggested here that we might use our present leverage to try to push the GOG further in the direction of a Cyprus solution, perhaps by pressing for agreement on a sovereign Turkish base on the island, or perhaps on the transfer of Grivas. We doubt we have enough leverage to move the GOG very far on Cyprus, even should we decide to accept the disadvantages inherent in trying.

9. Most of these are difficult questions to judge with any sense of certainty, and we feel the need of your wise counsel in helping us consider them.

Rusk

284. Telegram From the Embassy in Greece to the Department of State[1]

Athens, May 5, 1967, 1130Z.

5117. Ref: State 186592.[2] For Battle from Ambassador.

1. We are keenly aware of fact we risk slipping into normal relationships with GOG without specific assurances of concrete progress toward reestablishment of democratic government in Greece. It would be equally foolhardy to break off all contacts when major interests are at stake. We try to walk the tightrope.

2. Our contacts with new government have been limited and exploratory. We have reported our conversations with Kollias, Spandidakis, Patakos and Makarezos. We expect to make contact with Papadopoulos shortly.

3. Our impression is that the coup leadership is pro-US, pro-NATO, rigorously if not fanatically anti-Communist. It apparently regards itself as revolutionary with a mission of cleansing and reorienting Greek economic, political and social life on new and wholesome basis. We find little evidence it believes its mission can be accomplished within a short period of time.

4. Since the coup, information has gradually become available indicating that coup group has existed in some form or other since 1957 under aegis of Papadopoulos. Group considered itself as reformist element whose objectives were to seize power and revitalize Greek institutions generally in line with principles which governed IDEA. They considered IDEA, however, to have lost its dynamism. According to reports, Papadopoulos has long been known as "Nasser" to some of his colleagues because of his intriguing nature and his concept of role which army under leadership of aggressive middle-grade officers could play in modernizing the Greek society.

5. This junta or revolutionary group is reported to have been comprised of about 40 officers. This group seems to consider King useful symbol with which it will cooperate but is unlikely to subject itself to his control. Although vast preponderance of Greek officers are probably genuinely loyal to King, coup leadership has moved swiftly to retire a number of senior officers. They have successfully established their members in many key commands and have exploited the natural tendency for the mass of the officer corps to be responsive to command channels. Army promotions to be made in next week or two will provide important

---

[1] Source: Department of State, Central Files, POL GREECE. Secret; Priority; Limdis.
[2] Document 283.

evidence as to whether traditional hierarchy has regained measure of control or whether partisans of coup managers will be advanced to key positions without regard to seniority and fitness.

6. Our contact has been too limited to form a valid conclusion as yet whether this leadership will be prepared to divest itself voluntarily of the responsibilities of government in foreseeable future. Some observers believe Papadopoulos and perhaps other officers will eventually leave army and form new political party. However and whenever current phase terminates, Greek political life in future will be vastly changed in structure and personalities.

7. We are concerned about internal political implications of current situation and its impact on long term US position here even though coup was in fact greeted with certain amount of initial satisfaction by an undetermined portion of population disgusted with protracted political instability and low public morality.

8. It is difficult predict how much time may elapse before leftist and militantly democratic elements of population recover from shock and reaction sets in. Tenor of broadcasts from bloc radios suggests Communists may consider that coup provides them unexpected opportunity to enhance their position in Greece. A large number of Greeks believe United States concurred in or tolerated coup. Many Greeks assert only Communists dispose of an organization capable of leading resistance against a dictatorship and warn that Communists must not again be permitted to become leaders of democratic resistance as in World War II. We accept essential validity of these latter points although it is difficult to weigh precise force in current situation.

9. We recognize, nevertheless, that almost any kind of government which could be created at this time would depend ultimately on Greek military for support and that consequently we must seek accommodation with them. Moreover, we are sensitive to fact that split in Greek armed forces (with possibility of actual conflict) would be extremely dangerous for Greece and for US position here. Although Greek armed forces are ostensibly solidly behind new government, there is probably growing number of officers who are aware that King did not in fact initially concur in coup and who privately feel character of coup (extensive suspension of civil liberties, seizure of control by middle-grade officers etc.) has not in fact produced type of solution to political crisis which they may have hoped for. Such sentiments, if confirmed, might exercise important moderating influence on policies of coup managers.

10. In these circumstances I believe we must attempt create situation in which coup managers will feel compelled by their own personal interests to give precise assurances and take concrete actions to implement program aimed at restoration constitutional government. These interests include GOG expectation of continuing foreign assistance of varying

sorts (military, development credits, etc.) as well as general foreign and domestic reputation of the regime and support for it.

11. With no early alternative to present regime in sight, problem is how to achieve the sort of turn around to civil rule that ultimately followed the Turkish military coup of 1960. This would involve a GOG commitment to constitution-drafting to create some sort of government based on consent of governed. It should include progressive restoration civil liberties, establishment of committee of jurists to revise Constitution, plebiscite on constitutional revisions, encouragement to coup leaders to yield office to qualified civilians, elections within specified time frame, etc. Dept will have noted CAS reports indicating Papadopoulos group has in past devoted serious effort to question constitutional revision.

Crux of problem is endeavor insure through public commitments that specific action is taken as part of more or less irreversible process before this government is permanently embedded in dictatorial form. We are attempting to develop points that could be pressed, and I assume Department is also working on this in response to our request (Athens 5000).[3]

12. It is to these ends that Embassy is pointing its efforts. Specifically:

(A) I propose to continue urging King to maintain a position vis-à-vis the government that would clearly reflect his reserve but without ostensible hostility. Last week our immediate goal was to save King for some useful future role. Yesterday we discussed this role as well as steps he might take to overcome growing impression he may have come into full accord with coup group.

(B) We propose maintain only limited contacts with government and coup leaders and continue to emphasize that USG cannot easily carry forward programs with Greece until constitutional situation clarified. Yesterday we spelled out to Admiral Avgheris, FonMin Gouras and King that delivery main important types of military equipment has been suspended pending review of MAP and that concrete evidence that GOG sincerely moving restore constitutional government would greatly aid USG resume program on previously established basis.

(C) We probing GOG economic policies also. In view of adverse balance of payments prospects (Athens 5066)[4] I anticipate upcoming requests for help at least in supporting Greek applications to international lending institutions. These will give further opportunities to point to moral.

---

[3] Telegram 5000 from Athens, April 27, requested guidance from the Department of State on ideas to pass to the Greeks regarding a return to democracy. (Department of State, Central Files, POL 23–9 GREECE)

[4] Dated May 3. (Ibid.)

(D) Washington could support this approach in several ways. For example, USG should continue to emphasize in its public statements that it is awaiting concrete steps toward reestablishment of democratic government. I recommend that in near future President Johnson make statement roughly along lines of that made by Secretary. Secretary's statement was briefly alluded to, but not quoted, in only one Athens newspaper and ignored in others.[5] Also, Secretary or Under Secretary could usefully call in Greek Ambassador and set forth importance which we attach to return of democratic government as a condition for full and intimate cooperation with GOG.

(E) I hope you and I can keep in closest communication on question of resuming delivery of major items of MAP equipment. In general, they should not be delivered until we are satisfied with programs developed by GOG for return to representative government. We in Embassy will make sure GOG understands this. As you know, however, I am anxious that we not get into bureaucratic bind that would impede MAP shipments when conditions are right. There is a fine line between using MAP deliveries to press for constructive policies and dismantling keystone of our mutual security cooperation with Greece. We weathered military coup in Turkey without damage to our strategic interests. We must have same objective in Greece.

(F) If Department finds above lines acceptable, we should consult with other Western powers, particularly UK and Germany, with a view to having them adopt a posture similar to ours.

13. I believe it would be premature for us to take initiative with regard to Cyprus problem at this time. Gouras and Caglayangil had 90-minute talk at Bonn and presumably will go on from there. We can add little until our own relations with GOG are worked out. There are, however, intimations Cyprus occupies very important place among preoccupations this government.

14. Initially we must speak candidly in private while in public making clear not only expectation as to line GOG will follow but also our confidence that they intend to follow such a course. Leaders of this coup are doubtless very sensitive having risked greatly and won handsomely in first phase of their program. Presumably they are also dedicated men. Although politically relatively unsophisticated, they also are probably convinced they are acting not only in interest of Greece but of West and NATO.

Talbot

---

[5] For text of Secretary Rusk's April 28 statement, see Department of State *Bulletin*, May 15, 1967, pp. 750–751.

285.   Telegram From the Embassy in Greece to the Department of State[1]

Athens, May 5, 1967, 1600Z.

5136. Athens 5047.[2]

1. During my call on King Thursday evening I told him in confidence of Mrs. Papandreou's assertion that her husband is being administered drugs and of her description of medical history of Andreas and attendant dangers of any regime of drugs. He could anticipate consequences if Andreas' health should suddenly deteriorate while in detention. Even at propaganda level, it could do Greece no good if drug charges should be aired abroad and some international committee be formed to examine his condition.

2. King said he had heard nothing that indicated Andreas had any health difficulties. Cy Sulzberger, who had seen him last Saturday, had described Andreas as in normal health and in good spirits.[3] However, King thought he could emphasize to Patakos great importance of avoiding any chance that political prisoners would lose their health and vitality while in detention. If his probing should pick up any indication of drug administration, he would be in position to pursue question in detail.

Comment: King said he and Sulzberger had agreed to tell no one they had met. Please protect.[4]

Talbot

---

[1] Source: Department of State, Central Files, POL 29 GREECE. Secret; Limdis.

[2] Telegram 5047, May 1, reported that Margaret Papandreou was concerned that her husband's captors were "brainwashing" him through the use of dangerous drugs. (Ibid.)

[3] For Sulzberger's account of his meeting with Papandreou, see *Age of Mediocrity,* pp. 331–333.

[4] For Sulzberger's account of his meeting with the King, see ibid., pp. 336–341.

286.   Telegram From the Mission to the North Atlantic Treaty Organization and European Regional Organizations to the Department of State[1]

Paris, May 9, 1967, 2018Z.

17886. NATUS. Subject: Sec McNamara's talk with General Spandidakis. Following is memcon, still subject to clearance with SecDef:

1. Minister of Defense Spandidakis, accompanied by Ambassador Palamas and an interpreter, called on Secretary McNamara in his USRO office at 1630 immediately following conclusion of the Defense Ministers meeting. Ambassador Cleveland and Assistant Secretary McNaughton were present. Spandidakis initiated the conversation by saying he assumed McNamara wanted to know why the military acted in Greece. He then talked through the interpreter for 15 minutes.

2. He said that from 1964 things had been deteriorating in Greece, that the political parties had been corrupted, that there were a number of liaisons with the Communists, and that there was a Communist build-up everywhere including the army. It was clear the country was going to fall in Communist hands, so the army, to prevent this, took over on April 21 despite the Constitution. Spandidakis referred at this point to the need to prevent a return to guerrilla warfare ("another Vietnam") in Greece. He said the ease with which the revolution was carried off in a few hours proves it was accepted by the Greek people. He said there were no "victims" (he would not count as victims the two people who were killed in violating the curfew). He pointed out that peace reigned in Greece two days after the action. He said the population, except for a Communist small (12–15 percent) minority, accepts the action.

3. Spandidakis said the attacks on the Greek action are mainly from foreign countries, by Communist governments or by groups associated with the Communists. He referred also to false rumors such as the alleged kidnapping of the King's daughter to put pressure on the King, and the rumors about the regime's intentions to execute Andreas Papandreou and Communist leader Glazes. But he said the "greatest bitterness is in the rumor that the US would revise its assistance to Greece." He said this made no sense because the alternative was to surrender to Communism. He said that, as it is, the ties between Greece and NATO are stronger now than before.

4. He said it is true that some people have been detained, including George Papandreou—who, he says, is now being treated better than he

---

[1] Source: Department of State, Central Files, POL GREECE–US. Confidential; Priority. Repeated to Athens, USCINCEUR, and EUCOM for POLAD.

would be in his own house. He referred to others being kept in hotels, in comfortable circumstances as the press could see for itself. He said such detentions were necessary to stop their stirring up trouble.

5. Spandidakis said the government had a four-point program: (1) to reorganize the government mechanism, (2) to establish economic control, (3) to revise the Constitution to "bring it up to date", and (4) to "return the country to a constitutional order." He said no one knows how long the program would take, that it depends on the depth of the preexisting disorganization. He said, "All of us are of a democratic point of view; we are not going to establish a Fascist regime in Greece". He added that today there is no Parliament but, except for that, there is more democracy today than before April 21; he said they had anarchy at that time. He pointed to the interest taken by the new government in the farmers and low income groups, who have expressed their appreciation.

6. Secretary McNamara said he was grateful for the explanation and for Spandidakis' frankness (which frankness, together with sincerity, Spandidakis had emphasized on three occasions). McNamara said he would likewise be frank. He said it was unnecessary to tell a Greek of the admiration that the American people have for the Greek people: we have had a very close relationship with them over the past two decades; and our civilization is based upon theirs, dating back 2500 years. He said it is completely natural for our young people to expect to travel in Greece; indeed, his daughter had spent the last year there and is still there. He said it concerns us greatly that Greece has moved away from constitutional processes.

7. McNamara said it would be unbecoming of him to comment on Greek internal affairs, but that it was not inappropriate for him to comment on US internal affairs. He then said that the American people could never understand a statement that there is more democracy today than before April 21—with the press suppressed, assembly prevented, people restrained, no free speech, and other constitutional guarantees suspended. Also, important to the view by the American people was the absence of any schedule for resumption of constitutional processes. These, he said, are strong feelings of most of the people in the US, and he and other government officials are servants of the people. He said it would be extraordinarily difficult to maintain the Greek military assistance program without modification if there is no acceptable time schedule for the resumption of constitutional processes.

8. McNamara said that he believed Spandidakis' statement that he opposed a Fascist government, but that the American view would be greatly affected by the degree to which the Greeks indicate (a) a desire to make the change, (b) a schedule for the change, and (c) actions toward the change. McNamara said the US would be willing to try to help—e.g., by avoiding any public denunciation. But he said, the Greeks should not

underestimate the concern of the US and the strong hopes for movement back toward constitutional processes.

9. Spandidakis at this point said, "Then you must explain the facts to the American people". McNamara responded that, unfortunately, the facts seemed to be as stated earlier—people detained, constitutional processes suspended, etc. He said that the US looks to the future with hope along the lines he had described.

10. Spandidakis said that a revision of the Military Assistance Program would be dangerous, spelling out the Greek reliance on US aid. McNamara said that the whole Greek situation is dangerous, and that, until action is taken to remedy it, the dangerous situation will continue. He hoped the Greeks could see a path for return to constitutional government which would make progress in that direction obvious to outsiders. He added his view that the greatest deterrent to the Soviets and the thing most likely to encourage support from the US would be a demonstration by the Greeks that they can return to constitutional processes.

11. Spandidakis said that continuation of MAP will shorten the time required. McNamara answered that, as Greek plans along the lines he had described became firmer, we can be informed of the progress, and public support for MAP in our country will grow.

12. Spandidakis asked what if the election had taken place and Greece had gone Communist. McNamara said he would not speculate but did not believe Greece would vote the Communists into power. After Spandidakis explained that only 12–15 percent of the population are Communist, but that more than 50 percent of the people were going to make the mistake of following them, Palamas said that the political parties had been behaving in such a way as to let the Communists take over. McNamara repeated that the important thing was to lay out a course of action to return to the constitutional processes.

13. The conversation was concluded at 1720 with a short exchange on reliability of NATO as an ally of Greece in trouble—both Spandidakis and Palamas suggesting that NATO was in such disarray that it could not be counted on to come to Greece's aid. McNamara said that, in his view, NATO is in much better condition today than it was a year ago, pointing to a year of "tremendous accomplishment" in both the political and military sense, pointing to the way the Allies had successfully survived the French withdrawal and eviction, and to the birth and apparent good start of the NPG. He added that we need (and will, in his view, be doing) more NATO planning in support of defensive actions on the flanks.

Cleveland

287. Telegram From the Embassy in Greece to the Department of State[1]

Athens, May 10, 1967, 1658Z.

5209. NATUS.

1. Col Papadopoulos, member of ruling military triumvirate, repeated to me last night government's brief public policy statement on Cyprus, i.e. enosis with protection for Turkish Cypriots through peaceful means, specifically through dialogue with GOT. Papadopoulos added that he is firm believer in need for close and harmonious relations between Greece and Turkey and that he hopes these relations can be restored to what they were before crisis over Cyprus. No decision has yet been taken, he said, on date for resumption of dialogue.

2. These comments confirm our impression that new regime leaders have been so engrossed in consolidating their position within army and in familiarizing themselves with numerous domestic problems that they have not yet begun to focus seriously on Cyprus.[2]

Talbot

[1] Source: Department of State, Central Files, POL 27 CYP. Confidential. Received at 2:19 p.m. and repeated to the Secretary of Defense, DIA, JCS, USDOCOSouth, USCINC-EUR, Ankara, London, Paris, and Thessaloniki. The meeting described in this telegram was the first between Talbot and Papadopoulos. The Ambassador reported on their discussions relating to the Greek internal situation in telegram 5191 from Athens, May 10. (Ibid., POL 15 GREECE)

[2] In telegram 193045 to Athens, May 12, the Department of State noted that the situation in Greece made an initiative on Cyprus premature. (Ibid., POL 27 CYP)

---

288. Telegram From the Department of State to the Embassy in Greece[1]

Washington, May 10, 1967, 3:55 p.m.

191368. NATUS. Ref: Athens 5135, 5144, 5148, 5182.[2]

[1] Source: Department of State, Central Files, POL 15–1 GREECE. Secret; Priority; Limdis. Drafted by Owens and Brewster and approved by Rockwell. Repeated to Ankara, London, Nicosia, Paris, USCINCEUR, and USDOCOSouth.

[2] Telegram 5135 from Athens, May 5, reported King Constantine's view of the Greek internal situation. (Ibid.) Telegram 5144 from Athens, May 5, reported a conversation with King Constantine regarding changes in the Constitution imposed by the Junta. (Ibid.) Telegram 5148 from Athens, May 6, reported Pattakos' comments on constitutional reform plans. (Ibid.) Telegram 5182 from Athens, May 9, reported on Embassy efforts to push the Junta to a return to civilian rule. (Ibid.)

1. Your excellent telegrams over weekend have been read carefully here. Dept deeply appreciative your thoughtful analysis.

2. We agree that our approach to new Greek Govt must be to walk tightrope and that problem is essentially how to show people in Greece and elsewhere that U.S. (and King) not attached to new govt, while at same time working with GOG to get Greece back on constitutional road. As you state, our chief effort now must be to create situation in which coup managers will feel compelled by their own personal interests to give precise assurances and take concrete actions towards restoration of constitutional govt.

3. As we see it, major problem of next few days and weeks is to convince GOG that it must take specific, concrete steps to demonstrate to world that it sincerely plans to return to constitutional govt. As you have pointed out to King, vague assurances of good intentions will not suffice. Govt plan to appoint committee of eminent jurists to revise constitution, as announced by Pattakos, is step in right direction but, as DCM emphasized to Makarezos, to be fully effective must be accompanied by announcement of dates when revision will be completed and when plebiscite will be held to approve final document. Your suggestion that King use occasion of birth his child to announce timetable for return to constitutional rule is excellent one and you should encourage King to attempt obtain GOG approval such move. Also important will be nature of persons appointed to revision committee. Ideally, they should be persons of international stature; in this connection, govt may wish consider appointment of some eminent foreign jurists to such committee.

4. We are somewhat encouraged by your description King's policy of cooperating with new govt at same time retaining image of separateness from them. We also feel his effort to encourage senior officers of known loyalty to reconsolidate their command authority is wise move and could be crucial factor at later stage. You should continue to encourage King to apply pressure on new govt by selective non-attendance at certain functions (as described to you in Embtel 5135) and we share your view that Embassy should follow King's lead and thus indicate clearly to coup managers our support for King's efforts.

5. In addition to positive steps by govt we wish to encourage, we should also use our influence with King and Kollias to discourage further repressive measures by govt, such as establishment special military courts, abolition political organizations, and recently announced elimination of municipal elections. New govt has real public relations problem which could be alleviated somewhat by more restraint by coup managers in public announcements.

6. Most urgent question as far as American and international public opinion is concerned remains, of course, fate of political prisoners and particularly of Andreas Papandreou. We fully aware of deep opposition

on part of coup managers to release at this time of Andreas Papandreou and other political prisoners. However, you should continue to impress upon them at every opportunity fact that to large extent world image of new govt will be based on its handling of prisoners' question and trial of Andreas.

7. As occasions arise where such action can serve useful purpose, we plan continue press GOG in desired direction through public statements. Concerning the calling in of Greek Ambassador here to stress importance of early return of GOG to democratic processes, Amb. Matsas has been recuperating from recent operation and thus far has not been available. We will do so when he returns to duty.

Rusk

289. Telegram From the Embassy in Greece to the Department of State[1]

Athens, May 14, 1967, 1435Z.

5265. For Battle from Talbot. Ref: Athens 5264.[2]

1. Reftel conveys Country Team impressions of situation here three weeks after coup. To these let me add some personal thoughts as you face new rounds on Hill.

(a) Rather astonishing extent of acquiescence to coup can no longer be explained just as stunned reaction. Mood of relief has osmotically spread through community. As when power suddenly fails in boiler factory, only in this unexpected moment of quiet are many people realizing how much strain they had felt in normal high-decibel political din. Many now admit, too, to having feared destructiveness of impending electoral clashes. I'm reminded of Pakistan in 1958, when first reaction to Ayub's coup was also sheer relief. This is a real phenomenon, not a shibboleth.

(b) How long this mood will last, we don't know, certainly not indefinitely. Greeks are Greeks and will come to resist. But while it does, it has two major consequences: (1) it gives coup group almost ideal climate in which to consolidate control, and (2) it insulates many Greeks from

---

[1] Source: Department of State, Central Files, POL 23–9 GREECE. Secret; Immediate; Limdis. Passed to the White House and USIA.

[2] Telegram 5264, May 14, summarized the situation in Greece 3 weeks after the coup. (Ibid.)

impact of European and American outcry against "rape in cradle of democracy". I am surprised at how widely we are getting rejoinders that Americans should understand it was Papandreous, especially Andreas, who strangled democracy here.

(c) This all heading, I fear, into major breakdown of genuine communication between important segments of opinion in Greece and in US. It is not merely matter of American disbelief of Greek feelings of relief at recent developments or of Greek wonderment at American lionizing of Andreas. More basic is fact that Americans and Europeans think Greece is clothed in Athenian values, while Greeks themselves remember how often in past 3,000 years—and in past 145 years since independence— they have been shuttlecocked between Athenian and Spartan concepts of government. Veterans in this century of seven wars, five military coups and at least two other attempts, one Royal assassination and three Royal withdrawals, at least three dictators, and more than 20 parliamentary governments since 1950, five of them in past 21 months, modern Greeks have enjoyed stable parliamentary rule really only between 1952 and 1965 (Papagos–Karamanlis–Papandreou). Thus I encounter reactions of "Well, here we go again. Wonder what it will be like this time. Hope it won't be too bad; at least they've been rather soft to start with— no killings or anything like that". This is very different attitude from outrage at rape of democracy, and perhaps more in keeping with cynical ennui of Eastern Mediterranean.

(d) Defining this attitude doesn't solve our problem, nor does it suggest that present nonparliamentary regime will remain popular; far from it. But it does suggest that when volatile Greeks as usual look for some other path after some time, we should try to be ready to encourage and help them on realistic basis that neither they nor we want Greece soon to sink back into parliamentary tumult characteristic of pre-1952 period and of recent past.

(e) How to do this? Just pressing GOG to set precise dates for plebiscite and elections will not be enough, I fear. Based on previous Greek experience with plebiscite promises, date setting would not necessarily assure early return to representative government. In any event, GOG has proven resistant to our advice not only because military Ministers have already come to enjoy power but also because they seem to have persuaded themselves that setting early date (only kind they think would interest us) would inhibit their carrying through essential reforms. Despised politicians, they believe, would then merely hole-in and await time they could regain control of moneybags and patronage. And the one thing these military Ministers are determined not to do is to turn country back to same old hacks they stole it from.

(f) If Papadopoulos and company are to be diverted from road Nasser took after deciding Wafd could never again be trusted to govern

Egypt, therefore, Greeks and we need to concentrate on how to get parliamentary democracy that avoids anarchy. Several Greeks, including Karamanlis and Pipinelis, have long been thinking about this. Ideas we could feed in from experience in other countries (requested in Athens 5000)[3] would be helpful.

(g) In long run, I doubt we could cooperate efficiently with a Papadopoulos-dominated GOG. Frontal effort to break him now would, however, be without guarantee of success and if successful could well shatter Greece. Task as I see it is to try to restrain him and his coup associates from excesses, wrap more talent and disciplined organization around them, and keep pushing in direction of a constitutionalism that will work. Meanwhile, I believe we should continue supporting King and stay as much as possible in posture of neither giving Greeks what they most want—full aid and recognition—nor coming to definitive break.

2. I am not so presumptuous as to think all this will be useful to you, but writing it has helped me clarify my own thoughts. Good luck in arduous chores you face.

Talbot

---

[3] See footnote 3, Document 284.

---

290.   Memorandum From the President's Special Assistant (Rostow) to President Johnson[1]

Washington, May 15, 1967, 11 a.m.

Mr. President:

You will have seen Marquis Childs' story (Tab A)[2] in this morning's *Washington Post* on our alleged involvement in the Greek coup.

The story is about as inaccurate as it could be.

The facts are these:

—On March 8 and 13, 1967, the 303 Committee considered a proposal that [*less than 1 line of source text not declassified*] put $200–$300,000

---

[1] Source: Johnson Library, National Security File, Intelligence File, Greek Coup, 1967. Secret; Sensitive. A note on the memorandum reads: "rec'd 5–15–67, 3:30 p.m." The memorandum is marked with an "L," indicating that the President saw it.

[2] The May 15 article was entitled "A Coup in Greece; A Bit of Blackmail."

into the Greek elections which were then scheduled to back candidates who would be anti-Andreas. Although, as indicated in the attached minutes (Tab B),[3] we all felt considerable reservation about the proposal, we examined it carefully because the Ambassador recommended it. We finally decided that Foy Kohler should take the matter up with Sect. Rusk, and if the Secretary felt the proposal was vital, I would raise the matter with you. On March 14, Kohler reported as follows:

"He (Sect. Rusk) comes down negative. In the Greek case, he believes the possible political gain is outweighed by the security risks. He commented that if the dual-national Greek-Americans are concerned about the prospects and if $200–$300,000 will make the difference, they should have no trouble raising that sum themselves without involving the United States Government."

In general, the view we took was that it was becoming less and less appropriate for us to try to influence elections in places like Italy[4] and Greece [*less than 1 line of source text not declassified*]. Moreover, there was considerable skepticism—shared by me—that the outcome in Greece would be much affected by this kind of money.

In any case, the issue before us was not 'what should we do or not do about a coup': it was, 'what should we do or not do about an election which at that time we all believed was more likely, rather than less likely, to take place'; although we knew there was considerable anxiety in certain Greek quarters about that election.

I have already asked State to undertake an investigation of who might have spoken about this matter to Marquis Childs. The problem in tracking down this particular inaccurate and distorted leak is that, because Ambassador Talbot came in with a cable,[5] a considerable number of people in State probably knew that we were considering something to do with Greece. I have every reason for confidence in Foy Kohler, who is an exceedingly tight-lipped man.

I will let you know the results of our investigation.

Walt

---

[3] See Documents 259 and 261.

[4] For documentation on Italy, see *Foreign Relations*, 1964–1968, volume XII.

[5] Document 255.

291.   Telegram From the Embassy in Greece to the Department of State[1]

Athens, May 21, 1967, 2323Z.

5377. NATUS.

1. In my first discussion with him since April 26, Prime Minister Kollias Friday revealed GOG's sensitivity to official American view of situation in Greece. Our exchange started with some rather starchy references by Kollias to United States "misunderstanding" of Greek military action to save Greece. After my assertion that our biggest question is what direction new GOG will take, Kollias concluded with assurance that formation and operation of constitution-revising committee will proceed promptly. On the whole, I believe exercise was useful.

2. At first Kollias was edgy and visibly upset by what I gather was well-embellished telegram from Ambassador Matsas describing talk with Secretary May 17.[2] Greeks, Kollias said, are "very sorry" and he feels "great bitterness" because American friends do not seem to realize great necessity for change and continue unfavorable criticism on top of which they also cut military assistance. Greeks many times have shown they can live on cats and mice rather than betray ideal in which they believe. Greece even if left in lurch by its allies will continue to fight for real democracy and continue to love Americans and be grateful for support they have given since 1947. Greeks understand liberty and they understand need to overcome corruption of recent parliamentary process in order to restore true liberty to their country. He himself had starved and fought as simple soldier in cause of liberty and had now given up judicial career of forty years to assist in service of his country. He would never agree to serve a cause whose purpose was imposition of a dictatorial regime. Rather this government's purpose is to establish real freedom and democracy in order to save country from chaos and catastrophe that was about to befall it. Revolution of April 21 was perhaps most civilized, most liberal and most bloodless revolution ever to occur. All information government has received from interior of country is extremely satisfactory. Eighty per cent of people share enthusiasm for change.

3. After twenty minutes of similar oratory I managed to riposte that having listened with close attention I was greatly disappointed to realize

---

[1] Source: Department of State, Central Files, POL 15–1 GREECE. Secret; Limdis. Repeated to Ankara, Nicosia, Paris, and USUN.

[2] Telegram 196553 to Athens, May 17, reported that Rusk had pressed Matsas on the issues of the fate of political prisoners and political repression by the Junta. (Ibid., POL 23–9 GREECE)

that GOG apparently had not understood major points USG has been seeking to make. We have our views on what has occurred before April 21 and thereafter. American people had not believed recent conditions in Greece ideal, but it would be unrealistic to think Americans would not have reacted to what has happened.

4. Events of April 21 raised questions which need sorting out before future U.S. road can be determined. Thus the military assistance review (whose details I spelled out to correct his assertion that aid had been cut off but also to leave him in no doubt that review could ultimately be concluded in any of several directions). However, I went on, USG is not concentrating on the past; it is not suggesting that clock could be turned back. Rather, it is looking to present and future. What direction is this government going to take? If it is to move along lines of military governments fastened on some Arab countries, for example, Americans could be expected to react. ("No, no," Kollias objected.) If on other hand this government pursues objective of restoring representative government as quickly as possible, we could expect American policies to move in another direction. Problem is one of being convincing. As Prime Minister aware, announcement of plan to form constitution-revision committee and submit its product to plebiscite after review by government was favorable step. Yet that simple declaration not enough to persuade international opinion in face of other things that have happened in Greece.

5. We know, I continued, that Greeks can fight their battles, alone if necessary. But we do not want to see GOG isolated from world. We have been privileged to be closely associated with Greeks in their struggles, especially in past twenty years. That is why we are so much interested in persuasive evidence that GOG will indeed move briskly toward constitution revision and representative rule.

6. Speaking personally, I told Prime Minister that my colleagues in Washington had made great efforts to persuade influential Congressmen and others not to heat up American reaction before receiving firm evidence of GOG intentions. This was a difficult exercise, and I did not know how much longer it could be carried on. Assurances given now by GOG could be much more helpful in calming international opinion than same assurances given after some weeks when adverse attitudes may have grown.

7. With his adrenalin still running, though less vigorously than at first, Kollias declared that it is and has always been the desire of this GOG to have country return to normal political life as soon as conditions will permit. GOG said so in its initial proclamation to the people, and has since repeated its pledge. Prime Minister could categorically assure me that names of twenty members of committee which will be charged with revision of Constitution will be announced by end of this month. Com-

mittee will be given up to six months to prepare revision and after study by GOG this will be submitted to plebiscite. He could also assure me that with help of God and with aid (unspecified), government would be in position within one year to proclaim elections. He made it clear, however, that without aid GOG would not be in position to establish conditions that would make elections possible within this time.

8. I commented that public statement along lines he had just set out to me would in my opinion have beneficial effect. He said he could make announcement about constitution-revising committee members' appointment without delay, but that talk about elections would be different matter since that would depend not only on GOG. Full memcon being pouched.[3]

Talbot

---

[3] Transmitted as an attachment to airgram A–656 from Athens, June 3. (Ibid., POL 15–1 GREECE)

---

292. Letter From the Ambassador to Greece (Talbot) to the Country Director for Greece (Brewster)[1]

Athens, May 26, 1967.

Dear Dan:

In view of the distribution given even Exdis telegrams, I would prefer for some time to report to you by letter some of the more sensitive items that emerge from my conversations with the King. This will give you direct control of distribution of this sort of information in Washington—a control that I believe to be essential in these circumstances.

Yesterday the King described further steps in his thinking about how to meet a confrontation with Col. Papadopoulos and the Revolutionary Council, should one occur.[2] His visits to military units scheduled for June will, he hopes, give him a chance to test the loyalty and discipline of units to which he might want to turn. He thinks that the 20th Armored Division (General Erselman) and other Third Corps elements along the

---

[1] Source: Department of State, Greek Desk Files: Lot 69 D 553, POL 15–1. Secret; Exdis.
[2] Talbot reported on his May 25 conversation with King Constantine in telegram 5466 from Athens, May 26. (Ibid., Central Files, POL 15–1 GREECE)

Evros River (Gen. Zalocoris) might provide him a welcome in case of need. His tentative idea in the event of a confrontation would be to get his family out of the country and then make every effort to get to the north by plane or ship (presumably Royal Hellenic Navy ship) in order to base himself with loyal units, broadcast to the nation, and announce that he was moving south toward Athens to reassert his command over the Armed Forces and his headship of the nation. The success of such a plea, he feels, would depend in part on the loyalty of the Greek Armed Forces, but very substantially also on United States actions. He would hope that we could work out a plan between now and early June which I could then discuss in Washington. He continues to think how fine it would be if the Sixth Fleet could be in the area at the time of confrontation. Its mere presence would probably turn the tide, in his view. He hopes that he and I could also talk, however, about the possible availability of Marines to come ashore peacefully as in Lebanon in 1958, should the need arise. I immediately cautioned him against expectation of any involvement of U.S. forces. It is a long time since 1958, conditions are different, and any such action could be taken only on the express instructions of the highest levels in Washington. I would not want him to draw false encouragement from anything I might either say or not say in response to his comments. He said he understood this but that "we should think of some plan before you go to Washington, so that you can discuss it there in detail."

This is the King's second foray with me on the question of his own contingency plans if it should become impossible to carry on with the present government. Presumably he will raise it again when I see him sometime in the first week of June. We are working on some thoughts here, which I hope to get to you promptly, but I will urgently need the Department's instructions and guidance in coping with further stages of development of the King's ideas.

With best wishes,

Yours sincerely,

Phillips Talbot[3]

---

[3] Printed from a copy that bears this typed signature.

293.   Telegram From the Department of State to the Embassy in Greece[1]

Washington, May 31, 1967, 5:17 p.m.

205238. Ref: Athens 5521, 5509, 5510, 5486.[2]

1. While we consider appointment of committee to revise Greek constitution as positive step towards eventual return to constitutional processes, we are nonetheless disturbed by other steps taken by new government, as well as by comment by Min Papadopoulos and press organs close to him, which appear to indicate that govt. does not intend to return to parliamentarianism in near future. We recognize that somewhat contradictory developments may represent split within coup leadership as to ultimate aim of April 21 "revolution." Therefore, as part of continuing U.S pressure towards return to parliamentary government, as well as to encourage those elements within govt. supporting return to constitutional processes, we recommend that you call on PriMin Kollias at early opportunity to set forth following points:

(a) U.S. is encouraged by May 30 announcement of appointment of 20-member committee which will revise constitution and submit it to govt. within six months. This step is consistent with earlier statements by King and govt. leaders of an intention to return to constitutional processes, and we hope that it will soon be followed by announcement of date completed document will be presented to Greek people for approval.

(b) However, we are disturbed by certain other developments which seem to suggest a step-up in repressive measures. Among these is arrest of additional non-Communist politicians, including John Tsouderos, as well as delay in release of several thousand political prisoners, as earlier promised in govt. statements. We are also concerned by statements in newspapers reflecting govt. opinion that return to parliamentary democracy will be far in the future, as well as by articles in such papers seemingly aimed at discrediting parliamentarianism. Also disquieting is Papadopoulos statement that "termination of life of revolution before it fulfills its tasks would be act of highest treason both to nation and to people (Athens 5509).

(c) Degree to which new govt. moves (or does not move) towards restoration democratic institutions is closely followed by American pub-

---

[1] Source: Department of State, Central Files, POL 15–5 GREECE. Secret. Drafted by Owens, cleared by Brewster, and approved by Rockwell.

[2] Telegram 5521 from Athens, May 30, reported on membership in the Greek constitutional committee. (Ibid.) Telegram 5509 from Athens, May 29, noted that the Junta had no intention of an early return to parliamentary rule. (Ibid.) Telegram 5510 from Athens, May 29, reported the arrest of two former Ministers and regime opponents. (Ibid., POL 29 GREECE) Telegram 5486 from Athens, May 27, reported other arrests of former political figures. (Ibid.)

lic and Congress. (U.S. press and public concern at recent developments in Greece is illustrated by May 30 *NYTimes* editorial "Backsliding in Greece.") Possibility of returning to normal Greek-U.S. relations, including resumption of MAP, will be directly influenced by new govt.'s progress in returning to constitutional processes and its handling of political prisoners. To extent govt. steps up repressive measures it lessens chances of early return to normal relations.

2. You may wish to draw on above in discussions with other key govt. leaders.[3]

3. We would also appreciate your assessment of recent developments as indicative of split within coup leadership over question of future return to constitutionalism.

Rusk

---

[3] Prior to his return to the United States, Talbot held meetings with Prime Minister Kollias, Pattakos, Makarezos, Spandidakis, and Papadopoulos. Memoranda of these conversations are ibid., Greek Desk Files: Lot 69 D 553, Coup Managers.

---

294.   Telegram From the Department of State to the Embassy in Greece[1]

Washington, July 7, 1967, 5:58 p.m.

2763. Following summary FYI only and Noforn. It is uncleared and subject to revision upon review.

1. The Secretary received Greek Foreign Minister Economou-Gouras July 7.[2]

2. Gouras said that he brought good news re Greek internal situation. New government being supported by people. Examples were attendance at ceremonies in Piraeus municipal theater and Athens stadium. Gouras had thought first might have been arranged but was certain enthusiastic stadium crowd spontaneous.

---

[1] Source: Department of State, Central Files, POL 1 GREECE. Secret; Limdis. Drafted and approved by Rockwell and cleared in S/S. Repeated to Ankara, Nicosia, and Belgrade.

[2] A summary report of the meeting, sent to President Johnson, is ibid., Greek Desk Files: Lot 69 D 553, President's Evening Reading.

3. Foreign Minister recalled he had discussed with Secretary at Luxembourg GOG plans to return to constitutional situation.[3] He happy reaffirm GOG will keep this promise perhaps in an even shorter time frame, a year and a half or two years at latest. He hoped constitutional committee would have finished work before end of year. Gouras explained previous constitution did not have moral support of people since it permitted abuses by political parties. New one will imitate U.S. constitution in that members of government will not be permitted at same time be members of Parliament. Number of deputies will be cut from 300 to 150. Not yet decided whether will be one chamber or two.

4. Gouras alleged Greek financial situation encouraging. Savings in banks and post office accounts last month up 18% over corresponding month 1966.

5. Secretary suggested one or two members of committee considering revision constitution come to U.S. to talk about how provisions of U.S. constitution work; drafters of constitution thought weak executive better than a strong one and result their work is that carrying on business of government requires lots of time and willingness to cooperate between branches thereof; implications of this should be carefully studied. Secretary also suggested that committee make public statements from time to time to show that effort a serious one which making real progress. He thought this would be helpful in counteracting impression that work of revising constitution only window dressing.

6. Foreign Minister said change in Greece was not simple military coup designed merely to change a government but was true revolution similar to that which occurred in 1909 when elder Venizelos came from Crete; military members GOG were not ambitious but modest men who would return to barracks after they had achieved a healthy democracy for Greece. Contrasted their attitude with what he described as previous conspiracy between EDA and leftist branch of CU to establish Communist dictatorship in Greece.

7. In discussion of time which might elapse between plebiscite on new constitution and elections Gouras said difficult be precise. One problem would be revision of electoral lists, as those who have taken part in conspiracy against Greek values will be deprived of right to vote.

8. In response to Secretary's question Gouras said Greek economic situation strong; there was public confidence in government, the drachma had been stabilized, and export-import situation good.

9. Foreign Minister complained of "aggressive" campaign being carried out against Greece by Iron Curtain countries. Mentioned his own

---

[3] No memorandum of conversation has been found, but Secto 19 from Luxembourg, June 14, forwarded the text of a Greek paper on the return to constitutional government. (Ibid., Conference Files: Lot 68 D 453, CF 191)

past role in bettering relations with Greece's Balkan neighbors. Maintained matter of agreement with Yugoslavia not important and new one would be negotiated.

10. In discussing position of King, Gouras said he more popular than ever. Maintained he has accepted revolution and told government he would support it in its task of strengthening Greek democracy. When Secretary inquired who exercises real power in government, Gouras said Prime Minister has very strong position. Military members of course have material power but Prime Minister has decidedly powerful influence over them. Gouras denied rumors of discord between three military members.

11. In response Secretary's question re trade unions, Gouras asserted situation all right now. At Geneva meeting ILO Greek representatives gave unsatisfactory explanation. Nonetheless malicious reports re trade union situation continue to be circulated in order influence international opinion against Greece.

12. In subsequent private session with Secretary Gouras took up MAP. Said military members GOG might "do something crazy" under pressure USG exerting by suspending shipments. Secretary said he going before Senate next week at time when latter very upset by whole U.S. arms policy as result India-Pakistan and Arab-Israel wars and Greek coup. Would jeopardize entire Military Assistance Program if, Secretary said with regard to Greek program, more than that situation continuing under study. Thus Secretary could give Gouras no assurances beyond saying policy under continuing review. Gouras disappointed but said would do best to explain in Athens.

13. Re Cyprus Gouras said GOG had offered 60-year lease on Dhekelia base to Turks but they had turned down. GOG very disappointed. Gouras had had three-hour discussion with Caglayangil in New York with no positive result.

Rusk

295. Circular Airgram From the Department of State to the NATO Capitals[1]

Washington, July 12, 1967, 11:35 a.m.

CA–263. NATUS. Ref: Paris' 275; Moscow's 98.[2]

1. There has been cumulative but still inconclusive evidence over past few weeks that current authoritarian GOG may be giving consideration to plan for ending Cyprus stalemate irrespective of position Archbishop Makarios and those around him. However, we have no concrete evidence to indicate GOG contemplating "coup" despite circulation coup rumors in Athens and Nicosia during last two weeks.[3] Recent radio and press attacks on Makarios and those around him might well have been designed to bring pressure on Archbishop to abandon his position on "genuine enosis" and we now inclined believe GOG will continue pressures on Makarios to obtain his acquiescence in GOG/GOT agreement or his resignation.

2. GOG thinking seems to comprise following elements:

a. Because of its character, it is better able than democratic Greek Government to make settlement which would meet GOT desiderata. Offer of 60-year lease to Turks suggests that GOG may go all the way and offer GOT a sovereign base.

b. Settlement perplexing and frustrating Cyprus problem would satisfy nationalistic aspirations most Greeks, and would add to GOG's own internal and international prestige. This government more than most Greek Governments likely view honorable Greek settlement, i.e., some form enosis, as essential.

c. Makarios and some of those around him either are not prepared to accept form of enosis which would satisfy GOT, but may even prefer continued independence. GOG concerned about growth of anti-enosis sentiment being encouraged on island.

d. Existence of crypto-communist AKEL and its satellite organizations on island is threat to Hellenism as a whole. GOG also clearly con-

---

[1] Source: Department of State, Central Files, POL 27 CYP. Secret; Limdis. Drafted by Horner and McCaskill, cleared by NEA and EUR, and approved by Rockwell. Also sent to Moscow and Belgrade and repeated to Nicosia and Istanbul.

[2] Telegram 275 from Paris, July 6, requested guidance regarding Cyprus in the wake of a July 5 Soviet statement by TASS. (Ibid.) Telegram 98 from Moscow, July 7, reported on the Soviet propaganda offensive charging Western plans for action against the Makarios government. (Ibid.) The Soviet statement expressed concern about U.S. backing of a coup in Cyprus; for text, see *Weekly Digest of the Soviet Press*, July 26, 1967, p. 20.

[3] In telegram 17 from Athens, July 1, Talbot reported that while no evidence existed of plans for a coup against Makarios, the Junta was planning some action regarding Cyprus. (Department of State, Central Files, POL 27 CYP)

cerned about Lyssarides and his influence on Makarios, and about Clerides and others who have vested interest in continuing independence of Cyprus.

3. We assume essential element in any GOG planning would be prior agreement with GOT, possibly in some detail. Thus far there no indication any such agreement reached. In fact, GOG FonMin Economou-Gouras, now in US, has informed us[4] that in recent talks with GOT FonMin Caglayangil he still attempting to prevail upon Turks to accept long lease on Cyprus base, whereas GOT insistent on sovereign base area. In this connection, of course, it possible Gouras not privy to thinking of Athens coup group which may be willing transfer sovereign base area.

4. If GOG thinking along these lines, sequence events envisaged may be something along following pattern (though not necessarily in that order):

a. Secret agreement with GOT, providing for (1) Turkish possession of a sovereign base area in Cyprus, either at Dhekelia, or Karpas Peninsula (but presumably the former), and (2) stipulated guarantees of communal rights of Turkish Cypriot minority.

b. Neutralization, using Greek military units on Cyprus as necessary, of Archbishop Makarios, other Greek Cypriot leaders not clearly in favor of enosis, and, of course, Communists (AKEL) and others of left-wing persuasion. Such neutralization would accord with self-proclaimed objectives of current Greek leadership, and recent official statements from Athens would seem to pave the way towards, or foreshadow, some such action.

c. Placing in positions of power in Cyprus of Greek Cypriot elements in confidence of GOG.

d. Announcement, possibly in collaboration with GOT, of some form of union between Cyprus and Greece. This might take form of Commonwealth relationship, with King Constantine acting as sovereign of Cyprus, GOG assuming responsibilities for foreign affairs, defense, and perhaps also internal security, and, for the rest, internal self-government for Cyprus including careful delineation of role and privileges of Turkish minority.

5. Depending upon kind of action GOG may take, we would expect particularly strong reactions within NATO, which includes three contributors to UNFICYP—Denmark, Canada, and UK. Scandinavians are consistently critical of what they consider shortcomings of fellow NATO members (e.g., Portugal), and Danes have already raised question of Greek internal political developments. These members might well recall

---

[4] See Document 294.

reiterated Greek insistence over past three years in NATO that solution to Cyprus problem was responsibility of UN. More recently, Belgium, Italy and UK have pressed for cancellation of NATO military exercise in Greece for fear of domestic reaction against cooperation with military junta.

6. Soviet Union has initiated considerable diplomatic and propaganda pressure in attempt forestall any change in Cyprus status. Formal TASS statement July 4 expressed Soviet concern with developments around Cyprus and with attempts aggravate again situation in area endangering existence Republic. Statement alleges implementation old plans for coup d'etat not accidental but result NATO plan to exploit situation in Greece extending antipopular militarist dictatorship to Cyprus. Soviet diplomats made virtually identical oral démarches to US (Depcirtel 2553)[5] and UK expressing concern that attempt planned to liquidate sovereignty GOG asserting "certain circles NATO" are behind it. Soviet opposition was reaffirmed to liquidation Cyprus' independence, its dismemberment, and conversion into NATO military base, noting such developments could lead to "significant sharpening already strained situation in area." Démarches cite previous UNSC resolutions on Cyprus and call on receiving governments as permanent members UNSC take all measures to thwart these dangerous plans. Other East European communist states expected to follow USSR in strident and probably drawn-out propaganda campaign. Yugoslavia, already claiming security threatened by advent authoritarian government in Athens, would probably view anticipated events as extension "imperialist" plot. President Tito alleges has shaped diverse developments such as revolutions in Ghana, Greece, Indonesia and recent events in Middle East. We would anticipate considerable Soviet and East European efforts gain non-aligned support for moves keep Cyprus question alive, even if anticipated actions were carried out effectively and quickly and with agreement Turkish government. Recourse to Security Council may be expected.

7. US position on Cyprus is that we are ready to agree to any arrangement acceptable to the parties concerned, i.e, Cyprus and the three guarantor powers (UK, Greece and Turkey). We have urged the Turks and Greeks to continue talking, but have not asked them to keep us informed about these talks.

Rusk

---

[5] In circular telegram 2553, July 7, the Department of State informed posts that Deputy Under Secretary of State for Political Affairs Kohler had denied any NATO plans existed for intervention in Cyprus in a July 6 meeting with Soviet officials. (Department of State, Central Files, POL 27 CYP)

296. Memorandum From Secretary of State Rusk to President Johnson[1]

Washington, July 21, 1967.

SUBJECT

Normalization of US-Greek Relations

We have had a number of interdepartmental discussions recently on the subject of normalizing our relations with the Greek Government.[2] Both in the Regional Group under Assistant Secretary Battle and in the Senior Group chaired by Under Secretary Katzenbach, with Ambassador Talbot present on both occasions, certain steps in this direction have been agreed upon. I am in accord with the conclusions reached.

From the point of view of our relations with Greece, I consider the steps outlined below important to our interests. Ambassador Talbot is returning to Greece at the end of next week and should be able to tell the Greek Government something positive on this score shortly after he arrives.

Recommendation: That you approve the actions described below:[3]

Foreign Policy Aspects

1. Since the April military coup we have withheld delivery on certain major arms to Greece and been quite cool in our relations with the Government with the idea not only of exhibiting disapproval of the methods by which the junta seized control but also, hopefully, of encouraging some return, however gradual, to more constitutional processes.

2. We now believe these tactics are no longer useful and that, if continued longer, may be counterproductive. The King has come to the same conclusion. Ambassador Talbot considers it quite possible the Greeks, although highly desirous of close relations with us, may adopt the same tactics by causing certain difficulties with some of our facilities there.

3. We have in Greece facilities important to the Air Force, the Navy, [*less than 1 line of source text not declassified*] and USIA; they have increased

---

[1] Source: Johnson Library, National Security File, Memos to the President—Walt Rostow, Vol. 35. Secret; Nodis.

[2] An interdepartmental regional group discussed the issue on July 6. A July 13 memorandum to Rusk from Battle reporting its recommendations is in Department of State, Greek Desk Files: Lot 69 D 553, Org. 3. The Senior Interdepartmental Group (SIG) discussed the recommendations on July 19. A July 24 memorandum by Brewster summarizing the conclusions of the SIG meeting is ibid., Lot 71 D 6, DEF 19.

[3] Rostow endorsed the recommendations of Secretary Rusk in a July 22 memorandum (attached to the source text), but President Johnson took no action on the recommendations. (Johnson Library, National Security File, Memos to the President—Walt Rostow, Vol. 35)

in value since the Arab-Israeli war. That war underlined the importance of Greece (along with Turkey and Iran) to U.S. interests.

4. We propose that Ambassador Talbot be authorized to inform the Greek Government of certain relaxations as set forth below, making clear that future actions in this regard will be related to progress in the restoration of constitutional processes: (a) a coastal minesweeper ($2.9 million); (b) one F–104G trainer ($1.5 million); (c) sidewinder missiles and related equipment which are excess to the needs of the Netherlands (no charge); and (d) 175mm cannons (8–$1.05 million). These items were chosen (a) as having a clear NATO context and (b) as obviously not lending themselves to the suppression of civil disturbances.

5. We believe we should not release just yet either tanks, helicopters, or other heavy equipment. (With respect to FRG shipment of military assistance to Greece, particularly including tanks, we believe we should give the Germans the go-ahead signal in the near future but not just at this time.)

Congressional Problems

1. Although the timing of this action is not particularly favorable given the concern in Congressional quarters with respect to arms programs, both sale and grant, nevertheless, we believe we must proceed and that the over-all interest of foreign policy requires that we do so as soon as possible. We judge that although there will be some adverse reaction in Congress and elsewhere, it will not be great and can be reasonably contained by stressing the following:

a. This is a minimum step.
b. Greece, like Turkey and Iran, emerges as particularly important to the U.S. given the uncertainties in the Middle East and the Soviet thrust in that area.
c. It is essential that we maintain Greece as an active and functioning member of NATO under whose umbrella the arms programs are developed.
d. We must avoid pressing Greece in the direction of the French with their lukewarm and unhelpful posture in a NATO context.

2. If you approve the above course of action, we will undertake a certain amount of educational work on the Hill. How much can perhaps better be determined after the appearance on July 26 of Secretary of Defense McNamara before the Senate Foreign Relations Committee in a hearing on military assistance programs.

Dean Rusk

297.   Letter From the Ambassador to Greece (Talbot) to the Country Director for Greece (Brewster)[1]

Athens, August 7, 1967.

Dear Dan:

Having heard nothing further on the limited military assistance items whose transfer was recommended by SIG and IRG, I assume that the process of getting White House and Congressional clearance has, as we had more or less anticipated, proved difficult. I also assume that my extended presence in Washington would not have changed this situation, and that it was wise for me to leave the Capitol and return to Athens on schedule.

At this end my impressions are gradually taking shape, but I have hesitated to express my views on the changing scene before fresh talks with the military members of the Government as well as with the King and the Prime Minister. Later this week I would hope that process would be sufficiently advanced to permit me to express fresh opinions with confidence.

My tentative impressions are that internal consolidation by the coup group has substantially advanced during my absence and that as more prospective difficulties have become apparent there is greater sensitivity and some change in the wider public mood.

Specifically, purging of persons on whom the coup leaders cannot confidently depend has proceeded not only through the upper reaches of the Air Force and Navy (but not yet the Army) but also into the gendarmerie and police as well as civilian ministries and agencies. Some changes are distinct improvements, e.g., ETVA and GAEC. Elsewhere replacements have either proved undistinguished or, indeed, unavailable. While the departure of Zolotas and John Pezmazoglu will undoubtedly attract the most international attention, with Galanis at the helm this shift may be less important than changes in other areas.

Distasteful developments include the tightening of the screws in the fields of education and the arts. The Embassy's airgram (A–68)[2] spells out these details. Nor is it encouraging to hear that Papaconstantinou is running into increasing frustrations so that instead of an early end to press censorship we could just possibly see an early end to Papaconstantinou as a Government official.

---

[1] Source: Department of State, Greek Desk Files: Lot 71 D 6, Letters from Athens. Secret.

[2] Airgram A–68, August 3, reported on education and the arts under the Junta. (Ibid., Central Files, CUL 2 GREECE)

As the Embassy has reported, the economy shows many signs of weakness including spreading unemployment in the industrial sector. You have seen our reports of labor restiveness. Businessmen, too, seem more acutely aware now than in June of the prospect that this reform government will put a sharper tax bite on them than has been their past lot.

On the constitutional front there is a good deal of confusion and of skepticism. We should get deeper into this question during the current week. In any event, I hear numbers of people now discussing matters from the implicit assumption that the coup group will attempt to stay in power indefinitely.

By and large, however, my impression is that a good many influential Greeks believe the country still has open options and that perhaps the King with American encouragement can bring this Government to a recognition of the need for constitutional progress. Since this is so central a question in the United States, I would rather hold off for some days before making a current estimate of the prospects. As the Embassy's recent reporting has made clear, there are a good many difficulties.

All this should not, I believe, be interpreted to mean that we should go slowly on the limited moves agreed to by IRG and SIG. On the contrary, my fears have been strengthened that the Greeks are moving into a prickly and negative mood and that it will not be easy to persuade them to wait quietly while we sort out our domestic policy issues. The argument in favor of flexibility in handling military assistance remains very strong indeed. If we are to have any chance of pulling Greece into the direction of constitutionalism, this one limited bit of leverage should certainly be available to us.

I recognize that an interim letter of this kind may do more to raise the level of your concerns than to clarify your analyses of the situation here. I will have to try to be better based and more explicit in communicating with you later in the week.

With best wishes always,

Yours sincerely,

Phil

August 8

P.S. After dictating the above paragraphs yesterday, I had a reception last evening for Archbishop Iakovos which brought into the open a disturbing note of which we were already generally aware. None of the invited Ministers turned up. (Nor, it appears, did either Kollias or Papadopoulos attend the Fourth of July reception.) In the course of the afternoon, when Papadopoulos' staff man, Major Lambropoulos, telephoned the Minister's regrets for the evening, Geoff Ogden told him that Congressman Brademas would like to see the Colonel and suggested a drink at the Residence sometime today. Lambropoulos was exceedingly curt in explaining the Minister was busy today and in any event a request to see the Minister should be made through the Protocol Office of the Foreign Office. He had earlier given Stephen Calligas a similar answer to a request by Malcolm Forbes for a meeting. It is evident that we have a problem. Whether resistance to social relations is a harbinger of further counter-irritance to our policy of coolness and non-decision on military matters is a question we will try to probe promptly though deftly.

298.   Telegram From the Embassy in Greece to the Department of State[1]

Athens, August 7, 1967, 1130Z.

684. Ref: Athens 604.[2]

1. During my conversation with King July 30 he referred once again to the possibility that in end he might have to come into confrontation with present regime. As Dept aware King's view of inevitability or desirability of confrontation has varied in past several months depending generally on temperature of his cooperative relationship with Junta (read Papadopoulos). More recently King has indicated he views immediate period after submission of draft Constitution as sensitive one in which confrontation may be unavoidable if regime does not keep faith with its assurances re Constitution and early referendum [document number not declassified].[3] This same three-month period is also considered one of incipient crisis by a majority of Greeks who for present are willing to give regime chance to prove its intention.

2. King spoke of contacts he had made with senior Generals and others, and seemed reasonably expectant that in event of showdown he could get adequate support to oust Junta. He did not want to precipitate action, however, unless US knew and approved of his purposes. He did not ask, as he had done in the past, about prospects that he could count on American fleet presence or logistic assistance.

3. In replying, I pointed out that at present US heavily committed in many parts of the world. I tried to get him to understand that US should

---

[1] Source: Department of State, Central Files, POL 15–1 GREECE. Secret; Exdis.

[2] Telegram 604, July 31, reported King Constantine's impressions of the internal political situation. (Ibid.)

[3] Not found.

not be looked to for participation in any change in governmental arrangements. This sort of decision could be made only by him. King said he understood, but if it should become necessary to move he would advise USG in advance.

4. As example of influences now being brought to bear on King, I was interested in his account of secret visit to him by retired General Gennimatas, former Chief of HNDGS. Latter had reminded him there had long been suspicions that Papadopoulos and other colonels had been plotting and that he, Gennimatas, had dispersed them to distant commands whereas subsequently Gen. Spandidakis had permitted them to reassemble in Athens posts. He thought this could mean Spandidakis was in on plot, though he hoped not. In any case, colonels are more known than respected by armed forces, who now accept their authority for lack of current alternative. Gennimatas proposed that when new Constitution ready King move to dispose of colonels. They could be thanked for their role in saving country from Communism, decorated, and returned to dispersed units or retired. From then on, armed forces would pay no attention to them. Alternatively, they could be forced to resign from army in order to stay in politics. Here, again, they would lose grip over armed forces. Key point, he said, was not to permit important further changes in the army before the new Constitution readied. It would then be essential to move before Junta consolidated control over army commands. Whatever course King might choose to pursue in ridding country of these colonels, Gennimatas was convinced armed forces would support him absolutely. King had listened with interest but without commitments. He said he did not know whether Gennimatas was organizing a movement among senior military people against the colonels, but in any case he would not interfere. (*DATT comment:* Gennimatas' views are correct but he is not known to be in any particular contact with any group.)

5. *Comment:* We have recently had reports of preliminary plotting by several groups of officers (mostly recently retired) [2 *document numbers not declassified*].[4] We believe some of this is motivated by their belief King would support a countercoup. (It is fairly generally assumed that his trips to north were for purpose polling amount of support he could count on in such event.) Some may also believe that American attitude of coolness toward a "colonels" regime implies we would support a countercoup by other military. However, we see no evidence yet that plotters pinpointed so far would be an improvement over current regime, either as scheduling early return to constitutional processes or acting with more leniency in repressive measures. This estimate would, of course, be revised if regime gave indications of betraying assurances both to US and Greek public re return to parliamentary life. We will also have to

---

[4] Neither found.

watch carefully what, if any, progress various groups make in coalescing to point they undermine regime's control of key units in Attica area or consolidate their control of sufficient other ones (Larrissa and the north) to neutralize regime's superiority in Attica.

6. *(Comments cont'd)* Some of the plotters are known to have been awaiting my return and any comments I might make, either directly or around town, to get nuances of latest Washington attitude toward present regime. To extent there are incipient coup ambitions in Greek military, we face tricky period of attempting to avoid giving impression either that we firmly endorse present regime or that we would encourage some countercoup.

7. *[less than 1 line of source text not declassified]* DATT concur in comment.

Talbot

---

299.   Telegram From the Embassy in Turkey to the Department of State[1]

Ankara, August 29, 1967, 1620Z.

966. Report No. 1. Subj: Cyprus and the dialogue.

1. Following must be fully protected as Caglayangil intended his comments only for my ears.

2. I have now had two conversations with him[2] and expect follow-up tomorrow with Asst SecGen Turkmen, following which expect to present more complete report containing suggestions for President's future conversation with King Constantine in Washington. In interim it is clear that:

A. GOT and GOG are and have been in contact throughout last month regarding Greek proposal for PriMinister level meeting. There is no lack of contact. Proposal has been under intensive review and apparently considered by National Security Council evening Aug 29. Ambassador Tuluy here from Athens as an advisor. Further details by separate message.

B. GOT is not well impressed with proposal for PM-level meeting which it sees as reflecting GOG desire for "gesture" to show to NATO Al-

---

[1] Source: Department of State, Central Files, POL 27 CYP. Secret; Priority; Nodis. Repeated to Athens and Nicosia.

[2] Reported in telegram 967 from Ankara, August 29. (Ibid.)

lies that it is legitimate govt by appearing to negotiate major question with its neighbor. On substance GOT sees no signs GOG prepared to take real step forward. Caglayangil adversely impressed by "bargaining tactics" of Greek Govt, failure to make progress on substantive preparations for high-level meeting. GOT concerned over position in which would find itself in proceeding to such meeting (which could not be held without publicity) in face recent Greek public pronouncements that only solution for Cyprus is enosis. If Prime Minister Demirel went to meeting under present circumstances his political opposition would galvanize general Turk public around suspicion he meeting Kollias "to discuss enosis."

3. I made point that our assessment of King Constantine, with whom Ambassador Talbot enjoys particularly close relations, is that he is deeply committed to find Cyprus settlement which would lay basis for permanent friendship with Turkey; and that he could and would be sort of guarantor or underwriter of any agreed settlement, thus legitimizing it for an elected successor Greek Govt. Caglayangil agreed with our assessment of King but stated GOT does not feel same confidence toward rest of GOG, which in discussions continuously raises the ante "from two to eight" in its own favor. GOT has emphasized to GOG that on basis its four principles "there are 20 ways" to settle Cyprus problem: federation, cantonment, adjustment of Zurich agreements, etc. Greece on other hand offers Turkey "lease for sixty or eighty years". Former US Ambassador Warren (believe he meant Amb. Hare) had supported such offer to Inonu who replied that even if Parliament accepted it he would refuse for "only a big power can keep a base on foreign territory." In answer my query about personalities he said Economou-Gouras is a technician and ineffectual. Kollias much better but controlled by, not controlling, the military leaders. I said this left question of how dialogue could be carried forward but I expected that King Constantine would mention privately to President at Washington GOG's "unanswered" proposal for PM level meeting. As it possible that King is not fully informed on GOT–GOG exchanges proposal, was there something useful President could say in rejoinder?

Caglayangil suggested might be emphasized to King that in view tension in Middle East now is time for rapid solution of Cyprus problem. Greece should recognize that Turkish attitudes conditioned by former possession of Cyprus and by allegiance of Turk-Cypriots to Turkey. It should therefore take into account not just what is in Turkey's interest but what is within Turkey's range of possibilities, in negotiating Cyprus settlement. Then he hesitated and said Turkmen would let me have more closely reasoned suggestion August 30. (This being Turk holiday I expect it may be August 31.)

I also stressed that we also felt that now was time to reach such agreement since present Govt of Greece, if it could be galvanized to take substantive steps would not need concern itself as much with press or public position as would a successor elected government. Latter in fact would probably be unable to tackle such basic decision but on other hand would find it hard to reverse or declare illegitimate such agreement if it carried King's endorsement. Caglayangil and Turkmen seemed to agree.[3]

Hart

---

[3] In telegram 972 from Ankara, August 31, Hart reported that a meeting between the Greek and Turkish Prime Ministers would take place September 9–10. He added that Demirel had expressed pessimism about chances of a breakthrough. (Ibid.)

---

300.   Memorandum From Secretary of State Rusk to President Johnson[1]

KCG/G–2   Washington, September 7, 1967.

SUBJECT

    Your Meeting with King Constantine of Greece

King Constantine is coming to Washington at his request.[2] While the main purpose of his visit is to explain the aims of the Greek Government which came to power in the April 21, 1967 coup and to obtain U.S. understanding and support for the Government, at the same time he will seek Presidential assurances of U.S. backing in any confrontation he might

---

[1] Source: Department of State, Briefing Book Files: Lot 69 D 553, Visit of King Constantine. Secret. Talking points for the President's meeting with the King were attached but are not printed.

[2] King Constantine had been scheduled to make a good will tour of Europe and Canada. Following the April coup, the Western European portion of the tour was cancelled. Telegram 589 from Athens, July 30, reported that the King hoped to utilize some of the days originally scheduled for Europe to make an informal visit to the United States and had requested a meeting with the President. (Ibid., Central Files, POL 7 GREECE) President Johnson approved an invitation on August 4. (Johnson Library, National Security File, Country File, Greece, King Constantine) Telegram 876 from Athens, August 18, reported that the King had expressed the desire for a private meeting with the President to discuss Cyprus and internal Greek developments. (Department of State, Central Files, POL 7 GREECE)

have with the Greek junta. The King views his role as one of continuously pressing the coup leaders in the direction of a return to democratic processes. He also believes that his standing with the junta, as well as Greek-U.S. relations, will be enhanced by the resumption of U.S. military assistance to Greece. The very fact that you have agreed to receive him will strengthen his position with the Government.

We share the King's view that he can play a constructive role in encouraging the Greek Government in the direction of constitutionalism. However, we believe we should caution him against pushing the regime to the point of provoking a confrontation, since we do not want to see armed conflict in Greece and would not wish to intervene militarily in his behalf. We realize that walking such a narrow line is a difficult course to follow, and believe that the visit offers the occasion to reassure the 27-year old King of our recognition of the importance of the monarchy as well as our appreciation of his vital role in returning the country to constitutionalism. On military assistance, we believe that you should inform the King that full resumption of MAP is out of the question at this time because of strong public and Congressional sentiment against such a move; however, we are prepared to consider releasing a few of the items now currently suspended. In this way we can bolster the King's position vis-à-vis the coup leadership as well as prevent our own relations with the Greek Government from becoming frozen.

In sum, we believe that the visit of the King can serve a useful purpose in making clear our profound desire for continued close relations with Greece as well as our belief in the necessity for an early return to constitutional government. It also provides an opportunity to reassure the King of our support for him and at the same time to discourage him from moving into a confrontation with the junta.

Dean Rusk

301. Memorandum of Meeting Between President Johnson and King Constantine[1]

Washington, September 11, 1967.

King Constantine of Greece in his conversations with the President described developments in Greece and pointed to two times at which the confrontation with the coup leaders might occur: (1) at the time the committee report on the constitutional revision was reviewed by the coup leaders, and (2) at the time of a plebiscite on the constitutional revision. The first might be in December, the second later in 1968. The King was not certain that a confrontation would occur on the other hand—it might occur at any time if a "second round" were attempted—but these two times were obvious potential points when the crunch might come. The King elaborated on the fact that if a confrontation were to occur, it would be on issues of real substance, not on such questions as, for example, military appointments.

The King expressed a lack of confidence in the coup leaders' ability to come up with coherent government policies. He did not think that they had the talents to govern. He was evidently by no means confident that they would stick to the constitutional commitment and schedule.

Speaking of return to constitutional government and the King's relationships with the military in general, he noted that he had some support of certain military leaders in the northern areas but he recognized that as time went on the coup leaders were attempting to infiltrate all commands with officers of absolute loyalty to them.

The King spoke at some length about the question of confrontation and his relationships with the coup leaders. He gave the impression of being serious-minded and devoted to the concept of returning Greece to constitutional procedures and democratic processes. He stated that he was willing to get his family out of Greece if tensions between him and the coup leaders grew, and to go so far as to risk his life if a confrontation were unavoidable.

---

[1] Source: Department of State, Central Files, POL 15–1 GREECE. Secret; Nodis. The source text, which bears the handwritten dates "9/13" and "9/15/67," bears no drafting information but, according to a September 25 covering memorandum by Benjamin Read, it was prepared on the basis of Walt Rostow's recollections. According to the President's Daily Diary, he met with King Constantine alone in the Oval Office from 12:37 to 1:30 p.m., when they joined Vice President Humphrey, Secretary Rusk, Secretary McNamara, Walt Rostow, Assistant Secretary of State for Near Eastern and South Asian Affairs Lucius Battle, Greek Chargé Alcibiades C. Papadopoulos, and Grand Marshal of the Greek Court Leonidas Papagos for a luncheon. The King left the White House at 2:35 p.m. (Johnson Library)

During his Washington visit, the King also met with members of Congress. A memorandum of this conversation is in the Washington National Records Center, RG 84, Athens Post Files: FRC 72 A 5030, POL 7 Visits, King Constantine.

He inquired as to what we were prepared to do in the case of a confrontation and spoke of the possibility of (1) the landing of marines as a show of force, (2) the positioning of Sixth Fleet units in Greek waters, and (3) a sympathetic U.S. posture and a public statement reaffirming the U.S. support for the King's efforts to return the country to constitutionalism.

The President explained the problems growing out of such a request and noted that a military intervention would not be feasible. The question of a public statement would be studied in the light of circumstances at the time, but he could not commit himself in advance on this question.

Addressing himself to the question of military aid, the King made a plea for restoration of military aid, noting that the continued withholding of aid was not achieving the U.S. political objectives and causing serious irritation to the coup colonels. Some military aid linked to continued loyalty to the constitutional scenario would be helpful.

The President made clear that he could make no commitment until legislation was passed but indicated that he understood the King's argument.

In terms of specific requests, the King pointed to the need to be in a position to communicate with his people in the event of a confrontation and asked for a possible use of VOA radio facilities (either Thessaloniki or more likely Rhodes). Secondly, he asked for more efficient two-way communications facilities between the Palace and the US Embassy in Athens. His third request was for US support of a program loan of $70 million for Greece to assist in the reconstruction of the earthquake-damaged areas. On this subject Mr. Rostow explained the problems involved in reopening the question of a program loan for a country that had graduated from the AID school and had achieved the economic growth rate which Greece had over the past years. Speaking to the question of the earthquake, it was stated that the needs on that front could be examined with a view to any assistance of a humanitarian nature that might be given to relieve the temporary housing needs in the stricken areas. There was talk of examining the possibility of obtaining Nissen huts but it was understood that this matter would have to be explored more fully with Athens.

The King explained the legal position with Andreas Papandreou, and the President explained our political problem with him and other political prisoners. It was clear the King did not rule out an amnesty once the legal procedures had been followed.

The King explained his deep disappointment in the failure of the Cyprus talks. Secretary Rusk volunteered that he would take the matter up with the two Foreign Secretaries in New York.

THE CYPRUS CRISIS OF 1967 AND THE VANCE MEDIATION, SEPTEMBER–DECEMBER 1967

302. Telegram From the Department of State to the Embassy in Greece[1]

Washington, September 15, 1967, 0019Z.

37758. NATUS. Ref: Athens' 1266; Ankara's 1220.[2]

1. While Department had not expected weekend talks between Greek and Turk Prime Ministers would lead to immediate or dramatic results, we are disappointed learn that two parties were so far apart. We had felt earlier Toumbas–Caglayangil conversations were leading in direction "compensated enosis" and had believed GOG willingness offer GOT sovereign base area on Cyprus would be main ingredient in Turkish acceptance enosis. On other hand, Greek delegation probably went Kesan/Alexandropolis meeting with somewhat exaggerated expectations. One can speculate that becoming aware of Greek junta's desire achieve settlement for political reasons, GOT has somewhat raised its price for agreement. We would appreciate views Embassies Athens and Ankara this point.

2. We are concerned lest this setback could lead to loss momentum and dissipation of favorable atmosphere which has existed. Both sides seem be weary of prolonged stalemate since December 1963. In talking with senior officials of GOG and GOT, we hope you will convey our strong belief that Prime Ministerial meeting, although lacking in concrete results, represents act of statesmanship and sincere endeavor to frankly come to grips with Cyprus problem. We hope that both countries will avoid taking rigid or intransigent positions, and will not rake over past grievances. Important thing now is that talks continue, and that real effort be made compromise on differences which, if substantial, do not seem be irreconcilable.

Rusk

---

[1] Source: Department of State, Central Files, POL 27 CYP. Secret; Exdis. Drafted by Horner, cleared by NEA, and approved by Rockwell. Also sent to Ankara and repeated to Nicosia, London, and Paris.

[2] These telegrams, both dated September 12, reported Greek and Turkish impressions of the September 9–10 meetings of Prime Ministers Demirel and Kollias. Telegram 1266 from Athens is ibid., POL GREECE–TUR; telegram 1220 from Ankara is ibid., POL 27 CYP.

303.   Telegram From the Department of State to the Embassy in Turkey[1]

Washington, September 18, 1967, 2249Z.

39286. 1. NEA is considering recommending to the Secretary that in his forthcoming talks with Turkish and Greek Prime Ministers at 22nd GA he raise the possibility of an approach to Cyprus problem which might by-pass the major difficulties which we believe Greeks and Turks have been encountering in their bilateral talks. We would suggest that if this initiative seemed to evoke interest on the part of the two Foreign Ministers, the Secretary might agree to the discreet presentation of such possibility in more concrete form at a time and place to be mutually agreed upon. It would be made clear we not offering to mediate, but rather to assist efforts of parties concerned which we continue to regard as best road to solution.

2. Substance of the proposal we have in mind is the creation of a form of commonwealth relationship between Greece and Cyprus, with substantial guarantees for the Turkish Cypriots and advantages for Turkey. This follows along the lines of Wehmeyer paper which you have seen.

3. If our calculation is correct, the atmosphere making for a settlement is better now than it has been for some time. We believe there is mounting weariness on the part of all concerned with the existing stalemate, the expense involved and the damage to the Greek and Turkish security situation in the Eastern Mediterranean. At the same time we think we detect disappointment and uncertainty on the part of the GOG. A proffer of good offices on our part would, we think, be well received, although we cannot of course predict that it would have tangible results. It should be emphasized that we are thinking of a careful, discreet and cautious approach to the matter, so as minimize possibility misinterpretation of our motives. On balance we tend to think possible gains overbalance predictable disadvantages.

4. Department would appreciate comments of three Ambassadors by C.O.B. Tuesday, September 19.[2]

Rusk

---

[1] Source: Department of State, Central Files, POL 27 CYP. Secret; Immediate; No Distribution Outside Department. Drafted by Horner, cleared by NEA and L, and approved by Rockwell. Also sent to Athens and Nicosia.

[2] Telegram 1364 from Athens, September 19, reported that the Greek Government would welcome active U.S. intervention in the Cyprus negotiation process. (Ibid.) Telegram 355 from Nicosia, September 19, responded that while Makarios and other Greek Cypriots would welcome a more active U.S. role, the Turkish Cypriots would be highly mistrustful. (Ibid.) No reply from Ankara has been found.

304. Telegram From the Embassy in Greece to the Department of State[1]

Athens, September 20, 1967, 1525Z.

1382. NATUS Info.

1. King Constantine last night expressed to me his "fed-upness" with hardened Turkish position which had brought to naught Prime Ministerial meeting on which he had pinned strong hopes. Acknowledging Greek side might have bungled discussions, King doubted even extreme Greek ineptness could have caused such sharp change in Turkish position. He could not understand how Turkish side could say enosis had not been contemplated when even word enosis was included in paper jointly signed by Toumbas and Caglayangil last December. Col. Papadopoulos and his associates now believe British probably responsible for Turkish intransigence.[2] (I expressed doubt British could or would have played that role.) King himself could think of no reason except Turkish desire to trim sails to Soviet winds on eve of Demirel's Moscow visit. In any case, King saw no point in further efforts to deal with Turkish Government at this stage. Perhaps when Turkish reasoning clarified, somebody (presumably meaning U.S.) could help get Turks back on rails. In meantime King would have no further interest in "this kind of game."

2. I commented that out of our own sad experiences with international disputes we had repeatedly been taught necessity for patience and persistence. Continuation of dialogue could be very important. King heard me out but without further comment turned to other subjects.

Talbot

---

[1] Source: Department of State, Central Files, POL 27 CYP. Secret; Priority; Limdis. Repeated to Ankara, Nicosia, London, Paris, and USUN.

[2] Queried by the Department of State in telegram 41302 to Athens, September 21, about the apparent discrepancies in Greek versions of this meeting, Talbot responded in telegram 1431 from Athens, September 22, that enosis was mentioned in the "Basic Principles" document initialed by the Foreign Ministers at the beginning of the meeting and that this had been inserted by the Greek side as one of its objectives. In initialing, the Turkish Foreign Minister was simply acknowledging he understood the other side's basic principles. (Both ibid.)

305.   Memorandum of Conversation[1]

SecDel/MC–16   New York, September 28, 1967, 4:15 p.m.

SECRETARY'S DELEGATION TO THE TWENTY-SECOND SESSION
OF THE UNITED NATIONS GENERAL ASSEMBLY
New York, September–October 1967

SUBJECT

Cyprus Problem (Part I of V)

PARTICIPANTS

US	Cyprus
The Secretary	Foreign Minister Spyros Kyprianou
Robert A. Stein, NEA Adviser	Ambassador Zenon Rossides, Permanent Representative to UN
	Mr. Andreas Jacovides, Director of Political Division, Ministry of Foreign Affairs, Nicosia

The Foreign Minister declared at the outset that the Cyprus problem, of course, was by far the major issue for them. He said that Cyprus was not surprised at the result of the Evros talks, because the Cypriots had always had reservations with regard to the Greek-Turkish dialogue. He said that now that the dialogue is ended Cyprus is considering what should be done next. He said that the situation in Cyprus is improved over what it was a year ago, and it is time to strengthen efforts for peace by finding another procedure to follow. Could common ground be found within a UN framework? He commented that the Cyprus Government is thinking in terms of "good offices". Possibly something along this line might make it easier for the Greeks and the Turks. A vacuum may be dangerous, he said. We are in a period of reconsideration, and are ready to consider anything.

The Secretary said that he knew that U Thant was concerned about the cost of the UN force on Cyprus. He said that U Thant had mentioned it at his dinner for the Big Four Foreign Ministers but there was not much reaction from the Ministers. The Foreign Minister said that the annual cost is about $8 million.

The Secretary said that the US has no fresh ideas on the subject, and asked the Foreign Minister if the Cyprus Government is in a hurry for

---

[1] Source: Department of State, Central Files, POL 27 CYP. Confidential; Exdis. Drafted by Stein and approved in S on October 2. The meeting was held in the Secretary's office in the U.S. Mission. Memoranda of other portions of this conversation dealing with trade with Cuba, the Middle East, U.S. facilities in Cyprus, and United Nations affairs are ibid., Conference Files: Lot 68 D 453, CF 216.

action. The Foreign Minister replied that there is no particular hurry, but the situation cannot continue on indefinitely. He observed that some procedure such as good offices would have a calming effect. He mentioned that the UN force on the island had a peacemaking as well as peacekeeping role. The Secretary asked if the presence of the force causes problems, and the Foreign Minister replied in the negative, saying that an absence of the force would, however.

The Secretary asked whether the Foreign Minister thought that a new procedure would lead quickly to a solution. Mr. Kyprianou did not think so, but he believed it would be helpful in eliminating impractical ideas. The Turks, for instance, are thinking of a condominium. In reply to a question the Foreign Minister said he believed there is a consensus among the people of the island for enosis. He thought the use of good offices would be a way of clarifying many of the issues involved. The Cyprus problem is affected by the situation in Greece, he said. With regard to the Turks, is it a problem for them of security or of the Turkish Cypriots? Do the Turks want partition? Under good offices this could all be discussed in a logical way.

The Secretary told the Foreign Minister that in his meeting yesterday with Turkish Foreign Minister Caglayangil[2] the word Cyprus did not come up once. The Secretary added that it would be convenient if the US could take the same position the British did for three years back in the 40's with regard to the Palestine question. Their position was that Britain would go along with anything the parties concerned decided.

The Secretary ascertained that the Foreign Minister had spoken to U Thant about the possibility of a new procedure being adopted. He said that U Thant would like to stop spending that $8 million a year, and he is certainly entitled to try to do so. The Secretary commented that there might be two or three procedures: to find a solution, to keep things in hand until a solution is found, or to keep things in hand without anything further in mind. He said he would talk with his colleagues in the Department on the subject of a new procedure.

---

[2] Memoranda of Rusk's conversations with Caglayangil are ibid.

306. Memorandum of Conversation[1]

SecDel/MC–17   New York, September 29, 1967, 10 a.m.

SECRETARY'S DELEGATION TO THE TWENTY-SECOND SESSION
OF THE UNITED NATIONS GENERAL ASSEMBLY
New York, September–October 1967

SUBJECT

US-Greek Relations (Part II of III)

PARTICIPANTS

U.S.	Greece
The Secretary	Foreign Minister Paul Economou-Gouras
Robert A. Stein, NEA Adviser	Ambassador to the US Christian Palamas

The Foreign Minister said that work was going forward on drafting a Greek Constitution. When the Secretary asked if there was something on paper, the Foreign Minister said it is too early since work is now only in the pre-draft stage. It is hoped that a working draft will be available in about a month and that there will be a final draft before the end of the year. He said that the Greek Government would be sending a committee to the US, France, and the Scandinavian countries to consult with constitutional experts.

The Foreign Minister declared that the Greeks are concerned about the weakening of the security situation in their area. He said that in addition to the threat from the north, Soviet naval forces now in the Mediterranean to the south make the country feel insecure. He mentioned that Greece has a long border—850 miles—with communist territory. He said that he would like to see NATO concentrate not only on the defense of its flanks but also on the interior lines. The Secretary said that there should be no worry in a military sense because of the Soviet naval force. They are in an exposed position, and would go back into the Black Sea if trouble were in the offing. The Foreign Minister agreed that the Soviet naval force was more serious from a political than from a military aspect.

The Foreign Minister declared that Greece wanted to be helped by its friends. The Secretary said that the Greek regime caused a big problem in US, and our whole aid bill is having difficult passage in Congress as a result. The Secretary explained that the President and the Executive

---

[1] Source: Department of State, Central Files, POL GREECE–US. Confidential. Drafted by Stein and approved in S on October 2. The meeting was held in the Secretary's office in the U.S. Mission. Memoranda of other portions of this conversation dealing with Cyprus and Vietnam are ibid., Conference Files: Lot 68 D 453, CF 216.

branch of our government get no money at all to spend that is not authorized by the Congress. The King's visit and his discussions with members of Congress helped, but we will not know for a while what funds will be authorized. Perhaps we will have more of an idea in two weeks or so.

The Foreign Minister said that the Greek leaders are not ambitious. They are patriotic men who want to see Greece out of the mess it is in. The Foreign Minister said that he is afraid they would become desperate when Greece's friends do not show an understanding attitude. He pointed out that Greece had voted with the United States yesterday in the debate in the General Assembly on the question of defining aggression. Turkey and Cyprus had abstained in the vote.

The Secretary said that the Greek coup d'etat was the sixty-fourth to occur in the world since he became Secretary of State. He observed that there had been no prior consultation with us, and the coup had created serious problems for us. While we recognize that the matter is an internal one for Greece, it does cause the US problems. The Secretary said that we are friends and allies, and both of us would like to see our relations improve, but it will take time.

The Foreign Minister remarked that he and Ambassador Palamas continue to have hope, and that is why they are serving this government. The Secretary replied that we take note of the fact that men like the Minister and the Ambassador are in the Greek Government and draw encouragement from this fact. The Foreign Minister mentioned that he and others are fighting to keep Greece in NATO. He asked why there was so much criticism against Greece and not Portugal. The Secretary answered that probably people expect more of Greece.

307. Editorial Note

Fighting between Turkish Cypriot military formations and Greek Cypriot police and National Guard units broke out on November 15, 1967, at Agios Theodoros and nearby Kophinou. On November 16, the Turkish Government demanded that Greek Cypriots immediately cease their attacks and threatened military intervention. The following day, a Turkish note to the Greek Government demanded the removal of its troops on Cyprus, the recall of General Grivas, compensation for victims of Greek Cypriot attacks, and the end of restrictions on Turkish Cypriots.

After consultations with the involved states and at the United Nations, the United States decided to send a special envoy to the area to support the efforts of U.N. and NATO representatives to avoid a military clash over the island.

On November 22, President Johnson asked former Under Secretary of Defense Cyrus Vance to serve as his envoy. Vance arrived in Ankara at noon the following day. Between November 23 and December 4, Vance shuttled among Ankara, Athens, and Nicosia in an effort to secure a peaceful settlement. Documentation on the Vance mission is in Department of State, Central Files, POL 27 CYPRUS, and ibid., POL 7 US–VANCE, and Johnson Library, Tom Johnson's Notes of Meetings.

Also on November 22, U.N. Secretary-General U Thant announced that he was sending José Rolz-Bennett to the three capitals as his Special Representative to convey directly to the governments his grave concern and his "urgent appeal for utmost restraint." For text of his statement (U.N. Doc. S/8248/Add.3), see *American Foreign Policy: Current Documents, 1967*, pages 365–366.

---

308. Memorandum of Telephone Conversation[1]

November 15, 1967, 8 p.m.

SUBJECT

Cyprus Situation

PARTICIPANTS

Ambassador Parker T. Hart, Ankara, Turkey

Stuart W. Rockwell, Deputy Assistant Secretary, NEA

Mr. Rockwell said that the highest authorities here were very much concerned by developments on Cyprus. He asked the Ambassador whether there were any recent indications of what the Turks intended to do.

Ambassador Hart explained that his last information was that the Turkish Government was still trying to decide what to do. He, Hart, had informed (Turkish Foreign Ministry Secretary General) Kuneralp that the fighting had stopped in accord with orders from Athens. Kuneralp

---

[1] Source: Department of State, Central Files, POL 27 CYP. Secret. Drafted by Draper.

was "very happy" at this news. He was also gratified by information that UNFICYP was endeavoring to bring the situation at the "villages" back to the status quo ante. The Ambassador had also informed Kuneralp that UNFICYP wished to remove the National Guard from the villages. Of course, he said, we did not know how future developments might emerge, and we therefore could not be certain how the Turkish Government would behave.

Ambassador Hart said there was a good deal of activity and meetings in Ankara. The heads of the Turkish military forces had been meeting that night, for example. He did expect, he said, certain precautionary moves. The Ambassador thought it rather unlikely that the Turks would take any "particular action" with matters quiet on the island. He reiterated that he did not now anticipate "forceful action" but quickly made clear that this estimate was good only as long as there was quiet and no further spread of fighting.

The Ambassador went on to mention that some 30 percent of the Turkish Cypriot population was in the Nicosia triangle and that an estimated 10,000 Turks were in the region affected by the fighting. Whether quiet would remain in that region was still a question, he admitted. He said that, sharing what he understood was also the US opinion, the Turks were firmly convinced that General Grivas was behind all the trouble. Cabinet meetings had taken place on this subject and he understood that the Cabinet Ministers and the service chiefs had held a joint meeting.

Mr. Rockwell at this juncture said he had just received a message from Athens (Athens 2148)[2] concerning the GOG request to the GOC to withdraw the National Guard. He conveyed the substance of this message to the Ambassador. He reiterated that the point of his call was to register the real concern in the highest quarters in Washington over these developments. These quarters were gravely concerned that the interests of all parties were endangered. Ambassador Hart said that this message from Athens was most welcome and he thought it would assist him in his own efforts.

Note: The telephone call was made in the expectation (and hope) that the Turks would monitor it.

---

[2] Dated November 16. (Ibid.)

309.   Telegram From the Embassy in Greece to the Department of State[1]

Athens, November 17, 1967, 1452Z.

2186. NATUS.

1. I took occasion of delivery of Secretary's message to Prime Minister (State 70871)[2] to weigh in heavily with him (and later with King) on potential further serious explosion unless Grivas is removed from Cyprus scene immediately, even though temporarily.

2. PriMin thanked me for Secretary's message and said that GOG is determined to show greatest wisdom and restraint in order to preserve peace between two countries. He reverted to his suspicions of Turkish intentions, referring to following: Turk overflights, Turk armored brig being moved towards Everos triangle and demonstrations in Istanbul when anti-Greek and anti-American slogans heard. GOG had strictly forbidden any intervention of RHAF in connection overflights and movement of Greek troops toward Evros from Alexandropoulis had been halted. I congratulated him on this restraint and said that as one who is deeply concerned about situation I must say that today looks worse than yesterday did, particularly with the renewal of patrolling in Agios Theodoros. He did not appear aware of this development. I passed on our reports from Nicosia (Nicosia 638 and previous).[3]

3. I said I was afraid that this resumption would not be taken by Ankara as indication of restraint and peaceful inclinations on part Cypriot Govt.

4. I then turned to Grivas problem and said that I did not like to refer to individuals when discussing policy matters yet as one who had lived through Cyprus difficulties in 1964, I felt that Turks would no doubt take the traditional attitudes and look upon Grivas actions as having been ordered by GOG since both Grivas and other Greek officers serving in Cyprus are all active officers of Greek forces. PriMin insisted this was not correct because as soon as GOG had learned of Grivas actions it had at once made strong recommendation and on next day requested GOC to refrain from any further action re Agios Theodoros. Grivas and other regular Greek officers in Cyprus take their orders from GOC not Athens govt. I said I was not speaking under instructions but had been mulling

---

[1] Source: Department of State, Central Files, POL 27 CYP. Secret; Immediate; Limdis. Received at 1602Z and repeated to Ankara, Nicosia, London, Brussels for the Mission to NATO, USUN, USCINCEUR, and USDOCOSouth.

[2] Telegram 70871 to Athens, November 17, transmitted a message from Rusk for Kollias congratulating Greece on its restraint over the Cyprus issue. (Ibid.)

[3] Telegram 638 from Nicosia, November 17, reported on further fighting in Cyprus. (Ibid.)

over ways which might help reduce tension. It had occurred to me that one way might be to invite Grivas to Athens for consultations. Such gesture could be taken in Ankara as sign of good faith of GOG and its desire to reduce tension on island. I continued that there are hawks and doves in Ankara and we do not know what decisions and discussions are being held there nor what has been said during last 24 hours that GNA has been meeting behind closed doors. PriMin promptly replied that GOG had already thought of this. He regrets that his thoughts coincided with those of the American Ambassador. Now if this action is taken it will be presumed that it is result of American pressure. I replied I would be more than glad to withdraw suggestion at once.

5. I assured PriMin I was aware that many people feel that American recommendations for restraint are made only in Athens. All one could say to them is that they do not know what has been happening in Ankara during the last week. PriMin said he understood that and certainly recommendations for moderation from US to two allies who are in difficulty cannot be interpreted as intervention. He reverted to another recount of his suspicions of intentions of Turks to create yet another pocket and cut off Nicosia–Limassol–Larnaca road. He then appealed to US to use all possible means to convince Turkish side of good intentions of GOG because he feels that good faith on part GOG only may not be enough. I assured him that USG is well aware of good intentions of GOG and we would be happy to help in any way that PriMin feels would be helpful to both parties.

6. Although our conversation laid sensitive problem on the line in frank tones, PriMin did not react in scratchy, near irascible manner he sometimes does. He appeared to be deeply worried man seeking way out of dilemma.[4]

Talbot

---

[4] In telegram 2182 from Athens, November 17, Talbot reported that King Constantine had informed him that the Greek Government had ordered Grivas' withdrawal. (Ibid.)

310.   Telegram From the Department of State to the Embassy in
       Cyprus[1]

Washington, November 17, 1967, 1846Z.

70960. NATUS. Please deliver following message from President
Johnson to President Makarios by fastest available means:

"Your Beatitude: Developments on and relating to the Island of
Cyprus during the last few days have created a situation of utmost gravity. As I see it, the issue is war or peace and not the rights and wrongs of
any specific problem. I appeal to you, as I am appealing to King Constantine and President Sunay,[2] to do everything within the power of your
Government to reduce the threat to peace now hanging over your region.
In particular it seems to me that in this explosive situation the continuation of patrols in the areas of the current conflict is extremely dangerous,
for peace in Cyprus and the eastern Mediterranean.[3]

Sincerely, Lyndon B. Johnson"

Rusk

---

[1] Source: Department of State, Central Files, POL 27 CYP. Secret; Flash. Drafted by
Howison; cleared by Battle, Rockwell, and Rostow; and approved by Rusk. Repeated to
Ankara, Athens, London, USUN, the Mission to NATO, USCINCEUR, and USDOCO-
South.

[2] A similar message was transmitted to the Embassy in Ankara in telegram 70962,
November 17, and to the Embassy in Athens in telegram 70961, November 17. (Both ibid.)
King Constantine's reply, pledging his efforts to ensure peace, was transmitted in telegram
2215 from Athens, November 18. (Ibid.) President Sunay's reply, outlining the Turkish
position including its fundamental demand for the withdrawal of Greek forces from
Cyprus, was transmitted in telegram 2407 from Ankara, November 18. (Ibid.) See also Document 311.

[3] In telegram 650 from Nicosia, November 17, Belcher reported that he had delivered
the President's message and believed that Makarios would attempt to reduce tensions by
calling off patrols by Greek Cypriot police. (Department of State, Central Files, POL 27
CYP)

311. Telegram From the Embassy in Turkey to the Department of State[1]

Ankara, November 18, 1967, 0200Z.

2393. Ref: State 70962.[2] Subj: President's message to Sunay.

1. Delivered President's message to Caglayangil at FonMin at earliest he could receive me, approx 1235 am. Kuneralp and Turkmen were present. I delivered it verbally but left them copy at their request. (I did it this way so that if necessary they could say technically that I had not delivered a "letter" or note or any formal written communication which could be subject of controversy within govt or between govt and Parliament as was case from June 1964 to Jan 1966).[3] Turkmen translated immediately into Turkish and Caglayangil immediately dictated following provisional reaction:

"I would like to thank President Johnson and the US Govt for the interest they have shown in the matter but I would like to point out that the problem is no longer a problem of passions or good will. You know that the incident of the Greek patrols to Bogazici (Ayios Theodoros) has caused very tragic events. Twenty-four of my kinsmen have been killed. One thousand Turks had to flee their homes and live under deprivation. An 80-year old man, a Turk, has been burned alive in Gecitkale (Kophinou). Tortures like the ones used in the Middle Ages have been applied against the Turkish community, and after all these tragic events we have seen that the Greeks have again sent their patrol yesterday and today in a very ostentatious manner. This example of the 80-year old man who was burned alive which has shocked you (he referred to my facial expression) is only one incident among many others. If you can read them without being shocked and without feeling nausea, I can give you other accounts of events which have been witnessed by the UN forces. The Turkish public opinion and the Turkish community have been incurably aroused against the Turkish Govt. We have sent today to the people of Gecitkale some relief goods through the Turkish Red Crescent and these people are people whose houses have been destroyed, whose belongings have been pillaged and who had barely escaped a massacre. They were all hungry and despite the fact that they were hungry they have refused all the relief goods and they said:

---

[1] Source: Department of State, Central Files, POL 27 CYP. Secret; Flash; Exdis. Received at 0332Z and repeated to Athens, London, Nicosia, the Mission to NATO, USUN, USCINCEUR, and USDOCOSouth.

[2] See footnote 2, Document 310.

[3] In telegram 2396 from Ankara, November 18, Hart amplified on the reasons for delivering the message orally. (Department of State, Central Files, POL 27 CYP)

"'We don't want anything from Turkey. Get out of here.' This is not a sad story I am telling you, it is what happened today in the island.

"We, as the Turkish people, have a love for the American people because we feel they are our friends, because we share their philosophy and their democratic principles and it is for this reason that we have formed our destiny with that of the United States. Because we believe that it would bring no good to the world we are struggling together against an ideology and since many years we are the sentinels of the struggle on the very frontier. At such an hour I had expected that a message coming from a country with which we have a common destiny would be different. Since 10:00 PM today Erenkoy (Kokkina) has been surrounded by Greek forces and subjected to heavy firing. I had expected that given this situation (the entire present situation) our American friends would come and tell us that they regret that they have prevented in the past a Turkish initiative and that they would say: 'Now the decision is yours.'

"This message, the message you have brought is addressed to our head of state. We will, of course, convey this message to its high destination. We will, of course, study it and evaluate it, bearing in mind its importance and in the spirit of Turkish-American friendship. We shall weigh carefully each word. During the time we have worked together I have seen, Excellency, how much value you attach to Turkish-American friendship and I know also your tireless efforts to promote this friendship. I would like to thank you for the interest you have shown for our national issue.

"Some one and half hours ago I have called in the Greek Ambassador. I told him that we were holding the Greek Govt responsible for everything that happened. I told him that we were definitely determined not to allow the Greek Govt and its puppet in Cyprus to continue to undermine the interests and prestige of the Turkish state.

"Seeing that these brutal actions in Gecitkala have not received any reaction the Greeks do not any longer recognize the influence of any authority and all of them by individual initiatives are attacking at any occasion our innocent people. The Turkish Govt cannot condemn its 120,000 kinsmen to live like cattle while waiting their turn in a slaughter house. I believe that from now on it's not what we want but what God wants that will happen. This, Mr. Ambassador, is what I wanted to tell you." (It is interesting that there was no mention of Czech arms.)

2. I commented that I much appreciated his remarks concerning my devotion to Turkish-American friendship. I would continue to apply myself with all my energies to furtherance of this relationship and to assistance in finding some way out from fearful problem which Turkey faces today in such manner as to avoid further loss of human life. I deeply admired statesmanship and restraint shown by FonMin in present crisis,

as well as his attitude and attitude of rest of govt throughout last two years. Prospect of a war between two allies was a nightmare for us all. It was in spirit of foregoing that President's message should be read and understood. As I had indicated, messages had been sent to King Constantine and to Archbishop Makarios. These were strong messages. Up to time these messages had been sent tremendous efforts had been spent to stop patrolling in stricken villages of Cyprus and otherwise ease situation by every means. Some progress being registered, as shown by fact, still very secret, Grivas being recalled to Athens and due to depart 2:00 AM or 10:00 AM today. We hoped very much his recall would be permanent. Patrols also had been suspended temporarily and we hoped suspensions could be made indefinite.

Caglayangil replied: "You have rightly referred to the prospect of a war between two allies as a nightmare, but to go through this nightmare once and for all is preferable to seeing a nightmare every night." At this point I felt Caglayangil was not being quite as serious as before.

I said that without trying just to have the last word I must say that he and I both knew that a war would not be a nightmare for one night but for an indefinite number of days and nights and with incalculable consequences.

Caglayangil who had been very tense at start of meeting, appeared much more relaxed as I left. He and I agreed I would refuse all comment to press and I did so when they surrounded my car a few minutes later.[4]

Hart

---

[4] In telegram 2224 from Athens, November 20, Talbot commented that he believed Turkey was trying to force the United States to adopt its position on the troop issue by the use of an ultimatum. (Ibid.)

312. **Telegram From the Embassy in Greece to the Department of State**[1]

Athens, November 22, 1967, 0205Z.

2296. Ref: 2294, 2295.[2]

1. At 0230 local King summoned me to Greek Pentagon where he meeting with senior Cabinet members and Chiefs of Staff. He asked that I urgently inform USG that GOG had reached several conclusions tonight:

A. PriMin and FonMin now completing draft reply to Turkish note of Nov 17. Reply which hopefully will hold door open for Greek-Turk talks expected to be ready for delivery in morning.

B. GOG will welcome Brosio's injecting himself more actively in relieving Greek-Turkish differences and is so informing him.[3]

C. Idea of joint GOG–GOC approach to UNSYG was considered but discarded for tonight because of doubt UN would act fast enough or that Turkey would agree to participate in talks at this stage with GOC as well as GOG.

D. GOG would welcome invitation from President Johnson to King Constantine and President Sunay, with their Prime Ministers and Foreign Ministers, to meet together in United States to discuss peace between Greece and Turkey.

2. In course of evening King had grown enthusiastic about this last idea. I suggested that since I could not know how President would feel about this suggestion or whether it would be realistic in relation to all other considerations he must have in mind perhaps we could start by exploring idea hypothetically. For example, could Greece accept not just simple invitation but something suggesting specific direction of talks? Earlier in evening, King had mentioned demilitarization of Cyprus. Turks talking about removal of Greek forces before bilateral talks. Would it be feasible for President, if he should extend invitation, to indicate he understood Greece and presumably Turkey looking toward demilitarization of Cyprus and was inviting their highest representatives to talks on how to achieve this and other steps necessary to resolve current difficulties and restore friendly Greek-Turkish relations?

---

[1] Source: Department of State, Central Files, POL 27 CYP. Secret; Flash; Limdis. Received at 0327Z and repeated to Ankara, London, Nicosia, USUN, the Mission to NATO, USCINCEUR, and USDOCOSouth.

[2] Telegram 2294 from Athens, November 21, reported that the King had suggested that President Johnson invite himself and President Sunay to Washington for talks designed to head off a clash over Cyprus. (Ibid.) Telegram 2295 from Athens, November 21, reported that King Constantine assured Talbot that Greece would not launch a preemptive strike against Turkish invasion forces but warned that the time for effective diplomatic intervention was short. (Ibid.)

[3] On November 24, NATO Secretary General Manlio Brosio announced that he would go to the crisis area in an effort to find a solution.

3. King felt this might give GOG difficulties but excused himself for few moments to consult PriMin and FonMin. On his return he said government shared his feeling it would not be appropriate to have agreement to demilitarization as a condition of meeting, which should be called to discuss urgent issue of peace between Greece and Turkey. However, acceptance of demilitarization would certainly be important question for discussion, along with adjustment of treaty provisions relating to unilateral intervention and other questions. He said again that most of his Ministers and Chiefs of Staff want to get Greek forces out of Cyprus.

4. I promised to convey his ideas to Washington immediately. He hoped that response could be prompt.

5. In absence of Canadian and British colleagues I made no reference to Turkish ideas of basis for settlement that we expect to put to Foreign Minister in morning. Perhaps phrasing can be found which will meet Turkish minimum needs for indication for action before talks but also get top level talks going rapidly.

6. On another subject, King mentioned that Makarios has proposed plans which GOG studying tonight for partial mobilization and full mobilization in Cyprus.

Talbot

313.   Telegram From the Embassy in Cyprus to the Department of State[1]

Nicosia, November 22, 1967, 1245Z.

710. Reference: State 73069.[2]

1. As suggested reftel saw Makarios noon today local to present modified draft message (text septel)[3] for his consideration. Made somewhat lengthy introductory remarks enlarging para 2 reftel and referring in particular to his oft repeated remarks desire see reduction of military forces on island and indeed eventual demilitarization. Also referred our

---

[1] Source: Department of State, Central Files, POL 27 CYP. Secret; Flash. Received at 1347Z. Also sent to Athens and repeated to Ankara, London, USUN, the Mission to NATO, and Ottawa.

[2] Telegram 73069 to Nicosia, November 22, instructed Belcher to press Makarios to take action that would facilitate the removal of excess Greek forces from Cyprus. (Ibid.)

[3] Telegram 711 from Nicosia, November 22. (Ibid.)

expressed desire play useful role as non-aligned power and suggested he might add to his stature as statesman by some timely action in keeping with his acceptance speech of December 1959. At critical juncture in history of Cyprus and of Greece and Turkey, if he could take initiative in calling for reduction, if not elimination of military forces in Cyprus, he would be making real contribution to defusing present crisis which of utmost gravity and at same time make significant contribution to overall settlement of Cyprus problem. I then gave him text describing draft message as combination State Department and Embassy thinking which I had no time to clear with Washington and therefore had no official USG status but was merely an effort put down some thoughts which might be useful if he considered concept our suggestion valuable.

2. Makarios commented that we were correct in our assumption that he favored demilitarization through a phased reduction of forces but that for him to take the initiative without reference to Athens was out of the question. He said he personally would have no hesitation in telling me that he agreed with the concept and indeed the text of the proposed message. However in view of present crisis and state of public opinion both here and in Greece, he feared he would be accused of being a traitor and selling out Greece. I attempted argue that a private and confidential message of this sort might actually assist Greece in reaching decision regarding reply to Turkish note. The injection of a statesmanlike suggestion such as this at this time might have most significant bearing on outcome of crisis. He agreed but again said he could not take initiative. Archbishop then said he could, however, respond affirmatively to any Greek initiative along these lines and asked that we consider making presentation in Athens along lines mine to him. I said I would pass his observations back to Department and to Embassy Athens and I assumed I would hear something further which I would then communicate later today or this evening. In meantime I urged him give further thought to our proposal. He replied that he intended discuss it with Clerides and Kyprianou and in event of any change in his view as result these discussions, he would call me.

3. *Comment:* I think significant point to come out of somewhat discouraging conversation is that Makarios and his government would not only oppose reduction and eventual withdrawal of Greek forces, and indeed further steps toward demilitarization, but that he willing respond affirmatively to any possible GOG proposals along lines reftel. Realize that initiative along these lines in Athens would complicate if not counter efforts now being made there on wider concept of Turk five points. However, certainly in event Greek rejection present tripartite initiative, foregoing could conceivably be used as next move in our efforts avoid conflict. Prior to seeing Makarios discussed proposed approach

654 Foreign Relations, 1964–1968, Volume XVI

with Canadian HICOMer and he very much in accord. Had no time inform UK HICOMer but doing so now.

Belcher

---

314. Telegram From the Embassy in Cyprus to the Department of State[1]

Nicosia, November 22, 1967, 2030Z.

717. Ref: Nicosia 716.[2]

1. During 45 minute meeting with Makarios UK and Canadian HICOMers and myself, Canadian was spokesman and read prepared text including Turkish five points[3] (being sent reftel).

2. Makarios commented that first three Turkish points were acceptable to him if accepted by GOG. Speaking to me he remarked that as he had said earlier today (Nicosia 710)[4] he was in favor of complete demilitarization including removal of Greek and Turk contingents. He went on to say that presence of any foreign military troops would be source of constant friction and suspicion and therefore would be best include them in withdrawal as well. UK HICOMer remarked that for time being perhaps Turks would feel their contingent's presence required in order give some sense of additional security to Turkish community. I remarked that this aspect of course could be included as one of items to be discussed further as suggested in last paragraph of document which Canadian HICOMer had given him.

---

[1] Source: Department of State, Central Files, POL 27 CYP. Secret; Flash. Received at 0100Z on November 23. Repeated to Athens, Ankara, London, Ottawa, USUN, the Mission to NATO, USCINCEUR, and USDOCOSouth.

[2] Telegram 716, November 22, transmitted the text of the paper read to Makarios. (Ibid.)

[3] Presented to the Greek Government on November 22, the five points were: 1) Turkish reaffirmation of the inviolability and integrity of the Cyprus Republic, 2) withdrawal of Greek armed forces on Cyprus in excess of the numbers permitted by the London–Zurich Agreements, 3) expansion of UNFICYP's role to pacify the island, 4) payment of indemnities to Turkish Cypriots, and 5) security arrangements for Turkish Cypriots not dependent on Greek Cypriot police or military formations. (Telegram 2303 from Athens, November 22; ibid.)

[4] Document 313.

3. After first saying that if five points acceptable to GOG he could accept also, Archbishop expressed reservations with regard (D) and (E) which he felt were matters purely concerning the GOC. He would require time to discuss these two points with his Ministers. He said he would call in Greek Ambassador Alexandrakis for further discussion of five points. I reminded him that these five points and numerous other aspects of problem had been discussed at great length in Ankara by our three colleagues and GOT representatives. These had emerged as basic points in Turkish position. They had been presented today noon by our three colleagues in Athens to FonMin Pipinelis who had said he would refer them at once to Greek Cabinet. I doubted whether Alexandrakis would have word as yet although at some point hopefully very soon, there would be some consultation, at least on last two points. I said that we would be informing Athens at once of his favorable views on reduction of forces covered in points (2) and (3) and I felt sure this would be major factor to be taken into consideration by Greek Cabinet in reaching its decision. Speed was of the utmost importance at this most critical time and he could be assured we would send this word by the fastest possible means.

4. Makarios closed meeting by commenting that ref in last para of document to "other interested parties" meant primarily Cyprus. Said that presumably discussions between Greece and Turkey could not go further into ultimate solution without involvement of GOC at early date.

Belcher

---

315. **Telegram From the Embassy in Cyprus to the Department of State**[1]

Nicosia, November 23, 1967, 1020Z.

723. Reference: State 74021.[2] Subject: Possible Makarios–King Constantine message.

---

[1] Source: Department of State, Central Files, POL 27 CYP. Secret; Flash. Received at 1206Z. Also sent to Athens and repeated to Ankara, London, Ottawa, the Mission to NATO, and USUN.
[2] Telegram 74021 to Nicosia, November 23, instructed Belcher to make the strongest presentation possible to Makarios to ensure a peaceful settlement of the crisis. (Ibid.)

1. Makarios saw me 9:30 AM (local). As expected, however, he reiterated his position as set forth Nicosia 710[3] that he could not get out in front by sending unilateral message. I then urged him consider proposing to GOG that joint message be sent. This would avoid either King or Makarios being singled out as one who "sold out Hellenism". Makarios' initial reaction was that this idea had merit. He wondered if message might be sent by himself and King jointly to UNSYG who then could take further action on it. I said that such a proposal could well fit in with presence of Rolz-Bennett in Ankara later today. If offer inherent in proposed text could be made to U Thant as response SYG's appeal and then forwarded by him to Rolz-Bennett in Ankara, latter might be able make excellent use of it in his conversations with Turks. This might well be instrument for defusing situation and getting Turk finger off the button.

2. Makarios asked if I thought presence of high-level emissaries in Ankara might result in defusing situation. I had feared Vance and Rolz-Bennett Missions might be seized upon by him as excuse for further procrastination. I am sure this is what was in his mind. I told him in very strong terms that we convinced all they could do was buy some time by their presence and that Turks would require some sort of response from Greeks. I said we convinced that reduction of armed confrontation on island was central to their basic position as set forth in five points.[4] If no move made at least in this direction, I could see no hope in situation. Since he accepted in principle concept set forth in proposed message and King accepted in principle and since concept of demilitarization encompassed points two and three of Turk five points, surely sensible thing to do at this stage was to move along these lines. He said he would have to consult his advisers and I asked him notify me perhaps through Clerides as soon as possible since time was of the essence. Also offered transmit any message for him if this would facilitate matter.

3. I immediately called on Clerides and Alexandrakis and made similar presentation and believe have won their support. Also tried impress on both of them need for swift action in order take advantage Rolz-Bennett presence Ankara. Alexandrakis had one important modification to suggest in proposal. He believes that message if agreed to by Makarios and his government should be from Kollias and Makarios rather than from King. He fears that public reaction in Greece to message would be very adverse and he did not want to risk institution of monarchy in this connection. As he put it, we can sacrifice Kollias in the interests of peace but not the King.

4. Ambassador Talbot may wish proceed put these same ideas to GOG without awaiting for Makarios' final reaction. Could be that

---

[3] Document 313.

[4] See footnote 3, Document 314.

Greeks might wish take initiative in developing joint message. Believe they may be more aware of need for speed than is Archbishop who is characteristically a procrastinator.

Belcher

---

316.   **Telegram From the Embassy in Greece to the Department of State**[1]

Athens, November 23, 1967, 0330Z.

2330. Ref: Ankara 2501.[2] For the Secretary from Talbot.

1. With all respect, another way to stop war is for Turkey not to start it. I do not now comment on specific plan suggested reftel, which I assume being studied in Ottawa, London, and Washington, but rather on general idea that only way to keep peace is for Greece to meet Turkey's terms within hours.

2. For full week now Turkey has been bullying Greeks to accept capitulation on an issue that all sides now believe could be resolved by negotiation not under gun. In process, Turkish actions and demands have engaged maximum energies of USG, British, Canadians, NATO, and now UNSYG. Virtually total resources of major Western powers and international organizations created since World War II to provide alternatives to war for settlement of international disputes are now available to Turkey and Greece. If wrongs have been committed by Greek and Cypriot forces (and they have), Turkey has access to full panoply of international machinery for redress. If in these circumstances it nonetheless concludes that its case can be carried only by its own military power, case must be weak indeed. Especially as in present circumstances Turkey has no treaty justification for military action in another sovereign country, since Article 4 of Treaty of Guarantee which Turkey usually cites authorizes unilateral action only in absence of common or concerted action, which certainly is now occurring and could be complete if Turkey itself would join.

---

[1] Source: Department of State, Central Files, POL 27 CYP. Secret; Immediate; Limdis. Received at 1221Z and repeated to Ankara for Vance, Nicosia, London, Ottawa, USUN, and the Mission to NATO.

[2] Telegram 2501 from Ankara, November 23, suggested that the Greek Government inform Turkey of its interest in a speedy and effective mutual demilitarization. (Ibid.)

I well understand Turkish rationale for present course is "Turkish honor." When in history of aggression has national honor not been reason advanced for military attack on another country? One week ago Greece through Grivas-led Cyprus National Guard attack had lost any claim to international support of its position. Today I suspect Turkey by its tactics has raised doubts in many governments about justness of its cause. Has not time come to make this fact plain to Turks?

Knowing importance of our interests and delicacy of current relations with Turkey, I am full of admiration for way Ambassador Hart has been handling task which substantially more difficult than mine here. Nonetheless, I hope instructions given Vance Mission will permit him to make forceful case to GOT that this dispute must now be committed to international machinery designed to deal with threats of war. Against this, who can argue that there is excuse for escalation to war actions whose inescapable result would be killing of many more Turk Cypriots than have yet been casualties of communal strike on Cyprus, not to mention anticipated Turk and Greek casualties and other costs?

Talbot

317.   Telegram From the Embassy in Greece to the Department of State[1]

Athens, November 23, 1967, 1220Z.

2338. NATUS. Ref: State 74022.[2]

1. I called on King at 1200 local just before meeting convened at Palace of "little Cabinet" (PriMin, FinMin, 5 military Ministers) and outlined points in paras 2 and 3 reftel. King grimaced at idea of recalling Greek military personnel under heat of Turkish military pressure. I suggested Makarios initiative, if it forthcoming as we now urgently recom-

---

[1] Source: Department of State, Central Files, POL 27 CYP. Secret; Immediate. Received at 1331Z and repeated to Ankara, London, Nicosia, Ottawa, USUN, the Mission to NATO, CINCEUR, and USDOCOSouth.

[2] Telegram 74022 to Athens, November 23, instructed Talbot to suggest to the King that Greece immediately offer to withdraw 500 troops from Cyprus and indicate its readiness to discuss further withdrawals. (Ibid.)

mending, ought give good basis for Greek token withdrawal as earnest of good will. Discussion revealed Royal firmness on point that any Greek action would have to be matched by comparable Turkish de-escalation action. I came away with impression that if Vance can get Turkish pledge of some visible pullback we can expect to be able to persuade Greeks to order withdrawal of some troops. However, in matters such as these King both influences Ministers and is influenced by them. I may be able to get better reading of Greek mood today after Cabinet meeting.

2. I have impression mood developing in Palace and "little Cabinet" to go for complete demilitarization of Cyprus as part of settlement this crisis if war avoided. In [King?] says military Ministers now tending to want to get rid of Greek and Turkish contingents as well as all forces put on island since 1963. In their developing view, internal security could then be maintained either by reinforced UNFICYP or by merging Cypriot National Guard and Turkish-Cypriot military and paramilitary units into single national Cyprus force.

3. I mentioned USG concern over protection of minorities in Greece and Turkey as tensions heightened. King immediately suggested Greece would welcome American or other international observers during period of crisis in areas where Turkish ethnics congregated, on assumption Turkey would offer similar facilities.

4. I also noted importance of obtaining from GOG assurance that Greeks will not initiate military action during period of discussions, and said I had already communicated his pledge that there would be no pre-emptive strike by Greek forces. "Never", he replied.

Talbot

---

318.   **Telegram From the Department of State to the Embassies in Turkey, Greece, and Cyprus**[1]

Washington, November 23, 1967, 1857Z.

74061. Literally eyes only for the Ambassador from the Secretary. I wish to express to each of you my deep appreciation for the round-the-

---

[1] Source: Department of State, Central Files, POL 27 CYP. Secret; Priority. Drafted and approved by Rusk.

clock effort you have been making to avoid catastrophe over the Cyprus question. I need not emphasize the scope of the catastrophe for all of us and for NATO if Turkey and Greece should get into a war with each other. What we should keep in mind is that such an event would mean that our bilateral relations with both countries would approach zero for the foreseeable future. Therefore, in dealing with your host country about these issues, you should concentrate on what your host country can do to prevent war and not be unduly worried about whether subsequent bilateral relations will be as comfortable as you would hope. Each one of you should concentrate on how you can persuade your own host government to make a maximum effort to preserve the peace. The stakes are such that the future of our bilateral relations is secondary to the prevention of hostilities between Greece and Turkey. My colleagues back here could write memoranda explaining why this is not necessarily so. Indeed, I admit that I have in mind certain irrational factors which ought not to be there. But the events themselves and the predictable reactions of the American people and the American Congress will take the play away from us diplomats. We need not apologize to any of your host governments for the harshest pressures we may put on in the interest of maintaining peace. The issues in Cyprus itself are, strictly from the point of view of the US national interest, trivial compared to peace between Greece and Turkey. Our responsibility is to support that central US national interest.

My personal regards to all three of you. The President and I are grateful for your dedicated effort in these trying moments.

Rusk

---

319. Telegram From the Embassy in Greece to the Department of State[1]

Athens, November 23, 1967, 2322Z.

2354. Vanto 6. For the President, Secretary Rusk and Secretary McNamara.

1. I have completed my first round of talks in Ankara with President Sunay, Prime Minister Demirel and Foreign Minister Caglayangil.[2]

---

[1] Source: Department of State, Central Files, POL 7 US/VANCE. Secret; Immediate. Received at 0434Z on November 24 and repeated to Ankara.

[2] A complete record of these talks was transmitted in Vanto 9 from Athens, November 24. (Ibid.)

Throughout the Turks maintained a consistently hard position which apparently reflects a concerted Cabinet decision.

2. While the dangers of a military confrontation are acute, none of us believe the Turks will attack while my mission remains in the area, thus, we probably have some time to try to find an effective handle to this problem but the grip is short.

3. The Turks are clearly in a dangerous, fatalistic mood. After four years of what they consider to have [garble] painful salami tactics on Cyprus, they claim they will pay no more. The situation is described in simplistic terms of Greek illegality and villainy and Turkish suffering. They assert that their honor is at stake, and popular passions in the country are so high that a catalytic explosion is in the offing. The only possible way out, in their opinion, is a virtually immediate Greek decision to commence withdrawing its "illegal" military units on Cyprus.

4. This is heady stuff. Yet, throughout we were received with courtesy and friendship. Beneath the harsh description of the imperatives of the situation we sense a Turkish hope that we can pull a rabbit out of the essentially ultimative hat they have presented to us. This is going to take some doing but we are still in the ball game.

5. Detailed account of conversations follows. Septel submitted from Ankara in Vanto series on Sunay conversation.

Talbot

---

320.   Telegram From the Embassy in Greece to the Department of State[1]

Athens, November 24, 1967, 1718Z.

2395. Vanto 11. Subject: Vance's meeting with Greek Foreign Minister Pipinellis November 24. Secretary Vance, accompanied by Ambassador Talbot and John Walsh, had lengthy discussion with Foreign Minister Pipinellis this morning. Throughout conversation Pipinellis was courteous, calm, thoughtful, and somewhat fatalistic.

---

[1] Source: Department of State, Central Files, POL 7 US/VANCE. Secret; Flash; Exdis. Received at 1824Z and also sent to Ankara and Nicosia.

In response to Pipinellis' inquiry, Vance frankly outlined his impression of the mood and position of the GOT and the Turkish people. He summarized situation as very grave with war fever running and GOT flatly insisting on immediate withdrawal of illegal Greek forces as sine qua non for easing of tensions. He pointed out that he had been rebuffed when he suggested that solution might be found in simultaneous Greek withdrawal and GOT steps to lower mobilization levels. While some moderate forces exist within GOT, he was uncertain whether they could withstand mounting war pressures.

Pipinellis said he was not surprised by Vance's assessment. Greece and her allies were faced by gravest dangers. All Greek information pointed to probability of Turk attack. He had taken position as Foreign Minister determined to find peaceful solution but not at the price of national humiliation. What Turkey asks, he said, no self-respecting government could accept. They wish Greece to give up all its assets before talking. If Greek forces are withdrawn from Cyprus, he predicted communal clashes would occur followed by a Turkish landing. Turkey would then exercise its will without hindrance on Cyprus. If clash with Turkey is unavoidable, he preferred it to occur under existing circumstances. Despite his conviction that Greek forces are factor of stability on island and their elimination would create vacuum inviting Turkish intervention, he was prepared consider phased withdrawal connected with establishment of some other type policing force, providing Turks would accept formula which would not humiliate Greece. This, he said, is all Greece can do. If it is not acceptable to Turkey, situation is hopeless.

Vance then turned to possibility of solution to impasse if U Thant issued call to Greeks to start withdrawing and to Turks to take action reduce tensions. He felt this plan could prevent war without humiliation and stated he authorized to inform Pipinellis that UKG shared this view. Greeks would respond first to SYG and then Turks would respond. Under this plan SYG would provide umbrella protecting dignity each country. In eyes of world, Greece would benefit if it responded first to SYG. Furthermore, chances of peaceful settlement are slight unless Greece moves first, since GOT has presented complete stonewall when we raised possibility simultaneity in decisions both countries.

Vance pointed out that his proposal had not been discussed as yet with U Thant but he would raise it with his Special Representative Rolz-Bennett, if Pipinellis considered plan had merit.

Pipinellis responded that idea appeared reasonable, but felt GOG would require at least simultaneity in notifications to SYG and timing of commencement of specific actions. Furthermore, there would be no Greek withdrawal from Cyprus unless Turks withdraw. Movement outwards must be on staged basis and accompanied by build-up of UN or other replacement forces. Ensuing discussion indicated Pipinellis unaware numbers of Greek and Turkish illegal forces on island and apparently assumed approximate equality these forces. He emphasized that principle of complete withdrawal must be accepted by both sides. This should not be linked, however, to London–Zurich Accords because of Makarios.

Pipinellis said he would work out written statement for consideration with Vance in afternoon and subsequently with Cabinet.

He then summed up his views by saying he was prepared to go far in search for peace but he would not yield to Turkish pressure. If Turks not prepared make slightest gesture of understanding feelings of a free people, war will result. Finally, any Turk landing on Cyprus would speedily escalate into full war between Greece and Turkey.[2]

Talbot

---

[2] Following the meeting with Vance, Pipinellis submitted a draft paper for submission to Turkey. The paper, with modifications suggested by Vance and his comments on the draft, was transmitted to the Department of State in Vanto 13 from Athens, November 24. (Ibid.)

---

321. Telegram From the Embassy in Greece to the Department of State[1]

Athens, November 25, 1967, 0317Z.

2410. Vanto 16. For Secretary Rusk and McNamara. In the course of a busy day I have met with King Constantine, Prime Minister Kollias, Foreign Minister Pipinellis, and the UN Special Representative, Rolz-Bennett. I have found in Athens none of the raucous war hysteria which prevails in Ankara. There is no evidence of panic by the people or the government.

In my opinion, the Greek Government remains cool and determined as the war clouds thicken. They have a real desire to find a peaceful solution to the crisis. The King again today reaffirmed his commitment that there would be no preventive military actions by Greek forces. The Greek Government has also accepted certain military risks in limiting military call-ups and military movements in order to avoid provocation of the Turks and exciting the populace. They have leaned over backwards in an effort to formulate a proposition for me to convey to the Turks tomorrow

---

[1] Source: Department of State, Central Files, POL 7 US/VANCE. Secret; Exdis. Received at 0356Z and also sent to Ankara.

which would be compatible with Greek national dignity and Turkish demands for Greek troop withdrawals. I could not ask them to do more. Signed Vance.

Addendum by Talbot:

Revisions of Greek statement which we declared necessary encountered considerable resistance in lengthy "little Cabinet" meeting with King tonight. We understand Greek military command—but in end not military Ministers—strongly resisted compromises they described as capitulation. When Vance and Talbot met King, PriMin, FonMin at 0115 local, GOG still wanted simultaneity in public announcement of acceptance of UNSYG appeal by GOG and GOT. Nearly two hours of discussion ensued, with King's decisive interventions finally turning tide.[2] At last Vance headed for airport at 0330 with documents he could fairly present to Turks.[3]

Talbot

---

[2] The Embassy reported on this meeting in telegram 2419 from Athens, November 25. (Ibid.)

[3] The text of the Greek proposal was transmitted in Vanto 17 from Ankara, November 25. (Ibid.)

---

322.   Telegram From the Embassy in Turkey to the Department of State[1]

Ankara, November 25, 1967, 1445Z.

2561. Vanto 24. Subject: Vance meeting with FonMin Caglayangil—November 25. At 0800 Vance, accompanied by Ambassador Hart and John Walsh, met with Foreign Minister Caglayangil to discuss results of mission's discussions in Athens. Implications of meeting were ugly. Caglayangil was churlish in manner and cavalier in his comments on various aspects of the mission's proposals. It was difficult to avoid conclusion during meeting that USG had been tricked into a Turkish charade

---

[1] Source: Department of State, Central Files, POL 7 US/VANCE. Secret; Flash; Exdis. Received at 1525Z and also sent to Athens and Nicosia.

which would come to an abrupt end at Turkish National Security Council meeting scheduled later in morning. As Caglayangil left for NSC meeting, he told Ambassador Hart that our proposals were hopeless.

Vance opened session with description his activities in Athens, including problems persuading Greeks to agree to formulation which would satisfy Turk demands that Greeks take initiative in accepting proposal plea by YG [SYG?] and in beginning withdrawal Greek units. After considerable persuasion this had been accomplished in form of draft action paper (Vanto 17)[2] and side minute signed by FonMin Pipinellis.[3]

After glancing at documents presented by Vance and briefly discussing them with his FonOff colleagues, Caglayangil's subsequent comments quickly chilled the atmosphere.

The Vance products were not, he said, as good as the five points presented by the US–UK–Can Ambassadors.[4] In his opinion, they seemed to represent an effort to save Greek prestige without regard for Turkish prestige. The provision for total demilitarization was unacceptable to him because it conflicted with the London/Zurich Accords establishing fixed levels for Greek and Turkish contingents. The interrelation between paras and the balanced relationship between Greek and Turkish actions seemed incomprehensible to him. Furthermore the Pipinellis side note to Vance cited above was surprisingly described as a Greek ultimatum. When Vance proposed to clarify individual points Caglayangil opined that it might be helpful but would not change his assessment that Vance proposals were not acceptable to GOT.

Speaking in a more general sense, he launched series of rockets. Turkey, he said, is not faced with simple choice of peace or war. If at present acute phase of crisis, GOT is unable safeguard its kinsmen on Cyprus the damage to its social structure will far exceed costs of war. Country would collapse in anarchy if people lost confidence in army and government.

Evidently responding to yesterday's strictures by Ambassador Hart that a Turkish war decision would seriously affect US-Turkish relations, he said he did not share this point of view. Nobody with sound mind would be shocked by Turkish use of MAP equipment against ally after the events of November 14–15. Vance responded vigorously at this point, outlining inevitable American reactions to such an event.

After Caglayangil's departure for Cabinet meeting, Vance requested FonOff pass message to him requesting urgent meeting with President Sunay and informing Caglayangil that, if Cabinet took deci-

---

[2] See footnote 3, Document 321.

[3] Transmitted in telegram 2408 from Athens, November 25. (Department of State, Central Files, POL 7 US/VANCE)

[4] See Document 314.

sion turn down Vance proposals, USG would conclude it had been tricked by GOT and entire exercise had been Turkish charade. This resulted in quick response that President would see Vance at 1230 today.

Hart

---

323.   **Telegram From the Embassy in Cyprus to the Department of State[1]**

Nicosia, November 25, 1967, 0810Z.

770. 1. I hesitated use this precedence for following message but it will give you all some indication what we are up against in dealing with Byzantine mentality so prevalent in GOC.

2. Makarios called me to Palace 8:00 P.M. local. Foreign Minister was present. Makarios said that they had information to indicate that Caglay-angil had made what purported be serious proposal: GOT would land troops in Cyprus but with no intention open hostilities unless opposed. Their idea would be to secure a beachhead and hold it and then negotiate from a position of greater equality vis-à-vis Greece and Cyprus. President wanted me to know and get word to GOT that such an action would be considered an act of war and would of course be opposed with whatever forces GOC could muster.

2. I told the Archbishop that we had had similar information but from military contacts and not from anyone in authority on the civilian side of the government and we had already commented from this Embassy that such a hope on the part of the Turks was out of the question. He asked nevertheless to report this information and to make clear the position of his government.

3. Our discussion then turned to the Vance Mission and the central theme of demilitarization. I reminded His Beatitude of our conversation when the UK and Canadian HICOMers were present the other night[2] at which time I had said that I doubted very much whether the Turks would be willing to go the whole way and remove their contingent. I understood that the Greek position was similar to his and that they both supported complete demilitarization and the removal of the contingent was

---

[1] Source: Department of State, Central Files, POL 7 US/VANCE. Secret; Flash; Limdis. Received at 2057Z. Also sent to Athens for Vance as Tovan 4 and repeated to Ankara, USUN, London, and the Mission to NATO.

[2] Reported in telegram 699 from Nicosia, November 21. (Ibid., POL 27 CYP)

an integral part of this concept. Kyprianou interjected that unless the Turks could agree to removal of their contingent, the whole proposition was hopeless. I turned to the Archbishop saying that his words to me the other day were graphic in describing the situation as not merely one of war or peace but rather one of peace or survival. This being the case would it not be better for the time being to accept a limited demilitarization which would involve the removal of non-Cypriot forces in excess to the London/Zurich treaty levels? Surely this was a question which could be decided in the talks which must take place subsequent to settlement of the present grave crisis. The modification of London/Zurich would be central to any such talks—even the Turks agreed to this. For the sake of preserving peace could this aspect of the problem not be postponed? Both the Archbishop and Kyprianou said this was out of the question.

4. Our conversation then turned to other aspects of the Turkish five points with emphasis on internal security. We discussed at some length the problem of policing and whether there would be joint UN-Greek and Turkish patrols. I had the strange feeling of being somewhere else engrossed in [garble—irrelevancies?] while the central point of avoiding war was being argued. I could not seem to impress upon them their fate hung in the balance no matter how many times I tried to bring the conversation back to the central issue.

5. As I took my leave I reminded them that Mr. Vance's first conversations in Ankara had been discouraging and that we were now awaiting a report of his conversations with President Sunay. In response to Makarios' question I assumed the reason Mr. Vance was not coming here at the present time was that the Turks had not accepted the Greek position as he had presented it after his consultations in Athens yesterday. I reminded him that I did not know any of the details except that the Turks had objected to the removal of the two contingents but that I would try to keep him informed if we learned of any other points of issue. In the meantime, what was needed was a miracle and I wished them good luck in finding one.

6. For the first time in my five years of knowing Makarios he was using his worry beads (I might add that the Foreign Minister and I had ours out too!).

Belcher

324. Telegram From the Embassy in Greece to the Department of State[1]

Athens, November 25, 1967, 2057Z.

2431. Vanto 29. For Secretary Rusk and Secretary McNamara. Vance meeting with Foreign Minister Caglayangil—November 25.

1. Secretary Vance, accompanied by Ambassador Hart and John Walsh, met with Foreign Minister Caglayangil late afternoon. By end of one and one-half hours frank exchanges, Vance had obtained GOT concurrence to revised draft text containing both advantages and serious problems for GOG viewpoint. While process formulating accord agreeable GOT and GOG is painfully slow and mission has no illusions about capacity Makarios government to place spanner in works, it has impression after long and hard day with Turks that they may have turned the corner in a policy sense in the direction of trying to obtain peace.

2. Mission returns to Athens with flat assurance of President Sunay, with Prime Minister and Foreign Minister hearing his words, that no military action will be taken while mission efforts continue.[2] Furthermore, in course of day, Caglayangil's mood and manner shifted dramatically. In morning session he verged on rudeness and ugliness, with much dark muttering about potential collapse of Turkish society unless war decision were made. At productive noon session with President Sunay he said nothing. In late afternoon he was again courteous and friendly, speaking of desire for peace, cooperatively working out textual changes, voicing confidence in Greek intent carry out withdrawal pledges, and warmly praising peace efforts our mission.[3] Why this shift occurred is not clear but we suspect that it reflects the personal intervention of President Sunay and the weight of persistent U.S. and international pressure to hold the Turkish hand. In addition, there may be a growing belief in GOT that arrangements short of war can be made for departure Greek forces. While not sanguine about final results, we remain hopeful.[4]

Talbot

---

[1] Source: Department of State, Central Files, POL 7 US/VANCE. Secret; Flash; Exdis. Received at 2119Z and repeated to Ankara and Nicosia.

[2] The meeting with Sunay was described in Vanto 28 from Athens, November 26. (Ibid.)

[3] Discussions with Caglayangil were the subject of Vanto 32 from Athens, November 26. (Ibid.)

[4] Ambassador Hart transmitted a summary of Vance's discussions in airgram A–292 from Ankara, December 7. (Ibid.)

325. Telegram From the Embassy in Greece to the Department of State[1]

Athens, November 27, 1967, 0105Z.

2446. Vanto. Subj: Vance meeting with FonMin Pipinelis, November 26.[2]

1. Vance, accompanied by Ambassador Talbot and John Walsh, called on FonMin to receive Greek reactions to draft accord as modified in November 25 meetings in Ankara. Pipinelis reported Cabinet had reviewed draft in long and difficult session and had prepared revised draft which he requested Vance to present to GOT tomorrow. Text contained in immediately following cable.[3]

2. After quick review Vance said he would of course carry out wishes of GOG but it was his judgment that their draft could not be sold to GOT. With time running out, it is imperative to minimize textual changes. With this thought in mind he had prepared draft which represents fair balance between desires of two countries and which has reasonable chance of acceptance in Ankara. Text follows:

"1. The Secretary General of the United Nations would address an appeal to the Governments of Turkey, Greece and Cyprus, such an appeal to include, inter alia:

a. An invitation to the Governments of Turkey and Greece to reaffirm the independence and territorial integrity of the Republic of Cyprus.
b. A request that the Governments of Turkey and Greece take immediate steps to remove any threat to the security of each other and of Cyprus and as a first step along the line of my previous appeal to bring about an expeditious withdrawal of Greek and Turkish forces, in excess of those present in 1963.

2. The Governments of Greece and Turkey would declare their readiness to comply forthwith with the appeal of the Secretary General.
3. Thereupon the Greek Government will withdraw expeditiously its military forces from Cyprus. Accompanying this, the Turkish Government will take all the necessary measures for removing the crisis.
4. In response to the appeal of the Secretary General, the three countries undertake to seek from the Security Council an enlarged and

---

[1] Source: Department of State, Central Files, POL 7 US/VANCE. Secret; Flash; Exdis. Received at 0157Z and repeated to Ankara, Nicosia, and USUN.

[2] When Vance met with Pipinellis shortly after midnight on November 26, he reported on his talks with the Turks and offered a revised draft of an accord on troop withdrawals. Vance carried a letter from Caglayangil containing assurances that Turkey would reduce its mobilization levels parallel with Greek force withdrawals. (Vanto 30 from Athens, November 25; ibid.)

[3] Telegram 2445 from Athens, November 27. (Ibid.)

improved mandate for UNFICYP giving it an increased pacification role and calling upon it to assist in setting up expeditiously new practical arrangements for the safeguarding of internal security (including the safety of all citizens) and the supervision of disarmament."

3. In explaining text, Vance emphasized that his object was to stop outbreak of war and not to solve all problems of Cyprus. Therefore, text could not be as inclusive as either party might wish. On other hand, text seems fair to both and could provide medium for resolution present crisis.

4. After discussion number elements of Vance draft, Pipinelis said it would not be feasible to reassemble the Cabinet to review paper before Vance's departure. He then proposed a "gentlemen's agreement." Vance should present the Greek draft to GOT tomorrow. If it is rejected, Vance should then present his draft. If Turk concurrence is obtained, Pipinelis pledged himself to support the draft in Cabinet. He also authorized Vance to inform GOT that he had reasonable confidence that GOG would approve the draft.

5. In discussing GOT plans for reduction mobilization levels, Pipinelis said GOG placed high priority on removal invasion fleet which had been assembled in Turk ports and would like to obtain letter from GOT covering reduction schedules comparable to their letter on withdrawal schedules. Vance said he would urge GOT to provide such a letter.

Talbot

---

326.   Telegram From the Embassy in Turkey to the Department of State[1]

Ankara, November 27, 1967, 1625Z.

2589. Vanto 33. Subj: Vance meeting with FonMin Caglayangil—November 27. Vance, accompanied by Ambassador Hart and John Walsh, met at 0800 with FonMin Caglayangil and Turkmen. Although speaking in somewhat bewildering rococo style, Caglayangil was courteous and friendly throughout the two-hour session. Vance opened the substantive section of the talks by conveying to Caglayangil the deep

---

[1] Source: Department of State, Central Files, POL 7 US/VANCE. Secret; Flash; Exdis. Received at 1717Z and also sent to Athens, Nicosia, and USUN.

appreciation of Greek Foreign Minister Pipinellis for the personal message from Caglayangil.[2] He then said that he had discussed with Pipinellis the GOT concern about the schedule for Greek force removals. In an effort to meet this problem, Pipinellis had written letter to Vance containing a specific schedule which would move all Greek forces in excess of London–Zurich levels within a three-month period. He had authorized Vance to pass this letter to Caglayangil.[3]

Having established a favorable frame of reference, Vance then turned over a document containing the GOG's formulation of a draft accord, which he had received from Pipinellis on the previous evening.[4]

After carefully reading the document, Caglayangil said he would take it to his government. He went on to say that Greece and Turkey were faced with two problems, the Cyprus question and the crisis born out of that question. In the past hectic week the GOT, aided by the US, had tried to resolve the crisis and had not wished to bog down in the vast ramifications of the Cyprus question. Vance had convinced him that, while the GOT had not given an ultimatum, world opinion believed that the GOT had cornered Greece.

Vance had found an ingenious way out in the form of a response to an appeal from the SYG. This idea would have solved the crisis. Greece could have reacted positively, contributing to an eventual atmosphere in which the basic question of Cyprus could have been solved. However, the Greek document is designed to show the public that the GOT has renounced the London/Zurich Accords, thus prejudging the Cyprus question. This is unacceptable to the GOT.

In response, Vance said that when he first came to the area he had felt that it would be wise to let the parties find a solution within the concept of an appeal by the Secretary General. In a sense, he had acted as a postman.

After reading the Greek draft last evening, it was clear to him that it would not be acceptable to the GOT. He felt the time had come for him to synthesize the ideas of both sides. The object of the document which he had prepared was to solve the immediate problem, and to leave to future negotiations the overall problem of Cyprus.[5] He could contribute little to the solution of that complex issue.

While largely based on the GOT draft of November 25, it does not include certain elements included in the Greek and Turk drafts. It is,

---

[2] See footnote 2, Document 325.
[3] Not found.
[4] Quoted in Document 325.
[5] The Vance draft was transmitted in Vanto 34 from Ankara, November 27. (Department of State, Central Files, POL 7 US/VANCE)

however, a fair and honorable formulation which, if approved, would resolve the immediate crisis.

In response to Caglayangil's question, Vance said the GOG had [garble—not?] seen the draft text presented to him but he has discussed the concept in the draft with the Greek Foreign Minister. Vance said he believed there was a reasonable chance that it would be accepted by the Greeks and he would bring all his energy to bear on the Greeks if the text were accepted by the GOT.

At the conclusion of certain clarifying comments by Vance, Caglayangil said he could easily discuss Vance's draft and would take it promptly to the Prime Minister and to the Cabinet. However, he was troubled by the Greek three month time table.

Vance said the important thing is the written Greek commitment to withdraw. Since it takes time to move troops, a three-month broad schedule was not unreasonable. When Vance asked what the GOT schedule was for reducing the mobilization rate, Caglayangil stated there is no time-table. However, if the Greeks begin to withdraw, the GOT could return to the November 15 levels immediately.

President and Prime Minister have been meeting with party leaders. We will not receive any word before 2000 local.

Hart

---

327.   Telegram From the Department of State to the Embassy in Greece[1]

Washington, November 27, 1967, 2110Z.

75051. Tovan 30.

1. We have hesitated to offer any specific comments re tactics your negotiations on assumption those officers on spot who are advising you are in position best fulfill this function.

2. As we follow evolution of draft proposal however we are impressed with extent to which ultimate success your mission could

---

[1] Source: Department of State, Central Files, POL 27 CYP. Secret; Immediate. Drafted by Wehmeyer and approved by Rockwell. Also sent to Ankara, London, Ottawa, Nicosia, the Mission to NATO, and USUN.

depend on reaction in Nicosia in view built-in veto Makarios might have by declining join proposed tripartite approach to SYG. We unaware whether you have discussed this Makarios problem with GOG.

3. For what it may be worth as supplement to what you may have heard and may hear, consensus here among officers experienced Cyprus affairs, is that even if you go to island with draft omitting express reference to London–Zurich and without direct reference to Turkish contingent you will not be able avoid substantive discussion with Makarios in which it will presumably become clear to him that settlement envisaged will include continuance Turkish contingent on island and Turkish insistence on validity London–Zurich agreements.

Belief here is that in such situation Makarios can be expected either reject proposal outright or attempt finesse by counter proposals. Unless Greek Cypriots have been intimidated by assigning high degree credibility danger Turkish attack, which appears not to be case, officers here consider Makarios likely will continue rely on his basic assets, namely, (a) status of Cyprus as sovereign independent state with all that implies; (b) membership in UN giving Makarios access to SYG and UN organs for protection; (c) psychological ties with Greece which can be exploited to inhibit action by GOG in connection such matters as unilateral withdrawal Greek forces from Cyprus over opposition of Makarios.

4. There arises accordingly question whether tactics can be developed to deter Makarios from reverting to his classic waltz around ring tightly clutching the UN. Only approach which has occurred to us is based on premise Makarios more likely attempt torpedo or evade your proposal if he is in doubt about ultimate political consequences than if he has fairly clear idea where it would lead. If he can be persuaded that political situation beyond your immediate proposal would be satisfactory from his standpoint he may be willing accept proposal. Our thought is that you might discuss this aspect of the problem frankly with Makarios and refer to Declaration of Reconciliation[2] as type of settlement which would appear possible in near future and which would establish political environment in which GOC, its officials, and its people could prosper, politically, economically, and socially. Ambassador Belcher would have coordinated this ahead of time with Canadian Ambassador, and you would say Declaration is Canadian proposal.

Rusk

---

[2] Reference is to a proposed appeal by the U.N. Secretary-General to the involved parties.

328. Telegram From the Embassy in Greece to the Department of State[1]

Athens, November 28, 1967, 0930Z.

2473. Vanto 36. Subject: Vance meeting with FonMin Caglayangil and Prime Minister Demirel—November 28.

1. Vance, accompanied by Ambassador Hart and John Walsh, had a five and one-half hour meeting beginning at 0200 this morning with Fon-Min Caglayangil who was assisted by Turkmen and Bulak.[2] At 0900 the mission departed for Athens, carrying a draft to be presented to the GOG on an "accept it or accept war" basis. This paper is final Turkish position which you will note rejects most of my draft.

2. We have grave doubt Greeks will agree to this document. Even if they do paragraph #4 as insisted upon by Turks does not provide basis for SYG to act unless three countries agree to paragraph #4 and Makarios would agree. In addition time running out and if Makarios did not agree within very short period of time Turks may move. We are trying to find some way around this problem but have no answer yet. Perhaps SYG could issue appeal based on points 1, 2, and 3 of current draft and act uni-laterally along lines of paragraph #4 of draft Vance presented to Turks which was rejected. This would take great courage on part of SYG and would carry risk that it would not be accepted by Turks who already have rejected it, or by Cypriots. (Request flash comments of Department and Goldberg.) Will continue to seek better alternative.

3. In addition Turks rejected Greek time table and have insisted on total withdrawal within 45 days. (Text of pertinent Caglayangil letter to me is attached.) We do not know whether Greeks can swallow this.

4. Plan to meet with Greek Foreign Minister immediately on arrival. Then plan to see Rolz-Bennett to get his views and help.

5. As result of last night's session which will be reported in detail in cable to follow we have question as to Demirel's ability to control his Cabinet. He appeared shaken and under great strain. We were informed he was turned down on more than one occasion in urging acceptance by Turks of some of points in Vance draft.

Text of GOT draft accord handed Vance Nov 28 as follows:

"1. The Secretary General of the United Nations would address an appeal to the Governments of Turkey, Greece and Cyprus, such an appeal to include:

---

[1] Source: Department of State, Central Files, POL 7 US/VANCE. Secret; Flash; Exdis. Received at 1131Z and repeated to Ankara, Nicosia, London, the Mission to NATO, USUN, and CINCEUR.

[2] Vance reported on his meeting with Caglayangil, in which he requested and received an audience with Demirel, in Vanto 39, November 28. (Ibid.)

A request that the Governments of Turkey and Greece take immediate steps to remove any threat to the security of each other and of Cyprus and as a first step along the lines of the Secretary General's previous appeal to bring about an expeditious withdrawal of those forces in excess of the Turkish and Greek contingents.

2. The Governments of Greece and Turkey would declare their readiness to comply forthwith with the appeal of the Secretary General.

3. Thereupon the Greek Government would withdraw expeditiously its military forces and military personnel and equipment from Cyprus. Accompanying this, the Turkish Government will take all the necessary measures for removing the crisis.

4. In response to the appeal of the Secretary General, there should be an enlarged and improved mandate for UNFICYP giving it an increased pacification role, which would include supervision of disarmament of all forces constituted after 1963 and new practical arrangements for the safeguarding of internal security including the safety of all citizens."

6. Following accompanying letter dated Nov 28 from FonMin Caglayangil also given Vance:

"Dear Mr. Vance:

Recognizing the great importance of reducing tensions between Greece and Turkey expeditiously, it is suggested that the proposed timetable for the withdrawal of the Greek forces contained in the letter of the Greek Foreign Minister to you be reduced from three months to 45 days. It is also stressed that this withdrawal should take place in a continuing process and carried out in good faith.

On its part the Government of Turkey will take in parallel all the necessary measures for reducing the crisis. This means that with the commencement of the withdrawal of Greek forces the Government of Turkey will stand down the current state of readiness of its forces, and in parallel with further Greek withdrawals will reduce the military preparedness of its forces to levels in effect prior to November 15, 1967.

Ihsan Sabri Caglayangil"

Talbot

329.   Telegram From the Embassy in Greece to the Department of State[1]

Athens, November 28, 1967, 1215Z.

2475. Vanto 38. Ref: Vanto 37.[2] Subject: Vance meeting with FonMin Pipinelis—November 28.

1. Vance, accompanied by Ambassador Talbot and John Walsh, called on FonMin Pipinelis at 1130, shortly after their return to Athens. Theodoropoulos also present.

2. Vance opened discussion with statement situation very grave. He then ran through events and meetings in Ankara reported septel, reporting that Greek draft accord had been badly received. After summarizing the very difficult meeting that he had in early morning hours with Caglayangil[3] he handed over the two GOT documents emitting from that session, namely letter to him from Caglayangil limiting Greek withdrawal period to 45 days and GOT draft accord representing "final" Turk position.

3. Vance said honesty compelled him to state time is very short and Turks will not accept any change in draft. This is fact of life.

4. Pipinelis said this was ultimatum which he instinctively inclined reject. From beginning to end of Vance process he had tried to settle issue. With each exchange, however, Turks had raised the price.

5. While he did not seem to boggle over 45-day limit on withdrawal and did not have particular difficulties with operative paras affecting Greece–Turkey relations, para 4 concerning UNFICYP operations appeared impossible to him. Greece, he said, could take steps on its own but it cannot make decisions for Cyprus. Furthermore, he was convinced that chaos would result if Greek forces were withdrawn and the National Guard was disbanded before some other force were constituted. He said he could not recommend this to his government, since it makes no sense. Furthermore it would be impossible to carry the Cabinet with this proposition or to get Makarios to accept it.

6. Talbot then pointed out that para 4 as drafted by Turks was not operative and furthermore language implied parallelism between phasing out National Guard and constituting new force. Vance pointed out

---

[1] Source: Department of State, Central Files, POL 7 US/VANCE. Secret; Flash; Exdis. Received at 1457Z and repeated to Ankara, London, Nicosia, USUN, the Mission to NATO, and USCINCEUR.

[2] Vanto 37, November 28, reported on negotiations with the Turks on Vance's proposals for a settlement. At the end of the discussion, Caglayangil stated that the U.S. effort was at the "end of the line" and that Turkey would accept no further modifications of the proposal. (Ibid.)

[3] See Document 328.

that provisions of para would be implemented by UN not by GOT. Therefore, parallelism and timing was in hands of UN. In addition, he had made perfectly clear to Turks that para as drafted was not operative. Turks have also specifically stated they have no time limits in mind re [garble—para 4].

7. This exchange somewhat buoyed Pipinelis who said he would discuss letter and draft accord with Cabinet. At Vance's urging he agreed withhold negative decision until he talked to Brosio and to us. Vance told him we had some ideas which might help.

Talbot

330. Telegram From the Embassy in Greece to the Department of State[1]

Athens, November 28, 1967, 2143Z.

2486. Vanto 43. Subject: Vance meeting with FonMin Pipinelis— November 28.

1. Vance, accompanied by Ambassador Talbot and John Walsh, met with FonMin Pipinelis at 2130. Pipinelis came directly to the issue. He said Cabinet had accepted GOT proposals and he would present letter to that effect to Vance. Decision was reached after moving scene in Cabinet. It was not easy but it was right. He hoped this would be the beginning of end of sad story of conflict with Turks over Cyprus.

2. Pipinelis said he also hoped Turks would not try score propaganda victory as result GOG decision. Said he had prepared lengthy statement emphasizing no value in winning or losing in Greek-Turk relations, and pointing out agreement will not settle everything but it will open the door to direct contacts between two countries.

3. Vance said he wished express his deep personal admiration for Minister. His decision had been very courageous.

4. Pipinelis said GOG wished seek certain clarifications and would request Brosio visit Ankara tomorrow morning. First of these concerned Makarios. GOG accepted Turk proposals in good faith but could not

---

[1] Source: Department of State, Central Files, POL 7 US/VANCE. Secret; Flash; Exdis. Received at 2227Z and also sent to Ankara, London, Nicosia, USUN, the Mission to NATO, and CINCEUR.

commit Makarios re para 4. Government was prepared, however, to try bring him aboard. Second concerned relationship in some paras between elimination of National Guard and constituting new force. Government believed these actions should be parallel. Third concerned definition of military personnel in para 3. Vance interrupted at that point to express belief each side should hold own interpretation that issue. Fourth was GOG desire stretch withdrawal period from 45 to 60 days in order provide logistical and elbow room.

5. Vance suggested that once withdrawals began issues like this should be practical subjects of discussion with Turks. Pipinelis ended discussion by expressing firm conviction that war would have occurred [had not] President Johnson sent the Vance Mission to search for a peaceful solution. On behalf his government he expressed deep appreciation to President.

6. Text of letter from Pipinelis to Vance follows: "I have the honour to inform you that the Greek Government accept the proposals contained in the attached text, on the understanding that the measures to be taken by the Turkish Government to remove the crisis in accordance with the letter of the Foreign Minister of Turkey, dated November 28, 1967, shall be implemented in good faith.

The Greek Government wish to point out that, as far as the provisions of paragraph 4 are concerned, which they read as also covering the question of the National Guard, they cannot engage the responsibility of the Government of Cyprus, whose rights must remain by necessity reserved."[2]

Talbot

---

[2] In Vanto 41, November 28, Vance requested that Hart inform the Turkish Government of Greek acceptance. (Ibid.) In Vanto 42, November 28, Vance reported that he was flying to Nicosia to secure Makarios' agreement. (Ibid.)

331. Telegram From the Department of State to the Embassy in Cyprus[1]

Washington, November 29, 1967, 0113Z.

76019. Tovan 37. Ref.: Vanto 41.[2] For Vance from Secretary.

1. Problem all along with Makarios has been that US does not have much of a handle on him. We have no economic or military aid program, and communications facilities, for which we are to pay rent, are distinctly to our advantage.

2. Makarios has never wavered in his conviction that US will not permit Turkey to invade Cyprus. Your present mission is probably seen by him as further convincing evidence of this. In current crisis Russians have complicated matters by telling GOC that Turks are bluffing. You would wish to disabuse him on this—in fact, if you can scare him it might be helpful.

3. In circumstances best tactic would appear be to attempt play on Makarios' vanity by stressing his positive role as champion of peace. If this fails, you should try convince Makarios that if he tries torpedo Greek–Turkey accord, and Turks invade as result, GOC would be considered as bearing the principal responsibility for failure to avert a catastrophe. In such circumstances world opinion would be turned against GOC, and would regard GOC as having set political objective above peace. In such circumstances, moreover, GOC should not be assuming that US would intervene militarily. GOC will have noted that there has been no change in routine disposition of Sixth Fleet throughout this crisis.

4. Above is best strategy I can think of view lack of the instrumentalities of support we possess in other countries. In general you could stress that lack of cooperative action will inevitably have effect on our future relations, without being specific. I would caution you against suggesting any specific US action to help Makarios if he behaves, beyond renewed willingness to be helpful in attempt solve general Cyprus problem, in view well-known tendency of Makarios to use such gestures to his own advantage.

5. In the event you get indications that Makarios feels that he can disregard the Greek-Turk agreement by going to the Security Council on the assumption he could get a better deal, you should tell him bluntly that we would use every possible means at our disposal to prevent this

---

[1] Source: Department of State, Central Files, POL 27 CYP. Secret; Flash; Exdis. Drafted by Rockwell; cleared by Sisco, Katzenbach, and Battle; and approved by Rusk. Repeated to Athens and Ankara.

[2] See footnote 2, Document 330.

and to ensure that any action there would not go beyond the substance of the Greek-Turk agreement.

6. We would prefer that you use the above only if Makarios refers to this possibility; otherwise, we see no particular advantage in your taking the initiative in this regard.

7. The following points may be useful to you, subject to Ambassador Belcher's views. (He is real expert on Makarios.)

(a) I understand that Makarios reacts badly to strong words and a forceful approach.
(b) It should be made very clear to him that GOG has made a difficult decision and requires his support.
(c) Makarios does value his relations with the US, and could be encouraged anticipate more active effort on our part to tackle general Cyprus problem once this crisis over.

8. Congratulations on a superb job so far, and good luck!

9. By separate telegram we are sending revised text Presidential message to Makarios[3] which we have toned down somewhat in belief this likely be more effective and to make letter less susceptible of being used against us should Makarios decide complain in Security Council that he being pressed by US to give in to Turkish demands.

Rusk

---

[3] Transmitted in telegram 76018 to Nicosia, November 29. It called on Makarios to make the concessions needed to ensure a peaceful settlement of the confrontation. (Department of State, Central Files, POL 27 CYP)

---

332. Summary Notes of the 579th Meeting of the National Security Council[1]

Washington, November 29, 1967, 12:05–12:50 p.m.

Cyprus

The President opened the meeting by requesting Secretary Rusk to give a summary of the current situation in Cyprus.

---

[1] Source: Johnson Library, National Security File, NSC Meetings File, Vol. 4. Secret; Sensitive; For the President Only. Drafted by Smith.

Secretary Rusk: Cyrus Vance, the President's special emissary, has done a superb job and has warded off war between Turkey and Greece. He did not want to embarass Luke Battle but said that he was delighted to have had him as Assistant Secretary working on this problem on an hourly basis. He asked Mr. Battle to outline where we now are in our effort to end the Crisis over Cyprus.

Assistant Secretary Battle: Is optimistic that war between Greece and Turkey would be avoided. To Mr. Vance belongs the credit for the astonishing progress which has been made in keeping the Turkish-Greek crisis over Cyprus from turning into hostilities. Provisions of a statement which both Greece and Turkey have accepted (copy attached)[2] were summarized. Mr. Vance is now in Cyprus trying to persuade Cyprus President Makarios to accept this agreement. Makarios could cause trouble in many ways, but the expectation is that he will not block the Vance effort.

The problem of Cyprus will be with us for some time to come, difficulties will rise in the future, for example, reaching an agreement to expand the role of the United Nations, but for the moment a Greek-Turkish war has been avoided.

Secretary Rusk: Turkey wants the United Nations Security Council to approve a new and expanded UN mandate covering Cyprus. We do not think Council action is necessary but the problem is in the hands of the Secretary General and the heat is off us. The Turks can more easily live with the failure of the Secretary General to obtain a new mandate from the UN Security Council than they could if we had agreed to get a new mandate and had been unsuccessful.

Everyone is appreciative that the President made Vance available for this assignment, adding that without his activity, Turkey would now be at war with Greece.

The President: Asked General Wheeler to summarize the military situation.

General Wheeler: Tension between the two countries has somewhat abated, pending the outcome of the Vance negotiations.

1. Turkey had an advantage over Greece in the air and on land. The Greeks have an advantage at sea because of their greater naval strength.

2. If Greeks [Turks?] chose to invade Greek Thrace, they could advance rapidly, probably as far as Salonika.

3. The Turks could put several divisions in Cyprus, probably on the north side in the Kyrenia area, in two to three weeks. They could gain control of the island, only some 40 miles from Turkey, despite Greek opposition.

---

[2] Not found.

4. If the Turks attack, it would take them 24 hours to gain air superiority by pre-emptive air strikes on Greek bases. They would probably invade Cyprus but probably would not invade Greece from Thrace.

CIA Director Helms: We have no reports of Soviet military activity in the area. However, the Russians are fishing in troubled waters by egging on the Turks and telling the Cypriots that Turkey was bluffing.

[Here follows brief discussion of the Soviet Union and Vietnam.]

Bromley Smith

---

333.   Telegram From the Embassy in Cyprus to the Department of State[1]

Nicosia, November 29, 1967, 1700Z.

817. Vanto 50. Reference: Vanto 46 (Nicosia 812).[2] Subject: Vance's meeting with Archbishop Makarios and FonMin Kyprianou—November 29. Vance, accompanied by Amb. Belcher and John Walsh, met at 0930 with Archbishop Makarios and FonMin Kyprianou for 75 minutes. Vance again reviewed the events of the past week, stating that his mission is to prevent a war and not to solve all the complex issues of Cyprus. War has been very close this week. Had he not reached Ankara on November 23, the Turks would have gone to war. In the course of intensive discussions with the GOT, President Sunay had assured him that Turkey would not invade Cyprus. However, time ran out last night and, if Greece had not accepted the proposals, the Turkish units would have been on shores of Cyprus this morning. Intelligence estimates indicate they could put close to 50,000 men ashore with heavy equipment in 48-hours under cover of complete air control. Carnage would result.

In response, Makarios expressed his deep gratitude for the U.S. effort to preserve the peace. He fully understood the critical nature of recent days and was happy that war had not occurred. He had slept while Vance worked in Ankara, confident that nothing would happen.

---

[1] Source: Department of State, Central Files, POL 7 US/VANCE. Secret; Flash; Exdis. Received at 1759Z and also sent to Ankara, Athens, USUN, London, the Mission to NATO, and USCINCEUR.

[2] Vanto 46, November 29, reported on Vance's 8:30 a.m. meeting with Kyprianou, during which Kyprianou outlined his government's objections to the proposed accord. (Ibid.)

Makarios said he understood the Greek Government had accepted the agreement document but he had not heard directly from Athens as yet. While GOG could properly make its own decisions, he had, of course, difficulties with the document, particularly para. 4.

Cyprus, he said, is plagued by the presence of foreign troops. His basic objective is the total demilitarization of the island, including the Greek and Turk contingents. Under those circumstances he would also disband the National Guard which was costing too much money. With help of UNFICYP, he would try to disarm everyone. Only police force would remain and his government would have talks with Turkish community about this.

In view of need for total demilitarization it would be difficult for him to agree that Greek and Turk contingents could remain on the island. They were source of infection and should be rooted out now.

Vance said he realized the Archbishop's view this subject and had insisted that language relating to the withdrawal of Greek and Turk forces be qualified "as a first step along the lines of the SYG's previous appeal." Since the SYG's appeal called for ultimate demilitarization, acceptance of the document in no way impeded movement toward final goal of elimination of all military forces. Therefore, removal of contingents was in no way precluded by language of document. However, GOT will not agree discuss this issue at this time. Approval of document as it stands is vital step in avoidance bloody war.

Makarios then shifted to dangers of foreign intervention, saying he hoped guarantee could be obtained from U.S. and UK on behalf of Security Council. Vance responded, saying he had no authority to give USG security commitments. He suggested Makarios look to Security Council in this respect.

Turning to para. 4, Makarios said UNFICYP already had adequate mandate and call for enlarged and improved mandate unnecessary. Vance agreed and emphasized that GOT had insisted on this language over his strong objections. Makarios then said that the para could not be accepted unless a reference were made to elimination two contingents. Vance responded that GOT would not agree and that war would be certain outcome of GOC unwillingness accept agreement. Progress on broader issues possible if war is avoided.

Vance then gave Makarios message from President Johnson. Although Archbishop read carefully and made wry comment about reference to his wisdom, he did not respond substantively.

Vance then suggested Makarios could write letter to him, stating GOC approved proposal but reserved views re removal of contingents and ultimate demilitarization. Makarios said he would draft a letter clearly indicating his views these matters. Vance pointed out that message would have to be restrained in tone or it would be read as rejection by GOT. This might trigger invasion with dire consequences.

Session ended with Makarios statement that he would take proposals to Cabinet and would meet with Vance later in day.

We now have 2000 local appointment with Makarios.

Belcher

---

334. Telegram From the Embassy in Greece to the Department of State[1]

Athens, November 30, 1967, 0405Z.

2501. Vanto 53. Subject: Vance meeting with Archbishop Makarios—Nov 29–30. Vance, accompanied by Amb. Belcher and John Walsh, met with Archbishop Makarios, President of the Parliament Clerides and FonMin Kyprianou in 6 and 3/4 hour marathon session, ending at 0245. Mission left for Athens at 0345.

Makarios stubbornly and cleverly defended a defective GOC written commentary into the early morning hours.

Finally, His Beatitude gave way sufficiently to permit the completion of a draft which seems sufficiently forthcoming to contribute to the overall defusing effort. Negotiating with him under circumstances threatening existence of his country can be fairly described as unique experience.

Text of the secret written GOC comment signed by Spyros Kyprianou, Minister of Foreign Affairs, follows:

"Dear Mr. Vance

We welcome the many and strenuous efforts which have been made in recent days to preserve peace in this area.

The Government of the Republic of Cyprus, referring to the proposals contained in the attached text, wishes to state its position as follows:

1. The first three paragraphs of the said proposals concern primarily the Governments of Greece and Turkey and have already been agreed

---

[1] Source: Department of State, Central Files, POL 7 US/VANCE. Secret; Flash; Exdis. Received at 0946Z and also sent to Nicosia, Ankara, London, USUN, the Mission to NATO, and CINCEUR.

upon by them. The Government of Cyprus acknowledging the aforesaid agreement between the Governments of Greece and Turkey considers it as a first step on the lines of the Secretary-General's appeal of November 24, 1967, for the phased withdrawal of all forces and complete demilitarisation.[2] It, therefore, maintains that such phased withdrawal should include the Greek and Turkish contingents because it firmly believes that, in this way, the cause of peace would be best served.

2. The pacification measures stated in paragraph 4 are objectives of the Cyprus Government.

3. The Cyprus Government questions the need for 'an enlarged and improved mandate for UNFICYP.' It suggests that the three governments discuss this issue with the Secretary-General of the United Nations in New York.

4. The Government of Cyprus will ask the Security Council for guarantees against military intervention in accordance with the last paragraph of the Secretary-General's appeal of November 24, 1967. Yours sincerely, Spyros Kyprianou, Minister of Foreign Affairs."

Detailed report on meeting will be submitted in septel.[3]

Talbot

---

[2] U.N. Doc. S/8248/Add.5; for text, see *American Foreign Policy: Current Documents, 1967*, pp. 367–368. This was Secretary-General Thant's second appeal; his first was on November 22 (see Document 307).

[3] Not further identified.

---

335. Telegram From the Mission to the United Nations to the Department of State[1]

New York, November 30, 1967, 2144Z.

2672. From Goldberg for Vance. Rossides, Cyprus Rep at UN has advised SYG that Kyprianou letter to you constitutes rejection by Government of Cyprus of the agreement. I have been at Rossides myself for two hours telling him that he is absolutely wrong and insisting that he go

---

[1] Source: Department of State, Central Files, POL 27 CYP. Secret; Flash; Exdis. Received at 2240Z. Also sent to Athens and repeated to Nicosia, Ankara, London, Ottawa, the Mission to NATO, and USCINCEUR.

back immediately to his government for positive instructions to advise SYG that Kyprianou acknowledgment language means GOC supports agreement as Kyprianou stated to you before you left Palace in Nicosia. I have also insisted that SYG not accept this statement as final.

I shall advise you again upon hearing from Rossides having impressed upon him necessity for affirmative response forthwith.

Rossides action here is in character. In handling of Cyprus problem at UN he has consistently been more hawkish than Makarios or Kyprianou. It will be highly important to get to Makarios and Kyprianou so that Rossides can be instructed to consent to SYG issuing his appeal tonight.

If it will help with Makarios you can advise that both Turks and Greeks are willing to revise para 4 to meet Makarios view, as well as our own, that new and enlarged mandate is not required. Governments of Turkey and Greece are willing to agree to following revision of para 4:

"In response to the appeal of the SYG, UNFICYP, under its existing mandate, would be available to undertake an enhanced and broader pacification role, which would include supervision of disarmament of all forces constituted after 1963 and new practical arrangements for the safeguarding of internal security including the safety of all citizens."[2]

Goldberg

---

[2] In telegram 77716 to Nicosia, December 1, the Department of State instructed the Embassy to convey its strong request that Makarios correct the mistaken impression created by Rossides, warning that his actions might be placing his nation in danger of attack. (Ibid.)

---

336.   Telegram From the Embassy in Turkey to the Embassy in Greece[1]

Ankara, November 30, 1967, 1515Z.

2638. NATUS. Ref: Ankara 2637.[2]

1.   FonMin asked me to call at 1500 Nov 30 and reading from notes conveyed following points representing decisions of Cabinet.

---

[1] Source: Department of State, Central Files, POL 7 US/VANCE. Secret; Flash; Exdis. Received at 2317Z. Also sent to the Department of State, Nicosia, and USUN and repeated to London, Ottawa, and the Mission to NATO. The source text is the Department of State copy.

[2] Telegram 2637, November 30, reported on the meeting at which Hart presented Caglayangil with a summary of the Vance–Makarios talks and reported on the draft text agreed to by Makarios. (Ibid.)

A. GOT will accept substitute langauge for para 4 of agreement as recommended by Ambassador Eralp and reading: "In response to the appeal of Secretary General, UNFICYP under its existing mandate would be available to undertake an enhanced and broader pacification role, which would include supervision of disarmament of all forces constituted after 1963 and new practical arrangements for the safeguarding of internal security including the safety of all citizens".

B. GOT reserves right to return to Security Council to seek enlarged improved mandate for UNFICYP if operations under existing mandate prove unsatisfactory.

C. Turkey's NATO allies and especially US, UK and Canada should declare immediately after appeal issued by SYG that they support appeal as a whole but giving particular support to para 4.

D. At Security Council meeting on Dec 15 concerned with prolongation of UNFICYP consensus of members should be sought by Turkey's allies to obtain approval of new role for UNFICYP envisaged para 4 SYG's appeal. (This most important to box in Makarios.)

E. GOT insists that withdrawal of Greek forces start in shortest possible time and be carried out in continuous and uninterrupted fashion and in good faith. (FonMin explained this is essential to avoid complications and to establish a basis for an improvement in Greek-Turkish relations.)

F. Repetition of incidents such as those of Nov 15–16 on Cyprus must be avoided at all costs. Absolute security must be maintained on island.

G. Greek Cypriots must avoid provocative acts. GOT has given like instructions to Turkish Cypriots.

H. Makarios must be prevented from playing role in New York in connection with SYG's appeal that would sabotage Turkish-Greek agreement. NATO allies, especially representatives of US, UK and Canada, who took part in working out "five points", should play efficacious role to this end in Nicosia. Interval during which SYG's appeal issued and replies given is especially critical. Makarios should not say appeal is unacceptable to GOC, should not be allowed to interpret it so as to sabotage it.

2. FonMin then said that under above conditions, and once agreement with SYG on new formula for para 4 seemed assured, he saw no need for Vance to hurry to New York. On the contrary, he could usefully remain in Athens and endeavor to plan with Greeks accelerated withdrawal of Greek troops in manner indicated above. (Implication was GOT would do its part on standdown.)

3. Caglayangil said that as soon as SYG makes his appeal GOT would like to have clear affirmative answer from GOG without qualifications or interpretations. Makarios could say GOC accepts appeal of

SYG reserving always its own viewpoint regarding final solution. He should say nothing more. If style and content SYG's appeal conforms to agreement GOT will immediately respond that it accepts and is ready to conform to it. GOT will point especially to para 4 saying that it approves and supports this provision.

4. I said would immediately report FonMin's remarks.

5. Septel follows on conversation and supplementary points.[3]

Hart

---

[3] Not found.

---

337. **Telegram From the Embassy in Cyprus to the Department of State**[1]

Nicosia, December 1, 1967, 0220Z.

831. Tovan. Ref: USUN 2672.[2] For Goldberg and Vance from Belcher.

1. I have just come from meeting with Makarios and Kyprianou. Kyprianou has spoken with Rossides on telephone and given instructions on following lines: he is to support an appeal by the Secretary General based on para one of the GOG–GOT agreement. He told Rossides that he and Makarios agree as set forth in para one of his letter to Vance.[3] He told Rossides on phone (in my presence) that they could not agree to have anything in this first appeal on the basis of para four. He said that the Secretary General should do as suggested in para one USUN 2673.[4] That is to discuss with the three governments the question of para four or as he put it, "This question of additional pacification measures and the role of UNFICYP".

---

[1] Source: Department of State, Central Files, POL 7 US/VANCE. Secret; Flash; Exdis. Also sent to Athens, USUN, and Ankara and repeated to London, Ottawa, the Mission to NATO, and CINCEUR.

[2] Document 335.

[3] The text of the letter is included in Document 334.

[4] Telegram 2673 from USUN, November 3, requested an immediate approach by the Secretary-General to the Turkish Government and transmitted an agreed text of the Turkish reply. (Department of State, Central Files, POL 27 CYP)

2. While waiting for call to Rossides Kyprianou had suggested this course of action prior to our receipt of USUN 2673. When I received word by phone by Embassy along lines USUN 2673, I explained Vance and Goldberg apparently now thinking along these lines too. I warned him however that we had no indication as yet that Turks would be willing go along with this suggestion. I reminded him that originally GOT had informed Vance that document stood or fell as a unit. Whether they could be persuaded to follow this suggestion was matter we could not answer at this time. We would try get their concurrence.

3. I showed Kyprianou new text para four per last para USUN 2672. He commented that if GOC accepted the revised language, would mean that GOC would agree that what the Turks want can be accomplished under the present mandate. He said in presence of Makarios GOC would reject language of para four unless qualified as per letter to Vance.

4. With regard to Kyprianou's commitment to Vance as latter was leaving Palace, Kyprianou claims that what he said was that Rossides would be instructed not to oppose the Secretary General's appeal as it was his understanding that para four would be subject to further discussion between Secretary General and three governments and would not be included in appeal.[5]

5. Rossides instructed contact Goldberg and SYG along these lines at once. He is also to give copy of Vance letter to SYG.

6. Additional re para four Kyprianou went over same ground as in our lengthy discussions with you night of 29th in Nicosia. Said if they had to give categoric reply to question of accepting or rejecting para four as then drafted (or as presently revised) they would have to reject. "For this reason we devised formula which appeared in letter to Vance".

7. "GOC could not 'sign away sovereignty' by giving to UNFICYP undefined powers over internal security and other concepts included para four. For this reason they could only go along with statement accepting objectives of para four as being those of GOC too and agreeing to discussions in New York of role of UNFICYP in meeting between GOC, GOT, GOG and SYG."

Belcher

---

[5] Vanto 55 from Athens, November 30, reads: "Prior leaving Palace in Nicosia early this morning, ForMin Kyprianou commented to Vance that reference in para 1 to GOC 'acknowledging' the agreement between Greece and Turkey should be construed to mean that GOC will support the agreement." (Ibid., POL 7 US/VANCE)

338. Telegram From the Embassy in Greece to the Embassy in Turkey[1]

Athens, December 1, 1967, 0625Z.

2531. Vanto 62. We are manifestly in a dangerous bind. At this early morning hour, our options appear limited in numbers and attractiveness. Unless we get some glue into the situation in a hurry, the agreements between the Greeks and Turks which we brought about may quickly fall apart and the Turks may proceed with their landing plans.

We seem to have two possibilities: (1) US, UK, and GOG make combined, or separate, effort to persuade GOC to agree to an SYG appeal which includes the revised para 4 language, contained USUN 2672.[2] We would inform GOT of this attempt. We would provide GOC assurances that we would be conscious of their sovereignty problems. (2) Same combination would exert maximum pressure on GOC to agree that SYG issue appeal, which includes request that interested parties meet with him to work out improved pacification measures. GOT would have to be brought aboard on this approach expeditiously. US, UK, and GOG would promise GOT we would use our full influence to reach agreement in New York on those measures.

Request comments soonest from addressees on these or other possibilities.[3]

Talbot

---

[1] Source: Department of State, Central Files, POL 7 US/VANCE. Secret; Flash; Exdis. Also sent to Nicosia, USUN, and the Department of State. The source text is the Department of State copy.

[2] Document 335.

[3] In telegram 841 from Nicosia, December 1, Belcher suggested that Vance return to Cyprus in an effort both to increase pressure for settlement on Makarios and to avoid a military intervention. (Department of State, Central Files, POL 7 CYP)

339.   Telegram From the Embassy in Cyprus to the Department of
State[1]

Nicosia, December 2, 1967, 0222Z.

848. Vanto 72. Ref: Vanto 71 (Nicosia 847).[2] Subj: Vance meeting with
Archbishop Makarios—December 1–2.

1.   Vance, accompanied by Ambassador Belcher and John Walsh,
had 4-hour meeting 0215, December 2, with Archbishop Makarios, Parliamentary President Clerides, and FonMin Kyprianou. Although maintaining his customary stubbornness in face of pressure from any quarter,
Makarios was less dominating figure than in previous meetings. Kyprianou and Clerides tended to dominate the discussions on the Cypriot
side. As in Ankara, the Cabinet was in session in an adjoining room and
was reported by Kyprianou to be in negative mood. Ministerial opinion
showed signs of stiffening against Turkish pressures, probably reflecting
irritation at Turkish overflights of Nicosia and a growing belief that the
US would hold the Turks in check.

2.   Vance opened the discussion by endeavoring to impress the
Archbishop with the sincerity of the US peace effort, the seriousness of
the Turkish threat, and the necessity for Cyprus to pay for the events of
November 14–15. This set the stage for the presentation to Makarios of
the revised draft of para 4 and a draft letter of confirmation. Text follows:

"Dear Mr. Vance: You have informed me that the Governments of
Greece and Turkey would be prepared to revise the language of para-
graph 4 of the document, annexed to my previous letter to you, dated
November 30, 1967, as follows:

'In response to the appeal of the Secretary General, UNFICYP, under
its existing mandate, would be available to undertake an enhanced and
broader pacification role, which would include supervision of disarmament of all forces constituted, after 1963 and new practical arrangements
for the safeguarding of internal security including the safety of all citizens. The Secretary General's good offices would be available to work
out the specifics with the interested parties.'

If this language were approved by the Governments of Greece and
Turkey, and the Secretary General were to address an appeal along the
following general lines:

'On November 24 I emphasized the need for the UN through its
appropriate organs to do all it can to reverse the trend toward war result-

---

[1] Source: Department of State, Central Files, POL 27 CYP. Secret; Flash; Exdis. Also
sent to Ankara, Athens, USUN, London, the Mission to NATO, and USCINCEUR.

[2] Vanto 71, December 1, forwarded a Cypriot proposed redraft of paragraph 4 of the
agreement. (Ibid.)

ing from the Cyprus question. The Security Council met and on November 25 called upon all the parties concerned to show the utmost moderation and restraint and to refrain from any act which might aggravate the situation in Cyprus and constitute a threat to the peace. The Security Council further requested all concerned urgently to assist and cooperate in keeping the peace and arriving at a permanent settlement in accordance with the resolution of the Security Council of 4 March 1964.[3]

'In the light of the Security Council consensus and the continuing tension in the area, as Secretary General of the United Nations, I now urge the Governments of Greece and Turkey to take immediate steps to remove any threat to the security of each other and of Cyprus, and as a first step along the lines of my previous appeal to bring about an expeditious withdrawal of those forces in excess of the Turkish and Greek contingents. In addition UNFICYP under its existing mandate would be available to undertake an enhanced and broader pacification role, which would include supervision of disarmament of all forces constituted after 1963 and new practical arrangements for the safeguarding of internal security including the safety of all citizens. The Secretary General's good offices would be available to work out the specifics with the interested parties.'

The Government of Cyprus would accept such appeal."

3. Vance said the revised para 4 had been approved by the GOT, GOG, and SYG. Furthermore, it satisfactorily met the GOC belief that it would be unnecessary to request a new and broader mandate for UNFICYP and also would clarify for the GOC the extent of an enhanced and broader role for UNFICYP since it called for discussions with the SYG of the specifics of the new effort.

4. Makarios replied in his customary loving style. He was grateful for US assistance but could not accept ultimatum. If a "yes or no" answer was required, the answer was "no". The revised draft was somewhat worse than the earlier draft with which he had had serious difficulties. If asked what the GOC response was to para 4, it was clear "unacceptable." Furthermore, he could not understand why the SYG did not issue an appeal limited to the first three paragraphs.

5. After this opening salvo, it was clear that the mission's expectations of a long and difficult evening had been fully justified. Having made his mark, the Archbishop was relatively quiet thereafter.

6. Kyprianou was center stage through most of the remaining period, worrying the draft and the problem like a terrier gnawing a bone. Occasionally, Clerides joined the game.

7. Fundamentally, Vance tried to explain to them that his mission was to prevent a war, not to solve the overall problems of Cyprus. It was understandable that the Cyprus Government resented discussions con-

---

[3] For text of the November 25 Security Council statement (U.N. Doc. S/8266), see *American Foreign Policy: Current Documents, 1967*, pp. 368–369.

ducted under the pressure of a gun. But the revised agreement, if approved, could put an end to the guns, and could set the stage for subsequent discussions of the basic issues of the island.

8. Finally, Kyprianou drafted a bare-boned para 4 which he asked us to try out with the Greek and Turk Perm Reps in New York (see reftel).

9. It was agreed the group would reconvene at 08:30 for further discussions. Clearly it was going to be very difficult to obtain agreement of Makarios to a para 4 which makes sense.[4]

Belcher

---

[4] In Vanto 76, December 2, Vance reported that if Makarios remained adamant, he intended to tell him he would be returning immediately to Athens for passage to the United States, effectively ending the mediation effort. (Ibid.) In a December 2 memorandum to the President, 10:45 a.m., Bromley Smith explained that while Vance remained in Athens to prevent an outbreak of war, U Thant would issue a short appeal that would serve as the basis for an immediate token withdrawal of Greek forces from Cyprus. The United States hoped this approach could avoid recourse to force. (Johnson Library, National Security File, Memos to the President—Walt Rostow, Box 26, Vol. 53)

---

340. Telegram From the Embassy in Cyprus to the Department of State[1]

Nicosia, December 3, 1967, 1517Z.

875. Vanto 86. Subject: Vance meeting with Archbishop Makarios—December 3.

1. Vance, accompanied by Ambassador Belcher and John Walsh, had a two-hour meeting beginning 1300 with Archbishop Makarios, President of Parliament Clerides, and FonMin Kyprianou. Makarios was adamant, rejecting para 4 as revised during the night, and refusing any further efforts at compromise. He said Greece and Turkey can do what they want but it was impossible for him to accept anything that resembled commitment prior to discussion in Security Council. He said during course of our meeting Greek Government had urged him not to

---

[1] Source: Department of State, Central Files, POL 7 US/VANCE. Secret; Flash; Exdis. Also sent to USUN, Ankara, Athens, London, the Mission to NATO, and CINCEUR.

reject the draft para 4 but he had refused. In final statement, he expressed great appreciation to President Johnson, Vance, and USG for untiring effort to safeguard the peace. You have done the utmost, he said, and we will always be grateful no matter what the future may bring. When Vance pressed him to ponder again and to withhold a final decision, he responded negatively. He did, however, agree to refrain from press comment, although GOC had already begun to circulate background statement that it would never knuckle under Turk pressure. Thus there was no give in the rigid GOC position as time ran out in Nicosia for the Vance Mission. Vance will leave approximately 1800 for Athens.

2.   Vance opened the discussion by reading the following prepared statement:

"We have been working throughout the night and this morning in a desperate attempt to get acceptance of the proposal which we transmitted on your behalf yesterday to the Government of Turkey.

In the early morning hours the Government of Turkey flatly rejected your proposal.

Through the rest of the night our Ambassadors in Ankara and New York with almost superhuman effort endeavored to get the Turks to change their position. They have been successful in getting the Turks to agree to the fundamental issues contained in your proposal, namely, that the matter should be considered by the Security Council and that the Secretary General's good offices would be available to work out the specifics with the interested parties. In doing this the United States has made great sacrifices. In June 1964 the United States at great political cost sent a letter from our President to the Government of Turkey in order to preserve the peace at that time. Last night in obtaining the concessions that I have referred to from the Turks, the United States again expended an important element of its influence and prestige.

The situation as we see it is as follows:

A. The Foreign Ministers of Greece and Turkey have publicly announced that Greece and Turkey have reached an agreement.[2]

B. Therefore, insofar as the world is concerned an agreement for peace has been reached subject only to the possibility that it may be frustrated by the unwillingness of the Government of Cyprus to permit that agreement to be implemented. This all hangs on paragraph 4.

C. With respect to paragraph 4, the Government of Turkey has said that it will return to the original language of paragraph 4 as contained in the document attached to your letter to me, and will also agree to the addition of the last sentence with respect to the good offices of the Secretary General.

---

[2] Greece and Turkey each stated on December 2 that they had reached an agreement on a settlement to the Cyprus crisis; see *The New York Times*, December 3, 1967.

D. Thus we are faced with a situation where the decision for war or peace hangs on the difference between the words 'should be' and 'will discuss in the Security Council'.

You and your government are thus faced with the opportunity to go down in history as the man and the government which made the decision which preserved the peace in this area, or the decision which plunged it into war."

3.   At the end of this statement, Vance handed to the Archbishop the following revised text of para 4 negotiated during the late night hours in Ankara:

"In response to the appeal of the Secretary General there should be an enlarged and improved mandate for UNFICYP giving it an increased pacification role, which would include supervision of disarmament of all forces constituted after 1963 and new practical arrangements for the safeguarding of internal security including the safety of all citizens. The Secretary General's good offices would be available to work out the specifics with the interested parties."

4.   He pointed out that last night the GOT had flatly refused to accept the text of para 4 proposed by the GOC. Under our heavy and politically costly pressure, the GOT had agreed to revised para 4, cited above, which would meet GOC desires to debate issue in Security Council and to act under good offices of SYG. Turks had accepted this despite their fears that GOC would have enormous advantage in SC. We firmly believe this would protect GOC interests and would lift the terrible threat of war from the region.

5.   This statement ran into a stonewall of Cypriot opposition. The Archbishop said he could not accept it because it would only create misunderstandings in the future. Greece and Turkey could do whatever they wished but he would not agree to do more than discuss the issues encompassed in para 4.

6.   Kyprianou stated the Turks wished the GOC to accept certain principles and then to discuss them. Why, he asked, should the GOC make concessions. Furthermore, if the GOC agreed to the formulation as presented it would limit its freedom in the Security Council. This was a matter of substance and not merely protocol.

7.   Vance then restated the familiar line of argumentation for GOC acceptance: The agreement between Greece and Turkey was a three-legged stool which would fall without GOC cooperation; the differences between the GOC and GOT drafts were largely semantical in nature; the position of the GOC in the SC would be fully protected and the GOC would have an enormous advantage in any SC debates on this issue; and finally, the world would never understand if this opportunity to prevent war were not seized.

8. This was not persuasive to the Cypriots. When Clerides, who had played a helpful role throughout the discussions, said that the world should not be surprised if the GOC does not agree, we decided to take a walk in the rose garden in search of inspiration and to buy time for Ambassador Goldberg's efforts in New York. As we stepped into the garden, the Archbishop sweetly advised us not to work very hard since he had already made up his mind.

9. After 45 minutes, Vance resumed his advocacy of peace, reworking the argumentation and hammering at the point that the GOC was refusing the safe path to the SC and away from war simply over a matter of words which were of little consequence.

10. He went on to say that the Turks and the Cypriots were locked into rigid positions over words, and, tragically, they were going to go to war. He emphasized that, while not defending or condoning Turkish war hysteria, the GOC had to recognize that the present situation developed from the tragic incidents of November 14–15. A price must be paid by the GOC for those events. He beseeched the Archbishop to show the flexibility now required to prevent the misery of war and the loss of countless innocent lives.

11. Kyprianou then said the GOC could not accept. Their only recourse now was to go promptly to the Security Council to show the world who the aggressor was.

12. At that point, there was little more to say. Vance expressed great personal sadness about the evident failure of the search for peace in which so many people have engaged. President Johnson and he had been convinced that a just settlement was imminent and now it appeared that no one in the world would understand or appreciate.

13. He then asked with great solemnity that the Archbishop not give him a final negative answer but rather to ponder once again. Our plane would depart for Athens in a few hours and Vance could be reached there.

14. Makarios then said he had no need to ponder. He had made up his mind. Vance's words had raised a delicate issue for him, since he was deeply grateful to President Johnson, to Vance, and to the USG who had done their utmost to preserve the peace.

Whatever the outcome of the present situation he would never forget what the United States has done. He then concluded with the words: "I know my answer".

15. In departing the Palace, Vance, by agreement, limited his comments to the assertion that he was returning to Athens.[3]

Belcher

---

[3] In Vanto 85, December 3, Vance requested that the Secretary-General be asked to immediately release his appeal. (Ibid.) For text of this appeal (U.N. Doc. S/8248/Add.6), see *American Foreign Policy: Current Documents, 1967*, pp. 369–370. The decision to request the release of the Secretary-General's appeal was made after a telephone conference among Rusk, Vance, and Goldberg. A transcript of their discussion is in the Johnson Library, National Security File, Country File, Cyprus, Vol. 4.

On December 3, the Greek Government, in a brief note, accepted the Secretary-General's appeal. The Turkish Government also accepted on the same day. (U.N. Doc. S/8258/Add.7)

---

341. Telegram From the Embassy in Cyprus to the Department of State[1]

Nicosia, December 4, 1967, 1414Z.

888. Subject: GOC reply to SYG appeal. Reference: Nicosia 883.[2]

1. Issuance SYG appeal without prior GOC approval forced Makarios' hand tactically. Archbishop was required to respond in apparently positive manner since he could not very well reject UN initiative for peace once such initiative was taken. However, tone of GOC letter to SYG is guardedly affirmative at best and clearly reserves GOC positions on fundamental problems that plagued Vance discussions.[3]

2. Letter highlights GOC positions which will be basis for SC battle that is shaping up, viz:

A. GOC goal is "ultimate and complete withdrawal from Republic of Cyprus of all non-Cypriot armed forces" (other than UNFICYP). This includes both Greek and Turk contingents and doubtless GOC will seek tie disarming and disbanding of National Guard to withdrawal of contingents.

---

[1] Source: Department of State, Central Files, POL 27 CYP. Secret; Immediate. Also sent to USUN, Ankara, and Athens and repeated to London, Ottawa, and the Mission to NATO.

[2] Telegram 883, December 4, transmitted the text of the Cypriot reply to the Secretary-General's appeal. (Ibid.)

[3] On December 3, the Cypriot Government made an interim reply to the Secretary-General's appeal. (U.N. Doc. S/8248/Add.7)

B. GOC will demand "effective guarantees against military intervention in affairs of Cyprus" probably from SC. Makarios will not miss opportunity to seize upon SC discussions of Cyprus problem to bring into question Turkish treaty right of intervention in Cyprus.

C. Expanded role for UNFICYP must be considered in terms of GOC "sovereignty, territorial integrity and independence." This raises question of who is going to be policeman on Cyprus: GOC with sovereignty over whole island or expanded UNFICYP to which some of GOC sovereignty would be given in trust at least temporarily.

D. Pacification and permanent peaceful solution are to be "within framework of Charter and relevant resolutions on Cyprus by SC and GA" (an obvious reference to GA resolution of December 1965 inter alia).[4]

3. In above points we can see emerging general lines of GOC strategy. Building case on sovereignty of government, UN Charter and favorable UN statements on Cyprus (March '64 SC Resolution, December '65 GA Resolution, Galo-Plaza Report), Makarios through his forensic Foreign Minister, Kyprianou, will attempt to achieve complete demilitarization of Cyprus, effective guarantee for inviolability of the Republic, and extension of sovereignty of his government to all parts of island including Turkish enclaves where his writ does not now run.

4. Intensity of Turk and Turk Cypriot reaction to such GOC strategy in SC can easily be imagined. Basing legal position on London/Zurich Turks will wage bitter fight for what they regard as basic elements permitting peaceful existence of Turk Cypriots on Cyprus. We have already had full plate of suspicions from Kuchukery, even before they had read letter of "acceptance." Our next meeting, after they have digested in full the GOC reply, should be even more revealing of Turk and Turk Cypriot fears.[5]

Belcher

---

[4] General Assembly Resolution 2077 (XX).

[5] The Cypriot Government, in a December 4 note, accepted the Secretary-General's appeal and offer of good offices. The note specifically accepted the proposal for demilitarization and withdrawal of unauthorized military forces. (U.N. Doc. S/8248/Add.8)

342.   Notes of Meeting[1]

Washington, December 5, 1967, 1:18–2:37 p.m.

NOTES OF THE PRESIDENT'S MEETING
WITH
THE VICE PRESIDENT
SECRETARY McNAMARA
SECRETARY RUSK
CYRUS VANCE
CIA DIRECTOR HELMS
WALT ROSTOW
GEORGE CHRISTIAN
TOM JOHNSON

The President congratulated Mr. Vance for an excellent job and an excellent report.

Secretary Rusk said a case study should be made of this. He called Cyrus Vance's actions an example of diplomatic excellence.

The President explained that he thought General Chapman would make an excellent Marine Corps Commandant. Dick Helms called it the "right" man for the job.

Mr. Vance then reviewed his report to the President, stressing the need that the report not be made public or any acknowledgement that a written report was submitted. (A single copy of this report is attached.[2] It is not for redistribution.)

Secretary Rusk said the most important impression that Mr. Vance brought back from his trip was that both Greece and Turkey were anxious to reduce their commitment to Cyprus. The Secretary said Greece could do this only under a dictatorship so we should try to get this disengagement from Cyprus before a democratically elected government comes into office in Greece. Otherwise, the Secretary said public opinion would not permit a democratically elected government to reduce its commitment.

Mr. Vance said he appreciated the fact the President gave the widest latitude possible in handling this situation.[3]

[Here follows discussion of unrelated subjects.]

---

[1] Source: Johnson Library, Tom Johnson's Notes of Meetings. No classification marking. The meeting was held at the White House. These notes are printed with the permission of Tom Johnson.

[2] Not printed.

[3] For text of President Johnson's statement issued after the meeting with Vance, and of Vance's remarks, see *American Foreign Policy: Current Documents, 1967*, pp. 370–371.

RELATIONS WITH THE GREEK MILITARY JUNTA AND CONTINUING DISCUSSIONS ON CYPRUS, DECEMBER 1967–DECEMBER 1968

343. Letter From the Ambassador to Greece (Talbot) to the Country Director for Greece (Brewster)[1]

Athens, undated.

Dear Dan:

With the Cyprus issue having survived the war threat, the domestic Greek political pot is boiling once again.

Twice in recent days King Constantine has expressed to me his anxiety about the Junta's intentions. On November 30, when he and the Queen came to the Embassy residence for dinner with my wife and me and Cy Vance and John Walsh, he told me in an aside that he feared the Junta might move that night to arrest Defense Minister Spandidakis and Generals Kollias and Perides. The King had met each of the three earlier in the day and had been concerned that the Generals expected to spend the night in Athens. He had advised General Spandidakis not to sleep at home and the other two to find places other than their usual quarters in Athens.

The difficulty as the King understood it was that Generals Kollias and Perides had been furious at the government for agreeing to pull back the Greek troops (in excess of the contingent) from Cyprus and that Spandidakis as a hawk had also resisted the government's decisions. The Junta ministers, as leaders of the government, had accused all three generals of insubordination and talked of dismissing them. Should they try to arrest them that night there would be a first-class crisis. From other sources we had understood that at the same time the Junta leadership was bracing its security mechanism out of fear that the King might be organizing a countercoup. I put our political and [*less than 1 line of source text not declassified*] people on an all-night alert to watch the situation, which was complicated later in the evening when a homemade bomb was thrown into a crowd in downtown Athens and a woman killed. She was the first casualty of the anti-regime terrorist campaign mounted sporadically in recent months, apparently by very small groups of provocateurs.

At about 3:30 a.m. we thought the King's foreboding might have substance. The Royal Gendarmerie Commander for Attica put out a hur-

---

[1] Source: Department of State, Greek Desk Files: Lot 69 D 553, Countercoup. Secret; Exdis.

ried call for numbers of his best men, who on arrival at gendarmerie headquarters were armed with tommy guns and hand grenades and dispatched in squads of five or six to various sections of the city with the mission of protecting various ministers in their homes. It was only with the arrival of daylight that we were certain that "protect" did not mean "arrest." Later information suggested that the Junta was in fact worried that the evening's bomb incident might be followed by more bombing attempts directed at the homes of certain ministers. It was in this general atmosphere that the King that evening muttered to me that "I'm going to have to get rid of these people (the Junta) one day soon." He was not more specific, however. (He made this comment while attempting to reach Junta ministers by telephone to get the details of the downtown bombing incident. The last time he had used my telephone to call ministers was on the night when I told him that a court martial had given a five-year sentence to Averoff.)[2]

As you perceive, the dicey part of all this is that those generals whose military pride was most hurt by the decision to withdraw Greek forces from Cyprus under Turkish pressure are precisely the ones on whom the King has been most counting for support against the Junta in any future showdown. An oddity of recent days, in fact, is that on Cyprus questions the King, Pipinelis and Col. Papadopoulos have supported the same policy lines while opponents of the Junta and natural supporters of the King's role in Greece have opposed Greek "capitulation."

On December 5, when I called on the King to recapitulate developments during the final days of the Vance Mission,[3] we had some further conversation about the domestic situation. He was preoccupied with difficulties he foresaw on the immediate horizon. He senses that with the easing of the Cyprus crisis the Junta will attempt to move very rapidly to recoup its diminishing prestige and consolidate its hold on power. Specifically, he anticipates that the Junta will promptly press for the appointment of Col. Papadopoulos as Deputy Prime Minister and will also try to get rid of Spandidakis and those senior generals (the King's supporters) who had opposed the government's decisions on the Cyprus question.

The King also asked whether I had seen the Caramanlis statement.[4] I had, and I commented that we had been approached by a friend of Caramanlis who had recently seen him in Paris (but I did not identify the source as Athanasios Tsaldaris) to urge that we encourage the King and

---

[2] Averoff was arrested on July 12, charged with violation of a rule against gatherings of five or more persons. He was tried and sentenced to 5 years in prison on August 15 and pardoned on August 16.

[3] A memorandum of conversation is in Department of State, Central Files, POL 15–1.

[4] In a November 29 interview in *Le Monde*, Karamanlis had strongly criticized the foreign and domestic policies of the Junta.

Caramanlis to get into communication, since they were the only two men
who, working together, could resolve the situation. The King rather
abruptly changed the line of the conversation without commenting on
this point. Nor did he echo my praise of the performance in recent days of
Pipinelis; on the contrary, he observed that Pipinelis had made some mistakes in dealing with the Greek governmental and military elements
which were saved only by the King's intervention.

It was obvious the King did not wish to discuss political personalities who might be available as alternatives to the Junta, and on this occasion I did not press him. I can only conclude that either the family's
antipathy to Caramanlis remains strong or they are in a deep-covered
relationship that he did not want to discuss with me. Unfortunately, the
former is the more likely possibility.

Meanwhile we have been hearing from all of our political contacts
that now is the time for the King to move against the Junta and that he
would be certain to have the support of practically all of the old crowd,
from George Papandreou to Harry Rendis. Some of the reports indicated
they would support a move by the King to create a government of military figures responsive to him or even on the basis of another year or so of
martial law or a variant thereof. We have also heard from these sources
that the Junta is losing credibility in the country. Certainly it has blun-
dered in foreign relations and now in relations with press proprietors,
and these missteps have not gone unnoticed. It may be that skepticism of
the Junta's effectiveness will spread through wider segments of Greek
society and even that that most potent non-military weapon of all, ridi-
cule, might come into play. This could undermine the Junta's public support but not, at least for sometime, its command of the military units that
control the Athens area and its grip on strategic units in the northern
commands.

As of today, we don't know what impact the new constitutional
draft will have, nor even its thrust. Since the beginning of the Cyprus crisis I have not heard anything (nor have I pushed to seek it) about the draft
now presumably approaching completion and the government's plans
for dealing with it. However, it could become a factor in the new situation, just as could the open campaign of opposition to the Junta that
seems to have been launched by Caramanlis.[5]

---

[5] Printed from an unsigned copy.

344. Telegram From the Embassy in Greece to the Mission to the North Atlantic Treaty Organization[1]

Athens, December 13, 1967, 0915Z.

164. For the Secretary.

1. King Constantine summoned me to Tatoi Palace at 0915 local and stated he has decided to move against Junta today.[2] He planned to leave Tatoi airport this morning in his aircraft with entire Royal family, Prime Minister Kollias and General Antonakas and fly to Kavalla where military commanders in north prepared to receive him. He will assume command of Greek armed forces, and call for resignation of government so he can reform it to carry forward "Greek renaissance."

2. King asked that we pass his instructions through our channels to Ministers Pipinelis and Spandidakis ordering them to support his move with NATO allies and then proceed immediately to Thessaloniki to join government.

3. King said he would be grateful if President and USG could endorse his move as step toward constitutional government.

He also asked that we use all available persuasion to convince colonels it would be unwise for them to seek to oppose his action and thus thrust Greece into civil war. He asked that USG do what it can to keep Greece's neighbors from taking advantage of situation. He asked if American stations in Greece could broadcast statement he has taped stating he has gone to Macedonia in order to exercise freely his initiative for reforming of government in order to bring about return to democratic normality. He hoped we could do this if forces loyal to him fail in effort projected for this hour to seize Athens radio facilities. Finally, he also asked me to request our Ambassadors to advise King and Queen of Denmark and Princess Sophia in Madrid.[3]

4. *Comment:* Whether or not King is prepared, die is cast. I will send further flash when we hear whether he has safely gotten away from Tatoi airport. I do not plan to have King's statement broadcast on American

---

[1] Source: Department of State, Central Files, POL 23–9 GREECE. Secret; Flash; Nodis. Repeated to the Department of State. Secretary Rusk was in Brussels December 10–15 to attend the NATO Ministerial Meeting. The source text is the Department of State copy.

[2] Talbot provided a more complete report on the meeting and the events surrounding it in telegram 2749 from Athens, December 13. (Ibid.) In a letter to Brewster, December 18, Talbot provided a postmortem of the counter coup attempt. (Ibid., Greek Desk Files: Lot 69 D 553, Countercoup)

[3] The message was transmitted to the Embassy in Copenhagen in telegram 49, a repeat of telegram 2721 from Athens, December 13. (Ibid., Central Files, POL 23–9 GREECE)

facilities at least until it clear his maneuver has reasonable chance of success. Please inform Pipinelis and Spandidakis.[4]

Talbot

---

[4] The Greek Foreign and Defense Ministers were also in Brussels attending the NATO Ministerial Meeting.

---

345.   Telegram From the Embassy in Greece to the Department of State[1]

Athens, December 13, 1967, 1158Z.

2730. Ref: Athens 2721.[2] At Greek Pentagon at 1230 local I was taken to office of Chief, Hellenic National Defense General Staff and ushered into presence of Ministers Papadopoulos and Makarezos, Generals Angelis and Zoitakis and Col. Paleologos (KYP). Papadopoulos states that General Angelis had received this morning message from King dismissing him as Chief, HNDGS, and stating he (King) would address message to Greek people. Papadopoulos claimed King had left Tatoi airport one and half hours ago, but he did not know King's present whereabouts. He presumed King had gone to north. According to Papadopoulos it is clear King is attempting to overthrow revolution. He asked me specifically whether I had any knowledge of this action "from any direction." I said there was certainly nothing I could tell him and that if he was implying question whether U.S. involved I could assure him flatly that it was not.[3] In response to my question, Papadopoulos stated that he presumed that Prime Minister Kollias had gone with the King and he stated that Pattakos was now out of Athens but would return within one-half hour. Papadopoulos expressed hope that I would do everything possible to avoid bloodshed in Greece. I responded that through the mission of Mr. Vance the United States had recently made great effort to avoid conflict in this part of the Mediterranean and that we

---

[1] Source: Department of State, Central Files, POL 23–9 GREECE. Secret; Flash; Limdis. Repeated to the Mission to NATO for Secretary Rusk.

[2] See footnote 3, Document 344.

[3] In telegram 4097 from Athens, December 13, Talbot requested that the press be informed that while he had frequently seen the King in previous weeks, the "U.S. Government has no advanced knowledge of this undertaking." (Department of State, Central Files, POL 23–9 GREECE)

naturally had every wish that civil strife could be avoided inside Greece. I informed Papadopoulos and others that I would immediately inform my government and that I would be available in Athens throughout day if they wish to communicate with me again.[4]

Talbot

---

[4] Telegram 2739 from Athens, December 13, reported that at 12:30 p.m. local time Papadopolous and Makarezos called Talbot stating they had no knowledge of the King's whereabouts. The telegram also described military maneuvers in the city of Athens. (Ibid.)

---

346.   Telegram From the Embassy in Greece to the Department of State[1]

Athens, December 13, 1967, 1647Z.

2751. 1. Suggest I be given standby instructions, to be executed at what seems appropriate moment, to attempt to make contact with King and with Junta leaders to express USG's strong hope questions of government in Greece can be resolved without bloodshed. I would like to say US as ally and friend of Greece not intervening in domestic issue but, as recent Cyprus crisis demonstrated anew, warfare in this part of world can redound to benefit only of Communists. We do not know what plans either King or Junta may have, but we should exceedingly deplore any conflict between elements of Greek armed forces that have been assiduously built up in the past two decades with our substantial assistance. However difficult it may be for contending groups to settle their differences peacefully, we urgently request both sides to find ways to solve present crisis by negotiation.

2. Although it will presumably not be practicable to get this message to King in immediate future, there could be utility in conveying it to Junta leaders. As I see our interests, first object is to get quick resolution with minimum of bloodshed. Whatever we may think of King's wisdom in making this move today, our interests now lie on side of his success since his failure would probably not only destroy monarchy but fasten extreme military Junta on Greece for years to come.

3. If and when we satisfied that King has gained full loyalty of northern army, so that preponderance of Greek armed forces committed

---

[1] Source: Department of State, Central Files, POL 23–9 GREECE. Secret; Flash; Limdis. Repeated to the Mission to NATO for the Secretary.

to his side, I would wish to add to above message strong appeal to Papadopoulos to make deal with King rather than attempting to fight it out. By then he would know military odds against his success. He would know we have strong interest in seeing all elements in Greece accept peacefully government constituted by King. I could say we understand King's broadcast offered Junta forgiveness if they capitulated immediately, and promise that we would strongly urge King to honor this offer even at this late hour if Junta agreed. Alternative, I would point out, could be nothing but disastrous destruction of fabric of Greek society.

4.   There could be moment in immediate future when passive presence of Sixth Fleet units in Greek waters could have powerful psychological impact here (notably on Papadopoulos). I will withhold recommendations until we see how situation clarified.[2]

Talbot

---

[2] In telegram 84028 to Athens, December 13, the Department of State authorized Talbot to act as suggested in paragraphs 1 and 2, but instructed him to avoid any action suggested in paragraph 3 at that time. Any use of the Sixth Fleet would be delayed until developments in Greece were clearer. (Ibid.)

---

347.   Transcript of Teleconference Between the Embassy in Greece and the Department of State[1]

December 13, 1967, 5:20 p.m. (EST)

SecState item 1.

Participants

Amb. Battle
Mr. Rockwell
Mr. Brewster

Subject: Greek crisis

Classification: Secret–Exdis

End Item.

Athens item 1.

We face new situation tonight with Papadopoulos having in effect declared King deposed and new government of which he Prime Minis-

---

[1] Source: Department of State, Central Files, POL 23–9 GREECE. Secret; Exdis.

ter, etc.[2] My inclination continues to be try to see him and argue issue out on basis Athens 2751[3] (to which we have received no response). However, Athenians may take a call by me as de facto recognition of this regime which I assume we must consider to be a rebel regime. We are attempting to get some Embassy [*less than 1 line of source text not declassified*] officer to Kavala tomorrow to establish contact with King, whose movements and plans continue to be unknown to us. Question arises, however, whether USG should now make its choice and cast die in favor of King. This might involve USG declaration of support of King and instructions to me to join King and his Cabinet wherever they may be at earliest opportunity. You will understand gravity of this decision, involving as it does our total presence and all facilities in all of Greece. My own view at this moment is that in best of circumstances USG will find it extremely difficult to deal with Papadopoulos controlled govt of southern Greece. I cannot say for certain how best civil war can be averted.

My sense, however, is that rather than attempting straddle issue we might do best by opting strongly on side of King as soon as we have any information that he has in fact won loyalty and support of preponderance of Greek armed forces. As of this moment, we have no assets to learn true situation in north of Greece, nor has King yet established contact with Greek people or with US. Request your comments.

End item 1.

SecState item 2.

Following statement drafted for issuance this morning and delayed in view sketchy info then existing. Please comment on wisdom issuing this or similar statement:

"U.S. statement

King Constantine of Greece has departed Athens and arrived at Larissa in northern Greece. He has issued an appeal to the people of Greece asking for their support for the restoration of democracy.

Since the change of government in Athens on April 21 the United States Government has urged that steps be taken in Greece to bring about a return to constitutionalism. The United States Government has believed, and continues to believe, that it is essential that this be accomplished by peaceful means. We urge the people of Greece to work together for the re-establishment of democracy, avoiding bloodshed and civil strife.

---

[2] During the evening of December 13, the Junta announced the deposition of the King, his replacement by a Regent, and the formation of a new government with Papadopoulos as Prime Minister. The Regent, General George Zoitakis, and Papadopoulos were sworn in by the Archbishop of Athens that evening.

[3] Document 346.

End item.

Item 2. Answering SecState item 2.

Your statement is excellent and I recommend it be put out immediately. You will see that King has been reported by VOA source as seen in Kavala this evening. Rather than "arrived at Larissa" I would suggest "arrived at Macedonia."

My own inclination is to make last appeal to Papadopoulos, along lines of Athens 2751 if you agree, and laying on line our probable position if they persist in partition. We could opt for King early tomorrow when we know better what his situation is.

End item 2.

Athens item 3.

While I was dictating previous item Brigadier Pattakos telephoned Embassy and asked to speak to me. If you agree, I will phone back in few minutes and arrange to see him shortly to make pitch suggested in previous item.

End item 3.

SecState item 3.

We understand that King's statement has been repeated four (4) times today. Is this correct?

End item.

Item 4 Athens answering SecState item 3.

We understand King's message was broadcast 4 or 5 times on Larissa radio between 1430 and 1800 hrs today, and also on Thessaloniki radio. We have not yet heard any broadcast from Kavala or any other from King or forces presumably supporting King.

End of item 4.

Item 5 Athens

State 84028 answering Athens 2751, has just arrived.[4] I will proceed on basis this instruction with any modifications conveyed in present telecon in response to foregoing items.

End item 5.

Secstate item 4.

We agree you should make pitch in first two paras your message and had already so authorized. Agree you should so speak to Pattakos. Suggest you not use last sentence para 2 in view danger that King would consider U.S. had undercut him by emphasizing negotations which he may not consider acceptable.

---

[4] See footnote 2, Document 346.

End item.

Item 6 Athens.

We doing everything possible to increase flow of information. All elements contributing all intelligence available to Embassy Sitreps.

End item 6.

SecState item 5.

We agree we cannot straddle issue very long, and must support general goals of King.

However, we prefer to finesse for time being question of state of regime in Athens and group with King. We are inclined prefer standing on position we have taken since April 21 which implies support of King but without making entirely clear difficult legal situation.

There are advantages in your remaining in never-never land for day or so particularly if it appears likely contact with new new govt can produce useful result.

We agree subject approval Secretary and President to adherence purposes of King but without going all way with your withdrawal to his at present unknown destination.

Decision your move to north would likely depend on ability of King to control army and generate public support.

End item.

SecState item 6.

Assume your call on Patakos obviates your call Papadopoulos for moment. In general, however, you should avoid paying calls on high level officials if possible unless you have some important reason to do so. If it is possible to hold necessary contacts at low level this is desirable.

End item 6.

Athens item 7 answering SecState item 6.

Thanks, but if we are to attempt to influence Papadopoulos, Pattakos, and Makarezos tonight I fear no Embassy officer but me can establish contact. I will try to do as much as possible in one call, presumably on Pattakos.

End item 7.

SecState item 8.

We understand and concur.

End item.

SecState item 7.

Is it your recommendation that statement (our item two (2)) be issued immediately or do you wish await further info strength of King with army and public.

End item.

Athens item 9.

Suggest you issue statement immediately.

End item 9.

Athens item 8.

I have just talked with Pattakos who asked me to come to Greek Pentagon to meet with "us". I assume he means Papadopoulos, Makarezos, General Anghelis and he are there together. EmbOff and I will go there as soon as this telecon completed.

End item 8.

SecState item 9.

From Amb. Battle

I have just talked with Secretary who interested having all information as soon as possible especially with respect situation in north. He suggests possibility Embassy send someone to north to ascertain facts. NATO Council adjourns in 12 hours. There is strong sentiment there for what King is trying to do provided he has any base of support and there is anything to back up. If we want Secretary to take any action he must have guidance within 8 hours.

Secretary's inclination at moment is that statement should await clarification of situation in north.

End item.

Athens item 10 answering SecState item 9.

We are trying to [get?] officer from CG Thessaloniki over to Kavala. [*3-1/2 lines of source text not declassified*] At first light we will see whether there any chance attaché plane can take off from Athens airport for north. US military units in north have been quartered on bases, and we have no other active assets in eastern Macedonia or Thrace. [*2-1/2 lines of source text not declassified*]

End item 10.

Athens item 11. Further to SecState item 9.

I will flash recommendations for Secretary at NATO after returning from forthcoming meeting with Junta colonels.

End item 11.

Secstate item 10. Re Athens item 4.

Larissa armed forces radio announced 2001 GMT on behalf Premier that by decisions King, Ministers Papadopoulos, Zoitakis, Pattakos, etc. dismissed. All armed forces in Thrace, Macedonia, Epirus, Thessaly—90 percent of army and all air and naval forces obeying King's command.

End item.

SecState item 11.

From Amb. Battle

In your message for Secretary you should also include your recommendations re public statement by USG. Secretary still bearish at present time.

End item.

Athens item 12.

SecState item 11 understood and will do.

Do you have anything further?

End item 12.

SecState item 12.

We have nothing further. Thanks.

End item.

---

348.   **Telegram From the Embassy in Greece to the Department of State**[1]

Athens, December 14, 1967, 0250Z.

2771. 1. At request of Pattakos, I went to Pentagon at 1:15 a.m. local to meet with Generals Angelis, Zoitakis, and Pattakos and Colonels Papadopoulos, Makarezos, and Paleologopoulos [*Paleologos?*] and Under Minister of Foreign Affairs Christopoulos.

Papadopoulos, in his new role of Prime Minister, began conversation by asking whether I had heard this evening's radio announcements of government and whether I had any comment to make on today's developments. I replied that I heard not only announcements of government but also message of King. Then, as authorized by Department, I proceeded to read verbatim from first part of Embtel 2751.[2] Elaborating on themes in this message, I reminded Papadopoulos and others that only recently my government had exerted great effort to prevent conflict in this part of Mediterranean, at times bloodshed had seemed inevitable but was avoided only at last minutes. Now once more we have reached

---

[1] Source: Department of State, Central Files, POL 23–9 GREECE. Secret; Immediate; Limdis. Repeated to London, Nicosia, the Mission to NATO, USUN, the Secretary of Defense, JCS, DIA, USDOCOSouth, USCINCEUR, CINCUSAFE, CINCUSAREUR, CINCUS-NAVEUR, and Thessaloniki.
[2] Document 346.

point where blood could be spilled—this time in a civil conflict which would be even more tragic. Surely something could be done to avert such a catastrophe. I also said I was under instructions to convey this same message to the King and to urge both sides to resolve differences peacefully through negotiation.

3. In response, Papadopoulos adopted self-righteous position that his government had in no way misbehaved and that it was King and Kollias who, suddenly without warning, left Athens to overthrow revolution. His government, on other hand, had acted properly, even following Constitution in appointing regent. It was King's, not Athens government, which had created present crisis and danger of bloodshed. Papadopoulos, backed by several of his colleagues, repeatedly insisted they had complete control of Greek armed forces, as well as support of all social classes.

4. I commented we are now faced with critical situation involving what are claimed to be two governments, each side claiming loyalty and support of people and armed forces. We are not in position to judge merits of conflicting claims, but existence of two governments obviously would create potential disaster for Greece, as well as legal questions for USG. For example, what is position of King? Has he abdicated, in their view?

5. Papadopoulos argued that, by leaving Athens and disappearing, King had "abandoned" his duties as Monarch. Therefore, according to Constitution, government had appointed regent in his place. I replied that this interpretation would be difficult for me to persuade my government and others to accept, particularly since King had left Athens only some hours earlier and, as far as I knew, is still in Greece and is acting in accordance with Constitution. Christopoulos broke in to assert that there might be legal question if two governments should actually exist, but events would soon prove there is in fact only one government, i.e., that of PriMin Papadopoulos. I warned them, however, that I could foresee difficult legal problem.

6. Immediate issue, though, was how to avoid internal conflict and strife in Greece. How did they believe it could be avoided? Pattakos' first reaction was that it was not their responsibility as they had not created problem. I reminded them that Vance had heard this same remark twenty times a day for twelve days during Cyprus crisis. As he had repeatedly answered, need was not to apportion responsibility but to avoid tragedy. Pattakos then indicated that they would be willing to communicate with King if they knew where he was. General Angelis, however, immediately tended to knock possibility of negotiations by stating flatly King had crossed river and burnt his bridges behind him. Papadopoulos implied that there was no need for negotiation as his government had complete control of country. I again stressed that, though

we are not in position to judge rival claims, my government, including specifically Secretary Rusk who now at NATO table, is most anxious about danger of bloodshed and that we hope every effort can be exerted to avoid strife. I would naturally inform USG of this meeting and would be available any time for additional talks.

7. Junta officers, as well as Angelis, Zoitakis, and Christopoulos, gave the [no] sign of friction among them and attempted portray air of confidence. Pentagon itself was reasonably calm, though additional guards were posted inside and outside building.

Talbot

349. Telegram From the Embassy in Greece to the Department of State[1]

Athens, December 14, 1967, 1915Z.

2807. First installment possible effects of King's abortive counter-coup.

1. This estimate will doubtless be revised as the specific events of December 13/14 become known.

2. King Constantine's abortive attempt to overthrow April 21 coup government has wrought change on Junta's future options. The new Papadopoulos government would now appear to be undisputed master of Greece, with no potential internal check on its tenure or its programs.

So long as the King remained a factor in internal political equation, there existed possibility that King could exercise a certain measure of control over Junta and in extreme circumstances it was believed that he had capability to oust Junta with support from certain loyalist army elements in the north. With King now out of country, and clear demonstration that Junta is in ultimate control of armed forces that count, hardliners in Junta will doubtless conclude there is no obstacle to indeterminate rule by Papadopoulos and company.

---

[1] Source: Department of State, Central Files, POL 23–9 GREECE. Confidential. Repeated to Ankara, London, Nicosia, the Mission to NATO, the Secretary of Defense, USUN, JCS, DIA, USDOCOSouth, USCINCEUR, CINCUSAFE, CINCUSAREUR, CINC-USNAVEUR, and Thessaloniki.

714 Foreign Relations, 1964–1968, Volume XVI

3. Other pressures that existed before December 13 which were being exerted toward a restoration of constitutional representative government in Greece continue with undiminished potential: US Government, NATO, Western opinion in general, and international climate. Presumably these can have some effect on Junta's program for a restoration of normality. However, there is no ace in hole, no possible alternative to coup group, since a different government could only be imposed by military intervention from abroad, which is apparently inconceivable. Some elements of Junta therefore will now attempt more confidently to enjoy prospect of setting own timetable, with assurance that no one can forcibly change schedule or "force" them to do anyone's bidding.

4. Question which should become more clear in next several days is whether Papadopoulos and company will now take a more relaxed attitude toward constitutional reform and an eventual return to a parliamentary system through elections or feel "events" have put them on their metal. First inclination will doubtless be to think that since they can't be forced out, why should they be in a hurry to leave. And therefore they would probably focus on trying to carry out their revolutionary program of reforming the administration, making bureaucracy efficient, changing habits and working methods of Greek people, and generally "shaping up" country. Regime's leaders might be more willing to use strong measures to effect changes they desire, since they no longer need be as sensitive to anyone else's opinion. Alternate pressure will be that "incident" has challenged "honor" (filotimo) of national government and Junta must prove Constantine was wrong in prognostication in his appeal that they were not interested in constitutional reform and implementation.

5. Effect on Greek people of more stringent measures being used by Junta and apparent lack of any realistic alternative to present regime may be to polarize populace increasingly into regime supporters and opponents, with a diminishing category of apathetics. This would not in immediate future mean activation of larger group of activists (bomb throwers etc.) in opposition. Oppositionists who looked to King to "do something" or expected that foreign pressure would eventually cause government to fall or give up power will now, in some numbers, decide they must turn to direct action against government in one fashion or another. However even elements who favor comparing dangers of WW II resistance and now—when Communists took over active resistance movement in mountains—find it difficult to forecast development activist resistance movement of this type. This particularly true since Greeks of WW II resistance forces were not necessarily from sophisticated urban groups (who are trying be "articulate" opposition at present) but from peasants who had double motivation—foraging for food and shoot it out tradition with "government" of whatever mark existed. In the end,

Papadopoulos government, by its new demonstration of strength, determination and staying power will probably gain tolerance of many Greeks whose primary political instinct is to find which way the wind is blowing and then to bend with it, in other words to join ranks with the apparently winning side.

Talbot

---

350.   Telegram From the Department of State to the Embassy in Greece[1]

Washington, December 19, 1967, 2339Z.

86871. 1. King Constantine telephoned to Secretary at 9 a.m. EST December 19 to report that messenger Ch. Potamianos returning to Athens. King's views were that there should be firm date for plebiscite on constitution and date for elections set by the junta. Constitution was not an issue because he did not know what was in it. He had to insist on precise dates.

2.   King expressed hope US would not recognize GOG unless he returns as safeguard that things will be implemented. He hoped UK and others would also put pressure on GOG using means at their command.

3.   He said he was considering possibly going back without further negotiation. (*Comment:* This brainstorm may have grown out of his talk with Caramanlis and others who have advised him to go back before it was too late.)

4.   Secretary did not comment on this idea. He also did not commit himself concerning King's request to link US recognition with King's return to Greece, saying that question would require study.

5.   King concluded conversation by stating he would not be making press statement today.

6.   We have reviewed carefully question of US-Greek relations and do not want to get into the middle in negotiating question of King's possible return. Obviously the Greek Government is in the driver's seat and not ready to pay much of a price, if any, for King's return. At same time we want to strike a blow with Greek regime for principles of early plebiscite on constitution and a firm commitment concerning elections. We want to use leverage of US relationship with Greece in current circum-

---

[1] Source: Department of State, Central Files, POL 30 GREECE. Secret; Priority; Exdis. Drafted by Rockwell and Brewster, cleared by Battle and Katzenbach, and approved by Rusk.

stances to maximum degree as an additional tool in achieving our basic goal of bringing Greece back to democratic life as soon as possible, irrespective of what King may decide to do.

7.   We would like you to get in touch informally and quietly with Papadopoulos or Pattakos (rather than Pipinelis as suggested Athens 4175 [2859]).[2] Say that current developments have complicated for us our relations with Greece, but that this was already difficult for basic reasons which remain a serious obstacle to the kind of relations we would like to have with a NATO partner and traditional friend. We see little chance for a satisfactory relationship until progress is made on removing these problems, which can be described in general as the continuing lack of convincing movement toward the restoration of a constitutional situation. Involved are such issues as firm and early dates for a plebiscite on the constitution and elections, restrictions on the press, and the resolution of political prisoner cases in accordance with due process of law. Add that the strength of opinion of the American people and their elected representatives on these issues prevents the USG from having a normal relationship with Greece, and that accordingly we are anxious to see Greece make decisive progress toward constitutionality.

8.   If you are asked whether the US intends to recognize the GOG, you should say that no decision has been taken pending clarification status of King; you should leave no doubt that basic problem for us continues to be undemocratic nature of regime itself. FYI. We prefer leave situation imprecise for awhile, although we recognize contact with Papadopoulos or Pattakos might be considered a step toward recognition; we hope it can be done in a manner to minimize such an interpretation.[3] End FYI.

Rusk

---

[2] Telegram 2859 from Athens, December 20, recommended that the King make no statement until Ambassador Talbot had sounded out Pipinelis on future relations between Constantine and the Junta. (Ibid., POL 23–9 GREECE)

[3] In telegram 2892 from Athens, December 20, Talbot reported that he had been unable to secure a meeting with Papadopoulos and suggested delaying further efforts while awaiting further moves by the King and the Junta. (Ibid.)

351. Telegram From the Embassy in Cyprus to the Department of State[1]

Nicosia, December 30, 1967, 0940Z.

1056. Subject: Turk Cypriot Provisional Administration.[2]

1. Acting FonMin Araouzos called me to Ministry half hour ago as first of Chiefs of Mission all of whom he will see today. Subject, as we expected, was government decision to consider further visits by Chiefs of Mission to officials of new "Administration" as recognition of "flagrantly unlawful act" by Turk Cypriots. Araouzos said that GOC "cannot agree to any visits by Chiefs of Mission to officials of the new executive council." If the GOC were to give assent to "official visits" this would merely encourage Turks to take further steps of separative nature. He said that in past visits by Ambassadors and Chargés to Kuchuk and other "officials" had been considered for convenience as merely visits to leaders of Turk Cypriot community. The GOC could no longer maintain this fiction and therefore could not agree to any further visits. There could only be one government in Cyprus and that government could not condone recognition of the "new Turk Cypriot Administration."

2. In response my question Araouzos said that this rule did not apply to members of the staff of the Embassy. I remarked that I thought this was essential since I believed in the past our contacts with Turk Cypriot community had been of value in defusing various incidents and in general reducing tension.

3. Araouzos said somewhat apologetically that he recognized this action by the GOC would present us with certain difficulties but that the decision had been taken with the feeling that they had no choice. Speaking personally and without instructions I offered the opinion that this action might prove to be ill-advised in that it gave unwarranted recognition to an action which I and my government did not consider very much more than a mere institutionalizing of a situation that had existed de facto for some time. This was in fact a recognition of the existence of a separate entity in the Turkish Cypriot sector and in that respect at least the action in a sense strengthened the Turkish position. In accordance State 91488,[3] I expressed our view that timing of Turk Cypriot move regrettable in view of hoped-for implementation of pacification program

---

[1] Source: Department of State, Central Files, POL 18 CYP. Confidential; Immediate. Repeated to Ankara, Athens, London, USUN, and the Mission to NATO.

[2] In telegram 1052 from Nicosia, the Embassy reported on the organization of the "Turkish Cypriot Provisional Administration" and the issuance of regulations by that organization. (Ibid.)

[3] Telegram 91488, December 20, commented on the impact of the creation of the Turkish Cypriot Provisional Administration. (Ibid., POL 27 CYP)

which had now been postponed. I said that for once I agreed with Communist newspapers this morning which had urged government to proceed with normalization despite Turk action. I hoped that now that government had apparently reached decision that normalization in its best interests it would not allow this unfortunate event to interfere with implementation of program.

4. I closed our conversation with statement that I would report GOC decision to my government and would presumably receive instructions.

5. *Comment:* Have just talked to UK HICOMer who followed me to FonMinistry. Costar said he had same record played to him and was requesting instructions from his government. Of course this poses greater problem to Brits in view their status Guarantor Power. Nevertheless, Costar agrees with me that there would appear to be little choice but to acquiesce in GOC ruling. He, however, is not offering opinion to London and will merely await their decision. He reminded me that we will have to face problem Jan. 1 when Kuchuk gives his traditional Bayram "at home." Members of corps have in past paid their respects and as matter of fact, I have traditionally gone to sign his book on New Year's day after calling on Archbishop. Under circumstances I consider it inadvisable to make calls this year and DCM will sub for me.[4]

Belcher

---

[4] In telegram 91621, December 30, the Department of State expressed its concern over the latest examples of intercommunal tensions and instructed the Ambassador to seek a reversal of the Cypriot Government's ban on Ambassadorial contacts. (Ibid., POL 18 CYP) In telegram 91622, December 30, the Department of State reported that it had also conveyed its concerns to the Cypriot Chargé with a request for the lifting of the ban. (Ibid.)

352. Letter From Prime Minister Papadopoulos to President Johnson[1]

Athens, January 6, 1968.

Dear Mr. President,

I deem it imperative today to expose to you officially and with due responsibility the causes, the aims, and the prospects of the Revolution of April 21st, 1967. I take this step, prompted by the hope that certain misunderstandings as to the nature of the change that has taken place in Greece will thus be cleared. These I consider detrimental to the interests of both nations concerned, as well as to the Free World.

Our country is honored as the cradle of Democracy. This very fact has placed all powers friendly to Greece, as well as all champions of Democracy in an embarrassing position. The regime which existed before the present change, however, had no relation whatsoever with Democracy. It was a regime of factious debauchery, unrestrained demagogy and disintegrating corruption.

It had three basic characteristics: a steady fall toward economic collapse, an ever-increasing deterioration of all institutions, and the menacing erosion caused by Communism in political parties, in the press, in a part of society, and in the government itself. In this corner of Europe, as you well know, Communism has thrice tried to seize power by revolutions which steeped the country in blood. The last (1946–1949) would have inevitably made a captive of Greece behind the Iron Curtain if the United States of America had not materially helped my greatly menaced country.

The Revolution of April 21st, 1967, took place on the eve of certain civil war—the inevitable result of the elections set for May 28. These elections, whatever the verdict at the polls, would not have solved the ever growing crisis. On the contrary, they would have brought it to an explosive climax. And in the midst of the nightmarish chaos that would have ensued, only the Communist Party—the sole organized power besides the Army—would have prevailed. Its persistent attempts to descend to the Mediterranean and annihilate the eastern flank of the Atlantic Treaty would have been crowned with success.

---

[1] Source: Department of State, Greek Desk Files: Lot 71 D 6, POL US. No classification marking. A covering memorandum from Bromley Smith of the NSC, attached to the source text, notes that the letter was "brought by hand from Greece and then delivered to the White House through a private citizen." The citizen was Tom Pappas, President of Esso–Pappas. In a January 10 memorandum for the President, Rostow commented that the letter was a plea for recognition and endorsed the Department of State's suggestion that the President delay a reply until "a useful time." (Johnson Library, National Security File, Country File, Greece, Vol. 3)

Those who undertook the responsibility to restrain this process at the very last minute, have an individual record of more than ten years' struggle against every shade of Totalitarianism in favor of Freedom and Democracy. They have never thought of imposing a personal regime. Their awareness of responsibility—so lacking in others—as well as their sensitiveness as perceptors of the people's anxiety, due to their origin as members of the armed forces, urged them toward this venture.

The success of this venture, without any bloodshed—a success unique in the annals of world history—is clear proof that the imposed change was an expression of the wishes of a great majority of the Greek people. The latest events (the counter revolution of December 13, headed by the Sovereign of the State himself) constituted a second test for the Revolution, proving once more its necessity, its sway over the people, and its absolute de facto stability.

On the solemn occasion of this my written communication with you, I wish to assure the President of the United States of the following:

It is not the intent of the Revolution to impose a permanent regime, at variance with the fundamental principles proclaimed and championed by the Free World—headed by the United States of America.

The suspension of only a certain number of articles of the 1952 Constitution is temporary. A new Constitution, brought up to date, will eventually be given to the Greek people, no later than 1968.

The regime of this country—Democracy together with a hereditary Sovereign (Constitutional Monarchy)—will remain unaltered.

As soon as the Revolution has accomplished its mission, that is, as soon as it has set the foundations for the economic development of the country, brought the functions of the government up to date, and safeguarded the democratic institutions from the Communist menace, it will call upon the Greek people to elect its deputies in a free, general and secret vote.

The National Government would willingly set the date of the country's entrance into the smooth course of representative government, rid of all the ugliness and dangers of the past, if this were practically possible and psychologically advisable.

Mr. President,

When the Revolution of April 21st took place, Greece was much in the same state as Czechoslovakia had been before February 1948. Ever since World War II, Communism has coveted Greece for strategic and other reasons. This is why Communism has so actively stirred world propaganda against our National Government, thus influencing—as you know far better than myself—a large number of non-Communist elements who shape politics and form public opinion in the Free World.

In this address to you today, the Greek Government hopes that both its professions and its assertions will be duly estimated, and that its sincere devotion to its allies and to the principles of the Free World will meet with due response from the Government of the United States of America.

On the occasion, please allow me to express my best wishes for the New Year.

With kindest personal regards,

G Papadopoulos

---

353. **Telegram From the Embassy in Greece to the Department of State**[1]

Athens, January 9, 1968, 1315Z.

3099. 1. Mr. and Mrs. Andreas Papandreou called on me at home January 8. Andreas seemed well, vigorous, responsive and as articulate as ever.[2] He dismissed his fainting spell several days earlier as not important or serious but rather as an incidental effect on his metabolism of excitement of being released. Similar incidents had occurred in past years. He said he had not been mistreated in jail but that eight months of confinement with armed guards always physically present has inevitably taken their toll and his strength and energy were naturally reduced. He was now rebuilding them. Worst period in prison was last twenty-four hours after amnesty had been announced but before he was certain it would apply to him.

2. Since his release he had discussed possible future plans with his family but not with anyone else before this conversation. He found many reasons to stay in Greece, but he would then have to remain close to home and concentrate on writing since any serious contacts with old friends and associates would be subject to misunderstanding by regime. Also so long as he remained in Greece he would be a factor and possibly an embarrassment to regime causing it to act more defensively. Thus without

---

[1] Source: Department of State, Central Files, POL 30–2 GR. Confidential; Limdis.

[2] On December 23, 1967, the Junta announced that it would be releasing Andreas Papandreou and other political prisoners. On January 2, Margaret Papandreou requested a meeting with Talbot in order for her husband to discuss his future plans. In telegram 2929 from Athens, December 23, Talbot raised the likelihood that Andreas would request a visa to return to the United States and outlined means of arranging the most "expeditious" issuance of a non-emigrant visa. (Ibid.)

inflating his own importance, he had come to feel that perhaps the regime could move more freely toward constitutionalism once he had left the country. In any event, he had decided to return to United States. He had applied for a Greek passport and had reason to think it [garble—would] be forthcoming shortly. If so, he would like to start promptly for the United States. I told him we could give him visa quickly. We also discussed possible effect on him of Supreme Court decision in Afroyim case. I explained that Court had not ruled on questions involving a citizen who took Ministerial oath of allegiance to foreign sovereign and that therefore decision could not be presumed to have given him fresh claim to U.S. citizenship. Any administrative or further judicial interpretation could, of course, modify this position, but as of this date no such finding had been made. Andreas asked if his acceptance of Greek passport now would reduce his prospect of resuming American citizenship in event of later broad construction of Afroyim decision. I responded that to best of my knowledge it would not.

3. Papandreou said he had decided that for indefinite future, "which could be very long time," he would abandon political activities and return to academic career which would now be focussed on broader developmental economics than on his earlier mathematical econometric specialty. With several university offers in hand, he had ruled out Middle Western possibilities (Minnesota, Northwestern) but had not yet decided whether to go back to California or another West Coast institution or to settle on East Coast. It would depend on kinds of contacts he might have in one place or other.

4. Our talk, which has relaxed and friendly throughout, also included candid discussion of some of Andreas' past activities and his appraisal of present prospects in Greece. Ostensible purpose of call, however, was to express thanks for Embassy's intervention "to save my life" on first night of April coup and thereafter. Andreas said he was aware of my approaches to coup leaders and Embassy's concern for his family and deeply appreciated our interest. I commented that Embassy had been prepared to offer assistance to his family if need arose, particularly if he or they should ever appear to be in imminent danger, but happily this had not been necessary. We discussed how much he may have been in actual danger of being killed. I suggested that although I was grateful for his appreciation of Embassy's efforts, in fact maximum danger had probably come immediately during his arrest, before Embassy knew what was going on. Once regime had him in custody and world knew it, any physical attack on him would have been hard to justify. Certainly we had not discovered any indication that regime ever planned to execute him. Papandreou agreed with this assessment. Pattakos had told him junior members of Junta wanted to get rid of him but that Pattakos had overruled them. When after forty-eight hours or so Andreas under-

stood that there were no political killings, he felt his own situation much safer. It could however have been different story if top coup leadership had lost control to more activist juniors.

5. Throughout this phase of our conversation, Andreas made repeated references to comfort he had gained by knowing USG and Embassy maintained lively interest in his situation.

6. While in prison Andreas had thought through events between July 15, 1965 and April 21, 1967, he said. He had come to see situation from perspective of Greek state as a whole without partisan distortions. Now that that phase had passed, and he could talk without sounding as if he were trying to make marks for future, he wanted to make clear what position he had held vis-à-vis United States, since he felt there had been misunderstandings between him and American Embassy and perhaps some bias in reporting. Ever since 1961 he had believed Embassy and State Department had favored Greek rightists and strong role for King. He reminded me that he had asserted this to me in Washington after Greek elections of 1961, which he felt had been distorted not by domestic influences alone (a delicately-phrased assertion that CIA had intervened in those elections). Whatever Embassy may have thought in 1965–66 and 1966–67, he had never advocated departure of King from Greece but merely limitation of King's ambition to play de Gaulle by precise delimitation of Royal powers. Also, he had never advocated departure of Greece from Western Alliance; on contrary, Greece unlike Tito's Yugoslavia could not survive neutralism because its position would not permit this. Finally, whatever criticisms of United States policy he had made, he had not attacked U.S. policies as an enemy but rather as member of family. Having been an American citizen, he had felt he could be as frank as Senators Fulbright and Morse without putting into question his basic belief that United States and Greece must continue closely together.

7. I told Papandreou I accepted these statements. From our point of view, Embassy (and I as former newspaperman accustomed to importance of separating news from editorial opinion) had tried to maximum extent possible to avoid bias. His father and he had asserted to me early in my tour in Greece that Embassy had neglected importance of Center Union[3] without discussing prior situation which I had not known at first hand. I was confident he would agree that in 1965–67 period Embassy had maintained close contacts with Center Union and I personally had seen his father quite frequently as well as other prominent members of party. Andreas acknowledged that. I went on to observe that he should know that in 1960's, at least (which only period I could speak of personally, not having previously been in government service), both Presidents Kennedy and Johnson had determined firmly that there should be one

---

[3] See Document 214.

United States policy in a country. It was thus unrealistic to speak of separate diplomatic, military and intelligence policies. Papandreou interjected that he was glad to hear "this important statement." I continued that while Andreas and his father had both assured me that they followed same policies despite differences in style, I had subsequently concluded that in fact there were substantive differences between them. Andreas acknowledged that he and his father in the end had disagreed on policy points. He reiterated, however, that this had nothing to do with their joint view of the importance of the American connection. His own strategy had been to try to detach as large a faction as possible from the Communist-front EDA Party in order to assure an electoral victory for the Center Union. He admitted this was a risky policy, but felt that he could have carried it off despite his father's doubts.

8. Andreas spoke of American influence in Greece and the importance of getting this country back on constitutional lines. I responded that in early Truman Doctrine and Marshall Plan period American influence had apparently sometimes been used tactically, to extent of insistence upon broad-based government to carry out reconstruction and development programs. However, as with other countries well along development trail, in recent years we had held that Greece itself (rather than outsiders) must be mainly responsible for its political, economic, and social development, and that we could no more take responsibility for its failures than for its successes. It was on this basis, that we had not intervened with King last spring to set up temporary government that would have sidetracked elections and presumably averted military coup. Similarly, at present stage, we are not in position to tell Greece what kind of government it should have. Papandreou commented that in many ways this is a pity, since present rulers of Greece need advice. I noted that no one in Greece is unaware of fact that Americans would find repugnant any permanent military dictatorship in Europe in 1960's. Key policy question for us, I added, is whether gradual restoration of democratic and parliamentary rule is more likely to be accomplished if allies turn their backs on Greece at present juncture of work with government of day. Papandreou said that not even while in prison had he ever suggested U.S. should not recognize this Greek government, nor would he now. In his view delicate task for U.S. would be to work with present regime while letting Greeks know our purpose is to urge country toward restoration of constitutionalism. I noted this is precisely posture we developed after April 21 coup.

9. I noted that in U.S. Andreas would find American public opinion toward Greece sharply divided, with important elements of academic community taking different line from other significant groups such as major Greek-American organizations. On how best to deal with present situation, Andreas again said he had been doing much thinking in pris-

on, and that we could count on him not to exacerbate policy attitudes in U.S. He recognizes that present regime is well in saddle, that any immediate opposition would seem likely to be generated only by more extreme elements within revolutionary group, which would be worse than present leadership, and that restoration of constitutional patterns might take long time. I mentioned Turkish experience of plebiscite on first anniversary of military takeover in 1960, followed by elections six months thereafter and then for some time by a civilian government under shadow of military veto before parliamentary institutions firmly reestablished. While Greece is not Turkey, I hazarded view this country might be in for similar process. If constitutional referendum held within next six to eight months and first elections within year thereafter, this would not necessarily be bad. Andreas commented that process should not be allowed to lag too long but also that there danger in trying to push it too fast because junior officers might react to strong pressures by refusing to permit any progress at all. He felt present group, despite its power position, is insecure and uncertain. Because of this, I said we had for some time felt it important that the regime commit itself to constitutional progress at least one step at a time. Now a constitutional draft had been produced practically within promised six months framework, and inclusive dates had been announced within which referendum would be held. This constitutes progress of sorts though we can make no substantive judgments about prospects without seeing constitutional draft as produced by Mitrelias Commission and as revised by government. Before chance to appraise rigidity or liberality of government's draft, I personally would doubt wisdom of pressing for fixed date for elections. Andreas said he agreed fully.

10. The Papandreous promised to let me know as soon as they get definite word about his passport. Department will be advised when visa application received.

Talbot

354.   Telegram From the Embassy in Greece to the Department of State[1]

Athens, January 11, 1968, 1150Z.

3129. Ref: State 95291.[2]

1.   In response to intimation I would be glad see him privately and informally, FonMin Pipinelis invited me to his home January 10. We talked two hours, covering both Cyprus (septel)[3] and Greek domestic situations. Pipinelis was as friendly and forthcoming as he had been during our intensive discussions in November and early December. He grasps our concerns about status and intentions of current GOG and I believe will be helpful in Cabinet discussions.

2.   Pipinelis first reviewed his own movements after moment at NATO Ministerial when he learned of King's attempted countercoup, whose illogicality had flabbergasted him. Papadopoulos telephoned him three times and King once in Brussels. En route home he stopped in Rome to see King, whom he found dispirited yet still defiant. Pipinelis urged King to return to Greece immediately, as Papadopoulos had proposed on day following King's departure. King's refusal was mistake, in Pipinelis view.

3.   On return to Athens Pipinelis found reorganized government already proceeding with business and committed to pursuing agreement with Turkey. Pipinelis agreed to continue in government because he believed its leaders were sincere in their announced intentions to cleanse country and restore parliamentary rule. He still believes they are. Indeed, his relations with governmental leaders have become not only friendly but even easier than with his colleagues in Kanellopoulos government last year.

4.   I told Pipinelis we regret even temporary break in close and cordial relations we have enjoyed with Greece for many years. We continue to regard our association with Greek ally as important, and I personally am confident way can be found over present barriers to resumption of normal business. It was in that spirit that I had wished to discuss situation with him.

5.   As background to questions I wanted to pose, I described repugnance found in United States to idea of any military takeover in Europe

---

[1] Source: Department of State, Central Files, POL 23–9 GREECE. Secret; Limdis.

[2] In telegram 95291 to Athens, January 9, the Department of State recognized the "difficulties caused" by the U.S. posture but stated it hoped to use the irregular nature of the diplomatic relationship to apply pressure on the Greek regime. The telegram instructed Talbot to seek an informal meeting with Pipinelis. (Ibid., POL 16 GREECE)

[3] Telegram 3131 from Athens, January 11. (Ibid., POL 27 CYP)

in 1960's, extra difficulties caused us by apparent withdrawal of Royal umbrella that had more or less legitimized April 21 revolutionary government, and uncertainties being expressed in US about reality of constitutional progress. I noted that many of those who would most strongly oppose any USG decision to work normally with present GOG were drawn from same circles as opponents of President's Viet-Nam policy and that this added sensitivity to problem. In these circumstances it would be helpful if we could be enlightened on specific plans accepted by GOG for constitutional advance as well as precise information on status of King and Regent in relation to government.

6. In response Pipinelis made following comments:

(1) Constitutional draft. Draft produced by Mitrelias commission was surprisingly close to Karamanlis draft constitution of 1963, he said. In basic concepts it introduced few—too few, in Pipinelis view—changes from existing Constitution. Any fair-minded person would call it not only democratic but liberal. After draft was presented to government December 23, copies were circulated to Ministers with instructions to make comments in writing by January 6. This had now been done. Pipinelis himself had recommended inter alia some changes designed to draw higher quality persons into Parliament. He does not yet know what others have recommended. He believes Ministerial proposals would be studied very rapidly and is fairly confident that a final draft will be promulgated in near future—meaning some weeks rather than months. I commented on rumors that government has now decided to hold back plebiscite until last possible date mentioned by Papadopoulos, September 15. Pipinelis responded that on contrary he believes GOG would find a way to hold plebiscite perhaps not on first declared date, April 21 (which is Orthodox Easter), but near then. I told Pipinelis it would be helpful to us to be able to see Mitrelias constitution. He took note.

(2) Date of elections and initiation of parliamentary government. Pipinelis thinks leaders themselves have not yet settled on date of initial elections. Many uncertainties remain, such as whether revolutionary Ministers will create their own political movement and run for office. Moreover, in his view, it would be very serious mistake to set election date at this stage of present government. From moment elections declared, no matter how distantly, political elements in country would start jockeying for advantage and moral authority of present government would be lost. It always happens thus in Greece. But this would be great misfortune in present circumstances, because this government has much important work to accomplish before leaving office—work of cleansing and reconstruction that an ordinary political government would probably not have will or strength to tackle successfully. To Pipinelis, for allied governments to press for precise date for Greek election would be error both for foregoing reasons and because it is a superfluous

issue. Once new Constitution adopted in national plebiscite, process of return to elected government would be automatic and irreversible. *Comment:* From Pattakos statement in interview with Bavarian radio correspondent (septel) and other sources, we understand that ultimate date for elections is integral part of struggle now under way in revolutionary committee between Papadopoulos/Makarezos and Ladas groups. This tug-of-war appears centered on kinds of revisions to draft Constitution which the hardliners are pushing (see Athens 3122, para 4).[4]

(3) Relaxation of press restrictions and establishment of judicial proceedings for detainees. New press law being prepared. This very important, since Greece must have strong and independent press but cannot afford to go back to morass that was Greek journalism until last April. He could not say when law would be ready, but thinks it likely to come fairly soon. He had nothing specific to report on judicial process for detainees.

(4) Roles of King and Regent. For himself, Pipinelis said, it is apparent that government needs King and King needs government. Therefore, he should return soon. He has repeatedly and vigorously made this point to Cabinet. Papadopoulos has now taken firm line, however, that King should return to Greece but not now because of highly antipathetic feelings in army and general population.

Pipinelis has been unable to shake government leaders on this point, though he still trying. But this is domestic Greek issue. It is true there was a fault in manner of inducting Regent but this was due to force of circumstances and is domestic question not affecting government's support of monarchy or acceptance of Constantine as King. If any other government has legal problems, it should be enough for that government to perceive that King has explicitly addressed leader of this government as Prime Minister and thus has implicitly also accepted Regent who swore him in. Moreover, if another government should agree that King's role continues important, question is whether it can better help persuade GOG of this fact by avoiding contacts or by reopening working relations. He would strongly argue for latter as more fruitful course. Pipinelis added that question of King's return is exclusively matter of timing. Neither side has put up conditions that it would be difficult for other to accept. Once decision made on date of King's return, it would be simple to find a formula to suit interests of both him and government.

7. Pipinelis concluded with statement whose import was that he hopes USG can see way clear to restoration of normal business while there still time to influence present group constructively. He sees no reason to make prominent announcement of resumption of business. It

---

[4] Dated January 10. (Ibid., POL 16 GREECE)

would be possible just to pick up quietly again where matters had left off. This was what German Ambassador had done in calling on him day or two ago, and he hoped others might do it as well.

8. I mentioned having heard rumor that Papadopoulos is under pressure from his associates to make speech this weekend critical of posture of allies and pointed out it would be regrettable if public statement by high official should further complicate already difficult situation at this stage. Pipinelis understood, and promised to speak to Papadopoulos. I also mentioned that in situation like present one we find ourselves approached by variety of volunteer intermediaries, as presumably does GOG. One current example is Tom Pappas, who is understandably worried by interruption of direct communication between our two governments. While we appreciate desire of others to be helpful I would like GOG to understand Embassy is not using any non-official as intermediary but prefers to give and to get its impressions in direct contact with leading GOG personalities. Pipinelis took note of this as well.

9. We agreed to be ready to meet again in weeks ahead at instance of either of us.

Talbot

---

355. Telegram From the Embassy in Cyprus to the Department of State[1]

Nicosia, January 12, 1968, 0730Z.

1137. Reference: Ankara 3187.[2] Subject: Cyprus planning.

1. Ambassador Hart's point that delay in US initiative creates opportunities for both Greek and Turk Cypriots to make moves that narrow negotiating room is well taken. In fact, establishment of TCPA represents just such a preclusive move by Turks-Turk Cypriots.

2. Whether GOC redrafting of Constitution which now underway is designed as preclusive move or not is moot. Certainly there are those

[1] Source: Department of State, Central Files, POL 27 CYP. Secret; Limdis. Repeated to Athens, Ankara, London, Ottawa, USUN, and the Mission to NATO.

[2] Telegram 3187 from Ankara, January 9, discussed possible U.S. responses to preclusive moves by either Greece or Turkey in Cyprus. (Ibid.)

within GOC (including, we suspect, Kyprianou) who will prefer unilateral use of redrafted Constitution, no doubt with appropriate bows in direction of Galo Plaza report, as propaganda and negotiating ploy.

3. Less cynical (and probably less likely) interpretation is that Makarios is sincere in his comments to Ambassador that exercise in which GOC now engaged is one of putting thoughts, including autonomy for Turk Cypriots, into revised Constitution which will be advanced as negotiating document and not unilateral initiative. Makarios' desire to use UN forum and his need to to be ready for SYG's good offices make preparation of working paper consistent with this interpretation.

4. Experience indicates that we should incline to cynical interpretation. Fact that GOC working on revised Constitution leaked to press reinforces view that GOC does intend to proceed in unhelpful manner to rally public support for new Constitution before any talks with Turks-Turk Cypriots can begin.[3]

5. In any case, sooner U.S. offer of good offices made and opportunities for unilateral initiatives foreclosed the better. If Makarios' redrafted Constitution contains serious elements of compromise, it can always be used in context U.S. good offices effort.

Belcher

---

[3] In telegram 1152 from Nicosia, January 12, the Embassy reported that Makarios had called for Presidential elections. The telegram evaluated his speech announcing this decision to renew his mandate as a "sincere" effort to improve the situation on Cyprus. (Ibid.)

---

356. Telegram From the Department of State to the Embassy in Greece[1]

Washington, January 13, 1968, 1:46 p.m.

98446. For Ambassador.

1. We have decided to move in the near future to a working relationship with the regime in Athens. Our plan is first to consult during the

---

[1] Source: Department of State, Central Files, POL GREECE–US. Secret; Exdis. Drafted by Rockwell, cleared in substance by Katzenbach, and approved by Battle. Repeated to the Mission to NATO and Rome.

coming week in Washington with NATO reps [2] and then to authorize you to pay a formal call on Pipinelis. Formal contact with Junta Ministers would not be authorized for time being but is envisaged as following step.

2. Decision is based on fact regime in control of country, belief we have extracted as much benefit as we likely obtain from present policy, and fact we have interests in Greece which require attention.

3. We do not intend make formal announcement, and will seek avoid publicly discussing question of whether we have recognized GOG. We plan say we resuming working relationship based on de facto situation of control.

4. During your future meetings with FonMin you should continue press for progress toward constitutionalism.

5. If you believe it would be helpful you authorized informally convey to FonMin, without awaiting occasion of formal call, acknowledgment of message which PriMin sent to President via private channel. Text being sent you separately.[3]

6. In light above we believe it preferable you remain Athens for time being.

7. At luncheon with Palamas January 15 Battle will be generally encouraging re US–GOG relationship.[4]

Katzenbach

---

[2] In telegram 98588 to Athens, January 15, the Department of State reported that Rockwell had begun a round of meetings with representatives of the NATO allies to explain the change in the U.S. position. (Ibid., POL 15–1 GREECE)

[3] The Prime Minister's letter is printed as Document 350. In telegram 3248 from Athens, January 19, Talbot suggested that the appropriate line of approach would be a direct response from the President. (Ibid., POL GREECE–US) In response to a January 19 memorandum from Rostow outlining Talbot's reasoning, President Johnson wrote: "OK Talbot call on PM. Isn't this sufficient." (Johnson Library, National Security File, Memos to the President—Walt Rostow, Vol. 3) In telegram 101277 to Athens, the Department of State authorized Talbot to convey orally to Papadopoulos an acknowledgement of his letter and to state the President would soon reply. (Department of State, Central Files, POL GREECE–US) In telegram 3246 from Athens, January 19, Talbot reported that Papadopoulos had been informed by an Embassy official. (Ibid.)

[4] In telegram 100451 to Athens, January 18, the Department of State reported that Rockwell had called in the Greek Ambassador on January 15 and explained the proposed changes in the U.S. position toward Greece. (Ibid., POL 15–1 GREECE)

357.   Memorandum of Conversation[1]

Washington, January 16, 1968, 10:30 a.m.

SUBJECT

Review of the Cyprus Situation

PARTICIPANTS

Cyprus:
Foreign Minister Spyros Kyprianou
Ambassador Zenon Rossides, Permanent Representative to UN
Mr. Andreas Jacovides, Director of Political Division, Ministry of Foreign Affairs,
    Nicosia
Mr. Costas Papademas, Counselor, Cyprus Embassy

U.S.:
The Secretary
Mr. Joseph J. Sisco, Assistant Secretary, IO
Mr. William J. Handley, Deputy Assistant Secretary, NEA
Mr. Robert S. Folsom, Country Director, Cyprus Affairs

Foreign Minister Kyprianou opened the conversation by stating that he wished to acquaint the Secretary with his views on the Cyprus situation and to learn in turn the Secretary's views. He said the Cypriot Government has sought seriously to find a solution since the November crisis within the framework of procedures established by the Security Council debate. He added that the Cypriot Government has always sought a solution within the UN context and that since the end of the Galo Plaza mediation this effort has been made through the Secretary General.

We are now faced, he said, with a situation in which the Cyprus Government supports the Secretary General's initiative on both long-term and short-term solutions, but that the Turks are seeking to restrict discussion to "internal security" matters which they say must precede any long term discussions and even then such long term discussions should be outside of the UN.

Cyprus, he said, cannot separate internal security from external security though the Government is prepared to start with internal security matters while working for a package deal. Prerequisites he said are (1) removal of Greek Cypriot fears of an attack from outside, and (2) removal of the fear of the Turk-Cypriot minority. He said his Government had presented the Secretary General with four points as comprising the basis of the Cyprus Government plan:

---

[1] Source: Department of State, Central Files, POL 27 CYP. Secret. Drafted by Folsom and approved in S on February 2. The meeting was held in the Secretary's office.

1. A guarantee against external attack.
2. Complete withdrawal of Greek and Turkish troops including the contingents.
3. Disarmament of all Greek-Cypriot and Turk-Cypriot forces, leaving only the police and UNFICYP.
4. Discussion of arrangements for effective internal security.

Adoption of these four points, he said, should remove the fear of all parties concerned.

The Secretary pointed out that a guarantee against external aggression may be necessary but may not be possible.

Mr. Kyprianou responded that as long as there is danger of external attack there is increased danger of internal incidents and that if the guarantee is necessary, a way must be found to make it possible. He then said he wished to note new developments: (1) the untimely establishment of the Turkish Cypriot Provisional Administration (TCPA), established by the Turk Cypriots and Turkish Government officials, which has disturbed the possibilities for internal improvement and evidences continued plans for partition; (2) the decision of President Makarios to seek a new mandate and to offer new solutions for the Cyprus problem to be offered to the Secretary General (these steps, he said, have been necessitated by the aftermath of the crisis and the withdrawal of Greek troops); and (3) a Turkish Aide-Mémoire addressed to the UNSYG on the subject of current UN negotiations on Cyprus.[2]

Mr. Kyprianou said that his Government took a negative view towards the Aide-Mémoire, because it fails to deal with the external danger to Cyprus, makes no mention of withdrawal of Greek or Turkish national contingents, and deals only with internal security, and even in this, tends to affect the substance of the problem by appearing to lead towards partition. He said the Cypriot response to the Aide-Mémoire was being postponed until after his talk with the Secretary.

The Secretary asked if bilateral Turkish-Cypriot talks had been considered.

Mr. Kyprianou agreed that the real question lay between Cyprus and Turkey, but said his Government prefers to deal through the UNSYG. He noted that the issue no longer was enosis, but the independence of Cyprus and the rights of the Turkish minority—a fact which the Turks recognize, while at the same time, they do not want to confirm their recognition of the Cyprus Government.

The Secretary then asked how Mr. Kyprianou saw the question of guarantees.

---

[2] Reference is presumably to a January 8 Turkish communication to the Secretary-General. (U.N. Docs. S/8330 and S/8331)

Mr. Kyprianou said this was a very difficult problem, while suggesting: (1) a special Security Council resolution of guarantee, (2) a U.S. or other single nation guarantee, or (3) a multi-party guarantee; he noted his preference for (1).

The Secretary then asked whether UNFICYP would be required for a protracted period.

Mr. Kyprianou said that even if demilitarization could be completed, the presence of UNFICYP would be required, on a reduced scale, in a symbolic sense until a final solution was achieved.

The Secretary asked how the viability and rights of the Turkish Cypriot minority could be assured.

Mr. Kyprianou replied that this could be achieved along the lines of the Galo Plaza report though not so identified because of Turkish objections.

The Secretary asked if Makarios' reference to the Turkish Cypriot "Community" was significant.

Mr. Kyprianou said use of the word "community" was not significant, that the word was used frequently, that what his government objected to was any reference to "two communities" so implying separation or equality. His government, he added, was ready to apply full guarantees and was willing to accept international guarantees for the minority, but Turkey was unwilling.

Mr. Sisco, after being called on by the Secretary, said that our role in the UN to date has been to support the SYG and that we have felt it best to concentrate on the internal problem as a means of achieving lasting peace and creating the right atmosphere for peace.

Mr. Kyprianou insisted that the internal problem is part and parcel of the whole, that the National Guard, for example, cannot be dismantled without assurances of a guarantee from external attack and withdrawal of the two national contingents. He asserted that a vacuum had been created by the withdrawal of Greek troops and that this vacuum must be filled. He said his government had done much towards normalization and pacification already but cannot go all the way to disarmament without taking care of external dangers first. He said informal talks with Mr. Vance had clarified that withdrawal of Greek troops is only the *first* step so there must be a *second* step, but that the Turks deny this, saying the national contingents are not concerned. He dismissed the Turkish assertion that its national contingent is part of the London–Zurich settlement by asserting: (1) that they had violated the Agreement by moving their troops and (2) in any case, that they were not obliged to keep any troops on Cyprus under the Treaty of Guarantee. He then quipped "What we need is a guarantee against the guarantors", stating his inability to see why the Turks could object to a formula embracing neither enosis nor partition.

The Secretary asked what will happen when the SYG sees the Cypriot reply to the Turkish Aide-Mémoire.

Mr. Kyprianou said he expected that either the SYG would continue his negotiations in an effort to find common ground or call a Security Council meeting. He then asked if the U.S. supports the SYG's good offices and whether the U.S. has proposals for him.

The Secretary noted that in good offices proposals are usually not made and, that when made, are offered very quietly in an effort to bring the two parties together.

Mr. Kyprianou asked whether if a quick agreement on the external and internal security issues cannot be reached, the substance of the problem might not be attacked. In this respect, he noted that President Makarios is proceeding along these lines.

In reply to a series of questions posed by the Secretary, Mr. Kyprianou clarified that the Cyprus elections are scheduled for February 25, that the Turks can take part in the elections under the 1965 law, but that they do not have to, that he did not expect violence in the elections, that only the office of President will be at issue and that if opposition candidates wish to run, they must announce their candidacies by February 15.

Mr. Sisco asked if there was any way out of the current ban on ambassadorial contacts with the Turkish Cypriot leaders in the TCPA, pointing out that the situation requires such contacts.

Mr. Kyprianou said the issue is delicate, that he would hope that the Turks could be convinced to abandon the TCPA—that if what they say is true, all they need is a committee, not an "administration" including Foreign Affairs, Commerce, Agriculture, Defense, etc.

Mr. Handley asked if contacts were possible, if it was clear that these were not with the TCPA as such.

The Secretary asserted that it was not very agreeable for Ambassadors to be told that they can't have contacts with others and suggested that maybe we should tell Ambassador Rossides not to have certain contacts here. He stressed that such a ban is contrary to diplomatic custom, except behind the Iron Curtain, and stated his hope that the Foreign Minister would take steps to correct the situation.

Ambassador Rossides interjected that since all agreed that establishment of the TCPA was a faux pas and since it was deprecated from all sides, the Turks might be persuaded to "climb down" eliminating Foreign Affairs, Defense, etc.

The Secretary replied that, due to the ban, we have no Ambassadorial contacts.

Ambassador Rossides then suggested that we talk to the Turks in Ankara.

Mr. Kyprianou next quoted from the past to prove that Kuchuk does not speak for the Turkish Cypriots and that authoritative statements can come only from Ankara. He went on to point out that the Turkish Government refers to the Cypriot Government as the "Greek Cypriot Administration" and to the TCPA as the "Turkish Cypriot Administration", so trying to equate their roles.

The Secretary, at this point, said the U.S. has much more serious problems with Turkey than this and reemphasized the seriousness of the ban, adding that we will be in touch on this matter further.

He then asked what Mr. Kyprianou wanted from us with regard to the SYG's negotiations.

Mr. Kyprianou replied by asking what should be done if negotiations failed to develop and whether a Security Council meeting should be called.

The Secretary said he didn't believe a meeting of that type with debates would deal effectively with solutions.

Mr. Sisco said that it is necessary for the Greek Cypriots to talk to the Turkish Cypriots and that it is inappropriate for us to become involved with the SYG's negotiations at this point. He stressed the need for progress, noting that an impasse might cause a new crisis, that the UNFICYP mandate expires March 26 and that the troop contributors are restive.

The Secretary, noting that the Greeks invented diplomacy, asked if it were not possible for two private individuals to get together for talks.

Mr. Sisco inquired as to Cypriot delegation's contacts with the Turkish delegation.

Mr. Kyprianou replied that contacts were only informal, but were not excluded, even talks with the Turkish Foreign Minister.

The Secretary observed that we will remain in touch with the situation and wish to be helpful. He then asked if the Turkish Aide-Mémoire was public and how the Cypriots would reply to it.

Mr. Kyprianou said it was not public and that depending on how the SYG posed it, they might reject it outright or reject it leaving the door open for further discussion.

The Secretary asked whether if the SYG proposed Turkish-Cypriot talks, the Cypriots would agree.

Mr. Kyprianou said yes, they would.

Ambassador Rossides then brought up the subject of the TCPA again, remarking that it was unfortunate, too formal and a cloak for a "'government" administration.

The Secretary stated that we were not informed about it in advance and would have counselled against it had we known in advance.

Mr. Kyprianou again said that if the TCPA is what the Turks claim, it could be reorganized as a committee. He went on to say that a logical solution to Cyprus must be found, that the mere expectation that one side or the other would reject a solution must not be allowed to jeopardize a solution and that a breakthrough to a logical solution is necessary. This he described as an independent unitary state with rights for the Turkish minority or community. The solution, he said, cannot include both independence and no independence, Greek-Turkish involvement and Greek-Turkish non-involvement, nor any other seeds of division. He asserted that, while the Turks officially reject partition, they always work towards this end and that partition cannot solve the problem.

The Secretary asked whether if all the Turkish Cypriots had lived in one area, federation could have been possible.

Mr. Kyprianou simply replied this is not the case.

The Secretary then asked, since geographical division is not possible, whether some form of vertical division is possible, noting that a "unitary state" implies to the Turks their own disappearance.

Mr. Kyprianou asserted that equal rights for all plus special rights for the Turk-Cypriots is possible, but that Cyprus cannot go back to the London–Zurich settlement, that the seeds of division must be removed.

The meeting closed with the Secretary emphasizing that we will keep in close touch with developments.

---

358. Memorandum From Secretary of State Rusk to President Johnson[1]

Washington, January 17, 1968.

SUBJECT

Strategy for Negotiation of a Cyprus Settlement

Recommendation:

That you approve our taking an active part in promoting an early settlement of the Cyprus dispute, by supporting mediation efforts by the

---

[1] Source: Department of State, Central Files, POL 27 CYP. Secret. Drafted by McFarland and cleared by Folsom, Rockwell, and Battle.

United Nations Secretary General or by taking steps that would involve us directly in the mediation process.[2]

Discussion:

In the last four years we have twice intervened diplomatically to stop a Greek-Turkish war from developing out of the Cyprus dispute. For the last several years, we have refrained from involving ourselves substantively in the issue, preferring the parties to reach agreement among themselves.

After Cyrus Vance's skilled mediation last November succeeded by the narrowest of margins, we have concluded that a new effort must be made to reach a permanent solution of this dangerous problem, and that a major role for the U.S. in this effort is indicated.

Shortly after the November crisis ended, a Cyprus Study Group, headed by former Ambassador Charles W. Yost, was formed to make recommendations on how the United States could aid in bringing about a settlement. The group's recommendations, which are attached,[3] have been approved by the Interdepartmental Regional Group headed by Assistant Secretary Battle and by the Senior Interdepartmental Group under the chairmanship of Under Secretary Katzenbach.

The basic recommendation that emerged is that the United States Government do all in its power to bring about a long-term Cyprus settlement. We believe that the risk of war has increased to the point that our interests are served best by actively promoting an early solution, despite the resentment that our role could conceivably produce in Greece, Cyprus, and Turkey. The parties are still very far apart, and it may well be that only the United States has the influence to bring them together. Chances of settlement are now somewhat better than before the November crisis.

Our first step would be to consult with the British and Canadian Governments, which also are strongly interested in settling the Cyprus dispute, and with the United Nations Secretary General, who has already begun discussions with representatives of Greece, Turkey, and Cyprus. Depending on the Secretary General's plans for continuing his discussions and his prospects for success, we would then follow one of two courses: strong support for United Nations mediation of a long-term settlement, or support for its mediation of interim measures while we take over the search for a long-term settlement. In the latter case, we would review the situation again before appointing a United States mediator.

---

[2] There is no indication on the source text whether the President approved or disapproved the recommendation.

[3] Entitled "Strategy for Negotiation of a Cyprus Settlement," not printed.

Because the need for action is urgent, we would like to begin the course of action recommended by the paper as soon as possible.

Dean Rusk

---

359.   Memorandum for the Record[1]

Washington, January 24, 1968.

SUBJECT

    NSC Meeting Held January 24, 1968, at 1:00 p.m. in the Cabinet Room

PARTICIPANTS

    The President
    The Vice President
    Secretary of State, Dean Rusk
    Secretary of Defense, Robert S. McNamara
    Secretary of Treasury, Henry H. Fowler
    Chairman, Joint Chiefs of Staff, General Earle G. Wheeler
    Director, Central Intelligence Agency, Richard Helms
    Director, U.S. Information Agency, Leonard Marks
    Deputy Secretary of Defense, Cyrus R. Vance
    Under Secretary of State, Nicholas Katzenbach
    Under Secretary of Defense, Paul Nitze
    Assistant Secretary of State, Joseph Sisco
    Assistant Secretary of State, Lucius D. Battle
    President's Special Assistant for National Security Affairs, Mr. Walt Rostow
    Executive Secretary, Mr. Bromley Smith
    White House Press Officer, George Christian
    White House Press Officer, Tom Johnson
    Nathaniel Davis
    Harold H. Saunders

[Here follows discussion of the *Pueblo* incident.]

II.   The President, in introducing a *discussion of the Cyprus problem,* welcomed Mr. Vance to the Council table and said he wanted to thank him publicly for his efforts last November and December in avoiding a war between Greece and Turkey. He then asked Mr. Battle to summarize the problem for the Council.

---

[1] Source: Johnson Library, National Security File, NSC Meetings File, Vol. 4. Secret. Drafted by Saunders. At the beginning of the meeting, President Johnson noted that it had originally been called to deal with the Cyprus question but that the seizure of the U.S.S. *Pueblo* necessitated a briefing on that matter as the initial order of business.

Mr. Battle said that, while Mr. Vance's mission had saved us from war, the Cyprus problem remains. New small incidents occur weekly which heighten tension on the island. Next time it will be impossible to hold Turkey back, especially while the Greek internal situation is what it is. Ambassador Yost had reviewed the situation after Mr. Vance's return. He concluded—and the IRG and SIG have concurred—that the situation is unstable and that it is important that we be ready to move in if required. Via the Vance mission, we have involved ourselves again in the Cypriot problem. The UN is now discussing how to tackle the long range problem and we must let the UN effort run its course, but we are not optimistic about what U Thant can achieve and should not let him fail without having something of our own ready to put in his place. Mr. Battle concluded by saying that he did not want to step into this problem, but he felt we had no choice but to be ready.

Mr. Helms noted that the Greeks have withdrawn their troops as agreed with Mr. Vance, although there are still some 1500 on the island as a regular part of the National Guard. He noted that the Greeks claim that 300 Turk officers remain in a similar capacity. There is still no inter-communal cooperation. Makarios' declaration of a Presidential election at the end of February might further inflame the situation.[2] In sum, the situation is still extremely uneasy.

In response to the President's request, Mr. Vance summarized his feelings as follows: "The situation is still held together with paste and glue, and more paste than glue." If it flares up again, war cannot be avoided. The majority of Turks had wanted to go to war in November. The Greek people felt humiliated and many of them are anxious for a chance to have a go at the Turks. The Cypriots are fatalistic.

He believed that the US should take an active role in trying to achieve a settlement. The pace of the problem is quicker than the pace of the UN Secretary General. He hopes the problem can be solved within the framework of the UN, but he is "not sanguine."

Mr. Sisco agreed that the UN would not be able to do the job. He noted one slight opening in the last 24 hours—that Makarios has apparently agreed to discuss his own draft Constitution with the Turkish Cypriots. He shared the prediction that U Thant would be at the end of his road in a few days. The President asked whether there is more that Ambassador Goldberg could do. Mr. Sisco said the Ambassador had made clear his support of the Secretary General and had urged Cypriots and Turks to get together. He pointed out, however, that the Turks distrust U Thant. The Cypriot Foreign Minister wants to tie the pacification efforts envisioned in the Vance agreement to replace the withdrawn

---

[2] Makarios made the announcement of elections in a January 12 national radio broadcast.

Greek troops with Cyprus' protection against Turkish invasion. The Turks want to concentrate on pacification alone.

Mr. Sisco pointed out that the governments contributing troops to the UN peacekeeping force are restive and may be reluctant to renew their contributions when the current mandate for the force expires at the end of March unless there is some progress in further implementing the Vance agreement and moving toward a more permanent arrangement.

Secretary Rusk noted that it is time for serious talks with the Turks and Cypriots. He hoped we could move some diplomatic chips in before the next crisis—before we "get to the end of the road."

Under Secretary Katzenbach agreed that the time fuse is shorter than the UN process. He noted that we are concerting with the Secretary General in order to avoid being blamed for his failure.

In response to the President's request to summarize, Mr. Battle said that we would be in touch with the Secretary General and the parties concerned over the next few days. However, we would like to get our mediator appointed and briefed quietly in order to have him ready to step in the moment he was needed.

[Here follows discussion of Vietnam.]

Harold H. Saunders

---

360. **Telegram From the Embassy in Greece to the Department of State**[1]

Athens, February 2, 1968, 1600Z.

3425. Ref: State 108450.[2]

1. In friendly, frank 35-minute session with Prime Minister Papadopoulos, following are significant points established:

2. Prime Minister warmly accepted invitation for luncheon aboard USS *Roosevelt* February 15.[3] This will include underwater operations demonstration.

---

[1] Source: Department of State, Central Files, POL GREECE–US. Secret; Priority; Exdis.

[2] Telegram 108450 to Athens, February 1, provided instructions for Talbot for his discussions with Papadopoulos. (Ibid.)

[3] In telegram 3394 from Athens, February 1, Talbot suggested an invitation to visit the U.S.S. *Roosevelt* as a means of etsablishing "a more confident relationship" with Papadopoulos. (Ibid.) The Department approved the suggestion in telegram 108612 to Athens, February 1. (Ibid.)

3. New Constitution—PriMin said expects be ready to publish new constitutional draft and announce precise date of plebiscite very soon. Decision "almost made" to publish for full public consideration and comparison texts present Constitution, Mitrelias committee's draft, and government draft based on latter. Following full discussion and possible changes suggested by local and foreign public opinion, and by US Government and/or foreign constitutional law experts if they wish, final text to be submitted to plebiscite within time period previously stated.

4. Reorganization of state machinery—progress is slow because difficult get at truth amid welter of charges against individuals—"Greek mentality has not changed." PriMin said he does not wish do injustice to individuals. However, he determined move ahead and if mistakes are made, will not hesitate rectify even though accused of retreat.

5. Resumption full military assistance—PriMin said, while he believed it unjustified, he understood how USG could afford "luxury policy" of MAP suspension prior emergence of Soviet fleet in Eastern Mediterranean. Believes USG cannot now afford such policy. Greece, he said, can be relied upon, in its geographic area, to do its full share in defense of free world but must have assistance from its friends.

6. Cyprus—No new developments, but PriMin somewhat anxious about Turkish motives concerning paragraph 4 Vance agreement. He emphasized that on basis historical evidence Turkish policy not based on sincerity. USG, he said, must advise Turks appropriately to prevent future crisis which could only help the Communists.

7. I explained and PriMin said he understood President and administration extremely busy with other matters.[4] I commented, however, on encouraging signs shown in GOG's recent progress on number matters (experimental relaxation press restrictions, signs increasing attention paid to trade unions, etc.) on which there continuing interest in US. I expressed optimism that accomplishment of various constructive steps by GOG would ease current unfavorable attitude in some sections US Congress and press, thus permitting US and Greece get back on most friendly basis established since 1947.

8. PriMin assured me he understood and would continue be completely frank and sincere in our future discussions for which he said he will always be available. He agreed that it would be mutually helpful to discuss and closely follow step-by-step progress towards GOG achievement of conditions making possible full US support. But, he said, this "step-by-step" progress should not be met by a continuing "wait-and-see" USG attitude.

---

[4] In telegram 108701 to Athens, February 1, the Department of State informed Talbot that a reply to the Papadopoulos letter was under consideration and instructed him to tell the Prime Minister, if queried, that he had no reply to date. (Ibid.)

9. Discussion ended when PriMin expressed assurance that USG could count on his government's sincere desire for frank and friendly relations and on his own friendly feelings toward me. I assured him that USG and I reciprocate the desire.

10. Believe that a good beginning was made to eliminate whatever residue might remain of Prime Minister's resentments, hurt feelings, and suspicions created after December 13. He was in affable mood, seemed genuinely pleased with visit, and made no comment on my remark at outset that I was pleased to be meeting with him under conditions and at an hour much more pleasant than the last time (January 12). He continues to be aware that Greece's earliest possible return to democracy is our desire.

Talbot

361. Telegram From the Embassy in Greece to the Department of State[1]

Athens, February 9, 1968, 1615Z.

3507. 1. FonMin Pipinelis, suffering from thrombosis incurred after strenuous recent activities and affecting his right leg, summoned British Ambassador Stewart and me to his home this noon to describe his recent secret meeting in Switzerland with Turk FonMin Caglayangil and a new initiative on Cyprus. He mentioned that he had seen Canadian Ambassador on same subject earlier today and that Caglayangil was giving similar information today to our colleagues in Ankara.[2]

2. According to Pipinelis, he and Caglayangil agreed to tackle long-term Cyprus settlement by focussing first on getting for an independent Cyprus a constitution that would be acceptable to both Greek Cypriots and Turk Cypriots. Plan they drew up calls for joint secret request to Canada to convene and chair a four-cornered conference of Greek and Turk FonMins with Makarios and Kutchuk to settle constitutional questions but not deal with other outstanding issues. Questions of

---

[1] Source: Department of State, Central Files, POL 27 CYP. Secret; Priority; Exdis. Repeated to Ankara, Nicosia, Ottawa, London, and USUN.

[2] Hart reported on his talk with Caglayangil in telegram 3742 from Ankara, February 9. (Ibid.)

Greek military personnel serving with Cypriot National Guard and of treatment of minorities in Greece and Turkey would meanwhile be dealt with under separate procedures that Pipinelis and Caglayangil also discussed.

3. Pipinelis emphasized that Canada would be asked to present conference idea as exclusively its own, and that no Cypriots would be informed of secret prior Greek-Turk understanding. He hopes Canada will see its way clear to lead this initiative despite preoccupation of government leaders with forthcoming elections. As he sees desirable scenario, approaches to Makarios and Kutchuk would be made after some days, to reduce chance of Canadian initiative being linked to rumors of Pipinelis–Caglayangil meeting, but four-way meetings would start after Cypriot elections later this month. Pipinelis believes UNSYG will welcome Canadian initiative as alternative to his own flagging efforts to exercise good offices.

4. It was improved climate following November crisis that led to his meeting with Caglayangil, Pipinelis said. Feelings had calmed down in Greece and Turkey, tenseness on island had relaxed, and on January 12 Makarios had taken constructive step of announcing plans to present a new constitution for Cyprus. However, it became apparent new storm clouds gathering and conditions might again deteriorate. Both he and Caglayangil concluded, therefore, that time had arrived for action. Caglayangil had been good enough to suggest they meet secretly, and Pipinelis had readily agreed despite his doctor's efforts to prevent him from traveling.

5. In considering next steps on Cyprus, GOG had reasoned that a final settlement would in any case be so difficult that parties must start by concentrating on what aspect most likely to succeed, or least likely to fail. With Makarios' plan to present Constitution, this had become obvious starting point. Caglayangil agreed with this reasoning, and they had no difficulty in deciding to focus on how to get a constitution for an independent Cyprus that would be agreeable to both Greek Cypriots and Turk Cypriots, leaving all other issues to be handled separately or later.

6. At first Pipinelis had proposed that constitutional talks be conducted between Greek Cypriots and Turk Cypriots under aegis of UNSYG. But Caglayangil had rejected this because of Turk distrust of U Thant. Then Pipinelis had proposed that Greek Cypriots and Turk Cypriots be stimulated to meet together by themselves. Caglayangil has found this idea unsatisfactory because "you have a strong advocate on your side and we don't on ours." Finally they reached agreement on a conference at which Turk and Greek FonMins, Makarios and Kutchuk would all sit together. Caglayangil noted that this was first time a Turkish Foreign Minister had agreed to negotiate directly with Makarios.

7. How should such a conference be convened? Pipinelis was definite that Makarios should not have reason to think this a put-up job between Greeks and Turks. Initiative would need to come from outside. After considering whether US or UK would be well situated to play this role, Pipinelis and Caglayangil had concluded it would be better for initiative to come from Canada which naturally interested and involved through UNFICYP. Thus their secret request to Canada today. Meanwhile they hope US and UK can stand ready to help as needed. In particular, they hope US and UK can encourage Makarios to see importance of proceeding carefully toward agreement with Turk Cypriots on new constitution.

8. In response to our questions, Pipinelis told Stewart and me that he and Caglayangil had also discussed question of Greek officers and noncoms with Cypriot National Guard. Caglayangil had explained pressures GOT is under to get action. Pipinelis had replied that throughout crisis he had known that this was a question Greece could not resolve without agreement of Makarios and that premature removal of leadership would leave National Guard dangerously undisciplined. However, it of little importance to Greece itself whether few military involved stay on island or return home; he would be prepared to try to get Makarios' agreement to progressive withdrawal of Greeks. GOG would prefer that in any case as soon as conditions safe and Makarios agrees, Sir Michael Stewart then told Pipinelis of Kyprianou's statement to HMG January 30 that Cypriots acknowledge GOG right to withdraw its military personnel from Cypriot National Guard, and also that Makarios wants to reduce size of National Guard. Pipinelis welcomed this news, especially as Makarios told him he would not agree to removal of Greek personnel at this stage. Pipinelis indicated he might have another try on this with Makarios after Cypriot elections.

9. Finally, Pipinelis said he and Caglayangil had agreed to establish Ambassadorial-level commission to examine each country's complaints about treatment of minority in other country. Precedent for this exists in Averoff–Zorlu agreement of 1959 that activated Bitsios–Kuneralp investigations. These had proved useful though intrusion of Cyprus crisis of that era prevented their implementation. Pipinelis thinks similar approach may help Greece and Turkey deal with complaints now being raised about difficulties experienced by Greeks in Istanbul, Imbroz and Tenedos and by Turks in Thrace.

10. *Comment:* Pipinelis was obviously pleased with results of meeting, whose accomplishments appear to have exceeded all expectations.

Pipinelis repeatedly warned us of importance of avoiding leaks.

Talbot

362.   Telegram From the Embassy in Greece to the Department of State[1]

Athens, March 2, 1968, 1428Z.

3777. Subject: Cyprus.

1.   Pipinelis expressed great satisfaction to me today that Canadian initiative now launched.[2] As Makarios had seemed ready to go to U Thant in next few days, Canadians have moved apparently just in time. Pipinelis reasonably hopeful Canadian effort will bear fruit, though he said he spends his nights worrying about what could go wrong.

2.   Pipinelis hopes Canadians can obtain not merely acquiescence from UNSYG but solid support which may become necessary to persuade Makarios to accept proposal. He hopes U.S. can also help influence Makarios. I expressed confidence that after idea surfaced we would do what we could within limits of our influence. Pipinelis commented that limited influence is everybody's problem in dealing with Makarios, most especially Greece's.

3.   Pipinelis saw no serious problem about mid-April date for first meeting, though he agreed with my expressed concern that each passing week could give more opportunities for difficulties and accidents. Pipinelis showed little concern that either Makarios or Turk Cypriots would take separate initiatives in immediate future. While Canadian proposal should give Makarios pause, Pipinelis evidently counts on his understanding with Caglayangil to hold Turk Cypriots quiet.

4.   Makarios, in Pipinelis' view, has shifted his ground now that all agree enosis not practicable and he can therefore work openly toward independent solution he has privately always favored. Pipinelis sees Makarios as clearly preparing for direct talks with Turks—either with Turk Cypriots or, in end, with Turkey itself with which he must ultimately reach agreement. This is why Canadian initiative stands a chance.

5.   Pipinelis relatively optimistic on ability of parties to reach agreement on terms for a new Cyprus Constitution. Earlier Greek-Turkish dialogue had broken down over international issues, but substantial and useful areas of agreement had nevertheless been achieved on constitutional concepts for Cyprus. These understandings, which Turkish Gov-

---

[1] Source: Department of State, Central Files, POL 27 CYP. Secret; Exdis. Repeated to Ankara and Nicosia.

[2] Canadian proposals for a quadripartite conference on Cyprus were presented to the Government of Turkey on February 29, and to the Government of Greece on March 1. (Telegrams 4186 from Ankara, March 1, and 3753 from Athens, March 1; both ibid.) A copy of the Canadian proposals was transmitted in telegram 3749 from Athens, March 1. (Ibid.) On March 1, the Canadian Government also informed the Secretary-General of its proposals and its intention to sound out the Cypriot Government. (Telegram 3999 from USUN, March 2; ibid.)

ernment had shown courage in agreeing to, are now available to be built upon.

6. Real difficulty ahead, Pipinelis feels, will be question of international guarantee of new Cyprus Constitution. He anticipates Turkey will assert continuing unilateral right of intervention as under London–Zurich treaties, although it knows this would be impossible for an independent Cypriot Government or for Greece to accept. Yet some form of international guarantee or assurance will probably be necessary. This is a void to be filled, and a question to which Pipinelis said he is giving much anxious thought.

7. Department please pass to other addressees as desired.

Talbot

---

363. **Telegram From the Embassy in Turkey to the Department of State**[1]

Ankara, March 6, 1968, 1518Z.

4269. NATUS. Subject: Canadian initiative and Ambassadorial calls on Kuchuk. Ref: State 125137, Nicosia 1437.[2]

1. News reftels that Canadian initiative has stalled while UNSYG pushes forward proposal which Turk Cypriots cannot accept at this juncture bound to be very disappointing to FonMin Caglayangil. Considerable effort which he and Pipinelis made to set up framework for negotiations whereby all parties reasonably safeguarded has now apparently come to naught although four-sided talks may be revived for future use. FonMin will be inclined blame SYG again for coolness to Canadian initiative. He may also conclude he was right when he originally told Canadian Chargé (Ankara 4048)[3] he could not agree to having SYG briefed prior to approaches to four parties to be invited.

---

[1] Source: Department of State, Central Files, POL 27 CYP. Secret; Priority; Exdis. Repeated to Athens, London, Nicosia, Ottawa, Rawalpindi, USUN, the Mission to NATO, Adana, Izmir, and Istanbul.

[2] In telegram 125137 to Ankara, March 5, the Department of State reported that the Secretary-General had formally proposed to the Makarios government a conference between the two Cypriot communities. (Ibid.) Telegram 1437 from Nicosia, March 6, reported that Canada was taking a "go slow" approach to its initiative while awaiting developments on the Secretary-General's approach. (Ibid.)

[3] Dated February 23. (Ibid.)

2.   When Caglayangil finally agreed at Turkmen's insistence, it was on condition Canadians would not put pressure on him to accept invitation to discuss matter in some sort of UN forum. Turkmen also mentioned he wanted similar assurances from US and UK but these were never actually solicited. Nevertheless, we believe US, after strong commitment to Canadian initiative, should not turn around and pressure GOT or Turk Cypriots to agree to UNSYG's proposal. Such action would sit particularly badly with Caglayangil and would weaken whatever influence we have with him. We wonder why, if SYG sent instructions to Osorio-Tafall Feb 29 (Nicosia 1437), he could not have openly so informed Canadian PermRep Ignatieff during meeting Mar 1 (USUN 3999).[4]

3.   We have carefully considered whether this might not be good time for resuming Ambassadorial calls on Kuchuk. Following are factors in favor:

A.   Ambassadorial call would help us out in Ankara while FonMin digesting bad news on Canadian initiative.
B.   It would closely follow UN Rep Tafall's call on Kuchuk and could therefore be regarded as inquiring into Turk Cypriot views on and responses to Tafall's proposal.
C.   London 6939[5] suggests FonOff embarrassed by extent of delay in resuming calls.
D.   Excuses for not calling are running thin. First, we tried some kind of language to effect we do not accept legality of TCPA or recognize them as government (Nicosia 1143).[6] Secondly, we explored possibility of maximum numbers of Chiefs of Mission defying ban (Nicosia 1194).[7] Thirdly, we decided to wait until after Presidential elections. Fourthly, we waited until Canadian initiative launched in order to give it major support. Re Nicosia 1434[8] we do not feel we should wait until UNSC meeting.

4.   Factors against Ambassadorial call seem to rest on fear that possible consequences may be (A) PNG action or (B) deep-freeze treatment. Since calls at this time after considerable delay would not appear as challenging to Makarios' authority as in January, we wonder whether possibility of PNG action is not now reduced. On other hand, given SYG coolness to any outside initiatives while he still active in field, we think it may be some time before Canadian or other initiative can be started up

---

[4] See footnote 2, Document 362.

[5] Dated March 5. (Department of State, Central Files, POL 17 CYP)

[6] Telegram 1143 from Nicosia, January 12, described the instructions that U.K. High Commissioner Costar had been authorized to present to the Cypriot Government to deal with the issue of Ambassadorial meetings with Turkish Cypriot representatives. (Ibid., POL 17 US–CYP)

[7] Dated January 19. (Ibid.)

[8] Not found.

again. In other words, deep-freeze treatment may not affect US contacts with Greek Cypriots as long and as adversely as once feared.

5.   We therefore suggest taking another and urgent look at problem of Ambassadorial calls. Voluntary issuance of disclaimer of recognition of TCPA might soften Makarios' retaliation, if any.

Hart

---

364.   **Telegram From the Department of State to the Embassy in Cyprus**[1]

Washington, March 8, 1968, 2259Z.

127157. NATUS. Subject: Cyprus: Renewal of Ambassadorial Contacts with Turkish Cypriots.

1.   Department believes interval between Makarios' lifting of restrictions on Nicosia Triangle and forthcoming Security Council meeting offers most propitious occasion we have yet seen for renewing ambassadorial contacts with Kuchuk. Although intelligence reports from CAS and British indicate that Makarios intends maintain ban on such contacts, appears doubtful he could take strong stand after announcing restoration of Turkish Cypriots' freedom of movement and while in need support in SC. Furthermore, it can be argued strongly that ambassadorial contacts at this point would be strong asset in getting discussions started with Turkish Cypriots on constitutional proposals. Additional point might be made that restrictions on Turkish Cypriots in Nicosia were maintained in January when restrictions elsewhere lifted because of formation of TCPA and logically lifting of ban on contacts, which also was response to establishment of TCPA, should be lifted in parallel.

2.   In addition, UK concerned that French and Italians may break ban before UK, which might prove embarrassing to British relations with GOT, and US in similar awkward position having attempted persuade other governments join in breaking ban.

---

[1] Source: Department of State, Central Files, POL 17 CYP. Secret; Immediate. Drafted by Folsom and McFarland; cleared in NEA, L, and IO; and approved by Battle. Repeated to Ankara, Athens, London, Ottawa, USUN, the Mission to NATO, Stockholm, The Hague, and Rawalpindi for Rockwell.

3. You therefore authorized to pay call on Kuchuk as soon as possible next week after call on Makarios per following para. You should do so in concert with your British, Italian, French and any other colleagues who may be able participate. You should also notify Pakistani, Dutch and Swedish Ambassadors through AmEmbassy Beirut re timing of call.

4. As preparatory step you should convey intentions to GOC, preferably Makarios if he available. We hope you can do this March 11 or at latest March 12 followed immediately thereafter by call on Kuchuk. In addition to explanatory statements outlined in State 109671,[2] which you may use at your discretion, you should take occasion express USG gratification over Makarios' lifting of restrictions on Nicosia Triangle and his expressed intention settle Cyprus dispute peacefully, as we have long advocated. Improved atmosphere should enhance chances for talks. If US support for peaceful settlement is to be effective, we consider it essential that Ambassadorial contacts with Turkish Cypriots be renewed. Last two sentences para 1 above may also be drawn upon. You may add that it should be clear from our cooperation since first of year, when ban on contacts was announced, that we have not wished embarrass Archbishop or take any step that would endanger our good relations. We hope that he will understand and concur with the reasons behind our desire to reestablish contacts with Turkish Cypriots.

5. Foregoing based on assumption per Nicosia 1299[3] that action outlined above would not result in your becoming PNG. If you believe this assumption incorrect, notify Department before proceeding consultation your colleagues per para 3.[4]

Rusk

---

[2] Telegram 109671, February 3, reported that the British Government felt it might be too far out front in its presentation to Makarios on the issue of Ambassadorial contacts, and stated that the Department of State shared these views. (Ibid., POL 18 CYP)

[3] Dated February 9. (Ibid.)

[4] Telegram 1439 from Nicosia, March 8, reported that the Cypriot Government had lifted all restrictions on contacts by Ambassadors except meetings with Kuchuk. (Department of State, Central Files, POL 27 CYP) In telegram 1454 from Nicosia, March 9, Belcher reported he had again pressed Kyprianou regarding the ban and was consulting with his Canadian and British colleagues. (Ibid., POL 17 CYP)

365.   Telegram From the Embassy in Greece to the Department of State[1]

Athens, March 27, 1968, 1747Z.

4087. Subject: US policy toward Greece. Ref: State 133784.[2]

Summary: In strategic terms I believe we have been on right track with Greece since April 1967 in emphasizing importance of return to constitutionality and representative government. Moreover, given US interests in Greece, absence of acceptable alternative to present regime, and our incapacity to legislate Greece's future, I see no practical alternative, barring accidents, to continuing on same course for at least next six months or so. If this is accepted, our current policy problems are primarily tactical. Here I recommend that we (1) release immediately certain selected defensive and training items on MAP suspension list, with further time-phased releases programmed for (A) June (provided GOG then publishes its own constitutional draft in reasonably acceptable form), (B) September (if plebiscite successful), and (C) as quickly thereafter as we can be confident of early implementation of Constitution, and (2) promptly open discussions with GOG on FY 68 MAP allocations and FY 69–FY 73 planning figures. If political process goes reasonably satisfactorily, MAP relationship could be fully restored before end of 1968, which in any case is probably earliest practical timing. In event of impasse or breakdown, MAP deliveries could if necessary be stopped again at any point. *End summary.*

1.   Looking ahead in Greece has rarely been easy but hardly ever more difficult than now. Malaise, as Department observes, currently characterizes both regime and wider public opinion. Strains within revolutionary group arise from growing awareness that it has achieved no glowing public success since its dramatic seizure of power, that its administrative inexperience and ineptness are now generally perceived, and that its continuing preoccupation with vigorous security measures, however necessary in its own view, is proving detrimental to constructive programs and to public support. Public opinion is also influenced by current economic downturn (not wholly or perhaps even largely ascribable to Junta policies, though general malaise is a factor), and by expressions of hopes (by lower-ranking Junta members) or of fears (by opponents) that present "national government" will cling to power indefinitely. To extent any or all these trends may strengthen in coming months, strains will also mount.

---

[1] Source: Department of State, Central Files, POL 1 GREECE–US. Secret; Priority; Limdis. Repeated to EUCOM.

[2] Dated March 21. (Ibid.)

2. In these circumstances we sense Papadopoulos may not yet see his future course clearly, while facing challenges by Junta "hard-liners" that he is not being sufficiently firm and revolutionary. Their spokesmen frankly press for long-term authoritarianism and no nonsense about return to traditional politics. Outside government and army we detect little strong enthusiasm for this military-based regime, though number of big businessmen continue in vanguard of its support. We hear considerable though still disorganized and quietly voiced opposition, none of which it should be noted surfaced during November Cyprus crisis or King's countercoup. Most widespread reaction, however, seems still to be acquiescence by people who are either apathetic, or want to keep their heads down or, for lack of better solution and out of distaste for conditions before last April, are prepared to give regime more time to make discernible progress. Predictably, many Greeks seem to feel that in end Uncle Sam can be counted on to take lead in efforts to oust Junta.

3. At present our Greek contacts perceive no realistic alternative to present regime. Nor do we. Certainly neither King nor Caramanlis, Papandreous, or any other former political leader now commands assets necessary to re-establish leadership. Nor, so far as we can tell, are people now in mood to generate new civil war. While another military coup is conceivable either through split in present Junta or by group outside it, we have no evidence that a successful move of this kind is in offing; and another abortive attempt would have adverse effect of playing into hands of Junta hard-liners, whose reaction would be recourse to further authoritarianism and stricter security controls over populace.

4. It follows that I, for one, view with extreme skepticism risky thesis explicit in Andreas Papandreou's position that if all US support were withdrawn and regime ostracized it would "collapse of its own weight." Were we to act on basis of such an assumption I fear reaction, on contrary, would be one of intransigence, inverted nationalism and ascendancy of radical faction in Junta which would result in increased authoritarianism, worse image abroad, greater divisiveness of Greek issue in NATO and possible jeopardy to our important bilateral military facilities here. Even if, as [garble—contended?] by Junta's opponents, ultimate outcome of such a process would be present regime's downfall, time it would take to produce such a result is unpredictable and process would bring probable danger of civil strife before that corner could be turned. These considerations argue strongly in my mind against adoption of such a policy, especially at this stage when we do not yet know how far it may prove possible to push regime toward a return to more democratic ways or to enmesh it sufficiently in process so it will be unable to retain present degree of authoritarian control.

5. We face possibility that Junta under influence of hard-liners may in fact be pursuing constitutional process fraudulently and with design

mainly of misleading US and international opinion and masking under-lying aim of prolonging its exclusive hold on power. I see no way at present to guarantee against this possibility, which is what politicians fear. However, waiting for elimination of any chance of it before we make any responsive gesture to constitutional steps already taken would in my opinion be course most likely to bring result we least desire. Specifically, with reference to points raised in para 4 of reftel, continued frustration of regime over US failure to lift any of MAP restrictions could, in our estimate, have following adverse consequences: (1) strengthen hand of radical elements in Junta and thus slow down return to constitutionalism and reinforce authoritarian tendencies; (2) stimulate nascent GOG inclinations to look elsewhere—France, for instance—for military equipment, with attendant disruption of standardization criteria and probable prejudice to military efficiency and pro-American orientation of Greek armed forces, and (3) lead GOG to re-examine extensive military and VOA facilities rights it grants US (and continued to extend in highly cooperative fashion, it should be recalled, during 1967 ME crisis) and possibly to curtail those rights.

6. On other hand, adoption of even an imperfect constitution (comparable, perhaps, to Turkish Constitution of 1961) would be more likely to initiate process of return to greater measure of representative rule. Once a Constitution—indeed almost any Constitution not patently unacceptable—is adopted by plebiscite, I believe external and internal pressures are likely to build up on regime to permit its entry into force in reasonable period (12 to 18 months at the outside). If September constitutional draft should contain provision postponing application for two or more years while regime continued pursue unrealistic or unacceptable revolutionary goals, government would run risk of its rejection. We would in any case be afforded a further legitimate opportunity to put pressure on regime to get on faster with important business of return to constitutionalism.

7. As to what new advice and guidance we might give, I am not as sanguine as Iakovos and Pappas that Revolutionary Committee as whole is yet ready to listen to foreign counsel[3] though Papadopoulos might consider suggestions within limits. In next few months country's course will be importantly shaped by progress or failure along road to constitutionalism, economic betterment, and relations with Turkey. In my view most pressing problems for GOG now are (A) how to attract broader and higher range of skills to improve governmental performance and thus give flexibility and success image which are prerequisites for a transition to parliamentary rule; and (B) a political plan to find

---

[3] The Department of State reported on the views of Iakovos and Pappas in telegram 133260 to Athens, March 20. (Department of State, Central Files, POL 15 GREECE)

the exit gate from present narrowly-based governmental structure. New Constitution will presumably provide formalities of transition but, realistically, substance of transition is likely to be accomplished only when Junta has fixed upon its own future course from among several current possibilities. It could establish its own political organization with intention of contesting and presumably winning first elections, find strong civilian front man or group from behind which it could continue for some time to exercise real power (as happened in Turkey after 1961), or seek some other resolution of its obsessive determination not to turn country back to "same old corrupt politicians" who ran it before 1967. To extent we can contribute wisdom in solving these real issues of present regime, our advice could be welcomed.

8.   I sense that most leading Greek politicians have concluded they cannot afford to jeopardize their own future prospects by collaborating with present rulers. At least some realists among them, however, also hope Junta can be pressed by others to put forward for adoption a Constitution under which political life can be reactivated. To put it bluntly, they don't want to dirty their own hands by dealing with Junta but expect us to do whatever necessary to get show back on road. In past week such personalities as Papaligouras and Mavros have virtually admitted this to me even though they would not say so publicly. On other hand, the only political figures so far willing to help in this effort are asking extremely stiff price of Junta. Markezinis and Tsouderos, for example, have indicated willingness to join present government on condition they be given complete control of economic policy. Papadopoulos has not bought these terms. In these circumstances we have little choice but to follow policies dictated essentially by our own conception of what would be best for Greece and our own interests.

9.   On this question essential ingredients, as General Burchinal has put them, are solid and determined NATO membership on eastern flank and comparatively unrestricted availability of bases and facilities in support of US unilateral requirements in Eastern Mediterranean. These goals include further progress on encouraging beginning GOG has made in improving bilateral relations with Turkey and moving toward resolutions of Cyprus problem. Moreover, it is essential to pull Greece along to political posture with which other NATO countries can live. We have even more basic interest in attempting to prevent breakdown of Greek polity with all adverse consequences that would follow.

10. As I have suggested, in my view this means we must deal with present regime, supporting and focusing on its relatively responsible elements, and give it encouragement and not just lectures to get back on constitutional track. Therefore, I believe it is important for USG to make concrete move in acknowledgment of progress to date in constitutional process. First part of two-fold action should be to begin unfreezing MAP

suspension lists, starting with clearly defensive and training items, and to resume carefully time phased delivery MAP items. Current Soviet buildup in Mediterranean makes minesweeper natural initial candidate for early delivery. This could be justified on basis NATO requirement without increasing regime's capability in internal security. Training and transport planes would also have high priority. Then in June and September other items could be released. Presumably such lead time would be required under normal circumstances to deliver suspended items. By end CY 68, if all goes well, I would hope we could be past outdated posture of using selected restraints on MAP deliveries as tactic to achieve long-range political purposes. If things go badly, deliveries could again be interrupted.

11. Having taken this initial step, the second action which should be almost simultaneous would be to initiate discussion on FY 68 MAP and this year's 5-year planning exercise based on mix of grant aid and cash and credit sales. In discussing FY 68 program with GOG, we could make certain assumptions on lifting of all suspended items in current program. My advisors tell me very little time remains to meet current year deadlines. I believe it is therefore essential that we move promptly on this second action.

12. In my judgment course outlined above, while it does not guarantee success, represents most promising policy line available to USG for constructively influencing Greek situation in its present parlous condition. On basis recommended decisions USG and Embassy could safely lean harder on GOG than if we abstain from gestures responding to constitutional steps already taken.[4]

Talbot

---

[4] In a March 29 letter thanking Talbot for this analysis, Brewster reported that the question of resuming MAP aid to Greece had not yet been resolved. (Ibid., Greek Desk Files: Lot 71 D 6, Correspondence to and from Athens)

366.   Memorandum of Conversations[1]

London, April 22, 1968, 7:30 a.m. and 6 p.m.

SUBJECT

United States-Greek Relations

PARTICIPANTS

Under Secretary Katzenbach
Assistant Secretary Battle
Ambassador Phillips Talbot
Mr. Daniel Brewster
Mr. Laurence Eagleburger
Mr. Sidney Sober

Ambassador Talbot began by speaking of the recent SIG action[2] stating that the release of certain selected military items would be most helpful. He then sketched in recent developments in Greece including the government's action remitting agricultural debts, noting that the regime was obviously trying to curry favor with the farmer. It is conceivable that the Greek Government might be looking to a Peron-type situation basing itself on farm-labor support. He also noted that American Church-World Service representatives, who had been working with this Greek Government and previous ones considered this one, in fact, quite efficient. They also believed the Greek in the countryside was fairly well satisfied with his present lot.

Mr. Battle asked whether the business community and the "establishment" was not being affected by the Greek Government's rather spasmodic actions, particularly in the economic field. Ambassador Talbot replied affirmatively stating that the businessman is maintaining a "wait and see" stance and is annoyed with some of the government's more stupid actions. Even though the economy is in a "slow-down period", the government has moved effectively to collect taxes and direct tax receipts have been stepped up by 47% as against a year ago.

The Under Secretary asked what pressures there were internally on the Greek Government to return to political normalcy. Ambassador Talbot replied no effective pressures—basically those at work came from the outside world. He and the British Ambassador were the only two NATO representatives in Greece who were really pressing the Greek Government in the direction of Constitutionalism.

---

[1] Source: Department of State, Central Files, POL GREECE–US. Secret; Limdis. Drafted by Brewster and approved in U on May 16. The meetings were held in the U.S. Embassy.

[2] On April 16, the Senior Interdepartmental Group (SIG) reaffirmed its recommendations for resuming limited military assistance to Greece. Documentation relating to the SIG decision is ibid., SIG Files: Lot 74 D 265, SIG Memo 58 and SIG/RA.

Mr. Battle asked whether the proposed release of the military items listed in the SIG paper would make the Greek Government think that it could get away with less forward motion toward normalization. Ambassador Talbot replied "no". In his view they had not as yet settled in their own minds on the Constitutional question and the next two months were all important. It was during this time that our influence would be most meaningful, that is, while they were shaping their Constitutional thoughts. The Greek regime recognizes that it needs the West but at the same time is examining alternatives. It could also tighten up on the many privileges which the United States enjoys as, for example, the rights of overflight without advance clearance. The Government could generally take on a posture more like the present Turkish stance.

The Under Secretary said the problem he sees in the Greek situation is that the Greek regime is not interested in making genuine progress toward Constitutionalism. They may be prepared to say they are taking actions for the purpose of a facade, but we want to make sure that it is *their* facade not ours.

Mr. Battle, returning to the question of the timing of the release of certain selected MAP items, asked whether the best timing would be between now and June or between June and September. Ambassador Talbot said definitely between now and June.

Ambassador Talbot then spoke of two contingencies which (although considered remote by his colleagues) might call for a rapid decision as to a United States posture.

1. A take-over by the junior military.
2. A countercoup by senior military with possible participation of former politicians. Ambassador Talbot could foresee a situation where we would be called upon for help.

Mr. Battle responded by saying that we would have to look at the situation at the time, analyzing the composition of the group which was supporting the coup and those who were carrying it out, we would need to weigh carefully its chances of success, and its general acceptability to the Greek people. It was not possible to make any advance commitment.

Ambassador Talbot then described briefly three groups which might attempt to join forces to achieve a transitional changeover.

1. Karamanlis, former Prime Minister, plus ERE elements, the "apostate group" led by Stephanopoulos, and moderate Center Union elements.
2. Another group might include certain non-political "establishment" types, such as Professor Zolotas, former head of the Bank of Greece, Lambrakis, newspaper owner, and a variety of younger men including some former politicians.
3. A left-of-center group including from Andreas Papandreou to the far left. None of these groups are very far along with any planning or coordination of their efforts.

In response to questions as to whether a release of selected MAP items would deflect anti-junta planning by any of the political leaders, Ambassador Talbot thought it would not since the men recognized that the resumption of the shipment of selected MAP items was designed by the USG to press the Greek regime back to Constitutionalism.

The Under Secretary asked why Greek political figures (George Papandreou and Kanellopoulos) were boycotting the Greek regime's efforts to draw up a new Constitution. Ambassador Talbot replied that this stance on their part grew out of the fact that they as politicians could not afford to be associated in any way with the Greek regime's actions.

Finally, Ambassador Talbot raised the question of how active he should be in prodding the Greek Government. The Under Secretary responded that we should continue to push them privately and quietly, but not publicly. Mr. Battle pointed out that Ambassador Talbot could use the same theme he had used with the Greek Ambassador, namely that reestablishment of the traditional warmth in US-Greek relations would depend on the return to normal democratic processes.

In a second session at 6:30 p.m. April 22 (with all participants present except Mr. Sober) the question was raised by Ambassador Talbot as to the value we placed on Greece for the special facilities it offered. He also asked whether it was likely that we would be placing increased demands on the Greek regime for facilities as a result of any possible Turkish phasing-out of military installations. It was stated that on the basis of Ambassador Hart's assessment concerning facilities in Turkey there would be no call at present to absorb further DOD requirements in Greece. In this connection the Under Secretary requested that a memorandum be drafted to the Defense Department asking how valuable and irreplaceable the present DOD installations were in Greece.

There followed a general discussion on the contribution made by the Greek regime to a settlement of the Cyprus problem last fall and to an improvement in Greek-Turk relations.

Speaking of future MAP the Under Secretary noted the problems involved in anticipating the levels of 1969 MAP on a worldwide basis and determining what portion of the Military Assistance Program specifically be allocated to Greece. He thought Ambassador Talbot, on returning to Athens, should give the Greek regime a rather frank assessment of the mood in the United States. He should urge them to continue on the road back to political normalcy but not to the point where it would bring about a major crisis.

Speaking of the house arrest of the two former Prime Ministers[3] and the fact that forward motion on the release of selected MAP items in

---

[3] On April 15, Kanellopoulos and Papandreou were arrested for "excessive" political activity.

accord with the SIG decision was related to lifting this restriction, the Under Secretary stated that without instructing the Greek regime to release these two men, the Ambassador could describe the domestic problem created for us, both in Congress and with public opinion, by their continued detention.

367.   Telegram From the Embassy in Cyprus to the Department of State[1]

Nicosia, May 6, 1968, 1326Z.

1730. Subject: Cyprus: Local talks. Ref: State 158278.[2]

1.   We have previously reported abundant evidence that Turks at least considering implementation of some separatist projects. Nicosia's 1409, 1414 and 1615[3] spell out reasons for our suspicions about air-sea links with Turkey, development of economic autarchy and establishment of separate Turkish Cypriot government. In fact, TCPA itself could be regarded as first step in separatist movement.

2.   More recently we would cite following as casting further doubt on Turk-Turk Cypriot "good faith" regarding compromise solution to Cyprus problem:

A.   Fact that Turks have not made even minor reciprocal move in areas of normalization and military disengagement in spite of real concessions by Greeks (removal of 7,000 illegals) and Greek Cypriots (lifting economic and travel restrictions and limited withdrawal of National Guard from certain areas);

B.   Manner in which GOT torpedoed UNFICYP efforts establish verification procedures in response GOT request (Nicosia's 1710 and 1716);[4]

---

[1] Source: Department of State, Central Files, POL 27 CYP. Secret; Noforn. Repeated to Athens, Ankara, London, Ottawa, the Mission to NATO, and USUN.

[2] Telegram 158278 to Nicosia, May 3, expressed Department of State concern about the disagreement over venue and requested further information on factors motivating the Turkish Cypriot stand. (Ibid.)

[3] Telegram 1409 from Nicosia, February 28, expressed concern that future moves by the Turkish Cypriot community might heighten tensions on the island. (Ibid.) Telegram 1414 from Nicosia, March 1, reported increasing signs that the Turkish Cypriots would form an independent administration. (Ibid.) Telegram 1615 from Nicosia, April 13, reported that Turkish Cypriot radio was signaling a hardening of position by Denktash. (Ibid.)

[4] Telegram 1710 has not been found. Telegram 1716 from Nicosia, May 3, reported Turkish Cypriot demands that UNFICYP verify that Greek nationals were separated from the Cypriot National Guard. (Ibid.)

C. Statement made last week by Denktash to officers of UK HIGH-COM that Legislative Council of TCPA would soon have to meet to "formulate" regulations on certain matters (which is bound to elicit agonized howl from GOC and to be regarded as another step on way to provisional Turk Cypriot government); and

D. Withdrawal last Tuesday morning of compromise offer on venue made Saturday by Turk Cypriot leadership (on basis of timing and Bulak's statement—Ankara 5577[5]—it appears withdrawal ordered by Ankara).

3. *Comment:* We feel question not so much one of determining "Turkish intentions regarding Cyprus talks" but one of determining Turk Cypriot-Turkish intentions regarding entire Cyprus problem. Key to latter question is, of course, GOT. In this connection our analyses of GOT intentions must necessarily be speculative. What might be done of positive nature is for USG to clarify views (by calling in Esenbel and by démarche in Ankara) to point out that we opposed to unilateral moves by either side that would worsen situation; that we feel it now up to Turks to make some positive response in areas of normalization (UK took such action when Stewart saw Caglayangil in London—London 8477),[6] and that we hope GOT will be able to accept some form of compromise on venue problem.

4. We see much to be gained by telling GOT officially of our interest in and views on current developments in Cyprus dispute and specifically our belief that time is ripe for positive reciprocal action by Turks-Turk Cypriots. Makarios has little room left for unilateral compromises. In Saturday speech he struck pessimistic tone by commenting that prospects for talks not bright and that, although door for talks open as far as Greek side concerned, "frequent recent Turkish statements do not permit great margins of optimism." In addition, hints are beginning to creep into Greek Cypriot press that because of Turk intransigence perhaps best policy for GOC is return to confrontation with Greece's help.

5. To regain momentum lost in past ten days we believe reciprocal move by Turks in areas of normalization, as well as willingness by both sides to compromise on venue seem necessary.[7]

Smith

---

[5] Telegram 5577 from Ankara, May 2, reported apparent Turkish willingness to consider Cyprus as a venue for later intercommunal talks. (Ibid.)

[6] Telegram 8477 from London, April 26, reported British suggestions for use of Beirut as a venue for talks. (Ibid.)

[7] Representatives of the Greek and Turkish Cypriot communities met on May 21 at a Nicosia dinner party hosted by Osorio-Tafall. This meeting initiated the intercommunal talks. The Embassy in Nicosia reported on the meeting in telegram 1825, May 22. (Ibid.) Formal talks began in Nicosia on June 24.

368.   Telegram From the Department of State to the Embassy in Turkey[1]

Ankara, June 17, 1968, 2005Z.

184458. Subject: Cyprus: Turkish Economic Aid. Ref: Nicosia 1939.[2]

1. In light of Makarios' comments on GOT economic aid to Turkish Cypriots (reftel), it seems evident that initiation of aid program which GOT reportedly now considering could, if not handled carefully, have effect comparable to that produced by last December's sudden announcement of Turkish Cypriot Provisional Administration.

2. Believe would be wise precaution if Embassy could find opportunity to note to FonOff need for handling aid issue so as to preserve climate of confidence necessary for success of communal talks. Aware as we are of Greek Cypriot misgivings about objectives of aid, we hope that if GOT decides initiate economic aid program in Turkish Cypriot community it will inform GOC well in advance of public announcement and will make sure that GOC has full and correct understanding of purpose of aid.

3. We will seek opportunity make same point with Turkish Embassy after you have approached FonOff.

4. If approached on possible US economic aid for Turkish Cypriots, Embassy should offer no encouragement. We have consistently turned down such proposals for several years. Embassy may point out that we no longer give aid to Cyprus; if we did, it would have to be on government-to-government basis; and aid funds are now more severely restricted than ever.[3]

Rusk

---

[1] Source: Department of State, Central Files, POL 27 CYP. Confidential. Drafted by McFarland; cleared by NEA, IO, AID, and L; and approved by Rockwell. Repeated to Athens, London, Nicosia, Ottawa, the Mission to NATO, and USUN.

[2] Telegram 1939 from Nicosia, June 11, reported that Makarios had told U.S. representatives that he was willing to accept a Turkish aid program as long as it was not employed to encourage separatist tendencies. (Ibid.)

[3] In telegram 6704 from Ankara, June 19, the Embassy reported it had sounded out the Turkish Foreign Ministry on the issue of economic assistance prior to the receipt of telegram 184485 and had been informed that no problems had arisen when this plan was announced to the Greek Cypriots. (Ibid.)

369.   Telegram From the Embassy in Cyprus to the Department of State[1]

Nicosia, August 2, 1968, 1050Z.

2175. Subj: Cyprus: local talks and policy planning.

1.   Month-long break in local talks provides respite from rather frenetic pace of diplomatic activity maintained since last crisis, as well as opportunity for assessment of current situation and potentialities for further progress or new problems. Our starting point is same as it was in our immediate post-crisis analyses. In words of Yost report:[2] "... Unless and until long-term settlement (of Cyprus problem) is reached recurrence of ... crisis very likely; and ... if it recurs, war can probably not be avoided." Essential validity of this judgment should not be obscured by progress made in solving Cyprus problem since December 1967.

2.   After four years of immobility punctuated by periodic, bloody crises present 30-day hiatus in local talks permits leaders (and publics) of both communities to digest several new departures of past six months. In our view maneuvering starting in January and extending through first phase of local talks boils down to following:

A.   For all practical purposes Greek Cypriots have put aside enosis and Turk Cypriots have done likewise with partition. Both sides approaching problem on basis of independent Cyprus.

B.   In spite of real progress in normalization by Greeks and concessions by Turks in local talks, neither side has seriously compromised basic position designed to achieve equally basic goal. Greeks want power to determine destiny of independent Cyprus commensurate with their numerical and economic power. This they view as best achieved by unitary state responsive through new Constitution to will of majority. Turks want security of life and property which they feel best protected by (a) substantial autonomy in areas presently under their control plus (b) some form of background safeguarding role for GOT. Unilateral normalization measures instituted by GOC, although seemingly compromise, actually reinforced their position because to degree integrity of Turkish enclaves lessened by Turks coming out (or Greeks going in), by economic integration, etc., unitary state strnegthened. Only known Greek concession in talks is GOC agreement to pay same per capita amount for education of Turkish children as for Greek. This likewise strengthens unitary concept. By same token Denktash has offered to accept representation based on population (20 percent) for Turks in organs of government and

---

[1] Source: Department of State, Central Files, POL 27 CYP. Secret. Repeated to Ankara, Athens, London, USUN, Ottawa, and the Mission to NATO.

[2] See footnote 3, Document 358.

to relinquish right of veto in tax matters. However, neither concession impinges on concept of local autonomy.

C. Both Clerides and Denktash negotiating in good faith, though each trying to "get the most" for own side, to satisfy respective leaderships, to find a formula that will both work and be acceptable to public opinion of their respective communities. Each shows sympathetic understanding of problems other has with own communal leadership. Nevertheless negative pressures are great and increasing. However, negotiating position of both sides protected by fact that both have made it clear all compromises are contingent upon, indeed dependent upon, construction of "over-all agreement" including external guarantees of some sort.

D. UNSYG Special Rep Osorio-Tafall playing active (but still discreet) role by feeding compromise ideas into talks through his contacts with Makarios and Clerides.

E. Emphasis on "over-all agreement" has activated link between internal problems bilaterally solved and external problems to be solved by multilateral international accords.

3. Problems—We see following problems representing real block to further progress:

A. Loss of momentum—Momentum generated by November crisis—which has been a primary factor in bringing us to satisfactory conclusion of first phase of local talks—appears rapidly dissipating. We detect distressing signs of complacency in some Greek quarters. Certain Greek hardliners taking position they can afford to be firm in negotiations because economic and political factors operating in their favor, i.e., economic depression of enclaves and eventual necessity of Turks having to integrate economically with rest of island. (We suspect Makarios espouses this view.) Turk counterparts genuinely fearing erosion relative security they now enjoy argue they should stick to hard position in local talks, defend integrity of enclaves, and build economic and administrative separateness of their areas.

B. Constitutional differences—against this background of decreasing positive momentum real differences in substance must be considered. Two sides have arrived at point in local talks where they must begin to bargain on fundamentals if significant progress to continue. In pursuing goal of security Turks want autonomy, i.e., administrative and police control, in areas they now hold exclusively. Greeks in striving for unitary state prefer smaller Turkish administrative units based on towns and villages with less autonomy under centralized control. They emphasize common electoral rolls, elimination of executive veto, have suggested elimination of office of Vice President and other elements designed prevent Turks from obstructing responsiveness of government to will of Greek majority. Disposition of National Guard and TMT and related question of general disarming of population also obvious major unsolved problems.

C. Guarantees—International factor—in addition to problems of restructuring Cyprus state, both Clerides and Denktash have stated everything dependent on "over-all agreement." In short, hoped-for new constitutional arrangements will not go into operation until agreement reached on external aspects of problem, namely, for Turk Cypriots, some "adequate" provision for their security and for GOC elimination of GOT's claimed right of unilateral intervention.

D. Compensation—Agreement on reparations for losses suffered (principally by Turks), and how they will be financed is another knotty unresolved problem area.

E. Timing—Finally, question of timing is crucial. Most important dimension concerns position of Denktash in Turk Cypriot community. He is now at height of popularity and influence and is apparently strongly backed by Ankara and GOT Embassy here. Moreover, we feel Denktash has will to compromise, imagination to find ways and means to compromise and courage and position to push compromises with Kuchuk, GOT and Turk Cypriot community. However, longer local talks drag on, more subject he is to attack by hawks in own community and more his now practically unchalleneged position will be undermined. Already Turk Cypriot dailies *Bozkurt* and *Zafer* are challenging Denktash position by opposing in advance compromises he must make and by questioning usefulness of talks. Denktash has commented to us on opposition to him in TCPA and his method so far of dealing with it (Nicosia 2169).[3] Turkish Embassy (Nicosia 2142)[4] has also expressed concern about time element in connection with Denktash's leadership role. Other aspects of timing problem involve internal situations in Greece and Turkey. In former case, regardless of views about colonels' regime, appears to us here reintroduction parliamentary regime would in all probability mean Cyprus would become political football it formerly was. Basically, GOG is—at least for time being—out of Cyprus equation. Old-line politicians, if they return to power, might well bring Greece back into it. In case of Turkey federal elections are scheduled for 1969. It would seem almost inevitable that opposition will use Cyprus to berate present government if matter still unsettled when elections occur.

4. Recommendations—Given our analysis of problems remaining in current situation, potential which exists for failure of local talks, probably followed by swift deterioration of Cyprus problem, and limited time available to promote successful outcome of promising develop-

---

[3] Dated August 1. (Department of State, Central Files, POL 15–1 CYP)

[4] Dated July 26. (Ibid., POL 27 CYP)

ments to date, we raise following policy recommendations for consideration by Department and interested colleagues:

A. That Embassy Nicosia emphasize to GOC contacts at all levels our view that normalization by Turk Cypriots, disposition of Turkish contingent (see NKI 170 and 173),[5] and questions of guarantees are all linked to concessions by GOC on degree of autonomy Turk Cypriots will be given in restructured Cyprus state. As stressed by Denktash, the greater the degree of autonomy achieved by Turk Cypriots, more concessions they will make on normalization and guarantees.

B. That USG as appropriate encourage maintenance of GOG–GOT and GOC–GOT contacts on external aspects of Cyprus problem which so closely linked to internal problems. Progress on external problems such as contingents and guarantees could lead to progress in local talks as well as vice versa.

C. That USG join with Brits in effort to use December mandate renewal to maintain pressure on GOC and Turk Cypriots–GOT to compromise, e.g., by limiting mandate renewal to 3 months and joining other contributors in supporting further troop reductions (Osorio currently favors three-month renewal and further 25 percent troop reduction).

D. That Embassy Nicosia join at an appropriate time (probably sometime in second phase of talks this fall) with Osorio-Tafall in pushing for demilitarization, e.g., further deconfrontation and rundown of troop strength of National Guard and TMT.[6]

Belcher

---

[5] Not found.

[6] In telegram 216212 to Nicosia, August 6, the Department of State approved limited contacts to support the peacemaking process, commenting that it believed the most useful aid the United States could provide would be advice to the parties about the factors affecting the opposite parties' bargaining stance. (Department of State, Central Files, POL 27 CYP)

---

370.   **Telegram From the Embassy in Greece to the Department of State[1]**

Athens, September 19, 1968, 1440Z.

7008. Subject: Reappraisal of constitutional referendum. Ref: Athens 6963.[2]

---

[1] Source: Department of State, Central Files, POL 15–5 GREECE. Confidential.

[2] Telegram 6963 from Athens, September 16, reported Papadopoulos' statements at a press conference announcing the release of a new draft Constitution. (Ibid.)

1.   Embassy believes draft constitutional revisions announced Sept 16 are less important substantively than in their confirmation of emerging harder line of regime policies. Prime example is revision of Article 138. Earlier imprecise wording had given regime ample scope to control pace of return to full constitutionality. New formula, by specifying key articles that will not come into effect until government so decides, confronts Greek voters with Hobson's choice. Rejection of Constitution would put aside any early hope of getting constitutional rule. On other hand, acceptance of this Constitution now will mean explicitly approving regime as sole arbiter of dates when Greeks can once more have constitutionally-protected civil rights, political parties and elections. In other words, regime can claim affirmative plebiscite result (which we believe to be virtually certain) as public mandate to continue government in present authoritarian form under state of siege as long as government itself believes this necessary.

2.   As expected, many people here see revised draft, plus Prime Minister's explanatory remarks, as further strong evidence of military regime's unwillingness to relinquish power for indefinite period and that as a consequence constitutional referendum will be meaningless.

3.   Realistically, any prospect of forward movement after plebiscite depends mainly on appraisal by Papadopoulos and his colleagues that this is least disadvantageous course open to them. Their weak and divided opponents will not soon persuade them that it is. Nor in Embassy's judgment will continuation of MAP suspensions (which in fact will have consequences increasingly adverse to our interests). However, Embassy sees no reason to let regime believe we would regard favorable plebiscite result as genuinely meaningful step in itself unless accompanied by some concrete moves toward restoration of civil liberties and in direction of ultimate elections. We therefore believe it would be desirable to make these points clear to regime leaders in order to avoid any false expectations. Moreover, we would see some advantage if Department press spokesman in response to question about American views on final draft of Constitution should [garble] along lines that we continue to wish for Greece what we believe majority of Greek people sincerely desire— prompt restoration of their civil liberties and early return to representative government. Although such a statement would not be popular with regime it would advertise our continued adherence to goals we have supported since April 1967 coup.[3]

Talbot

---

[3] In telegram 7046 from Athens, September 21, Talbot reported he had informed Pipinelis that the resumption of U.S. military aid was dependent on the wording of a plebiscite proposal that permitted a free expression of will to the Greek people. (Ibid.)

371.   Memorandum From the President's Special Assistant for National Security Affairs (Rostow) to President Johnson[1]

Washington, October 8, 1968, 4:05 p.m.

SUBJECT

Partial Resumption of Military Shipments to Greece

Attached is Nick Katzenbach's recommendation[2] that you release about 40% of the equipment we've held in suspense since the April 1967 coup. Most of the items to be released would be replacement items for the air force and navy, though there would be some tank ammo and heavy guns. We would continue to hold the tanks and new F–5 aircraft.

The main argument is that the time has come to separate our NATO relationship from our disapproval of domestic Greek politics. The colonels have had their constitutional referendum, but they won't hold elections under it until they're ready. We can keep prodding them, but we can't make them. Meanwhile, it doesn't make sense to let our security relationships with Greece—NATO role, commo facilities, Sixth Fleet support—deteriorate further.

A vocal group on the Hill will object to any resumption. You have already had letters from Congressmen Edwards and Fraser, who are active with Melina Mercouri and other friends of Greek democracy. But if you approve, Nick plans to consult with key members—before telling the Greeks but after the foreign aid appropriation—and lay it on the line that we can't let our interests suffer further. He feels now is the time to face these people with the facts of the problem and tell them we have to move. He would like to do this before they go home.

The rationale for releasing only 40% is to keep some pressure on the colonels and to put ourselves on a more reasonable policy footing while leaving your successor room to move either way. I believe Nick is right that we've about run our course on the suspension. The question is whether you want to begin correcting course yourself.

WWR

Approve Nick's recommendation[3]

Leave it till January

Call me

---

[1] Source: Johnson Library, National Security File, Country File, Greece, Vol. 4. Secret.
[2] Not printed.
[3] The President checked this option.

372.   Telegram From the Embassy in Cyprus to the Department of State[1]

Nicosia, November 8, 1968, 1523Z.

2647. Subj: Cyprus: Impact of Georkadjis affair.[2]

Summary: Very tentatively, we evaluate fallout of Georkadjis affair in three areas. In Athens–Nicosia relations, Athens has emotionally demanded and won Georkadjis dismissal but without much heed as to consequences, not least of which is arousal of nationalist feelings on island in irritated reaction to mainland pressure. In local politics, affair has set kettle bubbling with strong pressures for new elections to House of Representatives which Archbishop, urged on by Athens, is resisting. As regards local talks, all right-minded elements are seeking isolate from fallout, but as result Athens–Nicosia tensions and domestic political repercussions, delays seem inevitable.

1. It is, of course, too early to predict with complete accuracy many internal and external ramifications of Georkadjis affair. Our preliminary analysis, however, indicates general lines of impact of Georkadjis problem in three aspects of political situation on island.

2. Athens–Nicosia relations—relations between GOC and GOG appear to have been affected on various levels. First, in terms of official government-to-government relations colonels' hand seems to be strengthened by obvious demonstration they can force Makarios to take action he supposedly reluctant to take. (Degree to which Makarios "reluctant" to fire Georkadjis is moot since His Beatitude may well have been looking for opportunity to dump increasingly powerful Interior Minister.) In any case, Makarios outwardly seems to have knuckled under to GOG demands for Georkadjis' scalp and this has disappointed many Greek Cypriots. Second, by forcing Makarios to accept Georkadjis' resignation GOG has further angered those politically powerful Greek Cypriot elements (i.e., city lawyer-politicians) who resent GOG meddling in GOC affairs, who are not pro-enosis and who are in favor of accommodation with Turk Cypriots (Clerides and Demetriades to name two), although they at least equally angry with Archbishop. On third

---

[1] Source: Department of State, Central Files, POL 27 CYP. Confidential; Priority. Repeated to Ankara also for Ambassador McGhee, Athens, London, USUN, Ottawa, and the Mission to NATO.

[2] On August 13, Alexander Panaghoulis, an anti-Junta activist and army deserter, attempted to assassinate Prime Minister Papadopoulos. On September 7, the Greek Government charged that the attempt had been engineered by Cypriot Minister of Defense and the Interior Polykarpos Georghiades in collaboration with Andreas Papandreou. Georghiades resigned on November 1, claiming innocence. Panaghoulis' trial ended on November 17 with a death sentence, but he was subsequently granted clemency on December 23.

level, however, Greek-Cypriot relations hardly disturbed at all. Great mass of villagers (as proved to Ambassador Alexandrakis' satisfaction during recent village visit) still regard "Mother Greece" as "Motherly Fatherland," welcome and support GOG presence on Cyprus, and regard Makarios as "Ethnarch" or leader of Greek nation in Cyprus.

3. Entire purpose of GOG in exposing Georkadjis and pressuring for his resignation may well have been to demonstrate to Archbishop (November 6 press carries stories stating that Archbishop ordered issuance of passport to Panagoulis) that there is point beyond which Junta will not tolerate His Beatitude's flirtation with left. According to some reports GOG will demand and get closer cooperation of Cypriot intelligence services (other reports including word from Clerides indicate Archbishop will pull intelligence function out of Interior Ministry and place it under his own direct control as part of apparatus of Presidential Palace).

4. GOG seems be proceeding from one precipitate action to next in Georkadjis/Panagoulis affair without thinking through implications. Initial demand for Georkadjis' resignation was achieved but only because Archbishop promised Georkadjis parliamentary elections before January as price for his final agreement to resign. Now faced with prospect of triumphant election of former MinInt to House, which would be real slap in face for GOG, they now exerting great pressure on Makarios to go back on promise to Georkadjis and according CAS info he has agreed to do so. We wonder if they have considered what implications this might have: i.e. mischief-making, not excluding violence from Georkadjis and supporters; more embarrassing leaks to press; and angry reaction from House members and others who now savouring election prospect. At moment Greek Ambassador thinks he has Archbishop's agreement to postponement of elections, but this may well be so only until His Beatitude next talks with Georkadjis, Clerides and other House leaders.

5. Domestic political situation—As mentioned above part of deal for Georkadjis' final resignation was undertaking by Makarios to hold parliamentary elections by end of January. Clerides informed various former EOKA-fighter groups who were demonstrating for Georkadjis of Archbishop's agreement to hold elections. It now appears that Georkadjis who has long called for formation of anti-Communist political party will organize his own party based on fighter groups with help and support (privately if not openly) of Clerides. Other members of House who support Clerides (floor leader Demetriades and Chamber of Commerce President Savvides) likewise favor early elections and probably would join Georkadjis–Clerides coalition. Believe Clerides would remain in background in order avoid any open clash with Makarios. He told

Ambassador (memcon pouched)[3] he considered role as negotiator in communal talks paramount and overruling any personal feelings re election. He would need all his influence with Archbishop for such time as talks require serious compromises. He would not jeopardize his chances of making contribution to solution merely to satisfy his own strong belief that elections necessary and party organization required.

6. We expect that Archbishop is reluctant to hold elections and prefers to stall. Among other things postponement of elections would probably cause erosion of Georkadjis' strength. Strong demand from Greek Embassy that Makarios prevent elections which would certainly install Georkadjis in House supports Makarios in own predilection to avoid or stall elections. Trouble is that Clerides and Georkadjis and fighter groups believe they have commitment for holding of these elections. Clerides, Georkadjis and his friends, and many Deputies who support Clerides will probably maintain pressure on Archbishop to hold elections. Clerides and Demetriades have even spoken to us of possibility of mass resignation of present members of House which would presumably force elections. (We doubt they would go to such extremes; no one voluntarily resigns in Cyprus.) In any case, tug-of-war between political leaders who would like to form parties and contest House elections and Archbishop who prefers House made up of political personalities without political party and dependent on him can be expected. If holding of elections becomes inevitable we anticipate His Beatitude will attempt to balance off various political factions (organized as parties) by urging all parties to unite in support of him and to agree on allocation of seats before elections. In short, net result of Georkadjis affair in domestic political arena will probably be to make political life much more "political."

7. Local talks—As we have previously reported both GOC and Turk Cypriots have gone out of their way to immunize Georkadjis affair from adverse impact on local talks (Nicosia 2638).[4] However, holding of elections is bound to complicate local talks even if there is prior Clerides–Denktash agreement. In first place, Greeks will only get Turk Cypriot agreement to holding of elections under 1960 Constitution which compromises Greek position on 1965 electoral law. In second place, Turks will hold their own elections (they would like to clean house as well) but question then arises will new Turk legislators start passing legislation for Turk Cypriot areas. Finally, any election campaign on Greek side risks resurrection of old nationalist war cry of "enosis and only enosis."

8. Georkadjis affair further complicates local talks because internal GOC crisis prevents Clerides from obtaining any clear guidance from Archbishop and Council of Ministers. Given fight shaping up over elec-

---

[3] In airgram A–371, November 11. (Department of State, Central Files, POL 15 CYP)
[4] Dated November 7. (Ibid., POL 27 CYP)

tions and possibility of new Council of Ministers if elections are held, further postponement of real progress in local talks seems likely. More and more concept of "third phase" of local talks (which would begin in January or later) appearing in press and conversation. As previously reported "third phase" seems to be quite acceptable to GOT Embassy here.

9. Needless to say, typically Byzantine political maneuvering in wake of Georkadjis affair is rife and some surprises may yet be in store—particularly since Panagoulis trial is not yet ended. Our regret is that villain of the piece, Archbishop's pro-Communist advisor, Dr. Vassos Lyssarides, at whose behest GOC apparently became involved with Panagoulis in first place, so far emerging unscathed.

Belcher

373.   Telegram From the Department of State to the Embassy in Turkey[1]

Washington, November 15, 1968, 2215Z.

272453. Subject: Cyprus: Tripartite Talks: Normalization and Local Talks.

1. Dept's discussions with reps UK FonOff and Canadian ExtAff held Nov 14 under chairmanship Dep Asst Sec Rockwell. Meeting produced striking similarity of views among three governments.

2. Following are conclusions reached on major points discussed:

a. Normalization and Pacification: all agree that progress in this field seems to have approached its limit with regard to major official moves, but that continuing minor steps taken in Denktash–Clerides forum and at local levels are encouraging and useful in improving atmosphere especially in eastern and central parts of the island. All agreed on continued need for such steps as well as for deconfrontation in such areas as Artemis Road.

b. Local Talks: Canadians and British pessimistic over prospects for local talks in view lack of progress in the second phase. We expressed

[1] Source: Department of State, Central Files, POL 27 CYP. Confidential. Drafted by McFarland, cleared by NEA and IO, and approved by Rockwell. Also sent to Athens, London, Nicosia, Ottawa, the Mission to NATO, and USUN.

view it is now too early to be either optimistic or pessimistic pending clear evidence of willingness of parties to compromise or similar evidence of obduracy. All expressed concern at lack of results so far but for moment see no need for outside intervention in talks. All would wish consult urgently with one another if talks in danger of collapse.

c. Relative Importance Normalization and Constitutional Talks: All agreed that normalization should not be overemphasized at apparent expense of constitutional talks and that the two should go "hand in hand".

d. UNFICYP mandate and renewal covered by septel.[2]

Katzenbach

---

[2] Telegram 272781 to Nicosia, November 16. (Ibid., POL 27–4 CYP/UN)

---

374.   Memorandum of Conversation[1]

Brussels, November 16, 1968, 9–10 a.m.

SUBJECT

Secretary's Meeting with King Constantine

PARTICIPANTS

King Constantine
H. E. Panayiotis Pipinelis, Greek Foreign Minister
The Secretary
Ambassador Ridgway B. Knight
Mr. Frank E. Cash, Jr., Country Director for Turkey

The King began by saying he welcomed the opportunity to discuss once more "the relations between our two countries." The constitution is a new development, and the question is where we go from here—what steps should be taken to encourage a return to "the right kind of system." He wondered what ideas The Secretary had as to how to promote the

---

[1] Source: Department of State, Central Files, POL 30 GREECE. Secret; Exdis. Drafted by Cash and approved in S on November 22. The meeting was held at the U.S. Embassy. Rusk was in Brussels November 12–16 for the NATO Ministerial Meeting. In telegram 7697 from Athens, November 5, Talbot endorsed the idea of a meeting between Rusk and the King to demonstrate continued U.S. interest in the King. (Ibid.)

return to at least the form of representative government as soon as possible. The King said he thought it would be impossible to go from the present system immediately to democratic government. This must be done gradually, but the process must be started soon. He would welcome The Secretary's ideas as to how to get the constitution into effect as soon as possible.

The Secretary said that although the United States has a great interest in this, he was not sure we had any recommendations as to how this should be done. He asked the Foreign Minister what plans existed.

Mr. Pipinelis replied that he had been in the hospital and unable to talk with the Prime Minister recently, but the latter clearly had the aim of reaching full implementation of the constitution by gradual and well-considered steps. Naturally there would be many, and the Finance Minister, who had attended the Cabinet meeting concerned, reported that the first very wise step has been taken in the appointment of a committee to draft the laws necessary to implement the constitution—a press law, a political parties law, a constitutional tribunal law, etc. After examination by the Cabinet, the laws will be put into effect at once, parties must be set up, and elections prepared. In his personal opinion, the Foreign Minister said, the most urgent matter now is the return of His Majesty, "not on formal grounds, but for political and psychological grounds." His presence would lend a new element of stability and enable His Majesty to exercise very important influence, which is essential. He expressed his personal conviction that the Prime Minister agreed with this idea completely, but that he had differences to contend with. No one influence is entirely predominant.

Here the King interjected, "Unfortunately!"

Mr. Pipinelis agreed and added that the Prime Minister's group, both inside the Government and without, is becoming predominant but is not entirely so yet. The Foreign Minister said he tried to find a way out. He supported the Prime Minister completely and is convinced the King's return will be advantageous to all. "Your advice," he said, "and your country's would be invaluable." "A formal démarche," he continued, "could do more harm than good, but you have a series of means to make your views known."

In response to The Secretary's question as to whether the differences he had mentioned were within the Cabinet or without, the Foreign Minister said "both", and the King said "mainly without."

Mr. Pipinelis said he knew how much importance the people—the revolutionary committee, and the people in general, attach to the opinion of the United States Government. He knew the United States had many official and unofficial contacts.

"You are aware," the King said, "of my planned meeting last May with the Prime Minister. Due to one thing and another, this has been postponed. It is very hard to know what is in his mind. I have told him through various people that it is far better to become master in his own house. I think he can't deal with the young people, who are tough. Immediately upon my return I'll work as hard as possible to get rid of them."

The Secretary asked where it had been contemplated the meeting would be held. The King said near Levkas, with the Prime Minister anchored in one cove and the King in another, with the meeting in between at night.

The United States, the King continued, carries great weight, but it's hard to tell how long this will last. It was very encouraging to hear that the drafting committee has been appointed, but the question is whether there will be delays.

Mr. Pipinelis said he did not think so. He was very happy that the committee had been appointed without his urging. The Prime Minister clearly intends to put the entire constitution into effect, but he is not alone. He has influence, but he must bargain. We have no alternative, the Foreign Minister said, but normalization through this Government and the return of His Majesty.

The King said he agreed, and both he and Mr. Pipinelis, and perhaps the United States, might exercise influence.

Mr. Pipinelis said he could safely say that with the King in Greece the possibilities would increase. The King initially should do nothing except permit his influence to grow.

The King laughingly said he'd play tennis.

Mr. Pipinelis said the King's influence would grow and become very important. The present Government is there to stay. It can be influenced but not thrown out without strife.

The Secretary said he had a few observations to make. During his tenure as Secretary there have been sixty-two coups in the world, none of which, he might say, had been engineered by the CIA. Wherever the United States has had influence, it has always been exerted toward return to constitutionalism. The United States has acquired a certain amount of experience in this area. Frequently there are two stages. First there is a restoration of basic civil rights and fair administration of justice, a removal of the fear of oppression, and this leads to the second stage, which, while not constitutionalism, is not totalitarian in its effect on individuals. An important step in Greece would seem to be the return of basic civil rights to prepare the way for constitutional elections.

As to the King's return, The Secretary said, he would be very candid. He could not, as a man of honor, advise the King to return, because to do so would imply assurances, which no one had given The Secretary. He could not make pledges he was unable to fulfill. He would not advise the King either to return, or not to return. The King should know to what he was returning. The Secretary could not advise the King to return to a trap.

Mr. Pipinelis said the purpose was to get advice to the revolutionary committee, not the King, who would have to make his own decisions.

The Secretary asked how much reliance the United States could put in assurances from the revolutionary committee concerning the King's return.

Mr. Pipinelis said it was not intended that the United States get assurances but rather that it give advice.

In response to The Secretary's question as to how much influence the United States could exert on the revolutionary committee, the Foreign Minister said, "considerable if properly done."

The King said it would be effective if Americans outside the Embassy "talked directly to the Colonels."

The Foreign Minister said there were also many other channels.

The King said he agreed The Secretary should not give him advice. He would make his own decisions. But the United States now has influence on the Colonels which may be lost in a year. Results would come from constant pressure on individual colonels for the return of constitutionalism and the King, because they always have in mind what the United States is thinking.

The Secretary said there was no question but that the United States would be glad to see the return to Greece of constitutional democracy, governmental stability, and progress. This advice, the United States has been giving and will continue to give. But in complete candor, the United States could not get involved in what might turn out to be a doublecross.

The King said he did not want his return discussed alone. The real issue is what happens to Greece. "I'm terribly homesick", he said, "but the important thing is, are the people going to get a better deal. I failed to push this Government out by force. Influence is the only possibility. We must persuade them to do the right thing. Then we must see if it's a trap—if I'm going back only as a puppet. It is very important that we— Mr. Pipinelis, the American Government, and I—press for the earliest possible return to constitutionalism. I have to go back to help the process. I'm absolutely confident of the loyalty of the people, but I'm worried about discipline in the armed forces."

The Secretary asked if there were any possibility of starting with local elections.

The Foreign Minister said this was the course he favored.

The King asked if The Secretary agreed that all should exert pressure on the regime and then see if a trap had been laid.

The Secretary said he would review this when he returned to Washington. There was no question but that the United States would be very glad to see Greece move quickly back to a constitutional system. However, it would not be the first time United States advice had been disregarded.

The King said he was "immensely worried about the armed forces." He was going to tell the armed forces chief that he fully supported his attempts to reinstill discipline. The captains are still ruling the colonels, and the colonels, the generals. There is still dissension between the forces. The armed forces must again earn the respect of the people.

The King said he hoped the United States Government and the new Administration would continue to have no dealings with the Regent, whom the King does not recognize.

In conclusion, the King said a determination would have to be made at some point as to whether or not attempts to exert influence on the regime were being successful. Allowing the situation to continue indefinitely would simply help the Communists, because eventually there would be an explosion.

The Secretary said this matter would be considered very carefully. He was inclined to agree that conditions could not be frozen, because this would be very dangerous. He hoped very much to see fast movement toward constitutional government and wished the King good luck.

The King and The Secretary then had a brief chat alone.[2]

---

[2] No record of this conversation has been found.

---

375. Letter From the Ambassador to Greece (Talbot) to the Country Director for Greece (Brewster)[1]

Athens, December 31, 1968.

Dear Dan:

My talk with Papadopoulos on December 28 was disappointing. So that you could get the full flavor, we decided to airgram Pete Peterson's full memcon rather than reducing it to more readable length.[2] If you can plow through it, you will see that the Prime Minister argued strongly for

---

[1] Source: Department of State, Greek Desk Files: Lot 71 D 6, Correspondence to and from Athens. Secret; Official–Informal.

[2] Transmitted as an enclosure to airgram A–2 from Athens, January 1, 1969. (Ibid., Central Files, POL GREECE–US)

military assistance levels to be judged on military grounds alone and virtually rejected my rather lengthy disquisition in support of the proposition that other factors have also to be taken into account even when military considerations are predominant.

I found the Prime Minister less forthcoming about his future plans than on any previous occasion. My effort to launch into a discussion of his plans for moderating the state of siege was turned aside by the comment that there was really nothing more to be said beyond his public address of December 14.[3] He was polite but firm in stating that he would be ready to discuss his future plans with me after the holidays if I desired but would regret it if such a discussion were really necessary to assure good relations between Greece and the United States.

I am not sure how to read this stiffening stance. One explanation is that Papadopoulos feels sufficiently secure in the saddle so that he can be a little more cavalier with us as well as with European countries. Another is that he has decided to get a reading on the new American Administration before defining his 1969 policies on civil liberties and constitutional implementation. If he has decided on a major forward step, he may prefer to hold it until its announcement could be expected to get him off on a good start with the new American Administration. Alternatively, he may have decided not to take any steps now that might prove not to have been necessary should the new Administration be substantially more relaxed than the old one in its attitude toward the Greek regime.

My own hunch is that his unforthcomingness resulted from a combination of these factors. It would be natural for him to regard the present American Administration, and its representative in Athens, as lame ducks and to hold off decisive moves until he can get a reading on the new Administration.[4]

If from your distance you have more illuminating insights, I shall be glad to know them.

With best wishes,

Yours sincerely,

Phil

---

[3] The Embassy analyzed this speech in telegram 8308 from Athens, December 16. (Ibid., POL 15–1 GREECE)

[4] In a December 27 letter to Brewster, Talbot reported that he had submitted his resignation effective January 20, 1969. (Ibid., Greek Desk Files: Lot 71 D 6, Correspondence to and from Athens)

Index

ISBN 0-16-045085-3

90000

9 780160 450853